W0069710

9/2017
STRAND PRICE
$2.00

HARVARD HISTORICAL STUDIES • 183

Published under the auspices
of the Department of History
from the income of the
Paul Revere Frothingham Bequest
Robert Louis Stroock Fund
Henry Warren Torrey Fund

KRIS MANJAPRA

Age of Entanglement

German and Indian Intellectuals across Empire

Harvard University Press

Cambridge, Massachusetts
London, England
2014

Copyright © 2014 by the President and Fellows of Harvard College
All rights reserved
Printed in the United States of America

Library of Congress Cataloging-in-Publication Data

Manjapra, Kris, 1978–
  Age of entanglement : German and Indian intellectuals across empire / Kris Manjapra.
    pages cm. — (Harvard historical studies ; 183)
  Includes bibliographical references and index.
  ISBN 978-0-674-72514-0 (alk. paper)
 1. India—Intellectual life—19th century.   2. India—Intellectual life—20th century.
3. Germany—Intellectual life—19th century.   4. Germany—Intellectual life—20th century.
5. Learning and scholarship—India—History—19th century.   6. Learning and scholarship—
India—History—20th century.   7. Learning and scholarship—Germany—History—
19th century.   8. Learning and scholarship—Germany—History—20th century.
9. India—Relations—Germany.   10. Germany—Relations—India.   I. Title.
  DS428.M36 2014
  303.48'243054—dc23   2013012269

For my father

Krishnan Variath Manjapra

Contents

Note on Style and Transliteration

In this text, historical figures are referred to by their full name or by their last name, except in a few special cases in which there is a strong convention in place to use the first name as the shortened form of identification, such as is the case with the Bengali personages Bankim (Bankimchandra Chattopadhyaya), Aurobindo (Aurobindo Ghosh), and Rabindranath (Rabindranath Tagore). Also, when referring to Bengali book titles or quoting from Bengali sources, the author has romanized Bengali words with diacritical marks using a standard system. Bengali-language personal names and place names have been transliterated without diacritics, using the most familiar and conventional spellings. Hopefully this goes some way toward balancing accuracy with readability. Unavoidably, variant spellings of Bengali terms appear in the text, as the romanization systems used in quoted sources sometimes differ from the one used by this book's author. To keep track of unfamiliar terms, please consult the glossary, which lists Bengali names with a large number of English-language variants, as well as important recurring Bengali and German keywords.

AGE OF ENTANGLEMENT

Introduction

There was a time when German nationalism was a prime force challenging the idea of Europe, just as Indian anticolonial nationalism was a prime force challenging the idea of Empire. In collaboration, although separated by a stark power differential, Germans and Indians sought to destroy the nineteenth-century world order organized by British power. In the late nineteenth century, Germans and Indians, positioned across multiple imperial systems, and across the colonial divide, began to use each other to pry apart and reorganize the world order. They used each other's intellectual institutions and each other's platforms of recognition to claim political distinction on a world stage.[1] In a time when the political coherence of Europe as well as the internal integrity of European empires was crumbling, Germans came to India, and Indians came to German-speaking countries like heirs apparent of a coming world system.

This idea of heirs apparent traveling between German Europe and India can be taken both as event and metaphor. To speak first of events: a thirty-year-old Archduke Ferdinand, heir presumptive to the Austro-Hungarian empire, made his regal tour of India in the winter of 1892. On his tour, he carried out an ethnological project of artifact collection, and had himself photographed exhibiting his colonial wares.[2] Two decades later, a thirty-year-old Crown Prince Wilhelm of Germany, the emperor's oldest son, great-grandson of Queen Victoria and heir to the German empire, traveled ostentatiously through Bombay, Allahabad, Delhi, Jaipur, Abbotabad, Benares, Hyderabad, and Calcutta. The prince made an extravagant display of German imperial science on his tour, driving around in a state-of-the-art

Siemens automobile at the Ahmedabad Fair that won the prize for industrial elegance. In this bit of *theatrum mundi*, the event of the German crown prince in India was meant to serve as a metaphor for the rising power of "German ideas in the world."[3]

German scientific pageantry in India coincided with intellectual displays by Indian nationalists. In February 1911, an Indian nationalist leader, Asutosh Mukherjee, the vice-chancellor of the University of Calcutta, bestowed an honorary doctorate upon the visiting crown prince in a ceremony that gravely angered the colonial administration. In his convocation speech, Asutosh spoke of the encounter with Crown Prince Wilhelm as a moment of recognition beyond empire. The visit, he remarked, "reminds us as well as the outside world that our University claims and acknowledges relations, interests, [and] sympathies wider than what is commonly understood."[4]

Ten years later, those words were strangely resonant with comments by Paul Natorp, prominent German philosopher, after the visit of Mukherjee's friend, Rabindranath Tagore. Rabindranath, the 1913 Nobel laureate in literature and the most prominent anticolonial cultural leader of India at the time, fashioned himself before German audiences in 1921 as a *viśvakabi*—a world poet—a wizard of universal truth. Natorp, who read Rabindranath's songs, poems, and dramas with his students and at home with his wife and children, hailed the Indian Prospero "as a brother and friend [who] has come to us and departed, and who is still close to us from afar."[5]

Both Germans and Indians embarked on projects of cultural and intellectual pageantry in each other's territories in this same historical period. Yet, a moment's reflection makes something obvious: the significance of German imperial travel to India cannot be equated with that of Indian anticolonial travel to Germany. In fact, these instances might even seem more opposite than alike, given that one group exercised imperial power, and the other group suffered it.

But similarities are not at issue here; *entanglements* are.[6] These vignettes of entanglement provide three important insights at the outset of this study. First, transnational scholarly and scientific encounters played an important role in sustaining a pageant of political recognition between German and Indian nationalists in the early twentieth century. Second, a particular alignment of international politics in the late nineteenth to mid-twentieth centuries facilitated new kinds of scholarly and scientific encounters across national and colonial boundaries. And finally, the transnational circulations and feedback loops of German and Indian intellectual life were kept in their array by the galvanic force of a third party: the lodestone of the British empire.

The British empire was the alpha empire of the nineteenth century, the first among equals, rising to world supremacy through a competition for spoils with the French.[7] By the mid-nineteenth century, it commanded the lion's share of martial, biopolitical, and institutional technologies needed to control a vast overseas empire. In the great nineteenth-century play of signifiers, the British empire came to serve as a master symbol for the white, gentlemanly West, just as the West served as the signifier for the civilizational ideals of Enlightenment universalism.[8] This chain of significations was held stable over the course of the nineteenth century by British naval dominance over the high seas, British control of worldwide communication channels and technologies, the unparalleled extent of British overseas colonial possessions, the global expansion of English as a language of trade and education, the de facto "sterling standard" that governed world trade, and the unquestionable world dominance of British financial services anchored by the City of London.[9] Even the synchronization of clocks around the world beginning in the 1880s took Greenwich's time as the meridian of universal time.[10]

A Eurocentric, and more specifically *Anglocentric*, world order legitimated by ideas about Enlightenment and Empire attained its fullest expression from about the 1830s to the 1870s. But beginning in the 1880s, this world order began to quickly crumble. In the decades after 1880, Britain lost its industrial prominence, even as it retained its role as world center of finance. The City of London sat at the center of a storm and in fact channeled the flows of invisible finance capital that helped drive the processes of global disintegration and reorganization taking place over the coming decades.[11] Observers in the 1880s witnessed the peak of the first "Great Depression," 1873–1896, when the optimism over the organization of the European world economy and the legal institutions of the *jus publicum europaeum* started to atrophy under the pressure of rising nationalisms and anticolonialisms inside and outside the European continent.

The period of "high imperialism" leading up to the Great War, often presented by historians as the apotheosis of the ideal of modern Empire, can better be understood as the disintegration of Empire as a collective aspirational project unifying Europeans.[12] In fact the ideal of Empire (with a capital *E*) fell apart beginning in the 1880s because the concept of a unified European identity sustaining it was quickly crumbling away. The ideal of

Empire devolved into many internecine imperialisms. Europe came to be increasingly de-Europeanized from the 1880s onward, just as the civilizational project of modern Empire came to be increasingly de-universalized. By de-Europeanization I mean the decline of the *ideal* of Europe as a unifying aspirational category of civilizational status. This did not mean the demise of European identities, or of imperial projects, but only their pluralization and increased internal conflict. The rise of the many "Pan" movements across Europe in this period—Greater Britain, Greater France, Mitteleuropa, Greater Greece, Slavic Universalism, Turanianism—shows that the aspiration for European integration, exalted after Waterloo in 1815, was debased by the fin de siècle. And this is not yet to mention the many universalisms that were arising across Asia during this same time.[13] Thus, in 1926, when Alfred Eckhard Zimmern, a political scientist at Oxford born of a German father, wrote his book on the "Third British Empire," his tone was anxious. He remarked that given the rising nationalisms of "non-white peoples" on earth, and the disappearance of the German, Austrian, and Russian empires after the war, the British faced "an age which seems destined to dissolve empires."[14] Trained briefly at the University of Berlin under the Philhellenic scholar, Ulrich von Wilamowitz-Moellendorf, Zimmern's reflections on the fate of British world power were informed by a deep awareness of the new clefts splitting up the world, but also by a perspective trained by German scholarly methods of that time.

The Concert of Europe fell into cacophony by the 1880s, a consequence of rampant intra-European imperial competition for Asian and African terrains that arose with the Berlin Conference of 1884–1885. Older historiography points to the rise of an "illiberal" German state after 1871, and the cunning of Otto von Bismarck who hosted the conference, as the first instigations for a tumble into strife leading to the Great War.[15] However, scholars such as Charles Maier, writing after the debunking of the *Sonderweg* thesis in German historiography, speak instead of a general process of "territorialization" that began in earnest in the 1860s and propelled political agendas around the world in increasingly protectionist ways up until the last third of the twentieth century.[16] To understand the distinctiveness of the period from 1880 to 1945, the concept of "entanglement" is especially valuable as it captures both the multiplication of boundaries and claims of difference, as well as the accelerated mutual implications and transnational feedback loops developing among discrepant national groups around the world in this period despite their power differences.

THE STUDY OF ENTANGLEMENT

This book examines the changing scope and quality of interactions between German and Indian actors across three historical periods. There was a time when German scholarly and scientific institutions, and German-speaking intellectuals, actually provided foundational support for the establishment of British colonial institutions in India. From about 1815 to approximately 1880, one might even say that British colonial science took on a markedly German character. This early phase of Germans in British India gave way to a second phase, lasting from about 1880 to 1945 and intensifying after 1918, when projects to destroy the nineteenth-century Anglocentric world order created unprecedented entanglements between Indian intellectuals and German-speaking thinkers. Finally, in the years after 1945, we witness a process of delinking between Indian and German intellectuals in the context of the Cold War and the emergence of the "Third World." Friends became strangers, and ideas of self and other were rearranged as historical circumstances changed.

When studying the history of Indian interactions outside the British empire and beyond the Indian Ocean arena, the focus on links with Germany serves an especially instructive purpose. Certainly, Indian connections with China and Japan, with the Americas, and with inland and coastal Africa deserve our further attention too. The German–Indian entanglement, however, provides the heightened expression of a family relation of collaborative revolts against the nineteenth-century Anglocentric world order. After all, German institutions were the most powerful disruptors of the "concert" of Europe in the 1880–1945 period. In this period, Germany became the European world power at the vanguard of projects for "de-Europeanization from within." German cultural and intellectual institutions provided the most forceful brake on the British imperial push for world hegemony. No wonder nationalists from around the world—American, Japanese, Korean, Turkish, Indian—all made contact with German scholarly institutions from the late nineteenth century onward to stimulate the growth of their own nationalist cultural institutions. Indian nationalists, on the other hand, and the Bengali intelligentsia in particular, played a vanguard role in breaking out of the conceptual framework of British multiethnic empire. The entanglement of Germans and Indians thus produced the strongest inflection of intellectual revolt against the nineteenth-century global status quo—a status quo constellated by discourses about Enlightenment, Europe, and Empire, and organized around the star of British world power.

The encounters of Germans and Indians must be studied in ways that reveal what *both* groups, given their power differences, were getting out of the interactions in terms of intellectual and social yield. In a specific historical period, 1880–1945, Germans used Indians to dispel a vision of nineteenth-century Europe in which they felt themselves subordinated to Anglocentric hegemony. Meanwhile, Indians used Germans to break apart the ideal of Empire in which they felt permanently trapped as colonial subjects on a seemingly endless road to imperial citizenship.[17] Entanglements occur when groups, alien from each other in many other ways, begin to need each other like crowbars or like shovels to break apart or to dig up problems of the most pressing concern for themselves. In other words, entanglements are always political—they have more to do with the realm of necessity and power than with the realm of freedom. And because they are political, they are also bound by historical conditions.

This book hopes to inject a necessary dose of realpolitik into the study of transnational intellectual history, through a focus on alliance building, political rivalries, and multilateralism. The study of intellectual history and international politics reinforce each other: aspiring social groups created alliances with other aspiring or dominant social groups worldwide in order to establish new communities of authority on the world stage. German and Indian nationalists sought each other's company in unequal alliances, and to divergent ends. The official and elite, as well as the interpersonal and popular interactions of Germans and Indians across the skein of empires in the nineteenth and twentieth centuries were partly tactics in international politics. But they were also acts of *intellectual* politics in an age when the ideals of Enlightenment, Europe, and Empire broke down as hegemonic, unifying signifiers.[18]

As opposed to studying encounters in terms of the pity of colonial domination, or else in terms of the charms of cross-cultural encounter,[19] a new study of entanglement would ask: what do different groups, some stronger, some weaker, get out of their political relations together? This question leads us beyond the study of perceptions and cultural representations, to the study of historical interactions.[20] How do groups use trans-societal interactions and linkages to satisfy their own specific local political interests? The study of entanglement in fact keeps different threads of history separate, just as it also traces the involvement of these threads together. Such a pursuit displays a multifocal interest in the politics, poetics, and practices of transnational relations.[21]

During a specific historical period, German and Indian thinkers needed each other in order to skew and transgress nineteenth-century ideals of Anglocentric Europeanness, on one hand, and ideals of imperial citizenship, on the other. The entanglements in this book show us that European and colonial intellectuals had much more in common than we have previously accepted—they shared intellectual and political projects. The epistemic transformations of what I define as the "post-Enlightenment," taking place over the decades from 1880 to 1945, did not simply involve the involution of Europe upon itself, but entailed geopolitical and intellectual alliances and circulations that stretched far beyond Europe, occurring among subordinated European thinkers and colonial thinkers alike.[22] Historians, writing after 1945, have represented the intellectual revolution that took place at the fin de siècle and up to the mid-twentieth century, detonating across the whole spectrum of the arts, sciences, and humanities, as the dialectic and the legacy of the West alone. But post-Enlightenment science and scholarship fed on the geopolitical disorder of the world up to 1945. What historians have mistaken as a product of the West's crisis of modernity in fact resulted from an unprecedented entanglement of intellectuals around the world, as they sought to break free from the "enlightened" concert of nineteenth-century Europe, and from the specter of British empire as the harbinger of Enlightenment universalism.

South Asian subalternist historiography devoted to the study of colonial cultural resistance can inscribe into the historical record a dualistic notion of historical agency—oppressor versus oppressed, the active versus the passive, the dominant versus the subordinate, the universal versus the particular. This obscures the actually existing *political* character of all social groups in the world, as Partha Chatterjee has brilliantly outlined.[23] Three decades of postcolonial scholarship in the Foucauldian and Saidian veins have taught us about the origin and scope of the imperial discourses of science and Orientalism, which supposedly engulfed all subjects, societies, and states in the modern period like poison gas. But what we still lack is a proper understanding of how discourses were practiced as dialogue—by whom and to what ends. In the analysis of knowledge/power and discursive regimes, we have tended to lose sight of the differentiated articulations of intellectual politics.[24]

Studying concentrations, circulations, intensifications, and rearrangements of intellectual power within arenas of transnational entanglement gives us the ability to see "westerners" and "colonial subjects" as implicated together in the affairs of globalization. The rivalry and alliance between different fractions of intellectual power around the world, manifested as dialogic action and "heteroglossia," are the main focus of the research in this book.[25] By taking the study of intellectual history in colonial India outside the exclusive gambit of the British empire, and by taking the study of German intellectual life beyond the familiar reference points of Western Europe and the transatlantic, this book studies a dimension of global entanglement that dualistic approaches inveterately ignore.

I use the term "German intellectuals" as shorthand to refer to the diverse group of central European Germans, Austrians, Moravians, Swiss, and others trained in German-speaking academia. On the other hand, I employ "Indian intellectuals" to identify the motley crew of thinkers from the Indian subcontinent associated with the powerful center of nationalist knowledge production located in Calcutta (Bengal), when Calcutta was still the most important British colonial city east of the Suez. The terms "German" and "Indian," then, are not used here to assume or connote ideas about territorial, ethnic, or cultural authenticity or identity, but to name the nationalism inherent in intellectual institutions in my period, expressed through modes of thought and scholarly inquiry, and associated with specific geographies of knowledge production. German and Indian intellectuals and their institutions of knowledge production chafed under the global hegemony of Anglo-Saxon power. But theirs was a struggle to redraw the world map of intellectual power, not to rend that map asunder. In order to challenge global symbols of power strongly associated with the norms of nineteenth-century British imperial culture, rising nationalist groups around the world found themselves envying the very power they sought to unmoor.

THE POST-ENLIGHTENMENT

At the core of the Enlightenment process in Europe, stretching in earnest from the seventeenth to the nineteenth centuries, was the search for rational universal laws that authoritatively categorized, arranged, and ordered the natural and the human domains.[26] Most of all, Enlightenment thought favored strong subjectivism: the idea of the "rational" individual as the observer, knower, and master of his or her environment. The discourse of Enlightenment underpinned a Europe-centered universalism, and to the extent that elite groups from around the world—mercantile, clerical, or mercenary—found their place within a Europe-centered world order in the nineteenth and twentieth centuries, they entered into conversation with the abstract concepts, concrete embodiments, and the material trappings of Enlightenment thought.[27] But what happened when the sign of Europe began to lose its global power after the 1880s?

In this book, the post-Enlightenment refers not to a reaction against the Enlightenment, and not to the Romantic movements of the late eighteenth and early nineteenth centuries that emerged on the heels of the *siècle des Lumières*. Masterful interpretations by H. Stuart Hughes and Isaiah Berlin have famously shed light on the "critiques of the Enlightenment" that began much earlier and ended much later than a tightly periodized Romantic Era, starting in the time of Vico in the 1720s and culminating in the intellectual upheavals of the "antipositivist" period from 1890 to 1930.[28] Interest in historical origins, in myth, in religion, and in language certainly characterized responses to the Enlightenment discourse of universal reason from the eighteenth century onward.

But here, by post-Enlightenment I specifically mean the sea change in scientific and scholarly production that began at the end of the nineteenth century and continued into the mid-twentieth century, marked by widening communication networks among white and colored thinkers across world regions, and by efforts to *work through* both the epistemic legacies of Enlightenment discourse as well as the political, social, and cultural consequences that the Enlightenment had brought to bear in the world. The scholarship of the post-Enlightenment critiqued, often in practice if not in theme, the great signifiers of nineteenth-century Western universalism: Europe, Enlightenment, and Empire.

The methods of post-Enlightenment sciences (both natural sciences and human sciences) of the late nineteenth and early twentieth centuries rejected conventional empiricism, and fused the heroically rational with the hermetically oracular in volatile blends of intellectual production.[29] Already by the 1880s, post-Enlightenment science—what Michel Foucault in the *Order of Things* called "counter-science"—constituted a unique bandwidth for scholarly production around the world. This new bandwidth interrupted the hegemonic Enlightenment broadcast, which was most forcefully disseminated at that time by British institutions in the world. Foucault, in his archaeology of the human sciences, noticed a group of scholarly practices that seemed to operate differently from the rest. "Psychoanalysis and ethnology are rather 'counter-sciences,'" he wrote, "which does not mean that they are less 'rational' or 'objective' than the others, but that they flow in the opposite direction . . . that they ceaselessly 'unmake' that very man who is creating and re-creating his positivity in the human sciences."[30]

Although Foucault did not identify the geopolitical dimension of these practices, he did show us the way some sciences of the later nineteenth century seemed to reverse their charge, and work through positivism to unmoor the positivistic subjectivism at the base of Enlightenment thought. The countersciences did not confirm the place of Enlightenment selfhood in the world, but confronted nineteenth-century ideals of selfhood with threats of unnerving insecurity and danger. Countersciences, wrote Foucault, "threatened the very thing that made it possible for man to be known."[31] They spelled the possible doom of Enlightenment selfhood in facts, numbers, and theories. But if countersciences broke old unities apart into smaller and smaller fragments, they also rearranged pieces together into newly enchanted wholes. And this work of rearrangement was constitutively transnational—carried out through relays of intellectual interdependence that brought Europeans and colonial peoples together into a strange interdependence. The post-Enlightenment was a time of unexampled political and personal alliance between those alien to one another, and of new affinities and communications between distant groups around the world.

The post-Enlightenment saw what David Lindenfeld usefully terms a "transformation," and not a rejection of positivism, with the rise of comparativist, expressivist, and perspectivalist views onto the natural and human realms.[32] Post-Enlightenment scholarship generated relativism, and what one thinker from the 1920s already called the "provincializing" of Europe's symbolic place in the world.[33] The post-Enlightenment that stretched from 1880 to 1945 formed a decades-long response to the "high" positivism and to the heroic subjectivism associated with nineteenth-century greats such as John Stuart Mill, Auguste Comte, and Rudolf Virchow. The new age saw the rise of scholarly practices that ferreted out differences, overturning prevailing presumptions of universal unity and conformity. Scientific and humanistic research in our later period uncovered hidden drives in the human realm, hidden order in the natural realm, invisible impersonal fields of language and culture that determined human activity, and visions of essence and depth that conventional European bourgeois scholarship could scarcely contemplate. Post-Enlightenment academic disciplines, with their comparativist, expressivist, and relativistic forms of knowledge production, not only sustained the national ideals of different groups worldwide, but also nourished alliances and new communities of recognition between distant groups in the world. The growth of national consciousness cannot be separated from the intensification of transnational bonds.

Post-Enlightenment scholarship fed off collaborations among intellectuals located in a disintegrating Europe and in disintegrating European empires. In this book, I consider a sequence of post-Enlightenment encounters between Indian and German thinkers stretching across the sciences, arts, and humanities, in fields of theoretical physics, international economics, Marxist criticism, geocultural studies, psychoanalysis, and expressionist art theory and practice. These scholarly fields facilitated the politics of *regional* power groups in Central Europe and in South Asia as they sought to contest the *global* nineteenth-century cultural hegemony of the British empire.[34] Germans and Indians, encountering each other across a sequence of scholarly arenas, used these interactions to assert new universalistic visions with themselves as the privileged spokespeople at the center.

If Max Weber proposed in his lectures of 1918 that the world had been "disenchanted" through nineteenth-century science, then his comments ring with a note of irony since the postwar years witnessed the crest in the wave of post-Enlightenment projects to scientifically enchant the world anew. Intellectuals around the world found new ways to gather "facts" about the natural and human worlds, new ways to arrange and group those facts, and new authority to glimpse universal patterns and meaning within those arrangements. As Theodor Adorno and Max Horkheimer observed and as Bruno Latour recently reminds us, science and mythmaking share much in common.[35] This book never loses sight of the fact that new scientific myths also produced new monsters with which the world had to contend.

THE COURSE OF ENTANGLEMENT

A word about the structure of this book. The chapters in Part I are macroscopic, focused on political and social stages, in both senses of the word, that led to an age of entanglement between Europeans and Asians from the 1880s onward. The first part of this book explores the underlying historical structures and processes that gave German and Indian intellectuals the ability to recognize each other as allies, and to speak shared languages especially in the aftermath of the Great War. In these chapters, I focus on British imperial modes of scholarly insourcing, the rise of German imperial competition, the popularization of Orientalism in Germany, and the origins of anticolonial internationalism in India.

Part II turns to the microscopic study of specific fields of encounter and intellectual entanglement ranging across the spectrum of the natural sciences, social sciences, and humanities. The second part provides a close study of the content and choreography of entanglements, including the construction of shared intellectual objects of concern, and practices of dialogue and cross-identification. The combination of macrohistorical and microhistorical approaches allows us to appreciate events and structures, texts and contexts, that characterized the transnational encounters at issue here.

A loose school of Indian nationalist intellectuals was formed by a group of young firebrands gathered around Rabindranath Tagore beginning in the early twentieth century.[36] Starting with the national *svadeśi* insurgency of 1905 and continuing into the interwar years, this group of scholars embarked on an internationalist program of anticolonialism. I take the Bengali internationalism of this Calcutta school as exemplary of a larger phenomenon that marked Indian intellectual activity across the subcontinent, and included Hindu and Muslim thinkers. Calcutta was the capital city of British rule in India over the course of the nineteenth and early twentieth centuries, and it became a hub for colonial education inside the British empire. A city that had once been the colonial metropolis of British rule in India became the epicenter of anti-British intellectual politics.[37] Bengali intellectuals inspired by Rabindranath led the way in forging encounters with German academics and institutions, even insourcing German intellectuals in their pursuit of new intellectual authority outside the frame of British empire.

It was in the interwar context that members of this Bengal group became deeply entangled with German-speaking institutions in Central Europe. Meghnad Saha and Satyendranath Bose encountered Albert Einstein and Walther Nernst, and Girindrasekhar Bose entered a long dialogue with Sigmund Freud. Karl Haushofer, the geographer, and Bernhard Harms, the economist, collaborated with Benoy Kumar Sarkar, and trade unionist Josef Furtwängler met M. N. Roy and Subhas Chandra Bose. In the interwar period, Rabindranath Tagore traveled three times to German Europe recruiting faculty for his new nationalist university in Bengal. Stella Kramrisch, a young Moravian-Austrian art historian, assumed the position of visiting professor at Rabindranath Tagore's university and organized a major exhibition of Bauhaus art for Calcutta audiences. And the actor and producer Himanshu Rai hired German director Franz Osten to help establish the Bombay Talkies film studios in Bombay. These exemplary encounters—

just a few of the knotted itineraries considered in this book—occurred across disciplines ranging from the sciences to the creative arts and humanities. And these threads of travel and thought point to an underlying pattern of entanglement specific to the 1880–1945 period.

By combining the specific study of intellectual and social encounters with the study of broader historical contexts, we put detail in its rightful place in the study of transnational history, avoiding facile assumptions about "global" sameness so as to trace the relations between differences. The period from 1945 until about 1960 gave rise to a new international dialogic order regulated by superpower rivalry. It was very different from what had existed in the period from about 1880 onward. The reconstruction of Europe, on one hand, and the rise of the Third World construct, on the other, confirmed the end of German–Indian entanglements in the political register they had once assumed. German–Indian interactions increasingly took the form of one-way donations of Western development aid to Third World peoples. The new normative paradigm was so powerful that it obscured the memory of the previous half-century of volatile entanglement and interdependence borne of late nineteenth-century transnational encounter, while also reconstructing the ideals of the Enlightenment, and the dialectics of Westernness as the engines of modern history. The West, now emblematized by the United States of America, asserted itself as a hegemonic aspirational category after 1945. Other kinds of aspirational categories and geographies thrived in people's minds in the preceding age of entanglement, 1880–1945.

The intensity of German–Indian interactions in the 1880–1945 period registers a seismic, though temporary, shift in international politics that distinguished it from the period before or the decades after. An age of global entanglement and recombination of identities and political power rose and fell between the nineteenth-century decline of the ideal of Europe and the post–World War II reconstruction of that ideal.

The *Age of Entanglement* is an entanglement of histories, and of historiographies, that describes and analyzes the global convolutions of decades when Fausts and Nāyaks—self-proclaimed German and Indian heroes of science and scholarship—arrayed themselves against the mythic archetype of the Anglo-Saxon "gentlemanly capitalist." German and Indian intellectuals found much to discuss when resistance to and rivalry with the global power of the British empire was still a galvanizing force in intellectual politics.

Stages of Entanglement

ONE

German Servants of the British Raj

German interactions with India date back more than 500 years and took place outside the bounds of a formal imperial relationship.[1] But the institutions of the British empire, and the place of Germans and Austrians within it, set the stage and established the parameters for sustained German–Indian historical entanglements that operated not at the level of occasional individual interactions and mere curiosity, but at the level of political interests and societal forces. German Orientalists may have never enjoyed firsthand the Orientalist grandeur of the British and the French empires, but they certainly contributed greatly to practices of British overseas empire in their role as service intellectuals, long before German projects in overseas empire-building ever began.[2]

Over the course of the eighteenth and nineteenth centuries, Europe's global identity developed around the competition between the two foremost European powers, Britain and France, followed by Britain's eventual supremacy in the period from the fall of Napoleon to the rise of Gladstone. The international order of Europe was transformed in the years from 1815 to 1819, from the concluding chapter in the Napoleonic Wars and the Congress of Vienna, to the Carlsbad Decrees that began the European "restoration." The Congress of Vienna of 1814–1815 lay the groundwork for a return to "stability from above," and the longest stretch of international peace in Europe since the Westphalian treaties. Over 200 delegates from almost every polity in Europe attended the conference convened by Prince Metternich. The conference established the parameters of European international law based on a condominium among "Great Powers," and a "concert" of their interests determined by their relative imperial strengths.[3] After 1815, Britain became the unquestioned dominant power at the center of the new international system.[4] Arrayed around British and French international dominance, and based on their imperial strength, the "Concert of Europe" began a crescendo in the 1830s and 1840s, persisted through the imperial competitions of the 1850s in the Crimea, and entered into a diminuendo by the 1880s.[5]

Heinrich Heine forcefully attested in 1844 that German-speakers, despite their geographic location within Europe and their contributions to the intellectual enterprises of the eighteenth century, felt themselves to be marginal to the ideal of "Europe" because of their late industrialization and the fragmented nature of the German polities. "The French and Russians have shared out the land," he jested," Britannia rules the oceans. We reign unchallenged in the realm of dreams and abstract notions."[6] Germans, lacking the industrializing process in any great measure in the early nineteenth century, felt themselves to be lagging behind the societies of the northwest European industrializing core. The hold of the old aristocracies and the German hometowns produced a strong sense of political backwardness and marginality. The "allochrony" that Johannes Fabian spoke about as a way that Europeans "denied coevalness" to colonial subjects seems to apply to the self-othering of Europeans within Europe as well.[7] If Europeanness was an aspirational identity, Friedrich Nietzsche diagnosed the pervading problem of *ressentiment* and Euro-inferiority among German-speakers in 1888: "how much tiresome heaviness, lameness, dampness, dressing gown dilatoriness—how much *beer* there is in the German intellect!"[8]

During the springtime of an enlightened European expansion in the world, spanning twenty-five years on either side of 1800, German nationalists often spoke of themselves as backward, and as suffering the arrested development imposed by absolutism and political fragmentation. In the early nineteenth century, German-speaking intellectuals sought alternative paths to grandeur and respect within the comity of enlightened folk. They turned to the East and to Orientalist scholarship as a way to contribute in the exploits of the foremost imperial powers.[9] The kind of Orientalist knowledge they produced through their Germanic philosophical and Orientalist pursuits also served to give the backward Germans a new geopolitical "soft power" to claim distinction vis-à-vis the powers to the west, Britain and France. Over the course of most of the nineteenth century, Orientalism, and the enchantments it produced, allowed the backward-leaning German nationalists to spring forward. It provided German nationalists a path both to bond with the heroic civilizational discourses of British world power, as well as a means to claim distinction for Germans as the most profound knowers of the East.

In 1771, Georg Forster and his father embarked on an expedition with Captain James Cook, the famed British explorer. The Forsters, a peripatetic family of German writers, traced their lineage back to Yorkshire.[10] A minor prefigurement of Darwin's travels on the *Beagle* decades later, theirs was a journey of British and German partnership through an Enlightenment endeavor of exploration in the South Pacific.[11] The team traveled on a ship called the *Resolution*. Forster kept a diary of the trip, and his spinning of European words around the islands and archipelagos visited by the ship provided a means for building an intra-European alliance through the assertion of enlightened European exceptionalism.[12] The Anglophilic Georg Forster, in his writings after the expedition, merged British pursuits and German interests into an integral effort to bring "primitive" peoples under the "public spirit" of Europe.[13] German mimicry of the styles of the English ruling classes, of their gardens, furniture, perfumes, salons, and dress,[14] not to mention the newfangled upper-class German practice of drinking black tea, also reflected the German desire to follow the British on the high seas to world significance.[15] In this period of European alliance-building after more than a century of strife, the roots of German Orientalism—an institution that grew to monumental proportions over the course of the nineteenth century—were steeped in Anglophilia.

German interest in ancient Indian texts grew from fascination with early British scholarship on India and the culture of British colonialism. Surgeons, jurists, lawyers, and army men made up the East India Company's first Orientalists.[16] Through the work of these British explorer-scholars, as well as that of their sundry French counterparts, such as Abraham Hyacinthe Anquetil-Duperron, German scholars first came into contact with ancient Indian and Persian texts.[17] The Orientalists of the British colonial administration in India, individuals such as Sir William Jones, Alexander Hamilton, John Zephaniah Holwell, and Henry Thomas Colebrooke, created the most important conduits of translation and transmission of Indian texts for German-speakers.[18]

After completing Cook's expedition, Georg Forster translated from English into German the two texts of greatest significance to British

Orientalists in the late eighteenth century. From original translations by William Jones, Forster prepared a German selection of the *Bhagavad Gita*, as well as the play, *Sakuntala*, by Kalidasa.[19] An important phase in the rise of a new German Romantic identity, the German appreciation of Sanskritic texts made German elites feel worldly like the world-traveling British, but also culturally distinctive as the foremost European interpreters of the East.[20] German romantics used the texts prepared by British Orientalists as tools to fashion a narrative of their distinct cosmopolitanism, or *Weltbürgerlichkeit*.[21] In the period of the Concert of Europe, groups that felt themselves on the margins of the ideal of "Europe" sought to reenvision the world order through Orientalist sciences and to position themselves as the privileged knowers of it.

The seventeenth- and eighteenth-century fascinations of the French philosophes and British deists with China, Persia, and the Arab lands, were superseded by an unparalleled German fixation on ancient India and Persia in the early nineteenth century. In the first decades of the nineteenth century, German Indologists revealed north India, in addition to ancient Greece, to be an ancient origin point of world civilization.[22] Stimulated by the philological discoveries of ancient texts by British Orientalists, this new Orientalism was chiefly marked by a shift of German attention from the peninsula of southern India to the Himalayan regions of the north. For German Orientalists in the nineteenth and twentieth centuries, the Himalayas would soon become the Sanskritic "navel of the earth," to challenge the Philhellenic "omphalos" of Mount Olympus.[23]

The rise of a new kind of enchanted Orientalism among German-speaking thinkers at the beginning of the nineteenth century took place within the integuments of rising British imperial force in India. In 1808, Friedrich Schlegel published his book *Über die Sprache und Weisheit der Indier*, in which he made radical claims about the relation between Sanskrit and European languages, highly inspired by William Jones's comparative method. Jones was the first to "claim kin in Calcutta" through the study of historical language families.[24] Going beyond Jones's more sober assertions, Schlegel maintained that Sanskrit was not only within the same language family as Greek, but was the original language out of which Greek emerged. Schlegel's work marked the beginning of a project for new enchantment by German Indologists that located global linguistic and civilizational origins in India. Schlegel's idea about Sanskrit as the original language of the East and the West laid the groundwork for viewing ancient India as a world center of civilization, and Europe as its ancient periphery. This claim was a "soft-powered" geopolitical ploy by German nationalist Orientalists. The special philosophical knowledge German scholars claimed to own about India and the Orient proved the superiority of German philosophies about the origins of world civilization vis-à-vis that of other Europeans.

Friedrich Creuzer, a German nationalist in the period of the Napoleonic invasions and chair in Philology and Ancient History at Heidelberg, published his *Symbolik und Mythologie der alten Völker* (1810–1812) in which he made the heretical proposition that north India was the origin place for the ancient myths of Asian and European civilizations, just as it was the origin of Indo-European languages. In the introduction to his *Symbolik*, Creuzer explained his interest in the comparison of the "figurative languages" of different ancient peoples in order to uncover shared mythological archetypes across the face of the earth.[25] His six-volume book on the genealogy of symbols in world religion began with the priestly castes of ancient India and the cult of Brahma. According to him, Brahmanism contained "simple and profound conceptions, and at the same time, the vast and bold system that explains with some success the religious symbols of most of mankind."[26] Indian deities such as Śiva and Vishnu, mentioned in the Brahmanas and Epics, and mythological symbols such as the lingam or the Kaliyug, became the archetypes for the rest of humankind's myths, including those of the Israelites, Creuzer explained.[27] The world's myths, rooted in Indian religions, began in the Himalayas. India was the center of an ancient world order that threw the modern Europe-centered world order into a world-historical relief. In making such sweeping and controversial claims, Creuzer was announcing a new distinction for German scholarship on the European stage. German comparativism claimed the intellectual power to rearrange knowledge, and upset the unidirectional diffusionist histories of Enlightenment progress.[28]

This power to geopolitically reorganize the history of world civilizations went by the name of "genius" *(Genie)* in German Europe in the nineteenth century—it was the key aspiration at the heart of elite German intellectual life.[29] To approach scholarship not just with the right technique but also with the right philosophy that looked beyond accidental forms and naked facts to the deeper actuality and the original causes preoccupied German thinkers from the time of Friedrich Schlegel to the time of Friedrich Nietzsche and beyond.[30] Comparativist methods provided ways for Germans to assert genius, to make German Europe into a center of knowledge and a source of power even without the overseas imperial trappings of the north-western European powers.

BRITAIN'S NEEDY EMPIRE

Rudyard Kipling tickled the fancy of his Victorian imperial readership when he wrote in 1899, "one of the few advantages that India has over England is a great Knowability."[31] The Victorian worldview was built on more than railroads and shipping lines; it was built on the Enlightenment hubris of universal knowledge of the world. A vast array of mechanical technologies, texts, managerial techniques, biopolitical strategies, and surveillance sciences were used to enhance and legitimate rule overseas.[32] So much so that the British empire had to regularly rely on the technical expertise of consultants in continental Europe in order to supply the needed managerial and scientific services for empire. German institutions across Central Europe supplied salient knowledge to Britons to enhance and expand the colonial project.

Finding the link between German-speakers and Indians need not limit itself to counting the relatively small number of Germans on the subcontinent, or the number of erudite German readers of ancient Indian texts back in the German-speaking countries. A more important, and yet generally understudied, entry point to understanding German–Indian political interactions relates to the overwhelming importance of German philosophies for the consolidation of British rule in India. Although Orientalism lost ground to "Anglicism" in the 1830s, managerial Orientalism returned with new force after 1857, as the British Crown Raj relied heavily on the comparativist methods of insourced German scholarship and consultants to govern the subcontinent as a whole.[33]

Franz Bopp was the most important scholar to cultivate, train, and temper a rising internationally recognized "school" of German Indology that contributed greatly to British empire, with their comparativist theoretical approaches and their search for the common origins of European and Asian languages. Boppian Indology honed the comparative method that envisioned all "Indo-European" languages as equal, parallel developments from a long-lost ancient ur-language. Bopp rejected the Schlegelian search for first origins. He instead focused attention on the codevelopment of different branches in a vast, ramifying language family. Bopp's detailed, comparative study of grammatical structures established "the Indo-European language family" on firm scholarly footing, stimulating the professionalization of Indology in German universities just at the time when Orientalist study in Britain flagged under the influence of Utilitarianism and Liberalism in the 1830s. After the Macaulay years in the 1830s, the British institutional commitment to Orientalist scholarship was largely discontinued.[34] German scholars picked up the slack.[35] A loose Boppian school of German Indologists soon came to provide specialized technical knowledge to British colonial officials, just as British institutions were disinvesting in institutions of Orientalist scholarship at home.[36] Bopp's students, not the least among them, Friedrich Max Müller, served as contractors of Orientalist scholarship both "on the spot" in India and at home in the British metropole. Müller served as the most authoritative Indologist at Oxford, receiving the chair of Comparative Philology in 1868.[37] Other Boppians in British service included Ernst Reinhold Rost as a librarian at the British Museum in London, Hans Roer, librarian at the Asiatic Society of Bengal, and Georg Bühler, originally from Vienna, who served as a library assistant at Windsor Castle before going to India.[38]

German-speakers felt a sense of distinction as intellectual contributors to an enlightened British empire. The first research chair in Sanskrit was established in Britain, at Oxford. And the first holder of the Boden chair was Horace H. Wilson, who had trained with Indian pandits, but not in professionalized academic institutions in Europe.[39] Germans, on the other hand, had been professionalizing the study of Indology for at least two decades. Herman Tull observed that the most renowned Sanskritists were found in German universities in the mid-nineteenth century.[40] Max Müller, in his inaugural lecture at Oxford, commented on the deficiency of British Indological methods. In comparison to British schools, Müller spoke of "[German] universities far more ready to confer academical recognition on new branches of scientific research [than Oxford]."[41] This created the groundwork for an alliance between British imperialism and German Orientalism, he proposed, and confirmed the "consanguinity between England and Germany."[42]

Especially after 1857, in the newly established British Raj, scientific management extended far beyond infrastructural sciences of road building, railroad laying, and canal dredging, into more scholarly programs of professional research, such as Indology, Geology, Forestry, Botany, and Archaeology that aimed to consolidate the intellectual institutions of a British–Indian Raj. But philosophical representations of the meaning of India in the context of British empire, and within the context of world history, only developed in fits and starts.

British colonial administrators looked outside the imperial bond, to third parties in German Europe and elsewhere, in order to supply methods and expertise on how to build up intellectual institutions in India. The British Raj insourced not just technique but, more important, philosophies about India's historical, cultural, and geological significance from the German Orientalist "geniuses."[43] Georg Bühler, Lorenz Kielhorn, and Martin Haug became the three most important bibliographers and paleographers in India, and all three were associated with Elphinstone College in Bombay.[44] Gustav Oppert and Eugen Hultzsch played important roles in the Educational Service of India in the Madras Presidency. Aloys Sprenger, a scholar of Arabic and Persian literature, came from Vienna to India as a medical doctor in 1843. He was named the principal of the Calcutta's prestigious Aliya Madrassa in 1850, after serving as principal of Delhi College.[45] When Sprenger left his position as principal of the madrassa in 1858, the year the British established direct rule, the position was filled by the India-born Indologist and son of German missionaries, Rudolf Hoernle.[46] Another Persianist, Heinrich Blochmann, from Leipzig, traveled to Calcutta as a mercenary of the East India Company, also in the *annus mirabilis* of 1858. He completed studies at Calcutta University, and joined the Aliya Madrassa in 1865 as a professor of Persian and Islamic texts.[47] Rudolf Hoernle led the madrassa until 1899, when the next principal, Aurel Stein, an Austro-Hungarian scholar who had studied with Georg Bühler and proudly thought of himself as an "English Citizen," took over.[48] As much as scholars from German Europe traveled to India to follow their research interests, they also came to fill the needs of the new knowledge-hungry British Raj.[49] German and Austrian Orientalist services, still without their own overseas imperial outlet in Asia, traveled through the military and political circuits of British world power.

IN THE METROPOLIS AND ON THE SPOT

Up to the late nineteenth century, German Indologists in both the British imperial metropole (under Max Müller) and on the spot in India (under Georg Bühler) claimed world-spanning intellectual authority on the back of British rule. German-speaking Indologists engaged in colonial projects as builders of institutions, catalogers of texts, and as revealers of invisible cultural patterns. These two groups differed from and complemented each other in the kind of work they contributed. The metropolitan group, gathered around Max Müller at Oxford, focused on correcting and translating texts. The on-the-spot group of German scholars collecting around Georg Bühler in Bombay occupied itself with acquiring texts from indigenous libraries, dating newly acquired manuscripts, developing catalogs of new sources, and eventually, carrying out archaeological expeditions. Both groups simultaneously contributed to reenvisioning the significance of India in the world as well as making the subcontinent more governable as an imagined cultural and administrative whole.

Müller served as an important cultivator of German talent in the British imperial metropole. For example, among the fifty volumes published in the Sacred Books of the East series supervised by Müller as chief editor, half were edited by German Indologists.[50] Müller enlisted a large group of younger German scholars as his assistants, including Theodor Aufrecht, Julius Eggeling, and Moriz Winternitz.[51] These scholars studied Indian manuscripts in London while serving as assistants to Max Müller. Georg Thibaut, born in Heidelberg, assisted Max Müller at Oxford before taking up a professorship in Sanskrit at Benares College in 1875. Richard Garbe, Hermann Oldenberg, and Heinrich Lüders also worked as Müller's assistants in Oxford before becoming eminent Indologists in Central European institutions.

If Müller worked from Oxford on the translation and publication of texts, German Indologists on the spot in India were especially occupied with paleography, epigraphy, and archaeology—the applied sciences of Indology aimed at discovering new source materials, and eventually justifying new philosophies about the ancient Indic past. More than Max Müller, Georg Bühler became the Indologists' Indologist, responsible for training some of the most important paleographers and archaeologists in nineteenth-century European Indological science. Georg Bühler trained more than thirty scholars from Germany, Austria, Britain, Holland, India, and America, and he fought to find jobs for them on the international market of Indological talent.[52]

Georg Bühler trained at Göttingen University. At age twenty-five, in 1863, he became a professor of Oriental Languages at Elphinstone College in Bombay after his stint as library assistant at Windsor Castle. He soon took on responsibility in the Education Department as an inspector of schools in the Bombay Presidency. Between 1870 and 1880, Bühler published annual reports on the standards of education in India.[53] Alongside Bühler's duties at Elphinstone College and the Education Department, he traveled widely throughout west and north India, acquiring manuscripts for the government from local Indian repositories, such as temples, monasteries, or the royal libraries of princely states. Bühler oversaw the project to acquire texts across Gujarat, the Punjab, and Kashmir for the purpose of building up a unified, rationalized, "enlightened" imperial library and archive. Bühler incorporated manuscripts and tablets from indigenous repositories into libraries owned by the British administration.

By and large, "discovering" new manuscripts meant taking them from collections of indigenous religious and state organizations, especially the collections of Indian princes. Georg Bühler did his job well, and was the first foreigner allowed to examine the princely library at Jaisalmer in Rajasthan.[54] He edited the Bombay Sanskrit series along with his colleague Lorenz Franz Kielhorn. The Bombay Sanskrit series systematically reproduced in print form all Sanskrit manuscripts in Western India known to the British administration. Bühler soon became known as the chief manuscript collector, epigrapher, and paleographer of the British Indian government. So far-reaching was his repute that in 1878 he was one of the first fifty individuals appointed to the Order of the Indian Empire.[55]

Bühler enriched the manuscript holdings of the imperial libraries, adding 2,876 manuscripts to government collections.[56] But he also looked out for the interests of German-speaking academics. He sent newly found manuscripts to German and Austrian universities. In 1873, he began acquiring manuscripts for the Königliche Bibliothek (Royal Library) in Berlin, and over the subsequent four years, shipped 485 Jain manuscripts to Berlin.[57] Both Heinrich Lüders and Richard Pischel called the tenure of Georg Bühler in Bombay, 1863–1881, the turning point for Indological scholarship in German Europe, opening doors for the expansion of professional Indology in German universities at the end of the nineteenth century.[58]

SCIENTIFIC OFFSHOOTS OF ORIENTALISM

German Orientalist scholarship uncovered not only textual and philological but also ecological, geological, and cultural frameworks within which the Indian subcontinent served as the focal point. Asserting power to see

India as part of a historical, cultural, and geophysical whole emerged as a feature of Britain's new, more grandiloquent, approach to rule in India after the establishment of the Raj. By linking India westward along the Hindu Kush and Altai mountain ranges, and eastward to the Taklamakan Desert and to the deltaic floodplains of Bengal and Burma, Orientalist natural and human sciences sought to reveal an underlying order to Asia. Comparativism made India look monumental, and the monumentality of the colonial possession made the British empire look more grand.

In 1854, three Bavarian brothers, Robert, Hermann, and Adolf Schlagintweit, under a commission from the India Office, began a project to reveal India as an integral interregional whole, culminating in their multivolume work, *Results of a Scientific Mission to India and High Asia* (1861). They completed the first all-India attempt to simultaneously survey the ethnography and natural geography of the subcontinent. The Schlagintweit survey recorded topological, magnetic, ethnographic, climatic, and barometric data taken from stations across the mountain ranges of the Himalaya, Karakorum, and Kunlun, and stretching down the Deccan to Sri Lanka.[59] The survey was dedicated to the Royal Society, and jointly funded by the King of Prussia and the East India Company. The Schlagintweit mission, 1854–1858, became a new standard for future British imperial work in geological, archaeological, and ethnographic surveying and intelligence gathering, setting a model for a slew of joint ethnographic and geographic survey trips by groups of British government officials over the coming four decades.[60] The eldest brother, Hermann Schlagintweit, had already visited the American Midwest where he wrote on the culture of the Mormons. The massive geographies of the American West and the Indian North constituted the two bookends of the earth for many German nineteenth-century travelers, such as Hermann, and the pairing of America and India in German world imaginings continued well into the twentieth century.[61]

The Schlagintweit mission was a diplomatic gesture, as no one other than Alexander von Humboldt communicated to the East India Company the willingness of Frederick William IV of Prussia to sponsor this major scientific mission.[62] Alexander von Humboldt's comparativist approach in his epic multivolume work, *Kosmos* (1845–1862), and his search to reveal *Naturganzen*, or interregional natural wholes, within which particular terrains cohered, directly influenced the Schlagintweit brothers. Humboldt was, for many Germans, a "New Columbus." The Schlagintweits were his Asiatic epigones.[63]

Scholars trained in German methods also took the lead in the archaeological study of Indian artifacts and the surveillance of the frontiers of
British India. The most important German-trained archaeologist for the
Raj was Aurel Stein. He brought the techniques and philosophies of Central European archaeological science to bear on British imperial research.
Aurel Stein was born in Budapest in 1862. He went to Leipzig in 1879 to
hear lectures by Georg Bühler.[64] Stein then traveled to Tübingen to complete his dissertation under Rudolf von Roth, professor of Indo-European
languages. Thereafter, Stein traveled to Britain in 1884, studied with Max
Müller, working on Sanskrit texts at the Bodleian Library at Oxford and at
the archives of the East India House.[65] After military service in Hungary,
he returned to London and assisted Reinhold Rost, a German-born Orientalist and librarian at the India Office Library. Stein met both Monier
Monier-Williams and Henry Yule, coauthors of the *Hobson-Jobson: A Glossary of Colloquial Anglo-Indian Words.* Through Yule, Stein heard of an
open position in the Punjab as registrar at Punjab University and principal
of Oriental College in Lahore.[66] Now in India, his first work was to compile
a catalog of manuscripts in the library of the Raghunathan Temple in Kashmir. In 1892, he published what came to be regarded as the most extensive
and scholarly English translation of Kalhana's *Rajatarangini,* or *Chronicle
of the Kings of Kashmir.* In 1896, he published a collection of Kashmiri
folktales recited by a professional storyteller, Hatim Tilawon.[67] And in 1900,
having served as principal of Calcutta Madrassa, Aurel Stein made his first
expedition from Calcutta to Khotan, greatly inspired by the earlier explorations of Sven Hedin and the travelogues of Huen Tsian.[68]

In 1902, Stein set out on his expedition to the Turfan oasis in Eastern
Turkistan on the frontier between British India, Russia, and China. This
would become the first of four prolific and internationally renowned archaeological digs, all under the aegis of the British empire and carried out
at the height of the Great Game. Stein returned with a valuable collection
of paintings, sculptures, and manuscripts that shed light on cultural continuities and the ancient history of peoples across the Himalayan valleys.[69]
Stein made other surveillance trips to Tibet, Balkh, and the Lop Desert
and the valley of the thousand Buddhas where he obtained a horde of sacred
manuscripts in March 1907. He envisioned the Taklamakan Desert and
the Tarim basin as part of an enchanted, integral, ancient Buddhist cultural world that also incorporated north India.[70] At the end of his exceptionally long active research life, Stein contributed new aerial photographic

surveying techniques to British intelligence gathering in Iraq and the Transjordan in 1938–1939, and in the Swat Valley in 1941–1942.[71]

Moriz Winternitz, an Austrian Indologist at Charles University in Prague who served on the examination board of the Indian Civil Service, believed archaeologists, like philologists, were in the business of revealing cultural wholes, invisible to the contemporary eye. This use of scientific methods to disclose invisible holism, believed Winternitz, was the great contribution of German Orientalism to European empire building. When confronted with a jumble of ancient texts not bearing dates or attributions, written in dead languages, the project of revealing the contours of the ancient cultural world that produced those texts matched the work of a natural scientist revealing "truths" about natural history. Winternitz mused, in a fashion both Alexander von Humboldt and Max Müller would have appreciated, "that Sanskrit literature would be made less and less a domain of chaos, that some benchmarks have already been established, that these cannot be overturned, provides us with the hope that one day we will have a cosmos before us, instead of the chaos . . ."[72]

If German scholars were busy collecting archaeological objects, cataloging dead or ritual languages, building up imperial library repositories of ancient texts, and integrating them into enchanted visions of civilizational holism all for the benefit of the British empire, they also turned their attention to the living regional languages of the subcontinent. George Abraham Grierson in carrying out the Linguistic Survey of India relied heavily on German expertise.[73] Grierson enlisted a young Norwegian scholar trained at Halle, Sten Konow, to prepare five of the nineteen volumes of the linguistic survey of India.[74] Grierson's contacts in German-speaking academia, especially Ernst Windisch in Dresden and Wilhelm Schmidt in Vienna, had recommended Konow to the Linguistic Survey, and from 1906 to 1908, Konow also served as epigrapher to the Archaeological Survey of India.[75] The portion of the Linguistic Survey of India on the Bay of Bengal region was almost exclusively based on German-language scholarship. Wilhelm Schmidt, a Viennese Jesuit priest, was a world expert on the languages of the Bengal-Burmese deltaic region. And the school around him, including Robert von Heine-Geldern, as well as the Austrian Jesuits, Johann B. Hoffmann and Arthur van Emelen, consulted with Grierson on the Linguistic Survey.[76]

Ulrike Kirchberger describes German geographers and geologists as the "Wegbereiter," or pathfinders, of British overseas expansion.[77] Geology and botany, not to mention cartography, were disciplines in which German-speakers made further significant contributions to the knowledgeable Raj. In the field of geology, the colonial administration made concerted efforts to recruit experts especially from German-speaking universities for the new Geological Survey of India in the 1860s and 1870s.[78] In 1861, Thomas Oldham, the inaugural superintendent of the Geological Survey of India, visited Vienna with the purpose of recruiting four new staff members for the Geological Survey.[79] Carl Diener, from Vienna, studied geology and paleontology and specialized in the fossils of the Himalayas and eventually became the head of geology in British India after Oldham's retirement. In 1878, the Austrian geologist Carl Griesbach (1847–1907) became assistant superintendent of the Geological Survey of India in Calcutta, and then went on to serve as superintendent from 1894 to 1903.

Ferdinand Stoliczka, a Moravian botanist trained at Vienna University, left Vienna for India in 1864 to join the Botanical Survey. He was named an honorary natural history secretary of the Asiatic Society of Bengal.[80] Wilhelm Waagen, also from Vienna University, worked in the Geological Survey and wrote on the Jurassic fauna of Gujarat.[81] Another Austrian botanist, Otto Stapf, became the assistant for Indian plants at the Kew Herbarium in London in 1890, and wrote an index of Indian ferns. Fritz Noetling served in the Geological Survey of India from the late 1880s to 1905.[82] Victor Uhling and Erich Spengler worked in India at the Indian Geological Survey between 1860 and 1890. The German topographer, Wilhelm Filchner (1877–1957), served as the head of the Magnetic Survey of Nepal, and led geophysical expeditions to Tibet in 1903. Bernhard Schmitt, a German missionary in Madras, published a work on Indian plants, while Immanuel Pfleiderer came to India as a missionary, and published his work on *Glimpses into the Life of Indian Plants* (1908).[83] British colonial geology and botany, at the level of scholarly administration, was a heavily German affair.

Vienna of the late nineteenth-century *Ringstraße* era was a world capital of geological and natural history research, as it was for art historical and anthropological research.[54] Eduard Suess, the eminent geologist at Vienna University, although he never stepped foot in India, popularized the influential theory of an ur-ocean, the Tethys, and an ur-continent, Gondwana, out of which he said the Indian subcontinent had emerged.[85] Suess's five-volume *Antlitz der Erde* (*The Face of the Earth*, 1893), styled after Humboldt's *Kosmos*, presented the earth as a system of oceans, not landmasses, and sought to describe the geophysical qualities of volcanoes, mountain ranges, deserts, and seas in their paleological historical perspective.[86] His text became required reading among British imperial geologists.

Suess's arguments about an ur-continent predating the Indian landmass drew on the work of German-speaking scholars in the Geological Survey of India. Ottokar Feistmantel published his four-volume treatise on the flora of the "Gondwana system" in 1876, arguing that the origins of India's plant life were shared with Antarctica, South America, and Australia.[87] German-speaking geologists and botanists focused their attention on northern India, and viewed the Himalayas as an almost magical bridge between the present and the prehistoric past. A similar fascination had long inspired German modes of comparative Indology, which saw not flora and fauna, but language, myth, and cultural artifacts, as umbilically anchored in the ranges of the Himalayas.[88]

The German sciences in India branched in still other directions. Dietrich Brandis, born in Bonn in 1824, envisioned the Indian subcontinent as an interconnected system of forests and woods. He trained in Botany at Göttingen and Bonn and joined the Indian service at age thirty-two in 1856. With a recommendation from Alexander von Humboldt, and the support of Governor-General Dalhousie, Brandis was named the first superintendent of the forests of Burma.[89] Brandis became the inaugural superintendent of Indian forests in 1864, appointed in order to solve nagging problems of mismanagement. The large-scale, unsystematic destruction of forests to supply wood for railway sleepers caused alarm in the colonial administration and the fear of an unsustainable demand for timber.[90] In total, Brandis spent twenty years in India, eventually accepting a position at Bonn University in 1883. He later joined the Cooper's Hill College in England from 1888 to 1896. In 1900, Brandis published his work, *Indian Trees*, a botanical encyclopedia. His theories of forest management became writ for the colonial administration.[91]

British colonial authorities appealed to Brandis's expertise and that of his German-speaking assistants to establish a scientific system for felling trees and for reclaiming forestland for agriculture. Ramachandra Guha notes that in the 1860s and 1870s, forest resources were so depleted in India that wood had to be imported from Europe.[92] Brandis developed a plan to make indigenous trees the main source for railway sleepers by sourcing Himalayan pines. Furthermore, he argued that "in selecting trees to be felled . . . more regard should be handed to the reproduction of the forest," and that a rotating system of felling should be instituted to allow for exploiting timber resources "without endangering the reproduction of the Forests."[93] Often enough, Brandis complained about the "narrow-mindedness" of the government, and rued the constant demand for surplus forest revenue.[94] Yet, Brandis and the forestry department also argued that a government monopoly on forestland was necessary in order to ensure successful planning.[95] Brandis insisted on the ultimate "right of conquest" held by the colonial state over the customary rights of forest dwellers.

In 1866, Brandis first recommended to the British Indian government that the model of forest administration in Germany should be used to train Indian forest officers.[96] In 1873, he wrote a memorandum in which he listed different continental European forests to be visited on a syllabus of practical study by British recruits to the Forestry Survey.[97] And in that same year, one of Brandis's assistants in India, Gustav Mann, published his textbook, *Extracts from a Report on Forest Management in Hanover and the Black Forest*.[98] Significantly, Brandis cultivated a group of German foresters around him who played an important role in institutionalizing Central European scholarship within the Indian Forestry Department. Wilhelm Schlich, who became the inspector general of forests to the government of India after Brandis's retirement, Gustav Mann, the assistant conservator of forests in Bengal, and Berthold Ribbentrop, special assistant conservator of forests, all worked under Brandis.[99]

The role of German-speakers as managers of British imperial science raised few eyebrows in the metropole in the period of Victorian self-confidence. For example, the figure of the German forester was even used to literary effect. That trope served Rudyard Kipling well in his short story, "In the Rukh" (1893), which featured a German forester, Muller, "the Gigantic German who was the head of the Woods and Forests of all India, Head Ranger from Burma to Bombay, [who] had a habit of alighting bat-like without warning from one place to another, and turning up exactly where he was least looked for."[100] The Victorian popular readership encountered the German presence in India as affable intellectual and scholarly service providers offering both technical know-how and philosophical perspectives to grasp India whole for British rule.

And German methods for studying India also had a strong reception among British intellectuals at this time. Henry Maine's work on the comparative study of Hindu legal systems explicitly drew on the comparative and historical methods of German scholarship, and his magnum opus built on German footnotes.[101] Only through the lens of German scholarship, Maine proposed in 1875, did ancient Indian texts appear as "the most exciting, as the freshest, as the fullest of new problems and [as] the promise of new discoveries."[102] Later on, the eminent British geographer and imperial strategist, H. J. Mackinder, explained that while the British were "pioneers" in methods of precise surveying, hydrography and climatology, they "fall so markedly below the foreign and especially the German standard" in terms of the "synthetic and philosophical" and "comparative" approaches to geography.[103] It was common among British scholars by the late Victorian period to think of the German-speaking countries as the benevolent source of philosophy and technique for managing the diversity of Indian geographies, languages, and cultures, and enhancing the strength of Empire.

THE GERMAN MODEL IN INDIA

German scholarship contributed to the British colonial enterprise both by supplying scientific techniques, such as manuscript collection and cataloging experience, paleographical dating, and forestry management, and by introducing comparativist and historicist philosophical perspectives to rearrange all the newly acquired information—India as the focal point of an ancient civilizational and geophysical world. But mastering India's ancient past did not resolve the problem of how to administer the colony's troubled present.

If Germans were taking study tours to an industrializing Britain in the eighteenth century in order to obtain firsthand knowledge of agricultural and economic planning, by the mid-nineteenth century, Britons were traveling to a muscularly industrializing German Europe for lessons in new forms of social and economic planning absent in Britain and its colonies.[104] Germany, in the latter nineteenth century, took the helm as an engineering and planning capital of the world as it sought to catch up with early industrialization and nationalization in Britain and France. This produced a feedback effect for the British empire, as industrial and social policy planners turned with increasing attentiveness to German models in order to develop planning strategies for the Indian colony.[105] Victorian Britons wanted to implement programs to reform and improve Indian society.[106] In order to do this they needed models, and they looked for models on the European continent. British administrators went to Germany to study the workings of educational programs, cooperative societies, artisanal organizations, fisheries, and leatherwork industries.

Long before German unification, the German states began organizing themselves for their industrialization and nationalization, thus inadvertently creating a set of templates for British colonial planning in India in the late nineteenth century.[107] Whether one thinks of the Zollverein movement beginning in the 1810s, or the organization of multitracked education to appeal to students with differing abilities, or ideas about the so-called internal colonization on the eastern frontiers,[108] or the Raiffeisen and Schulze-Delitzsch cooperative finance systems—all of these had the goal not only of reforming society but also of integrating a set of disparate early modern polities into a modern national whole.[109] British colonial administrators saw possible models for India in German methods of organizing political economy in the mid-nineteenth century. German-style social and industrial techniques could improve India and thereby help legitimate imperial rule by enhancing the efficacy of the colonial regime.[110]

Jeremy Bentham founded the University of London in 1829 on the German model in order to encourage scientific research, especially in applied subjects such as engineering.[111] Forty-five years later, Americans began a similar pursuit when Johns Hopkins University was established "for the providing of graduate instruction on the German model" in 1876.[112] As Daniel Rodgers's work shows, the established American Ivy League universities pursued their "Atlantic crossings" from the mid-nineteenth century onward by breaking away from the old patrician education models of Oxford and Cambridge, and adopting the professionalized and bureaucratized scholarly model of continental Europe.[113]

The famed social reformer Matthew Arnold, brother of a colonial administrator, wrote *Higher Schools and Universities in Germany* in 1874, and recommended the reform of British educational institutions along Humboldtian lines.[114] Echoing the findings of the Taunton Commission that met five years earlier, Arnold proposed that because Oxford and Cambridge were still only "hautes lycées," the British student was going off to "Paris, Heidelberg, or Berlin, because England cannot give him what he wants."[115]

Even the British colonial secretary, Joseph Chamberlain, complained in 1902 that Britain was at risk of "[falling] far behind in the race" of the "highest sciences." In that same year, famed British statistician, Karl Pearson, advised in a lecture, "we must aspire to the example of the German polytechnic."[116] Chamberlain's founding of Birmingham University, and the establishment of the London School of Economics in 1895, were partly studies in the emulation of German education.[117] And after completing his position in Curzon's Education Department, Arthur Mayhew returned to Britain with anxieties vis-à-vis Germany. He expressed his concerns by invoking a standard Anglocentric put-down describing German scholarship as overly systematic. "I was convinced, on my return that English schools and Universities, with all their anomalies and lack of arrangements, possessed the vital spark so sadly lacking in the precise systems of Germany . . ."[118] Mayhew assuaged the growing British sense of educational inferiority by asserting the exceptional capacity of Britons for the "vital spark."

German experts and German models played a role in stimulating the nineteenth-century social reform projects in India.[119] "Planning" in colonial India took on a Germanic tinge, as British colonial administrators looked to German methods of public works and city planning for models in administering the Indian colony.[120] It became common in the last quarter of the nineteenth century for British colonial officers to make study tours to continental Europe for advanced training in social entrepreneurship programs. Germany, France, Italy, and Denmark were generally taken as the models of emulation, but the German-speaking countries especially so. For example, the discussion about importing German techniques of cooperative banking to India was at the forefront of Frederick Nicholson's 1895 report on possibilities for "land and agricultural banks" in the Madras Presidency.[121] Frederick Nicholson wrote his two-volume report on continental land banks and cooperatives in 1895–1897, and implored the British Indian administration to "find Raiffeisen" in India.[122] In Indian economic discussion, cooperative banking received a great deal of attention among Indian and British planners and critics alike in the early twentieth century, and was strongly linked to the study of German models. V. Venkatasubbaiya, a member of the Servants of India Society, and Vaikunth Mehta, manager of the Bombay Central Co-operative Bank, in their report to the government in 1918, foregrounded the German model in which village cooperatives were to combine economic organization, financial assistance, and formal and ethical education.[123] Johann B. Hoffmann, a young German Jesuit priest and Indologist, began his own experiments in village cooperatives in Chittagong in the 1890s and later in the Chota Nagpur hill tracks, to the great consternation of colonial authorities.[124]

The science of social reform and economic planning also led British colonial officers to German Europe on other kinds of study tours. Ludwig Trick wrote on German paper production in 1886. E. S. F. Walker was deputized by the Indian Office to make a study tour of tanneries on the continent resulting in his report of 1892.[125] E. E. Fernandez wrote a report on forestry practices in France and Germany in 1897. In 1912, Frederick Nicholson published another memorandum on his study tour to German Europe, this time to explore the organization of German fisheries. There were a number of reports on childhood education from the late nineteenth century that took "the continent," represented by Germany, Sweden, and France, as models.[126] And Patrick Geddes, a Scottish urban planner in India, encouraged the colonial administration to study best practices in public works and public hygiene from the United States, Germany, and France. With the rise of systematic urban planning programs in India in the 1910s and 1920s, the town-planning legislation in German states was taken as an important precedent.[127]

THE SPLINTERING OF ENLIGHTENMENT EMPIRE

The partnership between the British and Germans relied on the universalist signs of Empire, Enlightenment, and Europeanness. But these signs began to disintegrate and fall apart during the imperial competition that emerged in the late nineteenth century. With the founding of the German nation in 1871, and the launch of *Weltpolitik*, or overseas imperial expansion, by the 1890s, Germans were seeking to stand out in the world and to establish their own endpoint in the "civilizing process" thus far defined by British and French cultural and political hegemony.[128] With the establishment of Bismarck's Germany, and the rise of the *Ringstraße* age of the Austro-Hungarian empire, many German-speakers had the sense they were coming into their own in the world, and that their intellectual institutions would play an important role internationally.[129]

Significantly, they were coming into their own not primarily as Europeans, but first and foremost as representatives of Germanic scholarship, and of German-majority empires. Just as the nineteenth century began with a grand project of European alliance building under the auspices of the Enlightenment, and under the northern star of the British empire, by the late nineteenth century, Europe was splitting apart along the fissure lines of its diverse traditions of knowledge and scholarship, and its disparate nationalizing projects—many of which entered into competition with each other.

British and German cousins, King George and Kaiser Wilhelm among them, were on the way to becoming blood enemies. Soon, German and

Indian intellectuals would increasingly see themselves as cousins-in-arms against Anglo-Saxon world power. The cohesive force of the Enlightenment myth of a single triumphant Europe could not hold. After the 1880s rupture, science became fissive, breaking apart the Republic of Letters. German-speakers began to use state power, industrial power, and intellectual power to claim their own place in the sun. New kinds of bonds began to form between German and Indian intellectuals in the context of British rule in India. Something other than a colonial relationship between German Europeans and Asian colonial subjects was at work here—something much more like the relationship between elective kin.

From 1894 onward, under the military guidance of Alfred von Tirpitz, Germany began constructing a naval battle fleet that clearly was meant to challenge the sea supremacy of the British.[130] Given German outspoken moral support of the second Boer War in South Africa and the inflammatory statements made by high-ranking Germans about Egypt, Britain came out of its "isolation," forming a mutual defense pact with Japan, followed by treaties with France (1904) and Russia (1907) in coming years. The German bankrolling of the Baghdad railway beginning in 1896 provided another instance that exacerbated Anglo-German rivalry.[131] Germany began "slicing the Chinese melon" in 1897 when it seized Kiaochow Bay.[132] The German overseas imperial experiment reached its high point in 1905 with the suppression of the Maji Maji Uprising in 1905 in German East Africa, the Herrero Uprising in 1904–1905 in German Southwest Africa, and the Moroccan Crisis in 1905 when Germans attempted to interfere with French imperial control.

German *Weltpolitik*, inaugurated in 1890 by the ascension to the throne of Wilhelm II, was a response to imperatives of imperialist competition and an expanding global economy. The volume of German world trade doubled between 1900 and 1910.[133] Germany became a world industrial center in these years, an importer of raw materials and an exporter of finished goods as well as technology.[134] But a feeling of inferiority laced German foreign policy, not to mention German national identity. German imperial expansion brought on attendant anxieties about the intentions and prowess of Germany's imperial competitors, especially Britain, France, and Russia.[135] In Julius von Pflugk-Harttung's map of "the development of the great cultural spheres [of] 1900," two-thirds of the world terrain was colored red, signifying the British sphere of influence, and the Russian empire took up a quarter of the earth. Germany, a small landlocked territory in the center of the image, was depicted as threatened on all sides.[136] In a 1904 *Gartenlaube* article, "Um die Weltherrschaft" (On world rule), Carl Falkenhort tallied the number of colonial possessions of various European countries. The results were provided in a striking pictogram. The image of a British soldier appeared as a giant, followed in size by images of a Russian and a French soldier. The German figure sat as a dwarf in their company.[137] German political observers, then, were particularly interested that the "old races" of the Orient were awakening, since this could have implications for the imperial status of Germany.

At the end of the nineteenth century, from the 1880s onward, Europe was increasingly de-Europeanized. Europeans often used Orientalist conceptions of Indic Asia in attempts to get away from their own Europeanness, as it had been constructed by Enlightenment discourse over the eighteenth and nineteenth centuries. As with any weapon, the soft power of comparative and historicist scientific methods and philosophies associated with the German study of India could help secure the grip of the British empire, but could also help subvert its rule when used with anticolonial intent.

German practices of science in India soon established pathways for striking intellectual alliances with Indian nationalists. The British empire, as opposed to a binding and unifying force in the world, became a focal point of global antagonism, and this new common enemy created new arrays of alliance. Because the British empire was a globe-straddling entity, its antagonists now could find common ground despite being geographically separated by great distances.

The mottos of *Wissenschaft, Kunst,* and *Technik* (science, art, and technology) would mark the project for German distinction in the world. In the time of *Weltpolitik* under Kaiser Wilhelm II in the 1890s, Germany's empire of scholarship was operating through the travels of German scientists around the world.[138] Paul Rohrbach, who along with Ernst Jäckh and Friedrich Naumann, made up the most formidable publicists for German cultural diplomacy *(Kulturpolitik)* at the turn of the century, proposed that Germany could offer the peoples of the world an alternative to British and French imperial society.[139] By the fin de siècle, German interest was seeking not only territorial expansion, but expansion in the invisible constellations of academic institutions and scholarly prestige around the world.[140] Knowledge, German imperialists emphasized, could be converted to power at the opportune time.

Coordination between German and Indian nationalist intellectuals eventually developed out of the very relays of an earlier German–British partnership. Orientalist interdisciplinary connections between philological study, geological discoveries, botanical exposés, and archaeological excavations marking German scholarship supported the cause of Indian nationalist protest. The German pen in India was like a double-edged sword. Against the backdrop of the vistas of ancient culture unveiled in the works of German-speaking Orientalists, British cultural supremacy could be made to seem illegitimate, placed in the shadow of towering visions of ancient Oriental civilizational grandeur.

Max Müller had once been highly supportive of the colonial system, even denying his Lutheran roots and converting to the Church of England in the 1850s.[141] But by the 1890s, he harped on the apparent superiority of German-language scholarship over the English, and also alluded to the legitimacy of Indian nationalist claims. Meanwhile, Georg Bühler embroiled himself in a scandal tainted with Germanic nationalism in the 1890s as he publicly championed the claims of a younger German archaeologist, Anton Führer, who erroneously claimed to have found the birthplace of Gautama Buddha at Lumbini.[142] Führer's false claims were revealed and Bühler was heavily criticized for promoting Führer's work. Soon thereafter, a disgraced Bühler mysteriously died in the midst of scandal, drowned in the Bodensee. Some thought he was driven to suicide by the embarrassment of his own pro-Germanism and by the "Führer Affair."[143]

Germanic Indological scholarship took Indian scriptural and religious traditions seriously—much more seriously than British scholars could or would. In turn, Indians responded by taking German Orientalist scholarship more seriously than British varieties. German scholarship was written all over the footnotes of late nineteenth- and early twentieth-century Indian nationalist scholars, from Bengal, Bombay, Lahore, Madras, and elsewhere.[144] Indian thinkers marked off Germanic philology as distinct from Anglo-Saxon science. In addition, the intellectual authority of German-speaking scholars in the fields of economics, politics, and history provided Indians with an evidentiary base to challenge many foundational Enlightenment claims of the British empire. German footnotes were mobilized for an intrascientific war by Indians to stand out in the world.

For example, in the 1880s, Bengali archaeologist, Rajendralal Mitra, used the supporting evidence of German philology to buttress his claims about "Indo-Aryan" stone architecture predating the invasion of Alexander.[145]

Mitra's argument proffered a direct critique of the Philhellenic and Anglo-centric views of the leading British archaeologist in India, Alexander Cunningham. German Indology, which had long sought to smash the clay feet of Classicism by asserting the origins of world civilization in Asia, not in the Mediterranean, was used by Mitra to attack imperial Anglocentrism. Meanwhile, P. C. Ray, Bengal's most celebrated chemist and influential nationalist leader, used Bühler's dating of the *Dharmasastra,* Rudolf von Roth's dating of the *Sushruta* (an ancient Sanskrit treatise on surgery), and Hermann Kopp's account of medieval origins of German chemistry, including the alchemy of Paracelsus, to establish the historical stature of "Hindu" chemistry.[146] The alchemical German middle ages, not the philosophical Hellenistic age, provided the main touchstone for his comparison of East and West.[147] Anagarika Dharmapala, the Ceylonese founder of the Maha Bodhi Society, an international Buddhist organization established in 1892, commented on the importance of Otto von Böhtlingk and Albert Weber's dating of Panini's grammar to the period after Buddha, and its significance for establishing the cultural importance of Buddhism in India.[148] These are just a few examples of intellectual alliance-building born of shared rivalries. German and Indian scholars, beginning in the 1880s, forged alliances against the incumbency of Great Britain as the hegemonic emblem of progress on earth, inheritors of the mantle from the Greeks and Romans.

By the late nineteenth century, Germanic scholars had split up with their British big brothers and were beginning to find new fictive kin among Indian nationalists. The kinds of entanglements that would arise were more complex than the colonizer/colonized binary relationship, unsurprising since the relationships of imagined kinship are far more muddy. Germans thought of groups outside Europe in relational terms, in terms of degrees and scales of proximity, not in terms of binary opposition.

TWO

Indian Subjects beyond the British Empire

The partition of Bengal, finally instituted in 1905, intensified an ongoing movement for nationalist resistance against British rule. The *svadeśi* (*sva-deśi* = for the native land, or home country) movement took shape.[1] The movement involved the boycott of foreign manufactured goods in domestic markets, militant attacks on colonial administrators and policemen, and the confident rise of a new kind of Indian anticolonial internationalism expressed as efforts in cultural diplomacy and alliance building outside the British imperial spatial regime.[2] The boycott and the radical militancy have become the focus of histories of *svadeśi* activism.[3] But in the context of the disaggregation of a nineteenth-century ideal of Empire into many competing twentieth-century imperialist visions, we must also grasp the dimensions of Indian anticolonial realpolitik as it sought to use the institutions of rising imperial forces to disrupt British world rule. In the midst of the Russo-Japanese War of 1904–1905, Indian nationalists solicited financial and institutional support for their cause from Japan, especially in terms of inputs of educational, transport, and print capital.[4] Indians also canvassed support among other colonized peoples and other nationalist movements in Morocco, Algeria, southern and eastern Africa, Egypt, Martinique, and China.[5] But given the framework of twentieth-century international politics, major cities in Germany and America became the most important centers for Indian anticolonial internationalism. As Europe fell apart into a Triple Entente led by Britain, France, and Russia aligned against a Triple Alliance led by Germany, Austria-Hungary, and Italy, Indian *svadeśi* internationalists worked to form cultural, educational, and military alliances especially with the great contender of those early decades, Germany. We observe not the apotheosis of concepts of European supremacy and Empire in the lead-up to the Great War, but rather the disintegration of Europe and Empire as universal signs, and the unprecedented political entanglements and conflicts that ensued. Indian nationalists dove headlong into that maelstrom of international politics, hoping to ride the winds out beyond the British world order.

Scholarship commonly assigns the "*svadeśi* era" to a three-year period from 1905 to 1908. Instigated by the partition of Bengal by Lord Curzon, the movement supposedly ended three years later due to massive repression by the colonial state, as well as the ineffectual political practices, including "terrorism" and cultural elitism, of the largely Bengali high-caste Hindu leadership.[6] But by viewing *svadeśi* nationalism within its proper international context, we notice how changing conceptions of the world in the 1905–1908 period actually led to the extension of *svadeśi* politics into the global arena in the following years. Beginning around 1910, Calcutta became an important node within an international network of Indian anticolonialism. In its second phase, from 1910 onward, once anticolonial networks were reconstituted in the aftermath of severe British colonial counterinsurgency measures, *svadeśi* was increasingly a phenomenon of diasporic nationalism, with *svadeśi* activists traveling throughout the world, in a routed, structured way. Despite their far-flung travels, *svadeśi* travelers remained within a transnational political network with those who remained at home in Calcutta and elsewhere in India. The nationalist movement cannot properly be studied without also considering its diaspora.

A highly articulated international imagination developed in the years after 1905, by which time Bengali thinkers saw their own experiences mirrored back in political events that had occurred, or were occurring, in China, Japan, the United States, and Germany. This international imagination produced a new mental map of the world based on comparisons that transgressed the framework of the British empire, in which Indians found affinities with other examples of nationalist struggle. *Svadeśi* activists were, as a group, great travelers. They expanded their struggle for anticolonialism much past the territorial boundaries of India, and established political nodes within a global network of activism.

The *svadeśi* movement was the culmination of a change in nationalist politics that was set in motion in the 1880s. After the period of *bhadralōk*, or Bengali high-caste "gentlemanly" Anglophilia, that marked the period before the 1880s, we see the rise of increasing anticolonial and anti-Anglocentric sentiment, which went along with growing Germanophilia.

Between the 1880s and the 1910s, the Bengali *bhadralōk* imagination transformed from one tied to the spatial regime of British empire to an internationalist mindset that extended beyond empire and forged circuits of travel and dialogue transgressing the imperial frame. In the fin-de-siècle period, 1880–1914, modes of transnational dialogue brought Indian thinkers into conversations with German-speaking intellectuals beyond the construct of Europe.[7] While an earlier generation of Bengali intellectuals, epitomized by Bankim Chandra Chattopadhyaya, spoke of Bengalis as confronted with the sign of *bilāt* (England, the West), Ramananda Chatterjee, of a younger generation, set Bengalis within a broader, more capacious horizon, which he called *bideś*, or the "world abroad."[8]

In his inaugural editorial in the *Modern Review* of December 1907, Ramananda Chatterjee invoked an "international brotherhood" that would destroy British imperialism. "We hold that there is a great international life of thought and action of whose glory Humanity as yet has caught but faint and feeble glimpses."[9] Participation in the international arena, both in terms of political and philosophical debate, inspired many *svadeśi* thinkers.

BRITAIN AS THE AEGIS OF EUROPE

Bengali intellectuals in Calcutta, by the 1830s, positioned themselves as intermediaries between the West and the native. In assuming that identity, the ideal of an abstract, unified Europe was formed in the minds of many Bengali intellectuals. Rammohan Roy, Henry Louis Vivian Derozio, and Ishwar Chandra Vidyasagar all saw themselves as intermediaries between the metropolitan and the native, a position Bankim Chandra Chattopadhyaya later called the *madhijaṣṭhā*, or roughly, the position of the colonial middle classes.[10] In Bengali, the civilizational categories of *bilāti* (English) and *iyurōpiyō* (European), as well as the imperial categories of *ingrez* or *inga* (the English), were used to name the new universality of "the West." The binary framing, the dilemma, of the indigenous versus the Western, was characteristic of the mental map of nineteenth-century Bengali *bhadralōk* political thought.

The last third of the nineteenth century saw the rise of a triumvirate of thinkers, Bhudeb Mukhopadhyay, Bankim Chandra Chattopadhyaya, and

Jogendra Chandra Ghosh, three high-caste intellectuals who invoked England as an apostrophe for the modern world order. They were reared in the Macaulayan Anglicist tradition, as well as in Comtean Positivism.[11] They came of age in the period of Pax Britannica, in a world in which the British empire played the hegemonic role as a symbol of modern Europe-centered universalism. Bhudeb Mukhopadhyay, for example, wrote two school textbooks in succession, *Iṃlander Itihās* (English history, 1862) and *Rōmer Itihās* (Roman history, 1863), linking the modern role of England in the world with the ancient, mythic grandeur of the Roman empire. Both England and Rome were taken to be centers of world civilization.

These later "Bengali renaissance" thinkers, as Sudipta Kaviraj has shown, forged the rudiments of an anticolonial Bengali *bhadralōk* nationalism, in which high-caste Hindu traditions became a repository for cultural resistance to British liberal imperial assimilation.[12] The resistance they envisioned took for granted England, or *bilāt*, as the sign of modern universalism, and this was counterposed in their writings by Hindu tradition, supposedly housed within an inner cultural domain of family life, religious practice, and personal commitment. Bankim spoke most powerfully about the dilemma of being between two worlds, the realm of *vijñān* (science) and the realm of *dharma* (very loosely, religious duty); between an outer domain ruled by the West and an inner domain of spiritual freedom anchored by Hindu culture and duty.[13]

In the early 1870s, Bankim published a series of essays on science (*vijñān*) in his journal, *Baṅgadarśan*. Bankim wrote on discoveries in astronomy, paleontology, and biology by American and European scholars and praised the "European astronomy" of the American scholar, Charles Young.[14] He discussed the bacteriological research of Irish scientist John Tyndall, as well as the work of scientists in France and Belgium attempting to date the age of the earth. He ended one essay arguing for the fusion of the West and the East—the rejection of neither but the harmonious combination of the best of both.[15] "Newton's science, Kalidasa's poetry, Humboldt or Sankaracharya's learning—these are fundamental contributions; Buddha's (*Śākyasiṃha*) wisdom, Akbar's valor, Comte's philosophy are each fundamental pathways," he concluded, establishing a course of reasoning about interculturalism that informed the writings of generations of Bengali *bhadralōk* thinkers after him.[16]

Yet, by the time of his late writings in the 1880s, Bankim began to withdraw from this "East meets West" narrative.[17] The spiritual concept of dharma now became an avenue to critique "Western" science.[18] Bankim contrasted science with the form of knowledge acquisition he claimed was native to Sanskritic tradition, which arose through philosophical contemplation *(darśan)* and cultural discipline *(anuśīlan)*.[19] Bankim asserted a persisting Sanskritic intellectual and cultural world that was both autonomous from and superior to the *vijñān* of the West.

What Subaltern School scholars valuably present as the "moment of departure" of Indian anticolonial nationalism, with the assertion of a "History 2" of cultural sentiment and affect against a "History 1" of Western capitalism, often takes Bankim's writings as principal evidence. In fact, the timbre of Bankimian political discourses of the 1870s and 1880s can be mistakenly taken as the uniform tone of Bengali anticolonial discourse generally, without appreciation for the transformations soon to take place.[20] In particular, the historical watershed of the 1880s remains invisible in an earlier mode of Subalternist analysis. If the sign of Empire came to break down into multiple imperialisms after that decade, and if the sign of Europe came to break down into many European nationalisms, so too did Indian national identity enter a phase of pluralization and multivocality from the 1880s onward—a process that ran in many more directions than the binary "home versus world" framework.

THE NEW INTERNATIONALISM

One of the most significant post-Bankimian statements of a new Indian anticolonial internationalism came in the work of Aurobindo Ghosh. At twenty years old, Aurobindo wrote *New Lamps for Old* (1893), a veritable clarion call by a new generation of colonial Bengali intellectuals. Aurobindo's *New Lamps for Old* emphasized the existential pursuit of new meaning for the modern Indian "self," which would place Indians in an international context and outside the framework of British imperialism. Instead of "eking out [a] scanty wardrobe with the cast-off rags and thread-bare leavings of [the] English masters,"[21] Indians had to transcend the intellectual niche that imperialism prescribed and associate themselves with the world outside. Aurobindo emphasized in 1893 that French politics offered a mirror for Indian anticolonialism. Both political cultures, he claimed, aspired to nationalism and universalism simultaneously. This linking of the inner with the outer, and the national with the universal, was more than a rhetorical strategy. It constituted the rudiments of a new habit of mind.

Young *svadeśi* activists, unlike the patrician colonial intellectuals of an earlier generation such as Bankim Chandra Chattopadhyay, had much in common with the anarchists of French and Russian *Attentat*. Aurobindo expressed great admiration for them, but also with the internationalist intellectual politics of the Japanese Meiji.[22] The effort to use global constellations of scholarship—bringing foreign experts to India and sending Indian scholars on study tour abroad, insourcing and outsourcing simultaneously— allowed Indian nationalists to build up new intellectual authority within an international context and outside a strictly imperial framework. *Svadeśi* intellectuals were attracted to radical post-Enlightenment epistemologies that blended indigenous knowledge traditions, Orientalist fascinations, and scientific discourse, and that challenged the normative claims of British liberal empire as the emblem of the world whole.

In August 1906, Aurobindo Ghosh started his famous *Bande Mataram* nationalist newspaper, which continued publication until mid-1908 when it was shut down by British colonial authorities.[23] The newspaper offered a veritable international compendium of political insurgency in Ireland, China, and Egypt, in addition to a sustained interest in suffrage activism in Britain.[24] But more occurred here than in the wide distribution of news from abroad through telegraphs and newsprint. *Svadeśi* thinkers established circuits of travel and affiliation that especially connected young nationalist Indians with the new industrial world centers of Germany, Japan, and the United States.[25] *Svadeśi* activists viewed Germany, the United States, and Japan as the major late-industrializing powers, and the major models for a muscular nationalism that Indians themselves had to cultivate. Indian fascination with the three industrial late-developers, and Germany especially, did not depend on the actual demographic size of Indian diasporic communities living in Berlin, Tokyo, or New York, but on the perceived goods nationalists believed might flow from making contact with the new strong nations of the twentieth century to loosen the nineteenth-century bonds with Great Britain.[26]

In the years leading up to World War I, Germany played perhaps the most important role as a node of extra-imperial internationalism for Indian nationalists. And the opening of German academic institutions to Indians in the fin de siècle had much to do with the geopolitical objectives of the German state. The Bengal Technical College, established in 1906, began sending students to schools in Japan, the United States, and Germany so they could return home from the foreign mountaintops of science as *kar-*

mabir, or heroes of national uplift. The *svadeśi* movement outside Bengal also made technical education one of its most important projects. J. R. D. Tata laid the groundwork for the nationalist Indian Institute of Science in Bangalore, which opened its doors in 1909 and first began teaching electrical engineering in 1915.[27] By contrast, the government engineering colleges only began to teach electrical engineering to Indian students in the 1930s. *Svadeśi* internationalists set out to insource techniques and expertise to accelerate economic and commercial development in India. They wanted cultural and intellectual replenishment, but also swift improvement in industrial sciences, market growth, and international recognition.

The Kala Bhavan, or the School for Art and Industry at Baroda, also took a lead in nationalist technical education.[28] The school relied on German machines, but more important, on contracting visiting German scientists to set up its programs. Hugo Schumacher, an expert from the giant dye manufacturing concern of Farben Fabriken AG, joined as a professor of chemical technology.[29] Meanwhile a German firm situated in Bombay sponsored scholarships for students to attend the Baroda Kala Bhavan.[30]

In the years leading up to World War I, Germany was portrayed in the *svadeśi* press as the chief geopolitical opponent of Britain, and the country that could best challenge its world power. An article from 1909 foretold the rise of Germany as the "most advanced nation" in the world.[31] Newspaper articles in the *Bande Mataram* newspaper celebrated the development of German naval power,[32] and argued that the hostile image of the German emperor disseminated in British newspapers was the result of British anxiety.[33] Bhikaji Cama, of the diasporic nationalist community in Paris, noted, "Berlin is the capital of the country which, at present, is most hostile in spirit to England."[34] And Manabendranath Roy wrote from New York in 1916, "the Indian people saw in Germany an ally whose interests were identical and in harmony with her own."[35] During the course of the war, there was a widespread belief among ordinary Indians too that Germans would help free India from British rule. In 1915, leaflets circulating in Calcutta pronounced that Britain was covering up the evidence of its impending defeat.[36] Those leaflets, it turned out, were written by Indians living in Berlin and funded by the German Foreign Office.[37]

Asutosh Mukherjee, *svadeśi* diplomat before the fact and nationalist vice-chancellor of Calcutta University, marked his nationalist predilections not in overt political displays, but in his personal habits of dress and his manifest political commitments.[38] Asutosh was responsible in the period from 1906 to 1924 for founding the University Science College of Calcutta University, for creating a spectrum of research chairs across the humanities, social sciences, and experimental sciences, and for reorienting Calcutta University toward nationalist aims right under the nose of anxious colonial administrators in the Education Department.[39] Asutosh Mukherjee, alongside Rabindranath Tagore, was the most important institutionalizer and organizer of intellectual politics in the *svadeśi* era.

In 1919, the Calcutta University Commission, led by a highly respected educational reformer, Michael Sadler, found Calcutta University to be "fundamentally defective."[40] German and American universities were named in the Commission Report as models for possible educational reform in India.[41] This continued a long-standing pattern, as has been noted, by which the British Raj turned to continental institutions and German European experts to resolve apparent deficiencies in knowledge management.

Brajendranath Seal, one of the most respected Bengali academics at the time and principal of Victoria College in Cooch Behar, told the commission: "Continental Universities [are] far more advanced than in English Universities. All University education in the Universities of France and Germany is in the nature of advanced study that lead to some sort of original work after graduation."[42] The 1919 resolution by the commission to study the model of German and American universities with a view to colonial educational reform was actually an echo of the proclamations made in *svadeśi* circles of intellectual politics ever since the turn of the century.

Asutosh Mukherjee had long been captivated by the model of the Humboldtian university, associated with the name of Wilhelm von Humboldt, Prussian minister of public instruction and the founder of Berlin University in 1810. The model of the Humboldtian university was associated with the professionalization of scholarly research, disciplinary specialization, the freedom to choose one's research topics, and autonomy of instructors over their choice of subjects to teach (*Lehrfreiheit*). The Humboldtian model of the research university fascinated *svadeśi* thinkers, especially as it seemed to encourage scholarly radicalism and academic renown.

The Indian nationalist university should not just be a place of applied industrial science alone, Asutosh Mukherjee insisted. The intellectual authority of Indians in an international community of scholars depended on contributions to fundamental knowledge and humanistic research. Asutosh was enamored of the Humboldtian research ethic because it aimed to cultivate intellectual authority. The Humboldtian model of the university could establish a nation's reputation for scholarly excellence and distinction within an international framework in a way that industrial or technical schools could not. The university was to be a center for primary research, allowing Indian researchers space and freedom for original work that did not necessarily relate to pragmatic industrial concerns.

Intellectual authority would earn more than foreign adulation or respect. It went beyond a pursuit of self-esteem and had a pragmatic intent. Growing in intellectual authority also involved growing in the ability to represent the social and physical world, and to use it according to Indian interests. Intellectual authority was needed to become *productive* in the world, and productivity, not dependence on British gifts and rationed provisions, was needed in order to establish a new horizon of meaning for Indian selfhood, these nationalists maintained. Identity formation was caught up with nationalist scholarship.

Asutosh Mukherjee's 1907 university convocation speech laid out a plan for ambitious reforms, in which the university would become a "center for the cultivation and advancement of knowledge," not just an examination and degree-granting institution.[43] "Every Professor must be a student . . . Unless the University can show a substantial amount of research, produced by the aggregate of its Professors, and unless it can show that it has trained a substantial number of able and willing workers to carry on research in the different branches of knowledge, the University can hardly be regarded as approaching the realization of its ideal."[44]

Asutosh Mukherjee organized a program to bring German scholars (and the occasional head of state, such as Prince Wilhelm) to Calcutta University, and to send young scholars to Germany with the expectation that they would return to help run a new nationalist research university according to the Humboldtian ideal. Such a program went far beyond the intentions and the mindset of the British Education Department. Indians gravitated toward German scholarship in the *svadeśi* period because the category of the Germanic stood out from that of the Anglo-Saxon in Indian eyes. Europe was not one but many for *svadeśi* internationalists.

The accomplishments of German Indology, ensconced in British colonial libraries, universities, and manuscript repositories since the 1850s, provided the starting point for Asutosh Mukherjee's fascination with German Europe. In 1912, he commented on the importance of the German style of Indology for Indian nationalists. He observed, "a generation of German Indianists . . . has rapidly extended itself over the whole field of Indian Research."[45] For

Asutosh, the *Germanness* of Orientalist scholarship on India was rooted in the criteria for empirical proof that German scholars employed and how they established their scope of inquiry.[46] At the 1911 convocation address, Asutosh stated, "we have, besides, had occasion to welcome here in our midst quite a number of German Orientalists some of whom have stayed in India as teachers for a long time, eminent men like [Martin] Haug, [Georg] Bühler, [Franz] Kielhorn, and one of our own graduates [Heinrich] Bloch-mann, and we readily acknowledge the excellent work done by these dis-tinguished scholars."[47] He went on to highlight the role of Franz Bopp in creating "totally new insight into the nature of languages."[48] In fact, during the 1910s, there was hardly a Calcutta University convocation address by Asutosh Mukherjee that did not single out German Indological research as the paragon of achievement in scholarship.

During the *svadeśi* years, Calcutta University convocations became cer-emonies to grant German Indologists honorary degrees. Richard Pischel was to receive an honorary degree in 1908, but passed away upon arriving at Madras harbor. Hermann Oldenberg received his honorary degree in January 1913, while Hermann Jacobi received his in December 1913. Praise for German scholarship during the degree ceremonies became a way of criticizing the deficiencies of British colonial science management.[49]

In 1913, in the context of the Balkan wars and the high-water mark of German–British imperial antagonism, Vice-Chancellor Asutosh Mukher-jee made three appointments of Germans to Calcutta University. This placed him on a collision course with British authorities. Otto Strauss, scholar of Buddhist studies, was named to the Sanskrit Department; Peter Brühl, who already taught in the Botany Department, was named univer-sity registrar. And Georg Thibaut, a German Indologist who had studied with Max Müller and traveled to Bombay at the behest of Georg Bühler, was named to the first professorship of Ancient Indian History and Culture.[50]

German academia provided templates and models for *svadeśi* interna-tionalists. An eminent Bengali educationist from this period, P. C. Ray, once remarked, "Germany's national struggle was an educational one."[51] And Asutosh certainly concurred, explaining in his 1915 wartime com-mencement address, "on the present occasion, the thoughts of us, the mem-bers of an Indian University, naturally turn most readily and spontaneously to Germany in one particular aspect—to the Universities of Germany as the chosen homes of learning and research . . . We, therefore, consider it incumbent on us to render ourselves acquainted with the characteristic features and excellences of the learned institutions not of Great Britain only but also of other Western countries; and among the latter, none, indeed, are more worthy of study and emulation than the great German Universities."[52] Benoy Kumar Sarkar, one of Mukherjee's young assistants, commented later, "Asutosh Mukherjee's internationalism, especially his faith in Germany (*Jārmānniṣṭa*), inspired the youth of all India."[53] Asutosh Mukherjee's Germanophilic internationalism flared up in the context of World War I. But only in the decade afterward did his program for anticolonial intellectual politics bear fruit.

Of the seven founding faculty members of the University Science College established by Asutosh Mukherjee in 1915 with private funds from nationalist philanthropists, almost all had obtained PhDs from Germany during the war years. Dhirendranath Chakravarty, Jnanendra Chandra Dasgupta, and Jogendra Kumar Chowdhury traveled to Berlin in 1910 to complete dissertations in chemistry, sponsored by the National Council of Education Bengal and the Indian Association for the Cultivation of Science. Meanwhile, Moreshwar Prabhakar attained his PhD in chemistry from Heidelberg in 1912. He remained in Germany during the war and became an important member of the diasporic nationalist organization in Berlin before his return to Calcutta.[54]

Arabindra Mohan Bose and Debendra Mohan Bose, two nephews of the iconic national scientist, Jagadish Chandra Bose, traveled to Berlin to begin PhDs in physics in 1913. D. M. Bose later became the first chair of Physics at the University Science College upon his return after the war. Presidency College student, Shankar Agharkar, originally from Bombay, was selected to study chemistry at Berlin University in 1914. He spent a number of years in German internment because of the war before being permitted to complete his degree. Agharkar returned to Calcutta as chair of Botany at Calcutta University in 1921. A period of German internment did not seem to sour his sentiments about German scholarship, as throughout the 1920s and 1930s Agharkar made the study of German language mandatory for his graduate students.[55]

Prafullchandra Mitra, having just returned from the University of Berlin in 1921, became the chair of Chemistry at Calcutta University. Ganes Prasad obtained his PhD in mathematics under Felix Klein in Göttingen and returned to Calcutta with a chair at Calcutta University in 1922. Meghnad Saha completed postdoctoral chemistry research in Berlin in 1922 before returning to teach at Calcutta University, and then became the first chair of Physics at the University of Allahabad. Suhrit Chandra Mitra completed his dissertation in psychology at Leipzig in 1926 in order to take up a position at Calcutta University following a reorganization of the university system in that year.[56]

In terms of Indological study, Germany was the favored destination among scholarly internationalists. Jodar Mall, from Lahore, traveled to Bonn to study under Hermann Jacobi. Manekji Davar completed his doctorate in Hebraic and Iranian philology at Berlin University in 1904. And later, Tarachand Roy, from Lahore, went to Leipzig on a state scholarship to complete his dissertation in Sanskrit in 1914. Meanwhile, Satish Chandra Roy finished his dissertation in Indology at Kiel under Paul Deussen in 1914, and Devadatta Ramakrishna Bhandarkar also completed his PhD in Indology at Heidelberg during the war years. Bhandarkar went on to serve as Carmichael Professor of Ancient Indian History at Calcutta University. His father, the renowned Marathi Indologist, Ramakrishna Gopal Bhandarkar, had obtained his doctorate from Göttingen in 1885, where he studied with the German Indologist, Martin Haug, recently returned from India.[57]

Asutosh Mukherjee's Humboldtian project at Calcutta University to create a research university with world-class pretensions, known for its original scholarship, led him to canvass scholars from around the world to join the university in the 1920s. He wasted no time in bringing international scholars to Calcutta. In 1922, Mr. Masuda and Mr. Kimura came from Japan to teach Chinese and Japanese. In 1923, he hired Stella Kramrisch away from Shantiniketan in order to establish Calcutta University's Department of Ancient Indian Art History. The nationalists in the university made special arrangements to expand Indology offerings to include not only the traditional study of Sanskrit and Persian sources but also "the far-reaching field of Buddhistic studies" as well as Tibetan studies. Meanwhile lectures in Indian philosophy were delivered in 1923 by Millicent Mackenzie from the University of Nebraska, and in Indology by the French scholar, Sylvain Levi. Asutosh Mukherjee's efforts in scientific administration at Calcutta University along Humboldtian lines served as an important model for the expansion of research programs elsewhere in India. Dacca University, the University of the Punjab, Benares Hindu College, Alighar University, the Indian Institute of Science in Bangalore, and Allahabad University all took research scholars from Calcutta in the 1920s.[58]

THE INDIAN MEIJI

One of the major aims of these travel itineraries was to make India an international center of intellectual and cultural life in its own right, independent of the British imperial institutions.[59] *Svadeśi* travelers were never just arms-carrying insurgents; they were almost always also students, teachers, authors, and speakers. They were epistemological radicals. The autobiographies and memoirs of a number of Bengali *svadeśi* travelers from the time highlight the relationship between scholarly activity and anticolonial insurgency. In 1922, Bhupendranath Datta recounted his involvement with the Bronx Socialist Club, his experience as a student at New York University, and his meeting with American intellectuals, such as W. E. B. Du Bois. Datta completed his first degree at New York University in 1913, and his doctorate in anthropology at the University of Hamburg in 1922 before returning to India in 1925. Hemendranath Dasgupta, who finished a PhD at the University of Michigan in 1921, wrote in his Bengali autobiography not just about interactions with Americans, but also about collaboration with Burmese radicals in the early twentieth century. And if Hemchandra Kanungo and his friend, Bapat, traveled to Paris to learn bomb-making techniques from French anarchists, they also met intellectuals and writers along the way in Colombo, San Francisco, New York, and London.[60] Kalidas Nag published his diaries from his years of PhD study in Paris in 1923–1924, during which time he went on study tour across continental Europe and met European anticolonial activists, such as Romain Rolland. And Abinash Chandra Bhattacharya, who temporarily settled in Berlin during World War I, recalled the dynamic teaching and publishing programs of Shyamji Krishnavarma in London, Bhikaji Cama in Paris, and Virendranath Chattopadhyaya in Berlin.[61]

The *svadeśi* movement used foreign relations beyond the British empire to effect domestic change. The travels of *svadeśi* itinerants buttressed the radical intellectual politics at home. Companies such as Bengal Pottery Works, Dabur, Duckback, and Bengal Chemicals arose as highly successful *svadeśi* enterprises, combining a "back-to-roots" ethic with the internationalist search for foreign technique and expertise. Bengal Pottery Works made terra-cotta, porcelain, and earthenware. Satyasundar Dev started the enterprise in 1906 after completing an apprenticeship in Berlin at the *Königliche Porzellanmanufaktur.*[62] The Bengal and Assam Pharmaceutical and Chemical Works, also established in 1906, arose from the work of nationalist scientist, P. C. Ray. P. C. Ray developed his company's lab products using foreign manuals and techniques obtained during his travels abroad to Europe and Japan.[63] Meanwhile B. N. Dasgupta, as an employee of Bengal Chemicals, traveled to Berlin in 1910 in order to complete his PhD in chemistry. A number of Bengal Chemicals' early top researchers also studied in Berlin, the world capital of chemical research, before returning to Calcutta with their German wives. Indian intellectual politics utilized foreign study tours and education in order to serve nationalist interests.[64]

The organization of student travel was a central objective of the Bengal National Council of Education (NCE) between 1910 and 1919.[65] Among the thirty sponsored studentships during that period, nineteen were sent to the United States, eight were sent to Germany, and six were sent to Britain. Upon closer investigation, we see a pattern in the way the NCE organized the study travel of its students. Almost all of the students sent to Germany obtained doctorates in chemistry, physics, or chemical engineering. Almost all the U.S.-bound students obtained higher degrees in the social sciences, such as economics, political science, and psychology. And almost all of the students sent to England, the smallest contingent in the group, studied industrial engineering.[66] Nationalist intellectual politics used foreign educational institutions, especially in the United States and Germany, in order to build up national programs in higher education—the sciences, arts, and humanities—at home.

The importance of America and Germany, alongside Japan, in the internationalist project of Indian *svadeśi* activists cannot be underestimated. In this post-Bankimian period of intellectual politics, Indian nationalists turned from imperial to international horizons. And within that international system, German institutions stood out as locales for acquiring technical skill and new kinds of scientific methods for an age in which Europe, and the ideal of a single Enlightenment universalism centered around the New Rome of British empire, was falling apart. "The German system of national education has been exercising greater influence on the organization and politics of modern times than any other system," wrote one observer in 1910.[67] Lala Hardayal, who lived for a time in Berlin, implored the Bengali youth to start learning German and French, for it was in these languages that a "very large proportion of modern research and intercommunication is carried on." Hardayal continued, "German is the language of science and research. Many of the books that are by students in England are mere translations from German."[68] Indian nationalists, in speaking about German-speaking Europe in such ways and traveling to its cities and institutions, were also registering the drastic change in the world order taking place in a post-Enlightenment age—in an age of entanglement.

THREE

German Visions of an Asianate Europe

Beginning officially in 1884 and occurring mostly within a fitful six years during the 1890s, Germany acquired colonial possession in coastal China, South-West Africa, East Africa, the Cameroon, and Togoland.[1] It also obtained territories in the Pacific, including Kaiser Wilhelmsland in New Guinea, and a number of islands in the Bismarck Archipelago.[2] The Britain–Germany relationship was already chilly when Queen Victoria was still alive, but it became overtly antagonistic and reached a symbolic watershed moment with the queen's death in 1901.[3] The struggle for the Middle East and the "Scramble for Africa" in the 1880s was followed by a "Scramble for Asia" in the following decade. The German overseas imperial experiment reached its high point, or perhaps its nadir, in 1905 with the suppression of the Maji Maji Uprising in German East Africa, the Herrero Uprising in German South West Africa, and the Moroccan Crisis when Germans attempted to interfere with French imperial control. German-speaking scholars went from being admirers of British imperial strength to being putative imperial "lords" in their own right. If Georg Forster in 1778 had nothing but admiration and awe for Captain Cook, as his travel narrative concluded with his finally joining Cook as a partner in the "discovery" on Ascension Island,[4] a later German scholar-traveler, Hermann Keyserling, in 1911 sarcastically spoke of the "dearth of [English] talents, the limitation of their horizon and the measure of recognition which every one of them extracts from me. . . . They alone are really perfect amongst all Europeans, and to their perfection every one bows the knee."[5] To parse this statement, and to understand the souring of feelings from Georg Forster to

Hermann Keyserling, we need to unravel the interworkings of German popular and scholarly discourses in the context of rising German imperialism in the late nineteenth century.[6]

Germans and Indians met at the intersection of British and German imperial competition in the late nineteenth and early twentieth centuries. Germans increasingly used images of Indic Asianness to break down the idea of Europe as a geopolitical domain organized around British world power. This process was driven by popular culture and percolated up into the realm of statecraft and elite intellectual discussions. Popular culture in Germany, not just the actions of scholarly elites, requires our close investigation in order to understand the de-Europeanizing process taking place over the course of the 1880–1945 period. Popularization, and what Norbert Elias called the "informalization" of society, meant that everyday Germans could claim intellectual authority to speak about the world in purportedly revealing and insightful ways.[7]

The cultural and philosophical resources of Indian civilization, as seen through German eyes, provided everyday Germans with resources to claim social distinction. Germans used Indian Asianness in order to make themselves stand out against the nineteenth-century aspirational norm of "the European," embodied in the image of the English gentleman or the French cosmopolitan. And the search for German distinction also had a gendered aspect, as women in popular culture led movements in Orientalist knowledge and aesthetics in order to break down the nineteenth-century norms of politics and art organized around bourgeois European men. The entanglement of German and Indian history, and the bonding of Germans and Indians as cousins-in-arms against British world power, was as much the product of pop culture as it was the result of university erudition.

Karl Bleibtreu, one of the many best-selling middlebrow intellectuals who wrote for a mass readership in the late nineteenth century, published *From Robespierre to the Buddha* in 1899, a collection of essays about radicalism in European nineteenth-century thought.[8] The end of Bleibtreu's book concluded with a series of essays on Buddhism, with the final chapter "Buddhism: Religion of the Future." Bleibtreu drew a parallel between the era of the French Revolution in the late eighteenth century, and the "new world order" at the end of the nineteenth century.[9] An intellectual revolution was afoot throughout Europe, he argued, centered in Germany, in which normative notions of history and Christian salvation were being supplanted by new worldviews; in which concepts of "eternal return," reincarnation, karma, and the rejection of the supposedly Judeo-Christian distinction between "good and evil" were on the ascent.

Bleibtreu was speaking, in the language of popular culture, of a rising post-Enlightenment. The rise of a post-Enlightenment age would emerge through many interpretive acts of German popular writers, and the 400 blows of popular modernism before engulfing lecture halls and academic research agendas. In the post-Enlightenment that welled up in the German-speaking lands at the fin de siècle, India—ancient and contemporary—was increasingly identified as a center of intellectual revolution and a world reservoir for geopolitical change.

The mountainous cultural geography of ancient India and Persia represented an archaic center of the world for German philologists and archaeologists over the course of the nineteenth century. By the late nineteenth century, Orientalism had left the study rooms of German universities and come onto the streets. It was not only through philological study, topographical surveys, and archaeology that the sacred domain of the Himalayas was explored and exploited for the German imagination. At the fin de siècle, popular Orientalists rediscovered the region as a site of planetary distinction. Going to that region either through physical travels or flights of imagination allowed Germans without PhDs or professionalized academic authority to nevertheless create authoritative meaning about the world via Asia.

In the 1920s, expressionist artists traveled to the Gangetic plains and Himalayan ranges of India in search of the spirit of the Vedic gods and the Buddha.[10] The Himalayas became the focus of German mountaineering expeditions, artist retreats, and, eventually, documentary and feature films.[11] Explorers such as Peter Aufschnaiter and Matthias Zurbriggen orchestrated well-publicized mountaineering expeditions to the Himalayas.[12] By the 1930s camera crews recorded documentaries of German mountaineers in Himalaya films such as Günter O. Dyhrenfurth's 1935 *Der Dämon der Himalaya* and Frank Leberecht's 1938 *Der Kampf um den Himalaya*, at the very same time as German scientific missions to the Himalayas brought back a vast quantity of new cultural materials.[13] The use of new media, especially art and cinematography, as well as popular writing, put the power of Orientalist enchantment in the hands of everyday woman and everyday man.

The Aryan Orient became a new Archimedean point to ground German popular identity in the world.[14] What has been described as a rampant unmooring of Germans from the best in European culture was really an attempt to reground the ancient origins of Germanness outside the conventional ideas about European primordial homelands in the Semitic Orient of the biblical lands, and to define a realm of German cultural empire against the contemporary fiscal, cultural, and imperial centers of northwestern Europe.[15] Counterculture and geopolitics propelled the rise of popular Orientalism.

And as Orientalism spread through popular culture in travelogues, popular novels, and film, representations of India were concentrated and made more acute. German-speakers became intellectually, emotionally, and personally involved in these projections about the subcontinent. This period of heightened entanglement between Germans and Indians from the 1880s to 1945 did not dissipate images and stereotypes, but rather enhanced them.[16]

SIBLING ENVY AND RIVALRY

Ever since the mid-nineteenth century, German-speakers, informed both by imperialist ardor and curiosity, felt an increasing degree of sibling rivalry with, as well as envy of, the British.[17] Paul de Lagarde traveled to London in 1852 to study Oriental manuscripts at the British Museum. He reported that his experience of mixing with the "British public," especially in aristocratic circles, greatly inspired his view of nationalist achievement.[18] Many other major colonial publicists and activists of the 1870s and 1880s began their careers in close connection with the British colonial administration. In the decades after 1871, three of the German *Kaiserreich*'s most vocal *Kolonialpolitiker*, advocates of colonial projects, had personal ties to Britain. Johann Jakob Sturz, a German businessman in Mexico and Brazil, studied engineering in London and worked closely with British advocates for free trade and antislavery regulation in the 1840s.[19] Wilhelm Hübbe-Schleiden, a publicist for German colonial interests in West Africa, had served as attaché to the German General Consulate in London.[20] And Carl Peters, the founder of the Society for German Colonialism and advocate for territorial acquisitions in East Africa, spent more than three years studying in London fascinated by British colonialism.[21] All three German colonial apprentices in London played important roles in defining the scope of Bismarckian interests overseas.[22]

Wilhelm Hübbe-Schleiden framed his arguments for a program in German overseas colonization in terms of catching up with the British, overcoming "passivity," and participating in the "cultivation of humanity" by amassing "sea power."[23] Carl Peters made a point of emphasizing his admiration for British imperialism as well as proposing a strategy for surpassing the British in the practice of colonialism. Germans, he explained, would use "rein wissenschaftliche Forschung" (fundamental scholarly research) as a tool to enhance German claims to overseas terrains and to outmaneuver competitors.[24]

With the advent of large-scale German immigration to the overseas territories and dominions of other European and American powers,[25] itinerant German experts, technicians, and businessmen across the colonial world were becoming self-conscious exponents of German national interests abroad.[26] Germans concentrated on extending what Dirk van Laak has suggestively called "technical internationalism."[27] As Paul Rohrbach, a publicist for German *Weltpolitik* at the turn of the century, put it, not only German capital and labor abroad but also the increasing influence of "German ideas in the world" would ensure German imperial ascendancy.[28]

In the period of Wilhelmine *Weltpolitik,* beginning with the fall of Bismarck and the rise of the young kaiser in the 1890s, the "Germanic" came to be juxtaposed to the category of the "Anglo-Saxon." And yet, the forging of a German imperial identity continually registered images of British dominance. For example, German thinkers Ferdinand Tönnies and Werner Sombart defined the popular conception of German *Kultur* as an equal and opposite reaction to British *Zivilisation.*[29] Alfred Wegener explained, "say what you will of the English, nobody can deny that they are the most experienced and successful colonists in the world. . . . We too have colonies and must learn as beginners. . . ."[30] He went on to praise "the quite extraordinary genius for administration which is peculiar to the English, as it formerly was to the Romans. Their greatest gift is not their business capacity; in that they have rivals. But they are unrivalled in their instinctive ability for organization and government."[31]

In some ways, the German mania for "finding its place in the sun" was an attempt to wrest recognition from the country "on whom the sun never sets." General Tirpitz, for example, justified his incendiary naval policy with the twisted aim of frightening Britain into becoming Germany's friend.[32] Tirpitz's naval extravagancies were echoed by the maritime militarization that the British put into play in 1902, when Admiral Fisher announced his plans to develop a fleet of new gunships, the Dreadnoughts, commanding unprecedented firepower and speed.[33]

Claims about the non-Englishness of German national identity constituted a source of pride, but also a cause of anxiety and envy. Just as steamships and travel technology played an important cameo role in German
popular literature about the Orient, so too did the persistent image of the
British colonial official. In German travel accounts to India, Germans often
mentioned being mistaken for Britons.[34] On the other hand, German travelers repeatedly asserted their difference from the British thanks to the
purported insights of German Orientalism.[35] At the level of international
politics, at least up until the Great War, German military and industrial
interests focused on emulating and surpassing the British ideal.[36]

This same theme of Germans using Orientalism to claim superiority over
the British repeats in the travel account of Hermann Keyserling in 1919. "It
seems to me as if by now [India] does possess me. I experience more and
more in the Indian manner, and more and more do I see the world and life
in the light of the spiritual sun of Hindustan."[37] Here again, the German
could do what the Briton could not. Bernhard Kellermann in his *Meine
Reisen in Asien* (1907) continually documented moments of being taken for
a Briton, only to proudly correct the misconception among his hosts. "When
the Rajah learned that we were not English, he slapped his thighs loudly,
jumped up in the air and began to laugh with joy."[38] Arthur Holitscher recounted his meeting with Gandhi in 1926, when the two "agreed" that
British capitalism could be overcome by spiritual struggle.[39] Again, embedded in German interest in India during this fin de siècle and early twentieth
century was the desire to be like the British, but also to overcome them.
And Orientalist literature was not only about European views of the Asian
other. In the age of imperial competition and twentieth-century European
wars, German Orientalism served a relational purpose, providing ways of
relating to one "other" (the Indic Orient) in order to register difference with
another "other" (Britain).

SCHOPENHAUER'S STAR STATUS

Representations of India, in the form of images, material objects, and cultural practices, permeated German popular culture in the last third of the
nineteenth century. Hindu or Buddhist texts, figurines, painted images,
and artistic impressions served the purpose of distributing the cultural
authority of the ancient Orient within popular culture. This authority of

Indic Orientalism gave everyday German-speakers the sense that they themselves could speak about contemporary cultural and political matters in sage and revelatory terms.

Arthur Schopenhauer was the great figure of extra-academic Indology in the early nineteenth century, and he inadvertently cultivated the mood of popular Indic Orientalism. His was an Orientalism beyond university walls. This "sage of Frankfurt" styled himself after the monks and priests living in the Himalayas, and used such affectation to authorize his claim that the world was divided between the realms of "will and representation."[40] Schopenhauer was a nineteenth-century neologian, with the French *philosophes* and the British deists as his inspiration.[41] Unlike the neologians, however, he not only challenged the traditional authority of Christian tradition, but actually converted to Buddhism. "Buddha, [Meister] Eckhart and I teach, in essence, the same thing," wrote Schopenhauer.[42] His immediate followers also took on a sage-like mood, which carried with it a sense of pessimism and disdain toward bourgeois European economic thrift and pluck, and a disdain for the rise of popular culture.[43]

This was Orientalism as antipopulism—the association of self-cultivation and ascetic introversion with disdain for "the crowd." In Schopenhauer's formulation, the mysticism of the early modern European Christianity of Meister Eckhart and Jakob Böhme provided a transition point in the history of world religions stretching from the Buddha to himself. Schopenhauer claimed to reject the Western religious tradition and turned to the East, thereby setting an extreme example of intra-European theological radicalism.[44] Many latter-day popular followers adapted his mood. Philip Mainländer and Eduard von Hartmann, both midcentury philosophers without university positions, and both eager to find some foothold to look down on normative bourgeois society, appealed to Indic wisdom and to Schopenhauerian posturing in their projects for self-respect.[45] Schopenhauer's claims were also amplified in the works of Friedrich Eugen Neumann, Karl Seidenstucker, Paul Deussen, even Friedrich Nietzsche and Carl Jung in the late nineteenth and early twentieth centuries.[46] Plenty of scholars, including Max Müller, Hermann Oldenberg, and Richard Garbe delved deeply into Sanskrit or Pali texts but maintained their commitment to the universal truth of Christianity.[47] But for Schopenhauer and his followers, the relationship was reversed. Eastern philosophy provided the fullest understanding of truths only darkly glimpsed by the Judeo-Christian scriptures.[48]

After Schopenhauer, people studied Eastern religion in order to perfect Europeanness, Germanness, and even Christianity, but in countercultural ways. Schopenhauerianism made understanding the Orient an integral pursuit in the effort to be a more profound and elite Christian, and a better German.[49] If Schlegel, Bopp, and the philologists found keys to European language in the East, Schopenhauer found the key to the European spirit and soul there.[50] The texts and culture of the Indic Orient, beyond the biblical lands, were identified as sources to rethink and redefine what it meant to be authentically German and modern. The reference to Sanskrit texts was part of a project to amass new intellectual authority outside Christianity, but for intra-Christian ends.[51]

It was left to popular intellectuals, then, to make Schopenhauer popular. Ironically, Schopenhauer, the snob and moody antipopulist, became a pop icon of late nineteenth- and early twentieth-century Germany.[52] The great innovation of popular writers such as Carl Langbehn and Paul de Lagarde involved making the Aryan Orient into a source and platform of authoritativeness and distinction in German popular culture. Paul de Lagarde was an Iranist, and considered himself the "only true student" of Friedrich Rückert, although Max Müller, who studied Persian alongside de Lagarde, respectfully disagreed.[53] In the writings of de Lagarde, the "Germanic" was not primarily a nation-state designation, but a composite of territorial, imperial, and traveling identities.[54] The "Germanic" evoked a territorial and cultural nucleus for the circulating flows of German-speaking people, German capital, and German intellectual production in the world. The Germanic was not a fixed, but a traveling, category—and it was used to define an intellectual character that could remain constant as people flowed out beyond the "Vaterland."[55] After de Lagarde, one did not need academic training or a professorship to comment authoritatively on contemporary cultural or intellectual matters. One only needed access to Indic sources to become a spiritual virtuoso and an everyday sage.

The 1850s and 1860s saw the rise of popular science and the articulation of Enlightenment rationality in everyday life associated with the writings of Rudolf Virchow, Ernst Haeckel, Charles Darwin, and Johannes Reinke. The popularization of science corresponded to the "reading explosion" and the rise of *freireligiöse* movements and popular revolts against traditional church authority.[56] The inkling of a post-Enlightenment ethos began to appear in the "table turning" craze of the 1850s and the beginnings of popular occultism. As Corinna Treitel aptly argues, the rise of the "irrational" was simply the inverse side of the expansion of "reason" in society.[57] The recently founded London-based Theosophical Movement, of which Hübbe-Schleiden was the main German representative, provided an important spur for the popularization of Indic Orientalism.

Theosophy was a movement started by Madame Helena Blavatsky, an aristocratic Russian émigré in London in 1875, and it arose at the height of popular science in Europe in the last quarter of the nineteenth century.[58] Theosophy validated the séances, nudism, vegetarianism, automatic writing, and occultist rituals among a segment of the respectable middle classes, and it became a conduit for the popularization of Schopenhauerianism in Germany.[59] German Schopenhauerians and German Theosophists—the two groups often overlapped—asserted their ability to comprehend the contemporary world from a superior perspective, rooted in Indian Vedic and Brahminical traditions.[60]

The Theosophical Movement in Germany played the most important role in disseminating Schopenhauer's ideas in popular culture. This allowed German thinkers to see themselves as positioned at the cultural center of the world due to their ability to interpret the significance of the archaic East for the modern West. Individuals such as Fritz Hartmann, a onetime army officer and coroner, Wilhelm Hübbe-Schleiden, the businessman and colonial trader, Theodor Schulze, a commissioner in the government of Dresden, and Mary Gebhardt, an Irish Theosophist married to a minor German aristocrat, played the most important roles initially.[61] They opened up pathways for everyone to become sages. Spiritualist Indology shared something in common, then, with German imperialism as it bragged of its world-historical perspective, and as it claimed to acquire spiritual goods from distant climes for the benefit of Europeans at home.

THE INTELLECTUAL POLITICS OF RISING SOCIAL GROUPS

At the end of the nineteenth century, the sociology of university scholarship entered a process of stark transformation.[62] New social groups, including people from working-class families as well as young middle-class women, were taking up university studies, and the rising number of academic professionals brought about increased specialization, and the "struggle over methods" as the traditional stakeholders sought to preserve their power within the academy.[63] The 1880s onward saw a rapid expansion of the educated middle classes in German-speaking society, measured especially by the demand for higher education. This period saw the steep rise in enrollment at imperial German universities. The number of university attendees exploded from 1865 to 1914, rising from 1.58 percent of nineteen-year-old males in 1869–1871 to 2.82 percent by 1914.[64] The "reader revolution" of the midcentury gave way to a university revolution by the late century.[65]

And the Humboldtian German university was at the zenith of its international repute in this period.[66] The number of American students in continental European universities peaked in the early 1890s, before beginning a slow decline as institutes for research-oriented graduate training were established at home.[67] Women and foreigners constituted a significant portion of rising enrollment at German universities. By 1905–1906, women made up between 6 percent and 8 percent of the student body, and 8.7 percent of university matriculates were foreign students.[68]

In the humanities disciplines, the influx of archaeological and cultural artifacts streaming into Europe created the need for new schools of art history, and here again, women played a pronounced role as experts. For example, in Vienna, at Josef Strzygowski's newly established *Kunsthistorisches Institut,* women wrote 63 of the 202 dissertations completed between 1909 and 1934.[69] Of those 63, 12 dissertations focused on Asian art, including Chinese, Indian, Iranian, and Ashkenazi.[70] Meanwhile, the 1910–1933 period saw the greatest number of dissertations published on India across all disciplines for any comparable period of time between 1800 and 1964.[71] The Orient created a new market for knowledge in German-speaking society and women played an important role in responding to that demand.[72]

Beyond academia, other professions that packaged and sold insight and enchantment emerged to make room for the large number of highly educated middle-class graduates.[73] Again, women were leading figures in new domains of popular Orientalist knowledge production. The partly Turkish and partly Egyptian Jewish spiritualist, Mirra Alfassa, who grew up in Paris, emerged as the leader of the Sri Aurobindo Ashram in Pondicherry in the 1920s.[74] In Dresden, Mary Wigman pioneered *Ausdrucktanz,* which combined the dramatic use of hand, body, and facial gestures to plumb spiritual depth.[75]

Konrad Jarausch's research sheds light on the "jettisoning" of liberalism by German academia, and the turn from cosmopolitanism to nationalism in the late nineteenth century.[76] But his argument must be read with awareness of the changing international context, as well as swiftly changing societal forces, especially the breakdown in hegemony of nineteenth-century ideals about a Concert of Europe and Enlightenment Universalism.

At the turn of the century, manifestations of Asian political activism made it into the German newspapers. Reports on India received pride of place alongside Japan. In 1905 the average number of monthly news articles dealing with Asia in the *Frankfurter Zeitung* was thirty-nine, already far more than what it had been five years earlier. But by 1911, the monthly average rose to fifty-six. The Boxer Rebellion (1898–1901) and the Russo-Japanese war (1905), as well as the *svadeśi* Uprising (1905–1908), caused fear of "yellow peril" to spread in the press. Kaiser Wilhelm II's outspoken fear about the "gelbe Gefahr" reminds us that the processes of asserting proximity to, as well as distance from, Asian political activism operated simultaneously in German official circles.[77]

Specifically with relation to India, the greatest coverage of Indian news was kindled in 1910 with the trip of the crown prince to India and China. The trip copied the opulent world-touring gesture of Franz Ferdinand of Austria, who visited India much earlier in 1892–1893.[78] The Archduke Ludwig von Hessen visited India in 1902, two years after Kaiser Wilhelm II undertook his *Orientreise* to Palestine.[79] In 1910, Crown Prince Wilhelm carried forward the ostentatious diplomacy on British geopolitical turf. During his visit to Calcutta, British surveillance reported that the German prince met with leaders of the Bengali revolutionary movement, including Bāgha Jatin Mukherjee, the "tiger" of Bengal, head of the radical *Yugāntar* underground anticolonial organization, and even promised financial and artillery support for the Indian resistance movement.[80] Apart from its coverage in the Bengali papers,[81] the trip spawned a number of book-length travel accounts in the German press.[82]

If Indic Orientalism had first descended from the dusty and hushed study rooms and libraries of philologists into popular culture in the late nineteenth century, popular writings about the Orient were filtering out of popular culture and into different fields of academia. In the early twentieth century, because the Indic domain signified a source of origins, sagacity and cultural authority in the German popular imagination, India soon also became a travel destination for German academics, political dignitaries, and middle-brow cultural figures with no direct ties to the discipline of Indology at all.

Travel tours to India were used by a surprisingly broad group of academics to project themselves into popular culture. Rudolf Otto, a professor of religion, first traveled to India in 1911–1912, in a year when many Germans seemed to be making the journey to the Orient. Later, in 1930, the anthropologist, Leo Frobenius, seemed to chase a popular audience when he called his book an "unphilosophical travelogue," based on his travels through South India and Ceylon. That same year, Hans Molisch, professor of plant physiology at the University of Vienna, published his travel book *Als Naturforscher in Indien* (As a natural scientist in India).[83] Some eminent German scientists, including Werner Heisenberg and Arnold Sommerfeld, also made world tours that included stops in India in the 1920s.[84]

Away from official circles, in popular culture, India was often considered to be one terminus for what Edgar Reitz once famously called German "Fernweh" (the longing for far-off places), while the vast Western frontiers of North America provided the other.[85] In fact, many German world travelers visited both America and India—as if these were the two terminals of a proper world tour.[86] Although Karl May traveled as far east as Baghdad, he mentioned the American frontier and the Orient in the same breath of exoticism. Hermann Schlagintweit, Hermann Keyserling, Josef Furtwängler, Arthur Holitscher, Bernhard Harms, Oskar von Miller, Alma Karlin, Elizabeth von Heyking, and Colin Ross are just a few of the disparate German-speaking popular intellectuals who traveled both to the United States and to India searching for new meaning in both lands. Keyserling's *Reisetagebuch eines Philosophen* began in India and ended in America,[87] although America signified superficiality, and India connoted spiritual depth.[88]

POPULARIZATION AND PUBLICATION

Popularization led Indic Orientalism to percolate and bubble through German literate mass culture as well as to seep through university walls and change intellectual cultures of research. India provided not only an object of study but also an ethos of study across various post-Enlightenment disciplines in the German universities of the 1910s. This included the fields of musicology, psychology, philosophy, history, anthropology, sociology, and physics, as the following chapters in this book will explore. Scholars in the interwar years claimed that Orientalist perspectives or fascinations could be applied to empirical data of different sorts, across different fields, in order to reveal profound insights.

Interest in Indian Buddhism in German Europe had arisen slowly from the 1850s onward.[89] The deciphering of the Pali language by Eugène Burnouf and Christian Lassen in the 1830s, followed by key archaeological discoveries of Ashokan pillars in the 1850s, provided the first impetus for the field. Highly influential scholars, popularizers of India in their own right, such as Max Müller and his student, Hermann Oldenberg, made as much of ancient Buddhism as of Vedic Hinduism in their writings. Buddhism was generally presented as a younger branch of the ancient Indic religious *Stammbaum*, or family tree.[90] It was younger, less constrained by archaic caste divisions, and more akin to the "salvation religions" that emerged later on in the Hebraic traditions in Asia Minor. By the 1920s, German Indologists such as Helmuth von Glasenapp began popularizing Jainism as another salvation religion from India.[91]

Even though Theosophy and Schopenhauerianism of the 1870s and 1880s were enamored with the Brahminical rituals and elite philosophies of the Vedas, there was a rising tide of interest in the supposedly more egalitarian, more accessible, and more Christianity-like Indic religion of Buddhism beginning in this same period. Buddhism was registered as an archaic, pre-Christian, popular religion that could serve twentieth-century Europeans. In the late nineteenth century, Germans began to convert to Buddhism, not to Theosophy with its Brahminical tinge.[92]

Buddhist scholar Hermann Oldenberg proposed that Buddhism provided a rendition of ancient Indic (*altindische*) thought that was more open to proselytization and conversion.[93] Buddhist scholars explained that Buddhism was inherently less elitist since it was an anti-Brahminical religion that developed when a prince (not a priest) decided to reject all his wealth and temporal possessions in an act of universal compassion and self-renunciation.[94] Oldenberg said that Buddhism was the most rational and advanced "technique of thought" to branch out from the Vedic tree.[95] Oldenberg sought to show that Gautama Buddha had been a historical person, just as Jesus had been.[96] It was not the lingam, the *devis*, and the elite Brahminical traditions or esoteric nondualist teachings that became the widespread symbols of spiritual renewal in German popular culture. Rather, concerns familiar to the Christian catechism, such as the personality of the prophet (in this case, the Buddha) and the moral injunctions of humility and self-renunciation, captured general attention.

Rudolf Seydel, a philosopher in Dresden and a Schopenhauerian, advanced claims about the influence of ancient Buddhism on the origins of Christianity. In 1892, Eduard Griesbach wrote his book on Buddha's life with the Wagnerian title, *The New Tannhäuser,* about the rejection of earthly pleasures and the achievement of grace available to every seeker, outside the limits of Judeo-Christian redemption history. Ferdinand von Horstein's play *Buddha* appeared in 1898. Joseph Victor Widmann published an epic poem in German devoted to the Buddha.[97] Max Vogrich and Adolf Vogl both wrote operas based on the life of the Buddha, inspired by Richard Wagner's aborted opera sketch about the Buddha, *Die Sieger.*[98]

Keyserling, in his *Reisetagebuch eines Philosophen* (1919), referred to Hinduism as the Catholicism of India—tired and replete with dead rituals—while Buddhism was Protestantism—alive, difficult, but rewarding. By contrast, Max Weber likened Hinduism to archaic Hellenism, while he proposed Buddhism had more the character of modern Europe's Parisian cosmopolitanism.[99] For some popular writers, Buddhism was related to a global German calling. For Keyserling, the proof of German difference from western Europeans was that they were aristocratically apolitical, a people of spirit and culture alone, like the ancient peoples of the Himalayas. Germans had a calling for depth because of their inherent honesty and "organic" mode of life.[100]

In 1915, the librarian Hans Ludwig Held, a friend of Thomas Mann, published his comprehensive bibliography of German-language Buddhist literature containing 2,544 entries.[101] The catalog was meant to display the vast number of treatises that used the "western epistemological method" to open up Buddhism to modern inquiry. It was also intended to provide a deep reserve of literature for those gripped by a "humane yearning and striving for spiritual insight."[102]

As Suzanne Marchand has beautifully shown, a number of free-floating intellectuals in the time of the "furor orientalis,"[103] with PhDs but without secure faculty positions, especially Karl Seidenstücker and Karl Eugen Neumann, contributed immensely to the popularization of Buddhist "wisdom" in German society thanks to their translations of sacred Buddhist texts, as well as their work as institutionalizers.[104] Their voluminous translations provided access to canonical texts that soon became New Testaments for twentieth-century anti-Christians, anti-Westernists, or anti-Semites.

While these categories often overlapped, they can also be disentangled because they colored outside of each other's lines often enough.

BUDDHA PRESIDING OVER THE POST-ENLIGHTENMENT

Popularized Orientalism created space for cultural producers from nontraditional backgrounds to attain high repute from inside and outside the university setting. Germans who converted to Buddhism, especially those who became monks, earned the authoritative status to speak about Indian religious tradition and to reveal universal truth. Religious converts in popular culture could distinguish themselves without having to go down the laborious and treacherous road to a PhD and Habilitation, while claiming a deeper understanding of the meaning of Sanskrit and Pali scriptures than the university professors themselves.[105]

Karl Seidenstücker, a pastor's son and philologist of Pali texts, founded the first German Buddhist Mission in Germany in 1903.[106] He completed his dissertation at Leipzig, but became involved in Buddhist missionary work and thus avoided the second ordeal of the Habilitation. Seidenstücker later collaborated with Georg Grimm, a lawyer and son of an ironworker, in establishing the Old Buddhist religious community at Ammersee, close to Munich.[107] Conversion from one religion to another, from one hierarchy of authority and tradition to another, was an important way of identity-formation for Germans in this early twentieth-century age of entanglement. In Berlin, Anton Güth, a well-known violinist, became Nyanatiloka in 1903, a German Buddhist monk.[108] In 1911 he established a hermitage for Western Buddhists on Dodanduwa Island in Sri Lanka. He later opened another hermitage at Kandy.[109] Sigmund Feniger converted to Buddhism and became Nyanaponika Thera in 1922.[110] Conrad Nell converted to Buddhism in 1924 and took the name U Nayanadhara, dying in Burma in 1935.[111] Ernst Lothar Hoffmann, a young archaeologist, became a Buddhist monk in 1928 and took the name, Anagarika Govinda, joining the monastery of German Buddhists in Ceylon.[112]

Perhaps the most important German Buddhist in terms of authority in popular culture was Paul Dahlke in Berlin, with his *Buddhistisches Haus* established in 1924 and his many brochures and books promising spiritual profundity and insight.[113] The combination of academic experts who sought to speak to popular audiences, free-floating intellectuals who translated

Eastern sacred texts as if life depended on it, and popular Schopenhauerians who wanted authority for everyman, brought about the German conversions to Buddhism at the turn of the century.[114]

Yet, aside from the converts to Buddhism, German conversions to ascetic Hinduism also took place. Ernst Georg Schulze and Baron Köth both
converted to Vaishnav Hinduism after meeting the charismatic Bengali
traveling preacher, Bhakti Hridaya Swami Bon, during his tour through
Germany in 1927.[115] Walther Eidlitz and Leopold Fischer, both from Austria and both Indologists, left for India in the context of World War II and
became Hindu monks.[116] These traveling German swamis provided the
complement to those Indian Hindus who converted to Christianity and became celebrated religious teachers and traveling saints. Sadhu Sundar
Singh, possibly the most celebrated itinerant Indian preacher in Europe in
the early twentieth century, achieved his fame as both an Indian sage and
as a convert to Christianity.[117]

The German Buddhism movement created a market for Buddhist *Welt-
literatur* among popular audiences.[118] Eugen Diederichs, a Nietzschean and
publisher of works for bourgeois audiences, began by purveying German
Romantic lyric poetry and translations of Giordano Bruno and Plotinus,
but his status was greatly enhanced in 1912 with the joint publication of
Leopold von Schroeder's *Bhagavadgita* and a collection of Persian mystic
poetry.[119] Diederichs came to publishing as an outsider, but his Indic focus
allowed his enterprise to amass considerable prestige and wealth by becoming the go-to press for popular Orientalist themes.[120] Meanwhile, Kurt von
Vowinckel, as well as Kurt Wolff, established the reputations of their presses
by publishing the first translations of Rabindranath Tagore's writings in
German.[121]

German Buddhists founded their own small presses. In Munich, the
converts Anton Güth and Georg Grimm established the Benares-Verlag.[122]
Paul Dahlke, who established the Buddhistisches Haus in 1924, also published from his own press, the Neu-Buddhistischer Verlag. But not only
small presses published Buddhist wisdom literature. Buddhism was big
business too, with Reclam and Insel in Leipzig and Piper in Munich publishing reprints of Karl Eugen Neumann's popular translations of the
Dhammapada and other Buddhist canonical texts.[123] Insel and Reclam
took their place as the two main publishers of works on Buddhism for general audiences, mostly not in the form of scriptural translations, but cultural
reflections by popular German writers such as Albrecht Schäffer and

Rudolf Delius. The huge popular success of Hermann Hesse's *Siddhartha* (1922) excited business-minded publishers, as much as it enamored its vast readership.

German Indic Orientalism, in the Buddhist key, reached popular audiences in its most accessible, literary, and least specialized form in the novel, *Siddhartha.* The author, Hermann Hesse, was an ardent reader of Karl Eugen Neumann's *Dhammapada* and Paul Deussen's *Upanishads*.[124] Hesse found inspiration from his tour of India in 1911, as well as from the memories of his grandfather, Hermann Gundert, an Indologist and missionary in India. Hesse's novella *Siddhartha* reached its sixth edition in just the second year of publication.[125] Keyserling's *Reisetagebuch eines Philosophen* was another popular success, reaching seven editions within four years of its publication in 1919. Around this same time, in 1921, Rabindranath Tagore's plays were appearing on the major stages of Germany in Berlin, Munich, and Frankfurt, and they continued to be produced on German stages for two years after his first visit in 1921.[126] German and Austrian composers interpreted Rabindranath's verse in music, such as Alexander Zemlinsky's *Lyrische Symphonie* and Hans Gál's *Phantasien.* In addition to the Central European reception, Rabindranath's poems were also put to music by a number of American composers.[127] Heinz Witte-Lenoir articulated a reading of Rabindranath Tagore's writings in visual form through paintings.[128]

The writers of belles lettres integrated Orientalism into their novels, novellas, plays, and poems, especially from around 1900 onward. Rainer Maria Rilke wrote his Buddha poems about the yearning for enchantment in the high-industrial age.[129] Stefan Zweig, who traveled to India and Burma in 1909, wrote a novella on the theme of sea travel to the Orient, and Lion Feuchtwanger set novels and plays on British ships sailing to India, or in British Indian courtrooms.[130] Thomas Mann's *Vertauschte Köpfe* evoked the erotic exoticism associated with the Orient in his story of a love triangle that ends in two decapitated heads and a woman who has to undergo a wife-burning ritual.[131] In high literature, the Orient was often used to connote themes of sexual transgression, narratives of personal integration, and stories about dissipation and the danger of distant travel.

All in all, high literature outside of academic Indology did not take the Indic Orient as seriously as did the vast compendium of registrations in either popular culture or academic writings. The early twentieth century was a period in which excitement for the accessible art of vaudeville and cabaret, as well as early cinema, outpaced enthusiasm for the *bürgerlich* opera stage, even in its monumental Wagnerian form.[132] The allure of wit and satire, and even the bathos of the little man, had increasing draw on audiences.[133] In popular culture, and among popular writers, the Indic became a way for the little man to travel the world and claim distinction vis-à-vis high bourgeois norms.[134]

The artistic avant-garde and the exponents of counterculture in postwar Germany and Austria chastised the bourgeois mainstream for its moribund liberalism and its epigonal neoclassicism.[135] What those with normative tastes called *Morgenländerei*, the fetish of the Orient, countercultural groups called insight and wisdom. It swelled up from below in the period from 1900 onward, calling forth its own literary mode, the "Indienbücher," or the "India books."[136] Authors such as Ida von Hahn-Hahn, Walter Heichen, and Thea von Harbou highlighted India's difference from Europe—as a wonderland of naked sadhus, beggars, and beyadère dancers.

For others, India was a place to find equivalencies in terms of political struggle and anti-British sentiment. The interplay between drawing distinctions and creating relations played out in the travel accounts of Hilmar Teske. Teske argued that Indians, in 1930, would not succeed in developing a true national feeling unless Hindu–Muslim divisions were healed and caste exclusiveness was abolished.[137] Only then could Indians do as the Prussians had done when they created the German empire, "serve the *Vaterland* . . . with one's whole soul."[138]

RESISTING THE EAST

As much as some Germans, riding a popular post-Enlightenment wave, asserted strong affinities between Buddhism and Christianity and used Buddhist identifications to mark German difference from western Europe, other Germans were intent on beating back *Morgenländerei* and locating Germany squarely on the side of the Judeo-Roman-Christian, the western and the European. Germany was part of the European geopolitical bloc, and as such was at the center of the modern world order, these intellectuals argued.[139] The destiny of Germany was connected to western Europe, the Mediterranean and the Semitic Orient, not pitched in opposition to it.

This was the argument at the heart of Max Weber's lengthy and masterful interpretation of the Indic tradition from the time of the ancient Vedas to the rise of Bhakti cults and modern Shaivism in the twelfth century CE,[140] *The Religion of India* (1916), which represented a sociological interpretation of Indic tradition. The study of the relationship between religious belief, social organization, and forms of collective discipline and productivity in Indian society was used to reflect upon what was unique about the European tradition, especially the development of "city religions" such as Judaism and Christianity. The study of India highlighted the unique family traits of Europe's "protestant ethic" in Weber's treatment.

Weber proposed that Brahmanism had sublimated the instinct-driven orgiastic tendencies of primitive society. But various revolts against the Brahminical tradition by "professional classes" of knights and "unorthodox intellectuals" produced disruptive readings of the Brahminical texts, creating religious innovations. The *Bhagavad Gita* and the Epic tradition stemmed from the work of warriors and knights to create a religion of duty and agency that challenged the quietism of early Brahmanism. Buddhism and Jainism, on the other hand, were religions that sought to reform archaic Brahmanism and create a more rational and democratic "religion of salvation."

In 1913, the philosopher of religion Rudolf Otto gave lectures on the "parallels and the different values between Christianity and Buddhism."[141] Otto, in a book dedicated to the maharaja of Mysore, claimed that Christianity and Buddhism could both be categorized as "unified" religions, or world religions.[142] The main difference stressed by Otto, however, was that in Christianity, salvation is obtained through communion, while in Buddhism, it is obtained through individualistic asceticism. Otto continually emphasized why Christian soteriology was superior to that of its Buddhist counterpart. He framed the Buddhism versus Christianity debate in world-historical terms. Every religion should have the chance to express its "Letztes und Tiefstes" (ultimate and deepest character) before dying out, Otto wrote.[143] He believed Christianity fit to win a global victory over the world-religion of Buddhism.[144]

Yet in the persistent engagement with the theme of Christianity's relative advantages over Buddhism from different disciplinary perspectives, the Eurocentrism of the discourse is less striking than the clear tone of anxiety that beset German-speakers as they contemplated their identity and relations as Europeans, Christians, and Westerners.[145] Where was German Europe and how far to the east was it really? That was an open question all the way up to 1945 when the *Morgenland* was finally dispelled like a bad dream, and the indeterminacy of the German-speaking lands was resolved within the geopolitical system of two superpowers. The question of German national identity within the German *Kaiserreich,* then the Weimar Republic, was defined by an age of global entanglement. Important approaches in German historiography tell us that the German national imagination tended to focus on *Heimat*—on hometowns and localities.[146] But the German identity also traveled and established moorings in discontinuous locations across the planet.[147] Germanness, *Deutschtum,* in the 1880 to 1945 period was an errant identity, and this created potentials not only for colonial interactions but also for ambivalent relations and entanglements with groups outside Europe and North America.[148]

RIGHT-WING ORIENTALISTS AND THE FEELING OF SMALLNESS

Anthropologists and philologists supplied two different definitions of the "Aryan" from early on. According to anthropologists, such as the Prichardian scholar, Brian Hodgson, in 1849, "Aryans were tall, light complexioned, meat-eating and vigorously monotheistic while the Dravidians and Turanians tended to be short, dark, vegetarian, polytheistic, prone to idolatry and indolence."[149] It was this rationale that guided the reorganization of the British Indian Army after 1857. According to British race theory of the time, the "Turanian" and "Dravidian" soldiery, that is, the infantry from Bengal and southern India, were demobilized, and the supposedly "martial" Aryan soldiers of the Punjab were heavily recruited along with Nepali Gurkhas.[150] But through the lens of philology, Aryans were not only fighters but also ancient poets, writers, artistic producers, and knowers; they were not only tall, well-built, and resilient, but learned and cultured.[151]

Arthur Gobineau's four-volume *L'Inégalité des Races* (1855) applied the concept of the "Aryan" in a new way—less as an anthropological or philological category, and more as a geopolitical one that asserted the place of the white man in the contemporary world. Gobineau introduced a theory of blood superiority of the *Ariens* (versus the "Melanians" and the "yellow races"), but he also viewed the contemporary white races as contaminated, and thus, in decline.[152] As Thomas Trautmann has so carefully shown, this kind of Aryanism was different from the purely philological kind articulated in Max Müller's work.[153] The geopolitical inflection of Aryanism hit

Germany and Austria-Hungary only during its age of *Weltpolitik* beginning in the 1890s, and much later than its receptions in France and Britain.[154]

The early twentieth century in Germany slouched toward Byzantium, but even more toward the Himalayas. Sheldon Pollock perceptively remarks, "in the German instance . . . Orientalism as a complex of knowledge-power has to be seen as vectored not outward to the Orient but inward to Europe itself, to constructing the conception of a historical German essence and to defining Germany's place in Europe's destiny."[155] A strong thrust in German Orientalism celebrated the decline of a nineteenth-century Europe and saw the recovery of the "Aryan" as a German–Asian identity that claimed geopolitical distinction. This was a vision of grandeur seen from the position of those who felt inferior. Friedrich Nietzsche, in the late nineteenth century, pointed to the rampant German social problem of inferiority complexes masquerading as displays of heroism. Thomas Mann diagnosed it in Germany in the 1940s, speaking of the problem of a small European nation demanding its own day in the sun.[156] Long before Oswald Spengler wrote his iconic *Der Untergang des Abendlandes* (The Decline of the West), other Jeremiahs dwelled on the theme of the death of Goethe's Germany, and the subsequent Orientalization of German Europe, which they associated with its geopolitical rise.[157]

This was a standard theme of the *Sylvester-Literatur* ("New Year's Eve" literature) published around 1899: in books such as Julius Hart's *Der neue Gott: Ein Ausblick auf das kommende Jahrhundert* (The New God: A Preview of the Coming Century), Karl Bleibtreu's *Robespierre und Buddhismus*, Ludwig Büchner's *Am Sterbelager des Jahrhunderts* (The Death Pangs of the Century), and Hermann Oldenberg's *Aus Indien und Iran*. Spengler famously proposed that Germans, and Westerners generally, were a dying people and a dying culture.[158] Spengler's book was anti-Hellenistic—he severed the connection between the ancient Greeks and modern European (and German) culture. The Faustian character of Western culture stemmed from the gothic and baroque culture of northern Christian Europe, he stated.[159] The insistence on struggle and industriousness that marked the Faustian character differed from the "Apollonian" resignation of the ancient Greeks and the Buddhist Orient, or the "Magian" exuberance of the Mediterranean Arabs.[160] The overall effect of Spengler's presentation was to minimize Europe's significance and to "provincialize" it.[161] Europe was just a "little part-world," he explained.[162] This was a Hegelian *Univers-*

algeschichte turned on its head, in which the world-historical gaze served not to inflate Europe's calling in the world, but to miniaturize its importance.[163]

Spengler's way of juxtaposing the Faustian, the Apollonian, the Magian, and the northern European to the rest of the world was at odds with a rising trend among other philosophers of history in the 1920s that fused northern Europe and the ideal of the Aryans, and set them in contrast to both the Mediterranean Greeks and the Middle Eastern Jews.[164] Both before and after World War I, the right-wing Orientalists in German Europe aspired to a Germanic identity that could extend itself over contiguous terrains of central, north central, and southeast Europe, as well as to discontinuous ports of call around the world.[165] These conservative middle-aged intellectuals, with patrician tastes and *völkisch* political aims, wanted a paradigmatic change in society that would return German Europe to rule by an aristocracy of intellectuals.[166] They wished to stand out in the world as the true wellsprings of culture vis-à-vis the French or British cosmopolitans.[167] Typical figures among the right-wing Orientalists were Leopold Ziegler, Karl Joël, Moeller van den Bruck, and Edgar Jung. These older nationalist thinkers helped establish the intellectual *piste longue* for the rise of National Socialism, but they also fell out of favor with the high command of the Nazi regime quite swiftly after the Nazi rise to power.[168]

The rise of scholarly interest in "Aryanism" in Germany occurred with the new academic research in mythography, archaeology, cultural studies, and "prehistorical" studies in the last third of the nineteenth century in the work of right-wing academic Orientalists. Mythographers in the late nineteenth century sought to uncover the influences of the Orient on the Occident, especially in terms of latent strands of paganism, heathenism, and mysticism in the European Middle Ages.[169]

Illusions of grandeur arise among those who fear smallness. Mythographers mixed the study of myth with archaeology and Vedic studies in their pursuit of the prehistory of the Aryans.[170] Beginning in the 1870s, Gustaf Kossinna, Carl Schuchhardt, Alfred Hillebrandt, and Julius von Negelein were the main scholars who made contributions to the German study of Aryan myth and the archaeology of "prehistoric" Aryan settlement sites in German Europe.[171] These scholars developed methods of *Siedlungsarchäologie*, or archaeological digs, in the German hometowns. Archaeological revelations were waiting in the backyard, not necessarily in the far-off Orient, these *völkisch* scholars claimed. And the artifacts that were uncovered in Saxony, Thuringia, the Rhineland, and elsewhere supposedly helped to reveal the history of an ancient racial group, a tribe of Aryan Germans. As Kossinna noted, "cultural areas that are sharply bounded archaeologically always coincide with completely distinct peoples or races [*Völkerstammen*]."[172] Edgar Dacqué, a paleontologist and Theosophist, compared myths around the world in order to define the supposed cultural characteristics of different racial groups, including the Aryan.[173] Scholars were seeking to reveal the morphology of cultures, the supposed integral and holistic worlds of particular racial groups on earth, of which the Germanic would be shown as superior.[174]

Beginning at the turn of the century, and especially after the Great War, German-speaking philosophers also turned increasingly to Aryan imaginings, this time for therapeutic effect.[175] Confronting the fear of inferiority and smallness, Karl Joël, the rector of Leipzig University in 1914, argued that the new philosophy of the twentieth century would require an appreciation of the holistic unity of life, gained from the study of Buddhism.[176] Leopold Ziegler, in his book *The Eternal Buddha* (Das Ewige Buddho, 1922), prophesied a German twentieth century that would see the return to genius through a fusion of Christian and Asian mysticism. Moeller van den Bruck, in 1923, foretold the return of German Europe to the rituals and inspirations of both Buddhism and the Byzantine Church.[177] A similar theme of renewal and cultural rebirth via Asianism concerned Paul Natorp in 1923 when he founded his Tagore Circle at Marburg University, placing the study of Rabindranath's *Gitanjali* alongside the study of *Aufklärung* thinkers.[178] In the context of violent imperial clashes, followed by the mutual destruction of World War I, as well as the fearsomeness of an anticolonial "Awakening East," older nationalist philosophers claimed distinction by relating themselves to the grandeur of Indic Orient, and by claiming to bring holistic insight into the bellicose rationality of the West.

The search for first origins amid the archaic Aryans provided the main thrust behind the work of right-wing nationalists in different disciplines. Leopold von Schroeder, a German Indologist from Dorpat teaching in Vienna, used the comparative method to reveal a supposedly "old Aryan" *Volksfamilie:* the Indians, the East Iranians, and the Germans.[179] These relations could be uncovered by comparing myths from the ancient mountain regions of the Himalayas. "There can no longer be any doubt that the Aryans once spread as undivided from *Mitteleuropa* all the way to southern Russia, before the Asian branch of the ethnic group [*Völkerfamilie*], the Indians and the Persians, separated themselves."[180] Schroeder's book,

Arische Religion (1914), claimed the Aryans as an ancient race bridging German Europe, Central Asia, and South Asia, effectively turning its back on and rejecting German ethnic ties to western Europe, and German cultural and religious ties to the biblical lands.

The right-wing anti-Westernism and anti-Semitism of Leopold von Schroeder's writing was rooted in a Germanic wish to matter, and the belief, mediated by a century of Indic Orientalism and philological study, that the wager required German-speakers to reject the old sacred world center of Old Testament history and to embrace what they believed was the sacred land of a greater Eden farther east.

And Josef Strzygowski, a Vienna-based art historian and right-wing nationalist, worked alongside Schroeder in this project to disrupt the normative classically oriented art history of the traditional Vienna school. "With my friend Schroeder," Strzygowski recalled, "I stood always alone in the world of Vienna."[181] Strzygowski published his *Krisis der Geisteswissenschaften* (Crisis of the Humanities) in 1923, soon after completing a tour of the United States and delivering the prestigious Norton Lectures at Harvard.[182] Strzygowski dedicated the lectures to his colleagues in the United States and claimed he wrote for the benefit of his "Jewish friends." He proceeded to warn against the rise of "Jewish projects" for intellectual world supremacy, which threatened to erase the distinctive cultural boundaries of Northern peoples and Northern art, by which he meant the Central Europeans.[183] Strzygowski's rhetoric showed the mix of fear, bigotry, and narcissism that characterized many of the right-wing nationalists in the interwar years: small individuals trying to defend a myth of their greatness.[184] And the tendency to Orientalize the Germanic in order to reject the West European and the Judaic provided important intellectual scaffolding for the Nazi rise.[185]

In the interwar years, a growing array of German-speaking scholars from different disciplines identified with the ancient peoples of the Eurasian Steppes, the "sacred" region lying between the Caspian Sea and the Himalayas. In the 1930s, Josef Strzygowski started referring in his work to this imagined community as "the Aryans."[186] In Strzygowski's "global" art historical project, all art could be understood in terms of an ancient, yet persisting, conflict between the art ideals of the North versus those of the South.[187] In his interpretation, the Greeks, the Renaissance Italians, and the Jews all belonged to the South, and the "Aryan" peoples of the Eurasian Steppes belonged to the North.

ARYAN STUDIES AFTER VERSAILLES

The Paris Peace Conference in 1919 and the Treaty of Versailles established a new international system based on the "ontology" of small states, in which the rhetoric of particularism was increasingly used to defend political legitimacy.[188] But if the war victors reconstituted an international system out of the wreckage of the Great War through the legal, economic, and moral institutions of the League of Nations, the new communist state of Russia pursued an alternate project for world reordering through the institutions of the Comintern, inaugurated in 1919.[189] Between the "Western" world system organized around Britain and France, and the "Eastern" world system organized around Russia, lay the defeated German-speaking polities. German nationalists, with resentment, thought back to a previous Conference of Versailles, in December 1870, when Bismarck triumphantly declared the unification of the German Reich.[190]

Right-wing Orientalists were enamored of the East as a geographic, genetic, and metaphorical location of lost purity and strength—as a fulcrum for leverage over western Europe and Christian norms. The central idea in Aryanist thought was the exceptionalism of ethnic Germans as a racial group in German Europe. The Aryan category provided geopolitical distinction to German-speakers vis-à-vis other Europeans, including the French and British, and the Latinate cultures of western Europe. It also drew a strict and deadly internal line of difference between "ethnic" Germans and German Jews.[191] "As the Germans first entered history, there still were no Italians, French, Spanish, [and] English nationalities; these only resulted from the mixing of Germans with other nations," wrote one eager Nazi anthropologist.[192]

To think of oneself as an Aryan after World War I was to still be at home in the world even after a world-historical war defeat. Egon Eickstedt, in his *Rassenkunde und Rassengeschichte* of 1934, said he carried forward Alexander von Humboldt's project of the encyclopedic description of the natural world through a complete overview of the world of human races.[193] "The aim is to create a world system of races, of human types," among which the "white Aryans" were the greatest.[194] As Klemens von Klemperer perceptively noted, "Aryan man is rooted in philology, not natural science."[195] The radical scholarship of post-Versailles Aryan scholars across German Europe was marked by the study of linguistic family relations, and the delineation of fanciful mythological and civilizational genealogies to blur the East versus West divide.

If Max Müller's invocation of Aryans in the 1850s served his wish to make Indian religions *more like* the Judeo-Christian tradition, the Aryanist scholars of the 1920s and 1930s, working in a wholly different historical and political context, had what seemed to be the inverse objective. Many Weimar and Nazi-period Aryan studies scholars sought to dissolve any sediment of Westernness or Judeo-Christianity from their identities in order to assert their cultural autonomy in the midst of war defeat, unbridled resentment toward the victor powers, and deep political embarrassment.[196]

Aryanism in Germany had no monolinear course from the nineteenth to the twentieth centuries. There is no straight progression of the "German mind" from Max Müller to Hitler.[197] Certainly, the popularization of Orientalism created the context in which the image of the "Aryan" could be used for vastly different ends by different kinds of popular and academic writers.[198]

In their orientation toward India after World War I, those on the political right returned to the debates of the *Creuzerstreit* from the early nineteenth century.[199] Right-wing Orientalism was intent on asserting the absolute distinction of German nationalist cultural identity through reference to Vedic primitivism and Himalayan heights. The Himalaya literature was vast, with authors writing about their travels to the highest mountains in the world. Herbert Tichy's *Zum heiligsten Berg der Welt* (1937) was a collection of travel writings by the author as he went on "pilgrimage" through Afghanistan, India, and Tibet. The book, with an introduction by the great Swedish explorer of Chinese Turkistan, Sven Hedin, spoke of the Himalayas as a terrain in which "one springs out of the everyday" and in which "one's thoughts become great and beautiful, just like the mountains."[200]

The German lands were different—and much better—than those of the war victors because of their myths, their language and their blood. Germans were purely related to the true, original world center, stretched across the Himalayas. If Britain and France were at the center of the current world order, their position was both illegitimate and illusory from an ancient Oriental point of view, claimed German conservative nationalists.

In 1923, Arthur Drews wrote in an article in the conservative journal, *Die Tat,* "ever since the West with its cultural center in Paris has taken an antagonistic stance toward us, its standing among us has been reduced, and the usual fad for Roman civilization has been greatly reduced. Ever since then, our view has turned increasingly to the east, as though salvation would come from there, and the ideas of those intellectuals from the *Morgenland* are now popular among us."[201]

The generational character of intellectual production by the "national economic boys" in the 1890s can be compared to the generational aspect of Aryanist thought in the 1920s, especially in the period of what Volker Berghahn calls "recivilization and its failure," 1924–1935, when Germans celebrated the return to economic and social stability and swiftly went about constructing ethnonationalist visions of grandeur born out of an inferiority complex.[202] In some ways, what economic discourse was to the 1890s during Germany's rise in the world was what Aryanist discourse was to the 1920s, during Germany's descent into political isolation and jingoism.[203]

In the context of postwar national embarrassment and the compensatory rise of the fascist Nazi regime, a young group of Indologists turned away from the study of Buddhist literature and Sanskrit, Pali, and Prakrit texts, and turned back toward the Vedas, and the supposedly original intellectual authority of ancient Hinduism. As Sheldon Pollock shows, some among this group, such as Bernhard Breloer and Erich Frauwallner, joined the NS-DAP before 1933 and were quick to enter Nazi state service as academic officials.[204] Pollock notes that of twenty-five or so Indology professors of the Nazi period, perhaps a third were active participants in the party.[205]

What I call, collectively, the "Aryan Studies boys" because of their generational specificity, were predominantly ethnic German scholars who identified their own rise in the profession with the work of reglorifying the Aryans, and expounding on ur-paganism and ur-heathenism as means to eradicate Hebraic, Christian, and Western philosophical and religious "impurities" in German Europe. By and large, those who contributed to the new interwar field of Aryan Studies came from conventional family backgrounds— with fathers who were bureaucrats, pastors, and professors.[206] But there were exceptions: Bernhard Breloer's father was a mill owner, and Hans Guenther's was a musician.[207]

Dominant figures among this cohort became leading officials and scientific managers of Nazi intellectual institutions such as the Ahnenerbe (Institute for Ancestry Studies) as well as programs involved in *Ostforschung* (research on the regions east of and contiguous to the German-speaking countries). Walther Wüst became SS Hauptführer and the leader of the Ahnenerbe after Herman Wirth and Richard Walther Darré, the two founding figures, fell out of favor with Heinrich Himmler in 1937.[208] In 1933, the Aryanist, Ludwig Alsdorf, was another member of the Ahnenerbe, while Jakob Wilhelm Hauer led the Nazi *Glaubensbewegung*, the German Faith Movement, a form of popular "German paganism" (*Deutsches Hei-*

dentum) envisioned as a new state religion by the Nazi party.[209] Hauer, a Tübingen Indologist and expert on Indian yoga practice, was an *Untersturm-führer* of the Nazi SS as of 1934. Breloer took up the prestigious chair in Indology at the University of Berlin in 1933.[210] Hermann Güntert, a scholar of Aryan linguistics, became rector of Munich University at age thirty-five.

In order to attain these high official positions, the Aryan Studies boys benefited from the convoluted patronage channels of the Nazi high command. Heinrich Himmler (who founded the Ahnenerbe), Rudolf Hess (who headed the Deutsche Akademie), Herman Göring and Alfred Rosenberg (who also vied for control of the Ahnenerbe) were all high leaders in the party involved in the oversight and internal struggles over Nazi scientific management.[211] If German Indic Orientalism lay close to state programs during the scientific institutionalization of the British Crown Raj from the 1850s onward, a new phase of Indological state service came in an undisputedly maligned form in the decade after 1933. Walter Ruben, a German Jewish scholar and the most important Indologist in East Germany after the war, called this the "nadir of Indology."[212]

Thanks to the post-Versailles young professionals born roughly between 1880 and 1907 the term "Aryan" came to be inseparable from Nazi rule. These Aryan Studies scholars generally studied under rigorous, empiricist and liberal *Doktorväter* such as Heinrich Lüders, Richard Garbe, Hermann Jacobi, Richard Pischel, and Wilhelm Geiger.[213] They addressed erudite questions about the grammar and paleography of the Vedas in their dissertations, before taking up more fanciful studies on the culture, beliefs, statecraft, and military strategies of the ancient Aryans in subsequent research.[214]

Erich Frauwallner followed in the footsteps of *Doktorvater* Paul Deussen in his study of ancient India through a history of "Aryan" philosophy.[215] Ludwig Alsdorf first followed in the path set out by his *Doktorvater* Hermann Jacobi with his work on Jainism.[216] But Alsdorf soon turned his attention to the history of vegetarianism and cow-veneration in the *Ṛg Veda* and the Book of Manu, as a cultural study of the ancient Aryans.[217] During World War II, Alsdorf penned a number of propagandistic accounts of Indian history, focused on the denigration of British colonial rule.[218]

Walther Wüst studied under the liberal Jewish Indologist, Wilhelm Geiger. Wüst completed his dissertation on the grammatical forms of the *Ṛg Veda* before branching out to the study of the history of Aryan beliefs.[219]

Bernhard Breloer, who studied under another positivistic and liberal scholar, Hermann Jacobi, published an essay on music in ancient India, before turning to the study of Aryan etatism and state centralization in the *Arthashastra*.[220] Herman Lommel and Johannes Hertel were others who turned attention after 1933 to the study of Aryan religion.[221] Of course, not each and every young Indic Orientalist in the 1920s was drawn into Aryan Studies. Helmut von Glasenapp, a student of Lüders, researched South India and Dravidian studies and kept far away from Aryan fixations.[222]

The Aryan Studies boys rebelled against their fathers in the post-1920s period by pursuing Nazism. Franz Altheim focused on the ancient Persians instead of the ancient Indians, and wrote a history of the "world war" of the third century BCE that followed after Alexander the Great. Now it was not the conquering Greeks, but the Ptolemies of Egypt and Seleucids of Syria who fought for control of monumental swaths of terrain stretching from the Himalayas to the Donau valley.[223] Altheim argued that with the rise of Egypt and Syria and with the new creed of Manichaeism, the ancient Germans as "Western Aryans" first began to play their role as *"Kulturbringer"* in southeast Europe.[224] Güntert wrote a cultural history of Aryan ancient history in the Stone Age, focused on a conquering group he called "Vorindogermanischen Bauernvölker" (Pre-Indo-Germanic peasants).[225] The book was based on homegrown, moonshine archaeological research carried out in Sweden and Norway as well as in Hungary, the Balkans, and Syria. These west Aryan peasant peoples, Güntert claimed, emerged from the Iranian, Khotanese, and Scythian peoples of the Himalayas, and their history since the Stone Age was marked by vigorous outward expansion.[226]

Hans F. K. Günther took Aryan Studies in the direction of ethnography and race science, and traced the racial type of the Northern European back to the ancient Hindus, Indo-Scythians, and Persians. "In Greece and Asia Minor, cultures originating in Western Europe went down before the incoming Nordic tribes."[227] Greece was invaded by fair-skinned, blue-eyed conquerors from the North, Günther wrote, basing himself heavily on Carl Schuchhardt's 1919 *Alteuropa*, but also on the works of Strzygowski. Günther's reasoning relied on the formal comparison of art objects as well as the comparison of phrenology and qualities of bodily traits, more than on the comparison of languages.[228] In turn, Egon Freiherr von Eickstedt cited Günther as he built his argument about racial determinants on psychology.[229] Aryan Studies relied heavily on interdisciplinary as well as freewheeling methodology, in order to make new, radical claims, and in order to marshal scholarly "proof" for seemingly outlandish, and blatantly chauvinistic, projects in intellectual politics.

The growing interwar field of Aryan Studies generated intellectual authority for Nazi rule. The fancifulness of many of the claims made by Aryanists was the very mark of their new paradigm. One of the goals of scholars in the field was to move the study of Aryans westward and to authorize the claim that the western Aryans were more evolved than eastern Aryans.[230] In the inferiorist reverie, Germans were the descendants of the more vigorous Aryan stalk that stemmed from the Eurasian steppes and then spread northward to invade Bronze Age Saxony.[231] This displaced the Greeks, Italians, Egyptians, and Jews as possible first-origin peoples, and made room for the German-speakers in the guise of "Western Aryans" to take their position at the center of the world.

Aryanism, and the intellectual institutions it legitimated, made neohumanistic sciences into annihilationist weapons. The rise of Aryan Studies as a field jolted the vast popular web of pro-Buddhist Indic Orientalism into disarray.[232] With the Nazi rise, the vast and diverse web of Orientalism that thrived in popular and academic institutions throughout German Europe and that expanded over the 1910s and 1920s was deactivated and cut off, except for a very narrow and fanatical nationalist segment.

FORCED EXILE

Aryanism did not cause Nazism, but Nazism was needed in order to activate and modulate a latent annihilationist potential in the Aryan idea. The rise of the field of Aryan Studies, especially after 1933, went along with the expulsion of vast numbers of German Jews from academia.[233] Yet, even in this period, some Jewish German scholars contributed significantly to the field of Aryan Studies. Among such Jewish German Indologists were Lucian Schermann, the scholar of Vedic and Buddhist literature; and Isidor Scheftelowitz, the son of a rabbi, who became a rabbi himself. Heinrich Zimmer, whose wife was Jewish, wrote on ancient "Aryan" mysticism. And Julius Pokorny, Indo-Germanist and Celtologist, wrote on ideas about time among the Vedic peoples and ancient Iranians.[234] The Jewish German ethnomusicologist, Erich von Hornbostel, and the Jewish Moravian art historian, Stella Kramrisch, both sought forms and spiritual integration in the "Aryan" ancient India.[235] Jewish scholars and other scholars with no inkling at all of anti-Semitism contributed to the study of "Aryan" literature to the extent that they too were interested in the scholarly investigation into first origins, and also sought enchanting and counternormative ways of thinking of relations between East and West.

Jewish Indologists and Orientalist scholars were among the many Jewish academics forced into exile after the "Law for the Reconstruction of the Professional Civil Service" of April 7, 1933. This law authorized the dismissal of government workers who were not of "Aryan" descent. The forced migration ensued of more than 2,000 academics over the coming five years.[236] Many of German Europe's best Indologists, Sinologists, Japanologists, Persianists, and Arabicists were forced out.[237] Across the disciplines, from physics to psychology to cultural studies, German, Austrian, Czech, and Hungarian institutions experienced a mass impoverishment of talent.[238] Recent scholarship provides a synoptic study of the diaspora of European Jewish Sinologists and Japanologists to East Asia.[239] Sometimes, European Jewish scholars with no particular scholarly interest in Asia nevertheless traveled East in search of safe havens to continue their scholarship. Erich Auerbach and Walter Ruben in Turkey, Karl Löwith in Tokyo, and Betty Heimann in Colombo are cases in point.[240] And, in the context of World War II and the beginning of the Nazi genocide campaigns, thousands of German and Austrian Jews traveled by sea to Shanghai out of sheer necessity.[241] Recently, Johannes Voigt and Anil Bhatti have added an important chapter to the study of German Jewish diaspora in the world with their book on Jewish exile in India.[242] As their work makes clear, refugees from Nazi terror traveling to India often did so because of preexisting Orientalist affinities. German Jewish émigrés to India were mainly philologists, writers, artists, and spiritual acolytes and converts to Hinduism, Buddhism, and Islam.[243] Stella Kramrisch, like other Jewish intellectuals, such as Betty Heinemann, Walter Kaufmann, and Hermann Goetz, moved to India. Many of them lost family members in the Nazi genocide.

A theme for further exploration in subsequent chapters is the contribution of exiled German-speaking specialists to Indian institutions of knowledge production beginning in the 1930s. Hermann Goetz, an art historian of Indo-Islamic traditions, left Berlin for India and began to work as curator for the maharaja of Baroda.[244] Stella Kramrisch taught art history at Calcutta University from 1921 until 1950.[245] Walter Ruben, the Indologist and student of Hermann Jacobi, obtained a position at the University of Ankara in 1935, and visited eastern Bengal for six months in 1935–1936.[246]

Ruben's trip to India was funded by the Turkish government, and also by a stipend from his teacher, the Frankfurt anthropologist, Leo Frobenius.[247] After the war, Ruben chose to return to East Germany where he headed the Indology Program at Humboldt University.[248] Betty Heimann, a scholar of Sanskritic philosophy, studied with Paul Deussen. She took up a lectureship in Sri Lanka in 1935. Heimann returned to teach in Germany at the University of Halle in 1957.[249] Meanwhile, Leopold Weiss, who converted to Islam and took the name Mohammad Asad, immigrated to the Punjab in 1932, and became a leading intellectual and statesman of the future Pakistan.

Central European Jews who escaped Nazi terror through migration entered the perplexing condition of statelessness.[250] Once scholars and intellectuals entered exile, the methods they used and the identity that came with those scholarly practices created lines of intellectual and disciplinary continuity with the German-speaking countries they had fled.[251] When German-speaking scholars entered diaspora, it was often their commitment to a set of practices, to an intellectual culture, and to a certain experience of self that marked their identity.[252]

The cooperation between the old right-wing Orientalists and the Aryan Studies boys shut down the vast dialogic domain of Indic Orientalism that had grown up in German popular and academic cultures as the ideal of nineteenth-century "Europe" fell apart. German-speaking scholars in exile continued to institutionalize Germanic modes of scholarship and habits of mind, especially ones that articulated post-Enlightenment scholarly perspectives.[253] The scholarly activities of exiled German-speaking scholars created entanglements with Indian nationalists in the 1930s and 1940s.[254] The rest of this book explores the relational webs that emerged. The rise of popular Orientalism and of Indian anticolonialism created a series of traveling itineraries that nation-state politics could not contain.

FOUR

Indian Visions of a Germanic Home

World War I brought Indians to Germany in large numbers. The Great War dealt a serious blow to the vitality of the British empire, and scholars have argued that the "decolonizing process" began as early as the time boots hit the ground in the Dardanelles. The increasing entanglements of Indian nationalists with societies and institutional spaces outside the British empire were symptoms not only of the decline of British power in India but also of the loss of Britain's magnetic force as the lodestar at the center of a world order. The multiplication of centers of world power in the lead-up to World War I—a regionalization of the earth—continued in accentuated form into the 1920s and 1930s. A measure of "deglobalization" pressed Indians into alternative migration patterns after 1918 as the "traditional Victorian economy crashed into ruins," and globe-straddling economic and cultural liberalism under the aegis of nineteenth-century British hegemony was replaced with a plurality of post-Enlightenment utopias.[1]

The German Foreign Office, under Max von Oppenheim, recruited high-profile Indian Hindu revolutionaries from Paris, London, and San Francisco to join the German war effort as consultants and propaganda czars at the very start of the belligerencies. A group of *svadeśi* internationalists, Virendranath Chattopadhyaya, Hardayal, and Bhupendranath Datta chief among them, collected in Charlottenburg in August 1914.[2] A Committee for Indian Independence was constituted as part of the newly established Nachrichtenstelle für den Orient (Information Bureau for the East) under Oppenheim's direction.[3] One of the main tasks of the Nachrichtenstelle was the production of anti-British propaganda in Middle Eastern and

Asian languages, including Urdu, Persian, Hindi, Arabic, and Chinese. Until the autumn of 1915, the two most important roles of the Nachrichtenstelle für den Orient involved attempts to provide massive amounts of weapons to revolutionaries on India's east coast via Hardayal's Ghadar network headquartered in San Francisco, and a simultaneous campaign to raise revolution throughout the Middle East that would spill into India from the northwest frontier.[4]

The number of Indian "sojourners" in Germany was augmented by the large number of Indian prisoners of war (POWs) from the British army, held at camps outside Berlin.[5] Prisoners were allowed to exit the camps if they entered the service of the German Foreign Office during the war. And after the war's end, some POWs chose to remain in Berlin rather than return to colonial India.

This contingent of radical anticolonial activists and ex-POWs formed the kernel for a significant Indian community in Berlin after 1918. The neighborhood of Charlottenburg became Berlin's "little Asia" partly because the Foreign Office had set up its Information Bureau for the Orient in that region during the war.[6] Hardayal recalled of his time in Charlottenburg in 1914 that "all the peoples of Asia could be seen on the streets."[7] The most powerful and respected Indian émigrés, especially Virendranath Chattopadhyaya and Bhupendranath Datta, established a center for diasporic anticolonial nationalist activity. The social imprint of wartime experience kept Indians in this same region of Berlin throughout the 1920s and 1930s. Social spaces that were established in the war years for anticolonial activists—dormitories for Indian students, community meeting houses, parks to play cricket, places of worship, the homes of the older generation of émigrés—now served a burgeoning community of Indian students in the Weimar period.[8]

The conduits of entanglements among German and Indian intellectuals were not random or diffuse, but were organized within fields of dialogue. There was choreography to transnational encounters. Entanglements and the institutions that structured them provided the frameworks and the media that gave shape to German–Indian interactions. These entanglements provided Indians with ways to resituate their place in the world. Discourses of the natural sciences, social sciences, and the humanities that connected Indians with German universities proffered a new kind of "soft power" for Indian nationalists to undermine the British imperial worldview.[9]

PATHS TO GERMAN EUROPE

Indians who traveled to Germany in the 1910s-1930s pursued anticolonial politics and obtained degrees of higher education before returning home.[10] Some made German society their new permanent home. In the time when the British empire was breaking down, Indians treated Germany, and German Europe generally (including Austria and Switzerland), as a reservoir of intellectual, cultural, and social resources to aid the nationalizing project.

Benoy Kumar Sarkar, one of the young leaders of the National Council of Education in Bengal, began a decade of world travel in 1914.[11] Sarkar, member of the Calcutta Dawn Society and disciple of Satish Chandra Mukherjee, led the project of building transnational linkages for *svadeśi* internationalists in the 1910s and helped plan which students were to be sent abroad by the National Council of Education.[12] Sarkar made a series of study tours across the world from 1914 to 1926 and wrote about his experience in books such as *Duniyār Ābhāoyā* (The atmospheres of the world) 1922.[13] He spoke about the need for study tours among Indian nationalists in order to ensure what he called the healthy "social metabolism" of the Bengali people.[14] He published five volumes on world touring, which included reports on his trips to Egypt in 1914, to England in 1916, to China in 1922, and to "Yankee-stan" (the United States) in 1923. Sarkar also published a 600-page work, written in Bengali, on his experiences in Germany, *Parājita Jārmānī* (*Defeated Germany*, 1932).[15] Sarkar developed a theory of touring and travel, which he called "digesting the world" (*duniyā hajam karā*).[16]

Benoy Kumar Sarkar repeatedly restated in his writings of the 1920s and 1930s that his views were produced from lived experience. He began his book, *Economic Development* (1926), by saying that "the papers were backed by a mass of concrete experience derived from visits to workshops and institutions as well as on-the-spot conversations."[17] Sarkar reported that he met Germans "in the flesh and blood" (*raktamāṃse*) and that he "condensed" all of these encounters in his work.[18] He proposed, "a unity of meaning could be bound together (*aikyer bandhan pāōyā jaibe*) by experiencing the flesh and blood of another people (*raktamāṃser gandhe*), and by being in exchange with their daily life (*mānuṣer prāṇer spandane*)."[19] His project was not only to experience the "world-forces" abroad but also to channel these forces to Bengal, and to "digest" them in particularly Bengali and anticolonial Indian ways. Between 1921 and 1936, Sarkar wrote twelve volumes of his *Bartamān Jagat* (Contemporary World) in Bengali covering some 4,000 pages.[20] "We cannot be satisfied with the still meager amount of research that Bengali researchers have carried out regarding today's world. Young Bengal requires more," Sarkar enjoined.[21] In an age of world touring, by Europeans and Asians alike, Sarkar inspired younger *bhadralōk* travelers.[22]

Kalidas Nag partook of Benoy Kumar Sarkar's travel ethos in 1923. While studying philosophy in Paris, he took the opportunity to make journeys through Italy, Germany, Sweden, Czechoslovakia, Egypt, and Palestine.[23] Nag published a set of travelogues on his experiences, especially focused on his encounters with continental European scholars. The way foreign experience could be socially distributed, almost as though it were an accruing and shareable kind of invisible capital, disrupts that hard-and-fast analytic distinction between the "rooted" and the "traveling" modes of anticolonial activity.[24]

Indians studying and touring abroad were interested in reaching the top of foreign disciplinary hierarchies. *Svadeśi* internationalists wanted to reach the most prestigious figures in German institutions in order to garner heightened international recognition for the Indian nationalist cause. By establishing relays with prestigious German science, Indians hoped to substantiate claims about their distinction vis-à-vis the British empire. Indian scholarly internationalists branched out to cover a wide spectrum of disciplines, from the natural sciences to the social sciences to the humanities: from physics to political science to art history.

ESTABLISHING AN INDIAN PRESENCE IN GERMANY

The diasporic community of Indians in Berlin during the 1920s numbered about 400 to 500 individuals.[25] But this small group also served as a wellspring of radical nationalism in the 1920s, a catalyst for politics back on the subcontinent. It was from these Central European connections, for example, that Indian anticolonial entanglements with European Marxist institutions first began.[26] Out of this group also came engineers, doctors, and business leaders for the nationalist movement.[27]

In 1921, the German consul in London wrote of his efforts to facilitate the travel of Indian students to Germany. He placed the advantages of Germany in comparative terms: "we are unquestionably in a position to offer a far better education [to Indians] than the English can provide."[28] Indian students often began working at British institutions and then from there obtained permission to take one or two years of study in Germany.[29] But the Indian Information Bureau begun in 1929 made it possible for Indian students to come directly to continental Europe, circumventing London's imperial nexus.[30] This project to send students to Germany for training came to be championed by Jawaharlal Nehru himself by the late 1920s, especially thanks to the work of the organizers in Berlin, Virendranath Chattopadhyaya and his assistant, A. C. N. Nambiar.[31] As of 1929, the Indian Information Bureau received funds directly from the Indian National Congress under Nehru's direction.[32]

Nehru wanted Indian students to go increasingly to Germany instead of to Britain for education, and this would help produce Indian intellectual elites with less dependence on British imperial institutions.[33] Within a two-month period from September to November 1929, for example, the Indian Information Bureau reported 68 inquiries, 219 visitors, and 17 new students, with 14 coming directly from India.[34] Around the same time, beginning in 1928, the Deutsche Akademie, an official agency for German cultural diplomacy, set up an Indian Department to facilitate the study travel of Indians to German universities.[35] This new program of 1928 and 1929, run both by diasporic Indians and by funds from the German state, responded to the rising trend in increasingly bold ways.[36] The policy of granting scholarships to Indian students expanded through the 1930s, and a Humboldt Medal for renowned visiting Indian scholars was introduced in 1936.[37]

Virendranath Chattopadhyaya was perhaps the most important organizer of institutions for Indian travel in German Europe.[38] He served the Information Bureau of the Orient during the war.[39] Virendranath was the son of an eminent Bengali literary family in Hyderabad.[40] He graduated from Oxford in 1903, and became an itinerant anticolonial nationalist between London, Paris, and Berlin in the period of *svadeśi* resistance to British rule.[41] Virendranath Chattopadhyay moved from one anticolonial underground to another, from the salon of Shyamaji Krishnavarma in London to that of Bhikaji Cama in Paris, embracing the program of springing the imperial lock by forging transnational alliances and cultural diplomatic ties in the diaspora.

The pursuit of study travel went far back in Virendranath Chattopadhyaya's family. His father, Aghorenath, had obtained a PhD in chemistry from Edinburgh University and had toured German and Dutch universities in 1875.[42] Aghorenath returned to India to join the Indian Civil Service, and became an influential educationist in Hyderabad as the first principal of Nizam College and the founder of a school for girls.[43] He passed on his enthusiasm for intellectual politics as well as a particular affection for both British and Central European education to many of his children. Aghorenath's son, Virendranath, his daughter, Suhasini Chattopadhyaya, and his daughter-in-law, Kamaladevi Chattopadhyaya, all studied in Britain and spent extended time living in Germany in the postwar years. The younger family members, in different ways, embraced communism in the 1920s as a powerful language for Indian anticolonial struggle.[44] Virendranath's older sister, Sarojini, was a celebrated All-India nationalist figure and the poet laureate of the Indian National Congress.[45]

In 1921, Virendranath established a new organization in Berlin, the Association of Indians of German Europe.[46] His main goal was to organize the many Indian students coming to Berlin, both to serve the diasporic student community and to coordinate students for anticolonial resistance. Virendranath founded the Hindustan Haus, a boarding house sponsored by the Deutsches Institut für Ausländer (German Institute for Foreigners) of Berlin University.[47] After the creation of the Comintern in 1919, Virendranath sat at the top of one of the three overseas Communist Parties of India, with the other two led by M. N. Roy in Berlin, and by Shapurji Saklatvala in London.[48]

By 1923, more than 300 Indians were staying in Berlin.[49] Among Indian students at Berlin universities, about a third studied natural and applied sciences, especially physics, chemistry, and engineering. A quarter studied the humanities, and a quarter pursued the social sciences.[50] Between 1928 and 1932, 140 Indian students matriculated at the University of Berlin, suggesting that the numbers of Indian students in Berlin remained relatively constant over the course of the 1920s.[51]

Many students lived in the Hindustan Haus on Uhlandstraße, in close proximity to the Berlin Technical University.[52] The majority of Indians living in Berlin tended to live close to the Hindustan Haus. There were also clusters of Indian students in the cheaper workers' neighborhoods of Moabit and Wedding.[53] Virendranath Chattopadhyaya's house at Georg-Wilhelm-Straße served as an epicenter for the Indian Association, and for Indian students and political activists. In May 1923, Virendranath hosted 225 students at his home on Georg-Wilhelm-Straße.[54]

In these early years, not many Indian students studied medicine. This was in contrast to the broader trend of foreign students who studied in

Berlin in the 1920s.[55] For example, of 2,578 foreign students matriculated at Berlin University in 1923, one-third studied either medicine or dentistry. Asian and African students (426 in total) made up about 15 percent of all foreign students studying at Berlin University in the 1920s. Indians were a small fraction of that number, and their studies tended to focus on the natural and social sciences.[56] A few Indian students also studied industrial arts, such as weaving and printing, although, in these cases, the students in question were generally already master craftsmen seeking advanced training.[57] Of the students in the sciences, physics, chemistry and engineering were best represented. Within the humanities, the majority of Indians studied Indic and Semitic philology, and German language and philosophy, while a few pursued photography or cinematography.[58] By the 1920s, Berlin's reputation in India as an arts capital rivaled the typical fascination with Paris.[59]

Within the social sciences, an overwhelming number of students studied political economy (*Nationalökonomie*).[60] In addition to university study, the Siemens enclave (Siemensstadt) in Berlin, a suburb of the city built by Siemens AG, sponsored a number of Indians to undertake industrial training.[61] As Siemens strengthened its presence in India in the 1930s, especially at the peak of an Indian electrification boom,[62] the Siemens enclave in Berlin became the scene for Indian cultural and educational diplomacy.[63] Both the Nizam of Hyderabad and the Prince of Baroda visited the Siemensstadt in 1931, receiving the red-carpet treatment.[64] The maharaja of Rewa visited in 1933, seeking an arrangement for Siemens to develop electrification and waterworks projects in his state.[65] The majority of Indian visitors to Berlin aimed, in some way, to acquire knowledge and methods that would further the political ends of anticolonial economic nationalization. Indians saw German Europe as a reservoir of know-how and technique in the arts and sciences.[66]

The Indian Association of German Europe organized nationalist meetings and social events for new arrivals to Berlin.[67] Over the years, luminaries such as Rabindranath Tagore, Motilal and Jawaharlal Nehru, the singer Dilip Roy, and Subhas Chandra Bose all sojourned in Berlin via Virendranath's institutions.[68] Virendranath set an example for others. Zakir Husain, who later became chancellor of Aligarh University and the third president of India after independence, studied political economy in Berlin beginning in 1924. Following Virendranath's example in anticolonial cultural diplomacy, Husain organized a major "gathering" of Indian students with German professors at the Hotel Bristol on Unter den Linden in 1926.[69]

Other younger Indian internationalists worked under Chattopadhyaya's leadership. Bhupendranath Datta, the younger brother of the Hindu spiritual leader, Vivekananda, helped organize one of the fledgling Indian Communist parties while completing his dissertation in anthropology at Humboldt University.[70] Meanwhile A. C. N. Nambiar, a Malayali intellectual and brother-in-law of Virendranath, joined the Berlin group in 1921 and later played a major role in setting up the Indian Information Bureau as a satellite organization of the Indian National Congress.[71] The "Indian News Service and Information Bureau," established by Virendranath Chattopadhyaya and A. C. N. Nambiar in October 1922, represents the first attempt to create a satellite office for the Indian National Congress.[72] Nambiar would later organize Azad Hind Radio, an anticolonial radio station transmitted from Berlin during World War II. He became the first Indian ambassador to West Germany in 1952.[73]

Virendranath Chattopadhyaya funded his operations in Berlin with a mix of funds from the Russian Bolsheviks and the Indian National Congress.[74] He tried to reconstitute an international anticolonial constellation in the postwar years from his Berlin base. Virendranath sent letters to H. N. Ghose in New York, Rash Behari Bose in Tokyo, Barakatullah in Kabul, and Jawaharlal Nehru in Delhi, proposing a renewed and organized traveling nationalist movement organized around the Berlin hub.[75]

Jawaharlal Nehru and his father, Motilal, visited Berlin in 1926 on Virendranath's invitation.[76] And when Virendranath became the general secretary of the Soviet-sponsored Brussels-based League against Imperialism, Jawaharlal Nehru agreed to serve on the executive council.[77] The Indian contingent to the League against Imperialism formed its own chapter with Jawaharlal Nehru and Shapurji Saklatvala as copresidents and with Jaya Surya Naidu, the nephew of Virendranath Chattopadhyaya, and Khwaja Abdul Hamid as Berlin representatives.[78]

A CATALYTIC CENTER

What ends were served by the organization of the Indian traveling nationalists in Berlin? Already in 1922, with the number of Indian students in Germany rising, the British government began raising concerns about the revolutionary leanings of the diasporic community in the city. An intelligence officer in British India reported, "the information recently received regarding the activities of Indian revolutionaries in Germany, and in particular the establishment there of a night school for the manufacture of bombs and explosives, has led the Government of India to consider further the question of the grant of passports for Germany to Indians."[79] In that same year, the Central Intelligence Department of the government of India began drawing up "blacklists" of Indians suspected of anticolonial activity on the continent, lists they revised yearly and maintained well into the 1940s.[80]

Indian students openly engaged in anticolonial activism by attending nationalist gatherings or by participating in even more direct involvement in political intrigue, including transporting Soviet-sponsored Marxist literature back to India and creating anti-British alliances with different levels of German officialdom. In Berlin, the line blurred between studying and engaging in radical politics. For example, while Ananda Mohan Bose completed his doctorate in physics in Berlin, he also associated with Virendranath's group and M. N. Roy's communist circle in 1924.[81] D. M. Bose, the nephew of leading Indian physicist Jagadish Chandra Bose, eventually returned to India as a communist agent carrying anti-British Soviet literature.[82] Or take the cases of Brajesh Singh and Tayab Shaikh who both came to Berlin to study engineering, but soon abandoned their studies completely in order to work exclusively in M. N. Roy's communist group.[83]

Indian doctoral students in Berlin often transformed themselves into radicalized leaders of Indian anticolonial politics. A diasporic center such as Berlin provided an important environment for their political formation before they returned home as nationalist leaders, ensconced in new dialogues about India's significance in the world. Zakir Husain, a reformer of university education associated with the University of Delhi and Aligarh Muslim University, later became president of India.[84] Ram Manohar Lohia completed doctoral research at the University of Berlin and returned home as a prolific political theorist of Gandhian socialism and as a leader of the Congress Socialist Party.[85] Gangadhar Adhikari, who arrived in Berlin to begin a doctorate in chemistry, soon involved himself with communist organizations in Berlin and went on to serve as one of the most influential theorists in the Indian Communist Party in the 1930s and 1940s.[86] And Meghnad Saha, an internationally renowned physicist who also studied in Berlin in the 1920s, returned home to Calcutta to play a major role as a nationalist organizer of science in India from the 1930s to the 1950s.[87] The biographies of many major Indian nationalist figures of midcentury bear the watermark of German diaspora.

But there was more going on than university matriculation and political radicalization alone. Diaspora led to German–Indian social interactions of proliferating sorts and outcomes. Many marriages between Indian men and German women developed.[88] Vikram Seth's *Two Lives* provides a touching biographical account of Indian–German intimacy in the 1930s.[89] The archives are less detailed, but the affective bonds of political, social, and intellectual entanglement between Germans and Indians in the war years is still obvious. Abdul Sattar Kheiri, Babar Mirza, Benoy Kumar Sarkar, Subhas Chandra Bose, and M. N. Roy all had German or Austrian wives.[90] The Bhaduri brothers, Anadhi Nath and Prasanta, both studied in Germany in the 1920s and also returned to Calcutta with German wives, Margrit and Gerta. British surveillance officers note that at Aligarh University in the 1930s, "at least six of the Professors have German wives," and these six professors had completed PhDs in Germany a decade earlier.[91]

The potentials of popularized Indic Orientalism in German society and the modes of relation that it produced could alternate from the seemingly sublime to the patently absurd. Indians could be represented as primitive, just as much as they could be represented as sage, or archaically exotic. Indeed, Orientalism and imperialism were different phases of a single kinetic force.[92] And this beam of German imperialist fantasies and German Orientalism seemed to intensify after the Locarno Treaties of 1925, just as Germany was beginning to reclaim a role in international politics after almost six years of enforced exclusion from the League of Nations.[93] As Germany was readmitted into the European international community, and as the economy stabilized, German colonialist cravings arose anew, in terms of the wish to reclaim German colonies abroad and the desire to annex contiguous land in the east.[94]

In July 1926 the billboards of Berlin were plastered with advertisements for "Indians in the Zoo!" John Hagenbeck, brother of the Hamburg circus magnate, Carl Hagenbeck, brought more than 100 South Asians from Sri Lanka to live in grass huts, charm snakes, climb poles, and dance in an "Indian Village" set up in the Berlin Zoological Garden. "The public gives the money," one observer remarked, "and seems delighted and astonished to learn that Indians can speak any language at all—they seem to think they are like apes in the forest, who only chatter."[95] The performers were paid only 20 to 50 marks per month, and gave up to six performances a day. They were not allowed to leave their compound and were instructed to collect around Hagenbeck when he made his appearance before the German

audiences. Human sideshows and exhibitions were not unique in this period, of course. In fact, ever since the exhibition of the "Hottentot Venus"
in the early nineteenth century,[96] but especially since the 1870s, European
audiences could celebrate their supposed place on the ladder of human
progress by viewing displays of "strange" peoples and "primitive" races in
purportedly indigenous dress at fairs, circuses, and exhibitions.[97] Carl
Hagenbeck, John Hagenbeck, and the Krone Circus were all involved in
bringing *Völkerschauen* to German audiences in the 1910s and 1920s.[98] In
1915, for example, some Indians who had come to Germany for study but
were then expelled from their courses due to war measures were forced to
don costumes and turbans and sell Ceylon tea at the Hagenbeck fair in
Hamburg.[99] By 1926, however, a diasporic community of Indians had taken
up residence in the city and was poised to launch an attack against John
Hagenbeck, and to criticize the German public for its ignorant depiction of
what was termed "Gandhi's people" in the German press.[100]

The first volley of protests came from the leaders of the Indian community in Berlin, Virendranath Chattopadhyaya and A. C. N. Nambiar. In an
article appearing in the *Berliner Tageszeitung*, the two argued on grounds
of human rights that the demeaning show should end.[101] They criticized
the racial hubris underlying the event.[102] Indian students protested the
show on two occasions. Letters were also sent to the British embassy in
Berlin demanding that Hagenbeck not be allowed back to Ceylon or South
India to recruit further. A German journalist, Rudolf Olden, noted the in-
humane conditions under which performers lived.[103] He spoke out against
the shows and called for an embargo on Hagenbeck's company by the British authorities.[104] The eruptions of protest in the Indian community confirm the presence of a highly organized, and vocal, Indian diasporic group
in Berlin during the 1920s.

INDIANS AND INSTITUTIONS OF TRANSNATIONAL ENTANGLEMENT

Rabindranath Tagore, in 1913, was the first Indian to win the Nobel Prize
in Literature.[105] With that prize, he stood out in the world. He rose to the
heights of international cultural prestige, and used his status in a project to
critique India's peripheral status in the imperial system. International literary audiences beyond the empire became important for Rabindranath's
project, and the most significant overseas audience at the end of World
War I was located in Germany.[106]

In his lectures across north and south Germany in 1921, Rabindranath emphasized the "spiritual" message of the East as contrasted with the "materialistic" and "exhausted" civilization of the West.[107] Such a prioritization of the Orient over the Occident resonated strongly with German postwar audiences. The whole trip was an affair in cultural diplomacy. Rabindranath's books became best sellers in Germany in the 1920s, published by Kurt Wolff Verlag. Because of popular Indic Orientalism, and because of the post-Versailles cultural shock, Rabindranath Tagore's books sold more copies in Germany between 1917 and 1924 than in other international markets.[108] In Berlin, beginning on May 29, 1921, Rabindranath delivered lectures, visited the Indian community living in the city, and even recorded a poetry reading on wax plate for the Wilhelm Dögen sound archive (which still exists).[109] Carl Heinrich Becker, the Prussian minister of culture, received the Indian poet.[110] From Berlin, Rabindranath traveled on June 5 to Munich, where Thomas Mann attended his lecture. The poet went on to Darmstadt, for the "Tagore Week" organized by Hermann von Keyserling. A visit was made to the Bauhaus School in Weimar where Rabindranath made the acquaintance of the school's art director, Johannes Itten.[111] The opponents of popular Indic Orientalism disparaged the extreme excitement over Rabindranath Tagore's visit as "Tagore-Mode" and "Tagore-Kult."[112]

But Rabindranath's efforts in cultural diplomacy involved as much the donation of wisdom and Indian culture to Germany as the solicitation of cultural gifts from Germans for the Indian nationalist cause. Rabindranath built institutional and personal friendships through complementary practices of gift-giving and gift-receiving.[113] If Rabindranath donated cultural goods in public, he was interested in receiving cultural goods in private. In Rabindranath's private discussions with German academics, he scaled the mountains of German science and sought to recruit German and Austrian scholars as visiting fellows to his recently inaugurated (1921) university, called the Indian International University (Viśva Bhārati).

He was pleased to receive a collection of 400 German books for the library of the new university presented to him at Darmstadt on the occasion of his sixtieth birthday. The book donation came with a laudatory birthday note signed by German scholars of national renown, including Adolf Harnack, Hermann Jacobi, Richard Wilhelm, Hermann Hesse, and Gerhart Hauptmann.[114] Rabindranath wrote from Darmstadt to C. F. Andrews, his colleague who was then in Shantiniketan: "Germans have done more than any other countries in the world for opening up and broadening the channel of the intellectual and spiritual communication of the West with India, and the . . . love, which she freely has given to-day to a poet of the East, will surely impart to this relationship the depth of an intimate and personal character."[115] Rabindranath was celebrated by the revolutionary conservatives, by the nationalist (bündische) Youth Movement, by the liberal bourgeoisie and belletrists, and by the Left, even if young critics such as Georg Lukàcs vituperated against the German fascination with Rabindranath's writings, which he saw as little more than a fetish of bourgeois Orientalism.[116]

Rabindranath's 1921 trip was widely covered in both the German press and the Bengali press.[117] In fact, the enthusiasm for Rabindranath Tagore in German newspapers was then reported in Bengali newspapers. Rabindranath, upon returning home to Calcutta, was hailed for "doing service to the mother country abroad (bideśe)."[118] Images of swarming crowds awaiting Rabindranath Tagore at Darmstadt and Berlin, as well as his portrait on the front page of the Berliner Illustrierte Zeitung, appeared in the Prabāsī magazine, the most important journal of the Bengali educated classes.

During Rabindranath's second trip to Germany in 1926, the popular cult around him subsided substantially. Economic stabilization, the rising antiromantic Neue Sachlichkeit (New Objectivity) artistic sensibilities, the resurgence of German imperial pretensions, but also the rise of the völkische variant of Aryan studies, meant that the coming of a dark sage from India sparked much less interest than it once had.[119] During this second visit, Keyserling again organized events in Darmstadt.[120] Indologists, especially Heinrich Lüders, Sten Konow, and Richard Pischel again hosted Rabindranath's lectures. Rabindranath met with a strong enough reception in 1926 to warrant a third and final trip to Germany in 1930. It was during the last trip that Rabindranath climbed to the top of the German magic mountain with his celebrated and much publicized summits with the icon of German physics, Albert Einstein.[121]

During his last tour, Rabindranath did not primarily come as a sage or a poet, but now in another guise—as an expressionist painter.[122] The exhibit of Bauhaus Art in Calcutta in 1922–1923, including the display of pieces by Paul Klee, whom Rabindranath so admired, stimulated a feedback response.[123] On this final trip, Rabindranath brought 400 of his watercolors with him and put them on display.[124] Rabindranath had already exhibited his paintings in Birmingham and Paris, and they now went up at the Moeller Gallery in Berlin, and then on to a subsequent show in Munich.[125] Before returning to India, Rabindranath gave a gift of six paintings to the Berlin Museum in his continued project to build international ties through giving gifts of Indian culture.[126]

Just as certain German scientists, for example, Albert Einstein and Sigmund Freud, became embodiments of Germanic monumental science with their gravitational pull felt as far away as colonial India, so too, for Germans, certain Indians, such as Rabindranath Tagore and M. K. Gandhi, became the charismatic embodiments of the Orient's monumental gravitas of myth and wisdom.[127] The 1920s, we should also observe, also saw a Gandhi craze in Germany.[128]

Rabindranath's efforts in transnational dialogue during his 1921 trip paid off. When he founded his new international university in 1921, his first order of business was to bring in prestigious continental European scholars as his founding faculty. Josef Strzygowski, an expert on non-Western art and founder of the Art History Institute at the University of Vienna, promised to come to Shantiniketan in order to set up a department there.[129] In the end Strzygowski did not come, but he sent his promising student, Stella Kramrisch, who remained in Bengal for thirty years helping to build up nationalist intellectual institutions. Meanwhile, in 1925, Ali Akhtar Ansari, a young Indian architect, began his dissertation on the architectural history of the Taj Mahal under Strzygowski's supervision in Vienna. Strzygowski also wrote five essays on Indian art for the London Indian Society in 1925, suggesting that the 1920s were Strzygowski's "Indian years," even if he remained an admirer at a distance.[130]

Sylvain Lévi, the leading Indologist at the Sorbonne, held a visiting chair at Shantiniketan in 1921. The linguist and German translator of Rabindranath's work, Heinrich Meyer-Benfy, assumed a visiting lectureship in 1922. Moriz Winternitz, eminent Indologist at Charles University in Prague, held a visiting Indology chair in 1923. The German-trained Norwegian scholar, Sten Konow, who had served as the deputy to George Grierson in the Linguistic Survey of India before World War I, came to Shantiniketan the following year, 1924–1925.[131] Rabindranath had wanted Paul Natorp to teach philosophy at Shantiniketan, and hoped also that artists from the Bauhaus school might visit to teach modern art.[132] Neither of those objectives was ultimately achieved. But Guiseppe Tucci, the Italian Indologist and specialist on Buddhism and Tibetan Art, arrived in 1926. And Vincenc Lesný, a Czech scholar and Winternitz's student, arrived in Shantiniketan in 1929. These scholars were brought in order to lend their prestige to

Indian nationalist learning, and to bolster Shantiniketan's academic status on the global stage. Rabindranath's anticolonial internationalist pursuit of cultural and intellectual distinction depended on alliance building. India had been centered in the world in the ancient past, Rabindranath argued, and collaboration with continental European scholars would allow India to again become a world center for the arts and humanities in modern times, just as "India's learning had once spread outside India, [and] the people outside accepted it."[133]

DIALOGUE UNDER DURESS

The relationship between dialogic action, epistemic radicalism, and anticolonial intellectual political power was not lost on British colonial surveillance. The British were concerned about Berlin as a crucible for political activism outside empire, against empire. By late 1924, the whole atmosphere in Germany had changed. In the national elections of that year, the German Communist Party had lost 1,000,000 votes. The Dawes Plan produced stabilizing results for the German economy: industrial production grew by 50 percent and the unemployment rate dropped sharply.[134] The year marked the conclusion of the revolutionary eruptions that haunted the young Weimar Republic. In this context, the German government cooperated with British requests to expel anti-British colonial activists in Berlin. The Berlin police suppressed the activity of Indian revolutionaries, apologizing to the British government for the "inconvenient guests" that took up residence in the city.[135] German officials turned on the tap of police aggression against Indians in the hope of securing the good favor of the British as well as the benefits of access to the Indian market for German industry.[136]

In 1925, at the insistence of the British government, the German government expelled twenty of the most influential Indian leaders in Berlin.[137] In 1925, the infamous traveling radical, M. N. Roy, moved to Paris (he was soon expelled from there too),[138] while others such as Bhupendranath Datta, Benoy Kumar Sarkar, and Abdul Jabbar Kheiri returned to India.[139] The business of Virendranath Chattopadhyaya's Indian Information Bureau ceased, and Chattopadhyaya was forced to move out of his spacious house on Georg-Wilhelm-Straße due to lack of funds.[140] He relocated to the suburb of Spandau before leaving for Switzerland.[141] Those leaders who did not return to India filtered back to Berlin in 1927, after the police onslaught subsided.[142]

As many Indian men in the diasporic community married German, European, or American women, the continuous political intrigue and fear of persecution strained, and often broke, relationships. The track record of Indian–German marriage was not one of perennial marital bliss or intercultural understanding. Evelyn Trent, an American, and the wife and political collaborator of M. N. Roy, wrote to a friend that she was "weary of being hunted from place to place, country to country, of having to hide and always to be rewarded by a thick fog of suspicion and fear."[143] Trent, in 1926, eventually decided to return home to the United States. Agnes Smedley, originally from the backwoods of Missouri, and eventually an important anticolonial political activist, was the partner of Virendranath Chattopadhyaya in Berlin at this time. She recalled the extreme difficulties, even neurosis, associated with the anticolonial cosmopolitan lifestyle. "We were desperately poor, and because Viren [Chattopadhyaya] had no possessions, I sold everything I owned in order to get money. . . . We met the problem by moving repeatedly and changing our name. But our debts and difficulties seemed to increase by geometric progression. More than death I feared insanity."[144] Smedley left Chattopadhyaya in 1928.[145] At least one German woman, Hilde Singh, was recorded as murdering her Indian migrant husband, Shiodeo Singh-Aluwaliya.[146] Indian–German romantic liaisons split up, as much as they joined together.

The ailments, psychological and physical, associated with traveling anticolonial life could be severe. Hardayal, one of the central Indian political activists in Berlin during World War I, retired in 1918 to a sanatorium to cure his nerves before leaving Germany for good and adopting a vigorous anti-German political stand.[147] A German official reported of Hardayal that "his nerves [were] so destroyed that, at times, he no longer [behaved] normally."[148] Life followed art. The theme was a favorite of Somerset Maugham in his writings on the fictional Indian radical, Chandra. After the war, Maugham served as a British intelligence officer investigating the dealings of Indian nationalists on the European continent. Meanwhile, W. E. B. Du Bois, in *Dark Princess*, wove together narrative threads of Indian diasporic political life, romance, and African American political travel through Europe.

Strain and paranoia can be traced through the biography of many itinerant nationalists in German Europe. M. N. Roy fell severely ill with an infection of the inner ear in 1929 just as he was being expelled from the

Comintern.[149] And Indian traveling nationalists suffered from dyspepsia. Subhas Chandra Bose, the renowned diasporic Indian nationalist in Germany in the 1930s, and Virendranath Chattopadhayaya both complained of severe stomach illness.[150] Although political activities and agendas differed in many ways, politicized travelers all had to face the depleting effects of continuous struggle and displacement. Severe physical and mental strain resulted from the condition of "statelessness."[151]

Virendranath Chattopadhyaya was said to suffer from paranoia. His German secretary, Lucie Hecht, recalled that he never took meals outside for fear of being poisoned.[152] Chattopadhyaya's second wife, the Russian Lidiia Kazunovskaia, remembered him as "always in a state of fleeing, full of disease, sorrow, awareness, always on the alert . . ."[153] Chattopadhyaya, a man without a sense of being at home, living in rented rooms paid for by the money of European patrons, entered a depressive state that eventually led him to abandon Berlin a final time in 1928.[154] After another period of wandering through Europe, he finally settled in Moscow in 1931.[155] He taught anthropology in Moscow for some years, but soon began to raise the suspicion of the paranoid Stalinist regime, which suspected him of deviating from "orthodox" Marxism-Leninism in his teaching. During the purges, a campaign began to prove his heterodoxy, and letters from some of his students, especially Archie Phinney, as well as from his ex-wife Agnes Smedley, accused him of being an Indian nationalist, not a "true" Soviet.[156] Chattopadhyaya disappeared in the Stalinist purges of 1938–1940, murdered by the regime.[157]

Adolf Hitler had already recorded his distaste for the Indian national movement in Germany in *Mein Kampf*, with its "fakirs" and "traveling jugglers."[158] And with Hitler's ascent, influential members of the Indian diasporic community in Berlin were immediately placed under arrest. In the midst of the Nazi crackdown on communists, on February 28, 1933, the Nazi paramilitary group, the SA (Sturmabteilung), stormed into the Indian Information Bureau and confiscated papers. By evening, the SA had taken the two administrators of the bureau, A. C. N. Nambiar and Jayasurya Naidu, Virendranath's nephew, as well as Taraknath Das and Soumendranath Tagore (Rabindranath Tagore's nephew), into custody.[159] The Nazi crackdown resulted in the imprisonment of thousands of communists during this same period.[160] Nambiar, Das, Naidu, and Soumendranath Tagore were released after ten days, following the inquiries of the British embassy in Berlin into their cases.[161] Indian activists fled the city. Nambiar took up residence in Prague.[162] Taraknath Das left Munich for the United States.[163] But conditions would again stabilize and Indian students once more started arriving for studies in Germany. More than 180 students came to study in Germany between 1928 and 1938.[164]

An Indischer Ausschuss (a new Indian Bureau), under the direction of Adam von Trott zu Solz, was established in order to oversee the activities of Indians in Germany. It had its offices in the Ahnenerbe headquarters in Berlin.[165] Trott zu Solz became the main Nazi government liaison to the anticolonial leader and representative of traveling *svadeśi,* Subhas Chandra Bose.[166] Bose spent much time in German Europe as a traveling nationalist in the 1930s, staying in Vienna. He made some visits to Berlin and Munich, but spent much less time in Nazi Germany than he did in Austria and Czechoslovakia.[167] Vienna was Bose's chief center of activity, partly because this was his first home in German Europe during his initial visit in 1933, and also for the important reason that his wife, Emilie Schenkl, lived there.[168] The Indian Central European Society, founded in 1934 in Vienna by doctoral student Brahmanand Agnihotri for the development of good relations between India and Europe (particularly Austria), was set up with an unusually large source of funding. British surveillance surmised that a leading member of the organization, Dr. Otto Faltis, was a "person of standing" in the Nazi Party, and that the support for Bose's organization was coming from "high places."[169] In the Foreign Office itself, there was an Oriental Department under the direction of Werner Otto von Hentig. Habibur Rahman was the main Indian representative to this arm of official Germany, along with other Indian Muslim leaders, including Hafiz Manzuruddin Ahmad and Zain ul Abidin Hassan. Habibur Rahman led the Muslim community in Berlin, located at the Jamiat-ul-Musslimeen in West Berlin.[170] These traveling nationalists also served as personnel in the Indian National Army established in Berlin under Subhas Chandra Bose. Zain ul Abidin Hassan helped to run Azad Hind Radio from Berlin. And Habibur Rahman, too, worked with Bose in that organization.[171]

Bose had an ambivalent relationship with German Nazism from the start. Already on his first visit to Germany, he voiced his shock and displeasure with the Nazi social policies.[172] He wrote to a friend after visiting Berlin, "Since I left Berlin, I have seen no indication of any good will towards Indians on the part of Germany. Recently another nasty Anti-Indian article has appeared in the 'Münchener Neueste Nachrichten.' In view of all these, I am thinking of starting an Anti-German campaign in the entire Indian press. I have waited sufficiently long for an indication of good will, but have been disappointed."[173] In 1934 when Hitler publicly derided the Indian nationalist movement, the Munich Indians protested to the German Foreign Office councilor.[174] Bose, again visiting Germany at the time, wrote to a German official, "the most serious factor threatening friendly relations between Germany and India is the unfortunate effect produced by the present race propaganda in Germany."[175]

After 1937, Indian students studying throughout Germany again came to be seen as unwelcome visitors by the Nazi regime. It is only in the crisis of World War II that the Nazi regime revisited its India policy and decided to support Subhas Chandra Bose and Azad Hind Fauj (Indian National Army) in a project to radicalize India from outside and thereby destabilize Britain on the Indian front.[176] This project followed the pattern already established in 1914, when the German government partnered with Indian anticolonial diplomats avant la lettre in attempts to disrupt British rule in India from outside.[177]

Beginning in 1940, the Indian Independence League in Berlin, using Nazi funds, published pamphlets attacking the British empire. A pamphlet written by the League stated, "England is responsible for starting the European war for the purpose of crushing rising Germany, in accordance with Britain's time-honoured traditional policy of downing her rival who may attain a position to challenge Britain's illegal world-supremacy secured at the cost of the happiness of millions of human beings."[178] The Germans were obsessed with dominating the "India work" within the Axis, and preventing Rome from becoming the main center for Indian strategy.[179]

Of the Indians living in Nazi Germany, a British Intelligence Department list of 1944 shows that a large proportion among that group had first arrived in the 1920s.[180] Some Indians such as the Sikh émigré, Dalip Singh Gill, had first come to Berlin as prisoners of war during World War I, and were thus members of the British Indian Army before that. The other main contingent of Indian settlers in Nazi Germany, however, traveled to Germany for university study in the 1930s. Indian students in Berlin and Munich continued attending the Indian Students Association, which had been established the previous decade. One British intelligence report from 1939 reported that thirty Indian students were studying in Berlin, remarking that the students association was "carefully nursed by the Nazis." Bengalis were also said to have formed their own group around Nalini Gupta's café in the Hindustan Haus in Charlottenburg.[181] Gupta had arrived as a traveling *svadeśi* activist back in 1919.[182]

The leaders of the Indian community in Berlin who represented the group to the Nazis were Habibur Rahman, Abdul Rauf Malik, A. C. N. Nambiar, and Subhas Chandra Bose. A Foreign Students Association in the city catered to students from the Middle East and Asia, and a significant Arab nationalist contingent collected in Berlin in the Nazi years.[183] The Nazis attempted to use the battle for territory in Palestine to win favor with Arab nationalists.[184] The mufti of Jerusalem took up residence in Berlin in 1941 and collaborated with Nazi officials.[185] In these cases, as in a similar scenario that played out during World War I, the genocidal Nazi regime tried to control non-European nationalists as if they were pawns in a "great game."[186]

Despite Hitler's stated dislike for the dark Orientals, there was a significant strand of Indic Orientalism among leading Nazis.[187] Some of these conciliating Nazis were inspired by notions of a distant Aryan brotherhood, while others identified with the ethos of anti-British struggle among contemporary Indian nationalist leaders. In 1935, a Deutscher Orient-Verein in Berlin was formed. It was associated with the Indian Students Association in Berlin, but also operated under the auspices of the German minister of propaganda.[188] The organization was formed by the government, but overseen by civic leaders, and was supposed to cultivate relations with Turks, Egyptians, Indians, Persians, Afghans, Iraqis, Syrians, and Palestinians living in Germany, as well as with their affiliates in the homelands.[189]

A large number of Indians were interned by the German military during the war. Indian sailors and British Indian troops formed the largest contingent among Indian POWs, and about 10 percent among their ranks chose to trade detention camp stays for membership in the Indian Legion.[190] In 1942, two military training camps for the Indian Legion were established, numbering about ninety men.[191] Meanwhile Hitler eventually directed Subhas Chandra Bose to seek out Japanese official support. The Nazi government sent him to Japan via submarine in 1943. Back in Germany, the Indian Legion continued its training, but its small infantry was eventually shipped to the southwest coast of France where it was employed to fight against the Allied troops.

During World War II, Indians who had returned home to India from German Europe tended to speak out against the British and in favor of the Axis powers. They shared the view that India might be sprung loose from the British imperial grip thanks to leverage from Germany, Italy, and Japan.[192] In 1940, Muhammad Obeidullah, who had sojourned as an anticolonial radical in Berlin in the 1920s, declared in a speech after Juma prayers in Delhi that Germans might soon invade India through Iran, thereby ending British rule.[193] Sattar Kheiri, a leader of the Indian Muslim community in Berlin during the Weimar years, organized pro-German meetings at his German society in Aligarh University. Kheiri also sought to obtain funding for university programs at Aligarh from the German consulate.[194] In Calcutta, Benoy Kumar Sarkar was president of both the Bengali German Association and the Bengali Dante Association, and Kalidas Nag presided over the Calcutta Japan Society.[195] Mahendra Pratap, the erstwhile president of the "Provisional Government of Free India" set up in Kabul with the aid of German funding and military support in 1915, now styled himself as president of a "World Federation" that advocated revolt against the British "overlords" during World War II.[196]

Indian traveling nationalists in Nazi Germany were seeking favors from their enemy's enemy.[197] This was partly the circumstantial politics of opportunism. But there was a great deal of historical momentum behind these alliances as well. Indians practiced forms of internationalism that had characterized their anticolonial movement over decades, stretching at least back to 1905. Both Indian traveling activists and nationalists at home in India worked together to mobilize international favor against imperial bonds. For some Indian immigrants in the 1920s and 1930s, Germany and Austria were no longer foreign lands and had become homes. A home of strife and division, but a place they identified with nonetheless.

Fields of Encounter

FIVE

The Physical Cosmos

The previous chapters have considered the social and political dimensions of rising entanglements between Indian and German travelers and their histories, especially in terms of the breakdown of the cohesive force uniting the ideals of "Europe" and "Empire" from the late nineteenth century onward. The second part of this book argues that this wreckage and rearrangement of geopolitics tracked transformations in the history of thought, and the history of transnational encounter. The rise of post-Enlightenment epistemologies across the range of the sciences and the humanities occurred over the course of this same period, 1880–1945. Post-Enlightenment discourses did not jettison the pursuit of scientific universalism based on modern scientific methods, but rather proposed new universalistic visions that challenged conventional positivistic views of the natural and the human realms.

Post-Enlightenment discourses of scholarship sought to enchant the world order in new ways, and it was within the fields of these scholarly discussions that German successionists from the nineteenth-century Concert of Europe and Indian rebels from the nineteenth-century ideal of Empire met each other as partners. These counterscientific fields were not *reactions against* positivism, but rather *transformations* of scientific positivism. They represented the pluralization of scientific worldviews from within—based on transnational exchanges of unprecedented format and scale.

A pattern of dialogue among German and Indian thinkers organized around the pursuit of new representations of the world as a totality worked across a diverse sequence of fields, including theoretical physics, international economics, Marxism, geocultural thought, psychoanalysis, and expressionist art history and practice. Post-Enlightenment thought created intellectual space to think through and beyond nineteenth-century notions of the world that were based on assumptions about the unity of Europe and the singular universal calling of European Enlightened Empire.

In each of these post-Enlightenment fields, colonial subjects and underdog Europeans sought to forcibly restructure their place in the world order using the power of philosophical thought. And these enchanting sciences served, sometimes inadvertently, as a source of soft power for geopolitical radicalism especially in the years after the Great War. Some kinds of European thinkers and some kinds of colonial intellectuals, while separated by a colonial divide along one dimension, were actually brought together along another intellectual dimension by their scholarly practices and their geopolitical radicalism. The revolutions in intellectual life in the early twentieth century that we are used to viewing as an apotheosis of Western science, as the dialectic of the (European) Enlightenment, were really the product of unprecedented entanglements and bondings across the colonial divide. Carl Schorske once famously noted that in the early twentieth century, "European high culture entered a whirl of infinite innovation, with each field proclaiming independence of the whole, each part in turn falling into parts."[1] But the epistemic innovation of this period not only led to a demolition into parts but also to a charged confrontation and overlap of new, discrepant, and often contending wholes.

*   *   *

The discourse of quantum physics in the early twentieth century sought to envision the physical universe in more accurate ways, and to reveal the truth about the cosmos in terms of the fundamental interwoven structure of time and space. Quantum physics constituted one important field connecting Indians and German-speakers after 1918. Theoretical physics was a kind of international Olympics of the mind in the age of high imperialism and in the postwar period.[2] At the same time, in India, the discipline emerged as one of the vanguard pursuits of anticolonial intellectuals.[3] Meghnad Saha, a lower-caste Hindu scientist from East Bengal trained in the nationalist educational institutions of Calcutta in the early twentieth century, traveled first to London, but then beyond the limits of the British empire to Berlin in 1921 to work in the laboratory of the world-famous German physicist who formulated the third law of thermodynamics, Walther Nernst. In Berlin, Saha publicized his original formulation of a new ionization equation for atomic particles that constitute the plasma around stars. The equation went on to carry the name in scientific literature of the Saha ionization equation. Saha's interests changed gears by the 1930s, as he moved away from theoretical physics toward policy debates about scientific organization.[4] If in the 1920s he probed the principles of thermodynamics, in the 1930s and 1940s, his attention turned to planning hydroelectric and nuclear energy programs for a prospective independent India.[5] Saha took models for his vision of scientific management for a prospective independent India from German Europe and North America, and later from Soviet Russia.[6]

C. V. Raman provides another example of Indian nationalist engagement with German physics. Raman, a Brahmin physicist originally from Tamil Nadu, also accredited himself in Calcutta's nationalist scientific institutions and crossed paths with Meghnad Saha in 1910s Calcutta. Raman won the Nobel Prize in Physics in 1930 for his original contributions to spectroscopy and observational techniques for studying the internal structure of atoms. Raman eventually became the director of the Indian Institute of Science in Bangalore. From that position, he developed collaborations with German physicists as he attempted to develop an institute for fundamental research in physics along the lines of the Kaiser Wilhelm Institute in Berlin. Raman cultivated a close relationship with the German Jewish quantum physicist, Max Born, even inviting him to Bangalore in 1934. In both cases, in that of the lower-caste Saha and the high-caste Raman, we see how German physics provided a kind of scientific mountain range that Indian nationalist thinkers sought to climb in order to situate themselves outside the intellectual constraints of British empire. Different kinds of Indian thinkers used dialogues with German thinkers to achieve political distinction in the world, and also to open up new philosophical perspectives on the order of things. And if Indians benefited from the alternative internationalism that emerged out of the revolutionary advances in the study of atomic structure, so too did Germans. Forging scholarly and political links with Indians and other scholars in the world beyond Europe became an important project among German physicists in the postwar years.

PHYSICS OLYMPICS

In 1932, in a lecture to the Prussian Academy, the Austrian physicist Erwin Schrödinger likened international science to international sport.[7] The

Olympic Games were, of course, both an ancient and a newfangled competition. The "new" games had just been inaugurated in 1896 as a dual spectacle of Greek nationalism and hegemonic European internationalism. Unsurprisingly, French and English were the official languages, and French and English sporting cultures set the standard for the games, with subsequent gatherings in Paris in 1900 and London in 1908.[8]

The science of theoretical physics provided another arena in which national champions could compete for international acclaim, Schrödinger explained, and in which the hegemony of the northwestern European powers could be challenged. Inherent in Schrödinger's metaphor was the assertion that the practice of science, like the training for a sport, displayed merit in a universally recognizable and measurable way (the strength and deftness of the human body likened to the brilliance of the human mind), and also that science's universal salience created possibilities for communication and competition appropriate to an international age. Of course, Schrödinger was himself one of the "Olympian" physicists of the German-speaking states in the 1920s.[9] But what was the recognition of science really good for, and who could put it to use?

Physics, like chemistry, was one of the sciences in which German-speaking European dominance was undeniable at the turn of the twentieth century, and in which revolutionary changes to scientific understanding were being made.[10] German-speaking physicists both before and after World War I, because of their immense prestige within this discipline, anchored a field of relation that interrupted the dominant world-shaping forces of the Anglophone and Francophone powers.[11] Indians sought to scale the mountains of Germanic physics institutions in order to make contact with the Zarathustra-like figures in the laboratories on top. Social interactions between German and Indian physicists based on research in thermodynamics and quantum physics provided Indians with high-profile ways to stand out in the world. On one hand, German-speaking physics made a name for itself by asserting fundamental claims about the subatomic level of the physical universe. On the other hand, theoretical physics research served as an arena in which Indians claimed recognition outside the center–periphery imperial framework and pursued their own centered position in an international field of knowledge production.[12]

In the 1910s and 1920s, German-speaking physicists, such as Albert Einstein, Max Planck, Werner Heisenberg, Max Born, and Erwin Schrödinger, established the field of quantum physics. The origins of the field lay almost exclusively in the originating work of German-speakers, in which Jewish intellectuals took the lead.[13] The field flourished and expanded internationally in the 1920s. Quantum physicists explained that the world could be understood only through probabilities and relativity—an insight that grew out of research in thermodynamics in the nineteenth century, and had deeper roots in seventeenth-century science.[14] Quantum physics, using pure mathematical reasoning, controverted the conventional Enlightenment view of the world associated with Newtonian physics. Quantum physics wielded power to reveal a new totality of the world at the most minute level of analysis.

Theoretical physics was one of the earliest and most important disciplines for the Indian pursuit of intellectual power. The iconic Indian scientist at the turn of the century was Jagadish Chandra Bose, a physicist.[15] He helped guide the Indian use of physics research as a road to anticolonial soft power. During Bose's world tours beginning in the 1890s, he often asserted to his European audiences that Indian physicists had a special ability to apply ancient Sanskritic wisdom to the study of modern Western science, especially in terms of a Hindu philosophical understanding of *advaita*, or the unity of all existence.[16] Indian physics, Bose claimed, had a special "power to reveal the invisible."[17] By "establishing himself at the metropolis of scientific research in Germany, France, England, America and proving many of their conceptions wrong he has not only honoured himself but has glorified the entire Indian nation," wrote one *bhadralōk* admirer.[18]

Theoretical physics research that questioned the conventional foundations of the field, by presenting a different view of the physical totality, offered Indian scientists in the early twentieth century a direct path to world repute.[19] Among the twelve Indian fellows elected to the Royal Society between 1918 and 1958, six were physicists and one was a statistician who had trained as a physicist.[20] The young physicists considered in this chapter, Meghnad Saha, S. N. Bose, and C. V. Raman, were three of the most successful and important Indian physicists to come out of Calcutta (although Raman was originally from south India). All three were elected fellows of the Royal Society.[21] Saha and Raman were both nominated twice for the Nobel Prize in Physics, and Raman won it in 1930.[22] Their historical significance can be understood not only in terms of their contributions to their disciplines, but also in terms of how they used their disciplines for Indian intellectual politics in the world.

SCIENTIFIC INTERNATIONALISM

The founding documents of the League of Nations devoted significant attention to academic internationalism between member nations as a means of strengthening postwar diplomatic channels.[23] The league inaugurated at least a "moment" of great optimism, not only between those in Western Europe and the United States but also among vast swaths of nationalists in the colonial world.[24] The organizers of the league hoped for a "vigorous interchange of professors and students" in the postwar years.[25] League institutions such as the International Research Council (for the natural sciences), and the International Academic Union (for the humanities) were established in 1920.[26] The Committee on Intellectual Cooperation became the umbrella organization in 1922,[27] and it provided the precedent for the United Nations Educational, Scientific and Cultural Organization (UNESCO) after World War II.

The British colonial administration made no provision for Indian scholars to take part in the league's institutions of intellectual exchange. Young Indian nationalist physicists, such as Meghnad Saha, from a lower-caste eastern Bengali family; C. V. Raman, from a Tamil Brahmin family; and S. N. Bose, from a Calcutta *bhadralōk* family of government clerks, each used the academic institutions of Calcutta to catapult themselves onto an international stage of fundamental physics research and scientific status competition.[28] They each broached discussions with eminent physicists abroad, thereby placing the Indian nationalist cause and their own identities within new fields of relation beyond Empire.[29]

In the 1910s and 1920s, Indians considered Germany as the great chemistry and physics laboratory of the world, and the United States as the great tool shop.[30] An article in the *Calcutta Review* of 1922 asserted that Germany was an "object lesson" for the world in how chemistry could be used in national uplift. "Both Germany and America recognized the fact long ago that education of a nation in advanced chemistry and higher physical science is the most paying investment that any country can make . . ." Physics and chemistry, for Indian nationalists, provided the high road to scientific and industrial development. In contrast to Gandhian *svarāj*, or "self-rule," projects in traditional handicrafts and cultural self-sufficiency, Calcutta-based modernists insisted that international fields of specialized science were a necessity for the prospective independent Indian nation, "since every industry imaginable has got to depend upon raw materials in which chemical science plays some role." The problem, according to Indian scientific internationalists, lay in the fact that "chemical research in our Universities, like that of England, is . . . greatly discouraged by making it most unprofitable for an average student."[31]

In colonial India, there was little support from the colonial regime for experimental chemistry within Indian institutions, and thus equally little scope for collaborations between universities and industry.[32] However, a debate began to develop, especially in the context of the *svadeśi* movement and the Great War, as to how anticolonial intellectual politics should work in fields of theoretical and experimental sciences. In order for scientific research to contribute to the nationalist cause, should efforts focus on applied questions related to industry, or should scholarship focus more on the arcane questions of fundamental and theoretical research, even when applications were not immediately obvious?

The main nationalist exponents of science in India seemed to prioritize theoretical research in the 1920s, but by the 1940s the tide had turned and emphasis was placed increasingly on applied and industrial science. By that time, the big infrastructural needs of new nation-states loomed large in terms of dams, electrification, irrigation works, radio wireless, industrial chemistry, and nuclear plants. The answer to the question of what kind of scientific labor was most needed for Indian and Pakistani nationalist projects changed over this period. That change had to do with a changing sense of South Asian national identity over the course of the decades under consideration. Both the technical and the philosophical dimensions of physics research played into Indic nationalist pursuits.

The Calcutta-based movement for nationalist science institutions emerged out of Bengali *bhadralōk* civil society, but participants were not limited to *bhadralōk* actors. In fact, the role of Calcutta as a subcontinental center for science research is important to note because figures such as C. V. Raman from Kerala, and S. P. Agharkar (botanist), Moreshwar Prabhakar (chemist), and Homi Bhabha (physicist), all from Bombay, came to Calcutta from great distances in order to pursue studies. Meanwhile Meghnad Saha's distance from the classic ideal of the *bhadralōk* has to be measured in a different way. Saha, as the son of a lower-caste family, came from a background far different from the majority of his colleagues and teachers who were generally part of the upper-caste Kayastha and Brahmin cultural elite.

Saha grew up in a small town near Dacca, in East Bengal, the son of a shopkeeper. The disadvantages, including the stigma he bore throughout his life by dint of his family name, played out in his political activities as he became a vocal proponent of secularism. He was a self-described member of the "democratic classes," and a critic of Hindu ritualism.[33] The institutions of the Calcutta metropolis, especially their internationalist scope for dialogue, provided him the means for his climb up from disadvantage.

Institutionalization of the natural sciences in Calcutta occurred not by the grace of British administrative planning, but from below, that is, from outside the official management of the colonial state. The knowledgeable Crown Raj of the post-1857 period was intent on developing its own programs of scientific management to fulfill the imperatives of long-distance colonial rule. It had few resources or imagination left for the organization of science within indigenous society. Civic scientific organizations first developed in Calcutta through the cooperation between local philanthropists and intellectuals. Mahendra Lal Sircar, a medical doctor and practitioner of homeopathy, established the Indian Association for the Cultivation of Science in 1876. Pramatha Nath Bose, who completed studies at Cambridge and served in the Geological Survey of India, founded the Indian Industrial Association in 1892. Jogendra Chandra Ghosh set up the Association for the Advancement of Scientific Industrial Education in 1904. The Bengal National College was started in 1906, led by Satish Chandra Mukherjee and Aurobindo Ghosh, funded by wealthy patrons such as Taraknath Palit and Rashbehari Ghosh. The Indian Science Congress was established in 1915, founded by Asutosh Mukherjee with C. V. Raman as chairman of the Physics Section.

Outside Calcutta, certain princely states also played important roles in nationalist scientific organization. Aurobindo Ghosh worked for the maharaja of Baroda before joining the National Bengal College. In addition, the princely states of Bhopal, Hyderabad, Mysore, and Travancore, in particular, showed a lively interest in cultivating research science, prompted in part by considerations for maintaining political legitimacy.[34] And Mokshagundam Visveswaraya, who organized science institutions in Mysore in his role as diwan, went on to play one of the most important roles in All-Indian nationalist science planning.[35]

SEEKING A MODEL

The Indian Industrial Commission carried out an extensive survey of the needs of technical education in India between 1916 and 1918.[36] The commission reported on the lack of indigenous systems for the production of steel and iron and large-scale manufacture. Madan Mohan Malaviya and P. C. Ray played central roles as native members of the commission.[37] P. C. Ray was responsible for developing a school of Indian chemistry at Presidency College and at the University College of Science. Ray encouraged his students to study abroad, just as he had done, but also to return to India to engage in the social labor of building nationalist intellectual institutions. Ray was famous, as David Arnold points out, for turning chemistry into a "subversive science" and aligning it with national objectives.[38] Madan Mohan Malaviya, nationalist leader from Uttar Pradesh, had recently founded the Benares Hindu University. He was fascinated both by Gandhi's *charkha*, or the use of the spinning wheel for homespun textile manufacture, and German mechanical and chemical industries.[39] As Shiv Visvanathan has shown in his study of the British Indian government's Industrial Commission Inquiry of 1916–1918, Malaviya felt Germany and Japan could provide Indians with the "relevant solutions" given the colonial penury of technical and technological capital.[40]

With the Montagu–Chelmsford Reforms of the British Indian constitution in 1919, the situation went from bad to worse in terms of the organization of both national education and colonial industrialization. Rajani Palme Dutt condemned the choice to make education and industrialization "transferred" subjects. This would mean that education departments in British Indian institutions would devolve into underfunded and disorganized provincial programs without any unified All-India organization.[41] D. H. Buchanan, an American observer, remarked in 1934, "since the funds available have been wholly inadequate, no very important policies could be initiated. Furthermore, the encouragement of industry requires a far-reaching unified government policy concerning not only raw materials and methods of production, but markets as well."[42]

But perhaps the real concern facing Indian nationalists was not the centralization versus decentralization of scientific organization, but the more fundamental issue of availability of funding, as well as the attentiveness of state planners to India's scientific needs. In 1921, following the Industrial Commission Inquiry, the government of India began deliberations on establishing a Government Department of Chemicals. But P. C. Ray, as founder of the Bengal Chemicals and Pharmaceuticals Corporation, deplored the idea, remarking that the government of India's vision of centralized science planning was a "glaring anachronism."[43] Ray believed that the development of science in India had to be decentralized, rooted in institutes and universities, and had to pursue the goals of fundamental research as well as those of building nationalist industry. Ray dreamed of a day when Indian scientists too could spend "a million dollars in the equipment of a laboratory."[44] He had in mind the model of "big science" pioneered in the German *Kaiserreich*, which culminated in the creation of the Kaiser Wilhelm Institutes in 1911.[45] The German model of the decentralized scientific institutes for fundamental research, coupled with generous state funding, inspired C. V. Raman when he assumed the directorship of the Indian Institute of Science in 1934, and attempted to create a national physics research institute in colonial India. The nationalization of science in India was a project to adjust the rules of the game such that Indians could see themselves as centered, and not peripheralized, in the scientific pursuit.

Meghnad Saha became one of Bengal's most eminent scientists, making fundamental contributions to the new field of astrophysics and thermodynamics with his "ionization equation." Saha also had outspoken anticolonial views, having been expelled from high school for boycotting a visit from the governor of Bengal in 1905, during the first *svadeśi* movement. He developed contacts with radical *svadeśi* revolutionaries when he arrived at Presidency College in Calcutta in 1909. He was also an admirer of the revolutionary leader, Jatin Mukherjee, the guerrilla leader of the Bengali underground insurgency movement.

Saha quickly proved himself to be a rising star of nationalist science. He received his doctorate at age twenty-six from the newly established University Science College, Calcutta. He had already mastered the German language in his student days in Dhaka, and he was well acquainted with Einstein's special relativity theory and his work on the photoelectric effect from 1905, as well as the general relativity theory of 1916.[46] Saha's early acquaintance with Einstein's work is attributable to the availability of German science magazines at the Indian Association for the Cultivation of Science in Calcutta.

There was another living connection to German Europe in Saha's vicinity, however. Peter Brühl, an Austrian botanist teaching at Calcutta University, played an important role in connecting both Meghnad Saha and Satyendranath Bose to the new scientific literature in Germany and Austria. Bose recalled that Brühl had Planck's *Theorie der Wärmestrahlung,* Laue's *Das Relativitätsprinzip,* as well as papers on quantum theory and relativity. "Since Saha and I had learned some German, we were glad to borrow these things from Brühl. Saha chose to study first thermodynamics, statistical mechanics and spectroscopy, while I decided upon electromagnetism and relativity."[47] By the time Saha obtained his PhD in 1919, he had already translated Einstein's paper on general relativity from German into English, and had published a number of articles explaining the new quantum theory to Bengali audiences.[48]

Saha's early interest was in the physics of the planets and the universe. Although Einstein theorized, in radical fashion in 1905, that the structure of space and time changed relative to motion, no experimental corroboration of that counterintuitive view came until 1919. In May 1919, Sir Arthur Eddington, the eminent Cambridge astrophysicist, led an expedition to Principe, an island off the west coast of Africa, to make observations of the sky during a total eclipse of the sun.[49] The techniques and tradition of leading "eclipse expeditions" arose in the age of colonial Victorian science, and relied on the access of metropolitan scholars to the equatorial terrains of the colonies. Eclipses could be best viewed and studied from the colonies.[50] Eddington followed the model of the famous Victorian astronomer, Norman Lockyer, who had made his observations and his name in India. When he was still a boy, Meghnad Saha's interest in astronomy was piqued by Lockyer's work.[51]

Eddington's observations, made on May 29, showed that during the 0.3 seconds during which the moon totally eclipsed the sun, the stars that appeared closest to the sun seemed to jump out from their expected positions. This suggested that light was being curved inward by the gravitational pull of the immense mass of the sun, thereby causing this effect. The observation provided the first experimental evidence in support of Einstein's general theory of relativity, which postulated something that scientists at that time found preposterous: that gravity could bend light.

The news of Eddington's observation first appeared in the *London Times* on June 5, 1919, but only in the form of a brief note that the photographs taken at Principe gave "reason to hope for some success."[52] It took until November for the evidence from the photographic plates to be sorted and verified. On November 7 and November 8, 1919, the *London Times* carried its report about the "Revolution in Science" heralded by Eddington's experimental corroboration of Einstein's general theory of relativity. In the context of the postwar armistice, this corroboration of a German scientist's theory of general relativity by a British scientist using the world-spanning imperial infrastructure of the British empire had the effect of making

Einstein and Eddington into internationally recognized heroes of science. But only Einstein's name entered the global popular imagination as a word synonymous with "genius."

Already three days before the *London Times* published news of Eddington's experimental confirmation of Einstein's theory, a Calcutta newspaper, the *Statesman*, carried a story titled "Time and Space—The New Scientific Theory."[53] Young Bengali scientist Meghnad Saha wrote the article, which explained the momentous significance of Eddington's Principe results to Calcutta audiences. Saha wrote, "The announcement conveyed in yesterday's Reuters' cable that Professor Einstein's theory of the equivalence of Time and Space has at last been verified by observations made during the last total solar eclipse, will be hailed with joy by scientific circles all over the world." Only on November 10, six days after Saha published his article in Calcutta and three days after the news broke in London, the *New York Times* published an article on the discovery, "Men of Science More or Less Agog over Results of Eclipse Observation." Imperial relays of information, and crosscutting transnational lines of communication, led to the popularization of Einstein's relativity theory to Calcutta audiences *before* London or New York audiences received the news. The chronology in which the news was publicized interrupts the center–periphery narrative of scientific communication. The newest physics scholarship was circulating in Calcutta with a higher velocity than it was in London itself.

After the announcement of Eddington's discovery, Saha began translating into English Einstein's 1905 paper on special relativity and Hermann Minkowski's 1908 paper on the fundamental equations of electromagnetic phenomena in moving bodies. Meanwhile, his friends, Satyendra Nath Bose along with D. M. Bose, who, recently returned from Berlin with his physics PhD, started translating Einstein's 1916 paper on general relativity into English.[54] The Saha translation would be the first English version of Einstein's famous paper (1920). Robert Lawson's translation from New York came out a few months later.

After translating the paper, Saha won a scholarship in 1919 to pursue two years of studies in Britain. Saha's own work brought astronomy together with the field of thermodynamics. Understanding heat, an invisible phenomenon that had neither weight nor substance, but could be transferred from one entity to the other at a distance, became a preoccupation of nineteenth-century scientists. If Newtonian physics studied visible physical processes, nineteenth-century scientists turned increasingly to the study of subtler, invisible processes that seemed not to have easy analogies in the mechanical universe. The study of heat as well as the study of electricity (electromagnetism)—that is, the study of two invisible forms of energy—prepared the way, logically and conceptually, for the even subtler revelations about the quantum level of the physical universe in the twentieth century. Quantum theory was also a form of post-Enlightenment scholarship, however, in that it not only extended the prior knowledge base but also challenged the very epistemic basis of prior understandings.

Saha's dissertation research sought to determine how heat energy could be measured in the gases around stars. On earth, the temperature of objects can be measured mechanically, for example, through the use of thermometers. But, in order to precisely measure the heat of high-temperature gases that collected around stars in the galaxy, other insights and methods had to come into play. Saha's equation allowed one to calculate the temperature and pressure of the gases that composed the photosphere of stars if one knew the percent ionization of those gases. And percent ionization could be determined experimentally through spectroscopy. With the "Saha ionization equation," as it came to be known, astronomers could more accurately explain the spectral classification of some kinds of stars in terms of the temperature, pressure, and percent ionization of stellar environments. "I prepared in the course of six months of 1919 (February through September) four papers and communicated them for publication from India within August to September," Saha reported.[55]

Saha received the direct support of Asutosh Mukherjee in the effort to leave the colonial periphery and to corroborate his research in metropolitan imperial laboratories. Laboratories in Britain had resources and data that the impoverished experimental labs in Calcutta did not. In Alfred Fowler's lab at the University of London in 1920, Saha used a large amount of spectroscopic data to proffer evidence for the theory he developed in Calcutta in 1919.[56] In 1921, Saha next took his wares to the center stage of research on thermodynamics, to Walther Nernst's laboratory in Berlin. Saha set off from London to Berlin not primarily to complete his research, but rather to display his work on the premier international stage of physics in his day.

In pursuit of discussions about "the new knowledge" of thermodynamics, as Saha put it, he traveled to Berlin, to one of the most prestigious laboratories of modern physics. There, fourteen Indians seem to have been working at Nernst's lab.[57] Walther Nernst was famous for inventing the

Nernst lamp, the grandfather of the standard incandescent lightbulb. He was an international representative of German science, as he had formulated the third law of thermodynamics in 1906 and won the Nobel Prize in 1920.[58] Nernst had a propensity to accept foreign students into his laboratory. Saha used Nernst's law in calculating the ionization energies of gases at very high temperatures.

In Berlin, Saha stood on a world stage of physics. Saha's work bridged the fields of thermodynamics, astrophysics, and the new quantum theory. Saha published a major contribution to physics research while there, capturing the attention of the physics world in 1921. Walther Nernst presented the "Saha ionization equation" at a meeting of German physicists at Jena in August 1921.[59] Saha's paper in the *Zeitschrift für Physik*, perhaps the most prestigious journal of physics research in the world at that time, appeared in September 1921: "Versuch einer Theorie der physikalischen Erscheinungen bei hohen Temperaturen mit Anwendungen auf die Astrophysik."[60] This provided an important advancement in what astrophysicists call the study of "stellar structure." For his findings, Saha was elected a Fellow of Britain's Royal Society in 1927, and nominated for the Nobel Prize in 1930 and 1937.

Saha spent one year at Nernst's lab in 1921 before returning to Calcutta as a professor at Presidency College. Soon after returning to Calcutta, he published an article in the Calcutta *Modern Review* describing the "luxurious life" of study in Berlin, where room and board costs were very low due to hyperinflation. Saha reported that many students from Eastern Europe, Turkey, China, and Japan were studying at the University of Berlin. Indian students would thus feel at home, he wrote. He recommended that more Indian youth take up studies in the fallen imperial capital of Berlin.[61] What he did not say in his article, but what would have been well known to his Calcutta readership, was that Berlin had become a global center of Indian anticolonial activity. Meghnad Saha had contacts with those revolutionary circles as well.[62] Back in Calcutta as of 1922, Saha became involved in the underground leadership of the Bengali anticolonial youth movement. He joined Subhas Chandra Bose as a copresident of the Calcutta Young Bengal Association, which had loose ties to the international communist movement.[63]

Saha soon took up a professorship at the University of Allahabad. He wrote consistently throughout the 1920s and 1930s of the new truths he believed were pouring out of German laboratories and institutes. "For we are living in an Augustan age of discovery in the physical sciences," he wrote. As president of the physics and mathematics section of the Indian Science Congress, he noted, "X-rays, radioactivity, the electron theory, the quantum theory of radiation, and the last, although not the least, the theory of relativity—all these taken together constitute a revolution in human thought."[64] Beginning his survey with Wilhelm Röntgen's detection of X-rays in 1894, Saha praised German scientists for showing that "beyond the knowledge of physical phenomena accumulated up to 1894, there were other vast fields as yet unexplored."[65] The important place of German physics in Saha's thought as a fount of radical knowledge and his intention to tap that source also allowed him to distance himself from British colonial institutions and conventions of knowledge. During and after the Great War, Germanic knowledge to many Indian scholars signified not only an alternative to British intellectual institutions but also a soft weapon to break the frame of British empire.

A GERMAN PROFESSORIATE FOR INTERNATIONAL SCIENCE

Satyendranath Bose was born in Calcutta, the son of a railway engineer, and was slightly older than Meghnad Saha. Bose also trained at the University Science College in mathematics and theoretical physics. With Meghnad Saha, he cotranslated Einstein's paper on general relativity. After completing his doctorate at Calcutta he departed for Dacca, where he was a member of Dacca University's founding faculty.[66] From his work desk in Dacca, Bose developed a new statistical technique for calculating the distribution of photons as wave particles over different energy states. Bose's statistical method helped describe the new kind of probabilistic world that was being revealed at the quantum level. His research contributed to the emergence of the post-Enlightenment episteme, and also to the building of radical intellectual bonds beyond the British empire.

Bose's scholarship contributed to the new probabilistic and relativistic understanding of the natural universe. He sent his work to Albert Einstein in 1924. Einstein immediately recognized the import of Bose's contribution, translating Bose's paper into German and publishing it in the *Zeitschrift für Physik*.[67] Walther Nernst had published Saha's paper in that same journal in 1921. Here again we note another case of an Indian scientist catapulting to international recognition thanks to the transnational leverage of German collaboration. S. N. Bose spent a year in Paris in 1924 and about six months in Berlin in 1925–1926 in order to work with Einstein and the physicists gathered around him.[68] Bose's method would later come to be known as the Bose–Einstein statistics, and represented a fundamental contribution in the march toward quantum mechanics, a new field of research that reached its full bloom by 1927.

Einstein's involvement with Indian intellectuals went beyond the curricular realm. He took significant interest in the Indian anticolonial movement. Unlike Walther Nernst, who operated as a nationalist representative of the German state, Einstein was more at home with counterculture and with the German Left. Einstein even attended the League against Imperialism conference in Brussels in 1927.[69] In 1930, Einstein had two highly publicized encounters with Rabindranath Tagore, in which both thinkers addressed fundamental philosophical questions about epistemology and ethics. Einstein also had written correspondences with M. G. Gandhi, Jawaharlal Nehru, and M. N. Roy.[70] German scientists, in this case, the iconic German physicist Albert Einstein, did not always interact with Indian interlocutors from the position of professorial superiority.[71] Einstein's interactions with Indian physicists and intellectuals came from an oblique angle, from the side and from below. Vectors that brought about intellectual and social relation and entanglement between German and Indian thinkers in the 1920s and 1930s could run in multiple, crosscutting directions.

In the German context of turn-of-the-century *Weltpolitik,* scholarship was power. Adolf von Harnack, theologian, national cultural spokesman, and founding director of the Kaiser Wilhelm Institutes, recorded the German professoriate's commitment in official briefings before the Great War, exclaiming, "for Germany the maintenance of its scientific hegemony is just as much a necessity for the state as is the superiority of its army."[72] Brigitte Schroeder-Gudehus situates the Kaiser Wilhelm Institutes in the context of a rapid "division of labor" in European science at the turn of the century.[73] Fields of research were being professionalized, scholars were becoming more specialized, and a vast workforce and huge new industrial laboratories emerged.[74] In this scholarly environment, scientists organized themselves around the most prolific and prestigious researchers in their field, but they also accepted their position as participants in a nationalist science condominium, cultivating close interlinkages with both state planners and industry. The Kaiserreich's ideal of science organization was not an organic model of a central brain directing the movements of many limbs, but rather the model of a decentralized national nervous system that worked together, from multiple locations, toward a shared pursuit.

Walther Nernst was a member of the Prussian Academy, and received the state honor of Geheimrat in 1913. He was a signatory of the "Manifesto of the Ninety-Three"—a document signed by leading German intellectuals, including Max Planck, Fritz Haber, Wilhelm Wien, and Adolf von Harnack, praising the German war effort.[75] Nernst sat at the helm of Berlin science and played the leading role in convincing Einstein to take up a research professorship in Berlin in 1914.[76] In 1921, the same year as Saha's arrival at his Berlin lab, Nernst became the rector of the University of Berlin. On the post-Versailles international stage of physics there was something particularly dramatic about Saha's decision to leave London for work in Nernst's prominent Berlin lab. There was something equally political about Nernst's decision to accept Meghnad Saha as well as the other fourteen Indians into his lab in 1920. In fact, Nernst wrote to Saha in 1920 that he would "allow him and his Indian colleagues to see the laboratories because the last blow to the British empire would come from India."[77]

Nernst saw himself as an international representative of German science, charged with the creation of an alternate world center for anticolonial scientists from the British dependencies. Nernst had already graduated one Indian doctoral student from his lab—Dhirendranath Chakravarty in 1913.[78] If only a minor theme in the years before the war, German transnational assistance to Indian nationalists became an avowed scientific policy after 1919. The changing German science policy toward the British colonial world reflects a major shift in the political contexts for scientific research between the Kaiserreich and the Weimar Republic.

In the years leading up to World War I, physics was closely associated with the building up of military and industrial prowess and with the amassing of *Macht*, or power. Arnold Sommerfeld's approach to the "physics of problems," as Suman Seth terms it, contributed to radiotelegraphy, wireless communication, and gyroscopic motion in ballistics research, all of which fed into war planning.[79] Meanwhile, the chemist Fritz Haber mobilized research to invent more effective means of chemical warfare, and to improve agricultural output in the context of economic blockade.[80] Max Born, who fled Nazi Germany as a Jewish refugee in the 1930s, had also played an important role in war research during World War I, earning him enemies in Britain when he first settled there after 1933.[81] And one of the aims of Nernst's lab during the war was to contribute, if only indirectly, to the science of "gas warfare, explosives, and ballistics."[82]

Paul Forman has argued that after the Great War, the role of German Olympian scientists changed. Science became "*Machtersatz*"—a means to substitute intellectual prestige and authority for the devastating decline in German political and military dominance in the world.[83] Before the war, Forman argues, German scientists conceived of themselves as "antipolitical," and merely "passive" in the pursuit of international prestige. Although functionally serving the national interests in many ways, German scientists perceived themselves as primarily driven by the rigors of their fields.[84] But in the midst and aftermath of the war, German scientists became self-proclaimed leaders of national uplift, "no longer [conceiving] of their political role in the classical passive terms. Rather they regarded themselves as agents . . . of the foreign policy interests of their nation."[85] Antipolitics was converted into overt politics after 1914.[86]

In the period from 1919 to 1933, before the Nazi seizure of power, German scientists proposed a new program of cultural diplomacy (*Kulturpolitik*) to ameliorate the political place of Germany in the world. As early as November 14, 1918, days after the signing of the armistice, Max Planck addressed a plenary session of the Prussian Academy of Sciences: "If the enemy has taken from our fatherland all defense and power . . . there is one thing which no foreign or domestic enemy has yet taken from us: that is the position which German science occupies in the world."[87] This continued the policies of the early twentieth century established by the likes of Karl Lamprecht, Carl Becker, Friedrich Naumann, and Paul Dehn. In 1912, for example, Lamprecht wrote that Germany had to excel in cultural diplomacy in order to succeed in its geopolitical mission, and had to supersede the projects of French, Americans, and Britons in spreading intellectual institutions around the world.[88] After 1918, German scientists carried out the nation's cultural policy in a more vocal and redemptive register.

The League of Nations International Research Council, founded in the aftermath of the war in 1919 with French scientists at its helm, implemented an official boycott of German scientists between 1919 and 1924. In 1922, German-speaking scientists were excluded from 86 of 135 international congresses, and in 1925, they were still excluded from 34 out of 68 congresses. In the 1920s, the discipline of physics helped Germany assert itself as a geopolitical world center despite the League of Nations boycott. German physicists, particularly in the decade after the war, perceived international collaborations and connections in physics research as critical exercises to counteract both the ignominy of war defeat, and the political and scholarly isolation that continued until 1926, when Germany was admitted to league institutions.[89]

In the 1920s, Fritz Haber played a leading role at the Kaiser Wilhelm Institutes in Berlin in cultivating international scholarly relations, especially with students from the United States, Turkey, and Japan, just as Walther Nernst cultivated ties with Indian students.[90] Haber maintained that "we know perfectly well that we lost the war and politically as well as economically no longer sit on the board of directors of the world. But scientifically we believe we can still be numbered with those peoples which have a claim to be reckoned among the leading nations . . ."[91] Informed by this same ethos of anti-isolationist internationalism, a group of leading scholars, in 1923, including Albert Einstein, Fritz Haber, Max Planck, and the president of the Kaiser Wilhelm Institutes, theologian Adolf von Harnack, formed a committee specially to promote contacts between German and Soviet scholars.[92] German scientists forged a policy of intellectual politics "by other means," skirting the International Research Council.

The residual effects of imperial rivalry between Britain, France, and Germany, and the German resort to a redemptive national science policy in the face of the league's boycott, created the transnational conduit for Saha's fateful and fruitful stay in Berlin. At an "Indian National Evening" at the posh Hotel Bristol on Unter den Linden on January 17, 1926, the directors of the Kaiser Wilhelm Institutes as well as fellows of the Prussian Academy gathered to show their support for the Indian nationalist cause. Fritz Haber, director of the Kaiser Wilhelm Chemistry Institute, Hermann Thoms, director of the Kaiser Wilhelm Pharmaceutical Institute, three members of the medical faculty, the dean of the mechanical engineering faculty of Berlin University, various faculty from the Technical University, as well as a representative from the ministry of education were all present. German scientists played the role of unofficial diplomats to Indian nationalist scholars.[93]

An official report prepared for the German Foreign Office by the members of the Prussian Academy of Sciences in 1926 emphasized that "the German academies are convinced of the usefulness and necessity of international science. They have never flagged from this conviction and never will. The progress of science is dependent upon the activities of a relatively small group of independent intellectuals . . ."[94] German scientists assert that the pursuit of knowledge was universal and yet also German. An internal report of the Kaiser-Wilhelm-Gesellschaft of August 1926, titled "Gedanken zu der Frage des Ausländerstudiums in Deutschland" (Considerations on the question of foreign students in Germany), called for Kaiser Wilhelm Institutes to do much more in the way of inviting scholars from abroad, especially those from outside Europe. Again, physics was a stage for Germans to perform internationalism in the context of the Western European boycott. Visitors from the United States, Eastern Europe, and Asia helped to demonstrate that Germans, functionally speaking, were not isolated in the world, even if nominally they were still a *gens non grata.*

Efforts in scientific internationalism had a measurable effect. In 1931, 242 international scholars came to the Kaiser Wilhelm Institutes in Dahlem, followed by 230 in 1932.[95] German scientists also traveled the world in the 1920s as cultural envoys for their nation. The Munich physicist, Arnold Sommerfeld, visited India in 1928 on a world tour that also took him to China, Japan, and the United States.[96] The quantum physicist Werner Heisenberg completed his world tour with stops in the United States, Japan, China, and India, in 1929. But both men traveled not just as scholars per se but also as exponents of German intellectual politics.[97]

Max Planck took up the directorship of the Kaiser Wilhelm Institutes for Physics in 1930, assuming the unofficial diplomatic role of an international representative of German science. He was already serving in another important administrative capacity, as the secretary of the Berlin Academy of Sciences.[98] At the behest of the German Foreign Office, which was persistently involved in the inner workings of the Kaiser Wilhelm Institutes, Planck conveyed a note of support to the newly restructured Indian Institute of Science in Bangalore. "We note with joy the special interest taken in the activities of the [Kaiser Wilhelm] Institute," Planck wrote to the institute's new director, C. V. Raman. "In principle, we place great import on collaboration with Indian scientific groups. At the Harnack-Haus, a number of Indian scholars have already taken up the invitation of the institute."[99]

A PRECARIOUS DECADE

The operation of the Kaiser Wilhelm Institutes changed drastically after April 7, 1933, when the racial restrictions on the civil service were introduced. The Nazi *Gleichschaltung* that began in 1933 had the effect of impoverishing the operation of the Kaiser-Wilhelm-Gesellschaft, as twenty-two researchers were removed from their positions in 1933–1934 on the grounds that they were "non-Aryan."[100] Albert Einstein left for Princeton in 1933, Fritz Haber immigrated to Great Britain in 1933, and Max Born at Göttingen was discharged and fled to Britain that same year. The number of foreign visitors to the Kaiser Wilhelm Institutes drastically declined after 1933.

The drastic changes in statecraft in German Europe occurred in the context of revolutionary developments in technology.[101] The interwar years saw the rise of radical research into the nature and uses of natural energy. Scientists and the states that controlled their activities clamored and competed to understand and then to master not just the old nineteenth-century energies of kinetic, electromagnetic, and thermodynamic energy but also the newly revealed "futuristic" kind of energy unleashed by the fission of atoms. If the 1920s witnessed the birth of quantum physics, the 1930s were the inaugural decade for nuclear physics. The "happy thirties," as Hans Bethe once called them, saw physicists claiming their utility not merely by pointing out applications for industry, but by demonstrating how they could change the world political order through innovations in using nuclear energy for medical equipment, urban planning, and most important, for military enhancement.[102]

In these darkening "happy years" of nuclear physics, in the lead-up to the genocide of the 1940s and the eventual dropping of the atomic bomb, German émigré scientists played a leading role in many of the conferences that skirted the Third Reich. The Rome conference (1931) organized by Enrico Fermi, the Solvay conference in Brussels (1933), the London conference (1934), and the famous Copenhagen conference, convened by Niels Bohr (1937), established the standards and the main tools and approaches that contributed to the 1938 discovery of uranium fission.[103]

Meghnad Saha returned to German Europe in 1927 and again in 1936. He attended the important Como conference, and also the Volta Centenary Celebrations in France and Britain.[104] In 1936, Saha, along with C. V. Raman, attended Niels Bohr's pivotal conference on nuclear fission in Copenhagen, and as a result of the discussions there, Saha resolved to construct a cyclotron for fundamental research in nuclear physics in Calcutta.[105] The international stage of science allowed Saha to think and act in ways that thwarted the British imperial regime of scientific organization.

Meanwhile, the German Foreign Office and the Ministry of Education intervened increasingly in the management of day-to-day operations of the Kaiser Wilhelm Institutes. After 1933, ethnic German scientists were enlisted in Nazi projects to build up the national scientific prestige of the Reich.[106] In 1937, a direct order arrived from the Ministry of Education stipulating that nuclear physicists Arnold Sommerfeld and Wolfgang Bothe of the Kaiser Wilhelm Physics Institute should represent German science at the Jubilee Anniversary of the Indian Science Congress Association in Calcutta, planned for January 1938.[107] In this period, Max Planck and Max von Laue, both Nobel laureates and both increasingly disparaged by Reich administrators, began their "inner migration," receding from public and administrative life.[108] Planck, in his last years, became an itinerant preacher on themes of science and religion, and inserted understated criticism of the Third Reich into his speeches.[109]

In the context of Nazi rule, Germany became less and less a terrain for actual Indian scientific activity, and more a remembered land for major Indian research physicists. Saha, like many Indian intellectuals, associated German scholarship with the Kaiserreich and Weimar periods, and as the Nazi regime progressed, the memory of that older Germany grew increasingly distant. For Saha, the dissonance between the ideal of German science, and the actuality of Nazism, led him to gradually turn away from German Europe as a focus of his transnational attention, and to find other fields of relation. By the 1930s, he had grown most fascinated with America and the Soviet Union.

INTERNATIONALISM FOR INDIAN BIG SCIENCE

Saha explained why he believed British colonial science policy was deficient. British colonial administrators gave "no indication that they have profited by the lessons obtained at the great European laboratories," he remarked.[110] Saha wanted Indian scientists to practice at the highest, internationally recognized levels, and the main technique of scientific development was the international study tour. In providing a work plan for the development of an Indian radio service, Saha proposed sending a band of six scientists abroad for "training on the technical side in factories and workshops. . . . The object will be to train a batch of men who can take charge."[111] From the 1930s until the 1950s, Saha formulated and advocated an "Indianized" program of scientific planning that relied heavily on insourcing expertise and gaining international experience for the benefit of nationalizing projects.

Saha looked internationally for models of rapid scientific development. Initially, Germany provided the chief model, but by the mid-1930s, the United States and the Soviet Union had already become more important. The political problems of science organization increasingly became Meghnad Saha's concern in the 1930s as he transitioned from original researcher to institution builder. He established the *Science and Culture* magazine in 1934 and the National Institute of Sciences in Allahabad in 1935. He served as chairman of the Association for the Cultivation of Science, and president of the Indian Science Congress. Beginning in 1938, Saha became an important member of the Indian National Planning Committee.

Saha, in the 1930s, spoke out as a leading exponent of big science and state planning in India, as the fall of British liberal empire in India seemed increasingly palpable. In the wake of a 1936 conference on nuclear physics convened by Niels Bohr in Copenhagen and before beginning his research tour of the United States, Saha became a major proponent of nuclear research. He was not alone. Homi Bhabha, a brilliant Bombay Parsi physicist, having recently completed a dissertation at Cambridge before working in Bohr's "inner circle" in Copenhagen in the 1930s, also attended Bohr's conference.[112] Both Saha and Bhabha would play the most important early roles in bringing nuclear physics to India.

In a decade-long project that developed in stops and starts, and without assistance from the colonial state, Saha raised money to build a cyclotron for nuclear research in Calcutta.[113] Meghnath Saha's student, B. D. Nag, studying at Berkeley in 1938, was responsible for shipping materials from the United States to build the cyclotron. Shipments of materials began arriving as early as 1940, and US$16,000 of purchases were made. The difficulty of obtaining spare parts from the big laboratories in the United States, and the fact that Bombay rose as the national center for nuclear physics research in the postindependence years, delayed the realization of Saha's grand plans.[114] Saha opened the Institute of Nuclear Physics research in Calcutta in 1949 with significant assistance from the independent Indian government.

The fact that Saha grew up in the riverine region of eastern Bengal also played an important role in forming his scientific imagination. He was preoccupied not only by the need for nuclear power and hydroelectric works for India but also by the need for procedures in flood control in East Bengal, and for the desilting of rivers in West Bengal. Especially after the great flood in North Bengal in 1923, Saha poured his popularizing talents into the theme of "river physics" and irrigation management. In 1933 he called for a hydraulic research laboratory in India, and proposed that it should emulate the famous Central European German river physics laboratories, the Wasserbaulaboratorium in Berlin Charlottenburg, and the Institut für Wasserbau in Vienna.[115] "Germany was the pioneer, as in many other enterprises, in the development of these laboratories, and the activities of her trained experts and scientists have done immense good to the development and improvement of her inland waterways."[116] In 1938, Saha called for scientific work to address the problem of the silting up of the Hooghli River. And in 1943, Saha played an important role in setting up the Damodar Dam project, modeled on the Tennessee Valley Authority, to lessen the threat of flooding.[117] Apart from the model of German and Austrian river physics institutes, the United States provided a major focus of emulation, since there too the government had taken "radical measures," especially after the great flood of 1913 in Ohio.[118] The Hirakud Dam in Orissa and the Bhakra Dam in the Punjab followed the Damodar experiment.

Saha, in the 1930s to 1950s, wanted a more organized as well as more regionally distributed system of scientific research, based primarily at universities and not at institutes directly administered by the state. The model recalled the ideal of scientific organization under the Kaiserreich. Saha also pursued technological self-sufficiency, so that India could have its own equipment and institutions to carry out original physics research. Saha wanted to learn from foreigners, but did not want to become dependent on them. India had to become a center of know-how and technique in its own right, not just a beneficiary of imported know-how from abroad, he argued. Saha maintained that Indian industry should not become complacently reliant on foreign scientific experts. If so, India would never develop its "technical autonomy." Speaking about the work of German engineers at the Rourkela Steel Plant in India in the 1950s, Saha explained to parliament, "I think that it is desirable that we engage a number of Indians of promise and ability to act as assistants to these Germans, in every phase of their work, so that when we wish to go for our next million ton iron and steel plant, we can do the planning and designing entirely with our own men, and we do not have to depend upon foreign technicians any further."[119] Saha called for the "Indianization" of science—Indians should eventually contribute the specialized knowledge and advanced techniques required for all Indian industrial needs. Yet even as Saha argued for the long-term technical autonomy of the postcolonial Indian nation-state, nothing was further from his mind than the outright rejection of international interdependence. He demanded, instead, a more strategic use of international scholarly alliances for the benefit of the Indian nationalist project.

C. V. RAMAN'S ASSOCIATION WITH MAX BORN

C. V. Raman was the second Indian to win the Nobel Prize after Rabindranath Tagore. He was born in a village in Tanjore District, South India, in 1888. After attending Presidency College in Madras, he worked for the government of India as a gazetted officer of the Indian Finance Department. Raman spent the years between 1907 and 1917 in this post in Calcutta, where J. C. Bose's presence in Calcutta deeply inspired him. Raman contributed articles and notices on experimental findings to the leading English-language international journal of science, *Nature*, from as early as 1907. He dedicated himself to the intense observation of natural phenomena, with a view to revealing properties that seemed previously invisible. He also showed a propensity to investigate objects and phenomena that were peculiar to Indians, and especially to the Calcutta environment in which he lived. Raman carried out his early experiments to explain the "wolf tone" of the violin, the colors in mica (of which the area east of Bengal is one of the richest sources in the world), the blue color of seawater, the wavelengths of the Indian tabla drum and vina, and the nature of vowel sounds.

Given his gifts, Asutosh Mukherjee invited Raman to take up the new Palit Chair of Physics at the new University Science College in Calcutta. In the laboratories of the University Science College, Raman carried out his experiments in light spectroscopy. Through close observation, he noticed a scatter effect that would later carry his name. Raman noticed missing bands in the scatter pattern of light as it interacted with various liquids. And studying the "Raman effect" in the spectrographic reading of a particular substance, the pattern of these missing bands, described that substance's intramolecular structure.

Raman quickly became an Indian cultural diplomat, a representative of science on the international scene. In 1921 he made a tour to Europe and

England. He traveled to the University of Toronto and to the California Institute of Technology.[120] In 1925, Raman was India's representative to the second centenary celebration of the Russian Academy of Sciences. In 1927, his contributions to *Nature* and other international journals reached a crescendo as he reported his findings on the diffraction of X-rays through different substances. Raman was knighted by the British king in 1928, obtained the Matteucci Medal from the Italian Society of Sciences in 1928, received an honorary doctorate from the University of Freiburg in 1928, and the Hughes Medal of the Royal Society of London in 1929.[121]

Raman's contributions to the prestigious London-based journal, *Nature*, peaked in the 1920s as he turned his attention resolutely to the study of the light spectra of liquids. He published seven papers in *Nature* between 1928 and 1929 on the Raman effect.[122] In 1929, twenty-five different articles appeared in the pages of *Nature*, by British, Russian, German, Italian, Dutch, American, Japanese, and Indian scientists on their own observations of the Raman effect, including a prestigious contribution by Ernst Rutherford.[123] Another twenty-five articles were published in *Nature* on the Raman effect in 1930. It was one of the most celebrated scientific discoveries of those years, and promised to experimentally corroborate the new quantum wave theory of the atom with observational findings. The work in spectroscopy earned Raman the Nobel Prize in 1930, and with that prize, Raman became a scientific superstar. The *New York Times*, for example, carried a story about "India's men of science leading a renaissance," in which Raman was taken as the main example.[124] In 1930, Raman made a tour of Germany, visiting the Zeiss Planetarium and the Deutsches Museum in Munich with its collection of scientific instruments.[125] In that year, Raman, along with seven other scholars from China, India, Japan, and Turkey, joined the international board of Germany's main organization for cultural diplomacy, the Deutsche Akademie.[126]

C. V. Raman, until 1933, was a professor at Calcutta University, and a member of the Indian Association for the Cultivation of Science. Upon his nomination to the position of assistant director of the Indian Institute of Science in Bangalore in 1934, he intended to make the Indian Institute of Science (IIS) into a center for fundamental research following the model of the Kaiser Wilhelm Institutes. The IIS had been established by funds from Jamshed Tata in 1909, after one of his secretaries, B. J. Padsha, had completed a study tour of science institutions in Germany and continental Europe.[127] The institute, since 1930, had attempted to obtain German physicists to take up temporary or long-term positions. The German consul in Colombo, who had been invited for an official visit to the institute in 1930, wrote to the German Foreign Office and to Max Planck, "I was received with great kindness at the famous Indian Institute of Science in Bangalore. It is built on the style of the Kaiser Wilhelm Institutes, with a talented group of scholars. It would like to cultivate a close relationship to German Wissenschaft, and has been attempting, although to no avail, to fill some of its empty positions with German scientists."[128]

Just as the Kaiser Wilhelm Institutes were typically built around the research agenda of an eminent scholar, Raman cultivated a group of young students who would carry on research on light spectroscopy and study the Raman effect of new kinds of substances. Raman rejected the view that Indian science should contribute only to industrial problems, such as synthesizing dyes, inventing machinery, or developing technologies for communications and transport. In this view, he differed starkly from Meghnad Saha, whose policy recommendations and research turned increasingly to irrigation and river management, geological surveying and research into new communications, and nuclear energy. Raman claimed he was happiest in his laboratory, making fine observations, pursuing science for science's sake. Although the concerns of international politics, and the wish to situate nationalized Indian scholarly institutions at the center of the world order, played a conspicuous role in his activities nonetheless.

In order to make Indian science stand out in the world, it had to make contributions to pure science, Raman insisted. Theoretical innovation could not be subordinated to the technical needs of national development. To make his point, he invited German theoretical physicists to join him in Bangalore to help direct the institution toward fundamental research. Raman contacted two theoretical physicists, Max Born and Erwin Schrödinger, directly, asking if they would serve as visiting professors.[129] He also wrote to the Deutsche Akademie in Munich, where he had an official affiliation, requesting names of German professors of engineering science.[130] In his letters, Raman specifically mentioned that he was interested in "non-English" scholars. Schrödinger wrote that he was not enough of an "Orientalist" to be comfortable in India, and could not settle in the "land of the Upanishads."[131]

Only one scholar accepted Raman's invitation. Max Born, who was without a permanent position in Cambridge after his forced migration from Nazi Germany, traveled with his wife to Bangalore in 1935–1936, and took up a position as visiting professor at the Indian Institute of Science. Born, after arriving in Bangalore, with its impressive infrastructure, its medieval Jewish synagogue, and its reputation for scientific advancement, seriously considered remaining in India permanently. Originally from German Silesia and associated with the Göttingen school of physics, Born wrote to a friend, "the situation in Europe looks pretty bad. Sometimes I think that this old continent is approaching the end of her splendid career. And then I consider staying in India."[132] There is some indication that his wife, Hedwig Ehrenberg Born, was the catalyst for Born's decision to move to India. And even after the ensuing embarrassment which forced Born to return to Britain, Hedwig Born seriously contemplated staying behind, especially as she had developed a devotion to the spiritual guru she had met, Swami Avinasananda, of the Ramakrishna mission.[133]

The colonial government was critical of Raman's project to establish an institute of theoretical physics research in Bangalore on the scheme of the Kaiser Wilhelm Institutes. A review of the institute began in 1936.[134] Raman's community of peers, especially Indian scientists from North India, as well as British scientists, began to bear down on Raman for his unorthodox and unilateral reorganization of the Indian Institute of Science. An organization such as the IIS, which had been originally conceived for industrial research, had now hired Max Born, a theoretical quantum physicist whose work focused on pure mathematical theorems alone without any pretense of industrial application. Meghnad Saha served on the Reviewing Committee and castigated Raman for creating a chair in "theoretical physics" in a field that did not have more direct practical application to industry.[135] The Indian Institute of Science, Saha insisted, was intended to contribute to industrial and applied research, not primarily to the study of either spectroscopy or quantum theory.

Saha's criticism of Raman stemmed partly from the assertion of a lower-caste intellectual (Saha) against the authority of a Brahmin scholar (Raman). It was also colored by the flair of a Bengali intellectual boast butting up against Tamil Brahmin pride. At the risk of reading too much into the conflict between Saha and Bose, or of reducing their strong disagreement to regional identity politics, one notes that these two scholars, both trained in the same Calcutta institutions, became avowed enemies in the 1930s just as Indian debates about the infrastructures of national science were on the rise. Raman and Saha started competing organizations: Saha's National Academy of Science in Allahabad was countered by Raman's National Institute of Science in Bangalore. Max Born, himself, was aware of the intensive intranationalist struggle between the two for authority over Indian scientific organization. Born wrote to Rutherford of a "terribly complicated system of intrigues, of real politics, connected with the jealousy between North- and South-India, of Bengalis and Mysorians, between low caste and Brahmins, and last [but] not least connected with the English-Indian relationships."[136]

Indeed, in addition to the Bengali and Tamil identities banging heads, the identities of Britons were also involved in the melee. The proposal to offer Max Born a permanent lectureship in India was turned down by the directors of the IIS, and in a manner that Born found most embarrassing. "This faculty meeting was one of the most awful experiences I have ever had," recalled Born. "I had to sit through a speech by Raman about my contributions as a scientist, a teacher and as a person, and I noticed that it was not well-received by some members of the faculty. The British professor Aston stood up and spoke in the most unfriendly way against Raman's speech. He explained that a second-rate foreigner, who had been expelled form his own country, was not good enough for him. That was especially disappointing [for me], since . . . we had been very friendly to the Astons."[137] William Aston was a British electrical engineer, who arrived one month after Max Born came to the institute. Aston believed his task involved "clearing up" the institute.[138] If the struggle between Bengali and Tamil, or lower-caste and high-caste identities, were of one kind, the assertion of racial superiority of British imperial administrators over the workings of the Indian Institute of Science was of another.

After the fiasco, Born recalled, "I was so shaken, and as I came back home to Hedi, I cried."[139] He convinced his wife of the urgent need to return to Britain. Max Born eventually found a permanent position at the University of Edinburgh in the winter of 1936. But this was not his last intimate encounter with C. V. Raman. In this case, however, absence did not make the heart fonder, and a major intellectual controversy developed between Raman and Born in the 1940s. If Raman could not relate to Born through cooperation in Bangalore, as he intently wished in 1935, Raman found another avenue for long-distance relations a decade later, but this time through the mode of long-distance critique and disagreement within the international field of physics research.

Raman stepped down from the directorship of the Indian Institute of Science in 1937, freeing himself from the oversight of the colonial government and from intrusions by the likes of Meghnad Saha. In April 1948, Raman founded the Raman Research Institute in Bangalore, again directly on the model of the Kaiser Wilhelm Institutes. It began with 65 fellows, and rose to 173 by year's end. Many critics complained that the new institute contained scholars who only did Raman's brand of work.[140]

Abha Sur writes insightfully about the way Raman's science exhibited a different "aesthetics" from European sciences, as it sought to create independent sources of institutional and personal authority for Indian nationalist scientific research. Raman continued to focus stubbornly on spectroscopy, and the vast majority of the essays by him and his students in the *Journal of the Indian Academy of Sciences* focused on that topic. Raman was concerted in his efforts to create a "school" of physics, meant to claim recognition not only in India but also on the world stage of science. He was asserting an Indian nationalist distinction in the world through the international practice of intellectual politics.

Indian intellectual politics on the world stage drove the late work of Raman in the 1940s, in which he aggressively embroiled himself in a controversy with Max Born over the lattice structure of crystals. As was so frequently the case in this post-Enlightenment age, battles over intellectual authority involved contests to disclose hidden worlds. In the case of the Raman–Born controversy, both Raman and Born made contradicting universalist claims about the true structure of atoms within crystals. Both thinkers used science to make conflicting assertions about the fundamental structure of the natural world. And the encounter that arose between Born and Raman in the 1940s, although based on disagreement, had the potential to enhance the international recognition of both men as well as the cultural worlds they represented.

Max Born predicted, using the mathematics of probabilities and the principle of uncertainty at the base of the quantum physicist's worldview, that the boundary conditions of chains of atoms in a crystal would be thought of as "looped" and infinitely repeating. Raman insisted that Max Born was wrong. The boundary conditions for crystalline structures could not be thought of as looped, and the oscillation frequencies of crystals occurred only at discrete energy levels. In effect, Raman claimed that his experimental and observational worldview—based on the belief that the world could be best known through close, deep observation—was superior to Max Born's probabilistic worldview—that theoretical models and statistical calculations could best disclose the world at the minutest scale.[141]

Raman's vocal opposition to Born's theories played out in a series of articles in *Nature* magazine.[142] Raman asserted the superiority of "Indian" methods of close observation against "European" methods of abstract theorization. In the 1940s, Raman's dissension from Max Born's theory contributed to his own efforts to maintain his stature on the international stage. Raman and his students continued to argue for their alternative view of the crystal lattice structure well into the 1960s, well after the period in which the international community had discredited their arguments. But Raman's arguments were soon judged to be much less plausible than Born's, and the "dynamical theory" of crystal lattices introduced by Max Born, Theodore von Krámán, and Born's Chinese student, Kun Huang, soon became the accepted view in the field, leaving Raman and his institute further and further behind.[143]

STRUGGLING FOR RELEVANCE

By the time the bombs fell on Hiroshima and Nagasaki, the justifications for harnessing nuclear energy were no longer framed in terms of extending the bounds of science, harnessing new sources of energy for national uplift, or performing physics like Olympic athletes. Nuclear physics was a matter of wartime defense and of strategic deterrence. The USSR acquired nuclear weapons four years after Hiroshima.[144] In India, the Atomic Energy Research Commission was established in May 1946, and Homi Bhabha's institute, not Meghnad Saha's lab in Calcutta, was identified as the national center for nuclear research in India. Homi Bhabha, sixteen years Saha's junior, established the Tata Institute of Fundamental Research in physics in June 1945 at the behest of Jawaharlal Nehru.

In 1951, Bhabha's laboratory in Bombay was the first Indian institute to carry out particle acceleration.[145] Saha's Calcutta institute had to wait until 1954, even though plans were set in place as early as 1934. Bhabha's institutionalizing work arose in a new world order in which science was controlled by the perceived security needs of the Indian postcolonial nation-state vis-à-vis Pakistan as well as by the constraints of the Cold War international order. In the post-Independence, Cold War period, the use of science changed. The ideal of the scientist as entrepreneur pursued by Saha and Raman before World War II increasingly became the scientist as administrator after the war.

It may be that the imaginations of both Saha and Raman belonged to an older world, and were out of sync with the new Cold War dynamics. Both men adopted the model of the scientist as entrepreneur—inspired by the model of the Humboldtian research university as well as by their respective direct engagements with the German-speaking academic world in the 1920s and 1930s. Both Saha and Raman engaged in science as a project to reveal a hidden natural order, and thereby alter the global order of intellectual power in which India figured. Saha also believed that the battle for new epistemologies closely allied with German institutions had also to be complemented by new technical advancement, inspired by foreign models but not dependent on them. The practice of physics, with its potential to make authoritative universalist claims about the structure of matter and its practical applications for industry and strategy, was closely connected with the assertion of national power (whether Bengal, Tamil, or Indian). In the anticolonial period, science gave Indians avenues to strike up new discussions in which their representations of the truth could demand recognition and win acclaim beyond the constraints of empire.

SIX

International Economies

After the Great War, Indians and Germans worked together to develop new universalist perspectives on the structure of world commerce—the flows and exchanges of trade and industry—that crossed territories and linked different regions of the earth together.[1] The claim of these sciences to special insight about the world economy served as weapons in the arsenal of both groups. The epistemic radicalism of some German-speaking economists after the Great War drew upon their attentive study of economic development in colonial and semicolonial Asia, for which India played an exemplary role. But German economists were also interested in engaging with the philosophies of Indian economists as they wrote from the periphery of the British empire. Research on world economics was mediated by scholarly texts and journals: sometimes Germans and Indians never met in person, but only via the personae of their internationally circulating written work.[2]

At the new Tata steel plant in Jamshedpur beginning in 1909, German engineers and laborers as well as a crew of American workers inaugurated production.[3] Jamshed Tata was long familiar with the importance of international study tours in order to solicit aid from foreign experts outside Britain and to guide the growth of Indian nationalist industry. The Tata family firm dealt initially in the cotton and opium trade.[4] But Jamshed Tata was intent on moving from trade to industry in the context of the Second Opium War. To that end, he went on a study tour to Europe and made several trips to continental Europe as well as to the United States, Japan, Australia, and Europe after 1863.[5] From these travels Tata developed his

143

initiatives in large-scale cotton production. But Tata had his eyes on a larger prize: steel manufacture to support the rise of Indian heavy industry.[6] Although he died in 1904, plans were already in the works for the establishment of a major steel plant. In 1912, Tata Works hired the German engineering firm, Siemens Brothers, to supply generators to the new Tata steel production plant at what came to be called Jamshedpur.[7] The original scheme provided for a normal operating crew of about 2,000, of whom around 175 were to be Europeans and Americans. Among that number of foreign steel workers and their superintendents were Germans, numbering about 60 men in total. During World War I, the German crew in Jamshedpur continued its work. Only after the war, in 1924, was the German crew sent home and 84 foremen brought from England to replace it.[8]

The persistent sense among Indian entrepreneurs and industrialists that the British colonial administration was providing insufficient support for industrial development was expressed in the Indian Industrial Commission report of 1916.[9] Madan Mohan Malaviya asked the British official, Mr. Hornell, in cross-examination: "is it a fact that England has been much more backward in the matter of technical instruction than Germany?"[10] In that report, Indian politicians used the example of Germany, especially its institutions of professionalized science, to highlight the deficiencies of British industrial education.

Siemens AG, after closing shop in India in 1915, reestablished a strong base in India selling machines, railway steel, and tools from 1925 onward. It thus built on the success of both its work in Jamshedpur and the construction of the Indo-European telegraph in the late nineteenth century. In 1932, an internal Siemens white paper on India explained that the company wanted to secure a major role in the industrial development of the subcontinent.[11] Until the late 1930s, German multinationals were involved in catering to industrialists in India.[12] Siemens in Calcutta became the regional center for the company in Asia. Borsig and Krupp contributed to technologizing Mahalaxmi Oil Mill of Shamsi near Malda in Bengal in 1926.[13] Bayer supplied chemicals, especially dyes, to India. By 1925, in terms of chemicals, the United Kingdom supplied 58 percent, but the major competitor, Germany, supplied 21.5 percent. In a series of reports from 1924 to 1927 on the status of British trade with India, "Report on the Conditions and Prospects of British Trade in India," Thomas Ainscough of the colonial Indian administration remarked, "the main reason why British manufactures are losing ground is that their prices are above those of their continental competitors."[14] The colonial planners lauded American producers and exporters for their "excellent production." British authorities, however, continually presented German goods as cheap and dirty, and for that reason, saw them as particularly threatening to economic dominance. Goods from Germany were gaining the dominant place in the lucrative, although less prestigious, bazaari retail sector. Germans dominated in bazaari hardware and cutlery. Germans were also the main competitors in glassware, and in drugs and medicine.[15] This was the peak of the "buy British" push in the colonies, and the glory days of Pears soap leading up to the 1932 Ottawa conference and the institution of the protectionist regime of imperial preference.[16]

In 1932 D. R. Gadgil offered a detailed analysis of the intrusion of other nations into British Indian markets. The degree of intrusion differed according to sector and specific commodity. It remained as true in 1932 as it was in the nineteenth century that the United Kingdom was the great purchaser of Indian primary goods, and the dominion countries plus the UK constituted the main market for Indian manufactures. Nevertheless, India maintained a trade surplus with Germany in the interwar years.[17] But especially in terms of imports to India (sheet metal, tools, chemicals, iron, steel, etc.), international competition was intervening in the imperial economic system. The United States supplied the most photographic apparata and machine tools to India. Germany was the leader in exporting musical, scientific, and surgical instruments. And the Germans and Japanese led in the export of cheaper paints that appealed to smaller Indian producers.[18]

ROOTS OF THE ENTANGLEMENT

By the postwar years, German institutions of economics research created major conduits for itinerant encounters between Indian and German scholars as they sought to rethink the world economic order to their own benefit. The Institute for Maritime Transport and World Economics (Institut für Seeverkehr und Weltwirtschaft) in Kiel was a humming center for German economic internationalism in the 1910s and 1920s.[19] By 1926, the institute had issues of 1,800 economic journals published worldwide, from New York to Calcutta. Research departments within the institute were dedicated to collecting paper clippings on different economic regions: North America, South America, Europe, East Europe, Asia, and Africa.

The professors and scholars associated with the institute also traveled internationally. The institute's founder, Bernhard Harms (1876–1939), completed a research trip to Calcutta and Tokyo in 1911, and a trip to the Balkans in 1916. Other founding members of the institute included Gerkens who traveled to India, Albert Schander to Algeria, Max Richter to the United States, and Carl Marx Mädge to Sweden.[20] The institute published a series of monographs, fifty-six in total, between 1910 and 1932. Many of these monographs were dissertations of students at the institute, and one notes the emphasis on German economic ties with the world outside Europe. Harms's students wrote on the Indian textile industry, on the Turkish cotton industry, on cooperative banks in the Dutch East Indies, and on the jute industry in British India.[21]

Germans and Indians in the crucible of the postwar years were seeking to reveal a more profound understanding of global commerce than the one upheld by liberal norms. They practiced economics research with a view to authoritatively shifting capitalism's geopolitical center from the trans-Atlantic region eastward. In this post-Enlightenment context, both German and Indian thinkers rejected the idea of a universal liberal economic realm that arose out of international comparative advantage. Instead, they took the British empire as a symbol of oppression and economic domination. German and Indian economic thinkers both felt they were held in orbit by the normative weight of Western economic dominance in the late nineteenth and early twentieth centuries. They suggested a variety of measures to redress geopolitical inequalities inherent to modern capitalism. They saw the world differently, and talked about it in new terms with each other.

Of course, the global economy had changed drastically over the past half century, especially because of the rise of the "late-developers," Germany and America, and their dominant share of the world market for industrial manufactured goods. Germany was the world capital of chemicals. But Britain, especially the southern and eastern regions and the City of London, secured its role as the major supplier of financial services to the world economy. If the German chemical factory and the American machine factory were ascendant, so too were the British financiers.[22] German and Indian economics in the nineteenth and twentieth centuries were responding to the ideology of laissez-faire universalism associated with Adam Smith—the ideology that directed British liberal imperialism.[23] Smith took up Newton's challenge to extend universal rules of action and reaction from the physical universe to the social one, and he was known in his own time as "the Newton of the moral sciences."[24] Adam Smith believed the economy had a natural order and coherence. The economy, unconstrained by vested interests and the lurid burden of customs, exhibits "the perfection of so beautiful and grand a system." For Smith, the beautiful order and design of a free political economy recalled the astronomical perfection of the "theater of nature" constellated by the stars above.[25] This assertion belonged to the eighteenth-century Enlightenment context of Kant's moral cosmology, Rousseau's law of human nature, the Newtonian physical universe, and Quesnay's economic tables.

Smith argued in terms of universally operating natural laws. The institutionalizers of German national economics, especially Friedrich List (1779–1846) and Bruno Hildebrand (1812–1878), relentlessly criticized Smithianism (Smithianismus), although for differing reasons.[26] List pointed out that Adam Smith assumed an economic universe in its last stage of development, thereby overlooking the developmental imperatives of distinct national economies. Bruno Hildebrand, one of the founders of the German Historical School, asserted by contrast that Smith's "atomistic" vision of world trade undermined the moral and cultural integrity of national communities.[27]

Friedrich List's economic thought sought to reveal the role of geopolitics in the world economy. As Keith Tribe notes, the basic elements of List's "post-Smithian" economics were shaped in the period 1825–1828.[28] List explained, "the object of the economy of mankind, or, to express it more properly, of cosmopolitical economy, is to secure to the whole human race the greatest quantity of the necessities and comforts of life."[29] Contra Adam Smith, argued List, "national economy aimed to increase not simply wealth, but power, and hence its principles go beyond the economy to the political."[30]

An internally renowned school of German national economics emerged in contrast to British liberal economics by the later nineteenth century. In 1897, Romesh Chunder Dutt, in Calcutta, praised German economists for challenging the claims of Smith's economic analysis and questioning the desirability of a Smithian "cosmopolitan" economy that only benefited the global top dogs. "[Adam] Müller first suggested that Adam Smith's system, as elaborated by his more dogmatic disciples, was essentially English and insular," wrote Dutt. Ranade wrote, "it succeeded in England, because the national life of England was preserved intact by its favored situation and past history and conservative instincts, while it was unsuitable to the

Continental Countries, because, with them the preservation of the National existence was a subject of greater importance than mere individual prosperity."[31] Dutt indicted the British for not improving Indian industry. "On the other hand, as India lost her manufacturing industry, she began to import British and other foreign piece-goods paying for it in food grains."[32] Dutt continued, "the industrial prosperity of a subject population was impossible when the settled policy of the ruling nation was to convert India into a land of raw produce only."[33]

The registration of Germanic economics as an alternative to British liberalism also appeared in the works of M. G. Ranade, of the "Bombay School" of economics. In 1899 he explained, "the work of positive exposition [of the critique of laissez faire] was, however, most successfully taken up by the German Professors. . . . Adam Smith's system . . . was essentially English and Insular."[34] List grounded his work in national economics with an episteme that took geopolitics and power seriously. "The function of the State is to help those influences which tend to secure National Progress through the several stages of growth, and adopt Free Trade or Protection as circumstances may require. In this view Free Trade may be good for a Country like England, but not for America and Germany."[35] Ranade spoke of "German teachers" who illuminated the arguments of national economics: Karl Knies, Wilhelm G. F. Roscher, Bruno Hildebrand, Adolph Wagner. It boiled down to a struggle between methods—the Liberal normative approach and the counternormative nationalist historical approach.[36] Ranade proposed that Indian economic thought had to attain "victory over free trade," and to irreverently embrace the "heresies according to English Political Economy."[37] Those heresies corresponded to enchanting German claims about the political flows of world commerce.

In 1910, V. G. Kale, representing the Bombay school of economic thought, laid out the case clearly: "Almost all our industries are in the infancy stage. How are they to grow in the face of the formidable rivalry of foreign manufacturers? On the contrary the modern school, the national and historical school of economists, has successfully demonstrated the abstract and impractical nature of the doctrines of the old school."[38] Kale went on, "Japan has demonstrated to the world what Protection can do for a backward country—and Asiatic country too, not to speak of Germany, the most formidable rival England has in Europe today."[39]

In order to create a different world order yanked free from the grip of the British imperial "world shaping force," central planning was required.

In other words, national protection was the best antidote to imperialism. Even Joseph Schumpeter, an Austrian defender of liberalism and classical economics, pointed out in 1914 that "protectionism" might indeed be an appropriate policy of a state in order to develop its young industries—something the British free-trade-oriented economist would not accept before the later influence of John Maynard Keynes.[40]

REINTERPRETING WORLD CAPITALISM

But protection could mean something other than a turn inward to autarchy and independence from international markets. One way in which both German and Indian economists revealed the world economy was as an energy field that could be tapped by different national groups worldwide. Nations had to fight for ways to best tap the flows of commerce. Protection might involve developing better strategies to alter and reroute the flows of commercial energy in the world.

There were two main schools of German international economics at the turn of the century. One was concerned with extending the German colonial empire overseas, and the other was intent on expanding markets in German Europe (Mitteleuropa), southward and eastward.[41] Bernhard Harms represented a different worldview, best described as a variety of German liberalism, which was nonetheless critical of Smithian laissez faire. Harms, like Julius von Soden and Georg von Cancrin in the early nineteenth century, criticized Adam Smith not for being too liberal, but for not being liberal enough. By remaining silent on the question of political power, especially the measures needed to keep it in check, Smithian economics was destined to create an imperial economic order for Britain under the guise of "free trade."[42] Harms was also a close reader of Heinrich Dietzel, another German liberal economist, who proposed that "the national economy should fuse with the world economy" (Nationalwirtschaft mit der Weltwirtschaft verschmelzen sollte).[43] Arthur Dix took a similarly optimistic view.[44]

The Institute for Sea Transport and World Economics received more than 300 foreign visitors and students in the 1920s. Of the 246 visitors to the institute up until 1926, the largest group (152) was from Europe, but the second largest group came from Asia (54). In addition 34 visitors came from the United States, 4 from Africa, and 2 from Australia.[45] One of these visitors was Benoy Kumar Sarkar from Calcutta, who had just completed an extended leg of world travel, which began in Japan in 1915 and ended in Berlin in 1920.[46] He came to Kiel to lecture on "Equations of Comparative Industrialism." Sarkar compared the industrial experience of India with the economies of what he called "Euro-America."

Over the course of the 1920s and 1930s, the institute collected almost every single essay and article written by Benoy Kumar Sarkar as well as essays by other eminent Indian economists such as Radhakamal Mukerjee, V. D. Kale, and Brij Narain. The institute held more writings by contemporary British Indian economists than did the British Imperial Library. And Bernhard Harms's journal, *Weltwirtschaftliches Archiv,* published original research articles by Indian and Japanese scholars abroad.[47] The rise of the institute in Kiel and the deliberate push toward a perspective that was simultaneously worldwide and also German was of a piece with similar developments elsewhere, such as the establishment of the Institute for Business Cycles (Konjunkturen) in Berlin, and the Institute for World Economics in Leipzig.[48] Bernhard Harms, like his nineteenth-century guru Friedrich List, was driven by the wish to make Germany into a global trading power and the hub of an alternative international economic and cultural order from the one anchored by London and the British empire.

Benoy Kumar Sarkar (1887–1954), for his part, was searching for a different internationalism in which Bengal, the old administrative center of British India, would play a prominent role. Sarkar believed that the world economy, especially the markets outside the British empire, had an important role to play in the economic development of India. "Everybody who brings capital and invests in the material and human resources of Bengal is a friend of the Bengali people," wrote Sarkar.[49] Both Harms and Sarkar believed that the structure of the world economy was changing in drastic ways and that the age of imperial economies was coming to an end. Nations required policies and planning in order to adjust to this epochal shift. The changes in the structure of the world order (what Harms called the *Strukturwandel der Welt*), especially the decline of the British empire and the rise of Asian economic national economies, would create new possibilities for German and Indian capitalism.

GERMAN *WELTWIRTSCHAFT* AND BENGALI *VIŚVAŚAKTI*

In 1912, Harms returned from a trip to India and Japan. He had visited Calcutta, and was impressed by the local knowledge, extensive contacts, and large official library of the German consul there. The consul in Calcutta, stationed at the "kernel" of the British empire, as Harms termed it, was widely perceived by German internationalists as holding one of the most important positions in the Germany Foreign Service. Harms wrote that Germany should have more people abroad like the German consul in Calcutta, who would "provide information on the world economy for German business."[50]

Harms wrote his programmatic and unorthodox textbook defining the terms and concerns of a new "Weltwirtschaftslehre" (study of the world economy). He insisted that the *Wechselseitigkeit* (reciprocity) of world trade could be used for Germany's national advantage, but state planning and the formulation of state and international law were required as protective measures. Without the creation of new laws, colonial empires, such as the British empire, would continue to grow in the world economy, and the chances for small nations would be curtailed.

In contrast to mainstream schools of German *Weltwirtschaft* that assumed the difference between a national economy *(Volkswirtschaft)* bounded by community and culture, on one hand, and an unbounded world economy of impersonal commerce, on the other, Harms drew on the work of Rudolf Kobatsch, who in 1906 proposed that national economies were only legally delimited zones of a global economic power grid, cordoned off by nation-state law.[51]

"Today, in some ways, Hamburg is closer to New York than it is to Munich," Harms remarked, arguing that it was neither culture nor shared history that tied Hamburg and Munich together into a "national economy," but only the legitimating power of German state law.[52] Resonant with the school of legal positivism that informed German discussions at the time,[53] Harms maintained that economic planners should think of "Germany" in terms of all the international domains worldwide in which its laws were at work, and not as some primordial cultural or historical entity set in contrast to the international realm. For Kobatsch, as for Harms, there was nothing natural or culturally rooted about the national economy, and Germany was a geopolitical economic and legal entity energized by the world economy.

Benoy Kumar Sarkar, on the other hand, had a communitarian vision of the nation, as a natural whole defined by shared kin relations, shared language, and shared culture. From the mid-1920s onward, the fascist ideal of voluntary association among a national kinship community seemed most promising to him—it represented the ability to mobilize collective institutions beyond those liberal ideals of the individual, the private corporation, or the political party, in projects of collective uplift. Sarkar explained, "after the war, the most enlightened politicians in all the countries of the world realized that the old Parliamentary conceptions of the State no longer corresponded to the crying needs of collective life and the new ways must be sought and found. . . . In the Fascist State, Syndicalism once an incitement to anarchy and to the dispersion of economic wealth, now becomes a public institution, a State organ, which regulates and guarantees the professional discipline of the different categories of workers."[54] For Sarkar, German cartels, agricultural planning, central banks, and state-directed trade unions provided his central examples of the benevolent state coordinating all productive factors.[55]

The Bengal National Chamber of Commerce was one outcome of Sarkar's return to India after almost a decade of travel across the United States and Europe. In Calcutta as of 1926, he resurrected the nationalist Indian Chamber of Commerce that he had previously founded in Berlin. The 1927 journal of the Bengal National Chamber of Commerce carried reports about the patriotic internationalism of other groups. A report appeared about a Japanese delegation that had traveled to Germany to study the organization of the German iron and steel industry in 1927. In particular, Sarkar celebrated the instrument of the cartel as a compromise of state and private interests. "In Germany, however, huge cartels or trusts have become almost natural or normal phenomena in business organization," wrote Sarkar.[56]

In 1928, Sarkar founded the Bangiẏa Dhana-Vijñan Parisad (the Bengali Society for Economics). In the period from 1925 to 1938, Sarkar went on to establish no less than eight other institutes (although they all had the same address at 9 Panchanan Ghose Lane).[57] In 1926, Sarkar began publishing his economics journal Ārthīk Unnati (Economic Progress), a series of the Bengal National Chamber of Commerce that continued until 1938.[58] It was published in Bengali, and focused on discussions of "techniques of capitalization and capital investment in India."[59] At Sarkar's peak, more than 100 scholars were affiliated with his various initiatives. All of these institutions put a special emphasis on the specifically regional Bengali wish to assert the geopolitical place of Bengal outside of liberal empire and to stand out in an international frame. If Bernhard Harms founded one institution, the Institute for Sea Transport and World Economics, Sarkar founded multiple organizations, and seemed intent on staging what sheer willpower could achieve in the pursuit of nationalist institutionalization contra colonialism. Other Sarkarian institutes included the Baṅgīya Samāj-Vijñan Pariṣad (Bengali Sociology Institute), Baṅgīya Jārmān Vidya Pariṣad (Bengali German Knowledge Society), Baṅgīya Dante Sabhā (Bengali Dante Society), Āntarjātik Baṅga Pariṣad (International Bengal Society), and the Baṅgīya Asia Pariṣad (Bengal Asia Academy). They were all conspicuously Bengali, and Sarkar insisted that the scholarship, journals, and discussions of the various institutes employ Bengali, and not English, as the working language. Sarkar wanted a "linguistic *digvijaya* [conquest], as conquest of the world by means of one's own language, or as absorption of the resources of human attainments in the *sarva-bhaumic* [universal] empire of one's mother tongue." Sarkar remarked that this politics of opening up to the world and translating new learning into Bengali "came into prominence with the birth throes of the National Council of Education in Bengal, in 1905."[60] Indian thinkers were thus breaking away from British colonial methods and institutions by turning to other major centers of modern science and scholarship.

The message of the journal was to develop an Indian program of protectionism, to create an India-centered, not empire-centered, world economic policy for Indian business. "India must remain open to trade in the world, but it must engage in trade in such a way that ensures capital is accumulating in India, and remains in the hands of Indians."[61] Sarkar's goal was also to enhance transnational dialogue and Indian anticolonial international relations toward this end.

By means of his various institutes, Sarkar wanted to "take as the field of researches not only Bengal and the Bengali people but other regions and races of the world as well."[62] In 1927, Oskar von Miller, a German engineer and the founder of the German Museum of scientific and industrial objects in Munich, was a guest of the Bengal Chamber of Commerce in Calcutta.[63] In 1932 Sarkar traveled to Munich as a visiting professor, accepting the invitation from the Deutsche Akademie, the main institute of Nazi academic internationalism.

Sarkar's radicalism was in contrast to the "village-economy school," later associated in the 1930s with Gandhians, such as J. C. Kumarappa. Sarkar's endeavor was more in line with the modernization economists of the late nineteenth century, such as Mahadev Govind Ranade, Gopal Krishna Gokhale, and Pramathanath Banerjea, who agreed that economic benefits had flowed from British rule, and called Indians to push forward toward a robust nationalized industrialism.[64] In an article that appeared in Harms's *Weltwirtschaftliches Archiv,* Sarkar proposed, "Indian Industrialism is already a power in the industrial commercial system today."[65] In order to continue India's rise, there would have to be an "energetic cooperation with the rest of the world." India would continue to be reliant on the machines and chemicals imported from the "older Industrial nations," but it should not be concerned with whether it received its machines from Britain, Belgium, or Germany. Foreign capital investment in Bengal, especially from sources outside Britain, counted as a "godsend" in Sarkar's view. India could not wait for the rise of *"svadeśi* millionaires" to "build the big factories, extract the minerals and petroleum, and create the global trade routes," he insisted.

India had to rely on the world's foreign capitalists to speed up the work of economic decolonization in India. The "leaders of German economy," Sarkar proposed, should send ten of their representatives to start enterprises in Calcutta, with the expectation of remaining in situ for about ten years. Such international cross-pollination would provide Bengal with technologies and skills that imperialism refused to give.[66] "Everybody who brings capital and invests it in the material and human resources of Bengal is a friend of the Bengali people. Capital does not know any nationality. It ought to be a part of our statesmanship to attract financiers from far and near,—British, American, Japanese, and even German, as well as, of course, Marwari,—to our villages and towns."[67] Such a message from Bengali nationalists was no doubt music to the ears of the Moravian entrepreneur, Jan Antonín Bat'a, who established his company's first shoe factory outside Calcutta in 1931, followed by the company town of Batanagar in 1934. The company was soon to become one of the largest shoe manufacturers in India, and a name synonymous with a postimperial Indian capitalism.[68]

The image of Germany had a double connotation for Bengali economists such as Sarkar: it represented both the most modern and advanced late developing economy of Europe (one that had outpaced the old great economy of Britain), and a subordinated and even "colonized" region of Europe— one that had been reduced to a semicolonized state after the Versailles Treaty and the occupation of the Ruhr valley. "The situation in Germany is exactly opposite to that in Great Britain and France and identical with that in the British colonies," Sarkar suggestively wrote.[69]

In 1936, Sarkar published *Parājita Jārmānī* (Defeated Germany), a compendium of all his writings on German Europe, including Germany, Austria, and Switzerland. The work extended over 600 pages and explained how the German historical experience, set within the very heart of Europe, could be identified with the Indian one. As a nation founded in 1871, Sarkar began, Germany achieved rapid industrialization and modernization in a matter of decades. In Sarkar's mode of Occidentalism, the longer history of German economic development was telescoped to the years between 1871 and 1914, and presented as the triumph of willpower exercised by great men, such as Bismarck and Kaiser Wilhelm. Germany developed strong economic and social institutions. Sarkar transposed himself into the German position. And what Germany did, India could also do.

In Sarkar's view, Germany resembled Bengal in other ways as well. Unlike England or France, which were nations organized around a great political and economic metropolis, Germany was decentralized, with Munich, Nuremberg, Düsseldorf, Leipzig, Hamburg, and many other cities playing an important role. But most important, the "Diktat" of the Versailles Treaty, the embarrassment of reparations, hyperinflation, breadlines, and penury all were analogies for the Indian colonial experience in the heart of Europe. The occupation of the Ruhr by French, Belgian, British, and American troops took place between 1923 and 1925. Sarkar called this *gōlāmi* (imprisonment) and *dāsatva* (slavery). It made Germany the India of Europe. "Between the [Ruhr] region and British occupation in India, there is no real difference."[70] The occupation engendered Germany's own *svadeśi*, or nationalist, struggle. "After the war, the Germans showed how a jāti (a people, a Volk), can rejuvenate itself."[71]

There was an important regional aspect to this discussion. In 1932 P. C. Ray delivered a series of lectures in which he regretted the "quill-driving careers" of Bengalis, vis-à-vis the Parsi, Gujarati, and Marwari traders. A Bengalification of industry was needed, especially in terms of the employment of the growing body of unemployed Bengali labor. Also needed was a total restructuring of the economy, which required interaction between the government and foreign experts. P. C. Ray referred to "the West," but evoked, in fact, a specific "West," associated with the German, Japanese, and American models.[72]

RADHAKAMAL MUKHERJEE AND GERMAN MODELS

If Benoy Kumar Sarkar focused on world economic trade, Radhakamal Mukherjee's interest was in the economy of smallholding farmers and small firms in India, and in the geopolitical difference between European economy and society, and that of India. Radhakamal Mukherjee began writing an agrarian history of India when such a project was still relatively unprecedented.[73] Radhakamal Mukerjee was a young member of Rabindranath Tagore's circle, and a student of Patrick Geddes, the urban planner and British (Scottish) critic of empire who traveled to India in 1914. Radhakamal completed his education at Presidency College and never traveled abroad to Germany except in the 1950s, when he helped found a program for Indian Studies in Berlin for the German Democratic Republic. In terms of Radhakamal's ideas, he practiced economics research as an enchanting science in order to claim the place for Indian forms of society and economy in the world. Beginning in 1921, Radhakamal became the chair of Sociology at Lucknow University.

Karl Kolwey, research affiliate of the Institut für Weltwirtschaft and specialist on the Indian economy, wrote a 1924 book contrasting the nationalist approach of Radhakamal Mukherjee with the liberal economics approach of Brij Narain. Kolwey praised Mukherjee for asserting the difference of the Indian case, and the "sociological factors" that show "that an industrialization of India on the model of the West would be disastrous given the danger that an excessive centralization and division of labor brings. [Radhakamal Mukherjee] is even of the opinion that an overthrow of the system is occurring in Europe."[74]

Radhakamal's entanglement with Germanic methods of radical science can be glimpsed from his reflections on his own intellectual pursuits. Radhakamal wanted to establish a "new science of Comparative Economics, which, along with the sister sciences of Comparative Jurisprudence, Comparative Politics, Comparative Aesthetics, and Comparative Religion, will explore the diverse zones of cultural distribution. For, indeed, all social and humanistic evolution, including the economic, is multilinear and diversely ramifying no less than the course of biological evolution; and, accordingly, we have to map human history, its institutions, its environment and habitat."[75] The study of economics was not to standardize one single economic model, but to differentiate and compare different regional economic worlds.

Radhakamal's worldview was comparativist, not assimilationist, in its objective. Radhakamal's "Comparative and Regional Economics" would move beyond the present "impasse and arrest" in economic thought, and would bring "harmony and reconciliation to the clamant strife and struggles of different peoples and regions in their blind career of competitive exploitation and aggressive self-expansion."[76]

Like so many other Indian scholarly internationalists, Radhakamal Mukherjee saw himself as the inventor of a new approach. "I have adopted an attitude of an innovator and experimenter, a disturber of the old order," he exclaimed.[77] It was his intent to disrupt the "old science" of British liberal economics using the comparative and historical methods. By doing so, he did not restrict himself to a part of the world's whole, but he claimed a superior, universal position to see an invisible world order of economic production. "I appeal only to a larger order, the coming cosmic humanism, which knows neither East nor West, neither white nor black." In that Rabindranath-inspired "humanist" pursuit was a geopolitical maneuver to break out from the British imperial periphery.

Radhakamal Mukherjee wanted to make India's cultural and economic characteristics stand out in the planetary frame. "In so doing I have sought to bring out the typical physiognomy of the Indian culture, and of the socio-economic institutions, instead of labeling these, as is so often done, under the indiscriminate catch-phrases and shibboleths of conventional economics."[78] Mukherjee was a student of Brajendranath Seal and of Asutosh Mukherjee. He positioned himself as a critic of "pre-evolutionary classical economists from Ricardo to Mill" and proposed that methods taken from sociology and psychology were important.

German Europe became the touchstone for Mukherjee's discussions about cooperative banking in India in the years after the world war.[79] Mukherjee observed in 1925 that "the magnitude of the results achieved in Germany as regards the development of rural industries was due not so much to coercive action on the part of the State in shepherding these industries, or to any direct or indirect assistance from tariffs, as to the steady and strenuous diffusion through specially created services of advice, information and education."[80] The German system apparently provided small nudges to economic actors through advice, information, and education, instead of via the bold gestures of tariffs or command. M. L. Darling declared in 1922 that "Germany is a splendid example of self-help . . . ," although "still adrift on the wreckage of her shattered empire."[81]

Radhakamal Mukherjee's approach to revealing the problems of Indian economics within a planetary frame of economic flows was to focus on the relationship between rural and urban economies. In elaborating his development economics, Mukherjee emphasized that Indian industry would not need to be like England's, but it need not be a cultural economy in the Gandhian mode either. His argument was greatly inspired by the urban planning theory of Patrick Geddes, who emphasized the need to study rural towns and villages and their agrarian economies on their own terms.[82] India's could be an economy of small-scale industry, Radhakamal proposed.[83] "In Germany, the small-scale industry continues to employ about two-fifths of the entire industrial population, and embraces more than 90 percent."[84] Radhakamal spoke of "rurbanization" and the "cityward drift" that would instigate the "improvement of the technical conditions of the village, which will satisfy the more intellectual and ambitious of village youths."[85]

In the 1910s and 1920s, still a decade before the rise of what came to be called "Gandhian Economics,"[86] Radhakamal Mukherjee was providing the most forceful argument for the power of the Indian village economy, and the "strenuous diffusion" of production factors as a geopolitical alternative to Western, city-centered, and finance-driven capitalism. Mukherjee praised the village and handicraft economies, while also emphasizing the ineluctability of the global economy, as well as the benefits it would bring to Indian society. In fact, the high merits of "communalism," or communitarian belonging, inherent in Indian culture, when married with the "steam engine," would allow India to reach a form of modernity that would surpass the alienation and social disintegration experienced in the West.[87]

In making his argument for "rurbanization," Radhakamal did not look to Britain, but to German Europe for models. He maintained that rurbanization and the use of rural industry based on small capital was mirrored in the German experience, not that of western Europe. Radhakamal's idea of the Indian economic character was a dialogic one, in which India's experience resembled other "small economies" in the world. The "co-operative credit" movements became one of his great interests. "Germany is the home of Raiffeisen. It is now a part of the peasant organization [in India], as it ought to be," wrote Radhakamal.[88] The agricultural reconstruction of German Europe, especially through cooperative credit, was appropriate for India. "In every country of Europe they have practiced handicrafts, and even now they or their womenfolk still knit, spin, make lace, embroider, plait straw, make baskets and pots, work wood and leather . . . [in] Germany, Denmark, Switzerland, Czechoslovakia, Russia, Hungary and the Balkan countries . . . In Germany, the small-scale industry continues to employ about two-fifths of the entire industrial population, and embraces more than 90 percent."[89]

Mukherjee wrote his prescient book, *Regional Sociology,* in 1926. The approach was to reveal social and political dynamics along the lines of Friedrich Ratzel, whom he directly quoted. In order to understand the economy and society of a people, one had to pay attention to the surrounding environment, and what happens when "genetic groups" move, relocate, and "fuse" with new groups. "The study of the relation between physical and social conditions, inspired by Ratzel's *Anthropogeography,* has corrected the old partiality for the one straight line in sociology," commented Radhakamal.[90]

From his sociological perspective, Mukherjee did not assert the unexampled uniqueness of India, but rather its relation to other groups in the world. The historical and comparative methods were both central to his emphasis on a new Indian identity beyond empire. Radhakamal claimed that agricultural economy in Belgium, Denmark, Switzerland, and Germany all exhibited "the grafting of processes of large co-operative business upon the small farming economy." And these conditions "are more easily applicable to India, where the solidarity of the family and the joint farm and homestead . . . make us unfit . . . for utilization of the full advantages of large and concentrative capitalism which inhere in countries of massive production like England and the United States."[91] The similarities between Germany and India in terms of their decentralized economic life became visible once a comparative lens was applied, and once their mutual differences with other forms of political economy were registered. The revealed world of global commerce that Radhakamal Mukherjee described was populated by bounded economies that nevertheless existed in global family relations. Radhakamal saw a world not of autonomous economies, but of far-flung economic family groups.

By the 1930s, Radhakamal came to a finalized formulation of his vision of the invisible kinship and community bonds that organize commercial flows. He articulated his final formulation in terms of "the humanization of industrialism through regionalism."[92] The ecologism, and the hints of eugenic science, expressed in these views were elements in Radhakamal's enchanting scholarship.

Radhakamal Mukherjee and Benoy Kumar Sarkar drew comparisons between German and Indian social types, but they pointed to diametrically opposite criteria for making comparisons. If Sarkar saw Germany as a land of cartels and central planning, Mukherjee insisted that the German example was most salient for its decentralized and distributed network of finance and expertise to rural areas. Scholars such as Gary Herrigel have pointed out that Central European political economy can indeed be understood as a combination of different kinds of economic order, with both decentralized and organized systems of capitalism working alongside each other.[93]

But beyond the accuracy of either R. K. Mukherjee's or Sarkar's way of revealing a different world of commercial life, we should not forget that the very practice of drawing comparisons had a political intent, as it allowed Indian identities to stand out from liberal empire *in relation to* other national groups. R. K. Mukherjee and Sarkar's epistemic radicalism was embedded in arenas of transnational encounter. Both spoke about world economics so as to assert relays of travel and association beyond British empire.

CAPITALIST ANTILIBERALISM

It was January 17, 1926. Sitting in the Blue Hall of Hotel Bristol on Unter den Linden, Werner Sombart (1863–1941), the famous national economist and social reformer, was preparing for one of his favorite pastimes: meeting with his Asian students. On this occasion, Zakir Husain, a Pashtun Muslim from the Punjab who would one day serve as president of India (1967–1969), had organized a dinner party for Indian students in Berlin with their German professors. Husain recently received his doctorate in economics with the grade of summa cum laude from the University of Berlin. He had studied under Werner Sombart. Husain completed his bachelor's studies at Aligarh University before departing for doctoral studies in Berlin where he also studied with Max Sering.[94] Husain finished his studies by 1926 and returned to India, eventually becoming the rector of Jamia Millia Islamia University.

Sombart's critique of Adam Smith fit into the long tradition of the German "Historical School" that argued against Adam Smith's "naive" suppositions that human societies could be studied according to one universal rule, and against the liberal assumptions of perfect individual agency. As German economists argued, the historical trajectories of a particular society were fundamentally important to the production of its economic life. "Language, literature, religion, art, moral, legal, and economic history" were all interwoven. There could be no understanding of the economy without an understanding of the cultural history of a people.[95] There was no proper understanding without an understanding of national difference. This assertion led Sombart to associate himself with other nationalists in the world who saw things in a similar way. Colonial nationalists were counted among that number.

Sombart's criticism of Anglo-Saxon liberal economics has earned him various epithets among modern historians: antipolitical, antimaterialist, anticivilizational, culturally pessimistic, illiberal, among others.[96] Still, he was remarkably open to interactions with colonial and non-Western thinkers, and his Indian students found much to engage with in his perspective. Although he seemed to repudiate German relations with western Europe (while adoring the United States), Sombart built relations with the Orient. Popular Orientalism provided modes of relation that caused him to cross-identify with and relate to the East.

Sombart's "antipolitical" critique of capitalism often found its way into the non-European "colored" circles of Berlin. Sombart had a strong reception among Russian economists, particularly in the period from 1905 to 1907 after the first revolution.[97] He had a voluminous correspondence with Indian, Chinese, Japanese, and Turkish students in the 1920s.[98] He was beloved enough by his Japanese students that the majority of his personal library, comprising 8,091 books, was purchased by the University of Osaka in the 1920s.[99] The Sombart Nachlass in Berlin gives evidence of the popularity of the economist among students from the non-West. Many Japanese students, such as Tsunao Miyajima, Kormosuke Otsuka, and Chuichira Gomyo; Indians including S. Sinha, Jabbar Kheiri, and Zakir Husain; Turkish students such as Achmed Naim Hakimbay, and Emmer Djelal; and Chinese students, such as Chao Feng, all wrote to Sombart in the 1920s asking for interviews with him, or for permission to attend his lectures.[100] This profile was in line with that of his great predecessor, Gero von Schulze-Gaevernitz, who also attracted a large number of non-European students. One of Sombart's Turkish students from the 1930s, Hilmi Ziya, recalled how Sombart would invite non-Western students to his villa in Grunewald for discussion. Ziya remembered Sombart's interest in the welfare of his student Ömer Celal, who had returned to Turkey some years earlier. Sombart said, "I still follow his work. But I want more Turkish students, especially given the social state of [their] country."[101] Sombart, a thinker often associated with the inward-looking antipolitical conservative circles of the Weimar era, wished surprisingly for contact with the world.

There were some 200 Indian students studying in Berlin in 1923.[102] And those who studied economics were likely to attend Sombart's lectures. Zakir Husain completed his dissertation under Sombart on "Die Agrar-Verfassung Britisch-Indiens" (The agricultural constitution of British India).[103] Husain's work recalled in its subject matter Sombart's own dissertation, which dealt with the agrarian economy of nineteenth-century Italy, focusing on the theme of technologization and reform.[104] It also recalled the dissertation begun by W. E. B. Du Bois under Gustav Schmoller a generation earlier in Berlin, "The Plantation and Peasant Proprietorship System of Agriculture in the Southern United States."[105]

Sombart portrayed the introduction of technology into the countryside in approving terms. But he also argued that state intervention had expanded communal property, introduced irrigation works, and tamed the pressures of trade capitalism. Sombart spoke of the organic nature of rural life centered on the family and local community, and he maintained that technology and state planning had enriched and strengthened the rural economic and moral order.

Husain's research under Sombart set a feedback loop in motion. Soon Sombart included Husain's scholarship in his footnotes. Sombart's *Das Wirtschaftsleben im Zeitalter des Hochkapitalismus* (1928), published one year after Zakir Husain submitted his dissertation, concluded with a discussion of peasant economies around the world. The exploitation of peasant labor to supply the world economy *(Gesamtwirtschaft)* typified a general economic order in "the East," Sombart argued. "I essentially follow the foundational work *(gründliche Arbeit)* of Husain, *Agrar-Verfassung*," he noted in a citation.[106] In the postwar period, the two thinkers, while interacting across a power differential of Eastern student to European teacher, saw each other as scholarly compatriots against liberal imperial capitalism.

German nationalists in the 1920s saw themselves simultaneously as teachers and compatriots of the East. Conservative newspapers, such as the *Preußische Kreuzzeitung*, featured many articles about anticolonial movements by Irish, Indian, Chinese, Egyptian, and Syrian activists. A common trope was that of Germans as a people of "poets and thinkers" now subjected to the materialistic forces of British and French imperialism.[107] While German scholars invited colonial intellectuals to "defeated" Germany to study and learn, they also adopted the language of anticolonialism to speak about their own experience in German Europe. Conservative organs, such as the *Deutsches Volkstum, Das Gewissen,* and the *Preußische*

Kreuzzeitung, published anticolonial, pro-Indian articles, even as they argued for the need for Germans to "take to the sea again" as colonialists.[108]

Max von Oppenheim, the former Foreign Office adviser who orchestrated German–Indian plots during World War I, and Ernst Graf zu Reventlow (1869–1943), conservative anti-Republic publicist, early Nazi politician, and later supporter of the German Faith Movement (*Glaubensbewegung*), attended the anticolonial meetings of Indian, Egyptian, and Syrian nationalists.[109] Reventlow was one of the sponsors of the Indian National Party of Berlin founded by Champakraman Pillai, a South Indian anticolonial activist.[110] Sten Konow, the Swedish Indologist teaching in Germany, published *Indien unter der englischen Herrschaft* in 1915. German Indologist Hermann von Staden published *Aufruhr in Britisch-Indien* in 1915, and A. K. Viator published *Deutschlands Anteil an Indiens Schicksal* in 1918. Many of these individuals were members of the *Bund der Freunde Indiens* (Union of Friends of India) in Berlin during the war years. But these same German figures were also often pro-imperialists in their own right, and harbored visions of German colonial reprisal and expansion into Eastern Europe, as well as into overseas territories.[111]

Ernst Bloch once commented that the old adventurous "pioneer spirit" of the United States, the anticolonial spirit of struggle in India, and the "triumph of the will" that was so central to German nationalism, and eventually to fascism, all shared a vague similarity in that they idealized the "moment of willing."[112] Indeed, it is certainly valid to ask how that fixation on oppositional "willing" arose in such different contexts, and how it related to forces rooted in Enlightenment science, not external to it.

Sombart, as one of the "national economic boys,"[113] expressed enthusiasm for modernization and technologization, while also deploring the depleting effects of "English" and "Jewish" capitalism. The chief elements of Sombart's postwar thought included an emphasis on the need for an ethical social order, a strong centralized state,[114] an assertion of the robustness of German culture, and a communitarian longing for the recovery of German *Gemeinschaft* in which "Volk, Vaterland, und Staat" would become "the source of heroism."[115] Sombart was said to be the Tönnies of German economics. He extrapolated the implications for economics of Ferdinand Tönnies's sociology of the modernization process.

Sombart's *Deutsche Volkswirtschaft* (The German National Economy, 1903) presented the German national story as one of development (social, economic, cultural, and political).[116] It is possible to track the change in

Sombart's perception of Asia from a period in which he spoke as a proponent of German imperialism, to the postwar period in which he spoke as a critic of western imperialism and self-perceived partisan of the global subaltern. A degree of identification across the colonial divide can be observed in Sombart's thought. In 1897, for example, he referred to the "inferior East European and Asiatic nations," and he especially emphasized the possibilities of German entrepreneurial spirit to colonize the contiguous lands of eastern Europe.[117]

By 1913, his study of economics addressed questions that related to the East. In *Luxus und Kapitalismus* of 1913, he wrote about the history of the production and shipment of sugar, cocoa, and cotton from the colonies to Europe.[118] In *Der Moderne Kapitalismus* of 1916 he criticized British and American economic expansion for the role it played in slavery.[119] In the same book, the economist identified the distinctiveness of Germany with the supposed absence of slave labor in its colonies.[120] Before the Great War, Sombart's concern was almost exclusively with German Europe and the Mediterranean, although the Boer War had also commanded his attention.[121]

In 1917, he published on British traders' extraction of precious metals from colonial territories.[122] In his 1920 *Der Bourgeois*, Sombart castigated the British colonialists, especially Cecil Rhodes, for their "rapine nature" *(Räubernatur)*.[123] By the time of *Zukunft des Kapitalismus* (1932), Sombart asserted that the "world economy of the period of high capitalism, the period of the white race's lordship of the entire world, has reached its end."[124]

The chief feature of the "English spirit" was imperialism, Sombart wrote. "The British Empire is an adding machine of acquisitions that are mechanically added piece by piece together: the parts are 'accumulated' and hang together in only loose connection with the motherland."[125] Throughout the work, Sombart ruminated on the "pump station" of the colonies,[126] on British success in making "colonial peoples fight their wars,"[127] and on Britain's laying of telegraph cable around the world in order to "spread lies" about Germany.[128] The "trader mentality" of the English is supposedly one that sought to destroy difference and spread the insipidity of commerce. Sombart's propagandistic tone in *Händler and Helden* (Traders and Heroes), a book dedicated to the German youth serving on the front, took the form of shrill attacks on British national character: "Nevertheless from early times the English character trait has been arrogance. It was no different in the sixteenth century than it is today. When they see a good-looking foreigner, they say: too bad it's not a Briton . . . The

English are very conceited about themselves and their work. They don't believe that there are actually other kinds of people [worth their interest] on this earth."[129]

A nonexploitative *Weltbürgerlichkeit* (cosmopolitanism), on the other hand, marked German culture.[130] Sombart became the proponent of a heroically *German* capitalism, just as other German nationalists, especially after the war defeat, would come to promote *German* music, *German* literature, *German* religion, or even the *German* atom. The construction of a *Germanic* identity that stood out in the world did not develop in isolation, but in relation to and comparison with other groups.

In contrast to destructive Western internationalism, Sombart claimed, "it is an aspect of German character that we have always approached foreigners with sensitivity and love. As some have put it, it is precisely *un-German* to want to be only German." But Sombart's writing on the German "heroic" spirit was full of contradictions. No sooner had he asserted the worldliness of Germans than he continued: "Ultimately, we Germans do not need the cultural or intellectual influence of anyone." And furthermore, "anyone who still speaks about the fruitfulness of foreign cultures for German intellectual life should consider what Goethe wrote about the German soul."[131] In the same text in which he proposed a German fascination with the "un-German," he also insisted on German cultural supremacy.

In Sombart's anti-Semitic, but also anti–Anglo-Saxon view, the Jews and the English were equated—both representing invisible, globally expanding threats to rooted German livelihoods. In his fanciful depiction, the "rootless" (*entwurtzelte*) Jews and the East India Company were the two forces responsible for establishing "high capitalism." Sombart drew the parallel multiple times throughout *Händler und Helden*, "but if the East India Company were the first to have a system of 'private obligation,' the Jews were the fathers of private obligation on a higher level."[132] Given the threat of British and Jewish internationalism, the German *Volk* could only respond by becoming international itself, Sombart seemed to contend.

Historian Karl Hardach proposed that the experience of "involuntary autarky" during World War I, when Germany was largely cut off from primary materials from the hemispheric south, "was to influence future German economic policy, especially after 1933."[133] The discourse on German *völkische* identity certainly owed something to a Romantic inheritance—to the nationalist philosophies of the likes of Johann Gottfried von Herder and

Johann Gottlieb Fichte. However, Sombart's construction of Germanness had much more to do with geopolitical tensions of the early twentieth century—first with German imperial hubris, and then with post-Versailles German resentment as a world power manqué.

INDIAN VILLAGE POWER

It is hard to know whether Sombart had a more tonic effect on his Asian students or whether their concerns, located in a different framework of politics and national struggle, may have tamed Sombart's tendency toward German nationalist excess. Zakir Husain, a young wunderkind of Aligarh Muslim University, wrote a dissertation closely aligned with Sombart's method of inquiry. It began with the claim that the modern economic life of India started with the arrival of the Mughals. Muslim rule broke the social stagnancy of Hindu village society by establishing a strong political center under Akbar, and "challenging local Brahman authoritarianism."[134] The resulting social order had its own disadvantages, however, and led to "the rule of land-rentiers, tenancy laws, [and] a poorly-equipped farmer-class, that lacked will and means to improve themselves."[135] But the coming of the British economic and legal system, Husain wrote, brought further enslavement of the Indian peasantry. In the period before the British, the moneylender had to mobilize the *"Dorfmeinung"*—the consensus of the village—in order to ensure payment of debt. Debtors who were late on their payments were pressured, and even shamed, by the community into financial responsibility. But under the impersonal legal order of the British, courts were established and court taxes and dues had to be paid. The authority of law now gave the moneylender the opportunity to extract all the concessions he chose.

With the coming of British colonial law came the death of community, Husain contended. British imperial capitalism caused the arrested development of India through "trade capitalism" *(Händlerkapitalismus)*. The Permanent Settlement, whereby the fledgling colonial state attempted to stimulate agricultural entrepreneurship in Bengal by rationalized titles to land in 1793, "was a measure implemented by traders—the English! They were indifferent to the well-being of the people; the first British occupation was of purely commercial character, and aimed only at economic profit."[136] Eventually taxes were increased, cash crops were introduced, and the great impoverishment and de-skilling of the Indian artisans and laborers in the countryside were set in motion, Husain wrote.

Husain concluded his dissertation, which Sombart highly praised, by addressing the political transformations taking place in India, and symbolized by M. K. Gandhi. The cosmopolitan forces of world trade had caused an "embodied de-nationalized intelligence . . . but the movement that carries Gandhi's name will produce strong currents which will bring about fundamental change. Here we find the will of India brought to expression—to live in its own land, and according to its own ideals."[137] The resonances with Werner Sombart's *Traders and Heroes* were strong. The village was the source of economic power and ethical and cultural rejuvenation in Husain's view. In making this argument, he was heavily influenced both by his German teachers and by standard claims of Indic Orientalism, as well as by the writings of Indian economic historians.

British political economists such as Henry Maine in his *Village Communities in the East and West* (1871) and B. H. Baden-Powell in *Indian Village Community* (1896), and German Indologists such as Heinrich Zimmer in *Altindisches Leben*, and Julius Jolly in *Grundriss der indo-arischen Philologie*, buttressed Husain's depiction of the cultural authenticity of Indian village life. And contemporary Indian economists, especially Radhakamal Mukherjee, in *Foundations of Indian Economics* (1916), supported Husain's argument for the need to preserve Indian village life as a source of nationalist power.

During World War II, Husain, by then vice-chancellor of Jamia Millia Islamia University, gave a series of lectures at Delhi University on "Capitalism." He began by observing that the neoclassical economists shied away from using the term "capitalism" to describe their own ideological commitments. But with a nod to his German *Doktorvater,* Husain said, "the popular textbooks of Gide and Marshall, Seligman and Cassel do not use the term. . . . But of late, specially through the influence of Sombart, the usefulness of the term to indicate with one word the economic life of a certain kind, has begun to be generally recognized."[138] Availing himself of the authority of Sombart's form of enchanting economics scholarship, Husain told his listeners that capitalism was a type of economic activity characterized by the "urge into the endless" and the transgression of bounds, by the push for rationalization, by entrepreneurship, and by the fixation on gain in monetary terms alone. World capitalism was marked by depletion and exhaustion, Husain asserted, by the proliferation of private economies, not public goods. In twelve elegant lectures, Husain demonstrated the range of his mature thought, covering themes such as the connection between militarism, slavery, and colonialism, and the capitalist wish for "the emancipation from the limits of space."[139] Husain concluded by forecasting the rise of an "Asiatic Capitalism" in India, which would be very different "from its Western predecessor."[140]

Abdul Jabbar Kheiri finished his dissertation in 1927, one year after Zakir Husain had completed his. Jabbar and his brother Sattar Kheiri were Khilafatists involved in the wartime activities to establish a political movement for Islamic universalism centered around the Ottoman caliph. They left India in 1916 and served the German Foreign Office at its reconnaissance and propaganda bureau in Istanbul during the war. After the war, the brothers traveled to Berlin, arriving in 1919. As recompense for their assistance to the German government during the war they received salaries from the German Foreign Office until 1922. Jabbar Kheiri matriculated as a doctoral student of Werner Sombart in 1922 and he also served as the imam of the Muslim community in Berlin until his return to India in 1927. He went on to teach at Aligarh University, and he and his brother became chief exponents for the Pakistan movement in the 1930s.[141] Aligarh University became a center of German-educated Indian Muslim economists, with six PhDs from Germany on their faculty during the 1930s.[142]

Kheiri's dissertation, "Indien und seine Arbeiterschaft: Ihre Entstehung und Bewegung" (India and its workforce: their development and movement, 1927), resonated with Husain's writing in many ways. Kheiri too praised the Indian village: "the Indian villages once were a collective for Indian well-being. They evolved long ago into a kind of commune."[143] While the Indian villagers were like German small towns, "marked by dignity [Erhabenheit] and obligation [Müssen], they were colonized by a people interested only in comfort and amusement and driven by greed," Kheiri proposed.[144] The British introduced "Finanzpolitik" to India, and thereby turned the land into a desert and the villagers into a proletariat. The British in Kheiri's narrative played the role of the Jews in Sombart's work. In Sombart's anti-Semitic narrative, it was Jewish cosmopolitans, with their supposed innate connection to trade, which disturbed the ethical Germanic Gemeinschaft of economic life.

In Kheiri's account, the fusion of Muslim and Hindu culture during the Mughal period led to a flourishing civilization. Unlike Husain, who saw the Muslim incursion as part of the process of rationalization, Kheiri focused on the development of "mosques, schools, universities, libraries, and study centers" during Mughal rule.[145] However, the British brought with them intellectual "anarchy," he claimed, as "the old learning was scorned, old customs and traditions were thrown out, and the old religion was laughed at as mere superstition."[146] Both Kheiri and Husain, then, spoke of culture as a source of ethical and social wholeness, destroyed by the incursion of trade. The Mughal rulers were portrayed as ending Indian Hindu stagnation in a way that did not occasion the moral degeneracy that came with Western capitalism.

As much as these Indian dissertation writers engaged with Sombart's perspective, it is also important to note that Sombart grasped the nettle and engaged with theirs. He was intent on observing the radical similarities between the experience of German economic and social development and that of India. A level of doubled identification, both as teacher and compatriot, was present in his interaction with the Indian students. In fact, Sombart was one among a whole group of writers and thinkers, the German revolutionary conservatives after the war, who readily identified with the experiences, history, and politics of the colonial world.

The claims to an ability to reveal hidden worlds of commerce and economy that disrupted the dominant northwestern European "liberal" international economy emerged within transnational discussions. Those dialogues gave voice to different authoritative assertions about the unseen economic flows that engulfed the whole world. In addition to the different truth-claims and the different spins of politics that marked the encounter between Bernhard Harms and Benoy Kumar Sarkar; or Radhakamal Mukherjee and German cooperative economic thought; or Werner Sombart and Zakir Husain and Sattar Kheiri, the fact that these politically unequal groups made claims *with* each other suggests something about the times. The German–British partnership, on the same side of the colonial divide, had persisted until the 1880s. After that point, transnational relays across the colonial divide were spun and became entangled. Especially after the Great War, an order of dialogue developed in which Germans and Indians often cross-identified, even as their manifest political and economic situations greatly differed. In the interwar years, German and Indian economic thinkers, with their radical globalist visions, registered each other as discussion partners, even elective kin, in ways that were highly transitory. Certainly by the end of World War II, economic discourse as a means to post-Enlightenment enchantment no longer created conduits for transnational interactions in this same way.

SEVEN

Marxist Totality

In the age of entanglement, radical Marxist thinkers struggled to conceive of laborers around the world as constituting a universal force—the consciousness of world history coming to self-recognition. In the words of the young Georg Lukács, the Marxist vision of totality is grasped when the proletariat becomes conscious of itself "as simultaneously the subject and object of the socio-historical process."[1] The workers of the world, Europeans and colonial subjects alike, formed a collective world-historical subject that would work out the universal, objective meaning of human history, radical Marxists believed. Marxism provided a worldview symmetrically opposed to liberalism: instead of the gentlemanly capitalist as the world-historical man, here it was the factory worker, the peasant toilers, and the colonial subaltern who together spoke for the universal. Institutionalized Marxism, in its "revisionist" mode under the Social Democrats after the Erfurt Program, promoted a worldview that affirmed the nineteenth-century ideal of Europe. After the Great War, Marxism-Leninism and communism created discursive arenas in which the uniform visions of Europe and of Empire were forcefully critiqued, and often through the dialogic feedback between spokespeople in Europe and in the colonial world. The post-Enlightenment discussions of radical Marxism constituted an arena in which both German and Indian social thinkers claimed universal and exclusive distinction as the only ones in the world possessing philosophical perspectives to reveal the totality of human history.[2] Itinerant Indian nationalists such as Virendranath Chattopadhyaya and M. N. Roy played major roles in establishing the rudiments of the Communist Party of India abroad, in Berlin. Figures such as Rajani Kanta Das and Ram Monahar Lohia found conversation partners among German and Russian Marxists, as they opened up epistemic arenas beyond the space of British empire and the aspiration of imperial liberalism.

INVENTING LABOR

Beginning in the nineteenth century, rooted in the radical work of two German scientific reenchanters, Karl Marx and Friedrich Engels, "labor" came to be seen as the quintessential invisible global force that surged through human society and world economy. Many commentators have shown how Marx's own stance toward the colonial question changed over time, from general admiration for British imperialism in the early 1850s, to outright critique of imperial force by the 1870s. By the 1870s, Marx defended modes of anticapitalist communism in Russia and began to look to the Russian peasants, not the industrial workers, as the likely source of revolutionary unrest.[3] In his later years, Marx hoped that a Russian revolution in the villages and farms would detonate a world proletarian revolution in the urban factories.[4]

Marxist views of Asia changed drastically at the fin de siècle. By the turn of the twentieth century, even before October 1917 in St. Petersburg, many Marxists imagined that the spark for world revolution would come from the Orient. By 1908, Vladimir Lenin spoke of Russia as an empire partly of Europe and partly of Asia.[5] As early as 1913, Lenin maintained the Russian experience would thus play an important role in "rousing" Asia to action. "World capitalism and the 1905 movement in Russia have finally aroused Asia. Hundreds of millions of the downtrodden and benighted have awakened from medieval stagnation to a new life and are rising to fight for elementary human rights and democracy," he wrote.[6]

The project of Marxists focused on how best to link the theoretical understanding of an invisible world of labor flows to the politics of social resistance and reform. The conceptual link of capitalism and colonialism as related forms of exploitation developed over time, and only in the context of high imperial competition in the late nineteenth and early twentieth centuries. In a way, what Marxism did in the early twentieth century was similar to what German comparative philology had done in the early nineteenth century. Marxism, using critical methods, threw suspicion onto the dominant and normative self-presentation of nineteenth-century European exceptionalism. Philology traced hidden familial connections across seemingly unrelated languages. Marxism traced hidden connections of labor and expropriation across seemingly unrelated economies. Instead of deep and unfamiliar family relations between languages, Marxism revealed deep relations among all those who toil for the modern economy. The discourse of Marxism thus granted intellectuals the ability to claim a privileged "historical materialist" worldview, and to claim a post in the central watchtower overlooking the world stage. Marxism allowed Marxists to construct universalist identities for themselves.

To appreciate the difficulty at stake in writing anticolonialism into the Marxist tradition at the turn of the century, one must only consider the conventional socialist discourse on imperialism at the time. Many socialists supported colonial projects, arguing that colonial economies benefited European workers. The Seventh International Congress of the Second International (International Socialist Congress) took place at the end of August in Stuttgart in 1907. H. M. Hyndman made a strong speech indicting the British empire. Both Lenin and Rosa Luxemburg were present, deeply dissatisfied with the reformist tone of the proceedings. As the largest international meeting of socialists in history to date, the meeting also drew members from around the world, including representatives from India, who equally expressed concern.[7]

The most important and controversial topic on the agenda of the International Socialist Congress at Stuttgart arose on the third day of discussion. The resolution submitted to be voted on read: "The congress observes that the use and necessity of the colonies for the working class have been highly exaggerated. It does not, however, denounce colonialism in principle or for all times, since it can, under a socialist regime, have civilizing effects."[8] But even this restrained critique of colonialism, still beholden to the universalistic nineteenth-century signifiers of Europe and Empire, was unacceptable to pro-imperial socialist leaders. Henri van Kol of Belgium and the elder statesman of socialist revisionist, Eduard Bernstein, expressed vocal opposition. Bernstein called for a "socialist colonial policy," since "it was necessary to give up the utopian idea that we can take a shortcut to letting go of our colonies. The logical end of such a policy would be that the Americans should give their land back to the Indians."[9]

On the other side, a minority of attendees vociferously opposed the resolution as an un-Marxist acceptance of the oppression of colonial peoples.

Georg Ledebour and Adolph Hoffmann of the German contingent insisted that the resolution be changed to condemn colonialism in the strongest terms. The radical left wanted to insert the statement: "The civilizing mission, on which capitalist society justifies itself, serves only as a cover for its lust for domination and exploitation."[10] Lenin and Luxemburg sided with Ledebour and Hoffmann, and their critique of the socialist stance provided the justification for the major break with the Second International in coming years. The original resolution was ratified with small amendments: 127 ayes, 108 nays, and 10 abstentions at the end of two days of heated debate. A fissure in the ranks of attendees appeared that would soon open up into a tectonic gap between the social democrats and those who would break away as members of a new "communist" party.

Rosa Luxemburg, of Polish Jewish decent, arrived in Berlin in 1898 and immediately entered the leading circles of the socialist left. She helped found the Polish Social Democratic Party two years earlier along with other leading figures, Julian Marchlewski (Karski) and Leo Jogiches. Luxemburg, in her *The Accumulation of Capital* (1913) argued, in terms that surpassed John Hobson's theory, not only that Europe existed in a world economy with colonial territories in which finance capitalists exploited European workers and colonial workers alike but also that European economy and society were affected by the political agency of those in the colonial world. This hinted at the possibility that political and economic upheavals outside Europe by non-Europeans could fatefully affect the lives of Europeans. Many Marxists at the time vehemently maintained that Europe had a responsibility to civilize the less sentient natural peoples *(Naturvölker)*.[11] German bourgeois society had rededicated itself to its colonial calling in Eastern Europe, the Middle East, and Africa at the very time Luxemburg wrote.[12] In this context, Luxemburg's views were heavily critiqued and subsequently dismissed by mainstream Marxists.[13]

Luxemburg reenchanted geopolitics, using the science of historical materialism to uncover a new coherence. Animated by the fact that the Orient (Russia) was leading the charge to revolution when Marx's own system had insisted that it would only begin in the West, Luxemburg sought to invert the relationship between peripheries and conventional centers of the world.[14] This intellectual motif was also noticeable in Luxemburg's masterwork, *The Accumulation of Capital,* where "the exterior" was mapped to the colonial world and "the interior," to the metropolis. Luxemburg, influenced by John Hobson's *Imperialism* and Rudolf Hilferding's *Finanzkapi-*

tal (1910), proposed the dependence of "internal zones" on "external" ones, or the economic dependence of centers on their peripheries.

While many socialist economists, including Marx and Hobson, had taught that colonialism would gradually lead to the expansion of capitalist modes of production throughout the world, Luxemburg instead suggested that capitalism in fact could exist only within a larger noncapitalist social environment *(nichtkapitalistische soziale Umgebung)*. The picture of capitalist organisms leeching off the social life of noncapitalist regions, be they peasant societies within Europe or in the colonial lands outside Europe, became the leading motif of the left Marxist critique of imperialism. Luxemburg's Orientalism gave her the leverage to make a connection with the East over the West. Instead of seeing the colonies as mere zones for the dumping of surplus capital, European colonies became spaces of disturbed and diminished social life through Luxemberg's lens.

RELATIONS BETWEEN EUROPE AND ASIA

If Rosa Luxemburg's work presented global labor in a single analytical frame by envisioning the collaboration and interdependence between "organized" and "nonorganized" workers, and between laborers in the "interior" and the "exterior" of a capitalist world, Luxemburg's student, August Thalheimer, proposed that comparisons could be revealed in the intellectual traditions with which Europeans and non-Europeans criticized and resisted social exploitation. Luxemburg maintained that solidarity between European and Asian toilers was possible. Meanwhile, Thalheimer proposed a way of broaching dialogue between Europeans and Asians to bring about global labor solidarity.

August Thalheimer was arguably the most important interpreter of Luxemburg's writings in the 1920s, and he served as leader of the German Communist Party from 1921 to 1923.[15] Thalheimer had a philological Orientalist background, having completed a dissertation on the grammar of the Micronesian language in 1908, and thus was a versed practitioner of comparative textual analysis.[16] Throughout his career, Thalheimer took a special interest in the application of Marxism to Asia and how the study of the Orient might alter the modern interpretation of Marxism. In Thalheimer's *Introduction to Dialectical Materialism*, originally delivered as a lecture series at the Sun Yat-Sen University in Moscow from 1924 to 1928 and then published as a book, Thalheimer argued that the revolutionary consciousness of laborers had developed within the Indic philosophical tradition. Echoing Max Weber's arguments about the traditions of "intellectual opposition" from within the Sanskritic tradition, Thalheimer argued that both Indians and Chinese need only look at the ancient history of their own indigenous high traditions to see that Buddhism had sprung from the social oppression of Brahmanism, and that Taoism had battled Confucianism. The Sanskritic tradition had also produced materialistic philosophical schools such as Nyāya, Cārvāka, and Sānkhya philosophy. Chinese and Indians could return to their own traditions, to Buddhism and Taoism in particular, and find the needed sparks for a revolution.

Thalheimer presented Marxism as a continuation of the Asian philosophical tradition. Marxism, he wrote, "incorporated and developed the results of two thousand years of natural and social science."[17] Thalheimer's approach involved first discussing the materialist philosophies of India and China, and then slowly showing how these modes of thought were improved upon and perfected by Marx. Marx, in Thalheimer's interpretation, was already Oriental.

Marxist Orientalism produced a repository of visual images, both static and moving, that aimed not just to unmask something true about the region of Asia, but to use Asia to make claims about the processes of capitalist exploitation affecting the whole world. Marxism, in addition to serving as a theory of political economy and as a means for social protest and mobilization, was also a transnational dialogue for the assertion of new intellectual authority—a means to challenge norms and to center new kinds of subjectivities within a global frame.

Orientalism on the left, in the works of scholars such as Jewish German philosopher and anticolonial activist, Theodor Lessing, provided a means to critique the idea of the West along cultural, political, and economic lines. The West represented modern commerce, world trade, territorial acquisition, and capitalistic rationality, and leftist Orientalists used Asia, especially India, as an anchor in their critiques of Western capitalism.[18]

Lessing published his book *Europa und Asien* in 1915. The book was a manifesto against Eurocentrism, and a rumination on the destructive "will to importance and megalomania of the European-American world."[19] A student of Edmund Husserl, and influenced by ideas about cultural holism current at the time, Lessing carried out his radical science of "cultural phenomenology," revealing the morphologies of the Chinese, Indian, Jewish, Islamic, Egyptian, and Persian civilizations in a comparative frame-work.[20] He argued for the greater richness and sophistication of these cultural wholes when compared with the crudeness of a warring Europe. "The book," recalled Hans-Georg Gadamer about Lessing's treatise, "rela-tivized what was, at the time, an all-encompassing horizon within which I developed through parentage, upbringing, and schooling," and contributed to a "provincialized Europe since 1914."[21]

Lessing was a firebrand of the Weimar years. His radical critiques aimed at laying bare Westernism, "Deutschtum," anti-Semitism, and the renewed imperialistic fervor in German society after postwar stabilization.[22] Orien-talism, as a cluster of cultural, social, geographical, and even geological associations, facilitated the claims of the German left to be able to repre-sent something deep and true about the world order and uncomfortable to Western capitalists. In 1925, after his harsh public criticism of the nation-alist, conservative president, Paul von Hindenburg, Lessing was removed from his teaching post at Hannover's Technical University. Lessing contin-ued his critique as a public intellectual, and received top billing as a speaker at the League against Imperialism conference in Brussels in early 1927.[23]

At the core of Marxist "Red Orientalism" was the idea that the study of imperial rule in Asia could make the injustices of the world economy more visible to the naked eye. Aspects of historical and social reality could be more easily perceived in Asia, since it preserved some of the archaic struc-tures of human society, Marxist anthropologists and historians main-tained.[24] Asia's primitivism intensified and magnified the social forms that determine human life across the globe, especially in those realms outside of the modern capitalism of the West.

A frequent commentator on the Orient in the pages of the German left literary magazine, the *Weltbühne*, vividly remarked, "the whole of Asia has begun to awaken from the hypnosis of British world rule."[25] Asia, in Marx-ist Orientalism, was a place of destructive vitality in the world. Arthur Holitscher wrote of "the Orient [as] a wrecked house."[26] And Egon Erwin Kisch in his *Asien gründlich verändert* (1932) insisted that no longer is it true that "the East is East and the West is West . . . we see the railways be-ing extended and the new silos being built, and the dark red Muscovite moon now shining over the once undifferentiated and colorless common property [of China]."[27]

This was the era of the *Kulturfilm*, the documentary style of educational films, which aimed at giving audiences a "scientific" understanding of distant cultural reality, especially through recourse to the ethnographic mode. Paul Zils, a German documentary filmmaker who spent the balance of his career in India, recalled, "I had a strong urge to see and discover the world for myself. I wanted the real men and women in their real surroundings, real things and real issues, and . . . I wanted to attempt the dramatization of the living scene and the living theme, springing from the living present." [28]

Egon Kisch's book of new objectivity, *China Geheim* (Secret China, 1933), spoke to the urge among many Marxist intellectuals to reveal the world in its social reality, and supposedly to get beyond mere artistic representation. His work contained 141 photographs by Wilhelm Thiemann. [29] These photographs suggested the critical Marxist hunger for proximity to once-distant, colonial peoples. The *Arbeiter Illustrierte Zeitung* (AIZ), founded in 1921 by Willi Münzenberg, was devoted to the dissemination of photographic representations of Asia and Africa. By 1930, the *AIZ* had a print run of 500,000 issues, making it the second-largest magazine circulating in Germany. [30]

The formal elements of Marxist Orientalism's visual expressions are striking. The pictures of Indians and Chinese portray them in acts of protest, or depict them as peoples in motion, on the way to class consciousness. Yet, even as they were in motion, they remained monumental and primitive, and thereby became archetypal for a modern global process. Between 1921 and 1925, the Soviets produced more than 100 educational films through the state-run Mezrapom agency. Films about the Orient made up a popular genre. Some of the most popular films were *Völker des Ostens* (1930), *Sturm um Asien* (Storm in Asia, 1926), *Das Erwachen des Orients* (The Orient Awakening, 1929), *Der Kampf um die Erde* (The Battle for the Earth, 1930), *Turksib* (1929), and *Gandhi* (1930). [31] In 1926, Vsevelod Pudovkin, the Russian director, produced *Sturm über Asien,* one of the most celebrated communist films of the decade. [32] In 1928, *The Shanghai Document,* by Yakov Bliokh, told the story of China after the civil war through a series of documentary street scenes. A German review of the film praised it for depicting "life itself, reality in its full breadth, its gruesomeness, its drama and its beauty are captured by the camera. This movie will even satisfy fanatics for reality." [33] Communist audiences wanted to see "the reality" of life in the East, and also to glimpse the archetypal forms of struggling, laboring "life itself." They believed Asia could reveal this for them.

Marxist Orientalists also looked to India and China for archetypes of mass mobilization and protest, which they perceived in the rising anticolonialism movements. German leftists studied the noncooperation movement in India as a method worthy of emulation. To be a European leftist meant to stand with the Toilers of the East, and this could connect with a variety of geopolitical assertions against Western Europe. Marxist Orientalism was infused with anti-Anglocentric, counternormative sentiment and with what Cemil Aydin has defined as "anti-Westernism."[34] This anti-Westernism on the left was alive within Europe itself, and it grew stronger the farther one traveled outside the northwest European power center.

REVOLUTION

News of the Russian Revolution of October 1917 reached India almost immediately and was greeted with enthusiasm.[35] Major newspapers and journals carried cheering stories about the Bolsheviks, and the colonial administration in 1918 worriedly remarked, "[Russia] has given an impetus to Indian political aspirations."[36] With its slogans of worldwide labor solidarity and its claim to having literally changed the course of history through concerted mass action, anticolonial radicals could not help but find inspiration in the Russian revolution. But the birth of mass labor movements in India came only in the early 1920s with major industrial centers such as Calcutta and Bombay erupting in strikes at cotton and jute factories.[37]

The Comintern International, established officially in Moscow in 1919, invited a number of prolabor members of the Indian National Congress to attend the Fourth Congress of the Communist International, held in Moscow in 1921. M. N. Roy, Virendranath Chattopadhyaya, Bhupendranath Datta, and Muhammad Barakatullah were all present for these discussions and debate. In this period, the Soviets saw India as the key to a larger revolution in the East. One Indian communist pamphlet from 1921 declared, "India is the universal meaning [for the communist struggle] . . . India is the citadel for revolution in the East."[38]

Indian Marxists identified with a larger Asian domain of labor struggle, on one hand, as well as with the European and American context of labor activism, on the other.[39] In 1921, Shripad Amrit Dange published his book, *Gandhi and Lenin*, in which he proposed that Bolshevism could provide useful modifications to Gandhian politics. And the month before the fourth meeting of the Comintern congress, Dange wrote in his new journal, the *Socialist*, "attacks from without have helped to consolidate the peoples of

Asia, as 'Asiatics,' without prejudice to their separate religious and national existence . . . It would indeed be a glorious thing for India to take the initiative and summon the first sessions of the Asiatic International in the pandal event of the Gaya session. Angora, Persia, Afghanistan, Asiatic Russia, the Far Eastern Republic of China and Japan would accept the proposal, we think, very gladly and send fraternal delegates to the International."[40] Asia, for Dange, was not to be understood as the colonial other of Europe, but as a geopolitical center of the world thanks to its revolutionary labor power.

Well-known Asian thinkers such as Sen Katayama, Tan Malakka, Semaun, Ho Chi Minh, and Zhou Enlai entered the upper echelons of the communist world, inducted as members of the Comintern in the 1920s. In total, sixty-four Asian and African members of the Comintern (1919–1935) were deputized to produce scholarly works and oversee political campaigns for revolution in the colonies.[41] Yet, while Moscow was the acropolis of the communist world in the 1920s, and a city where many high-profile Asian communists spent at least some amount of time, these individuals tended to spend most of their time in the European capitals of Berlin, Paris, and London.

The international infrastructure of the communist world was organized through the Western Bureau of the Comintern (WES) in Berlin. This was the "permanent representative of the Communist International in West Europe" and the liaison point for the coordination of communist networks worldwide. The bureau oversaw the distribution of funds to multiple groups affiliated with the Comintern from "Iceland to Capetown," at least up until the stabilization of the Weimar Republic in 1925 and the stabilization of the Weimar Republic regime,[42] Eduard Fuchs and Willi Münzenberg, the two German organizers of early communism, managed the millions of golden rubles that flowed in and out of the WES, the Western Bureau of the Comintern.[43] Housed at the Karl Liebknecht house, the headquarters of the German Communist Party before 1933, the bureau was also a major printing press for communist books, pamphlets, and brochures. It was here that M. N. Roy and Virendranath Chattopadhyaya, in Berlin, and the London group around Shapurji Saklatvala and Rajani Palme Dutt competed for funds from the communist administration, and vied to establish the definitive Communist Party of India. M. N. Roy printed his *Vanguard* and *Masses of India* weekly newspaper for shipment to India.[44] The Western Bureau was the major liaison point between Moscow and the world—organizations as diverse as the Far East Bureau of the Comintern in Shanghai and the Seamen's and Port Workers' International in Sweden were provisioned with funds through the Berlin bureau. Meanwhile, Indian communists based in London played an important role in forging the bond between Marxism and anticolonialism. Rajani Palme Dutt, Clemens Dutt, Shapurji Saklatvala, joined by Benjamin Bradley, Charles Ashley, and Philip Spratt, played particularly important roles.[45]

Marxism served as a way for Indians to claim global stature as revealers of globally applicable truths. It established causeways for Indian travelers across the planet, and beyond the institutions of British empire. Rajani Kanta Das left Calcutta for the United States in 1910, and started his studies of Indian settlers in southern California in 1912. Rajani Kanta Das served as a special agent of the U.S. Department of Labor. He earned a degree from the University of Wisconsin in 1916, and for some time was a lecturer in economics at New York University. He traced the first strikes in India back to 1882 and the first trade union to 1890.[46] Most of his works were published in Germany, however, because he was forced to flee the United States in 1923, after the anti-Asian immigration bill was passed.[47] As a stateless person, his American citizenship rescinded, Rajani Kanta traveled to Germany and soon began a career at the International Labor Office in Geneva in 1930.[48] From there, over the course of the coming six years he published a series of important works on Indian labor protest before returning to Calcutta.[49]

Ram Manohar Lohia, who formed the Congress Socialist Party along with Jayaprakash Narayan in 1936, completed doctoral studies in economics at Berlin University in 1932. Lohia, born in Uttar Pradesh and educated at Calcutta University, wrote his dissertation on "Gandhi's Salt March."[50] He completed the dissertation under the guidance of Hermann Schumacher, a scholar who worked on questions of Socialist economic thought. Ram Manohar Lohia developed an effective means of combining socialism and Gandhianism.[51] And his interest in a middle path to political mobilization and social justice, informed by the German Socialist movement, had a significant influence in Indian national politics as he returned to India.

In May 1930, Manabendranath Roy (1887–1954), along with a large group of Indian protesters, picketed the 1930 meeting of the executive committee of the Socialist Labour International in Berlin. M. N. Roy had just been expelled from the Communist Party because of his long-standing disagreements with the Stalinist regime.[52] Roy and his group carried placards bearing slogans such as, "Long Live Free India," "Long Live the Revolution," and "Down with British Imperialism." The Socialist International meeting was a public relations problem, given that the governments in power in Germany and Britain were the Social Democrats and the Labour Party, respectively. The reason for the protest was the complicity of the British Labour Party, in power for the second time since the end of the war, with the policies of British imperialism. At the meeting, Socialist International Chancellor, Gustav Stresemann, shook hands with Prime Minister Ramsay MacDonald. In M. N. Roy's open letter distributed during the summit, he criticized the British Labour Party for its attempt to "crush the anti-imperialist struggle," and for sanctioning the imprisonment of "thousands of men and women along with Mahatma Gandhi" for their protests against the upcoming Roundtable Conference. To the host members of the German Socialist Party, Roy wrote: "if you were true to your profession of socialism, then bring pressure to bear upon the British Labour Party too . . . release all political prisoners and repeal all repressive laws."[53] The presence of dislocated, diasporic Indian nationalists in Germany took many shapes and the itineraries pointed in many different directions. Marxism was more an arena of transit and entanglement, than an ideology.

THE LEAGUE AGAINST IMPERIALISM

Central European Marxists in this period experienced the penetration of their social world by itinerant Indian Marxist thinkers. Indian Marxists came, in particular, to Germany, for a host of reasons—to flee incarceration, to complete higher studies, to teach Europeans about the force of global labor as seen from the perspective of colonial labor. Although European history would record itself going out and bringing colonial peoples to Europe to initiate political collaboration, in many ways Asians, Africans, Black Americans, and others were penetrating the intellectual and social strata of European Marxism. This is particularly observable within Marxist cosmopolitan circles, where many colonial intellectuals congregated.

By the mid-1920s, European societies were no longer seen as the main sources or the vanguard theaters for Marxist social revolution. European Marxists increasingly saw Europe as "provincialized" in the world, to use a term from both Hans-Georg Gadamer and Dipesh Chakrabarty. Europe was nestled amid world regions that packed far more punch.[54] Asia, Africa, and Latin America were increasingly perceived as the centers of growing labor unrest and anticolonial resistance with global, not local, import.

The League against Imperialism was organized by Willi Münzenberg and Virendranath Chattopadhyaya based in Berlin, although the first meeting of the league was held in Brussels in 1926 due to intervention by German officials.[55] What S. A. Dange called the "Asiatic International" and Fenner Brockway termed the "Coloured People's International"[56] was not just an abstract ideal. It was a dialogic arena that convened the top leaders of anticolonial nationalist movements in the colonial and semicolonial lands across Latin America, Africa, and Asia. The first League against Imperialism meeting drew 174 delegates, and more than 104 of these were from the colonial world.[57] Criticized by liberal onlookers as a front organization for international communism, it was true that the organization was sponsored by Soviet funds, although the deliberations consisted not of Soviet diktats, but rather of speeches by anticolonial nationalists.[58]

Attendees included Jawaharlal Nehru of India, Lamine Senghor of Senegal, Mohammad Hafiz Ramadan of Egypt, Victor Haya de la Torre of Peru, Soong Ching-ling, the wife of the late Sun Yat-Sen, and Mohammed Hatta of Indonesia, among others.[59] The gathering provided an archetype for the Bandung Conference convened three decades later in 1955, as well as for a series of International Youth Congresses and Peace Conferences along the way.[60] Indeed, Jawaharlal Nehru and Mohammad Hatta were major forces behind the Non-Aligned Movement and the Bandung Conference.[61]

But not only the Asian, African, and Latin American but also the European delegates on hand are worthy of note. European envoys hailed from the pacifist fringe of Europe, including renowned German figures such as Albert Einstein, Theodor Lessing, Ernst Toller, and Alfons Goldschmidt, members of the anticolonial British left such as Fenner Brockway and Harry Pollitt, and the French Nobel laureate and pacifist, Romain Rolland.

At the conference, the heated political situations in China and India served as touchstones for the deliberations. As Frantz Fanon noted about the dynamic of recognition among colonized peoples, "the liberation of the new peoples are felt by the other oppressed countries as an invitation, an encouragement, and a promise."[62] Speakers as diverse as Jose Quijano of Argentina, Daniel Coltrain of South Africa, and Lamine Senghor of Senegal all welcomed the outbreak of political crises in China and India as the catalysts of a larger transcolonial struggle.[63]

In his speech to the league at its inaugural session in 1926, Nehru assured his audience, "Our problem [in India] naturally concerns us greatly, but I come to tell you, regardless of whether you come from China, Egypt, or other faraway lands, that your concerns are similar to ours and that the Indian problem is also of interest and importance to you."[64] There was a definite sense among the participants that solidarity was a feat of the imagination: the various colonial struggles worldwide had to labor toward common cause, and had to explain to each other wherein lay their interdependence. Mohammed Hafiz Bey Ramadan argued that since imperialism was a global phenomenon, the only adequate response had to be of global, not just national, proportions. "The hour has now come to close ranks and to battle policies that are leading to the common oppression of us all."[65] The league was a transcolonial declaration of allied autonomy from imperial domination.

In 1928, the Indian National Congress, announcing its commitment to anticolonialism in a transcolonial mode, declared, "the struggle of the Indian people for freedom is a part of the general world struggle against Imperialism and its manifestations."[66] The league met for a second time in Frankfurt in 1929. The historical consequences of the league meetings are noteworthy. In 1936, Nehru attended the First World Peace Conference in Brussels. On that occasion, he recalled the inaugural League against Imperialism meeting he attended in Brussels one decade earlier: "ideas of some common action between oppressed nations *inter se* . . . were very much in the air. It was felt more and more that the struggle for freedom was a common one against the thing that was imperialism, and joint deliberation and, where possible, joint action were desirable."[67]

FURTWÄNGLER IN INDIA

Franz Josef Furtwängler is a vivid example of the interpenetrations and feedback loops that developed between Central Europeans and Indians within the vast dialogic arena of Marxism. Furtwängler was one of the major spokesmen and popularizers of Gandhi within the German labor movement.[68] As he embraced Marxist Orientalism, Gandhi became Furtwängler's model leader of labor struggle and spiritual renewal.[69] Furtwängler, international secretary of the General German Trade Union Confederation as of 1923, was born into an artisan family in a small town, Vörhenbach, in the Black Forest. He trained as a mechanic and in 1911 began his journeymanship through various European countries, and on Italian and British steamships that visited North and West Africa, Egypt and Turkey. Upon return, he settled in Paris in order to learn French, but also to take his first steps into politics. After serving in the war, and being wounded at Verdun, he became a prisoner of war in a British camp, and was released in 1919. After his release from war camp, his real world travels began. Living in Calais, the great French emigration port, Furtwängler took up work as a translator on the docks for seamen from the East. Furtwängler recalled, "there I dealt with the many overseas and colored people who were seeking to travel to Germany after the war."[70]

In 1921, he returned to Germany, but this time to Frankfurt, where he joined the Metal Workers Union and enrolled in Frankfurt University for a yearlong course on economics sponsored by the union. The years following German economic stabilization were marked by an unprecedented swelling of labor activism, the growing fear of great disempowerment of German workers, and a new era of "überflüssige Menschheit" (superfluous humanity) brought about by rapid mechanization and specialization.[71]

Furtwängler attended lectures on labor law by Hugo Sinzheimer, a respected member of the Social Democratic Party. And Sinzheimer recommended that his talented young student begin serving on the organizing committee of the *Allgemeiner Deutscher Gewerkschaftsbund* (General German Trade Union Confederation) in Berlin. Especially given Furtwängler's facility with languages, and his unusual international experience, as well as his remarkable energy, he was named the international secretary of the German Trade Union Confederation (ADGB) at age twenty-six.

Furtwängler, the traveler, had a traveling career. His first "mission" as international secretary of the ADGB entailed an official research trip to the United States as a member of a fifteen-person delegation to study American industrial "rationalization."[72] The theme was important to Germans given the recent stabilization of their economy after three years of hyperinflation. As Mary Nolan and Daniel Rodgers have shown, Germans were looking to America in the 1920s for "models of modernity."[73] Josef Furtwängler was interested in the "white socialism" of Fordism, in American mechanization and assembly-line production. Upon return to Berlin he and his group completed their report, *Amerikareise deutscher Gewerkschaftsführer* (Tour of America by Leaders of German Trade Unions,

1925). It was a widely read and widely praised book, not only in Germany but also in Britain and the United States in translation.

But, even more important for Furtwängler than his research trip to America, was the one he took the following year to India. He was asked by the leader of the German Textile Workers Union to make a trip to India in order to understand "the extent and the outlook of new and blossoming [mechanized] textile industries in India that are already threatening the European labor market."[74] The trip defined the rest of Furtwängler's career, as he established his place as a specialist on Indian and Asian political movements. Furtwängler decided he wanted to encounter India with "sympathy and a will to understand the uniqueness of the Indian labor movement vis-à-vis its European counterpart."[75]

In 1926, the Textile Workers Union of England approached Furtwängler with the request to take another official research trip to India, in his position as international secretary of the ADGB. He thus planned a "similar, but even longer trip to India." He was determined to first learn Hindi, however, "so as not to rely on the information of the English officials in India."[76] The six-person delegation he headed in 1926–1927 visited textile factories in big cities like Bombay and Calcutta, as well as the tea plantations in Darjeeling and Assam where they reported on the de facto continuation of the "system of modern slavery," or indentured labor, even after its official end in 1922.[77]

The delegation traveled across India, from Bombay to Baroda to Calcutta to Madras. On the trip he met Subhas Chandra Bose, and encountered Gandhi at a distance.[78] Furtwängler proposed that with the end of World War I, the British empire "was no longer salvageable." He noted the increasing Indian demands for German machines and factors of industrial production.[79] In 1930, Furtwängler wrote that the Indian Swaraj Party and the whole Indian freedom movement was seeking to "break out of the trade monopoly of the British system and to push toward non-European markets."[80]

Upon return to Berlin in 1927, Furtwängler recalled, "I wrote more about my Indian experiences than about the American in newspapers and journals. I gave lectures on the topic on the radio."[81] In fact, Furtwängler published three separate books on India in the coming five years, each of which spoke of the subcontinent more as a locus of exploding "labor power" than as one of spiritual quiescence.[82] Furtwängler wrote essays on the "Insurgency of the Colored People of the World," "The Conditions of the Asian Labor Force," and a book on the *Competition by the Indian Labor*

Force on the World Market (1929). He saw Germany's aspirations as related to the rise of India. India was "on the move," and its labor force was vibrant, and defiant. And this dynamic of the young nations on the move offered a model for global development, in Furtwängler's view.

Like other German travelers of the 1920s, Josef Furtwängler identified with both America *and* India, simultaneously. For Furtwängler, both India and America were associated with labor optimism, and they both charted paths out of western European world dominance. Germany, after the war and the fall of the empire, entered a phase of "war in peacetime," Furtwängler noted. The rising German nationalism in the Weimar period became "white hot" in the face of external political threats and also international social crisis. "One would have had to understand the conditions in the colonized or half-colonized lands, such as India, China, or Egypt, to understand how similar the upheaval in [German] national and social life has been."[83] Furtwängler drew the comparison between Asian events and experiences at home in Germany in ways that show his cross-identification.

Franz Josef Furtwängler was a consultant to the German delegation to the Geneva International Labor Conference in 1929 and 1930. His main interest at the conference was the work conditions on British tea plantations in north India, which he had already castigated in *Das Werktätige Indien* of 1928.[84] By authoritatively discussing Indian matters, Furtwängler claimed attention at the international conference. He used Indian themes to stand out on an international stage. "We welcome the wave of national and social freedom struggles that are surging to Europe from Asia. We hail with deepest respect Sun Yat-Sen in his death, and the living Mahatma Gandhi. And we hail the thousands of industrious freedom fighters, who are now sitting in [British colonial] prisons."[85]

Furtwängler combined the roles of the anticolonial activist and German geopolitical radical. Beginning in 1929, he became the representative of the ADGB to the right-wing organization, the Association for Germandom Abroad (Verein für das Deutschtum im Ausland). Showing how sympathy for extra-European labor resonated with the extraterritorial commitment to protect, cultivate, and celebrate *Deutschtum* (Germandom), Furtwängler became the most active representative of the trade unionists in right-wing labor circles, eventually collaborating with the "Nazi Left" under Otto Strasser in the first years of the Third Reich.[86]

In 1934, Furtwängler defected to Hungary for four years. He returned to Germany in 1938 after failed attempts to immigrate to the United

States. In 1940 he received a position in the Special Department for India in the German Foreign Office, under Adam von Trott zu Solz. Trott zu Solz was the main liaison for Indian nationalist leader, Subhas Chandra Bose, from May 1941 onward, carrying on a family tradition.[87] The Special Department's role was to disseminate German propaganda, "to influence the international public, and the influential Indian diasporic communities."[88] Furtwängler was involved in preparation of fliers and handbills for distribution on the Eastern front. He spent three months on official travels through East Asia from January to April 1941, charged with distributing anti-British literature to Indian troops and inhabitants around Shanghai.[89] After the war and denazification, Furtwängler continued his writings on India, and even served as a member of the West German Parliament. The constant in Furtwängler's itinerary, as he wandered from Social Democratic politics, to anticolonial activism, to service to the Nazi state during World War II, was his interest in India as the home of models of labor resistance and heroism of the spirit that rejected the global assimilationist logic of British imperial liberalism.[90]

DIALOGUE IN EXILE

The mode of transnational dialogue on the theme of an unveiled world order of labor exploitation and resistance was central to the Marxists of the 1920s and 1930s. Even after the forced exile of Jewish and Marxist intellectuals imposed under the Nazi regime, and the mass imprisonments of Indian nationalists imposed by the British colonial regime in the early 1930s, clandestine transnational arenas still connected émigrés and inmates, at least for some time. Although Furtwängler continued his travels in the 1930s by veering to the right, the vast majority of those in Marxist anticolonial circles during the 1930s faced severe threats to their mobility and their life after 1933. The communist opposition was pushed into exile in 1933. August Thalheimer, Heinrich Brandler, and other main members left for France. From Paris, Thalheimer sought to reestablish connection with the trade union leaders in Bombay. Although M. N. Roy was in jail in India, other members of his group, especially V. B. Karnik, corresponded with the Thalheimer group.

In 1934, Thalheimer wrote to Karnik, "We have sent you a great deal of material, but apparently you never received it. . . . [I]n order to establish a regular correspondence between us, it is essential for you to find an address outside of India from which material can be sent to you."[91] The link ran from German Marxists in Parisian exile, to Indian Marxists in the anticolonial underground in Bombay. Thalheimer continued, "please send us copies of public statements made by your group recently. Send us publications and other important political documents. Can you give us a description of the general political situation in India?"[92]

The Communist Opposition Party (KPD-O) based in Paris thought of the Indian group as one more in an international constellation. In May 1934, Thalheimer again wrote, explaining his differences with Roy's views, "the fundamental principle of [Roy's] thesis is that it looks to Communists to revive the left wing of the Congress and with it to revive the Congress itself. We are of the opinion, on the contrary, that it is the task of the Communists, not to revive, but rather to bury the Congress. We have used the machinery of the Congress as long as the Congress had the outlook of bringing about revolutionary mass movement."[93] The old Marxist problem of nationalism versus labor universalism reared its head. Thalheimer spoke of the Indian political context, correctly or incorrectly, as if it were his own.

Thalheimer's letters reached Roy through clandestine channels. In three letters written from prison between 1934 and 1937, Roy made it clear that neither he nor his party in India would attempt to oppose the Congress from within as Thalheimer proposed.[94] He wanted "an organized left-wing of the Congress, acting, as such with no other party label."[95] Roy insisted that a separate party, such as the Congress Socialist Party then in formation and supported by Thalheimer in Paris, would divide the Congress into camps.[96] Roy placed emphasis on using Indian trade unions for educating workers and building the consciousness of solidarity. "The millions and millions of transport workers, plantation coolies and handicraft workers are not yet organized. . . . The Communist party must explain this [the proletariat's historic role] to the proletariat in popular literature, public meetings, trade union, clubs, etc."[97]

Meanwhile Jay Lovestone, the leader of the anti-Bolshevik communist faction in the United States, the so-called Right-Opposition of the Communist International, coordinated an international campaign calling for M. N. Roy's release from jail. Through his offices, figures of international repute including Albert Einstein, Fenner Brockway, and Roger Baldwin wrote to the Indian Office to protest Roy's twelve-year jail sentence. And Lovestone suggested in his letters to V. B. Karnik and the "Roy Group" that Indian trade unions apply for supporting funds from the American Federation of Labor. The institutions and intermediaries who created arenas of German–Indian entanglement on the left were forced into exile in the 1930s but relays remained durable for some time after the rise of the Nazis. However, by the time Roy got out of jail at the end of 1936, August Thalheimer had fled to Cuba, and other members of the anti-Stalinist German communists had migrated to the United States. Lovestone was negotiating his own kind of defection out of communism altogether, now as an anticommunist.[98] The discussion about unmasking and changing the world order through the study and organization of the global labor force that had connected Germans and Indians in the 1920s and 1930s came to a halt for the time being.

Marxist views of Asia, and of the links of global labor that crisscrossed the boundary between Europe and Asia, created webs of relation against Germans and Indians that differed from that of a classic colonial relationship. Orientalism in the twentieth century induced identification, more than estrangement, interrupting the normative relationship between center and periphery.[99] Radical Marxism's way of making the peripheries of European empires into world centers became an important means to mobilize counternormative claims about European culture, and about both German identity and Indian identity in the international order. Forging the imaginative link between the national labor politics of workers in European countries and the anticolonial struggle of elites and subalterns in colonial societies, took a great deal of transnational intellectual work and social interaction. But such a worldview was only possible because of a larger historical context at work as the age of enlightenment came to its final end at the conclusion of the nineteenth century, giving way to a more convoluted, more plural, and more contentious age of entanglement over the early decades of the twentieth century. But this historical age, although still young, was far from innocent. Even the universalist idealism of Marxism was steeped in different nationalist articulations and different thrusts for status on the world stage. Seeking to undermine the global hegemony of nineteenth-century Anglo-Saxon power led to new power plays and new universalist visions to legitimate them.

EIGHT

Geocultural Wholes

German and Indian nationalist thinkers used political geography and cultural history to make assertions about the expansive geographic dimensions of culture in ways that sought to regionalize the world. Especially after World War I, deglobalizing claims aimed to interrupt the normative nineteenth-century world map centered around the North Atlantic, diffusing outward to engulf the globe. Post-Enlightenment scholarship revealed maps of supposedly resilient flows of culture, history, and even race, and called for a revolutionary reorganization of space on earth. Projects in cultural geography were inherently interdisciplinary, and some of those projects were co-creations of Germans and Indians as they imagined together monumental world terrains in which they could respectively stand at the zero point. Entanglements developed as German and Indian nationalists defined new territorial boundaries and made new claims of difference, but in ways that actually increased interdependence and implicated each other in their respective projects.

The enchanting scientific discourse of geopolitics opened up another dialogic arena in which German and Indian nationalists affected each other's way of imagining a new world order, and legitimated each other as representatives of new holistic visions. Transnational dialogues brought together German and Indian folk historians such as those involved in the *Volksgeschichte* and *Shantiniketan* projects, put geopolitical thinkers such as Karl Haushofer and Benoy Kumar Sarkar into discussion in Berlin, and entangled political scientists Taraknath Das and Franz Thierfelder at the Deutsche Akademie in Munich.

These post-Enlightenment interlocutors tended to envision culture as a compass-like entity, with both a fixed and a ranging foot. Culture was depicted as rooted in a historical, indeed antique, community of kinship, language, and location. But culture was also seen to travel over geopolitical space, continually transgressing its own boundaries. In the 1920s, both Indian and German nationalist intellectuals envisaged a world map of expanding cultural regions spreading over both continuous and discontinuous space.

The armistice ending World War I was signed on November 11, 1918, and representatives of the Allied Powers gathered for the Paris Peace Conference at the beginning of January 1919. Germany, Austria, and Hungary were excluded from the negotiations, and at the conclusion of deliberations the territory of Germany was reduced by almost 10 percent. Alsace and Lorraine went to France, the Saarland became a League of Nations demilitarized zone under French supervision. Areas on the border with Belgium were turned over, northern Schleswig was returned to Denmark. In the east, large parts of what Germans viewed as Prussia were integrated into the resurrected Poland, most notably the territory of Upper Silesia with its rich iron mines.[1] Danzig was declared a free city, and all of German overseas territories in China, the Pacific Islands, and Africa were confiscated. The empire of Austria-Hungary was partitioned, following the nationality principle, into seven successor states. In addition, the "war guilt" clause and the associated sum of reparations shocked many Germans, and German conservatives began to see themselves as transposed into the position of a colonized and "subaltern" group of the new Europe.[2]

In response to the normative international order inaugurated by the Treaty of Versailles, counternormative nationalist identities developed.[3] Countersciences developed to articulate and defend the contrarian visions. Discourses of the social sciences emerged that critiqued the universal authority of the League of Nations to administer the postwar world order and claimed to disclose a deeper and truer world of cultural continuity that thwarted nation-state particularism. For Germans, studying the geographies of *Kultur* relativized and "provincialized" the geopolitical place of northwestern Europe in the world, and challenged the pretensions of the league to crown a new postwar universalism.[4]

Meanwhile for Indian nationalist thinkers, such as Ramananda Chatterjee, the idea of *Mahattvar Bhārat* or Greater India, designated an anticolonial Indian cultural geography—a region of planetary distinction for

Indians in the world. Greater India, said Chatterjee, was a world region that flourished in the ancient period of Hindu and Buddhist kingship across Asia, which omitted the kinds of imperialist "misdeeds" of universalist empires associated with the modern West.[5] Nationalists insisted that Greater India expanded through peaceful cultural interactions, unlike the expansion of "Britain and France." Greater India was most of all an oppositional category that facilitated the Indian nationalists' protest against western Europe's world-shaping force.[6]

GERMAN HEIMAT AND THE SHANTINIKETAN PROJECT

The nation of Germany was born, back in 1871, as a "nervous world power."[7] It was both a "newcomer and a latecomer," given that Britain, France, and Russia were already well along on their roads to creating overseas territorial empires. If English was the international language of commerce, French was the language of diplomacy.[8] The British and the French had made themselves universal in different ways, German geopolitical thinkers maintained—not just through their colonies but also through the spread of their languages and the extent of their "national ideas" abroad.

The Swiss scholar, Jakob Burckhardt in his *Weltgeschichtliche Betrachtungen* (posthumously published in 1905), proposed that the work of the German-speaking historian, simply put, was to make Germans at home in the world. "The best research of national history will see the Heimat as parallel with and in the context of the laws of the world-historical process. The Heimat will be seen as part of a world [*Weltganzen*], shone upon by the same stars that illuminated other times and other peoples."[9] Friedrich Meinecke, in his *Cosmopolitanism and the National State* (1908), concurred that national progress in Germany could be gauged by the gradual decline of a rootless, undifferentiated, cosmopolitan ethos among the educated classes, and the rise of a new traveling national identity, which remained German and worldly at the same time.[10]

The need to find global significance for the German national identity was not reduced, but exacerbated, by war defeat. The *Volksgeschichte* movement in Germany grew in force after 1918. It used the study of cultural history to preserve local identities, and also to reveal new expansive interregional and world-historical geographies of Germanic culture. Eminent German historians at centers in Leipzig and Bonn, among others, privileged the extensive category of the *volk* instead of the post-Versailles political category of the nation-state. Werner Conze, who would play an important role in German *Strukturgeschichte* after World War II, was a young member of the "school."[11] The *volk* was a category that had the advantage of being rooted in hometowns, or Heimats, as well as simultaneously being mobile and world traveling. *Heimatkunde,* the study of Heimats, was both fixed and mobile, and was as decentralized as the idealized German Reich was supposed to be.[12] There were organizations in the Palatinate, in the Rhineland, in Bavaria, in Saxony and Westphalia, and eventually in northeast and southeast German Europe that sought to reveal the extent to which the German *volk* had spread in ancient times. There were experts who devoted their lives to their hometown histories—Franz Thierfelder in Altenach, Georg Heeger in the Pfalz,[13] Günter Freyer in the Rheinland. Bavaria established a "Heimat- und Lebenskunde" ministry in 1921.[14] The Heimat movement was rooted in institutions of local civil society, in museums, clubs, and folklorist groups. Each scholar and organization contributed a particle to a vast cultural cloud. Heimatkunde played a major role in high school pedagogy after the world war, and much of the energy for the movement came from the Hochschule für Gymnasium Lehre, with its emphasis on teaching students the history of Germandom through local histories, as well as through narratives of German diaspora.

Rabindranath Tagore, much before the *Volksgeschichte* movement blossomed in Germany after 1918, had articulated a vision of education for Bengali youth based on a return to village culture and also on the embrace of interregional Asiatic connections. Rabindranath's interventions in education began with the founding of the Shantiniketan ashram in 1901 for the education of village boys. He published a series of essays over the coming decades that explained his pedagogical theory. Rabindranath wrote articles especially on the need for mother-tongue education, all the way from primary through to university education.[15] In 1904, he penned his famous "Svadeśi Samāj" essay that called for urgent social reform of the countryside, including rural education and artisan training. Rabindranath's turn to the village heeded Bankim's call from decades earlier to resist the tendency toward colonial assimilation, and to keep hold of the sources of Bengali identity unaffected by Western influence.

Bankim, in an 1872 essay about the importance of Bengali villages, harangued his urban *bhadralōk* interlocutors for not truly appreciating that the nation, the *deś,* was in fact constituted largely by its village communities and not by its municipal populations. Furthermore, Bankim wrote, "Britain gives money to the Indian city, but it takes the resources from the village. It takes its rice, silk, cotton, jute and indigo."[16] Such a view of the expropriation of India's natural resources and agricultural wealth was in line with the "drain theories" advanced by Indian economists such as Dadabhai Naoroji and Romesh Dutt, who spoke of the "exhaustion" of the "produce of the country."[17] The drain of natural wealth was portrayed in vitalist terms as the extraction of living energy from the Indian nation-body. Gandhi's call for *charka*, and his identification with the simple "thread-spinning" village craftsman, combined and extended these notions of the village as an embattled site of culture, and a depleted storehouse of Indian natural wealth. In both cases, the emphasis was on the endangered status of authentic Indian vitality vis-à-vis the cities.

Rabindranath Tagore, Kshitimohan Sen, Dinesh Chandra Sen, and Gurusaday Dutt all collected folk narratives and contributed to the ethnographic study of Bengali village life. But the village locale was not opposed to the cityscape in Rabindranath's view, nor was rootedness in the village placed in contrast to travel. The village served as the static leg of a traveling Indian nationalist geopolitical compass. The ranging leg of Indian culture moved across the whole interregional zone of south and east Asia, and also followed itineraries across the globe. A seismic shift was at work in the way Indian cultural geography was conceived by Bengali nationalists beginning at the turn of the century, and it differed from the nineteenth-century worldview of earlier thinkers such as Bankim Chandra Chattopadhyay. Now culture and travel went together, and identity was not linked to fixed, bounded territory alone. Greater India, *Mahattvar Bhārat*, as a self-construct and a discursive form was the geocultural expression of anti-Anglocentrism—and even deeper still, a protest against the hegemony of a liberal imperial world order centered around northwest European power.

CONTESTING IMPERIAL HISTORY

Ever since the 1880s, British imperial history writing had developed a consistent representation of the ancient Indian past, commencing with Alexander the Great conquering northern India, then passing to the Mauryan, Gupta, and Mughal empires, and concluding with the coming of the second Alexander, in the guise of the British empire. Neoclassicism in Britain as well as colonial preservationism in India was emblematic of the high age of Empire.[18] British historians in the late nineteenth century sought to draw strong continuities between the monumental kingdoms of India's past with origins in Alexander's Hellenic empire, and the stature of British empire in India's present. Historian E. J. Rapson positioned the British Raj in the line of "successors of Alexander the Great" in India.[19] V. A. Smith, a high-level colonial administrator and imperial historian, presented India's ancient past as a pageant of great conquering kings beginning with Alexander, and leading to Chandragupta Maurya, Asoka, Samudragupta, Harsha, and Akbar, before culminating in British rule.[20] D. D. Kosambi, the great Marathi Marxian historian, would later call Smith's book an "official and fashionable" history, built on "an incredible slender foundation of valid data, on which an imposing superstructure of conjecture, mere verbiage, and class-fashions [was] erected."[21]

But there was another reason for Rabindranath's turn to village vistas, as he responded to the Anglocentrist historical bravura of the Smiths and Rapsons of British academe. By turning to the village, Rabindranath, and the cultural historians and Bengali folklorists around him, were laying the groundwork for a different narrative of interregional continuity in South Asia. At the same time, the counterhistories of rural areas and localities were on the rise among nationalists.[22] The emerging Indian national responses to British imperial history defended the cultural worlds of ancient Hindu kingdoms, of Buddhist ecumenes, and of Islamic universalism. Indian historians at Calcutta University led the projects in such nationalist enchantment. K. P. Jayaswal worked on ancient Hindu polities, and Shaheed Hasan Suhrawardy studied Persian imperial history. Similarly, Anagarika Dharmapala embarked on the project of reconstructing Buddhism as a global religion. Buddhism was both regional and interregional, the work of the Mahabodhi Society explained.[23] Dharmapala, influenced by Al Afghani and by Okakura's vision of "Asia as One," maintained that ancient Buddhism encompassed the whole region of Asia and made it into an ancient interconnected cultural universe.

A windfall of new archaeological artifacts at the turn of the century—manuscripts, seals, tablets, columns, coins, and temple stones—provided Greater India scholars with what they believed was an ability to reveal an archaic cultural world that encompassed Asia from about 500 BCE to 500 CE. During that millennium, Bengali nationalists, relying on the authority of philosophy, numismatics, and archaeology, said the subcontinent, and especially northeast India, seemed to sit at the center of ancient inter-Asian relations. From the 1880s onward, ancient Buddhist manuscripts were recovered in Sanskrit and Pali, and also in a host of ancient and modern vernaculars, such as Kuchean, Agnean, Khotanese, Sogdian, Tibetan, Nepalese, Celanese, and Uyghur.[24] The interregional geography of ancient Buddhism became the spatial template for new Greater India research.

Indian scholars in the first two decades of the twentieth century relied on evidence from canonical Sanskrit texts, such as the Vedas, the Epics, and Puranas, as well as newly discovered works, such as the *Arthashastra* (purportedly from the fourth century BCE) and the *Sukraniti* (purportedly from either the fifth or eleventh century CE, but really from the nineteenth century), in order to argue that ancient Indian kings, the *sarvabhaumas* and *cakravartin,* ruled by "constitutional monarchy," not by martial conquest.[25] Greater Indian scholars argued that Alexander the Great's influence was minimal on ancient Asian societies. Kingship developed in a distinctive, Indic mode based not on war craft, but on alliance building. Kashi Prasad Jayaswal, in an influential essay of 1912, insisted that the ancient Hindu polities, or *sāmrājya,* were marked by benevolent kingship and constitutional monarchy.[26] A number of nationalist scholars wrote in a similar vein, including Pramathanath Banerjea, Narendranath Law, Radha Kumud Mukerjee, and the Malayali scholar, K. M. Panikkar.[27] Pannikar wrote his book on Harsha as the *cakravartī,* the Hindu world conqueror, who created a world center around which all Hindus, regardless of language or region, supposedly united.[28] D. R. Bhandarkar and Hemchandra Ray combined the philological study of ancient texts with the theoretical arguments of Central European political scientists, such as Johann Bluntschli and Adolph Wagner about state socialism.[29] Ray described a "similarity between the activities of the spies in Kautilya and State-Socialistic Germany, the child of Bismarckian policy."[30] Writers in the Greater India movement thus conceived of the world historical significance as well as the comparability of Buddhist and Hindu cultural worlds.

Kalidas Nag had completed a dissertation in Paris under Jules Bloch and Jean Przyluski in 1923. He wrote on a text that preoccupied the first generation of Greater India scholars, Kautilya's *Arthashastra.* In the 1920s, Kalidas Nag explained how the new nationalist conception of inter-Asian relations would build on the work of German-speaking scholars including Moriz Winternitz, Richard Garbe, Aurel Stein, and Albert von le Coq. Nag also noted the contributions of French scholars, such as Sylvain Levi and

Paul Pelliot, Russians, such as Dimitri Klements, and Japanese archaeologists such as Kozui Otani and Tachibana Zuicho.[31] In U. N. Ghoshal's comprehensive retrospective on the first decade of Greater India scholarship, ninety-six foreign academics were listed alongside Indian scholars in his bibliography, but only sixteen of these were British. In their footnotes and bibliographies, Greater India scholars flaunted their connections beyond the British empire.

In Nag's analysis, the *Arthashastra,* or the ancient text on the "Science of Profit" written around 300 BCE during the Mauryan period, was best understood as an ancient Indian diplomatic treatise. The text, said Nag, was a manual for kingly diplomacy in an era of ancient international war. In such a reading, Nag transformed the *Arthashastra* into an outward-looking treatise on diplomacy. The sleight of hand he employed earned him some swift criticism from scholars who noted that the main theme of the text related to conquest.[32] Indeed, Nag did not question the political rationality of conquest per se. He valorized both the geopolitical power to transgress boundaries through conquest, and the capacity to build new relations. These two principles of geopolitical power and diplomacy were woven through all Nag's writings as well as through the majority of Greater India scholarship.

Apart from the work of Kalidas Nag, a flurry of Greater India scholarship sprung up in the 1920s on Indian connections with China, Central Asia, Southeast Asia, and Afghanistan.[33] Each of these texts considered the transmission of Hinduism or Buddhism outside northern India through the mythic activities of Indian missionaries, settlers, and traders.[34] The loose "school" of Greater India numbered some fifty scholars and journalists based mostly in Calcutta and Shantiniketan in the interwar years.[35] In the period of the Khilafat movement, Muslim writers such as Shaheed Hasan Suhrawardy, I. H. Qureshi, Abul Kalam Azad, and Muhammad Shahidullah also wrote interregional histories focused on the Indo-Islamic universalism.[36]

Greater India was conceived as a hierarchical dominion of "culture-power," to use Sheldon Pollock's term.[37] Bengali-language histories of India commonly began with an account of the Aryans. Bhupendranath Datta's *Bāṃlār Itihāsa* (1935) covered the "Aryan era" to the Muslim, and then the British era.[38] The discourse on Aryanism had long taken hold in Bengali nationalist thought, especially through the reception of Max Müller's work. Rabindranath Tagore used the idea of the "Aryan" to propose a vision of cultural compromise and synthesis in South Asia. Beginning with his 1912 essay "Bhāratvarṣe Itihāser Dhārā" (The course of Indian history), Rabindranath proposed that in the ancient past, Aryan invaders had entered the subcontinent and had originally been derisive of the non-Aryan population they had found there. It was only in a later period, when Brahminical ritualism was checked by the caste of Kshatriya warriors in the time of the Indian epics, that the possibility for admixture arose. This mixture marked the beginning of *Bhārat,* Rabindranath proposed. Rabindranath Tagore, in his reading of history, claimed the age of the Ramayana represented a time of Kshatriya "amity" *(bhāv)* overcoming Brahminical ritualism. The meeting and fusion between the Aryans and non-Aryans, as expressed in epic literature, established the archaic roots of the Indian nation.[39] This mode of Aryan-oriented argumentation would continue in Rabindranath's work from the 1900s through the 1920s, and many of his articles in the *Visva Bharati Quarterly* of the 1920s focus on the theme of the "Aryan–Non-Aryan Synthesis." Aryanism, as ancient north Indian world-centeredness, reverberated through the Greater India conception, and it was strongly present in German discussions of cultural geography as well.

Not only the concept of the Aryans but also the comparative method tied Bengali thinkers in the Greater India movement to modes of German Orientalist scholarship. The study of texts could reveal hidden structures in world history, and these hidden structures could be used to center one's national group in the world. Suggestively, Rabindranath Tagore quipped in 1927, "one day some German scholar will do [the] work" of writing a comparative study of the Ramayana across south and southeast Asia.[40] Rabindranath recognized the disciplinary value of German scholarship in simultaneously asserting cultural identity and world-historical universality. It was an inherent methodological counterliberalism, one that did not begin with individualism and the diffusionism of a universalizing Enlightenment, but with notions of preexisting, historical holism and totality that could be rediscovered and disclosed in order to enchant the world afresh. Holistic notions of cultural geography in the early twentieth century sought to staunch the assimilationist tidal flow of Anglocentrist imperial liberalism that spilled over from the nineteenth century.

GEOPOLITICS AFTER DEFEAT

Here again, in this post-Enlightenment discourse of cultural geography, we have interaction and mutual borrowings, not one-way transmissions.

The Indian nationalist projects to invent "Greater India" in a world-historical mode caught the attention of German nationalists, especially after Versailles. Conversely, Indian programs in global enchantment often used German footnotes, and were directly inspired by German compensatory responses to the national embarrassment of war defeat. Karl Haushofer served as an officer in the Great War and experienced frontline combat as the commander of an artillery regiment. Previously he had traveled extensively through East Asia before the war as a military envoy of the German government. He went on a prolonged study tour of Japan between 1908 and 1910 to investigate the Antung-Mukden railway for the German government, and to study the organization of the Japanese Officer Corps.[41] During that trip, he also made a trip to India (Darjeeling and Calcutta), Burma (Rangoon and Mandalay), and Malaya (Malakka), and to China (Hong Kong).[42]

By the 1920s, Haushofer was also a popular writer, and Hitler read his writings on *Lebensraum* while in prison after the Beer Hall Putsch.[43] *Lebensraum* was the "Bereich der deutschen Ausstrahlung im Osten" (the domain of German emanation across the East), and it had no fixed boundary, only an advancing frontier.[44] Many German commentators at the beginning of the Nazi accession to power even saw Haushofer as the thinker who would define Nazi foreign policy.[45] A review of Haushofer's work in the conservative newspaper *Oberland* (1932) stated, "General Haushofer outlines the foreign policy of this 'Third Reich' . . . we must place much more emphasis on expansion into and maintenance of our bordering areas [*Grenzlandschaften*] than our overseas possessions. Likewise . . . the Greater German realm must protect and embrace any racially related [*rassenverwandten*] men. . . . All force working through space is political," he formulated.[46]

Karl Haushofer, in the first issue of his *Zeitschrift für Geopolitik* of 1924, stated that his aim was to follow in the tradition of Friedrich Ratzel's state organism and Rudolf Kjellén's state "life form." Haushofer defined *Geopolitik* as the "science of the political forms of life in their area relations, in their relation to the earth's surface, and as influenced through historical movements," and asserted that post-Versailles international relations had little to do with the wish for German *Lebensraum*. Perpetual struggle for territorial acquisition and dominance arose from the world-historical significance of Germanic culture.

Rudolf Kjellén, who died in 1922, was one of the leading modern proponents of the theory of the state as a living, "biological" organism. The influence of his writings, particularly of the *Staten som Lifsform* (1916) as well as the writings by Friedrich Ratzel on the correspondence between the territory and the historical organism of the state, set the foundation for *Lebensraum* discourse in the 1920s.[47] Haushofer wrote in a report in his *Zeitschrift für Geopolitik* of the "strengthening sense of protest of the whole earth [*Erdraum*] against the leading colonial, expanding powers, namely the Anglo-Saxons."[48] The German state became a symbol for the archaic world of German *Kultur*, and the imagined interregional past of German cultural greatness would take revenge on the territorial norms of the present.

The Orient, in particular, served Haushofer as the symbol of an archaic and archetypal stage in the world history of civilization. One of the main methods of geopolitics was to find metaphors for Germany's postwar difficulties on the world stage and in world history. "The study of foreign lands depicts [*zeigt*] the lost right to self-determination that has beset Germany."[49] Haushofer's special interest in the world-historical "Indo-Pacific Lebensraum" runs through his *Zeitschrift für Geopolitik*, as he wrote a report on the region in each issue. He conceived this "Indo-Pacific" region as consisting of India, China, and Japan as well as the islands of Southeast Asia. In Haushofer's conception, Asia as a geopolitical region would soon dominate world politics, and thereby the archaic would take revenge over the modern. The anticipated rise of the Orient, in Haushofer's mind, also charted the future of Mitteleuropa.

The discipline of geopolitics sought to divide the planet into interregional worlds based on climate, trade, and also spiritual and cultural affinities.[50] The key concept of "Raum," or space, was an extended "world region" that connected multiple disparate local regions and constituted the geography within which a dominant historical kinship community was said to hold mastery. The Nazi regime's concerns for mastering space, extending power, and legitimating itself through racial superiority combined to create "Raumforschung." The neologism, "Science of Space" became the main expression of the Nazification of university science, alongside another typically degraded compound word, "Gegnerforschung" (enemy research).[51]

Raum was the geography of the "Schicksalgemeinschaft" (a community of destiny). In order to strengthen his claim, Haushofer again made allusion to Asia. "When we concern ourselves with East Asian space and borders, we must also take into consideration the community of destiny of the three East Asian highly civilized nations [*Kulturländer*]: the 'three nations' [San-goku], as they have been known for thousands of years in Japanese: India, China, and Japan! Certainly, they are three separate cultures!—but they exist next to one another in a great community of destiny, in continual contact."[52] The "San-goku" idea was rooted in early modern Japanese political thought, but was popularized by Okakura Tenshin and the Japanese nationalists at the turn of the century. For Japanese nationalists, "Asia" became a connected domain of ancient world-historical dynasties, whose cultural power would come back to destroy the contemporary Western Eurocentric imperial map of the world.

Karl Haushofer "Orientalized" German Europe, casting it in the mold of Asia, in order to also claim the revenge of ancient dynasties over nation-states, and of ancient cultural organisms over contemporary European norms of international order. Haushofer felt that the East was more advanced than Europe when it came to its "sense of unity" [*Gemeinschaftsgefühl*]. "The sense of unity in Asia is much stronger than in Pan-Europe, despite the noble attempts of Coudenhove-Kalergi (of the Pan-European movement)."[53] For Haushofer, both Asia and Mitteleuropa were seen to promise the world-historical destruction of the newfangled small-state system of Versailles, as well as the notion of a worldwide federation of states.

Karl Haushofer cross-identified with Asia when he used the language of "the subaltern" to describe the German people. "Germans living outside of Germany [*Auslandsdeutschtum*], as is often being discussed today, are in danger in some parts of the world of *becoming subaltern* [*subaltern zu werden*] . . . What Graf Apponyi called an unbearable continuous strain [*unerträgliche Dauerbelastung*] on the pride of a people, can also be called the sinking into a subaltern disposition; and we have seen that the leaders of the Southeast Asian self-determination movements rose because they convinced their millions of followers to free themselves of this attitude that has now taken over Mitteleuropa."[54] Haushofer made the argument that a world order based on "self-determination" by the League of Nations was really an underhanded way for Western powers to extend their mastery of the world.[55] Continuing his self-Orientalization, Haushofer continued, "one would rather live on a peninsula that at least recognized the claims of Eurasia in the Pan-Asiatic sense, than in the slavery of imposed peace."[56] Indeed, some subaltern actors could nonetheless claim world-historical significance for their archaic past. They could use scientific disciplines to authoritatively evoke an earlier stage of world history in order to disrupt the present world-historical moment.

Germany could no longer suffice in its position as a second center, adjacent to Western Europe, given that it had once been the center of its own cultural world, the German subalterns claimed. It was destined to become a center in itself again.[57] As opposed to the juridical boundary system of the Versailles Treaty, in which "bounded political spaces" were to be constructed to accommodate the rights of ethnic minorities,[58] German geopolitical thinkers insisted on "natural" boundaries that would accommodate the world-historical cultures. German *Lebensraum* justified its expansionist project by asserting the autonomy not of different political groups who inhabited the contemporary world, but rather the autonomy of different cultural worlds that existed across world history. "In terms of the natural boundaries of cultural domains one thinks of landscape and irrigation, particularly mountains and rivers," wrote one German conservative thinker about Mitteleuropa.[59] The presence of the ancient past, supposedly embedded in the natural environment, called German subalterns to claim their autonomy not within a nation-state, but within the contours of a world-historical culture.

This project in German geopolitical radicalism connected claims about the continuities of cultural life with a variegated vision of coasts and hinterlands, steppes and riverine tracks, sea and land, cities and villages. *Lebensraum* and ecologism went hand in hand.[60] Mitteleuropa had to be freed, and had to attain planetary distinction, so the "spatial consciousness [*Raumbewusstsein*] of the German soul will never again be undone, like the recollection of the great Chinese and Indian Kingdoms, or of the common Japanese spatial consciousness that stretched to Asia Minor and lasted for 2000 years."[61]

German conservatives showed a strong and sustained interest in Indian anticolonial nationalism in the interwar period. Haushofer was a keen reader of Benoy Kumar Sarkar's work.[62] Haushofer called Sarkar's 1922 *Futurism of Young Asia*, "the new Bible of Young Germany,"[63] and he used the book in his university courses.[64] Journals such as *Deutsches Volkstum, Das Gewissen,* and the *Preußische Kreuzzeitung* published anticolonial, pro-Indian articles, even as they argued for the need for Germans to "take to the sea again" as colonialists.[65] In the late 1920s, the *Verein für Deutsche im Ausland* openly supported Indian nationalist struggle, just as it enthusiastically called for the renewal of German contiguous and overseas expansion. The geographer, Erich Obst, wrote in 1926, "The peoples of these regions would never turn down the offering of a friend and teacher. . . . We demand our right to our colonies, since without a German-overseas field of action, our people will be crippled. No other state in Europe is constrained on every side to the same degree as is the German. No one else feels what it means to be at the heart of a balkanized continent as do the Germans."[66]

German resentment sought its cross-identifications, its points of comparison and connection in the world. As much as German nationalists wanted to be colonizers again, they also saw themselves as the colonized. Ernst Graf zu Reventlow (1869–1943), a far-right patrician nationalist, helped establish the Indian National Party of Berlin with Chempakaraman Pillai in 1920, the Orient Verein in 1935, and he sat on the board of the Indian Association in Munich in 1950. Reventlow, a rabid anti-Semite and early contributor to the German Faith Movement, also expended much of his energies in anti-British propaganda.[67]

FIGHTING FIRE WITH FIRE

Some variants of German nationalist discourse in the 1920s and 1930s used Indic Orientalism to make claims about a revealed, benevolent, and pluralist imperialism that Germans could offer the world, and that differed from the oppressive Anglo-Saxon or Francophone varieties. Franz Thierfelder grew up in Saxony and began his life as a student at the University of Leipzig. Like many conservative revolutionaries, he served in World War I and was a prisoner of war in France. Later on, he went on to participate in the German militias that sought to put down revolutionary unrest by the communists in Germany in 1921.

Franz Thierfelder was a linguist and policy expert, and the founding president of the Deutsche Akademie in Munich in 1929, with its original mandate to protect the *Kulturgut,* or the cultural goods, of Germans living abroad. The Deutsche Akademie eventually supported German-language instruction in the United States, Britain, France, throughout Eastern Europe, and even in Shanghai and Calcutta.[68] Various country-specific committees were established, and in 1931, the Indian Bureau (Indischer Ausschuss) came into existence.[69] There were also American, Russian, Chinese, and Polish chapters. With the founding of the British Council in 1934, Thierfelder wrote a book warning against the rise of British imperial cultural diplomacy. He continually harped on the idea that the British, not the Americans or the French, should be viewed with anxiety and fear. Later on, after the war and denazification, Thierfelder served as the founding director of the Goethe Institute in the 1950s and as a leading proponent of policies of German-language reform and language cultivation.

Thierfelder's main writings focused on a view of the Balkans as the lost land of a land-based German empire, and the prospective role the German language could play in the region as the universal tongue to mediate national differences. The German language could serve as a "world language," he wrote, and could encompass the same kind of national pluralism in Central and Eastern Europe as French and English did in their overseas empires. But for the German language to fulfill this function, its inherent cosmopolitanism had to be cultivated. Thierfelder played an active role in the Deutsche Akademie from 1929 to 1937 in pursuit of that goal.[70]

Thierfelder's writings aimed in two directions: one focused on the Balkans, and the other on India. The immediate activities of the Akademie were to compile a "German biography" of all Germans living abroad and to establish a "German library" that would enshrine "the most important expressions of our people with regard to spiritual and material life."[71] Franz Thierfelder's writings depicted Mitteleuropa as a realm of pluralistic inclusion, held together by the universal language of German. The many cultural and linguistic groups of the Balkans as well as the interconnected economies of the former Austro-Hungarian empire and the seceded lands from the former German Reich could all be reconstituted as a single geopolitical unity of world significance if only the German language would be accepted as the lingua franca. At the height of resurfacing German imperialist reveries in the late 1920s, Thierfelder saw the enchanted vision of German-speakers sitting at the top of their own land and sea empire ranging throughout central and southeast Europe.

Thierfelder played an important role for the German Foreign Office as the "go-to" person on issues of cultural diplomacy, and he cultivated a particular interest in India. It was in part a matter of cross-identification—as he identified the geopolitical radicalism of postwar Germany with the anti-imperial struggle of Indian Orientals. But there was also a degree of imperialist role-playing at work, as Thierfelder sought to perform German patronage to the discontented peoples of the British liberal empire as a way of demonstrating that a German surrogate master would administer rule over the world's peripheral peoples in a kinder and gentler way than the original British colonial lord. It was as both subaltern and imperialist, compatriot and tutor, that Thierfelder gazed on India. This split identity seemed to haunt Germans throughout the postwar years.

Split identities haunted Indian nationalists too. Benoy Kumar Sarkar and Taraknath Das collaborated with Thierfelder to establish a scholarship program for Indian students through the Deutsche Akademie in 1929, and the program ran throughout the Nazi period, up until 1941. The Indian Bureau of the Akademie sponsored sixty-six Indian students to study in Germany between 1929 and 1936, thirty-four of whom received doctorates.[72] The academy also hosted eminent Indian scholars on guest professorships to give courses and conduct research in Germany. And the Akademie sponsored German students to take up research in Indian universities, and sent German professors on lecture tours throughout India.[73] Indian and German thinkers on the right envisioned revolutionary politics as involving the transfer of technological know-how from highly industrialized Germany to industrializing India, and also the exchange of gifts of enchantment, especially in terms of invisible goods of culture and spirit, between the German and Indian peoples.[74]

Taraknath Das, a *svadeśi* underground radical and internationalist from Calcutta, left for Tokyo in 1905, and boarded a Japanese ocean liner to San Francisco, arriving in April 1906. He became a leading Indian diasporic anticolonial diplomat in the United States, and obtained U.S. citizenship. During the war, he spent a year, 1918–1919, in federal prison for anti-British activities, Upon release, Das quickly returned to political life as leader of the New York Friends of Freedom for India Society, and he married an American progressive activist, Mary Keatinge Morse. He also earned a graduate degree at Georgetown University. In 1923, Taraknath Das was denaturalized as a U.S. citizen after the Supreme Court's anti-Asian decision in the United States vs. Bhagat Singh Thind case. He left the United States for Germany and set up his base in Munich.[75] In Munich, he entered a close collaboration with Franz Thierfelder from the late 1920s. Das insisted that British activities in India were caught up in attempts to defend a whole interregional arena, stretching across the Indian Ocean and the Bay of Bengal from Russian, French, German, and Japanese land and sea incursion during the nineteenth century. He asserted that world politics, from a realist perspective, was not based on the equal representation between nation-states, but consisted in the unrelenting battle between geopolitical power centers. He began *India's Position in World Politics* (1922) on this note. India was not a nation; it was an empire, and the first disservice to the Indian national cause came in assuming that it was on the way to the nation-state. Such a view neglected the essence and world-historical trajectory of Indian culture, Das maintained. "India is as big as Russia. India at the time of emperor Asoka was a more powerful empire than the Roman empire or the Greeks."[76]

The British used the language of liberalism in order to extend their own world dominance, he argued. Only this could explain why the British had been so intent on securing the Indian Ocean zone by assuming a leading role in administering the Suez Canal, by signing a treaty in 1903 to curb the construction of the Berlin–Baghdad railway, by the negotiation of the Anglo-Russian treaty of 1907 that allowed for the mutual sharing of spoils in Persia, by the Anglo-Japanese alliance in 1911, and by the seizure of Burma, Sikkim, and Tibet by 1915.[77] In Das's interpretation, the British empire was not a benevolent liberal force seeking to grant India national recognition, nor an agent of normalcy in the world. Das's mode of political science revealed the 1920s mandate system as a means for veiling British and French world power so that it could perpetuate itself.

Throughout the 1920s and 1930s, Germany served as the main mirror in which Das saw the Indian condition reflected, and in accordance with which he developed his views. Germany was "at the heart of Europe," he insisted, just as "India on the other hand is at the heart of Asia."[78] Das, like Thierfelder, was not a chair-holding academic, but made his mark through his political and educational institutionalizing activity and jour-nalistic writing. From the time he left India in 1903 to the time he died in America in 1958, Das did not once set foot in the territory of India. His politics was that of an itinerant nationalist, and a diasporic thinker who nevertheless imagined himself to be a traveling representative of India in the world.

The entanglement between German and Indian notions of cultural ge-ography began to have concrete geopolitical effects in the years leading up to World War II. The transnational arenas of dialogue created conduits for political action. World War I manifested the entanglement between differ-ent histories and political itineraries of groups seemingly distanced by planetary lengths and by the colonial divide. Now, as another great war was set to erupt between competing European powers, the entangled con-duits of collaboration between disparate groups arose in intensified form.

Eugene D'Souza has traced the wide reception of Nazi propaganda in India, especially in the form of Indian newspapers from Calcutta, Bombay, Poona, Gadag, Karnataka, Aligarh, and the Punjab that hailed the rise of German world power, and adopted ideological stances in line with the Nazi worldview.[79] D'Souza identified overseas Nazi party liaisons in a num-ber of Indian nationalist institutions.[80] In the period after 1937, India played an increasingly strategic role in Nazi preparations for international conflict. British intelligence in fact traced the push to create Nazi cultural institutions in India to 1936, when Georg L. Leszczynski first traveled to Bombay with the aim of establishing a Nazi party there.[51]

The German–Indian Institute in Bombay was eventually founded under Leszczynski's leadership.[52] Activities included the dissemination of propaganda literature, screening of German films, and the funding of Indian anticolonial organizations.[53] The Nazi party in Bombay also served as a conduit for Indians to travel to Munich to train as German instructors. In 1939, twenty-nine Indian teachers of German were being trained at the Deutsche Akademie in Munich.[54]

If Leszczynski worked as the main Nazi agent in Bombay, Horst Pohle played this role in Calcutta. British surveillance called him "one of the earlier apostles of National Socialism, [who] visited this country in 1933 and taught German at the Calcutta Y.M.C.A."[55] Some of the forty to sixty students regularly taking Pohle's classes in Calcutta studied at Calcutta University, and were required to study German by teachers such as the Berlin-trained biologist Shankar Purushottam Agharkar.[56]

Some Indians became closely connected with the official Nazi international project. These included Vinayak Damodar Savarkar, Madhav Sadashiv Golwalkar, and Keshav Baliram Hedgewar in Bombay. Savarkar, a Maharastrian nationalist and leader of the Hindu Mahasabha, took initiative in forging these ties.[57] He worked with Leszczynski in the pursuit of Axis aims. The Nazis in Germany sought to obtain Savarkar's assistance in establishing Hindu–Buddhist unity in China, Japan, and India.[58]

V. D. Savarkar promoted a vision of Hindu imperialism in India, or the revenge of world-historical Maratha conquerors in modern times. His book *Hindu-Pad-Padashahi* (1925) recast the history of the early modern Maratha Kingdom that arose after Shivaji not just as one of territorial expansion, but in terms of an "ideal of an independent Hindu Empire."[89] This was a geopolitical struggle of "dharma" and "desh" and the "fierce test that the Hindus were called upon to pass in their deadly struggle with the Muhammadan power." The Marathas under Madhao Rao, Savarkar said, "freed the Hindu seas" from the domination of the Muslim empire under Aurangzeb, allowing for Hindu trade and commerce that "humbled" English incursion. Savarkar wished for the creation not of a Hindu nation-state, but of a Hindu empire, fired by "Pan-Hindu" spirit. He continued that the two modern manifestations of this kind of empire building were "the German Empire of Prussia" and the Italian Risorgimento. "As the Italian kingdom of Piedmont, as the German Empire of Prussia, even so the Hindu Empire of

Maharashtra, in spite of civil feuds, is a national and Pan-Hindu achievement, for which every Hindu patriot must be grateful."[90]

Meanwhile, in Calcutta, under chief leaders Asit Krishna Mukherji and Vinaya Datta, a group of Hindu nationalists created the Bengal base of the German Nazi party abroad.[91] The *New Mercury* of Asit Krishna Mukherji championed Aryanism and anti-British sentiment. The curious personality, Maximiani Portas, of Greek and British parentage and of French nationality, became entangled with the Calcutta pro-Nazi group.[92] She was a Nazi enthusiast and a proponent of Indic Orientalism. She developed her own feminist-environmentalist brand of Aryan religion with Hitler as the savior figure. Portas traveled first to Bombay in 1932 and worked closely with Hedgewar and Savarkar's right-wing Rashtriya Swayamsevak Sangh (RSS).[93] She soon went on to Calcutta, where she married Mukherji.[94] Portas changed her name to Savitri Devi, returned to West Germany in 1945, and became one of the most outspoken post–World War II revivalists of the Hitler cult.

But, in Calcutta, Benoy Kumar Sarkar's pro-Nazi sentiment was of a different kind, filtered through the language of scholarly internationalism. Sarkar praised Nazism as a form of benevolent dictatorship. Dictatorship would bring about the end of the current experience of the colonial subject's "antithetical" relationship with the antagonistic colonial state.[95] Sarkar coined his phrase "despo-democracy" in 1938 in order to explain how the beneficent and therapeutic rule of an Indian strongman over his *jāti* (people, caste, or *volk*) would lead to a rewriting of the world map, and could win world recognition for Bengalis. Sarkar spoke of *jāti*, but it was not a Hindu (Aryan) nationalism that he invoked—as was the case for the Hindu Mahasabha and the Savarkar group—but a Greater Bengali ethnic nationalism. It included Hindus and Muslims. Sarkar's fascism was based on Hindu–Muslim unity within the cultural category of Bengaliness. And it is no wonder that Sarkar's great archetypal hero was Subhas Chandra Bose, who in 1941 began his campaign to both unify Hindus and Muslims and to destroy the British empire through close collaboration with Nazi and Axis powers.[96]

In Anita Desai's *Baumgartner's Bombay* (1988), the author imagines German prisoners of war at Ahmedabad passing their time in different pursuits derived from the repertoire of Indic Orientalism. "Some had ordered and obtained books and were studying Sanskrit, Arabic, astronomy or homeopathy; they organized a series of lectures and demonstrations of eurythmics, theosophy as preached by Madame Blavatsky, the Mary Wigmore [*sic*] style of dance, aerodynamics."[97] In this mise en abyme of German Indic Orientalism in British captivity, Desai captured how India had made it into German mentalities even as Germans made it into Indian ones. Transnational dialogues rooted in attempts to enchant the world order contributed to the heightening of nationalist resentment. Ernst Bloch, in 1954, was not the first to notice the possible kinship between radical anticolonialism and fascism based on what Bloch called the pursuit of false utopias. But one of the challenges for the historian is to distinguish potentials from preconditions. The post-Enlightenment field of geocultural studies connecting Germans and Indians generated potentials for liberation, for solidarity building, for retaliation, for jingoism, and even for genocide. The study of the scope and qualities of that dialogic field should be analytically separated out from the study of the various uses to which it was put.

The irony is that in the period of economic autarchy during the Great Depression we observe unprecedented levels of interdependence and entanglement all in the effort to re-envision the world order. In this historical period, the fascination with difference not with commonality, the ethos of confrontation and opposition, not of pacifism, brought "underdog" nationalist thinkers together. We observe here a situation in which groups used each other to get their own interests met and to pursue their own projects of distinction and universal relevance on an international stage. The age of entanglement cannot be understood in terms of the crisis of a singular liberal universalism, or fragmentation into myriad nationalist particularisms. In fact, we witness here a reversal of charge in the politics of difference, causing nationalist groups to become magnetically attracted to one another precisely because of their commitment to being different from all the rest. There was company to be found in nationalists' efforts at becoming the exceptional spokespeople for an enchanted world order of their own making.

NINE

The Psychoanalytic Universe

Psychoanalysis created a dialogic arena in which Germanic and Indian identities enchanted the human realm by disclosing hidden order not in the outer world, but in the inner world of the psyche. Postcolonial historical research has tended to consider psychoanalysis as a scientific discourse of the West, infused with the worldview of Empire, which once diffused to India, found new receptions and interpretations there.[1] But if psychoanalysis was more counterscience than conventional science, and if it was a child of the age of transnational entanglement not of European Enlightenment, then we must appreciate the specific place of psychoanalysis as one discourse among a spectrum of new countersciences in the early twentieth century emerging from a great decentralization and redistribution of power in the world order.[2] The psychoanalytic breakdown of unified notions of European bourgeois selfhood and the pluralization of forces at work in inner psychic life occurred just as the Concert of Europe and the sign of Empire broke down and were being pluralized.

Psychoanalysis, as a discourse, emerged out of the interactions between different centers of intellectual power in different parts of the world. It did not "travel" out into the world from "European" Vienna, but was rather co-constituted by a worldwide group of scholars who felt themselves to be exiles, castaways, or critics from the nineteenth-century vision of a progressing enlightened European universalism. Freud's early gamble to chart the dark continent of sexual life and the unconscious, to read hidden order out of the subterranean, Dionysian underground of bourgeois selfhood, and to study what he called the "basement" of subjectivity, threw the world into

211

relief in a new way. This was the original project of a "godless Jew," as Peter Gay described him, an in-between figure within a disaggregating Europe.[3] In colonial India at the turn of the century, Girindrasekhar Bose, a young doctor in Calcutta and student of psychology, was also an in-between figure, this time within a disaggregating empire. Bose began developing an original theory of psychoanalysis that differed from that of Freud, publishing a treatise on his alternative system in 1921. Bose had established the Indian Psychoanalytic Society in Calcutta in 1921. The space that stretched out between the Austrian-Jewish founder and the Bengali expert relied on the long-distance circulation of scholarly texts and on letter correspondence, as well as on the medium of the English language. When Freud and Bose addressed each other directly, it was in English. To a great extent, the spread of post-Enlightenment discourse in the 1880s–1945 period was not a reaction against, but a means of working through, the legacies of Enlightenment and Empire, which Britain played a dominant role in putting in motion in the peripheries of world power in the nineteenth century.

Wilhelm Wundt's approach to psychology, a sensation-based experimental psychology, and his establishment of the first laboratory for the study of the psyche, spoke to his positivistic background. His fundamental claim was that the psyche operated according to its own logic, which was different from that of a physiological system. But the psyche could still be studied empirically, through the use of performance tests, laboratory measurements, and statistics about mental activity. Mitchell Ash has pointed out how much this experimental approach to mental life fit in with the German experience of late nineteenth-century rapid, technology-led industrial growth.[4] Do students learn better in the morning or the afternoon? What are the best means to alleviate worker fatigue? How can employees assign the right worker to the right task? How can intelligence be measured, or enhanced?[5] These typical questions of applied psychology came out of the Wundtian school, and developed in the work of scholars such as Ernst Meumann at Zurich, Hugo Münsterberg at Harvard, and G. Stanley Hall at Johns Hopkins.

Major innovations in psychological sciences emerged in the last decades of the nineteenth century, and also became the main avenues for rethinking the psyche in the twentieth century. Gestalt psychology rooted in the work of Karl Hering and Carl Stumpf and the depth psychology propounded by Sigmund Freud were the two main post-Wundtian forms of mind sciences.[6] At the same time, Gestalt psychology, with its search for a holist perspective, emerged at the high period of *Lebensphilosophie* and the critique of the machine age of instruments and repetitive action.[7] It insisted that psyche and personality were an integral system and could not be understood through methods of scientific disaggregation, but only through understanding the organism-like wholeness of the mind.

Psychoanalysis claimed the authority to reveal a world of the mind that bourgeois normative conceptions about reason and the myth of the Enlightenment subject could scarcely perceive. Freudian psychoanalysis maintained that the dynamics of mental life could not be grasped with mechanistic conceptions either. Freud pointed to the inherent fractures and illnesses within the psyche and also to the textual or interpretive quality of mental life. The Freudian approach situated mental life within the irresolvable sexual dynamics of family and social life, and pointed to analysis and talking therapy as the only paths to provisional mental health. Psychoanalysis claimed the power to reveal the deep invisible psychic dimensions of the individual and society.

Both experimental psychology and psychoanalysis provided Girindrasekhar Bose and other Indians with an authoritative way to speak of the modern Indian psyche as well as psychological life in general, in a way that trespassed the constraints of British colonial science. In fact, the coming of psychology marked a stark intellectual intervention in the colonial knowledge order. In 1905, that is, at the beginning of intellectual *svadeśi* movement, Asutosh Mukherjee and Brajendra Nath Seal established psychology as an independent field of study at Calcutta University. It was not introduced by the colonial administration. The program floundered for a number of years, until these two planners of nationalist education policy sent students abroad to acquire the expert knowledge needed to establish new courses of study in Calcutta. They sent their students to the United States and Germany, that is, beyond the limits of the British empire.

In 1910, N. N. Sengupta still had three years of study ahead of him before he would attain his degree in history at Calcutta University. But a fund was set up with the aim of equipping the new Bengal National College with German- and American-educated professors, and Sengupta along with six other young students from Calcutta and Malda were selected to go abroad. Sengupta went to the United States as a student on a mission of transnational dialogue—he was going to bring back the latest methods of psychology research to India. Narendra Nath Sengupta was admitted to Harvard University in 1910 and began to study at Hugo Münsterbert's Psychology

Laboratory.[8] During his time at Harvard, he was present for Rabindranath Tagore's first lecturing tour in the United States in February 1913.[9] Narendra wrote articles and delivered lectures to fellow students explaining the national education program of Rabindranath Tagore.[10] Sengupta embarked on a study tour to the Psychology Laboratory of Edward Titchener at Cornell University. Titchener was also one of Wundt's students.[11] In 1915, Sengupta returned to Calcutta and immediately established the Psychology Laboratory at Calcutta University, later to be turned into the Indian Institute of Applied Psychology. The program employed Wundtian methods and used the Titchener textbook.

The Wundtian experimental psychology approach was the dominant one in the relatively new study of psychology, especially as it emphasized the interconnection between mental life and industrializing society. For intellectuals in Calcutta, one of the main allures of the study of social psychology was to assert their own modernism vis-à-vis European normativity, given that urban Indian minds were now as affected by city life and factory work as were European minds. Indians could carry out original research on the psychology of urban Indians, and their findings were as authoritative as that of European scientists, Indian Wundtians maintained.

One of the most influential Indian Wundtians was Suhrit Chandra Mitra, who traveled from Calcutta to Leipzig in 1923 to begin his doctoral studies under Felix Krueger, Wundt's student and his successor as director of the Leipzig Psychology Laboratory.[12] Krueger had met N. N. Sengupta in Boston a decade earlier.[13] Mitra's earliest work was directly related to experiments he observed or carried out at Leipzig, focusing on the Wundtian relation between perception and physiology.[14] In traveling to Leipzig, S. C. Mitra was making his pilgrimage to a center of new research. American psychologists had made similar study tours to the Leipzig laboratory, and to other German schools in the late nineteenth century as research programs at American universities developed. Stanley Hall, president of Clark University, wrote of his *Wanderjahre* in Germany, 1870–1882, in the age of Helmholtz, Hartmann, Fechner, and Wundt.[15]

The first volume of the *Indian Journal of Psychology* was published in 1926. N. N. Sengupta wrote the introductory essay and acknowledged his Harvard professor, Hugo Münsterberg, reserving special praise for the Leipzig school's "heroic effort at giving a portrait of mind as a unitary whole" after the "objectivism" of the nineteenth century that had not yet discovered the "mental context."[16] Significantly, Sengupta criticized the colonial regime for ensuring that the German and American "light" of psychological research only "faintly influenced the tenor or thought and culture on Indian shores." The methods of German scholars, of "Wundt, Stumpf, Lipps and Münsterberg," now opened up a "task that devolves upon the psychologist in India." This task "[was] not merely one of patient scholarly investigations but also of pioneering in our special field. It is our duty to dispel the delusions that circulate in the academic life; it is our duty to organize the energy wasted in the reiteration of text-book knowledge for the useful purpose of investigations," Sengupta wrote.[17] German methods would be used by Indians to disrupt British colonial intellectual arrest.

In 1929, Sengupta copublished a book on psychology and economics with Radhakamal Mukherjee. The book sought explanations for social displacement under conditions of industrialization. The authors argued that "regionalism," and the ability to remain rooted in the mother tongue, in local festivals, and local traditions was an important element for the cultivation of mental health of Indians in the context of colonialism and industrialization.[18] Sengupta and his student, M. N. Banerji, pioneered the psychological study of the workforce in Calcutta, especially focused on the Tata Works at Jamshedpur, the town constructed for the Tata steel plant not far from Calcutta. In 1931, Banerji wrote his essay on "Industrial Psychological, Fatigue Study, Reaction Time as an Indicator of onset of Fatigue at the Tata Works" in the *Indian Journal of Psychology.*[19]

The waves of Indian nationalist psychology in Calcutta soon began transmitting their effects to other institutions in the subcontinent. Dacca University saw the establishment of a Wundtian laboratory in 1921, thanks to the work of H. D. Bhattacharyya. And M. V. Gopalaswamy established the Mysore University laboratory in 1924. Psychology departments soon arose at Lahore under Parsa Ram, Mohammad Aslam, and Mohan Ganguli, and in Patna, Lucknow, and Aligarh in the 1930s. And feedback loops with German institutions were established.

A fine example of the transnational circulation that resulted is offered by the example of Kripal Singh Sodhi (b. 1911), the son of a doctor, who studied with one of N. N. Sengupta's students at Punjab University before going to Berlin on a Humboldt Scholarship in 1937. Sodhi worked on problems of cognitive psychology, studying how the brain creates depth perception. Sodhi eventually became the chair of the Psychology Department at the Free University in Berlin with a specialty in social psychology, especially the study of development of race identity.[20] The Free University's "Critical

School" of psychology became well known for its emphasis on the study of social minorities.[21]

Universalist claims of psychology were used to assert Indian cultural nationalism. Purported Indian cultures of family life, religious belief, or personality development were legitimated in a technical language of psychology, and placed in conversation with an international disciplinary field. The journal had a number of essays on emotion, instinct, and religious feeling that used Wundtian models to articulate the distinction of Indian culture. The nationalist project to claim recognition in the political domain was paralleled by the pursuit of recognition in international arenas of intellectual circulation.

In 1932, the Indian Psychological Association put out a Wundt special volume, edited by Suhrit Chandra Mitra, which celebrated the place of Wundtianism as a pillar alongside the new school of Pavlovian Behaviorists. A Pavlov Society was established in Calcutta in 1936.[22] The importance of the Wundtian approach in Calcutta is obvious from the kinds of essays that appeared in the *Indian Journal of Psychology* over the next twenty years, under Sengupta's editorship. The focus was experimental. Papers most frequently were devoted to intelligence experiments and to experiments in improving memory. The experiments aimed to better measure the learning capabilities of Indians in Bengal in order to improve national education. The next most frequent kind of research dealt with the physiology of perception, of sight, taste, and sound, which also related to this empiricist effort to understand perception through trials. Other research focused on fatigue and efficiency. Indian nationalist psychologists carried out research in Jamshedpur focused on improving the efficiency of workers and the stimulation and encouragement of native industry.[23]

Another important aspect of the journal presented surveys of international psychological literature and reflections on the state of the field. Disciplinary psychology fed into the different dimensions of scholarly radicalism, in terms of improving national education, enhancing commerce, and invigorating the mental power of nation. This faintly, and sometimes even boldly, eugenicist and vitalist pursuit also advanced ideas about inferior, undesirable, and unhygienic social practices within indigenous society, such as shirking on the job, or insubordination, which fit in with colonial Indian middle-class ideas of comportment. Most important in the present context, however, the radical scholarship of Indian experimental psychology practiced in the Calcutta laboratory allowed nationalists to utilize a language for reasoning and argumentation that had international salience and thereby could be employed to find recognition beyond the imperial context.

PSYCHOANALYSIS AS RADICALISM

Psychoanalysis received significant attention in the *Indian Journal of Psychology*, but it was not the main focus. Girindrasekhar Bose, a student of N. N. Sengupta, took up the task of using the disciplinary language of psychoanalysis as a new, and perhaps even more powerful, channel to attain intellectual authority for Indians outside the imperial frame. Psychoanalysis, in comparison to Wundtian experimental psychology, was a controversial science, and its enchanting claims about the world of the psyche were radical. The more controversial and anti-empiricist a disciplinary approach, the more enchanting authority it could potentially yield for those who utilized it. Girindrasekhar Bose used psychoanalysis to amplify the claims of Indian anticolonial internationalism, which placed Indian selfhood at the top and the center of the world order.

Sigmund Freud, the promulgator of psychoanalysis, made clear that his intensions diverged from that of the Wundtians. Wundtian science aimed to accommodate individual psyches to the pressures and stresses of modern life, while Freud's psychoanalysis took up a radical project of disclosure aimed at charting the Dionysian domain obscured by modern life. For Freud, the modern condition itself was the problem—conventions were the issue, not the rule. Freud insisted that the individual's illusions about the inner, personal realm and the outer, interpersonal realm had to be brought into view, recognized, and accepted. Only the cultivation of a self-reflective disposition, in which the patient accepted his or her own systemic internal conflicts, would allow for mental health in the modern world. Freud applied a cultural-historical method to the interpretation of the psyche, seeking to bring the primitive, irrational, and mythological—that which thwarts public reason—into the realm of the rational and modern.[24]

Freud's aim was not only to uncover uncharted "primitive" domains within the psyche but also to make that greater awareness into the source of responsible moral action. Freud said of psychoanalysis that "its intention is, indeed, to strengthen the ego, to make it more independent of the super-ego, to widen its field of perception and enlarge its organization, so that it can appropriate fresh portions of the id. Where id was, there ego shall be. It is a work of culture—not unlike the draining of the Zuider Zee."[25] Freud sought "the enhanced harmony of the ego, which is expected successfully to mediate between the claims of the instinctual life [the 'id'] and those of the external world; thus between inner and outer reality."[26] His notion of "Kultur," and of the taming of the id by the ego, certainly was informed by a belief in the superiority of European, male, and high middle-class social values. As much as Freud invented a counterscience that revealed a new aesthetics of the Dionysian inferno at the core of the self, he also maintained that these deep troubled waters could be dammed and drained, and European man's supposed cultural superiority preserved.

At the same time at which Freud was asserting his claims about the depth of the self and its inherent uncivilized and perverse nature in a way that confirmed Eurocentric presumptions, other fin-de-siècle European thinkers were taking the "inner journey" away from Europeanness in an Orientalist mode.[27] The search for psychic harmony was leading many in continental Europe to turn to the Orient and to popular constructs of Eastern spirituality. Romain Rolland, the French Nobel laureate in literature, and a celebrated pacifist, relied on the European construct of Indic spirituality to pave a path toward post–World War I spiritual awakening, especially in books such as *Gandhi* (1924), *Ramakrishna* (1929), and *Vivekananda* (1930).[28] Rolland was one of the main representatives of the wave of European Orientalist mystics in the 1920s.

For Sigmund Freud, Rolland's cultivation of the spiritual "oceanic feeling," achieved by turning toward the Orient, was futile and even dangerous.[29] Rolland had originated the term "oceanic feeling" to describe mystical experience. In letters to Romain Rolland, Freud explained his concerns about Rolland's Indic Orientalism. Freud explained that as a Jew, he "belonged to a race which in the Middle Ages was held responsible for all epidemics and which today is blamed for the disintegration of the Austrian Empire and the German defeat."[30] And given that position, caught within the ideals and projections of the German "compact majority . . . a great part of my life's work . . . has been spent [trying to] destroy illusions of my own and those of mankind," Freud wrote.[31] In the context of the outburst of virulent nationalist sentiment from the 1890s onward in the Austro-Hungarian empire, and the rise of Christian Socialism, both of which carried a strong anti-Semitic tinge, the position of Austrian liberals, and especially the Jews among them, became increasingly insecure.[32]

Freud criticized Romain Rolland's work for the false succor it provided to its readership, with its claims about inner personal harmony, and world unity based on spiritual awakening from the East. At a time in which "we continue to hate one another for minor differences and kill each other for petty gain," and in which it is "hard enough to ensure the perpetuation of our species in the conflict between our instinctual nature and the demands made upon us by civilization," Freud judged Rolland to be a votary of escapism.[33]

When Freud turned to metapsychology in his later works, he sought to diagnose the source of the "death drive" in modern European culture, which seemed to generate an irrational urge to self-destruction, perhaps best expressed in the climacteric of modern European warfare as well as rising fascist hatred of majority groups against minority communities. Ultimately, Freud argued that the otherness of the Jew was transformed by majoritarian Europeans into a symbol of the majority's own feeling of alienation from some imagined condition of plenitude. In the context of Nazi rule, Freud suggested that to achieve that "oceanic feeling" of union and wholeness, which had fascinated Romain Rolland so much, those of the compact majority would eventually seek to destroy the emblems of separation and estrangement from perfect communal union. And for *völkische* Germans, the chief emblem of alienation was the Jewish minority.[34] Freud was skeptical of both the escapism and the exoticism of Indic Orientalism. He also remarked on the degree to which Orientalist fascination was taken up by the radical right, especially in terms of the vindication of an ancient Aryan identity to supersede the Semitic.

But if Freud doubted the European constructions of India as a realm of archaic spirituality and the "oceanic feeling," he simultaneously had an interest in the events taking place in the modern East. As an Austrian Jew, a member of a minority group in an increasingly hostile ethnic German environment, Freud participated in a transnational community that crossed colonial divides, and that placed the "compact majorities" of Europe into question. His long-distance interactions with Girindrasekhar Bose in Calcutta as well as other practitioners of the "Psychoanalytic International" both inside and outside Europe, provided him an imagined global arena of recognition and interaction organized by counterscientific claims about social life. Freud had the idea of conquering the world through psychoanalysis.

Girindrasekhar Bose was responsible for the growth of an alternative approach to the study of the mind in Calcutta. Girindrasekhar viewed

Freud as a revealer of hidden truth. Freud "devised a special technique for probing the unconscious" that fascinated the Calcutta scholar since the early 1910s.[35] Girindrasekhar, since his college days, had been interested in hypnosis and in how magicians were able to manipulate their viewers' senses of perception. Beginning in 1917, Girindrasekhar began serving as a part-time lecturer in psychology at Calcutta University, in a department recently established by Asutosh Mukherjee. In early 1921, Girindrasekhar, upon completing his dissertation, "The Concept of Repression," at Calcutta University, sent a draft to Sigmund Freud in Vienna. The work was denigrated for its supposedly "defective style" by a British reviewer in the *Indian Medical Gazette*.[36] It seems Girindrasekhar's decision to send the work to Freud himself was a way of using the soft power of international correspondence against the patronizing dismissal of imperial institutions. This began a correspondence between the two that has been commented upon and studied extensively.[37]

The founding of a whole new science, an archaeology of the psyche, as Freud thought of it,[38] took less than a decade before descriptions of its methods reached the shores of Calcutta. In his autobiographical notes, Girindrasekhar explains he was introduced to psychoanalysis in 1909 not through the influence of a European teacher or envoy, but "mainly [through] magazine articles and scrappy references of information."[39] Girindrasekhar said there was "no systematic description of psychoanalysis in any book in English," and since he had no opportunity to learn German, he had to rely heavily on his imagination and his own introspective reasoning.

Girindrasekhar Bose did not see himself as adopting a European science, but as practicing a non-British one. Psychoanalysis did not have its roots in the Anglophone cultural world. Important for Girindrasekhar were the dialogues beyond empire that psychoanalysis allowed—psychoanalysis, far from being a discourse of "the West," actually opened up a path of enchanting science that also split apart the myth of a unitary Europe.

Girindrasekhar also saw the dialogic arena of psychoanalysis as one in which he claimed originality.[40] His induction into the discipline of psychoanalysis did not occur as if by appropriating European thought. He insisted that he worked out certain insights and then later found them corroborated. "Many truths which I then found out from my analysis of patients, and which I accounted as original, were in fact widely known findings as I discovered afterwards," he recalled.[41] He felt that the methods he discovered confirmed ideas he developed on his own, and truth he had already revealed through his own introspection and clinical practice. For Girindrasekhar, psychoanalysis expanded his scope for intellectual action and social interaction. For both the Austrian Freud and the Indian Girindrasekhar, the scholarly pursuit of psychoanalysis bestowed the aesthetic experience of being centered in a revealed world, even as they were on the margins of their respective manifest worlds. Although in ways that were discrepant, the claims of psychoanalysis gave both Freud and Girindrasekhar intellectual power to stand out against different kinds of social domination.

When their correspondence began, Girindrasekhar was thirty-five years old and Freud was sixty-five. In addition to the cultural and political differences that separated them, there was also a generational divide. Freud commanded the dominant position in their exchange given that he was the founder of this counterscientific field, and yet Girindrasekhar showed a remarkable scope to critique and challenge some of Freud's central theses within the psychoanalytic arena of discourse.

When Freud wrote to Girindrasekhar in February 1922, he articulated a remarkable degree of praise for the young Dr. Bose. "It was a great and pleasant surprise that the first book on a psychoanalytic subject, which came to us from that part of the world (India), should display so good a knowledge of Psychoanalysis, so deep an insight into its difficulties and so much of deep-going original thought." Girindrasekhar published the letter in both the *Calcutta Review* and the *Modern Review* during that same year. Recognition from Freud played an important role in the acquisition of status within Calcuttan intellectual circles, and also gave Girindrasekhar the sense of being a world player in matters academic, despite the institutional constraints imposed by the colonial condition.[42]

In an October 1922 letter, Freud asked Bose to allow his name to be printed on the cover of both the *Journal of the Psychoanalytic Association* and the *Zeitschrift für Psychoanalyse.* Freud wrote, "I beg your consent that your name may be printed on the cover of both journals as the leader and representative of the Indian group in the same way that other presidents are mentioned." Freud had the desire to establish an international circuit for psychoanalysis. The international journal, published in English, was started in 1920. Beginning in the third volume, Girindrasekhar Bose's name began to appear in the header, and he was listed as an assistant editor from Calcutta. Girindrasekhar Bose appeared alongside the editors in Berlin, New York, London, The Hague, Budapest, Zurich, and Vienna. For

Girindrasekhar, his international scientific affiliation was being used to blast apart the legitimacy of the British imperial bond. Calcutta was now a node on the international circuit of psychoanalytic science.

Freud too obtained some benefit from the encounter with the Calcutta scholar, Girindrasekhar Bose. After all, Freud wrote to Girindrasekhar in 1922, "my surprise is great that psychoanalysis should have met with so much interest and recognition in your far off country."[43] Psychoanalysis in Calcutta was proof for Freud of the "world conquest" (Freud's term) of his new science, which emerged on the margins of Europeanness. In the context of his debates with Romain Rolland, Freud saw Girindrasekhar Bose's scientific interest in psychoanalysis in India as the antidote to the illegitimate European spiritualist fascination with Orientalism, a fascination that could too quickly descend into escapism and even an inward-looking narcissism. For Freud, the intensive interactions with Girindrasekhar Bose confirmed the status of psychoanalysis as a new Europe-centered and yet self-reflective science with worldwide relevance. The transnational connection between Freud and Girindrasekhar served to bolster the self-perceptions of both individuals as well as their respective sense of having global salience.

DEBATES OVER METHOD

What was it about the method of psychoanalysis that attracted Girindrasekhar, and how did he put it to use? If there is anything Freud dramatically displayed in *The Interpretation of Dreams,* it was the aesthetic role of the scientist as a revealer of the hidden domains of psychic life.[44] Dreams were now texts that needed to be interpreted in order to disclose the depth of the psyche.

In addition the new aesthetic introduced by Freud for understanding mental life within a psychoanalytic framework, the methods of the talking cure, the interpretation of dreams and the case study, inspired Girindrasekhar Bose. Girindrasekhar accepted the main criterion of Freud's approach, that is, the priority of addressing sexual desire in understanding psychic life. But Girindrasekhar proposed a number of alterations and adjustments to the psychoanalytic method over the course of his career.

When Girindrasekhar embraced the project of developing categories of psychoanalysis for the Bengali context, he did something more than import or translate "Western" terms and methods to the Indian frame of reference. Rather, he used the tools of counterscience to disrupt imperial norms. During the first decade of his professional work as a psychoanalyst, Girindrasekhar wrote in English and analyzed his Bengali *bhadralōk* patients through the "free association" technique. He took copious notes on his patients. And he wrote up case studies of his cures, in which he applied the main categories of ontogenic analysis, searching for the dynamics of "repression" that could be revealed through the interpretation of dreams. "Every generalisation has been arrived at from a large number of specific cases," he reported in 1920 in the introduction to his pathbreaking *Theory of Repression*. Bose had a very active clinical practice, treating at least 1,000 patients by the time he wrote his major Bengali treatise on psychoanalysis, *Svapna* (The dream), in 1928.[45]

Freud envisioned the mind as caught in a pitched battle between three forces, the id, the ego, and the superego. And the outcome of therapy was a truce between these forces—a provisional end of internal struggle. Girindrasekhar proposed a different vision of the psyche's return to health. His aesthetic was informed not only by Freud's theories but also by the teachings about electric charge that were associated with Jagadish Chandra Bose, under whom Girindrasekhar had studied. Much of J. C. Bose's work revolved around the study of electrical conductivity in the realm of physics and biology. J. C. Bose worked on the polarization of electricity by crystals, and on the wireless transfer of telegraphic electric signals. Jagadish's most famous invention was the "magnetic crescograph," which magnified and recorded the magnetic impulses within plant life.

In the early twentieth century, if European scientists tended to make the analogy between the physiological and the psychological, Bose made a different parallel between the ecological and the psychological. Bose claimed that his observations with the crescograph could record a plant's response to the "trauma" of having been cut, or exposed to narcotics, or shocked by a change in temperature. The magnetic conduction in the plant was analogous to the nervous response in animals, he maintained. Girindrasekhar Bose was greatly influenced by this teaching about psychic "electricity." The unstopped flow of psychic energy was the image of mental health Girindrasekhar sought to disclose. "When there is no obstruction at any point of the circuit the wish is supposed to be free and unrepressed."[46] And later in his career, the philosophy of yoga as presented in the Yoga sutras and Saṅkhya, especially the vision of health as the free flow of energy and the importance of opposites and inversions as a means of cure, became increasingly important stimuli for Girindrasekhar's artistic innovations in the field of psychoanalysis.

As early as 1921, Girindrasekhar rejected the tripartite battleground of id, ego, and superego, and instead proposed a twin psyche composed of an "active" self and a "passive" self. He drew on the idea of the Purush-Prakriti, the male and female element, constituting each individual according to Saṅkhya philosophy. Repression occurs because the conscious wishes that belong to the active self, in their attainment, always repress the latent wishes of the passive self. This other, passive, side of the self had to be revealed through free association, and the psyche's passive wishes had to be brought to light and fulfilled through the practice of daydreaming. Only once the passive wishes were unrepressed could health be restored.[47]

Girindrasekhar first published an article on his original method in the *International Journal of Psychoanalysis* in 1925. Sándor Ferenczi, Hungarian psychoanalyst, member of Freud's inner circle, and famed clinician,[48] had begun to develop his own method of "forced fantasy" around this time. Girindrasekhar saw the need to assert the autonomous origins of his own methodological innovation within the psychoanalytic international. He insisted on his originality in prescribing daydreaming as a therapeutic practice, and maintained that the inspiration for his idea came from the Calcutta context. "I must point out that my ideas were developed independently of Ferenczi's suggestions. In fact I was using this method long before Ferenczi's paper on the subject appeared."[49]

Bose's amended mode of psychoanalytic analysis involved instructing his students to utilize the imagining of opposite types of daydreams to free up the channels of wish fulfillment. He created Bengali neologisms for technical terms of psychoanalysis, even inventing his own specialized terminology where needed, such as the "opposite wish" (*viparīta icchā*). As can be seen in the table of psychoanalytic language used by Girindrasekhar Bose, we are not dealing with a binary table of translation, from original language to target language. Bose worked within a matrix of translation between Bengali, English, and German words.

Svapna :: Dream :: Traum
Abādh bhābānuṣaga krama : Free association method :: Assoziation
Ūrdhvagati :: Sublimation :: Aufhebung
Histiriyā :: Hysteria :: Hysterie

Icchā :: Wish :: Wunsch

Kāmana :: Desire :: Begierde

Icchā Pūraña :: Wish fulfillment :: Wunscherfüllung

Paritṛpta kara :: Gratification :: Erfüllung

Abadaman :: Repression :: Verdrängung

Kāmabikār :: Perversion :: Perversion

Viparīta icchā :: Opposite wish ::—

This was not a case of the translation from Western origin-languages to Bengali targets, but one about the shifting matrix of relationship between Germanic, English, and Bengali linguistic and cultural authority. We note that English played the role of a trade language in this matrix. English operated in the middle as the language used by Freud in order to communicate with Girindrasekhar, and as the language that Girindrasekhar used to communicate with Freud. Furthermore, English provided the basis for Girindrasekhar to develop his Bengali neologisms. In cases such as "Free association method," Girindrasekhar translated from English to Bengali, or in his coinage of *viparīta icchā* (opposite wish), English served as the traveling language for his yoga-inspired psychoanalysis. Girindrasekhar only learned German beginning in the later 1920s, and never as a research or writing language.

And yet, given that terms such as "sublimation" and "repression" were themselves psychoanalytic neologisms in English, and carried the trace of the original German terms they translated, the authority of the English language was relativized within the international dialogic arena of psychoanalysis. English, here, was not a master language, but a trade language, and likewise, the discipline of psychoanalysis in Bengal was not based on master terminologies and interpreted translations, but rather on triangulations between different discrepant linguistic and cultural meanings. The dynamic of triangulation, not the dilemma of appropriation, characterized Girindrasekhar's semiotic task. He made use of the added degrees of freedom that came from the presence of third terms and English as a medium for trading outside the British empire.

Girindrasekhar always referred to Freud as a Viennese doctor, not as a Western or European one, and located Freud specifically in the atmospheric Viennese world of modernism. But perhaps by locating Freud in Vienna, not taking him to be an apostrophe for the abstract "West," and also by interacting with Freud in the trade language of English, the mother tongue of neither, Girindrasekhar obtained greater space to think along his own lines, and even to controvert some of the principles at the heart of Freud's own teachings.

If Freud recoiled from Orientalism as escapist truck, he also respected disciplinary disagreements. Freud explained to Girindrasekhar that the notion of the opposite wish seemed insightful and plausible, but Freud continued, saying that experimental evidence had corroborated the aesthetic of the classic tripartite view. Both separated and connected by the trade language of English and by the transnational dialogue of psychoanalysis, and still inhabiting two very different social and political worlds, Freud and Bose were free to partially agree with each other, while also keeping their differences in play.

PSYCHOANALYSIS BETWEEN IMPERIAL AND NATIONALIST IDENTITIES

In Calcutta in the 1910s, Bose was not alone in his interest in psychoanalysis. Another pioneer of psychoanalysis in India, working independently of Bose, was the British medical officer Owen Berkeley-Hill. Berkeley-Hill joined the Indian Medical Service and came to India after participating in the beginnings of the Psychoanalytic Society in London.[50]

Years earlier, as a student, Berkeley-Hill showed himself to be one of those young British cultural Germanophiles who proliferated at the fin de siècle. As a student, he had enrolled at the University of Göttingen because he was "disgusted" by the lack of rigor in the Department of Physiology at Oxford. "I went with another disgruntled fellow under-graduate, Edward Whitley," he recalled, when he first encountered the German study of psychology.[51] But after developing an illness in Göttingen and taking a cure in Hamburg, Berkeley-Hill was back in London.

When he returned, he became friendly with Ernest Jones, one of Freud's early British collaborators, and Berkeley-Hill joined the British Psychoanalytical Society as it was founded in 1913. This coincided with his entry into the Indian Medical Service. With his travel to India, first to a position in Hyderabad, followed by one in Ranchi, he developed a colonial administrator's appreciation for the psychoanalytic method.

In 1916, in his essay "Psychology and Pedagogy," Berkeley-Hill proposed that psychology provided ways to deal with the insurgency in India in the contemporary period of *svadeśi* radicalism. Berkeley-Hill's early articles focused on the mental hygiene of the "colored races," including what he uncovered as the anal-erotic factor that supposedly drove the supercilious-ness of Hindu ritualism, and the "parental complex" that he saw at the root of "fundamentalist" Islam.[52] He defied antigovernment activity as "anti-social behavior." Indian sedition was "as much a disease as is cholera, and, like cholera, is best treated by prevention rather than by cure."[53] The colo-nial administration was indeed very interested in the 1920s in the possibili-ties of exploring the new discipline of psychology for what it could teach about the prevention of anticolonial "neuroses" among the native popula-tion. Girindrasekhar Bose himself was hired to deliver lectures to the Cal-cutta police on the topic.[54]

Christiane Hartnack has shown that Girindrasekhar Bose's approach to the problem of "terrorism" was different from that of Berkeley-Hill, and Girindrasekhar openly refuted the view that radical political extremism should be treated as mental illness.[55] As Hartnack points out, in 1923, at the peak of British counterinsurgency in India, Girindrasekhar exempted "martyrs and patriots" from the category of those suffering from neurosis. "The sense of morality and duty often leads us to self-destructive actions e.g. the feeling of the patriot or martyr," Girindrasekhar observed.[56]

Identity formation under conditions of post-Enlightenment was in-formed by dialogic interactions and by the search to reveal hidden world order. In the age of entanglement, identities developed on a global stage, not a regional or a national one, even as constructs of regional and national identity were needed in order to anchor ideas about revealed worlds. Gir-indrasekhar's work to center Bengali Hindus within the international prac-tice of psychoanalysis, both as practitioners and as subjects, revolved around demonstrating originality in terms of the aesthetics of psychoanalytic diag-nosis and the methods of treatment. Through his innovations Girin-drasekhar wanted to make the Indian intellectual stand out in the world. And in his 1930s writings, he plied his path to intellectual authority and distinction in the world by connecting the science of psychoanalysis with traditions of Hindu philosophy. Girindrasekhar built an Indian nationalist identity by weaving together Germanic psychoanalytic science with high-caste Hindu modes of portraying the mind.

By the 1930s, a new phase in Girindrasekhar's career began as he wrote increasingly in Bengali. At the peak of his career he engaged in a split proj-ect, one written in English in which he participated in the international arena of psychoanalysis, and the other articulated in Bengali, in which he focused on centering the identity of the Bengali Hindu practitioner through appeals to Orientalist ideas about Indic tradition. The arguments Girindrasekhar made in his Bengali-language writings, which diverged strongly from his English writings, involved constructing a deep-rooted identity, anchored in history and philology, through readings of Sanskrit scriptures such as the *Bhagavad Gītā*, the *Yoga Sūtra*, and the *Purāṇā*. Girindrasekhar intended to show that these Sanskrit texts contained sources of psychoanalytic insight. In other words, he claimed that psychoanalysis was not foreign to Indians in the first place—it was already there at their origin of Hindu traditions. "A psychologist, therefore, is more in his element in the domain of Indian philosophy than in the province of western thought," he ultimately claimed.[57] This followed in a well-established tradition of Bengali scientists who sought to center themselves in modern science through claims about the deep-running continuity of ancient Himalayan and Gangetic cultural inheritances.

Pramatha Nath Bose, Brajendranath Seal, J. C. Bose, and P. C. Ray all wrote books on "Hindu" science, asserting the inherent rationality, and scientific nature of the Sanskrit tradition. Just as their intellectual politics led them to split up the West and to find other centers in Europe beyond Britain, another aspect of that effort was to transform their "periphery" into an intellectual center itself, through the innovative practice of enchanting scholarship, which often meshed the counterscience of German-speaking Europe with indigenous Hindu "high" traditions.

Bose shied away from having his Bengali books translated into English, insisting that they were intended specifically for Bengali audiences. He maintained, "if my works are of any worth, they will be translated by the foreigners in their own languages. No Englishman will write his works in Bengali for the benefit of the Bengalis!"[58] Girindrasekhar's project to use Bengali to make original contributions to scholarship in the Bengali language, and not in English, was part of the effort to make the Bengali mother language a "center of world culture," as Rabindranath Tagore had described.

Rabindranath's project of intellectual politics had envisioned a reversal of the imperial hydraulics of literary translation that always flowed in the direction from English to Indian languages. The Bengali language should itself be a source of world literature, in which art of global significance would be articulated in its original form. Rabindranath's *Viśvavidyālayer Rūp* (1933) proposed that mother-tongue education and research, at the highest levels, was necessary not only to advance intellectual development but also to ensure the ethical and aesthetic development of the Bengali people.

Scientific internationalism required placing domestic creativity in conversation with foreign styles, Girindrasekhar agreed. With his Bengali language psychoanalytic works, he proposed to establish the "particular footing" of Indian philosophies of the mind. The meaning of ancient *jñān* (wisdom) could be retrieved by modern *vijñān* (science). Psychoanalytic readings of ancient Indian texts could reveal the meaning *(byaṅgyārtha)* of the *Gītā* in a superior way to the philological exegesis of Bankim Chandra or Tilak.[59] Girindrasekhar's contributions to psychoanalysis in Bengali included a psychoanalytic interpretation of the *Bhagavad Gītā* (1931), a psychoanalytic reading of the Prāṇas, *Purāṇa Prabeś* (1934), a work on the chronology of Andhra kings, his magnum opus on the *Yōga Sūtras* (1938), and a book on psychoanalytic vocabulary in Bengali, *Manabyādhir Paribhāṣā* (1953).

Girindrasekhar drew comparisons between Patanjali and mystics and philosophers such as Plotinus, Erigena, Eckhart, Boehme, and Swedenborg.[60] Yoga was presented as a complement to the materialism of contemporary modernity—as the art that would complete the world of science. Surendranath Dasgupta's project in enchanting scholarship also involved speaking of ecstatic experience in scientific terms. The project to bring *jñān* and *vijñān* together also marked Dasgupta's writings, especially his large tome on Yoga philosophy in which he defended the Hindu world of philosophy against Buddhism. Dasgupta, professor of Indian philosophy at Calcutta University in the early twentieth century, was considered the most eminent Bengali scholar of Indian mythology. He wrote on "Yoga Cosmology," "Yoga Physics," and "Yoga Psychology," claiming to find equivalents for modern sciences in Patanjali's *Yōgasūtra*.

Girindrasekhar portrayed Hindu cultural distinctiveness in a way that asserted universal significance. Sanskritic traditions amplified the enchanting power of psychoanalysis, he insisted. "The philosophical systems of India, unlike those of the West, are not concerned merely with intellectual questions. All of them aim at the practical solution of the problem of suffering and misery."[61] Unlike Bankim Chandra's reading of the Gītā, which presented it as a religious text about disciplined action (*anuśīlan*), Bose interpreted the *Bhagavad Gītā's* teachings on ethics as a psychological prescription for reducing mental suffering (*duḥkhanibṛtti*). Reducing mental suffering came from "playing one's dharmic role as a member of a family and community," he maintained.[62]

Arjun's conundrum in the Gītā, Girindrasekhar wrote, arose from his "confrontation with the demands of *jātidharma* and *kulīndharma*—duty that comes from his position as part of the people, and his position as part of a family of esteem."[63] In Bengali, Girindrasekhar wrote that happiness and mental health are obtained by contributing to the "moral and material progress of the people."[64] Yoga, Girindrasekhar wrote, "shows that time is the purest entity that can only be grasped indirectly by the human mind. It has shown that the notion of multiple rebirths may in fact have some truth, especially as psychoanalysts are growing in awareness of the inter-generational continuities of the id. Our id is not our own, but from historical accretion . . . Hindu philosophy teaches the methods of permanently overcoming pain in this world and attaining a state of perfect happiness."[65]

In Bengali writings, not in his English texts, Girindrasekhar explained his work as a psychologist as being similar to that of an ancient Indian *ṛṣi*, employing introspection as a primary tool to make discoveries. "The great value of introspection in working out of psychological problems has not yet been truly appreciated," he insisted.[66] Indeed, the *ṛṣis* of old were psychoanalysts. "The *rishi*'s mind must develop empathy. . . . [T]he *rishis* utilized psychological thinking. . . . If the *rishi* ultimately came upon such an obscure entity as the Brahman it was only because his enquiry logically and quite naturally and inevitably led him to this point. It must be remembered, however, that he was mainly guided by his psychological sense, i.e. his own unsophisticated experience."[67]

If, in 1880, centering oneself in the world required that Bankim Chandra reject Western science for Indian culture, by the 1930s, the framework had changed. Now Girindrasekhar proposed that non-Western traditions could be found *within* science itself, but within the particular anti-positivistic science of psychoanalysis of fin-de-siècle Vienna. Whereas for Bankim Chandra, it was the overtly rationalizable aspects of Hindu traditions that attracted his attention, for Girindrasekhar, it was the opposite. The mystical elements that had previously proved too great a challenge to scientific understanding could now be unlocked, further revealing the deeper, hidden realm of the psyche. Yoga provided an internally consistent worldview of its own—not outside science, but from within it.

CARL JUNG AND OTHER GERMAN NEO-MYSTICS

Carl Jung provides a contrasting figure to Freud's aloofness from Orientalist mysticism. Jung's "avant-garde conservatism," as Jay Sherry terms it,
married myth and logos, soul and intellect, the spiritual and the scientific,
in a way that tended to assert the place of Germanic man in the world.[68] In
1938, Jung came to India to receive an honorary doctorate from Calcutta
University and to attend the Silver Jubilee of the Indian Science Congress
Association. He came full of expectation and eros, and left asserting that
he had to deny the urge to lose himself in the Indic, and had to stay true to
his Europeanness. In his narrative of temptation followed by renunciation,
Jung described his journey in a way rooted in Indic Orientalism. Orientalism and occultism were organizing interests. Jung began his career with an
interest in understanding occultism using scientific methods of psychology.[69] Séances were the focus of his PhD dissertation in 1902.

In India, Jung took the opportunity to travel, and visited temples in
Trichur and Amarkantak. His particular interest was in the structure of
temples and their altars. He visited Ellora and Sanchi, and also reported
being impressed by the beauty of the buildings of the Mughal period.[70]
Jung copied down mandalas he found at Ajanta and Madurai.[71] The study
of mandalas, visual representations of spiritual integration, had long fascinated him. He used the term "mandala" idiosyncratically in his own work
to refer to symbols, produced by the mind, that supposedly represent
unity while also laying bare all the oppositions and conflicts that unity
encompasses.[72]

As in much of his work, Jung coined new terms so as to make the most of
the symbols from the Orient. This also allowed him to brand his project as
different from and better than that of Freud, his teacher.[73] Enveloped in
the Aryanism of Central European Orientalists of his day, Jung saw in ancient Indian art "the Aryan unconscious [that] has a higher potential than
the Jewish; that is the advantage and disadvantage of a youthfulness that is
not yet totally alienated from the barbarous."[74]

Emphasizing the phylogenic, or inherited, factors that bear on life, Jung
proposed that archetypes, or broad ideational potentialities, were passed
on from generation to generation in a society until epochal change created
new archetypes for a subsequent age.[75] An epoch is known by its archetypes,
Jung proposed. Individuals in a single society tend to dream similarly. The

images that repeated themselves over and over again in the dreams of individuals are in fact generalizable across a particular society in a particular time. Those recurrent images related back to the large imaginative forms, such as the Mother Image, the Wise Old Man, or what he called the Anima.

If Freud was interested in zooming in on the individual psyche, Jung proposed to pan out, and to fit mental life within large social and historical categories. In the mandalas used in Hindu and Buddhist traditions, Jung saw the conceptual potential of a society in a particular historical period. This potential defined the scope for the expression of individual psychic life in a "primitive" age. In his reflections on his Indian trip, Jung wrote, "I am now going to say something, which may rather offend my Indian friends. As a matter of fact I am intending no offense. I think, I observed the peculiar fact, that an Indian inasmuch as he is really Indian, does not think, at least he is not doing, what we call thinking . . . He is like the primitive in that respect."[76] The Indian unconscious, Jung maintained, while great in its primitivism, had trouble accommodating itself to the modern world.

Jung accepted an invitation to lecture at Girindrasekhar Bose's institute in Calcutta, although Bose remained quite aloof from him. Bose had developed his own interpretation of the teaching of rebirth in terms of the intergenerational subconscious life of Indian Hindus. But this did not attract him to Jung. If anything, Bose was suspicious of Jung's approach. Bose was not interested in how monolithic images imprint themselves on individual minds, but rather in the ontogenic processes whereby individual psyches reorganize themselves through adjustments and practiced mental modifications, especially the personal and introspective work of imagination.

Girindrasekhar Bose disagreed with Jung's views from early on, but not primarily along the lines of cultural defense. The disciplinary controversy rather involved defending ontogenesis against phylogenesis, and defending the central place of sexual desire in psychic life that Jung and Oskar Pfister tried to replace alternatively with myth and religion. Bose explained, "[Jung] regarded the various instincts as issuing from undifferentiated primal life force, and to this primal life force he unfortunately applied the term Libido. His doing so introduced a quite unnecessary confusion into a subject that was already sufficiently complicated. Jung sees the primal libido as a will-to-live; adaptation to life, the fulfillment of a task, is the chief incentive; pleasure is obtained as a reward for duty done."[77]

Freud wrote with incredulity about the fascination with yoga among Central European psychoanalysts, mythographers, and Indologists. The "withdrawal from the world," the "regression to primordial states of mind" that he thought accompanied yoga, seemed of dubious value.[78] But scholars associated with Jung led the charge in fusing "depth psychology" with mythography and mysticism, as well as with a new prudery that substituted the lure of myth, for sex. The Eranos group that gathered at Ascona between 1933 and 1952 was specifically dedicated to these questions.

Chinese philosophy also provided scholarly potential for enchanting the fundamentals of everyday European life. Richard Wilhelm maintained that the wisdom of Chinese texts should no longer be the preserve of a small group of monks. In an "age of intellectual interchange between all parts of the world," the teachings should be disseminated broadly.[79] Wilhelm, as was typical of Germanic exegesis of foreign traditions, also found a profound resonance between the teachings of Lao Tse and Christianity. This recognition, not so different from the one that spurred Max Müller to translate the *Ṛg Veda*, impelled Wilhelm to finish his classic translations of the *I Ching* (1924) and the Taoist text, *The Secret of the Golden Flower* (1931).

This appeal to the intellectual authority of Taoism as a way of recentering the German self achieved a strong reception among the German literati. Through Wilhelm's highly popular German translation of Taoist texts, influential German writers also sought to assert new intellectual authority. Alfred Döblin's novel *Wang-lun* about an eighteenth-century rebellion in China was dedicated to the Taoist idea of nonaction, or *wu-wei*.[80] Marxist Orientalists enthusiastically discussed Taoism as an ancient precedent of historical materialist philosophy in the 1920s. Martin Buber, Hugo von Hofmannsthal, Albert Ehrenstein, and Bertolt Brecht all used Taoism to challenge "Western" philosophical conventions.[81] Germans used the intellectual authority of Asian literature in order to answer their own questions authoritatively.

Previously, in 1928 and 1929, Jung had a lively exchange with Richard Wilhelm, who established the China-Institut in Frankfurt, and instructed Jung on Tibetan mandalas.[82] The two were eager to extract the meaning of Buddhism and Taoism for Western audiences, and to make East Asian traditions applicable to Central Europeans outside the philological and theological faculties.

Heinrich Zimmer, son of an Indologist and a major German scholarly interpreter of yoga philosophy and tantrism, also joined Jung in this endeavor. Mircea Eliade, the Romanian scholar, treated Jung as his guru before their bitter split in 1950. Beyond Ascona, Giuseppe Tucci the Italian scholar of Tibetan Buddhism, Jakob Wilhelm Hauer at Tübingen, and Agehananda Bharati (aka Leopold Fischer) in India married psychoanalysis, philology, and mysticism. Hauer helped to popularize yoga as an esoteric form of bodily and spiritual practice in Germany in the 1920s. A main characteristic of his interpretation involved erasing the historical divides between different ancient Sanskrit textual traditions in order to treat Samkhya philosophy as a branch of a great Aryan Vedic tree.[83] The Vedas, for Hauer, constituted an "Aryan Bible."[84] Hauer spent four years, 1933–1937, directing the German Faith Movement which he described as the religion of new German paganism, purely Aryan and purged of the influence of the Jewish Jerusalem. The Jewish influence, in his conspiratorial and paranoid mind, was not that of a conspicuous minority, but that of an invisible great civilizational power, akin to that of British world power, that had engulfed the earth and against which German subalterns had to battle for livelihood.

Hauer's first anti-positivistic work on esoteric yoga practice combined philological study of the Patanjali yoga sutras with pseudopsychoanalytic traces of theosophical occultism. Hauer, who had studied with the empiricist Indologist, Richard Garbe, and devoted a number of books to his *doctorvater,* styled himself not only as a scholar but also as a sage.[85] Replicating the strategy invented by Schopenhauer in the early nineteenth century, Hauer employed ancient Indian scripture to stand out authoritatively as a German in the world, by asserting special access to Orientalist insight.

The Indian students who completed PhDs under Hauer, K. A. Bhatta and K. R. Dhawan, referred to him as their "guru," and wrote on the topics of Saivite tantric cults and reincarnation.[86] Hauer even had an extended correspondence with Shyamsundar Goswami, a young yogi from Santipur, North Bengal, who later became a yoga proselytizer in Sweden.[87] Goswami wrote to Hauer in 1932 about his yogic skills.[88] Hauer was intrigued by the yogi's offer to demonstrate. "Your demonstrations on Hathayoga interest me extremely."[89] But in the end Hauer could not offer funding and Goswami did not make his demonstration tour.

Magnus Hirschfeld, the Berlin sexologist, traveled through India in 1930. Hirschfeld was a German Jew, and also an early leader on research into the "third sex" and homosexuality. Although very different from Hauer in terms of his political orientation, he shared the fascination with the Orient as an entry point into a deeper science. Hirschfeld believed that the "primitive" art of Indian temples and religious objects represented a premodern relationship to human sexuality from which modern Europeans could learn.[90] Hirschfeld recalled that he "watched the ecstatic dances of the Vedas, especially the 'devil dancers,' who after rapid gyrations become cataleptic, the Yogis and Fakirs who rolled on their bodies instead of walking on their healthy limbs. The Hindoo gods and ceremonials show very interesting open and symbolic phallicisms; the Yon-Lingam abounds everywhere."[91]

The Indic Orient in the 1920s and 1930s was connected in the minds of many German psychoanalysts and mythographers with primitive sexual practices that brought to light the true sexual condition of Europeans. Jung joked in a letter to Heinrich Zimmer about the "phallic path" to the temple that he walked down.[92] Jung returned from India claiming to have realized what it meant to be European. "If you want to learn the biggest lesson India can teach you, wrap yourself with your moral superiority, go to the Black Pagoda of Kanarak, sit down in the shadow of the mighty rim, that is still covered with the collection of obscenities, read cunning old Murray's *Handbook of India* . . . then analyze all your reactions, feelings and thoughts. It will take you quite a while, but in the end, if you have done good work, you will have learned something about the white man in general, which probably nobody has ever told you before."[93] Jung's flirtation with the Orient in order to uncover what was authentically European was a common literary and intellectual trope among elite intellectuals. Johan Huizinga provided a similar account about his encounter with the Orient and his turn away from the study of Old India toward the study of the middle ages of Europe.[94] Mircea Eliade, who envied and even sought to emulate Jung, wrote his memoir *Bengal Nights* (1933) about his struggle to assert his authority against the famous Indian professor, Surendranath Dasgupta, under whom he studied in Calcutta in 1929–1931. Eliade also completed his Orientalist bildungsroman of European masculinity with the story of how he extricated himself from the seduction of the professor's daughter, Maitreyi Devi.[95] Thankfully, Maitreyi Devi, the young Bengali woman who became the Oriental muse in his memoir was to become an important Bengali poet and novelist in her own right. Decades later, she published her own literary account of her relationship with Eliade, which contrasted starkly with his own.[96]

Freud likened the "oceanic feeling" to "something like the restoration of limitless narcissism," a condition in which self feels itself everywhere, or feels all space available to it. Certainly Jung's travels to India, carrying his book on alchemy in his hand, and perhaps Eliade's travels too, suggests a Central European ego that felt an erotic pull toward the wider world. But that eroticism was indistinguishable from a narcissistic fetish for its own reflection.[97]

At the peak of his career Girindrasekhar Bose led a number of institutional projects. While serving as head of the Department of Psychology at Calcutta University in the 1930s, he also established his journal for psychoanalysis, *Samīkṣa,* which contained mostly English-language articles. In 1939, with the financial assistance of his wealthy brother, Rajsekhar, he established Lumbini Park Mental Hospital, an institution soon well-known for its use of shock treatment techniques.[98] In 1948, Girindrasekhar started a city clinic in Calcutta for the benefit of outpatients.[99] And a school was begun in 1949, Bodhyana, which attempted to implement general education along lines of psychoanalytic theory.

On the occasion of Freud's seventy-fifth birthday anniversary, Girindrasekhar and the Indian Psychoanalytic Society presented Freud with a carved ivory statuette of Vishnu. Freud kept the statue in a visible place on his desk and wrote that it reminded him of the "progress of psychoanalysis, the proud conquest it has made in foreign countries and the kind feelings for me it has aroused in some of my contemporaries at least."[100]

Sigmund Freud was interested in pointing out the fragmentation and the cracks within nineteenth-century European bourgeois culture, the fact that normative culture contained internal conflicts among pent-up, possibly self-destructive forces. In making such a claim he asserted the radical power of psychoanalysis to reveal an otherwise hidden dimension of social life, which had global validity. Girindrasekhar, who was working with different philosophical principles, and different political commitments from Freud, associated psychoanalysis with a reappraisal of Hindu Vedanta and Yoga philosophy, in which Hindu religious texts, at their intersection point with psychoanalytic science, provided globally salient insights into the inner psychic world.

Both Freud and Girindrasekhar practiced psychoanalysis to assert the existence of the hidden universe of the psyche, which conventional empiricism could not grasp. Their scientific work, and their social position, allowed them to enchant the world differently. Their respective contributions were counterscientific, giving voice to new visions of the world order—the inner world order—in which the signifiers of compact majorities of Europe and of Empire could be disassociated from the image of global universality, and rearranged in their place.

TEN

Worlds of Artistic Expression

In the years after the Great War, a Moravian intellectual educated in Vienna, Stella Kramrisch, played a crucial role in institutionalizing a new way of thinking of Indian art as an aperture into a hidden world of creativity. She was inspired by theories that originated at the Shantiniketan School of Art under Rabindranath Tagore, Abanindranth Tagore, and Nandalal Bose. Meanwhile, Franz Osten, a German film director from Munich collaborated with Himanshu Rai in creating a new aesthetics for Indian modernist cinema in the 1920s, in which Indian villages became the backdrops for dramas about social change and feminine individualism. Himanshu Rai, Franz Osten, and their collaborators, Niranjan Pal and Devika Chaudhury (later known by her screen name, Devika Rani), set out to communicate the universal drama in a feminine and Indic mode to Indian and international audiences alike.[1] In the fields of both art history and cinematic production, in the study and creation of still and moving images, collaborations between Indians and Germans sought to retrieve or to reinvent aesthetic norms that rebelled against the conventions of the nineteenth century. The discipline of Indian nationalist art history, and the production of nationalist art, challenged imperial notions of Indian "indigenous" art and culture as ethnic particulars lodged within an imperial British universal. Expressionism in Indian nationalist art was a coproduction of Indian–German collaboration in the years after the Great War.[2] Kramrisch and Osten were the two intellectuals who most contributed to the aesthetic rebellion in India as the ideal of Empire fell apart.

238

The ability to reproduce art images in mass numbers, which arose with the photographic revolution from the 1870s onward, allowed the imagination to travel farther and faster and it facilitated transnational dialogue and the synchronization of aesthetic sensibilities among groups around the world.[3] German thinkers used images to transport themselves to the world's peripheries, and Indian thinkers used images to move themselves to the world centers. And this occurred both as imaginative acts and as social action. Still and moving images, photography and cinematography, created the ability to distribute sensibilities on a global scale.[4] This chapter is concerned with the fields of entanglement that developed with these new methods of visual reasoning and aesthetic experience.[5]

Stella Kramrisch studied at Josef Strzygowski's famous Art History Institute in Vienna, completing her doctorate in 1919. She came to India as a postdoctoral student in need of a job, and she also had a fervent desire to obtain first-person contact with Indian Buddhist and Hindu temples, the focus of her dissertation research. Kramrisch stayed in India, first teaching at Rabindranath's University in Shantiniketan before moving to Calcutta University. She remained a member of the Art History Department in Calcutta until 1950 when she took up a position at Philadelphia University, later assuming the curatorship of South Asian Art at the Philadelphia Museum of Art. During the 1930s and 1940s, however, Kramrisch was forced to remain in India as a stateless person, unable to return to Austria after the rise of the Nazis and unable to find institutional entry points in Britain or the United States, despite her attempts. Kramrisch's position changed from that of a scholar-traveler to that of a forced migrant because of the violent reconfiguration of midcentury German Europe in the 1930s. India was transformed for her from a place of fieldwork and chosen identification, to a place of exile. Kramrisch was not alone.

The director, Franz Osten, although not of Jewish descent, also left Germany in 1934, and set sail for India. He, along with his German collaborators, the cinematographer Josef Wirsching, and the set designer Karl von Spreti, took up residence in Malad, a suburb of Bombay. They came at the invitation of producer Himanshu Rai and scriptwriter Niranjan Pal. The production house they established, Bombay Talkies, created the first mega hits of early Indian cinema in the 1930s.[6] Bombay Talkies became an institutional irrigator of the fledgling Bollywood film industry as the film house trained a set of important actors, set designers, and technicians who went on to consolidate the techniques and genres of Bombay cinema in the 1950s.

STELLA KRAMRISCH'S ENTANGLED INHERITANCES

The great master of visual reasoning in Indian art history was Ananda Coomaraswamy, a pioneer in the study of Buddhist art and in the inquiry into art history from an Indian nationalist perspective.[7] Coomaraswamy, born in 1877, was son of a Ceylonese father, Muthu Coomaraswamy, and an English mother, Elizabeth Beeby. His father died when he was two, after which his mother moved to Britain. He obtained his doctorate in Ceylonese mineralogy from the University of London in 1906. Coomaraswamy began writing on art in 1905 while still director of the Mineralogical Survey of Ceylon, and founded the Ceylon Social Reform Society. His first major publication, *Mediaeval Sinhalese Art,* was published in 1907. He styled his early projects after the work of William Morris. From 1909 to 1913, he participated in the circle around Rabindranath Tagore, and contributed to the Indian Society of Oriental Art in Calcutta.[8] In 1916, he went to the United States where he joined the research faculty of the Museum of Fine Arts in Boston.

Coomaraswamy was one of the pioneers in using photographic images as visual texts in art history books. His *Ars Asiatica* contained sixty-eight pages of text and sixty pages of high-quality full-page plates.[9] Another such pioneer, Victor Goloubew, edited the prestigious *Ars Asiatica* art journal of the École française d'Extrême-Orient beginning in 1912. That series revolutionized methods of argumentation with its high quality photographic reproductions. Kramrisch avidly read both authors in her student days.

Coomaraswamy used images as authoritative portals into an invisible world of creativity. In Coomaraswamy's view, images not only spoke about the subject matter in his work, but also were pointers to philosophical claims, to notions about government and polity, to fundamental ideas about society and social organization. Images even told the student how a people understand "time and eternity." His 350-page *Buddha and the Gospel of Buddhism* of 1916 provided an encyclopedia of Buddhist philosophy as well as images that explained Buddhism visually. Coomaraswamy took a number of the images in the book from the work of the Bengal school of Shantiniketan, especially the paintings of Nandalal Bose. Images were not like individual nouns in a sentence, each indexing a specific concept. Instead, visual images were much more powerful and composite symbols than words. They were pinholes into a universe. For that reason, images not only had to be read, they had to be deciphered. The history of art was, for Coomaraswamy, a scholarly pursuit to enchant the world.

Despite all the major art movements and approaches to art interpretation that Stella Kramrisch integrated into her work, Coomaraswamy's work provided the most important inspiration and she dedicated her last book and exhibition, "The Presence of Śiva," to him.[10] Her final 1983 show was a homage to Coomaraswamy's *Dance of Siva* of 1916. But Kramrisch actively engaged other influences in art historical scholarship. In fact, she moved between three major influences apart from Coomaraswamy. The comparative approach of Josef Strzygowski, the intellectual history method of Max Dvořák, and the artistic expressionism of the Shantiniketan school of art, also known as the Bengal School.

Kramrisch enrolled in the Institute of Art History of the University of Vienna in 1916, and completed her dissertation on the art of Sanchi and Bharhut in 1919.[11] As a student, she would visit the theosophical bookshop in Vienna regularly, especially in 1918, and also took up the new Orientalist-modernist style of *Ausdrucktanz*.[12] Kramrisch was impressed by Leopold Schroeder's *Bhagavad Gita* translation as well as Wassily Kandinsky's defense of theosophy and expressionism as the rejection of epigonal neoclassicism in *Concerning the Spiritual in Art*.[13] Kramrisch's adviser, the titan of art historical research, Josef Strzygowski, was a world-renowned comparativist. He began as an expert on Byzantine and Middle Eastern Art, but expanded his scope to encompass the "art of the Eurasian steppes" stretching from the Caucasus to the Himalayas. Later, he developed a newfangled notion of global art history based on race theory. He argued that global art history could be understood in terms of the creative opposition between Northern and Southern races.

But Kramrisch also worked closely with Strzygowski's nemesis, Max Dvořák, whose work emerged from and carried forward a different, historicist tradition in Viennese art history, leading back to Franz Wickhoff and Alois Riegl. That tradition emphasized the search for origins and for the sequences of cultural transmission. Dvořák maintained that "Art is the Gestaltung [the articulation in concrete form] of the philosophical ideas of a people," and that this articulation could be traced over long periods of time.[14] As a traveling intellectual, Kramrisch would assert her own creative authority and a different kind of identity on the world stage.

After completing her dissertation in November 1919, she left for Oxford University, accompanying her dissertation adviser, Strzygowski, on a postwar visiting fellowship apparently funded by the British Relief Fund.[15] That same year, Rabindranath Tagore began his fourteen-month tour of Europe and the United States in May 1920, partly in order to win support from foreign academics and intellectuals for his newly established Viśva Bhārati International University in Shantiniketan.[16]

Kramrisch first met Rabindranath in June 1920, either during his visit to Oxford or at the London home of his friend, William Rothenstein, principal of the Royal Academy of Art and president of the London Indian Society.[17] Kramrisch informed Rabindranath of her wish to study Indian sacred art in person.[18] Calcutta's Indian Museum housed the carved railings of the Bharhut Stupa. Meanwhile, Strzygowski dreamed of traveling to Shantiniketan to set up a department for art history on the model of his Kulturhistorisches Seminar (Institute for Art History) in Vienna.[19] Rabindranath was greatly impressed by the young scholar, Kramrisch, and was also banking on the support of world-renowned German-speaking academics, such as Kramrisch's *doktorvater,* Strzygowski. He asked both scholars to join the new university at Shantiniketan. Over the course of the next nine months, Rabindranath followed the progress of Kramrisch's application for a travel visa to British India.[20] The visa took time and required the intercession of Rabindranath's friends in London, such as William Rothenstein.[21] In 1921, Kramrisch enrolled in postdoctoral study at the School of Oriental and African Studies of the University of London, while she also became a long-distance affiliate of Rabindranath's circle in Shantiketan and Calcutta. She published an article based on her dissertation research in *Rupam,* an art journal edited by Ordhendra Coomar Ganguly and patronized by Rabindranath's nephew, Abanindranath—the main forces behind the *svadeśi* movement for a new national art for Indians. From London she published a second article in the *Calcutta Review* on general features of the Indian art tradition.[22]

When Rabindranath Tagore visited Vienna in June 1921, he met with Strzygowski. Now planning his visiting professorship at Bryn Mawr in the United States, Strzygowski bowed out of traveling to Calcutta, but proposed that his student, Stella Kramrisch, would go to Shantiniketan and pave the way for his guest professorship the following year.[23] In the end, Kramrisch departed for India and stayed almost thirty years, and Strzygowski never did follow.

INDIAN NATIONALIST EXPRESSIONISM

The struggle for independence was, of course, also a struggle for artistic and moral autonomy—a celebration of enchanted anti-empiricism in the face of imperial naturalism. Nationalist humanities sought to give Indians claim to independent political significance in the world. A traveling form of autonomy rejected British aesthetic norms through the exploration of other artistic styles. German art offered Indian national artists important horizons for exploration in the 1920s, just as Japanese art had offered and continued to offer since the turn of the century.

In the early twentieth century, Indian nationalists and their British advocates tended to champion handicrafts and "hand-made exotica" as the authentic specimens of Indian art that would showcase imperial pluralism and multicultural inclusiveness.[24] Orientalists such as the early Ananda Coomaraswamy and E. B. Havell viewed Indian art as a realm ruled by tradition, artisanship, and "immediate experience," quite unlike the "failure of energy" and enervation that they claimed characterized contemporary European art in the early twentieth century.[25] Art and crafts idealism and the desire to recover the great traditions of Indian religious art developed alongside the rise of popular bazaari art from the 1870s onward.[26]

In the period after the war, Indian nationalists championed not pluralism within empire, but geopolitical autonomy beyond the British world. Indian artists would not be satisfied with having their authenticity linked to minor arts and artisanal artwork alone, while British art and the "Western" tradition maintained a discursive grip on "fine art" and "modern art."[27] As Partha Mitter and Tapati Guha-Thakurta have shown, E. B. Havell, the principal of the Government School of Art in Calcutta, envisioned a project of Indian art cultivation that differed from that of the radical nationalists in that he championed Indian folk art against the naturalism of Western modern art. By contrast, Coomaraswamy's later work took inspiration from the nationalist Bengal School, and envisioned a great cultural region connecting India with Southeast and East Asia. Coomaraswamy moved from his early interest in artisanal arts to a new phase of more radical intellectual politics in which he sought to interpret the modern schools of Indian painting as centered within a monumental interregional terrain of ancient Asian cosmopolitanism.[28] Coomaraswamy moved from thinking like a citizen of the British empire, to thinking like a secessionist from the British empire. He no longer thought of Indian art in its own right as indigenous minority art within the world context of the British empire, but rather as a metropolitan art at the center of its own world. Stella Kramrisch would follow Coomaraswamy closely in this anti-imperial turn to redefine the meaning of Indian artistic production. Coomaraswamy was the trailblazer, Kramrisch the great consolidator of a new anti-Anglocentrist approach to studying Indian art.

The postwar nationalist project, already set in motion by Abanindranath Tagore in the 1910s in his break with Havell, began with the claim that Indian art had its own modernism, its own fine art, its own minor and folk arts, and its own world significance. Abanindranath "salvaged" the past in a new way, by reclaiming a "lost language of Indian art."[29] Indic aesthetics comprehended a total world unto itself, not just a peripheral piece in the larger imperial whole.

Importantly, a melding of Asianist and Orientalist claims about the spiritual depth of Indian art, arising out of ancient nondualist philosophies, served this enchantment project. Nationalists used Oriental distinctiveness in order to reveal a world of aesthetics in which Indians actors and audiences could feel centered. Tapati Guha-Thakurta points out that "European Romantic theories which defined art through certain exalted concepts of beauty, sublimity, emotion and idealism" were also at play.[30] But these theories were also counternormative and anti-Anglocentric. The "Europeanness" of these theories was not decisive, but rather their particular, anticonventional variety of German Europeanness. The expression of the German-speaking lands resonated with the distant cousin of the Bengal School movement—as a family relation.

Rabindranath Tagore's Viśva Bhārati was an institution for building transnational alliances, and Nandalal Bose, the director of the university art institute, wanted to learn the lessons of the contemporary German and Austrian experience.[31] He had already made great strides in creating linkages with Japanese artists. As the head of Shantiniketan's Kalā Bhavan, the art school established in 1919, he invited Yokoyama Taikan, Kampo Arai, Shunso Hishida, and Shokin Katsuta, among other Japanese artists, to give art demonstrations and master classes in Shantiniketan.[32] Now artists in Shantiniketan and Calcutta were interested in Stella Kramrisch's insights on the "modern movement in European art."

Artists in Shantiniketan and Calcutta waited expectantly for Kramrisch's arrival in 1921. She was quickly invited into the inner circle of the intellectual leadership at Visa Bharati University. Abanindranath Tagore soon started calling Kramrisch by the affectionate nickname, "Didi-mani."[33] Kramrisch delivered lectures both on European artistic modernism and on her specialty, Indian art history.[34] Bengali audiences expressed utmost interest in her insights on the "modern movement in European art."[35]

Kramrisch argued in her European art lectures that in the movement from impressionism to postimpressionism, cubism and Dadaism, European artists were searching for cultural renewal, and for an escape from Old Europe. European modern artists were breaking away from the naturalistic imitation of the outer world, which had surreptitiously constrained European aesthetics since the Renaissance. Artists in Europe turned increasingly toward representations of abstract inner human experience.[36] But if Kramrisch focused first on Europe, she spoke next of India. Her second set of lectures in India, beginning on July 27, 1922, carried the title, "The Expressiveness of Indian Art."[37] Here, she insisted that Indian modern art would succeed if it remained close to indigenous traditions, while also embracing influences from outside, from East Asia and Europe.[38]

Buttressing the intellectual anti-Anglocentrism of the *svadeśi* movement, Kramrisch argued that Abanindranath Tagore and the Bengal School helped initiate Indian cultural renewal by rejecting the "naturalism" of the British colonial Government Art College, and by returning to the "abstraction" of ancient Indic art traditions. This return to tradition was multifaceted, also involving engagement with Mughal miniature painting and Japanese wash technique.[39] Drawing the comparison between projects for new enchantment, she proposed that European, mainly German and Austrian, modernists increasingly rejected the "imitative approach" of nineteenth-century "Western art," and found renewal in "pure" abstraction.[40] Both Indian and Germanic modernists, then, were subjectivities shedding old skins, and looking for new ways to stand out in a reimagined world of aesthetics.

Kramrisch applied the comparative method. Creative endeavors in India paralleled German Europe: equal in aesthetic value, although different in form. According to Kramrisch's view, modern artists from East and West could find common ground, and enrich each other through mutual exchange. "The Indian outlook has a deep effect on modern Western spirituality, while at the same time the East accepts European civilization," she commented.[41] Franz Bopp's comparative linguistics, Wilhelm Wundt's psychological ethnology, Bernhard Ankermann and Fritz Graebner's idea of *Kulturkreise* (cultural circles), and Riegl's *Kunstwollen* (artistic will) were already well-established approaches to global comparative studies from the nineteenth century, and represented Germanic attempts to see the "big picture," the world-historical horizon, in ways that set "Europe" in a planetary context. Josef Strzygowski placed Europe in a global context so as to displace West European cultural hegemony. Kramrisch's comparativism drew inspiration from Strzygowski. He tended to blur the line between the Orient and Europe, and to upend the pieties of European artistic naturalism anchored in the Renaissance. The counternormative and anti-Anglocentric ethos of comparative study informed most of Kramrisch's essays in 1922 and 1923, and helps to explain her reason for organizing a major and unprecedented exhibition of Bauhaus artwork in Calcutta in 1922–1923.[42]

BAUHAUS IN CALCUTTA, BENGAL SCHOOL IN BERLIN

The Kramrisch project that had the greatest effect was the Calcutta Bauhaus exhibition. Kramrisch organized an exhibition of 175 pieces of Bauhaus School art that came to Calcutta in 1922–1923. In May 1922, Stella Kramrisch wrote a letter to Johannes Itten, director of the Bauhaus, whom she knew from the Viennese avant-garde milieu.[43] She inquired regarding the possibility of holding an art show and sale of Bauhaus art in Calcutta. Itten had likely met Rabindranath Tagore one year previously, in May 1921, when Rabindranath visited Weimar and recited poetry at the National Theater.[44] In an oral history that Stella Kramrisch recorded in 1985, she explained that she "suggested" the idea of the exhibition to Abanindranath Tagore. Writing from the "Shantiniketan International University," and "on behalf of Abanindranath Tagore," Kramrisch asked Itten for "some drawings, watercolors, lithographs or even wood carving . . . especially works by Mr. [Paul] Klee."[45] The show, she explained, would be part of an "international exhibition of living art" to be held at the Indian Society of Oriental Art in Calcutta in late 1922.[46]

Upon receiving Kramrisch's letter, Itten began canvassing the Bauhaus masters for contributions to the traveling art sale. In early August he wrote to Paul Klee, Lyonel Feininger, Gerhard Marcks, Oskar Schlemmer, Lothar Schreyer, and Georg Muche.[47] He also asked Wassily Kandinsky.[48] All of these artists, except Schlemmer, contributed a set of their works for the

Calcutta exhibition and art sale. Itten sent 60 of his own pieces, in addition to a selection of works by his students.[49] In addition, there were 35 Feiningers, 3 Kandinskys, 9 Klees, 29 Marcks, 9 Muches, 7 Schreyers, 2 pieces by the Bauhaus student, Sofie Korner, and 8 by another student, Margit Tery-Adler.[50] Each piece of art was marked with a price between £2 and £15. On August 30, 1922, Itten's secretary, Lotte Hirschfeld, mailed four large packets containing 175 pieces of Bauhaus artwork to Calcutta.[51]

The works of the German Bauhaus were not displayed in Calcutta to be fetishized as exceptional, but to be relativized and compared with contemporary Indian artwork. An article in the *Rupam* from early 1923 shows that the Bauhaus exhibition was "a section" of the Fourteenth Annual Exhibition of the Indian Society of Oriental Art on December 23, 1923.[52] Bauhaus art was displayed alongside works of the Bengal School. Kramrisch, in her catalog of the Bauhaus section, explained the intention to demonstrate, through images, how Indian artists "[framed] a form of expression from the Indian view of life," while also "[formulating] a language for which it is difficult to derive ancestry either in the East or in the West."[53]

And if Kramrisch adopted a comparative lens to interpret the Bauhaus exhibition, so too did Indian art critics. Abani Banerji, in a review of the Bauhaus exhibition in 1924, explained that just as modern European artists endeavored to clear away the "the cobwebs of anecdotic, literary association," Indian artists, such as Gaganendranath Tagore, were "leaping forward to further experimentation" in color and form.[54] In the April 1923 issue of the *Visva Bharati Quarterly*, Stella Kramrisch wrote her own comprehensive review of the Bauhaus exhibition. In this extended essay, she made her claim about the creative authority of Indian art, explaining that "certain qualities of pattern, of rhythm, of the relationship of part to part and of part to whole" central to Indian sacred art, were now also important to European artists.

But the Bauhaus exhibition in Calcutta figures as only one episode in a global scheme of circulating modernist artwork between India and German Europe in the early 1920s. In fact, at the very same time as the Bauhaus exhibition in Calcutta, a major exhibition of Bengal School artwork was shipped to Berlin for exhibition at the prestigious Crown Prince Palace of the National Gallery.[55] In Berlin, in February 1923, 113 pieces of Indian modern art from Shantiniketan and Calcutta greeted audiences at the Crown Prince Palace of the Berlin University. The show ran until March 1923. An inspection of the exhibition list shows an extensive selection of pieces by masters of the Bengal School, including Gaganendra-nath, Abanindranath, Nandalal Bose, S. N. Dey, K. N. Mazumdar, and Sunayani Devi,[56] as well as forty-two other artists. According to the list of artworks, "Rabendranath Tagore" even painted one of the pieces, titled "The Javanese Actress."[57] It remains to be determined whether this "Rabendra-nath" was actually Rabindranath Tagore, whose phase of painting and art exhibition is thought to begin only after 1927. What has often been presented as a history of iconic European art traveling to the East can more fruitfully be conceived as the circulation of modern artwork within enchanted networks of global interchange.

Benoy Kumar Sarkar organized the Berlin exhibition. As an itinerant nationalist, he once taught at the Bengal National College in Calcutta, but now coordinated activities on behalf of the sizable Indian diaspora in postwar Berlin through the offices of his Indo-Europe Trading Company and its journal, the *Commercial News*.[58] Over the course of 1922, Sarkar stayed in close contact with O. C. Ganguly, editor of *Rupam,* and published a series of articles on "futurism" and Indian modern art in that magazine. *Rupam* editorials from 1922 and 1923 show that Ganguly frequently rehearsed Sarkar's radical arguments about the need for Indian artists to free themselves from tradition, and to harness the power of *viśvaśakti* (world force).

Like Kramrisch's Bauhaus exhibition in Calcutta, Sarkar's Bengal School exhibition in Berlin was the culmination of an intensive period of interpretation and argumentation about the meaning of Indian modern art. Sarkar published his book, *Futurism of Young Asia*, in 1922, along with the series of essays in *Rupam*.[59] He even entered into a long-distance debate with Stella Kramrisch over the role of tradition in Indian modernism at the very time of their concurrent exhibitions.[60] If Kramrisch praised Indian modernists for remaining rooted in what she saw as an Indic tradition, Sarkar hailed Indian modernists for brazenly abandoning concern for tradition. "A certain intellectual unity organically binds the whole modern world of art," Sarkar insisted.[61] Kramrisch emphasized the comparability of Central European and Indian art in terms of "primitivism" and "tradition." Meanwhile, Sarkar also emphasized comparability, but in terms of what he called the shared "futurism" of European and Indian modernists. In the pages of *Rupam*, Stella Kramrisch, located in Calcutta, wrote critical rejoinders to Sarkar's essay on "futurism, and Sarkar, situated in Berlin, responded with his own critiques of Kramrisch. The transnational dialogue between the two also involved a curious transposition of physical locations, art objects, and identities. Not only did they argue from discrepant perspectives about the worldliness of Indian art, they implemented different programs to enchant the world and transgress the hold of old Europe and the British empire's hegemonic place within it.[62]

In order to address the dearth of comparative perspectives on Indian artistic modernism among German audiences, Kramrisch, in 1924, wrote interpretive essays about Indian art in German art journals, *Der Cicerone* and the *Jahrbuch der jungen Kunst*.[63] Her main thesis was that the "new art in Europe" derived its inspiration from the art of Asia. In this claim, taken from the toolbox of Central European Indic Orientalism, she inverted the center–periphery relationship. "The importation of the works of Art of the Far East into Europe, and their appreciation, meant but another step towards the depreciation of art ideals of the old European traditions and shook people's belief in the infallibility of the old standards."[64] Asian art brought modernism to Europe, Kramrisch argued, not the other way around.

ESTABLISHING ART HISTORY AT THE UNIVERSITY

Kramrisch's interpretations had a great effect on art criticism in Calcutta and Shantiniketan. Her lectures were well-received and integrated into the writings of the leading Indian art scholar of the Association of Oriental Art, O. C. Ganguly.[65] In 1925, Asit Kumar Haldar, a grandnephew of Tagore and an important artist at Shantiniketan, wrote an essay on "The Aesthetics of Western Art" ("Prācīn Śilpa-Kalār Rekhā-Chānda") in the 1925 *Prabāsī* journal. The article integrated many of Kramrisch's arguments about the correspondence between European expressionism and Indian art, including the shared elements of abstraction, dynamism, and primitivism. Indeed, art had long trespassed the narrow limits of naturalism—and this artistic power was only now being implemented by European modernists and expressionists, Haldar explained. The reception of Kramrisch's work in Calcutta was enhanced by her teaching. One of her favorite students, Prithwish Neogy, taught at Calcutta University before eventually becoming a professor at the University of Hawaii, where he would specialize in the study of traditional Hawaiian art. Another student, Devaprasad Bose, worked on Bengali folk art. And Niharranjan Ray completed his PhD with Kramrisch and went on to assume the Bhagishwari

Chair in Art History at Calcutta University.[66] Kramrisch and her students also challenged the idea that the great traditions of India were Aryan in origin. Niharranjan Ray spoke of "the Bengali people as a mix, not with the Aryans, but between Dravid and Mongolian."[67] This was in contrast to current Indian theories of Aryan origins, such as those proposed by Josef Strzyogwksi, Kramrisch's teacher, or else by the "Goethe of Poona," B. G. Tilak, when he claimed that in the prehistoric past, Aryans came down to India from the Arctic.[68] Kramrisch sought to uncover the unified philosophy of an archaic cultural world and to make that world speak again through its high art and folk art, and through its archaic artifacts and its contemporary expressionist art objects. By juxtaposing ancient terra-cotta with modern paintings of the Bengal School or by juxtaposing folk art or embroidery with high culture objects, Kramrisch argued that the essence and play, the *majā*, of the Indic cultural world remained alive and well, and towered over the normative liberal European aesthetics of the modern age.[69]

Kramrisch's influence was also felt thanks to her active and rigorous critique of the artwork coming out of the Kalā Bhavan, the art institute at Shantiniketan, as well as the artists of Calcutta. Kramrisch proposed that Indian art provided a stark aesthetic grammar, rooted in ancient Indic ways of conceiving the world that remained perennially modern. "Indian art in its elementary strength, in its untiring invention of crowded forms, in its endless rhythm, in its severe, abstract pattern of all the compositions participates in the primitive type of world's art," she explained.[70] The best Indian artists, the young Kramrisch maintained, were those who were most in touch with the primitive and unself-conscious Indian traditions. These artists, in her view, were women and children. "The simple craftsman, the child, the woman—all who are in fact not fully awake to the new age—possess still the synthetic vision, so distinctive of Indian art. Indian children, and Indian women too, are spontaneous in their artistic expressions."[71] Kramrisch took both Nandalal Bose and his students to task when she believed they produced inferior pieces. Panchanan Mondal, an art student in Shantiniketan in the 1930s recalled, "Stella brought a critical eye to the work of Kalā Bhavan. About Nandalal Bose's fascination with Chinese and Japanese modes of art, Kramrisch controversially proclaimed at one time that Nanda Babu 'had sold his soul China,'" because of his ardent Asianism.[72] At another time, she exclaimed of a piece of art by Ardhendu Bannerji, one of Nandalal's students, "the artist ought to be hanged!"

Abanindranath had to step in, asking Kramrisch to be gentler in her critique. On the other hand, Kramrisch unreservedly celebrated the "Indian cubism" of Gaganendranath Tagore and the "naiveté" and "spontaneity" of Sunayani Devi's work, both in Calcutta-based art journals and in international forums.[73]

Kramrisch played a leading role in helping to coordinate an international constellation of contributors and supports for the Bengali art movement. Thanks to her contacts, Coomaraswamy, from Boston, wrote for the *Rupam* journal, and Stella Bloch contributed from New York.[74] Hermann Goetz and William Cohn, specialists on ancient India and Indo-Persian art in Berlin, also regularly contributed articles.[75] Both entered forced migration after 1933, Cohn to London and Goetz to Baroda.

Rupam, begun under O. C. Ganguly, was renamed the *Journal of the Indian Society of Oriental Art* in 1934 when Kramrisch took over. In order to inaugurate her period as editor of the *Journal of the Indian Society of Oriental Art* from Calcutta beginning in 1934, Kramrisch invited Josef Strzygowski and Heinrich Zimmer to publish essays in the first volume of the journal published under her editorship. Strzygowski's article, "India's Position in the Art of Asia," appeared alongside Zimmer's article on "Aspects of Time in Indian Art."[76] Both Strzygowski and Zimmer wrote again in 1937, Strzygowski discussing the "northern roots" of Chinese art, and Zimmer the "trees, huts and temples" in Indian art.[77] Betty Heimann, once a student of Paul Deussen in Kiel, and now an exile in London, contributed an essay on the "Significance of Numbers in Hindu Philosophical Texts" in 1938.[78]

The journal focused on integrating archaeology and material culture with new nationalist interpretations of Indian art. Under Kramrisch's editorship, the journal cataloged new additions to the collections of Indian museums, described their attributes and features, and offered interpretations that emphasized the modern significance of the artwork and its sophistication.[79] The magazine sought to work at an all-India level, representing different regions and traditions, including Buddhist, Brahminical, and Muslim art, as well as art from Kerala, Nepal, and Cambodia. But as much as it delineated and constructed continuities for various ancient artistic traditions in India, *Rupam* devoted much of its work to identifying the rudiments of contemporary Indian artistic *modernism.* This project strove to assert a geopolitical and creative center for modernism outside northwestern Europe.

ARTISTIC INTERNATIONALISM

Internationalists in India were eager to keep track of how Indian cultural production was being received by international audiences, and to what extent Indian intellectuals were having success in gaining recognition abroad. Back in Berlin, reviews in the German press of "Modern Indian Watercolors" at the Kronprinzpalais were collected, translated from German to English, and published in the July 1923 issue of *Rupam* for the benefit of Calcutta audiences. Most reviews either extolled the "Romantic," "Oriental" spirituality in the Indian art pieces, or criticized them for being too "lyrical and sweet," or too rooted in "ancient dramas."[80] In other words, most reviewers emphasized the strict difference, instead of the comparability, between the Indian watercolors and European modern art. Only a review by Hermann Goetz, the young German-Jewish Berlin Indologist and specialist on Islamic art and a friend of Stella Kramrisch, argued that the Indian works were different but equal to the modern European specimens.[81]

The postwar period of intellectual politics connecting Tagorean institutions in Bengal with cultural institutions in Germany reached a celebrated culmination in 1930, when Rabindranath Tagore, by then a confident exhibitor of his own paintings, toured Europe and the United States with his artwork. Images and artistic exhibitions became new, and vital, features of Rabindranath's pursuit of anticolonial enchantment. Whereas he had long relied on the power of his words, he now counted increasingly on the effect of images to invite comparison and interaction with audiences abroad. Rabindranath first exhibited his artworks at the Birmingham City Art Gallery before taking them to the Galerie Pigalle in Paris in May 1930. In July, it was on to Berlin, where his show was held at the Ferdinand Moeller Gallery.[82] Käthe Kollwitz attended, as did Heinrich Lüders, chair of Indology at Berlin University.[83] The show of Rabindranath's art continued on to galleries in Dresden and Munich, and then to Moscow. Rabindranath's tour with his images was also a way of obtaining recognition for the contemporary international significance for Indian culture outside the frame of British empire.

Rabindranath's artwork was widely reviewed in the German press. Some German critics celebrated the affinity between his paintings and those of "Klee, Nolde, Rohlfs, and Kubin," and pointed to the comparability between Indian creative forces and the "newest painting of Western Europe."[84] But others excoriated the German organizers for presenting a show of "dilettantish kitsch," declaring it "unbelievable that an art gallery which has offered such service to the cause of German art should now put on such an exhibition!"[85]

For his part, Ludwig Justi, the director of the Berlin Museum, the individual who collaborated with Benoy Kumar Sarkar on the 1923 exhibition of modern Indian art, greatly admired Rabindranath's paintings. He inquired with the Möller gallery about the possibility of obtaining pieces from Rabindranath's exhibition for the National Gallery's contemporary collection. After hearing word of Justi's request, Rabindranath wrote to the museum director with news of his gift of five original watercolors to the National Gallery's collection.[86]

Along with twenty-eight other directors of German museums, the Nazis sacked Justi for his cultivation of "degenerate art" in 1933.[87] Rabindranath's art pieces remained in the collection of the National Gallery until 1937, at which point they were blacklisted as degenerate by the Nazi regime. Alongside works by Macke, Dix, Beckmann, Kandinsky, Kokoschka, Jawlenski, Braque, and many other modern artists, the paintings by Rabindranath were removed from the collection to make room for "German classics," such as Caspar David Friedrich's *Riesengebirgslandschaft*, acquired from Oslo with much fanfare in December 1937.[88] Over the course of the next two years, three of Rabindranath's paintings were returned to him, and two were traded at a Berlin art dealership for pieces of European art.[89] Rabindranath, who passed away in 1941, lived long enough to see his project of artistic internationalism come to an ugly end.

The image that most captivated Kramrisch, and to which she would return over and over again throughout her career, was that of Śiva. "The image of Siva surges with cosmic energy [depicting] one moment of the cosmic dance."[90] Kramrisch's search for images of enchantment was accentuated in the context of the 1930s, Nazi rule, and her exile from her home and family in Vienna. Kramrisch, still in Calcutta, continued to practice Germanic habits of mind while in diaspora, and she also turned to other institutions abroad with German links—especially the Warburg Institute in London where she began to cultivate strong connections. She formed increasingly strong ties with American institutions in New York and Philadelphia as well. For Kramrisch, it was not the search for radical Orientalist insight and the turn away from the norms of Westernness that characterized the Nazification of German scholarship. The rise of German fascism resulted from the misuse of a counternormative disposition among self-proclaimed underdogs—the pursuit of enchantment among the resentful, the uncouth, and the uncivil.

The Warburg Institute in London developed into the antithesis of Josef Strzygowski's *völkisch* Art Institute in Vienna, and represented the efflorescence of the "conservative" Viennese art history tradition in Britain, associated with the earlier work of Riegl and Dvořák. One of the leading scholars who set up the Warburg Institute alongside Aby Warburg was Dvořák's student, Fritz Saxl. Minority groups, such as the Jewish Germans who founded the Warburg Institute, sought ways of opening up and broadening the self-understanding of normative European culture. The Warburg Institute sought to understand the *Entstehung* of Western traditions especially by investigating the middle field between the European present and the "classical" past.[91] At the Warburg Institute, scholars turned critical attention to the understudied and underappreciated European middle ages and early modern period. They brought attention to the irrational and the ritualistic, especially the Hermetic tradition and the long continuities of European neo-Platonism and archaic paganism.[92] As a variation on the theme of studying comparative world regions from a cultural history perspective, some members such as Fritz Saxl and Erwin Panofsky also had interests in the Orient. The interests of the Warburg Institute ran orthogonal to that of Josef Strzygowski, who as a Germanic majoritarian, employed Orientalism and anti-Westernism in order to boost German Europe's geopolitical status, as well as to support claims about a purified Aryan cultural world rooted in the ancient East.

Stella Kramrisch began her association with the Warburg Institute and the Courtauld Institute in London between 1937 and 1940. During these years, Kramrisch would travel to London by ship in the summers, between May and September, and return to Calcutta for the winter and spring. In the summers of 1937 through 1939, she delivered public lectures at the Courtauld Institute, generally on themes related to Buddhist art and Hindu art. She provided "stylistic surveys" of major archaeological sites, such as Bharhut, Sanchi, Mathura, and Amaravati, and discussed Indian "iconography."[93] Kramrisch followed Coomaraswamy in arguing against the European hubris that presented Indian art, and the multiplicity of gods, as "iconolatry."[94]

During November and December 1940, Kramrisch organized a photographic exhibition "Aspects of Indian Culture" held at the Warburg Institute.[95] In London, surrounded by the diasporic German-speaking intellectuals of the Warburg Institute, Kramrisch put up a show for the British public. It was unique in its approach—a thematic show that sought to communicate abstract concepts and evoke a revealed cultural world of ancient Hinduism using photographic images. It was a show that was to explicitly resist the "archaeological and iconographical point of view."[96] Instead, Kramrisch saw images as views into a cultural universe outside Europe, in a similar way as Coomaraswamy. "Art is a language, and though we may at first need the symbols of our written language to initiate us into its secrets, essentially it is a language with its own symbols, and it cannot be properly understood unless we learn to read these symbols directly," she wrote.[97] The photograph created a new proximity of the view to cultic art. The show was to transport viewers from the Western world to a world of aesthetics centered on ancient India. This was a program in intellectual politics, imbued both with Indian anticolonial intent and the grand ethos of German scholarship to embrace the world *differently* from the order seen from the Anglo-Saxonist worldview.

The exhibition, called "The Meaning of the Hindu Temple and Its Decoration," was devoted to the Hindu temple as a religious environment. It formed the kernel of Kramrisch's later two-volume masterpiece, *The Hindu Temple* (1946). The show set out to give "a connected account of the meaning of the temple as a religious building, on the basis of its architecture and the relevant Sanskrit texts."[98] It was particularly the first section of the exhibition, "The Elevation of the Temple," that Kramrisch considered original. In it, she used images to explain, in her view, the fundamental unified philosophy of the Indian aesthetic tradition. This section included reflection on the temple as an image of the world, its different levels as symbols of the states of development, and the ritualistic objects in the temple as symbols of the "fullness of being."[99]

Kramrisch aimed to use photographic images not only as the substitutes for viewing material objects but also as carriers of enchanting experience for the viewing public. In particular, photographs were able to simulate the lighting in the temples, which viewing pieces in museums could not do. "It is essential that the photographs chosen should be modern and appeal to the wide public which has now grown accustomed to the latest photography brought by the daily papers, periodicals, etc.," Kramrisch proposed.[100] And in the catalog to the show, Kramrisch described her view of photographic reproduction, and how it actually added something to the original artifact. "Indian sculptures in museum collections are only fragments of a whole. They are detached from the body of the temple to which they belong, detached also from the setting in which they appear, from the light that envelops them and is reflected from them. The photographs show the light, or the darkness, in which the sculptures dwell on the walls and in the interior of the Indian temples, and help to visualize the original context to which they belong."[101] Kramrisch's interest in using images in pedagogy was certainly sparked by the immense popular reception of Indic Orientalism in German Europe in the 1920s. Ironically, Kramrisch's interpretations of the Indian Sanskritic tradition, and her project in using monuments for public education, nourished by Germanic methods of art history, would never reach a German or Austrian audience during the interwar years. Her work exemplified the thriving long-distance itineraries of German intellectual life cut off from their original home.

In 1946, from Calcutta, Kramrisch published *Hindu Temple* in book form. She recorded there her advanced method to study sacred images, emphasizing the close reading of images and also reflecting on the overall form, environment, and experience of encountering the images with a "warm heart." Her study relied heavily on self-reflection, addressing the internal experience on the part of the viewer of confronting Hindu religious architecture.[102] The ethos of the book *Hindu Temple* was both historicist and comparativist, as Kramrisch retrieved a great Hindu tradition, but then also insinuated throughout that the foreign world of the ancient Hindu past was of greater grandeur than that of the classical West. But the method of the book was also expressionist and anti-empiricist as Kramrisch not only relied on a great number of images to make her arguments but also spoke of the temple as a three-dimensional "being" that enveloped the visitor and spoke to her in a kind of mystical artistic language. Kramrisch placed personal experience of temple architecture at the center of the book in order to unlock what she called the "deeper meaning" of the temple environment and the cultural universe in which it belonged. In the Indian temple, Kramrisch's subjectivity was also centered in the world. To understand the temple, it had to be "reexperienced," perhaps in a way that Rabindranath would have understood best.

The later phase in Kramrisch's thinking focused on the expressionist wish to retrieve and reexperience a cultural world, not the historicist effort to trace the development of a particular artistic tradition. This shift reflects the intellectual distance Kramrisch traveled from the Vienna School of Dvořák to the Bengal School of the Tagores.

But by the late 1930s, signs had already developed that Kramrisch's relationships in Calcutta were under strain and that she felt isolated, or that she isolated herself from the social and cultural world of the city. Acquaintances recalled that she tended to keep to herself, focused maniacally on her work. When she visited families for the obligatory tea, she would bring her own powdered coffee and cookies.[103] She was in touch with Fritz Saxl at the Warburg Institute about possibilities of finding a lectureship there. There seems to have been some tension at the University of Calcutta that made her feel uncomfortable and unappreciated.[104] When she finally left the university in 1950, it was not on the best of terms. Had she been able to leave earlier, had she not been rendered stateless as a Jew from Vienna, she would likely have returned to Europe by the early 1940s. As things stood, she immigrated to Philadelphia first as a visiting professor at the University of Philadelphia, and later as the curator of Indian Art at the Museum of Philadelphia. Kramrisch brought all her tools for building intellectual authority with her to America.

Kramrisch's interest in the textual nature of artwork connected her to the Vienna School. Her focus on the experiential nature of artwork tied her to the Bengal School. But Kramrisch's insistence that the greatness of the Oriental world of art that not only contrasted with but also overshadowed the fragile and shallow aesthetics of post-Renaissance western European naturalism definitively connected her to the bellicose counternormative comparativist, Josef Strzygowski. Strzygowski, who maintained that the art of the Central Asian North had always towered over the cultures of the Mediterranean South, used comparativism to assert Central European global superiority. Kramrisch's means, and her objectives, in using the comparative method to reveal an Indian world of sacred art had nothing to do with Strzygowski's supremacist pursuit. Strzygowski spoke confidently about the East without ever going there. Kramrisch, on the other hand, remained in Calcutta for almost thirty years, and unlike Strzygowski with his self-involved monologue about world art, Kramrisch became deeply involved in dialogues and debates that drew her thinking somewhere into the middle field between Vienna and Bengal, somewhere between comparativism, historicism, and expressionism.

CINEMA AND INDIAN CREATIVITY

At the time of the *svadeśi* movement, Dadasaheb Phalke of Bombay was a pioneer of moving images in India. He was the first Indian to shoot film, and to critically reflect on the political significance of cinematic production.[105]

Another pioneering film producer, J. F. Madan, established the first large film house in Bombay. One of his sons, J. J. Madan, inspired by a concern for Indian intellectual power, wanted to make Indian film houses internationally competitive by acquiring first-rate expertise for Indian filmmakers and producers from abroad. Madan made a study trip to Hollywood in 1928. He brought American actors back to Bombay on a two-year contract to teach American-style acting.[106] The Madan studio was set up on the Hollywood model, which was also a blatant transgression of the limits of the British empire.[107]

By the end of the Great War, 85 percent of films imported to India were from the United States.[108] American films with chase scenes and gags entertained audiences.[109] German films, on the other hand, were known internationally for their technical expertise, expressionist lighting, and montage techniques. Special effects were popular in India, although difficult for Indian filmmakers to pull off given the technological chokehold imposed by British colonial rule. Indian audiences relied on imported films for their quota of advanced cinematography. The UFA (Universum-Film AG) film *Metropolis,* released in 1927, was a smash hit in India. But German films could not compete with the success of Hollywood films.[110] Americans producers had control of 90 percent of the Indian film market in the 1920s.

Yet Berlin and Munich, not Hollywood, were the most important suppliers of methods and technology to Indians by the late 1920s. As we shall see, the development of German methods and technology were themselves entangled with the myths of Oriental enchantment as well as the social and artistic contributions of Indian agents. As early as 1919, Himanshu Rai published an essay in the UFA magazine explaining the potential for worldwide recognition of Indian national cinema if it forged closer contacts in Germany.[111] Five Indians studied photography or cinematography at UFA in Babelsberg in the 1920s.[112] Zohra Segal studied at the Mary Wigman Dance School in Dresden in 1928 before returning to India to begin her acting career.[113] In 1933, V. Shantaram traveled to the AGFA laboratories in Berlin to develop his color film *Sairandhri.*[114] And in 1939, Suresh Chandra Das of Kali Films, Calcutta, also traveled to AGFA on a study tour for the benefit of his company.[115]

Devika Rani, a grandniece of Rabindranath Tagore, became one of the most celebrated Indian film superstars, known for enhancing the "prestige of the Indian screen in the eyes of foreigner[s]."[116] She represented the entry of "respectable" Hindu women into cinema after a first generation of mixed-race, especially Anglo-Indian stars, such as Ruby Myers, Renee Smith, and Beryl Cleason.[117] Devika Rani had worked as a set designer in London, and completed studies in dramatic arts at the Royal Academy of Dramatic Arts in London. She went on to Berlin to work under the Austrian film director, G. W. Pabst, in Babelsberg in 1928, and recalled holding the makeup tray for Marlene Dietrich during the shooting of *Blue Angel*.[118] In the 1930s, Devika Rani went on to star in and produce films for the Bombay Talkies studio—the first major Indian film house and the main source of talent and advanced cinematic techniques for the burgeoning Bombay film industry.[119] Devika Rani became one of the first superstars of the Indian silver screen, and an important patron of young talent.

THE GERMAN THREAT IN CINEMA

The Indian Cinematograph Committee (ICC), appointed by the government of India, studied the film industry in 1927–1928 with a view to preventing the monopolization of the Indian market by American and German firms.[120] The committee, chaired by an Indian lawyer, T. Rangachariar, consisted of three British officials and three Indian industry representatives. The ICC was asked to make recommendations to avoid the "lowering of standard[s] of social conduct" and the insulting of "religious sentiments."[121] During the committee's investigations, a total of 239 witnesses presented testimony to the committee, and the committee visited 25 cinemas. In 1927, Bombay far surpassed other Indian cities in terms of the number of permanent cinemas.[122] The second city of cinema in India was Calcutta. Madan Theatres owned the largest circuit of Indian theaters, and was Indian owned.[123] Witnesses tended to assert that Indian cinema still needed the development of modern technique and access to the latest technology.

The ICC remarked, with some concern, that German state subsidization was pushing German cinema ahead internationally. The *Kontingent* system, or the provision of state subsidies to German film houses, was making German film as internationally prevalent, and almost as cheap, as the American competitor. In the era of silent film, the matter of language was less of a barrier to international sales, only the intertitles needed to be changed. The ICC concluded that training in method and technology was sorely needed in India, and called for a more robust movie industry within India so as to curb the dependence on American and German productions. "There is urgent need for improvement in the stories, scenarios, acting, technique, photography—in fact, in all respects—although there has been some improvement, especially in photography," the report maintained. It included a number of proposals, including modifications of the tariff system, scholarships, and classes for training, and it noted the danger of "non-Indian" control.

The gravest concern according to the Indian Cinematograph Committee was posed by actor and director Himanshu Rai, a student of Rabindranath Tagore, and the scriptwriter, Niranjan Pal, son of the radical *svadeśi* leader, Bipin Chandra Pal.[124] Niranjan Pal settled in London after a stint as a gunrunner for the *svadeśi* activists abroad, and Himanshu moved to London after completing studies at Viśva Bhārati University.

Himanshu traveled to London to work with his friend Niranjan Pal in writing scripts and canvassing possible sponsors to produce Indian movies for international audiences.[125] The two comrades began their project on the heels of Rabindranath Tagore's tour to continental Europe in 1921. Rabindranath Tagore attended the Oberammergau play about the Passion of Christ in Munich in 1921, and he was greatly impressed by it. The play was reviewed in the Bengali press and this was the impetus for Niranjan Pal and Himanshu Rai to settle on the idea of making a series of films on the prophets of world religions.[126] The comparative approach behind their conception, placing different religious myths on the same footing, is striking both for its consistency with the ethos of *svadeśi* internationalism and for its cunning strategy for claiming Indian success in the expanding international film market. Their first film would focus on the life of the Buddha, they decided, followed by a second film on the Passion of Christ. The two cinematic colporteurs from India hoped such movies would win Indian actors and filmmakers global renown.

Pal was aware of the strength of popular Indic Orientalism in Germany, and saw an opportunity to respond to market demand. Plotlines that stuck to Buddhist and Christian themes would do well given the popular atmosphere of the time, both in Europe and America, as well as in India, potentially, where the "mythological" movie genre did well alongside the "social" and the "historical." In London, Himanshu Rai met Devika Rani, and, with Pal, the three formed a fateful liaison that would eventually include a set of close collaborators from Germany in the establishment of the Bombay Talkies film studio.

In 1924, Himanshu Rai and Niranjan Pal traveled to Munich to canvass for support from the South German production house, EMELKA, for movies about the Buddha and about Christ's Passion. It was in Munich that they met Franz Osten, the artistic director. EMELKA had just come under new ownership, and investors were excited about the prospect of a film about the Buddha, given the cresting Germany Orientalist fascination with Buddhism in the 1920s. Collaboration with Indians was sure to earn the film added cachet on the German market, setting such a collaborative film apart from the increasing number of exotic Orient films done in blackface or using African American actors as substitutes for Indians.[127] Stories about romance and myth in the exotic Orient were a standard genre of early German silent films.[128]

Exotic films about the Orient were big business from early on. The dominant tropes of early German Orientalist film featured wily Asian men seducing European women. The theme of the love triangle in the Orient played out in Robert Reinert's *Opium* (1919), Karlheinz Martin's *Die Perle des Orients* (1919), and Fritz Lang's *Das Indische Grabmal* (1921) based on the Orientalist pulp fiction novel by Thea von Harbou.[129] Other successes were Max Mack's *Die Lieblingsfrau des Maharadscha* (1920), Ernst Lubitsch's *Sumurun* (1920), Joe May's *Tiger of Eshnapur* (1921), and *The Indian Tomb* (after another novel by Thea von Harbou, 1921). EMELKA made its first attempt at the Oriental exotic film with *Der Brunnen des Wahnsinns* (1919), produced by Ottmar Ostermayr.[130] In German cinema, only the frontier films about Native Americans claimed pride of place over Indian film in the "exotic" genre.[131]

In the 1920s, German cinematic innovation fed off the fascinations of postwar popular Indic Orientalism, including Buddhism as a world religion, world-historical Indian epics, and the gargantuan geography of the Himalayas. Himalayan films, often in documentary style and focused on the triumph of the will, became big business in the Nazi years. Themes of philologically inspired Orientalism made their way onto the screen only from the late 1920s onward, and not least of all because of the efforts of Franz Osten and EMELKA. Rai and Pal's first collaboration with Osten and EMELKA resulted in *Light of Asia* (1925), an adaptation of Arnold Edwin's story of the Buddha's birth, *Wanderjahre*, and arrival at Nirwana.[132] It was a blockbuster in the German market in the 1920s.[133]

Franz Osten was born in Munich in 1876, and his family owned a photography business. He directed his first film in 1911, and during the Great

War, he served in the German army in South Tyrol, Galicia, and France. EMELKA was the production company of his younger brother, Peter, founded in April 1918. The company, situated in Munich's cultural milieu of stage and screen avant-gardism, was the south German equivalent of UFA in Berlin.[134] EMELKA was known for its extravagant historical costume dramas.[135]

In 1924, Osten was forty-four years old, and had already established his career as a nationally renowned German director. In the early 1920s, Munich was perhaps the center for German film, with Berlin's UFA taking the crown only by the later part of the decade.[136] *Light of Asia* was the first German-produced and -directed feature-length film to be shot on location in India. *The Light of Asia* ushered in a new style of the Orientalist film, first in terms of attention to ethnographic detail, second because of the use of Indian actors, and third, thanks to its adaptation of a plotline that incorporated the key enchanting themes characterizing Indic Orientalism of the postwar years.[137] The movie, with its mythic opulence, its extravagant set, and its religious theme intended to envelop its audience in a new world that was not only stranger but also more appealing than the everyday world of postwar realities. Perhaps for this reason the *Light of Asia* screened to only moderate success in Britain and the United States, while it became a blockbuster in Germany.[138]

The collaboration between Himanshu Rai and Franz Osten was quickly followed, only two years later, by *Shiraz: Das Grabmal einer großen Liebe*, inspired by the story of the romance between Shah Jahan and Mumtaz Mahal, and the building of the Taj Mahal. The film was also shot on location in India and met with immense success at the German box office. Given the role of Indian actors and screenwriters in these German productions, as well as the use of Indian landscapes and backdrops in making them (*Shiraz* was coproduced with a British company), both *Light of Asia* and *Shiraz* aroused the concern of colonial administrators. The influence of Indian actors and cinematographers abroad was out of imperial control. The imagined Orientalist world that gave German audiences a source of escape in the years after Versailles was produced from an actual world of global circulation and Indian creative contributions beyond the confining limits of an increasingly untimely British empire.

Rai was interrogated by the Cinematograph Committee about why he financed his films using foreign funds, why he sold his films in international markets, and why he used techniques and technology that were brought in from outside the British colonial world. The British Indian government wanted to keep Indians turned inward and set within the worldview of liberal empire. Himanshu Rai testified before the 1927 ICC, defending his work with German directors, cameramen, and production crews, as well as his acceptance of support from German production houses.

Himanshu appealed to pragmatism in responding to the committee's concerns. The greater the viewership for Indian films abroad, the more business Indian producers and directors would garner. Himanshu explained that Indian investors were reluctant to put up significant funds for new cinematic enterprises. "I cannot help it. I have no money. I went to one who was not of my nationality to get it."[139] It was necessary to canvass for foreign capital in these circumstances, he maintained. But this was a temporary pursuit, with the final goal of building up Indian film houses domestically and attracting the interest of Indian investors. "According to Mr. Himanshu Rai's evidence," a member of the Cinematograph Committee asserted, "had the original negotiations with German fructified, the predominant interest would have been German. If this sort of enterprise were considered deserving of encouragement what is there to prevent America from embarking upon such enterprises here? Is it true that Mr. Himanshu Rai says he tried to get Indians to take a financial interest in this venture of his and failed?"[140] The ICC expressed concern that foreign capital from Germany, and also from America, would handicap the successful development of an indigenous film industry. That is perhaps the more benign interpretation. From another perspective, colonial administrators were certainly anxious to keep the Indian cinema market safe from extra-imperial interests.

Rai insisted that his films were no less Indian and no less nationalist simply because they involved international collaborations. "I have not been sent by anybody. I am the producer of this picture. I have taken money from a financing corporation. I have my buyers and I engage my artists. It is my production. So it is an Indian production," he protested under heated grilling. "My films are swadeshi in the sense that the ownership, employees and stories are swadeshi."[141] The production of Indian nationalist cinema took place in India, for certain, but also at satellite locations abroad. Indian film reviewer Naval Gandhi wrote in an article published in Berlin's *Lichtbild-Bühne*, "the German film industry will have tremendous possibilities on the Indian market if they take their chance and take an active interest in this distant region. . . . There is certainly no dearth of beautiful scenic motifs and cheap labour which can easily be employed in the film."[142] Apart from the matter of finding investors for Indian filmmaking, those involved in the Indian film industry also had a general sense that German materials and technology were of superior quality, even to the products of Hollywood.

While the technology, techniques, and funding came from German Europe, Himanshu Rai pointed out that the movie plots were written by Indians and drawn from local themes, and that the acting styles were veritably Indian. Foreign techniques entangled with local talent and style constituted the mix that bolstered Indian creative potential in cinema and Indian internal renown in the anticolonial age. Himanshu stated, "we cannot express our sentiments in the same way in which the Englishman would express his and if you try to imitate that you would at once spoil the whole thing and it would be ridiculous and people would laugh. The time has come in cinematography for not showing any facial expression. It is done merely by the eyes. Facial expression is now confined to the stage. I am anxious that all expression that comes must be Indian."[143] Himanshu made the distinction between foreign technologies and indigenous styles. And he insisted that those Indian styles could travel the world and get mixed up with distant contexts, while still remaining *svadeśi*, that is, "of his own country."

Opposing values were at work in the confrontation between the members of the Indian Cinematograph Committee and Himanshu Rai. The committee members mobilized arguments about the need to keep Indian capital in India, and the need to develop Indian industries and not outsource to foreign companies. Himanshu Rai employed nationalist arguments about the urgency of making India a cultural producer of international repute. Earning recognition for Indian cinema would aid in this program. The geopolitical ambitions of Himanshu Rai were necessarily internationalist and relational—they required the recognition that foreign German collaborators, capital, and cinematographic techniques could be employed in the pursuit of Indian ends.

Himanshu Rai's working relationship with Franz Osten only strengthened after the Indian Cinematographic Committee expressed its official displeasure over his German collaboration. Rai and Osten's third film collaboration, *Schicksalswürfel* (A Throw of the Dice), was released in 1929. Again, shot on location in India, it was inspired by a story from the *Mahā-*

bhārata about mistaken identities, and a kingdom lost by a game of dice. With this film, Osten achieved his greatest popular success in Germany.[144] The three silent films that Osten directed in India in the 1920s were all in the mythological mode. They were set in the "eternal expanse of the jungle," dealt with maharajas and maharanis, drew on Indological themes from the *Mahābhārata* or from Buddhism, and sought to conjure the grandeur of myth. The team of Niranjan Pal, Himanshu Rai, Devika Rani, Franz Osten, and Josef Wirsching found a formula for popular cinematic success in Germany in this grand, Orientalist conceit that tapped into the broad popularization of representations of Orientalism in German society after Versailles.

POPULAR AUDIENCES AND INDIAN CREATIVITY

In Osten's writings in the German press, there was the usual tendency to present himself as a donor of European technique and the recipient of Indian cultural authenticity. The authenticity of India was the big selling point for the early Osten Orientalist films. "The task that I together with my loyal helpers . . . had to carry out was the production of an authentic Indian film with exclusively Indian actors, décor, costumes and accessories. Before us some American and European companies may have made films in India, but this shooting was meant only to complete their own modern feature films produced almost entirely in the studio with their own actors."[145] In promotional material, he pretended to bring his German audience backstage, so they could see how real all the actors, props, and sets were. "Since the film was set in Buddha's time, it was very important to use buildings that were from that period. To that end, we did most of the filming in upper Hindustan, north of Calcutta, which is about where Buddha came from, and where the villages are still untouchable by European influences. One of the richest maharajas showed a special interest in our work. He offered us all possible assistance and support, not only putting his people at our disposal for filming, but also about 30 elephants."[146] Osten even claimed that his Indian collaborators were "[dedicated] to preserving the ancient traditions of Indian theater." Over and over again, film reviews in the *Lichtbild-Bühne* and *Film-Kurier* acclaim the "spiritual authenticity" of Osten's films. While we might naturally focus on the projections and European imaginings that flickered through Osten's mind and the minds of his audience, we cannot lose sight of the fact that the teeth and grooves for Osten's cinema, and for some of the most popular German films of the 1920s, were cast from Indian sources and driven by Indian collaborations. In other words, to focus only on Osten's "German" mind and the Germanic features of Orientalist discourse is to ignore exactly that other half of the process that involves entanglement, coproduction, and the interdependence of dialogic action.

Historian Gerhard Koch has established the important German contribution to the Bombay Talkies endeavor, especially in terms of technological innovation.[147] Franz Osten explained in a biographical sketch that he organized the technical and administrative aspects of Bombay Talkies on a German model. "German machines and other materials" were bought, he proudly noted.[148]

In 1927, Osten moved to Berlin from Munich. In 1928 he traveled again to India on behalf of UFA in order to direct *Shiraz*. At that time, he published essays about on-the-spot directing in India in the main film journals, just as his three India films each had achieved great commercial success.[149] Meanwhile, between 1929 and 1934, Osten continued to work in Berlin for various German firms. He grew increasingly uneasy with the pressures to transform feature films into organs of propaganda for Germandom. In fact, Osten was known for the breadth of genres he covered. His film on Johann Strauss, *Der zerstreute Walzer*, and his film *Zu Straßburg auf der Schanz*, were musicals. He directed the *Kulturfilm* meant to provide historical edification, such as one about the life of Queen Elisabeth of Austria-Hungary, assassinated in 1898.[150] He made suspense films, such as *Die Damen in Schwarz*.[151] Meanwhile, a film such as *Der Judas von Tirol* had the nationalist flair of the *Heimatfilme* genre. The *Judas* film was a story about a German village in Tirol occupied during the Napoleonic invasions and the betrayal of a farmer against village *volk*.

After 1933, the National Socialists blacklisted over 2,000 German directors, producers, actors, and technicians. German cinema talent, like so many other types of talented individuals fortunate enough to escape, were forced into exile in the 1930s and 1940s. Directors from German Europe arrived in Hollywood in large numbers, as in the case of Fritz Lang and Douglas Sirk, or to Paris, as with G. W. Pabst and Lotte Eisner, or to London, as with Max Schach. Of all these destinations, Hollywood was the dominant one. More than 500 German-speaking film émigrés found work in American film and television studios after the rise of the Nazis.[152] If the majority of émigré talent traveled West to London and Los Angeles, Osten and his crew traveled east to Bombay.

Beginning in 1934, Osten, along with the exceptionally gifted Josef Wirsching, the young set designer, Karl von Spreti, and the film technician, Wilhelm Zolle, left Nazi Germany for chosen exile in Bombay. Osten was informed in a letter of June 1934 that his film company, Ideal Film, would not be allowed to operate because the required paperwork proving Osten's "Aryan roots" had not been submitted. Osten stalled in providing his information to the Nazi government's Reichsfachschaft Film.[153] He eventually joined the Nazi party in 1934, but had subsequently sought to create increasing distance from the German film market. His desire to avoid the Nazified German film industry, glutted with films about Heimats and fatherlands, mountaineering and geopolitical triumphs of the will, pushed him toward his Indian sojourn. Osten began an effort to Indianize his films and to shed the trademark Indic Orientalism that marked his Weimar work.

The Nazi regime cultivated films about Germanic world ascendancy in various genres. Filmic monumentality and world-historical movie plots became fixations of German cinematography in these years. During the 1930s, the German expedition films to the Himalayas superseded the popular genre of the Wild West films in popularity. *Kampf um den Himalaya* (1938) was a documentary about a team of German mountaineers, of whom seven members died attempting to climb the Nanga Parbat mountain peak in today's Pakistan.[154] Günter Oskar Dyrhenfurth's *Der Dämon des Himalaya* (1935) used the expedition to spin off a fictionalized account.[155]

The films of Karl Ritter, Leni Riefenstahl, Hans Steinhof, and Gustav Ucicky depicted fantasies of geopolitical struggle and German *völkische* supremacy. Ucicky's film in particular featured plots about the perilous return of *Auslandsdeutsche* (overseas Germans) to the homeland, sometimes from eastern Europe (*Heimkehr*, 1941), or even from Manchuria (*Die Flüchtlinge*, 1928).[156] But Colin Ross became the favorite director of monumental geopolitical documentaries during the Nazi years.[157] His movies focused on America, and the Asian Pacific Rim from India to Japan and Australia, including his popular film *Achtung Asien! Achtung Australien!*[158] He traveled as a family man, and featured his wife and children in many of his films, marketing himself as an Aryan world explorer and pater familias.

Josef Wirsching, Franz Osten's talented cameraman, worked on a variety of geopolitical films and *Heimatsfilme* in the late 1920s and early 1930s during the hiatus in the collaboration with Indians.[159] One of the most famous was *Kreuzer Emden im Indischen Ozean* (1926), a nationalist film about the German ship that fired shots at the Madras Harbor in 1915, precipitating a mutiny of British Indian troops at their base in Singapore. His *Stoßtrupp 1917* (1934) was a re-creation of the German front experience. *Unter Palmen und Pagoden* (1934) was a travel documentary to Thailand. After immigrating to India in 1935, his career in German film ended, except for one last German-language venture. Unsurprisingly, *An den Grenzen Tibets* (1943) deployed the tropes of Indic Orientalism in order to appeal to a German popular audience.

But the best was still to come for Wirsching. He went on to work with the biggest film stars and directors of Indian cinema, and became one of the legendary cameramen of Bollywood and a propagator of some of the most influential and successful camera techniques in midcentury Indian film. Wirsching specialized in bringing a 1920s German expressionist touch to many of his most famous films, especially with his signature deep field shots, and his use of camera effects to create a sense of ghostly and ethereal presences on the screen. Wirsching's camera also worshipped its heroines, capturing iconic images of female actors, including Madhubala in the haunting cinematic masterpiece, *Mahal* (1949), and Meena Kumari in the opulently filmed, *Pakheezah* (1972).

If Shantiniketan and the Kalā Bhavān infused Stella Kramrisch's study of still images and archaeological objects with a commitment to uncover the *rasa*, or the life force, expressed in Indian art, Himanshu Rai and Franz Osten's collaboration in cinema traced a different, but related, trajectory in expressionist cinema in the 1930s. Of course, Rai and Osten sought to appeal to popular audiences. If Kramrisch focused a large amount of her attention on religious objects and images of deities, Himanu Rai thought most persistently about the cinematic trope of romance, with all its popular appeal. In the 1920s, Rai and Osten used the mythological mode to appeal to German mass audiences with stories about romance and love affairs. Once Osten and his technical crew moved to Bombay in 1934, Rai and Osten reinvented the love affair using a different set of tropes, cultural forms, and styles in order to appeal to an Indian mass audience.

So the love story would make sense to Indian audiences, Himanshu, Osten, Niranjan Pal, and Devika Rani employed the artistic expressionism associated with Shantiniketan's Kalā Bhavan school of art. The village became the background and the context for a reinvented Indian modernity, and the romantic heroines became the main dramatic vehicles. This was Rabindranath Tagore's modernist aesthetic anchored by female protagonists, such as in the stories *Chārulatā*, *Strīr Patra*, or *Chitrāngadā*, but applied to cinematic media.[160] Himanshu Rai had studied at Rabindranath's university, and Devika Rani was a member of the Tagore family. The way Bombay Talkies plotted its love stories and the growing importance of Devika Rani's characters as the aesthetic and dramatic center of the movie plots suggest a distinctive project in Indian cinematic enchantment in which the female hero becomes a popular universal symbol for the human condition. In the Bombay Talkies films of the 1930s, at the start of what Ravi Vasudevan calls the "melodramatic mode" in Indian cinema,[161] the heroine does not so much serve as a symbol of Indian culture, as communicate, in an Indianized cinematic vernacular, emotions that claim to speak for the universal human drama.[162] In Bombay Talkies films, the expressionist replaced the mythological as the audience changed from German filmgoers in the 1920s to Indian filmgoers in the 1930s.[163] Roy was less concerned with making films about place than with using locality as a site to tell a story with worldwide, human currency.

NEW VILLAGE PLOTS

The films made by Bombay Talkies jettisoned the Indic Orientalist themes of Buddhism as world religion, the Himalayas as a center of world geography, and the Indian epics as sources of world history. Instead, the movies adopted the new theme of the Indian woman as the universal dramatic interpreter. This shift coincided with the end of the silent era and the coming of sound to Indian films. The Bombay Talkies plots of the 1930s period focused on the pulsing flow of romance, with special emphasis on universal human pangs of unrequited or unfulfilled love.

Bombay Talkies' early scripts, written by Niranjan Pal, were set in the town or countryside, but rarely in cities. Pal wrote eight of the scripts for the film house in the 1930s. His plots often highlighted feminine individualism as it butted up against social restrictions. *Jiwani Ki Hawa* (1935) is about an eloping couple and the mysterious murder of the girl's disapproving father as he tries to follow them. The blockbuster, *Acchut Kanya* (1936), tells the story of a Dalit girl who falls in love with a Brahmin boy, and tragically dies after suffering social ostracism. *Jeevan Prabhat* (1936) is a drama about a Brahmin girl, erroneously suspected of cheating on her husband in an affair with a Dalit potter. *Izzat* (1937) tells a Romeo and Juliet story set between two warring clans in a medieval Maratha kingdom. *Durga* (1938) relates the tale of an innocent village girl who suffers the death of her mother, and is subsequently mistreated by society and charged with a crime she did not commit. And *Nirmala* (1938) presents a pregnant woman who is told by an astrologer that she must run away from her husband in order to ensure a successful birth. Nirmala abandons her husband, only to then have her newborn son stolen from her by a village beggar. The film culminates with the ultimate reunification of mother, husband, and son just before Nirmala's tragic death.

The plots of the 1930s were channeled through the character of heroines played by Devika Rani. Just as Rabindranath's artistry sought to bring the world to the Indian village, so too Bombay Talkies set most of its 1930s films in the village. But the films focused on the universal coin of romantic suffering, not on the culturalist fixation on village life per se. Instead of drawing from high cultural texts such as the *Ramayana, Mahabharata,* or *Jatakas,* the 1930s Bombay Talkies films addressed everyday scenarios of romance, interrupted by family responsibilities and caste differences. The theme of heroic emotional struggle and suffering by Indian women returned to the plotlines.

Devika Rani assumed the role of heroine in nine successive Bombay Talkies sound films shot between 1934 and 1938. The new production house was in competition with two other houses, New Theatres in Calcutta and Madan Studios in Bombay. Stylistically, Bombay Talkies set itself apart with its more naturalistic style, its pioneering plotlines in the mode of the "Hindi Social," and also in terms of its high level of technical finesse. Devika Rani's heroines were often portrayed in sleeveless blouses, considered revealing and risqué. Plotlines often had her enter romantic liaisons with the wrong types of men, either because of their caste background or their community identity. She wore her on-screen makeup glamorously in the style of Marlene Dietrich. Devika Rani also sang and danced in some films (for example, *Durga*), challenging a taboo that kept Bengal *bhadhramahilā* (genteel women) away from Dionysian forms of artistry.

The overt depiction of romance in the early Bombay Talkies films from the 1930s, most often between Devika Rani and her costar, Ashok Kumar, made the movies stand out from the crowd. The love stories generally ended in tragedy, combining melodrama with social commentary. One disapproving reviewer wrote about the Bombay Talkies film brand, "the artistic, creative, and educative values of the film-shows are being thrown in the back-ground and most of the films are characterized by scenes and talks which are calculated to stimulate sex-desire among people and its effect on young minds."[164]

As early as the 1930s, Bombay Talkies established a style and a vision of Indian cinema that was popular at home, while also gaining esteem among international audiences. These Bombay Talkies films wielded a new artistic authority on an imagined global stage as they uncovered a world of human drama within the Indian village setting, and organized their plots around the powerful agency of embattled heroines. This institution of the Bombay Talkies served its purpose as another disciplinary effort to center both Indian and German creativity in the world in a shared project to tell universal stories about romance and tragedy differently. An article appearing in Berlin in 1939 called Devika Rani the "Greta Garbo of the miracle country." This kind of long-distance recognition was something that Indians had cultivated for more than three decades—it was rooted in intellectual politics.[165] As Koch points out, the presence of "foreigners" in the Bombay film industry drew critique in its time. The *Filmindia* magazine from 1938 railed against the "German experts . . . with their wives and children" who began to play such an important role in the industry.[166] On the other hand, Saadat Hasan Manto found the German involvement in the Bombay Talkies most natural, and recalled Himanshu Rai as the untiring, "single-minded," and unquestioned creative authority in the Bombay Talkies venture.[167]

The collaboration of Himanshu Rai and Franz Osten produced seventeen films in the course of five years, from 1934 to 1939.[168] The immense productivity of their interaction stemmed from the conviction among the collaborators that they were making a new kind of enchanted cinema for global spectatorship, in which India would be a modern global center of cultural production. With the coming of World War II, Franz Osten, already sixty-three years old at the time, was interned in a camp for enemy nationals. Osten remained interned for seven months until he was returned to Germany in April 1940. Because he was over sixty years old, he was quickly dismissed from internment and repatriated to Germany. But upon his return to wartime Germany, Osten was unable to direct again. Cut off from the German film industry both before and after 1945, Osten disappeared into obscurity, becoming the director of a spa facility outside Munich and a sometime instructor at a film school. In 1940, Himanshu Rai died unexpectedly, apparently brokenhearted both by the end of his marriage to Devika Rani and by the war internment of Franz Osten. Devika Rani went on to marry Svetoslav Roerich in 1945, the son of the Russian Orientalist and mystical painter, Nicholas Roerich, eventually immigrating to Australia.[169] Bombay Talkies, too, suffered the same kind of artistic dissolution as its creative leaders. By the mid-1940s, the company's best movies were behind it, even as the company fertilized Indian cinema in terms of theatrical, directorial, and technical talent for decades to come.

The film studios in Malad grew to an ensemble of almost 400 workers and artists.[170] Savak Vacha, a sound technician, later produced the blockbuster 1949 hit, *Mahal*. Ashok Kumar, Prithiwiraj Kapur, and Dilip Kumar, all three starting with Bengal Talkies thanks to the efforts of Devika Rani, became early leading men in Indian cinema. R. D. Pareenja the cinematographer, K. A. Abbas the important scriptwriter and director, and Saadat Hasan Manto the literary giant, were at the center of the Indian film industry in the 1940s and 1950s, and worked for Bombay Talkies.[171] Sashadhar Mukherji, the brother-in-law of Ashok Kumar, first worked as a technician with Osten and later became a producer of Bombay Talkies films in the 1940s. Other movie icons associated with the launchpad of Bombay Talkies included Leela Chitnis, Raj Kapoor, and Najmul Hussain. Meanwhile, Charu Roy, soon to be a famous Calcutta-based film director, worked with Osten as a costume designer in *Light of Asia*. But Satyajit Ray's work, beginning in the 1950s, most forthrightly pursued Bombay Talkies' simultaneous domestic and international artistic aspirations, with its outright challenge of the dilemma between authenticity at home and recognition abroad. Satyajit Ray's *Apu Trilogy* revealed the hidden life of human drama beginning in the village setting and transitioning to the city, capturing the imagination of both Indian and international audiences by revealing the universal in something seemingly particular. Ray's Bengali-language *Pather Panchali* (1955) aroused adulation and controversy throughout India, while also winning prizes at Cannes, Venice, London, Berlin, San Francisco, Tokyo, and elsewhere.[172] Satyajit Ray, along with other internationally renowned visual artists in the 1950s, such as Ramkinkar Baij and Benod Bihari Mukherji, with roots in Rabindranath's Viśva Bhārati University in Shantiniketan, also pursued an enchantment of the world through their art, which challenged the world order organized around Old Europe and the hegemonic claims of the Anglo-Saxon standard.

Historians of film in South Asia have chosen to grapple with the conundrum of whether Bombay cinema represented an assimilation, a rejection, or a vernacularization of "the West," especially in terms of the cinematic modernism of Hollywood. A more comparative, archivally based investigation shows that Indian–German collaboration also sits at the artistic and technological origins of Bombay cinema's distinction. And collaborations involving the entanglements of different histories and disparate historical agents were far more complex than processes of either vernacularization or negotiation with "the West." The history of entanglement and dialogic action in the pursuit of new intellectual authority is really at issue. Indian cinematic artists saw the pressing need to find ways to explore human drama outside the strictures of British liberal empire and its center of gravity, which tended to bend artistic taste around the world to fit with its own image.

Stella Kramrisch, a Viennese scholar originally from Moravia, worked to locate Indian artistic creativity on a world stage outside the framework of imperial art history. Himanshu Rai, Franz Osten, Devika Rani, and other collaborators in the Bombay Talkies film enterprise set out to shoot films that depicted the world of human drama from a proudly Indian, and feminine, perspective. These projects of artistic and scholarly efforts to enchant the world shared something in common with other programs for amassing intellectual authority that ranged across the spectrum of the arts and sciences. Indians in dialogue with German-speakers revealed hidden systems of thermodynamic and atomic energy, and new world orders of commerce, of labor, of cultural geography, of the psyche, and of aesthetics and drama. The post-Enlightenment arts and sciences depended on transnational dialogue beyond the scope and conventions of the nineteenth-century knowledge system anchored by the dominance of British empire. An obituary of Himanshu Rai in the Berlin *Film-Kurier* of

1940, eulogized the actor-producer as participating in a German collaboration that "conquered the entire world."[173] No commentary could be more fitting for its time—when the world was not a fixed, geographic entity, but rather a violently contested, and furiously and continuously counterimagined, domain.

ELEVEN

A New Order

This book has focused on intellectual projects to rearrange and recategorize the world—to do what scientific universalism had always done, but now in the service of the self-identified castaways, the vanquished, the rebels, and the exiles of the earth. Those were the types who most enthusiastically used countersciences in the early twentieth century. But the grand efforts to rearrange the natural and cultural worlds were not the result of acts of the will of individual actors. They were expressions of historical context—expressions of their times. The specific geopolitical conditions that arose with the seismic shift in world power between 1880 and 1945, and the great decentralization and redistribution of power to multiple centers worldwide in that period, produced the conditions necessary for collaborative, if threatening, projects to newly enchant the world. The sciences and scholarship of the post-Enlightenment were of a distinctive species, defined by their transnational dialogical scope and their rebellious and contrarian epistemic character. Science was not unified over the course of the nineteenth and twentieth centuries. It operated differently and served different masters depending on the historical period. In the years after 1880s, science was used to take the world apart and to generate a multiplicity of contending authoritative and conflicting world visions. Beginning in 1945, at the dawn of another process of rearrangement of world power, science started to play a new role.

Science became the standing reserve for emerging hegemonic powers—the United States and the Soviet Union—as they sought to put the world back together in their image. If the British empire promulgated a discourse of global enlightened integration before 1880, after 1945 both the American and Soviet world powers revived discourses of global integration and "competitive coexistence" through science.[1] After World War II, in the aftermath of Nazi imperial expansion, invasion, and genocide, the Potsdam Conference brought together the leaders of Britain, the United States, and the Soviet Union in 1945 to agree upon the division of Germany, and the protocols for its integration into an asymmetrically bipolar world order.[2] The Germanies were not only to be politically, but also epistemically, assimilated into the new world order.[3] The institutions and disciplines of German scholarship that had grown into a third center for imagining the world order outside the League and the Comintern in the 1920s had hemorrhaged into the form of the Nazi regime in the 1930s. The war victors would now dismember those institutions in order to ensure a new and stable world system.[4]

Given these large-scale political shifts, the dialogic order regulating the interactions between Germans and Indians drastically changed. Germans and Indians now encountered each other, respectively, as votaries of northern superpowers and as representatives of the Third World. Modernization theory, which evolved predominantly in institutions supported by the United States of America, as well as the United Nations' international apparatus, created arenas for knowledge production and for the exercise of intellectual power by German-speaking émigré economists. Almost a third of the scholars responsible for the emerging field of Development Economics after 1945 were German-speakers, the majority of whom were refugees from German Europe.[5] Detailed studies show that the universities of London and Oxford in particular, where Paul Rosenstein-Rodan and Kurt Mandelbaum settled, became institutional centers for the formulation of Development Economics.[6] These scholars had a strong impact on several of the most outstanding younger émigrés from German Europe who went on to make contributions to Development Economics, among them Heinz W. Arndt, Warner Max Corden, Gerard O. Gutmann, John H. Mars, Alexander Kafka, and Paul Streeten.[7]

For West German intellectuals, and for émigrés settled abroad who had been forced to emigrate during the Nazi period, becoming intellectual envoys of pro-Western economic and political integration was a way of reconstituting a new identity—one that was solidly located in the West, and that possessed the scientific means to make the rest of the world similar to the West. After 1945, many West German and émigré scientists would proudly claim the distinction to be more western than the West. And West German academia became the most America-friendly academia in Europe. Karl Jaspers's words in 1947 registered the sense of dispersal and negation that German intellectuals experienced after the war. This was the aftermath of a failed attempt at claiming planetary distinction by radical means. "We did not go into the streets when our Jewish friends were led away; we did not scream. We preferred to stay alive, on the feeble, if logical, ground that our death could not have helped anyone. We are guilty of being alive."[8] India and Germany had never been on parallel paths, politically or socially speaking. The discrepancies between their historical trajectories are just as important as the entanglements. Yet for the period from 1880 to 1945, many German and Indian intellectuals operated within shared horizons of nationalist anti-Anglocentric politics, and counternormative thought. After 1945, after the barbarism of the Nazis, no Germanic identity was left with which to seek jingoistic distinction on the world stage. Germans could attain world significance only via association with America, or the Soviet Union.

In the context of World War II, Alexander Gerschenkron, a Russian Jewish émigré, wrote of "Germany [as] the sore spot of Europe. The success or failure of its economic adjustment cannot be a matter of indifference to the outside world."[9] For Gerschenkron, it was the illiberal interventionism of the German state and the vested interests of groups such as the elite agrarian Junkers that had put Germany on the wrong course of development in the nineteenth and twentieth centuries. Gerschenkron explicitly cast Germany's nineteenth century in terms of the emergence of political and economic "backwardness"—a favored term among modernization theorists. Germany's path to modernization in the nineteenth century, he seemed to suggest, might foreshadow the Third World's modernization in the mid-twentieth. "The contingency of large imports of foreign machinery and of foreign know-how and the concomitant opportunities for rapid industrialization with the passage of time increasingly widened the gulf between economic potentialities and economic actualities in backward countries."[10] In Germany, backwardness propelled innovation not just in technology but also in organization: the blast furnace, the universal bank, cartelization, and so forth. But backwardness also encouraged corporatism, illiberalism, and ultimately, fascism.[11]

The University of California at Berkeley, the University of Chicago, and Harvard University became three of the main centers for modernization theory in the 1950s and 1960s. And these economics departments contained a large number of German émigrés, from both former Central Europe and the former Soviet Union. These scholars, in general, tended to emphasize modernization and the development of urban civil society as the proper avenue for aid to Asia. If German Orientalists cross-identified with Asia before 1945, this reflective dynamic was now reversed, and the decline of German Europe into totalitarianism during the interwar years was held up by many development economists as a cautionary tale for the new governments in Asia, the Middle East, and Africa. Pre-1945 Germany became a symbol of rapid development gone horribly wrong. While Germans identified themselves as set in Europe's Orient before 1945, the Third World became the Western Powers' Germany after 1945.

The main theme of development economics, one of the great disciplines of the Cold War era, became that of global integration, that is, of normalizing the world according to American and western European interests. Scholars such as Albert Hirschman and Harvey Liebenstein, focused on changing "attitudes, motivations, and incentives" in the Third World, and saw modernization as a grand educational project.[12] Gunnar Myrdal of Sweden was one of the most influential development thinkers to frame the question of Third World modernization in terms of a postcolonial, post–World War II, geopolitical shift, as well as the opposition between Cold War blocs. "There has been the rapid liquidation of the colonial power structure, accompanied by the craving for development in the underdeveloped countries themselves."[13] Myrdal's *Asian Drama* maintained that the West's development policies had to be explicitly conceived in terms of concerns for diplomacy, determent, and "winning hearts and minds" for the proper "alignment" of frontier regions of the world.[14] He concluded that investment in health, education, and poverty reduction policies would be the most important determinants of development. What the West had not successfully achieved in Germany in the 1920s, it now had to achieve in the Third World in the Cold War era.[15]

Otto Schiller, a West German agricultural economist at Heidelberg, became a consultant to the Indian and Pakistani governments between 1953 and 1958. He worked on village cooperatives as a method of agricultural development. Cooperative initiatives, which since the days of Raiffeisen and Schulze-Delitzsch in the nineteenth century had been one of Germany's most emulated models of development among foreign governments, reemerged as a major German brand of development strategy after the war. And as Corinna Unger has shown, West German delegations took up projects in village cooperatives and vocational training in India in the 1950s.[16]

"UNDERDEVELOPMENT" AS A GEOPOLITICAL IDENTITY

The years from 1947 to the mid-1960s were years of experimentation and possibility, especially within the emerging aspirational power bloc of the Third World, outside the direct influence of the two superpowers. The Pakistani state began forging diplomatic contacts with Arab and Central Asian nations in the 1950s.[17] Meanwhile, Indian officials in the 1950s were most excited about cultivating relations with China. K. M. Panikkar, India's first ambassador to China, spoke forcefully about what he termed the need for a new "regionalism," by which he meant the "recovery of Asia" as an interregional political bloc.[18] And India and Pakistan forged contacts with African countries, especially in the context of the Bandung movement. The two states had broken out of the orbit of British liberal empire, despite their formal membership in the Commonwealth, and the first two decades after independence were years of giddy exploration and experimentation in international politics.

In March 1947, the Asian Relations Conference met in New Delhi with representatives from more than thirty countries. Nehru followed this with the Inter-Asia Conference of 1949, which brought interregional Asian support to bear on the Indonesian freedom struggle. In May 1950, the emergence of an Asian bloc moved ahead with the Baguio Conference in the Philippines, which included the participation of India and Pakistan.[19] Between 1952 and 1955, various groups of Congress Party officials and National Planning Commission members, including Nehru and P. C. Mahalanobis, visited China both on diplomatic missions and study tour.[20] Meanwhile, an Institute of Asian African Relations was established in Calcutta in 1953.

In 1954, plans were put in place by Indonesia to hold an international conference of African, Arab, and Asian nations. The Panchsheel Agreement between India and China was signed in April 1954, controversially indicating India's recognition of China's claim over Tibet. And leaders of the "Colombo Powers," Indonesia, India, Pakistan, Burma, and Sri Lanka, met that same month in order to plan the Bandung Conference.[21] The inaugural

Bandung Asia–Africa conference convened in April 1955, bringing together twenty-nine countries across the southern hemisphere.[22]

From 1946 to 1965, the "spirit of Bandung" temporarily connected new nations across the global South.[23] The period came to an end with the rise of military conflict between erstwhile Bandung partners. The dialogues about "solidarity," "nonalignment," and "Third World nationalism" were not cohesive or adhesive enough to create sustainable diplomatic bonds across Asian state boundaries past the mid-1960s.[24] The increasing regional dominance of China, the Indo-China War of 1962, the Indo-Pakistan War of 1965, as well as the coincidental death of many of the main leaders of the Bandung Conference in these years, including Jawaharlal Nehru (1964), marked a shift in the prospects of Third World politics.[25] The direct American and Russian intervention in Asia, especially at the flashpoint of Vietnam, strained and antagonized broader inter-Asian relations.[26]

Still, in the age of decolonization, the transnational discourse of Marxism provided an alternative to the pursuit of global integration. Because of the Non-Aligned Movement and the rise of major Third World Marxist schools outside Cold War institutions, Third World Marxism served as an important mode for enchanting the world after 1947. Marxism from the South became one of the main sources of new intellectual authority among a young generation of the new Left in Europe and America pursuing social revolutions in the 1960s and 1970s.[27] The postcolonial nationalist Marxisms of Ghana, the Congo, India, Vietnam, Egypt, Cuba, Brazil, Argentina, and the Caribbean generated feedback loops in a post-Orientalist age. New forms of geopolitical entanglement and new waves of enchantment went together in the 1968 youth movements, for example.[28]

Manifestos of Third World Marxists sought to "delink" the Global South from the power blocs of the Global North. Akhil Gupta perceptively notes that the postcolonial irony of increasing dependence of Third World economies on northern powers, alongside heightened assertions of cultural autonomy, was often articulated in languages of Marxism. This created a new postcolonial predicament in which "underdevelopment [became] a form of identity in the postcolonial world."[29]

WEST GERMAN FUNDS, EAST GERMAN DIPLOMACY

After World War II, the first German Consulate General Offices were set up in Bombay in 1951, Delhi in 1952, Calcutta in 1954, and Madras in

1954. Plans for German companies, Krupp and Demag, to establish a steel plant in India emerged in 1953. The town of Rourkela was chosen as the site for the new plant.[30] Rourkela is located in the "iron belt" of India, and on the railway that connects Calcutta to Bombay. This was the era of the second five-year plan, overseen by P. C. Mahalanobis, in which the Nehru government sought to adjust its initial strategy, focused on agriculture, in order to develop heavy industries for India that would, in turn, produce the factors needed for building railroads and stimulating rapid industrialization.

Paul Zils, a German cinematographer, arrived in India in 1945, having worked at UFA in Berlin in the 1930s, and in Hollywood in the 1940s. Upon disembarking at Bombay, he was received by Lama Anagarika Govinda, a German Buddhist who had come to India in the 1930s.[31] The two men represented the encounter of two different eras, between the early twentieth-century era of popular Indic Orientalism in Germany and the midcentury era of West German First Worldism. In the last days of the British empire in India, Zils was hired by the Indian government to head the External Unit of Information Films of India. *India's Struggle for National Shipping* (1947), commissioned by Scindia's Steam Navigation Company, was Zils's first independent documentary. Zils combined advertising and documentary filmmaking, as he made a career of hiring his skills out to the firms or interest groups seeking to tell their story to an international audience. He played an important role in the development of Indian documentary film, as attested to by the Bombay journal he cofounded in 1955, *India Documentary*, along with colleagues Kamala Bhoota, F. R. Bilimoria, and others.[32]

In 1963, Zils made a documentary about the German-sponsored steel town in India—the "Ruhrgebiet of India" (the Ruhr valley).[33] The documentary, featuring scenes from the ore-separating, coke-smelting, and steel-finishing factories, depicted the message that both the Indian government and the West German firms wanted to send: West Germans were donating methods and technology so that Indians could develop themselves later on. Zils represented India as a nation of workers, producers, and productive technologies. His short documentaries also focused on the fishermen of Bombay, the tea-pickers in Darjeeling, and the textile industry.[34] In the immediate aftermath of World War II, West Germany was being reconstructed as a beacon of the normative West, and as a searchlight for modernization projects in the developing world.[35]

A plan was established for "mutual" collaboration between West Germany and India in economic matters, whereby Germany would give its expertise and its technology, and India would open up its vast market to German firms.[36] The order of transnational dialogue had changed. It was no longer the case that Germans and Indians were seeking to use each other's technology and philosophies to recenter the world around themselves. Those had been the terms of an earlier order of dialogic action structured by German popular Orientalism, on one hand, and Indian scientistic internationalism, on the other. Now, Germany offered India tools for global integration, while India offered Germans an "underdeveloped" terrain where their capital investments and cultural programs would associate West Germans increasingly with the West.

Popular Orientalism had died in West Germany, and Americanism took its place. Meanwhile, intellectual politics in India was no longer the project of insurgents against the colonial state, but of technocrats located within the postcolonial government. In 1959, a joint endeavor began between the government of India and the United Nations Special Fund, aimed to meet the shortage of trained industrial craftsmen, especially civil and mechanical draftsmen, electricians, mechanics, and sheet-metal workers. As part of this program, funds were set aside to send Indian students to Germany and Austria for technical education and science training. In addition, the Indian Institute of Technology, Madras, was founded in 1959 with West German funding and technical support. The German *Wirtschaftswunder* (economic miracle) made 1950s Germany into a magnet for students from Asia and Africa, just as German universities played a similar role in the 1920s. The German Developing Countries Foundation was established in Berlin in 1962, with the goal of giving visitors from the "developing world" the ability to study German industries for up to three months. It aimed at creating options for "international collaboration on German soil."[37] The *Wirtschaftswunder* also had the result that a number of German multinational companies expanded their interests in the Indian market.[38]

When West Germans did not establish firms, they donated technological culture. In 1941, the German Jewish architect Otto Königsberger, a nephew-in-law of Max Born, designed the modern city of Bhubaneswar.[39] Königsberger had a long-term interest in urban planning in India. He also contributed to the planning of the steel town of Bhadravati, and directed the design and construction of the New Town at Jamshedpur, an experiment in housing collectives for employees of the steel plant.[40] Of course, Chandigarh was designed and constructed in the 1950s by the French architect, Corbusier. German and other Western intellectual and cultural engagements with India in the 1950s and 1960s seemed stridently practical when compared with the kinds of pursuits in world enchantment from the interwar period.[41] Perhaps the cataclysm of World War II had a sobering effect on intellectual life in the postwar period. Certainly, Western geopolitical competition with the Soviet bloc under the threat of nuclear catastrophe added a degree of statist realism to West German involvements in India.

The kinds of dialogues that connected Germans and Indians took on a drastically transformed shape in the years after 1945. Germans and Indians no longer saw each other as bonded together in each other's projects to remake the world, and their cultural domains no longer fulfilled the role of outposts in each other's projects of knowledge production or identity formation. The kinds of transposition and cross-identification that marked German and Indian connections in the interwar years gave way to strict differentiation across the divide of the industrialized North versus Third World South. Discourses of post-Enlightenment gave way to discourses of modernization.

EAST GERMANY

Curiously, Indic Orientalism survived in East Germany in a much stronger way than in West Germany. In East Germany, the study of India served both to articulate geopolitical distinction and demonstrate the unique authority of Soviet-bloc scholarship and the Soviet worldview. If the Federal Republic of Germany followed a policy of development aid, under the aegis of American-centered internationalism, the DDR (Deutsche Demokratische Republik, or East Germany) eventually emerged as a leader in Soviet cultural diplomacy to the East. Nikita Khrushchev visited India in late 1955, the same year as the Bandung Conference. This inaugurated a phase of Soviet cultural diplomacy in India, and East German scholars played the major role in orchestrating the pursuit. From about 1957 onward, East Germany commenced a project of cultural diplomacy, leading to a "Day of the DDR" at the World Agricultural Exhibition in New Delhi in February 1960.[42]

A West German diplomat remarked at the time that the Eastern bloc was increasing its cultural offerings "like an unstoppable tide over India." In 1957, Mulk Raj Anand, C. B. Rao, Sajjad Zaheer, and Manoj Basu traveled to East Germany as members of a delegation to the Deutsche Akademie in Berlin. There they met Arnold Zweig, Bodo Uhse, and Günther

Deicke for an international summit of writers.[43] And in February 1960, a trade delegation from the DDR came to Calcutta. The East German presence in India was light on the ground—not marked by multinationals and development projects, but by cultural programs and conferencing.

Walter Ruben, Indologist at Berlin Humboldt University, became the most important DDR figure to develop cultural relations between East Germany and India. Ruben visited India in 1957, invited by the University of Delhi to deliver a series of lectures on Kalidasa and Samkhya philosophy. This same year, the DDR established an Indian–German Friendship Society in Nellore.[44] In December 1958 the society held the 135-year birth anniversary celebration for Max Müller, which commenced a cultural battle between East and West Germany to lay claim to the icon of German Indology in India. In 1960, West Germany renamed the Goethe Institutes for German language study in India as the Max Müller Bhavans, beating the DDR to the punch. Ruben wrote a dissertation on the Ramayana under Hermann Jacobi in 1926, and was greatly influenced by the African cultural anthropology of Leo Frobenius, with whom he also studied in Frankfurt. Ruben escaped to Turkey in 1935 and taught at Ankara University, then eventually went on to teach in Santiago, Chile, during the year of 1948–1949. In 1950 he chose to return to East Germany, where he served as the director of the Institute for Indian Studies at Humboldt University.

Ruben came to Marxism late, at age fifty-one, at Humboldt University. "I was [not] trained as a Marxist although I studied Marxism in 1952/54 as a student of the so-called Evening University of Marxism-Leninism," he recalled in a memoir.[45] The later Ruben was suspicious of Western spiritualists, whose interest in the Orient, he maintained, served to resolve inchoate and irrational compulsions. After return from exile, his writings were marked by a brilliant, if not maniacal, effort to reveal the dynamics of historical materialism at work in ancient and modern Indian cultural production. When he retired in 1965, he took up the work of summarizing "his knowledge about ancient India in five volumes," and the project took historical materialism as the overarching motivation from prehistory to the modern novel.[46] Walter Ruben sought to set the intellectual history of modern India within an economic frame of development, especially in terms of the rise of the Indian *Bürgertum* from 1885 to 1947.[47]

Characteristic of Ruben's approach was the focus on Rabindranath Tagore's importance for the historical development of Indian modernism. The DDR set up a festival to celebrate the poet's 100th birth anniversary.[48]

Ruben contrasted the East German approach to understanding Rabindranath to that of West Germany. The West presented Rabindranath Tagore as a spiritual sage, he maintained. The view from the Eastern bloc, with Berlin as the authoritative cultural observatory onto India, saw Rabindranath instead as a radical social thinker on questions of inequality.

Rabindranath, in Ruben's appraisal, was not significant because he shed light on the soul, nor because he presented Eastern spirituality. Rather Rabindranath perfected a new kind of cultural resistance to capitalism that ran through the whole Bengal renaissance and culminated in the nationalist movement. "One of the fundamental Vedantic concepts is 'truth.' In India this is not just a question of epistemology, but also a moral category," Ruben wrote.[49] Ruben carried out radical scholarship in a Marxist key, and sought to uncover a hidden world vision of global social equity at the heart of Indian nationalism.

In Ruben's view, Rabindranath fit into a triumvirate of "truth speakers" that included Vivekananda and Gandhi. Vivekananda, Rabindranath, and Gandhi all called for an anti-ascetic "affirmation of life [*Lebensbejahung*]." Gandhi's work, he argued, contributed to the anticolonial movements in Africa and Latin America, and set an example for the young nation-states.[50] Rabindranath recognized, however, the will to "progress" *(Fortschritt)* for the people. Because Rabindranath remained an active poet, and because he recognized the imperatives of socioeconomic development along with "truth speaking," he was truly world-historical, Ruben asseverated.

Ruben insisted that only Soviet perspectives could reveal the truth about Rabindranath Tagore's artistic creativity. Ruben continually reflected on the DDR's Indology and its different approach from the Orientalism of the Western scholars. "Among us there is no propagation of Yoga and other neo-Buddhist, theosophist or other sect liberators, as in the BRD [Bundesrepublik Deutschland]."[51] Meanwhile, West German Indologists expressed concern over East Germany's strength in Indological Studies, especially because Indology in the East seemed to have more visibility and general prestige than in the Federal Republic.[52]

Where the DDR could not invest resources into India, the regime did support some of the more fascinating scholarly research on the history of Indian society in the 1950s and 1960s. Ruben began a project on contemporary Indian novels written in English. By the late 1950s, his interest focused as much on ancient texts as on exploring forms of Indian modernism.[53] The Calcutta economist and social theorist, Radhakamal Mukherjee, came as guest professor for four years, 1953 to 1957, to Humboldt University in Berlin upon Ruben's invitation. And the collaboration between Ruben and Mukherjee created, in Ruben's words, the "foundation of the study of Modern India in Berlin."[54]

Ruben cultivated friendships with some of the most important Marxist historians of South Asia of the time. His longest and most intimate correspondence was with Debiprasad Chattopadhyaya, author of *Loyakata* (1959), a brilliant Bengali Marxist historian of science and a psychoanalyst who trained with Girindrasekhar Bose. In addition, D. D. Kosambi and Romila Thapar had extensive letter exchanges with Walter Ruben on materialist approaches to ancient Indian history.[55]

Orientalism remained strong in the DDR. In the West, Indic Orientalism receded into university precincts where it thrived, while the broad pathways into popular culture and state planning were largely shut down. For West Germans, the ideology of transatlantic integration and of Germany's European identity became de rigueur. There was no institutional or imaginary space to deploy ideas about mythic, spiritual, or linguistic origins as evidence of either the distinctiveness of Germanic science or the geopolitical destiny of German blood.

One might say that "the Germanic" was killed off in both West and East Germany after World War II. Indic Orientalism of the pre-1945 variety had defined Germanness in terms of positive identification with the Indic Orient, and opposition to other civilizational categories, such as the Anglo-Saxon, the Western, the Latinate, the Jewish, or the Christian. German ideas were perceived by British and American commentators as inherently dangerous. E. M. Butler asserted, in *The Tyranny of Greece over Germany* (1958), "the Germans are unique perhaps in the ardor with which they pursue ideas and attempt to transform them into realities. Their great achievements, their catastrophic failures, their tragic political history are all impregnated with this idealism."[56] After 1945, Germandom and Mitteleuropa became (and still are) bad words. As its oppositional identity with regards to Western norms died away, so too did "India" disappear as a focal concept in the German imagination.

Carl Schmitt perhaps represented best the intellectual tradition of the old German conservatives in the aftermath of World War II. He diagnosed the underlying concerns that had preoccupied the German nationalists at midcentury, and he boiled them down to the search for an underdog politics that could mitigate the feeling of subordination vis-à-vis normative western European force.[57] Looking back at Germany's career from its establishment in 1871 to World War II, Schmitt drew the comparison between Germans and the strapping figure of "the partisan," the practitioner of guerrilla warfare. Germany had been a partisan empire, he proposed, seeking to redress power relations in the world, just as guerrilla warriors had done within nation-state contexts over the course of the nineteenth and twentieth centuries. Schmitt pointed to Mao Zedong, Ho Chi Minh, and Che Guevara as the present-day inheritors of geopolitical radicalism that German Europe had once shared in.[58]

Indians, Pakistanis, and Bangladeshis also looked back at their forebears in the nineteenth and early twentieth centuries as partisans of the earth—rebels not just against one specific colonial power, but against what Britain's power signified more generally. The British empire over the course of the nineteenth and twentieth centuries, perhaps all the way up to the Suez Crisis, stood in for an interlocking Western universalism based on unifying ideals of Enlightenment and Empire, and centered around northwestern Europe. This was one kind of universalism from which the partisans of the earth, including German-speakers during a period in their history, wished to secede.

Epilogue

This book has argued that what people think must be seen in the context of whom they talk to, and the political interests that inform their talk. Political groups, despite their obvious alienating differences and power differentials, and despite immense material differences, will talk with each other *when they need help.* And the underlying subject matter of such transnational talk, in the particular historical age of interest here, 1880–1945, was the aim to reenvision the world order and enchant the world in ways that surpassed the nineteenth-century ideals of a "Concert of Europe" and Enlightenment Empire. Buried in these entanglements is the rebellion of a fledgling twentieth century against a nineteenth-century incumbency, and of regional interests against the self-reflecting satisfactions of a nineteenth-century British global hegemon.

Scientific and scholarly projects of enchantment in post-Enlightenment counterscience provided intellectual sources of soft power on the international scene. This book has studied diplomats and envoys active in worldwide intellectual relations. These individuals were often only a small step away from the overt concerns of international relations and power politics. An age of geopolitical entanglement and instability—a great international disorder—came to an end in 1945, followed by the Cold War reorganization that "normalized" the world into three geopolitical spheres, the Western, the Soviet, and the Third World.

In the specific age of entanglement from the 1880s onward, circuits of post-Enlightenment thought placed intellectuals situated across the colonial divide, in Europe and Asia, on the same wavelength, in ways that transgressed the spatial logic of Empire. The dual disintegration of the ideal of Europe and the ideal of Empire came to a head with German and Indian intellectual attacks on the position of the British empire as the totem of Western universalism. The struggle against Anglocentrist structures and symbols of world order was articulated from multiple positions, and this intensified the entanglements between the two groups. Indians sought to use the soft power of German science in intellectual pursuits against the British empire. Germans sought to use the soft power of Indian intellectual production in their rebellion against a European ideal in which the northwestern "Core" would continue its hegemony. In a word, in the transition to a twentieth-century world, it was the joint rebellion of Germans and Indians against the legacies of the nineteenth century that unified them and coordinated their activities for an extended span of time.

As geopolitical alignments changed during the catastrophic period of World War II, so too did patterns of transnational entanglement. Indians, Pakistanis, and soon Bangladeshis began speaking to other national communities in Asia and Africa as "Third World" compatriots. South Asians began addressing Germans in the mode of underdeveloped peoples receiving donations from industrially advanced "Westerners." The entangled projects of enchanting scholarship that characterized the late nineteenth and early twentieth centuries—focused on disclosing hidden worlds of natural energy, commerce, labor, culture, psyche, and artistic and dramatic expression as a means to interrupt power—came to an end. Intellectual, scholarly, and artistic institutions were increasingly absorbed into superpower blocs. Meanwhile, the rise of cultural history and Area Studies programs in the West helped stabilize the world order by highlighting "multiculturalism" as a feature of new normative Western universalism.

To frame the modern interactions between Asia and Europe within a center–periphery framework, in terms of European colonialism and Asian resistance, is to make a Cold War outcome stand in for an unpredictable late nineteenth- and early twentieth-century process. As theorists of interregional and transnational studies point out, the practice of taking sideways glances toward the constellations that transgress the colonial duality is the best way to disrupt the hemispheric myth that the globe was congenitally divided into an East and West (or North and South)—even in the modern period—and that ideas were exchanged across that fault line alone.[1] For a fateful short century from about 1880 to the end of World War II, German historical processes actually had more in common with

Asian history than we would suspect on first view. Germans and Indians, in their entanglement, expressed a heightened family relation of alliances across Empire aimed at destroying the nineteenth-century geopolitical status quo. This book has focused on the middle ground, and the blurring of Asian and European identities that arose when the nineteenth-century world order fell apart, and Europe-centered Enlightenment idealism went with it.

When we focus on the constellations of dialogic interdependence, not on monoliths of discourse, we are able to see how intellectual production, texts and media, disciplinary institutions and personal histories, often artificially sequestered from each other across national or neocivilizational divides, are in fact co-constituting, and implicated together in the struggle for new power on earth. Grasping that dimension of interconnection emboldens us to re-think periodization and our understanding of intellectual history within interregional frameworks. If a period of intellectual entanglement arose with the 1880s and reached a crescendo during the interwar years, then we are in need of new archival and theoretical work that can help us better conceive of the transnational era of creativity and wreckage, 1880–1945.

The Age of Entanglement reached back to the early nineteenth century and spanned 150 years of partnerships and splits between Germans and Indians put into array by the waning global power of the British empire in order to reveal dynamics that challenge conceptions of neat regional, national, and geopolitical divides. The study of historical entanglement exposes the connective tissue of transnational relations in nineteenth- and twentieth-century history.[2]

In the very project to build autonomy and distinction, groups continually mixed themselves up in the projects and the histories of others. German history is entangled with other people's histories and other people's interests. South Asian history is entangled with other people's histories too. The twentieth century produced complicated affairs, driven by the imperatives of presumed political needs. The Manichaean universe of black versus white, Self versus Other, German versus Jew, Asian versus European, and of high-contrast notions of "alterity" cannot do justice to the gradients of otherness and the spectrum of strange identifications that arose when alien groups started to feel the need to *need* each other in specific ways on a section of common ground, for a certain period of time.

Making sense of history in terms of entanglements also gives us perspective on our twenty-first century in which impermeable boundaries again seem increasingly less salient than the reterritorializing and reenchanting flows stimulated by global migrations and by the spread of digital media. In an age, after 2001, in which the attempts by the United States of America to establish itself securely at the center of a unipolar twenty-first-century world order have failed, and in which what was supposed to be an "American Century" has quickly begun to look like a century of rearrangement and redistribution of world power, of multipolarity and geopolitical competition, a Manichaean view of history will hardly do.

Selfhood and otherness are knotted things. The patterns of alliance building, intellectual creativity, and political connivance described in this book—patterns of entanglement—speak directly to our time.[3] More than a fortifying tale of finding common ground, however, the previous age of entanglement, 1880–1945, provides us with a sober reminder of the way attempts to overcome the monster of one hegemony can all too often give birth to new monstrosities. The enormity of the struggle for new universalisms, or more accurately, the efforts by particular power groups—be they white, brown, black, male, female—to stand out in the world and harness the intellectual authority to speak for new universalisms, continues to be the great inner demon that we all face, and with which we continue to reckon.

Notes

INTRODUCTION

1. Intellectual institutions, according to Thorstein Veblen, are "habits of mind" that predominate among the powerful fraction of society, and that perpetuate a coherence of tastes and values across generations associated with that power group. See *The Theory of the Leisure Class* (London: Macmillan, 1899), 116. Dietrich Rueschemeyer and Theda Skocpol locate intellectual institutions within the state apparatus as sources of "social knowledge" that establish parameters and semantics for crafting policy. See Rueschemeyer and Skocpol, eds., *States, Social Knowledge, and the Origins of Modern Social Policies* (Princeton, NJ: Princeton University Press, 1996), 5. C. A. Bayly draws on these sociological definitions, as well as the communication theory of Karl Deutsch, to trace the role of British intellectual institutions in the establishment of colonial rule in India, in *Empire and Information* (Cambridge: Cambridge University Press, 1996).

2. Regina Höfer, ed., *Imperial Sightseeing: Archduke Ferdinand of Austria-Este's Journey to India* (Vienna: Museum für Völkerkunde, 2010), 1.

3. Ferdinand Schrey, *Die Reise des deutschen Kronprinzen nach dem fernen Osten* (Berlin, G. Stilke, 1912); Paul Rohrbach, *Der deutsche Gedanke in der Welt* (Düsseldorf: Langewiesche, 1912), 123–148; on political theater in the Kaiserreich, see David Blackbourn, "Politics as Theater" in *Populists and Patricians* (London: Allen and Unwin, 1987), 246–261.

4. Asutosh Mukherjee, *University Convocation* (Calcutta: University of Calcutta, 1910), 130.

5. Paul Natorp, *Stunden mit Rabindranath Thakkur* (Jena: Eugen Diederichs, 1921), 25; see Letter of Helene Natorp to Rabindranath Tagore (1924) collected by Martin Kämpchen in *Rabindranath Tagore and Germany: A Documentation,* trans. S. V. Raman and Martin Kämpchen, ed. Jeanne Openshaw (Calcutta: Max Mueller Bhavan, 1991), 84.

6. I borrow from established work on "entanglement" and "crossed histories," but draw key distinctions with this corpus by focusing on alliance building by subordinated regional elites against global hegemons. See Marc Espagne and Michael Werner, eds., *Transferts: les relations interculturelles dans l'espace franco-allemand* (Paris: Editions Recherche sur les civilisations, 1988); Michael Werner and Bénédicte Zimmermann, "Beyond Comparison: Histoire Croisée and the Challenge of Reflexivity," *History and Theory* 45 (2006): 30–50; Gerhard Haupt and Jürgen Kocka, eds., *Geschichte und Vergleich* (Frankfurt: Campus, 1996).

7. C. A. Bayly, *Imperial Meridian: The British Empire and the World, 1780–1830* (London: Longman, 1989), 191–196; Linda Colley, *Britons: Forging the Nation, 1707–1837* (New Haven, CT: Yale University Press, 1992), 321–324, 363; Maya Jasanoff, *Edge of Empire: Lives, Culture, and Conquest in the East, 1750–1850* (New York: Knopf, 2005), 320.

8. See Ann Laura Stoler's seminal work on racialization and empire, *Carnal Knowledge and Imperial Power: Race and the Intimate in Colonial Rule* (Berkeley: University of California Press, 2002). A number of recent works have explored comparative racialization in regimes of empire. See Harald Fischer-Tiné, *Low and Licentious Europeans: Race, Class, and "White Subalternity" in Colonial India* (Delhi: Orient Black Swan, 2009); Satoshi Mizutani, *The Meaning of White: Race, Class, and the "Domiciled Community" in British India 1858–1930* (New York: Oxford University Press, 2011).

9. Gentlemanly capitalists are discussed by Anthony Hopkins and P. J. Cain, *British Imperialism: 1688–2000* (London: Longman, 2002), 177; Ian Clark, *Hegemony in International Society* (Oxford: Oxford University Press, 2011), 109; Pascale Casanova explores the global preeminence of French elite culture in the modern period, *The World Republic of Letters* (Cambridge, MA: Harvard University Press, 2004), 9. Also see Immanuel Wallerstein on the "core" of Northwestern Europe in his world-system analysis, *The Modern World-System,* vol. 2 (New York: Academic Press, 1974), 36.

10. Derek Howse, *Greenwich Time and the Discovery of the Longitude* (Oxford: Oxford University Press, 1980), 152–172; Ian Bartky, *One Time Fits All* (Stanford, CA: Stanford University Press, 2007), 82.

11. Paul Kennedy, "The Costs and Benefits of British Imperialism 1846–1914," *Past and Present* 125 (1989): 186–192.

12. Michael Adas, *"High" Imperialism and the "New" Imperial History* (Washington, DC: American Historical Association, 1993).

13. On "Islamic Universalism," see Ayesha Jalal, *Partisans of Allah* (Cambridge, MA: Harvard University Press, 2008), 179–191; on "Asian Universalism," see Sugata Bose, *A Hundred Horizons* (Cambridge, MA: Harvard University Press, 2006), 233.

14. Alfred Eckhard Zimmern, *The Third British Empire* (London: Humphrey Milford, 1926), 1; HUA File 2199/93. rectorat.

15. James Joll, "Liberalism and Its Enemies," in *Europe since 1870* (New York: Harper and Row, 1973), 133–150; Richard Langhorne, *The Collapse of the Concert of Europe* (Basingstoke, UK: Macmillan, 1981), 8–55; Norbert Elias, *The Germans* (New York: Columbia University Press, 1996), 162.

16. Charles Maier, "Consigning the Twentieth Century to History: Alternative Narratives for the Modern Era," *American Historical Review* 105 (2000): 807–831; David Blackbourn and Geoffrey Eley, *The Peculiarities of German History* (Oxford: Oxford University Press, 1984), 1–38.

17. Sukanya Banerjee, *Becoming Imperial Citizens* (Durham, NC: Duke University Press, 2010), 193; Daniel Gorman, *Imperial Citizenship* (Manchester: Manchester University Press, 2006), 205–215.

18. On transnational intellectual history, see Sugata Bose and Kris Manjapra, *Cosmopolitan Thought Zones* (Houndmills, UK: Palgrave Macmillan, 2010); Sebastian Conrad and Dominic Sachsenmaier, *Competing Visions of World Order* (New York: Palgrave), 1–28.

19. This might be generally portrayed as the tension between the approach of Edward Said in *Orientalism* (New York: Pantheon, 1978), versus that of Wilhelm Halbfass in *India and Europe: An Essay in Understanding* (Albany: State University of New York, 1988). Cambridge school historiography and subaltern school historiography have reprised this historiographic debate.

20. There is a rich and growing literature on German cultural representations of Asia, especially of India. The classic work by Leslie Willson, *A Mythical Image: The Idea of India in German Romanticism* (Durham: Duke, 1964), has stimulated many important refinements and elaborations. For an overview, see Jörg Esleben, Christina Kraenzle, and Sukanya Kulkarni, eds., *Mapping Channels between Ganges and Rhein* (Newcastle, UK: Cambridge Scholars Publishing, 2008).

21. See an important theoretical contribution in such a new approach in Jürgen Kocka, ed., *Comparative and Transnational History* (New York: Berghahn Books, 2009); and works by Andrew Zimmerman, *Alabama in Africa: Booker T. Washington, the German Empire, and the Globalization of the New South* (Princeton, NJ: Princeton University Press, 2010) and Susan Pennybacker, *From Scottsboro to Munich: Race and Political*

Culture in 1930s Britain (Princeton, NJ: Princeton University Press, 2009). For the classic example of intercultural studies, see Halbfass, *India and Europe*. A vast amount of new work is emerging in a new vein, emphasizing the political dimension of encounter. See Cemil Aydin, *The Politics of Anti-Westernism in Asia* (New York: Columbia University Press, 2007).

22. Partha Chatterjee discusses the "moment of departure" of Bengali nationalist thought during what he astutely identifies as the "post-Enlightenment" period of the late nineteenth century. See *Nationalist Thought and the Colonial World* (Minneapolis: University of Minnesota Press, 1986), 14–17, 58.

23. See Partha Chatterjee's argument, *Lineages of Political Society* (New York: Columbia University Press, 2011), 82–93.

24. In contrast to the dualism inherent in Edward Said's *Orientalism*, the fractional approach of Partha Chatterjee's *Lineages of Political Society* provides inspiration for my analysis.

25. Mikhail Bakhtin, *The Dialogic Imagination* (Austin: University of Texas Press, 1981), 259–422; on "dialogic engagement," see John Kelly and Martha Kaplan, *Represented Communities* (Chicago: University of Chicago Press, 2001), 6–9. Lydia Liu's notion of "translingual practice" is particularly germane to the following discussion. See *Translingual Practice: Literature, National Culture, and Translated Modernity—China 1900–1937* (Stanford, CA: Stanford University Press, 1995), 25. See the insightful discussion of *langue* and *parole* as it bears on the study of globalization 1850–1920 in T. N. Harper, "Empire, Diaspora and the Languages of Globalism, 1850–1914," in *Globalization in World History*, ed. A. G. Hopkins (New York: Norton, 2002), 155.

26. Emma Rothschild, *The Inner Life of Empire: An Eighteenth-Century History* (Princeton, NJ: Princeton University Press, 2011), 210.

27. Sebastian Conrad, "Enlightenment in Global History: A Historiographical Critique," *American Historical Review* 117 (2012): 999–1027.

28. Isaiah Berlin, *Vico and Herder: Two Studies in the History of Ideas* (London: Chatto and Windus, 1976), xxvi, xxviii.

29. David Lindenfeld, *The Transformation of Positivism* (Berkeley: University of California Press, 1980), 77–88; Anne Harrington, *Reenchanted Science* (Cambridge, MA: Harvard University Press, 1997), 23–30; Suzanne Marchand, *German Orientalism in the Age of Empire* (New York: Cambridge University Press, 2010), 4; Martin Jay, *Marxism and Totality* (Berkeley: University of California Press, 1984), 150, 174.

30. Michel Foucault, *The Order of Things* (New York: Pantheon, 1970), 379–381.

31. Ibid., 381.

32. Lindenfeld, *Transformation of Positivism*, 5–7.

33. Hans-Georg Gadamer, *Philosophische Lehrjahre* (Frankfurt: Vittorio Klostermann, 1977), 17.

34. For Anne Harrington's celebrated application of Max Weber's thesis, see *Reenchanted Science*, 29; Pierre Duhem, *German Science* (La Salle, IL: Open Court, 1991; orig. 1915); Daniel Rodgers, *Atlantic Crossings: Social Politics in a Progressive Age* (Cambridge, MA: Belknap Press of Harvard University Press, 1998), 367; Victoria de Grazia, *Irresistible Empire* (Cambridge, MA: Belknap Press of Harvard University Press, 2005), 159.

35. Theodor Adorno and Max Horkheimer, *Dialectic of the Enlightenment* (New York: Seabury, 1972; orig. 1944); Bruno Latour, *We Have Never Been Modern* (New York: Harvester Wheatsheaf, 1993).

36. The phenomenon of a "Tagore Circle," with a distinctive intellectual character, has already been perceptively observed by Mark Ravinder Frost, "The Great Ocean of Idealism: Calcutta, the Tagore Circle, and the Idea of Asia, 1900–1920," in Shanti Moorthy and Ashraf Jamal, *Indian Ocean Studies* (New York: Routledge, 2010), 251–279.

37. See Sumit Sarkar on "constructive Swadeshi," in *Swadeshi Movement* (New Delhi: People's Publishing House, 1973), 40.

1. GERMAN SERVANTS OF THE BRITISH RAJ

1. Vasant Kaiwar, "The Aryan Model of History and the Oriental Renaissance," in Vasant Kaiwar and Sucheta Mazumdar, *Antinomies of Modernity* (Durham, NC: Duke University Press, 2003), 31.

2. Susanne Zantop, *Colonial Fantasies* (Durham, NC: Duke University Press, 1997), 17–30.

3. Partha Chatterjee, *Arms, Alliances, and Stability* (New York: Wiley, 1975), 20.

4. L. C. B. Seaman, *From Vienna to Versailles* (New York: Harper & Row, 1963); Adam Zamoyski, *Rites of Peace: The Fall of Napoleon and the Congress of Vienna* (London: Harper Press, 2008).

5. On the crescendo of the 1830s and 1840s, see C. A. Bayly, *Imperial Meridian: The British Empire and the World, 1780–1830* (London: Longman, 1989), 1–25; Dieter Langewiesche, *Liberalismus in Deutschland* (Frankfurt am Main: Suhrkamp, 1988), 164–179; Langewiesche, *Nation, Nationalismus, Nationstaat* (Munich: Beck, 2000); Brian Vick, *Defining Germany: The 1848 Frankfurt Parliamentarians and National Identity* (Cambridge, MA: Harvard University Press, 2002).

6. Heinrich Heine, *Deutschland, a Winter's Tale*, originally published in 1844, trans. T. J. Reed (London: Angel Books, 1986), 45.

7. Johannes Fabian, *Time and the Other: How Anthropology Makes Its Object* (New York: Columbia University Press, 1983), 25, 31.

8. Friedrich Nietzsche, "What the German Lack," in *Twilight of the Idols*, originally published in 1895, trans. R. J. Hollingdale (Harmondsworth, UK: Penguin, 1968), 60.

9. Russell Berman, *Enlightenment or Empire* (Lincoln: University of Nebraska Press, 1998).

10. Michael Maurer, *Aufklärung und Anglophilie in Deutschland* (London: DHI, 1987), 370.

11. Berman, *Enlightenment or Empire*, 21–64.

12. Walter Mignolo, *Local Histories/Global Designs: Coloniality, Subaltern Knowledges, and Border Thinking* (Princeton, NJ: Princeton University Press, 2000), 51–60; Felix Driver, *Geography Militant: Cultures of Exploration and Empire* (Oxford: Blackwell, 2001), 26.

13. Maurer, *Anglophilie*, 253–291; Bayly, *Imperial Meridian*; Linda Colley, *Britons: Forging the Nation, 1707–1837* (New Haven, CT: Yale University Press, 1992), 147–194; Jörg Esleben, "'Indisch lesen': Conceptions of Intercultural Communication in Georg Forster's and Johann Gottfried Herder's Reception of Kalidasa's 'Sakuntala,'" *Monatshefte* 95 (2003): 217–229.

14. Maurer, *Anglophilie*, 50.

15. Maiken Umbach, "Visual Culture, Scientific Images and German Small-State Politics in Late Enlightenment," *Past and Present* 158 (1998): 110–145.

16. P. J. Marshall, *Bengal: The British Bridgehead* (Cambridge: Cambridge University Press, 1987), 26, 93.

17. George Sarton, "Anquetil-Dupperon (1731–1805)," *Osiris* 3 (1937): 193–223.

18. P. J. Marshall, *The British Discovery of Hinduism in the Eighteenth Century* (Cambridge: Cambridge University Press, 1970), 15–17.

19. Bradley Herling, *The German Gita* (New York: Routledge, 2006), 92.

20. Philip Stern, *The Company-State: Corporate Sovereignty and the Early Modern Foundation of the British Empire in India* (Oxford: Oxford University Press, 2011), 207.

21. Chen Tzoref-Ashkenazi, "India and the Identity of Europe: The Case of Friedrich Schlegel," *Journal of the History of Ideas* 67 (2006): 713–734. This is the classic theme of Edward Said, *Orientalism* (New York: Pantheon, 1978), and it applies in the German case to German relations with British imperial infrastructures.

22. Such was the claim of Josef Görres, the Catholic theological and nationalist scholar at Heidelberg in 1810, *Mythengeschichte der asiatischen Welt*

(Heidelberg: Mohr und Zimmer, 1810); Görres made the claim that archetypal mythic forms traveled from East to West, and that Western myths were derivative of Eastern originals. For a powerful argument advanced by Sheldon Pollock about the political interests of German *Wissenschaft,* see "Deep Orientalism: Notes on Sanskrit and Power Beyond the Raj," in *Orientalism and the Postcolonial Predicament,* ed. Carol Breckenridge and Peter van der Veer (Philadelphia: University of Pennsylvania Press, 1993), 76–133; Kamakshi Murti, *India: The Seductive and Seduced "Other" of German Orientalism* (Westport, CT: Greenwood, 2000), 11–33.

23. Frank Korom, "Of Navels and Mountains," *Asian Folklore Studies* 51 (1992): 103–125.

24. Michael Franklin, *Orientalist Jones* (Oxford: Oxford University Press, 2011), 38–42.

25. Friedrich Creuzer, *Symbolik und Mythologie der alten Völker* (Leipzig: Leske, 1810); Creuzer, *Aus dem Leben eines alten Professors* (Leipzig: Leske, 1840).

26. Friedrich Creuzer, *Religions de l'Antiquité,* vol. 1, trans. J. D. Guigniaut (Paris: Treuttel et Würtz, 1825), 132; George Williamson, *Longing for Myth* (Chicago: University of Chicago Press, 2004), 121–150.

27. Creuzer, *Religions de l'Antiquité,* 435; Williamson, *Longing for Myth,* 127.

28. See Suzanne Marchand's brilliant discussion of comparativism versus diffusionism, as well as the longer European legacy of the comparativist ethos in heremetic philosophy, *German Orientalism in the Age of Empire* (New York: Cambridge University Press, 2010), xxv, 62–66; Wilhelm Halbfass, "India and the Comparative Method," *Philosophy East and West* 35 (1985): 3–15.

29. This brilliant interpretation is offered by Louis Miller, "The Revelation of Genius," PhD diss., Princeton University, 1992, 119.

30. Heine, *Deutschland, a Winter's Tale,* 45. "The French and Russians have shared out the land,/Britannia rules the oceans,/we reign unchallenged in the realm/of abstract notions."

31. Niall Ferguson, *Empire: How Britain Made the Modern World* (New York: Penguin, 2004), 184.

32. See classic essays by Bernard Cohn, *An Anthropologist among the Historians and Other Essays* (Delhi: Oxford University Press, 1987), 224–254; 632–679.

33. S. N. Mukerji, *History of Education in India* (Delhi: Acharya Books, 1966), 65–67.

34. Morris Berman, "'Hegemony' and the Amateur Tradition in British Science," *Journal of Social History* 8 (1975): 30–50; Donald Clay Johnson,

"German Influences on the Development of Research Libraries in Nineteenth-Century Bombay," *Journal of Library History* 21 (1986): 215–227.

35. Lewis Pyenson, *Cultural Imperialism and Exact Sciences* (New York: Lang, 1985), 14–17; Dirk van Laak, *Imperiale Infrastruktur: Deutsche Planungen fuur eine Erschliessung Afrikas 1880 bis 1960* (Paderborn, Germany: Schöningh, 2004), 67–76.

36. Michel Foucault, *The Order of Things* (New York: Pantheon, 1970), 289–294; Tuska Benes, *In Babel's Shadow: Language, Philology, and the Nation in Nineteenth-Century Germany* (Detroit: Wayne State University Press, 2008), 76–95.

37. Salomon Lefmann, *Franz Bopp: Sein Leben und seine Wissenschaft*, vol. 1 (Berlin: Reimer, 1891).

38. A partial list of German-speakers, many who studied with Bopp (1791–1867), and who worked, even if temporarily, as librarians or assistants in British Orientalist libraries and institutions includes: Michael Solomon Alexander (1799–1845), Albrecht Hoefer (1812–1883), Aloys Sprenger (1813–1893), Theodor Goldstücker (1821–1872), Theodor Aufrecht (1821–1907), Ernst Reinhold Rost (1822–1896), Max Müller (1823–1900), Martin Haug (1827–1876), Ernst Trumpp (1828–1885), Gustav Oppert (1836–1908), Georg Bühler (1837–1898), Augustus Rudolf Hoernle (1841–1918), Carl Cappeller (1842–1925), Georg Thibault (1848–1914), Rudolf Hoernes (1850–1912), Hermann Jacobi (1850–1937), Eugen Hultzsch (1857–1927). See partial information on the theme in Valentina Stache-Rosen, *German Indologists: Biographies of Scholars in Indian Studies Writing in Germany* (Delhi: Max Müller Bhavan, 1981).

39. Rosane Rocher, "Sanskrit for Civil Servants 1806–1818," *Journal of the American Oriental Society* 122 (2002): 130.

40. Herman W. Tull, "F. Max Mueller and A. B. Keith: 'Twaddle,' and 'Stupid' Myth, and the Disease of Indology," *Numen* 28 (1991): 30.

41. Max Müller, *Chips from a German Workshop* (London: Longmans, 1867), 390–391.

42. Murti, *Seductive and Seduced "Other,"* 37.

43. Paola Palladino and Michael Worboys, "Science and Imperialism," *Isis* 84 (1993): 91–102.

44. Johnson, "German Influences." Lorenz Franz Kielhorn went to India in 1866 as a member of the Educational Department of Bombay Presidency after completing his dissertation under Adolf Stenzler at Breslau, and served as assistant to Monier-Williams at Oxford.

45. Ikram Chaghtai, ed., "Introduction," *Austrian Scholarship in Pakistan* (Islamabad: PanGraphics, 1997), 15; Nina Berman, *German Literature of the Middle East* (Ann Arbor: University of Michigan Press, 2011), 154–167.

46. "A. F. Rudolf Hoernle," *English Historical Review* 26 (1911): 795–796.

47. "Heinrich Ferdinand Blochmann," *Encyclopaedia Iranica,* http://www.iranicaonline.org/articles/blochmann-heinrich-henry/.

48. He was born at Secundra, near Agra. G. A. Grierson, "Augustus Frederic Rudolf Hoernle," *Journal of the Royal Asiatic Society of Great Britain and Ireland* 51 (1919): 119; "English Citizen" was inscribed on Aurel Stein's tombstone, at his behest. See Karl Meyer and Sharleen Blair Brysac, *Tournament of Shadows: The Great Game and Race for Empire in Central Asia* (Washington, DC: Counterpoint, 1999), 393.

49. C. A. Bayly, *Empire and Information* (Cambridge: Cambridge University Press, 1996), 142–179.

50. Max Müller, *Auld Lange Syne* (New York: Scribner's, 1898), 95.

51. Douglas McGetchin, *Indology, Indomania, and Orientalism* (Madison, NJ: Fairleigh Dickinson University Press, 2009), 107.

52. Moriz Winternitz, *Georg Bühler und die Indologie* (Munich: n.p., 1898), 22.

53. Georg Bühler, *Report on Sanskrit MSS 1874–75*, British Library.

54. Julius Jolly, *Georg Bühler, 1837–1898* (Strassburg: Trübner, 1899).

55. Johnson, "German Influences," 217.

56. Winternitz, *Bühler,* 55.

57. Johnson, "German Influences," 222; Indra Sengupta, *From Salon to Discipline* (Würzburg: Ergon, 2005), 136.

58. Sengupta, *From Salon to Discipline,* 113; Winternitz, *Bühler,* 19.

59. Adolphe, Robert, and Hermann Schlagintweit, *Results of a Scientific Mission to India and High Asia, Undertaken between the Years 1854 and 1858* (Leipzig: Brockhaus, 1863), x.

60. Kapil Raj, "When Human Travellers become Instruments," in *Relocating Modern Science* (Houndmills, UK: Palgrave Macmillan, 2007), 181–222.

61. Alexander von Humboldt, *Central-Asien: Untersuchungen* (Leipzig: Brockhaus, 1863), 203. Gordon T. Stewart, *Journeys to Empire: Enlightenment, Imperialism and the British Encounter with Tibet, 1774–1904* (Cambridge: Cambridge University Press, 2009), 245.

62. Schlagintweit, *Mission to India,* i.

63. Jürgen Osterhammel, "Alexander von Humboldt: Historiker der Gesellschaft, Historiker der Natur," *Archiv für Kulturgeschichte* 81 (1999): 105–131; Oliver Lubrich, "Alexander von Humboldt: Revolutionizing Travel Literature," *Monatshefte* 96 (2004): 360–387; David Arnold, *Science, Technology and Medicine* (Cambridge: Cambridge University Press, 2000), 24.

64. Jeannette Mirsky, *Sir Aurel Stein, Archaeological Explorer* (Chicago: University of Chicago Press, 1977), 22.

65. Annabel Walker, *Aurel Stein: Pioneer of the Silk Road* (London: John Murray, 1995), 19.

66. Frank Iklé, "Sir Aurel Stein. A Victorian Geographer in the Tracks of Alexander," *Isis* 59 (1968): 145.

67. S. N. Pandita, *Aurel Stein in Kashmir: The Sanskritist of Mohand Marg* (Delhi: Om, 2004).

68. Aurel Stein, *Serindia: Detailed Report on Explorations in Central Asia* (Oxford: Clarendon Press, 1921).

69. Iklé, "Sir Aurel Stein," 150.

70. Aurel Stein, *Innermost Asia: Its Geography as a Factor in History* (London: Royal Geographical Society, 1925), 495.

71. Aurel Stein, *Limes Report,* ed. Shelagh Gregory and Julie Kennedy (Oxford: British Archaeological Reports, 1985); Meyer and Brysac, *Tournament of Shadows,* 392–393.

72. Winternitz, *Bühler,* 10.

73. George Grierson correspondence with Ernst Windisch in Asia, Pacific and Africa Collections (APAC), MSS Eur E223.

74. S. N. Pandita, *Western Indologists and Sanskrit Savants of Kashmir* (Delhi: Siddharth, 2000), 218. See the Index of Papers published by the Archaeological Survey of India, APAC, V/14–21.

75. George Grierson, "Report on the Linguistic Survey of India," *Journal of the Royal Asiatic Society of Great Britain and Ireland* (1908): 1127–1131.

76. See "Linguistic Survey of India Records," IOR/S, APAC, British Library.

77. Ulrike Kirchberger, *Aspekte deutsch-britischer Expansion: Die Übersee-interessen der deutschen Migranten in Großbritannien in der Mitte des 19. Jahrhunderts* (Stuttgart: Franz Steiner Verlag, 1999), 312.

78. Andrew Grout, "Geology and India, 1775–1805: An Episode in Colonial Science," *South Asian Research* 10 (1990): 1–18.

79. V. Ball, *Scientific Results of The Second Yark and Mission: Memoir of the Life and Works of Ferdinand Stoliczka* (London: Eyre and Spottiswoode, 1886); Arnold, *Science,* 24.

80. See his diary in Ball, *Scientific Results,* 4–6.

81. Wilhelm Waagen, *Jurassic Fauna of Kutch* (London: N.p., 1873).

82. Ruth Struwe, "An Ambitious German in Early Twentieth Century Tasmania: The Collections Made by Fritz Noetling," *Australian Archaeology* 62 (2006): 33.

83. Immanuel Pfleiderer, *Glimpses into the Life of Indian Plants* (Mangalore: Basel Mission Book and Tract Depository, 1908).

84. Carl Schorske, *Fin-de-Siècle Vienna* (New York: Knopf, 1979), xviii–xxii.

85. Eduard Suess, *Das Antlitz der Erde* (Prague: Tempsky, 1883–1909); Erich Thenius, *Eduard Suess, Forscher und Politiker* (Vienna: Österreichische Geologische Gesellschaft, 1981), 53–82.

86. William Herbert Hobbs, "Eduard Suess," *Journal of Geology* 22 (1914): 811–817.

87. The term "Gondwana" was first used by H. B. Medlicott, superintendent of the Geological Survey of India, in 1872 in an internal report, and referred in that case only to the Deccan of India. Only in the work of H. F. Blanford and O. Feistmantel did the term come to be associated with an "ur-continent." Ottokar Feistmantel, "The Fossil Flora of the Gondwana System," *Palaeontologia Indica* 3 (1880): 1–77. See Erich Thenius, "Das 'Gondwana-Land' Eduard Suess," in *Eduard Suess— Forscher und Politiker* (Horn: Österreichische Geologische Gesellschaft, 1981), 53–60.

88. Arnold, *Science,* 53.

89. Herbert Hesmer, *Leben und Werk von Dietrich Brandis* (Opladen: Westdeutscher Verlag, 1975), 10.

90. Arnold, *Science,* 54.

91. Benjamin Weil, "Conservation, Exploitation, and Cultural Change in the Indian Forest Services, 1875–1927," *Environmental History* 11 (2006): 326–328.

92. Ramachandra Guha, *Forestry and Social Protest in British Kumaun, c. 1893–1921* (Calcutta: Centre for Studies in Social Sciences, 1985), 18, 19.

93. Dietrich Brandis et al., *Report on the Deodar Forests of Bashahr Punjab* (Simla: Forestry Department, 1865), 16, 17.

94. Indra Saldanha, "Colonialism and Professionalism: A German Forester in India," *Economic and Political Weekly* 31 (1996): 1266.

95. Dietrich Brandis, "Memorandum on Mr. Collins' Report on Caoutchouc," in *Edinburgh Report on the Caoutchouc of Commerce,* ed. James Collins (London: W. H. Allen, 1872), 48–54.

96. Dietrich Brandis, *Notes on Forest Management in Germany* (London: n.p., 1888), 1.

97. Campbell Walker, *Reports on Forest Management in Germany, Austria, and Great Britain* (London: George Eyre, 1873).

98. Hesmer, *Leben und Werk von Dietrich Brandis,* 136.

99. Ibid., 89; Ulrike Kirchberger, "Deutsche Naturwissenschaftler im britischen Empire," *Historische Zeitschrift* 271 (2000): 640; Berthold Ribbentrop, *Forestry in British India* (Calcutta: Superintendent of Government Printing, 1900).

100. Rudyard Kipling, "In the Rukh," in *All the Mowgli Stories* (London: Macmillan, 1993), 255; Saldanha, "Colonialism and Professionalism," 1265.

101. Henry Maine, *Village-communities in the East and West* (London: J. Murray, 1871), 7–8.

102. Henry Maine, "The Effect of Observation on India on Modern European Thought," in *The Rede Lecture* (Cambridge: Cambridge University Press, 1875), 39.

103. H. J. Makinder, *India* (London: George Philip, 1910).

104. Maurer, *Anglophilie*, 90–96, 238.

105. Kirchberger, *Aspekte deutsch-britischer Expansion*, 307–347.

106. Mike Davis, *Late Victorian Holocausts* (London: Verso, 2001), 311–340.

107. Peter Mandler, "'Race' and 'Nation' in Mid-Victorian Thought," in *History, Religion, Culture: British Intellectual History 1750–1950*, ed. Stefan Collini (Cambridge: Cambridge University Press, 2000), 224–244.

108. Abigail Green, "Representing Germany? The Zollverein at the World Exhibitions, 1851–1862," *Journal of Modern History* 75 (2003): 836–863. The developmental programs are clearly articulated in the journal of the *Verein für Socialpolitik*, especially in the 1880s, in particular, in terms of the "inner colonization" of German borderlands in writings by Gustav Schmoller and H. Rimpler.

109. Thomas Nipperdey, *Deutsche Geschichte: 1866–1918* (Munich: Beck, 1983) 2:649.

110. Gordon Cherry, "The Town Planning Movement and the Late Victorian City," *Transactions of the Institute of British Geographers* 4 (1979): 306–319; Manu Goswami, *Producing India: From Colonial Economy to National Space* (Chicago: University of Chicago Press, 2004), 31–72.

111. H. Hale Bellot, *University College London, 1826–1926* (London: University of London Press, 1929), 1; G. F. Daniell, "Position of Technical Instruction in England," *Nature* 88 (1912–1913), 320; Kurt Düwell, *Deutschlands Auswärtige Kulturpolitik 1918–1932* (Vienna: Böhlau Verlag, 1976), 70–103.

112. Colin Eisler, "Kunstgeschichte American Style," in *The Intellectual Migration*, ed. Donald Fleming and Bernard Bailyn (Cambridge, MA: Harvard University Press, 1969), 547.

113. Daniel Rodgers, *Atlantic Crossings: Social Politics in a Progressive Age* (Cambridge, MA: Belknap Press of Harvard University Press, 1998), 29–30.

114. Matthew Arnold was fond of quoting Wilhelm von Humboldt whom he called "one of the most beautiful and perfect souls that have existed." Nicole Staub and Kathrin Jost, eds., *Humboldt International: Der Export des deutschen Universitätsmodells im 19 und 20. Jahrhundert* (Basel: Schwabe, 2001), 238.

115. Matthew Arnold, *Higher Schools and Universities in Germany* (London: Macmillan, 1874), 229. See Ronald Hyam, *Britain's Imperial Century* (London: Batsford, 1976), 201, 274.

116. Karl Pearson, *The Function of Science in the Modern State* (Cambridge: Cambridge University Press, 1919), 55.

117. Hyam, *Imperial Century,* 274.

118. Arthur Mayhew, *The Education of India* (London: Faber and Gwyer, 1928), 208.

119. On the "gentlemanly" semiprofessionalized mode of social-scientific scholarship in Britain in the nineteenth century, see Dietrich Rueschemeyer and Theda Skocpol, eds., *States, Social Knowledge, and the Origins of Modern Social Policies* (Princeton, NJ: Princeton University Press, 1996), 230.

120. Paul Weindling, "The 'Sonderweg' of German Eugenics: Nationalism and Scientific Internationalism," *British Journal for the History of Science* 22 (1989): 321–333.

121. Frederick Nicholson, *Report Regarding the Possibility of Introducing Land and Agricultural Banks into the Bengal Presidency* (Madras: Superintendent's Office, 1895).

122. V. Venkatasubbaiya and Vaikunth Mehta, *The Co-operative Movement* (Allahabad: Servants of India Society, 1918).

123. Ibid., 21.

124. Walter Leifer, *Indien und die Deutschen* (Tübingen: Erdmann, 1969), 205. See P. Ponette, foreword in *Hoffmann on Mundari Poetry,* ed. Dineshwar Prasad (Patna: Joyti, 1979), i.

125. E. S. F. Walker, *Report of a Tour on the Continent to Inspect Equipment and Tanneries* (London: India Office, 1892).

126. Swire Smith, *Educational Comparison on Industrial Schools in England, Germany and Switzerland* (London, 1877); Friedrich Schenck, *Historical Sketch of the Rhine, in Connection with Education* (Edinburgh: Royal Scottish Society of Arts, 1876); Matthew Richards, *Continental Tours on Behalf of Sunday Schools in Sweden, France, Germany and Switzerland* (London: Sunday School Union, 1886); Mary Woods, *Report on the Teaching of History in the School of Germany and Belgium* (London: Macmillan, 1902).

127. Patrick Geddes, *Cities in Evolution* (London: Williams and Norgate, 1915); Narayani Gupta, "Urbanisation in South Asia in the Colonial Centuries," in *Dhaka: Past Present Future,* ed. Sharif Uddin Ahmed (Dhaka: Asiatic Society, 1991), 640.

128. Norbert Elias, *Über den Prozess der Zivilisation* (Basel: Haus zum Falken, 1939), 1:10–17.

129. Schorske, *Vienna*; Pieter Judson, *Exclusive Revolutionaries* (Ann Arbor: University of Michigan Press, 1996), 207–222; John Boyer, *Political Radicalism in Late Imperial Vienna* (Chicago: University of Chicago Press, 1981), 403–421.

130. Gary Weir, "Tirpitz, Technology, and Building U-boats, 1897–1916," *International History Review* 6 (1984): 175; Willi Boelcke, *So kam das Meer zu uns* (Frankfurt: Ullstein, 1981), 21, 22, 25.

131. Rudolf Ibbeken, *Das aussenpolitische Problem Staat und Wirtschaft* (Schleswig: Ibbeken, 1928), 196.

132. Akira Iriye, *The Cold War in Asia* (Englewood, NJ: Prentice Hall, 1974), 12.

133. David Blackbourn, *The Long Nineteenth Century* (London: Fontana, 1997), 250.

134. Carlo Cipolla, ed., *The Emergence of Industrial Societies* (Glasgow: Collins, 1973), 770–771.

135. Kwang-Ching Liu, "German Fear of a Quadruple Alliance, 1904–1905," *Journal of Modern History* 18 (1946): 222–240.

136. Johannes von Pflugk-Harttung, "Der Neuzeit," *Weltgeschichte,* vol. 6 (Berlin: Ullstein, 1908), 599–605.

137. Anon.,"Um die Weltherrschaft," *Gartenlaube* 101 (1904): 693.

138. Pyenson, *Cultural Imperialism,* 17.

139. Paul Rohrbach, *Der deutsche Gedanke in der Welt* (Düsseldorf: Langewiesche, 1912), 62.

140. Pyenson, *Cultural Imperialism,* 6–16, 312–316.

141. Johannes Voigt, *Max Mueller: The Man and His Ideas* (Calcutta: Firma K. L. Mukhopadhyay, 1967), 65–73.

142. Andrew Huxley, "Dr. Fuehrer's Wanderjahre: The Early Career of a Victorian Archaeologist," *Journal of the Royal Asiatic Society of Great Britain and Ireland* 20 (2010): 489–502; Charles Allen, *The Buddha and the Sahibs* (London: John Murray, 2002), 271.

143. Allen, *Buddha,* 73.

144. Wilhelm Halbfass, *India and Europe: An Essay in Understanding* (Albany: State University of New York, 1988), 287–309.

145. Rajendralal Mitra, *The Antiques of Orissa*, vol. 1 (Calcutta: K. L. Mukhopadhyaya, orig. 1873, 1961), 19; he especially cited the work of Goldstücker and Müller to contradict the British scholarly claims.

146. P. C. Ray, *History of Hindu Chemistry* (London: Williams and Norgate, 1902); see his opening references to Hermann Kopp's *Geschichte der Chemie* (1843); Friedrich Windischmann, "Über den Somacultus der Arier" (1846); Theodor Goldstücker, *Panini: His Place in Sanskrit Literature* (1861); Rudolf von Roth, "Indische Medicin" (1872); Georg Bühler, *The Laws of Manu* (1886).

147. P. C. Ray, *Hindu Chemistry* (London: Williams and Norgate, 1902), lvii, lviii.

148. Angarika Dharmapala, editorial, *Journal of the Maha Bodhi Society* 7 (1898): 95.

2. INDIAN SUBJECTS BEYOND THE BRITISH EMPIRE

1. *Svadeśi* is the standardized Romanization I use for the same word that appears as "Swadeshi" in many book titles and quotations that appear below.

2. Sumi Sarkar, *The Swadeshi Movement in Bengal* (New Delhi: People's Publishing House, 1973); Peter Heehs, *The Bomb in Bengal* (Delhi: Oxford University Press, 1993); Haridas Mukherjee and Uma Mukherjee, *Origins of the National Education Movement, 1905–1910* (Calcutta: Jadavpur University Press, 1957); Arjun Appadurai, ed., *The Social Life of Things: Commodities in Cultural Perspective* (New York: Cambridge University Press, 1986); Lisa Trivedi, *Clothing Gandhi's Nation* (Bloomington: Indiana University Press, 2007); Durba Ghosh, "Terrorism in Bengal: Imperial Strategies of Political Violence and Its Containment in the Interwar Period," in *Decentering Empire*, ed. Dane Kennedy and Durba Ghosh (New Delhi: Orient Longman, 2006).

3. Sarkar, *Swadeshi Movement*, 4, mentions the Maniktala arrests (May 1908), the deportation of nine leaders (December 1908), and the ban on the principal samitis (January 1909).

4. See Kris Manjapra, "Knowledgeable Internationalism and the Swadeshi Movement," *Economic and Political Weekly* 47 (2012): 53–62; Count Okuma, former prime minister of Japan, wrote in 1907: "the three hundred millions of Indians who were oppressed by the Europeans were looking for protection of Japan from the oppression of Europe. Indians were fomenting an agitation for boycott of European goods and if the Japanese failed to avail themselves of the opportunity they were disappointing the Indian people." Foreign Department Secret External, March 1908, no. 179.

5. Noor-Aiman Khan, *Egyptian-Indian Nationalist Collaboration and the British Empire* (New York: Palgrave Macmillan, 2011); Sareen, *Revolutionary Movement* (Delhi: Sterling, 1979), 25; James Campbell Ker, *Trouble in India* (Calcutta: Superintendent of Government Printing, 1917), 15; Cemil Aydin, *The Politics of Anti-Westernism in Asia* (New York: Columbia University Press, 2007), 142–168; Raouf Abbas Hamed, "Germany and the Egyptian Nationalist Movement, 1882–1918," *Die Welt des Islams* 28 (1988): 11–24.

6. Sarkar, *Swadeshi,* 14, 47. Sarkar calls this "Hindu revivalism."

7. See the argument for this 1880–1914 periodization of internationalist thought made by Tim Harper, "Empire, Diaspora and the Language of Globalism, 1850–1914," in *Globalization in World History,* ed. A. G. Hopkins (New York: Norton, 2002), 141–166.

8. See Bijoycandra Mazumdar's extended essay, "Iyurōpiyō Mahāsamar," on Prussia's challenge to England and France from the time of Bismarck to Wilhelm II in *Prabāsī* 15 (1915): 275–281; Kris Manjapra, "From Imperial to International Horizons," *Modern Intellectual History* 8 (2011): 327–359.

9. Ramchandra Chatterjee, "How to Help," in *Modern Review* 2 (1907): 483.

10. Bankim Chandra Chattopadhyaya, "Jaibanik," in *Vijñānrahasya,* ed. Brajendra Nath Bandyopadhyay (Calcutta: Bangiya Sahitya Parisat, 1938), 36.

11. Tithi Bhattacharya, *The Sentinels of Culture: Class, Education, and the Colonial Intellectual in Bengal* (Delhi: Oxford University Press, 2005), 153–191.

12. Geraldin Forbes, *Positivism in Bengal* (Calcutta: Minerva, 1975), 50–96; Sudipta Kaviraj, *Bankimchandra and the Making of Nationalist Consciousness* (Calcutta: Center for Studies in Social Sciences, 1989).

13. Bankim Chandra Chattopadhyaya, *Vijñānrahasya* (Calcutta: Bangiya Sahitya Parisat, 1938, orig. 1875).

14. Deepak Kumar, "The 'Culture' of Science and Colonial Culture, India 1820–1920," *British Journal for the History of Science* 29 (1996): 195–209; Irfan Habib and Dhruv Raina, "Copernicus, Columbus, Colonialism and the Role of Science in Nineteenth Century India," *Social Scientist* 17 (1989): 50–66.

15. Bankim Chandra Chattopadhyaya, "Āścarya Saurōtpāt," in *Vijñānrahasya,* ed. Brajendra Nath Bandyopadhyay (Calcutta: Bangiya Sāhitya Pariṣat, 1938), 79–81.

16. Bankim Chandra Chattopadhyaya, "Jaibanik," in *Vijñānrahasya,* 75–78.

17. Sudipta Kaviraj, *The Unhappy Consciousness: Bankimchandra Chattopadhyay and the Formation of Nationalist Discourse in India* (Oxford: Oxford University Press, 1995).

18. Ibid., 108–115.

19. Tapan Raychaudhuri, "Europe in India's Xenology: The Nineteenth-Century Record," *Past and Present* 137 (1992): 156–182.

20. Another important contribution in this vein is Andrew Sartori, *Bengal in Global Concept History* (Chicago: University of Chicago Press, 2008).

21. Sri Aurobindo, *New Lamps for Old,* essay five (Pondicherry: Sri Aurobindo Ashram, 1974), 37–39.

22. Robert Gregg, "Valleys of Fear: Policing Terror in an Imperial Age, 1865–1925," in *Beyond Sovereignty,* ed. Kevin Grant, Philippa Levine,

Frank Trentmann et al. (New York: Palgrave Macmillan, 2007): 80–102; Daniel Brückenhaus, "Every Stranger Must Be Suspected: Trust Relationships and the Surveillance of Anticolonialists in Early Twentieth-Century Western Europe," *Geschichte und Gesellschaft* 36 (2010): 523–566; Amit Kumar Gupta, "Defying Death: Nationalist Revolution in India, 1897–1938," *Social Scientist* 25 (1997): 3–27.

23. Sarkar, *Swadeshi Movement*, 68. Other founding editors were Subash Chandra Mullick and Shyam Sundar Chakravarti.

24. "Boycotting in Ireland," *Bande Mataram,* March 13, 1907; Barbara Southard, "The Political Strategy of Aurobindo Ghosh," *Modern Asian Studies* 14 (1980): 353–376; "The Awakening in China," *Bande Mataram,* April 4, 1907; "Seventy-six Suffragists Arrested," April 8, 1907; "France: The Strike Movement," *Bande Mataram,* May 22, 1907.

25. Manjapra, "Knowledgeable Internationalism and the Swadeshi Movement," 53.

26. Harald Fischer-Tiné and Carolien Stolte, "Imagining Asia in India: Nationalism and Internationalism (ca. 1905–1940), *Comparative Studies in Society and History* 54 (2012): 65–92.

27. Chitabrata Palit, *Science and Nationalism in Bengal, 1876–1947* (Kolkata: Institute of Historical Studies, 2004), 1–116.

28. Manu Bhagavan, "The Rebel Academy: Modernity and the Movement for a University in Princely Baroda, 1908–1949," *Journal of Asian Studies* 61 (2002): 919–947.

29. V. K. Chavda, "Development of Science Education and Growth of Scientific Institutions in the Native State of Baroda in the Nineteenth and Twentieth Centuries" (Delhi: NISTADS Seminar Papers, 1985), 4.

30. Dhruv Raina and Irfan Habib, "Technical Institutes in Colonial India Kala Bhavan, Baroda (1890–1990), *Economic and Political Weekly* 26 (1991): 2619–2624, 2621.

31. "The Rise of Germany," *Modern Review,* November 1909, 546.

32. "Germany's Fight for Sea Power," *Modern Review,* April 1907, 155.

33. "Character Sketch: Kaiser Wilhelm II: War Lord or Peace Emperor?" *Modern Review,* April 1907. Another article from April 1907 referred to "German Benevolence" and again complimented the kaiser for his good nature.

34. Panchanan Saha, *Madam Cama: Mother of Indian Revolution* (Calcutta: Manisha, 1975), 7–10.

35. M. N. Roy, "Letter to Woodrow Wilson," in *Selected Works of M. N. Roy,* ed. Sibnarayan Ray (Delhi: Oxford University Press, 1987), 1:80.

36. Samaren Roy, *Restless Brahmin: Early Life of M. N. Roy* (Bombay: Allied, 1970), 55.

37. German Foreign Office 1915, R27406, no. 1.

38. Syama Prasad Mookerjee, "Education in British India," *Annals of the American Academy of Political and Social Science* 233 (1944): 30–38.

39. Narendra Krishna Sinha, *Asutosh Mookerjee: A Biographical Sketch* (Calcutta: Asutosh Mookerjee Centenary Committee, 1966).

40. On Sadler's work in Britain, see M. Sadler, "The Unrest in secondary education in Germany and elsewhere," *Special Reports on Educational Subjects* 9, British Library, CD 836, London 1902.

41. Calcutta University Commission 1917–1919, APAC, V/26/864/6, 95.

42. Brajendra Nath Seal, *Indian Universities Commission: Abstract and Evidence* (Simla: Government Central Printing Office, 1902), 121.

43. Asutosh Mukherjee, "University Convocation 1907," *Addresses: Literary and Academic* (Calcutta: R. Cambray, 1915), 7.

44. Ibid., 20.

45. Asutosh Mukherjee, "University Convocation 1913," *Addresses by the Honorable Sir Asutosh Mookerjee* (Calcutta: University of Calcutta, 1913), 176.

46. David Lindenfeld, *The Practical Imagination: The German Sciences of State in the Nineteenth Century* (Chicago: University of Chicago Press, 1997), 264–322.

47. Asutosh Mukherjee, "University Convocation 1911," *Addresses: Literary and Academic,* 136.

48. Alexander Werth and Walter Harbich, *Netaji in Germany. An Eye-Witness Account of Indian Freedom Struggle in Europe during World War II,* ed. Sisir Bose (Calcutta: Netaji Research Bureau, 1970), 134.

49. See Mukherjee, *Addresses: Literary and Academic.*

50. Sinha, *Asutosh Mookerjee,* 81.

51. P. C. Ray, *Life and Experiences of a Bengali Chemist* (Calcutta: Chucker-vertty, Chatterjee, 1935), 262.

52. Mukherjee, *Addresses: Literary and Academic,* 132.

53. Benoy Kumar Sarkar, *Parājitā Jārmāni* (Calcutta: Oriental Book Agency, 1935), 656.

54. "Info zu Harish Chandra und Jnanendra Chandra Dasgupta," Humboldt Universität (HU) Archive, Phil Fak 532; Saloman to Auswärtiges Amt, September 21, 1915, Auswärtiges Amt (AA) Archive, 21077–2, 000105–107; Horst Krüger, "Indische Studenten in Berlin," Zentrum Moderner Orient (ZMO) Archive Berlin, File 89; Benoy Kumar Sarkar, *Futurism of Young Asia* (Berlin: Springer, 1922), 306.

55. "Information zu A. M. Bose," AA, 21101–2, 1916, 0000159; Arabinda studied physics, began his PhD in Heidelberg in 1914, and sought permission to continue his work throughout the war. Asutosh Mukherjee, "University Convocation 1914," *Addresses,* 251. Debendra Mohan Bose, a

nephew of Jagadish Chandra Bose, also studied physics at the University of Berlin in the laboratory of Erich Regener. S. C. Roy, "D. M. Bose: A Scientist Incognito," *Science and Culture* 76 (2010): 491–493; B. C. Kundu, "Professor Shankar Purusottam Agharkar, 1884–1960," *Taxon* 11 (1962): 209–211.

56. B. K. Sarkar, *Education for Industrialization* (Calcutta: Chuckervertty, Chatterjee, 1946), 49–51; Mukherjee, Convocation Address, March 27, 1914, *Addresses,* 135; S. C. Mitra to the Philosophische Fakultät, HUA, Phil Fak Prom 10035.

57. Vogel, Report to Foreign Office, AA, 21080–2, August 3, 1915, 107; "Info zu Manekji Davar," HUA, Berlin, 1904; Suzanne Marchand, *German Orientalism in the Age of Empire* (New York: Cambridge University Press), 192–193; Files of the Indian Committee, AA, 21072–1, September 30, 1914, 000086; Max Freiherr von Oppenheim, "Telegramm," AA, 21071–1, September 15, 1914, 000070; Bimala Churn Law, ed., *D. R. Bhandarkar* (Calcutta: Indian Research Institute, 1940); Files of the Indian Committee, AA, 21096–1, April 6, 1916, 000022; R. N. Dandekar ed., *Ramakrishna Gopal Bhandarkar as an Indologist* (Poona: Bhandarkar Oriental Research Institute, 1976).

58. Mukherjee, "University Convocation 1923," Convocation Speeches by Asutosh Mukherjee 1907–1924, Asutosh Mukherjee Papers, NMML, 503.

59. Rabindranath Tagore, *The Center of Indian Culture* (Madras: Society for the Promotion of National Education, 1919).

60. Hemchandra Kanungo, *Bāmlāy Biplab Pracestā* (Kolkata: Kamala Book Depot, 1928).

61. Bhupendranath Datta, *Amār Āmerikay Abhijnata* (Calcutta: Metcalf Press, 1926); Amal Chattopadhyaya, *Bhupendranath Datta and His Study of Indian Society* (Calcutta: Bagchi, 1994); Hemchandra Dasgupta, *Bhārater Biplabkāhini* (Calcutta: Jadavpur University, 1948); Peter Heehs, "Foreign Influences on Bengali Revolutionary Terrorism 1902–1908," *Modern Asian Studies* 28 (1994), 533–556; Hemchandra Kanungo, *Bāmlāy Biplab Pracestā* (Calcutta: Kamala Book Depot, 1928); Kalidas Nag, *Memoirs* (Calcutta: Writers Workshop, 1991; orig. 1921–1923); Abinash Chandra Bhattacharya, *Iijorope Bhāratiya Bilplaber Sādhana* (Calcutta: Bandana Impression, 1949).

62. "Report on the Working of the Indian Companies Act for 1896–1917," APAC, V/24/548.

63. Anonymous, "Girindrasekhar," *Samīkṣa: Journal of the Indian Psychoanalytical Society,* Special Number Bose Number Special Issue 9 (1955): 11; Taraknath Das, "A Programme for the Indian Nationalists," *Calcutta Review,* series 3, 7 (1927): 109–113.

64. Joachim Oesterheld et al., *Inder in Berlin* (Berlin: Ausländerbeauftragte des Senats, 1997).

65. Sarkar, *Education for Industrialization*, 46–48.

66. Ibid., 345–349. For example, four students enrolled at Harvard in 1910. Their enrollment was obtained through the offices of the Bengal National Council of Education. Their studies were funded by the Bengal National Council of Education: Jatindra Nath Set, H. L. Roy, N. N. Sengupta, and Benjoy Kumar Sarkar. See "Letter of Reshbihari Ghosh to the President of Harvard," April 8, 1910, Harvard University Archives, UAIII 15.88.10 1890–1968, Box 4371; "Letter by the Dean to the National Council of Education," July 24, 1911, UAIII 15.88.10, Box 4486.

67. Satis Chandra Basu, "Public Education in Germany," *Modern Review* 8 (1910): 167–170.

68. Lala Hardayal, "India and the World Movement," *Modern Review* 13 (1913): 185–188.

3. GERMAN VISIONS OF AN ASIANATE EUROPE

1. Andrew Zimmerman, *Alabama in Africa: Booker T. Washington, the German Empire, and Globalization of the New South* (Princeton, NJ: Princeton University Press, 2010), 5–15.

2. W. O. Henderson, *The Industrial Revolution on the Continent: Germany, France, Russia* (London: Frank Cass, 1967), 52.

3. Paul Kennedy, *The Rise of the Anglo-German Antagonism, 1860–1914* (London: Allen and Unwin, 1980), 157–205.

4. Georg Forster, *Entdeckungsreise nach Tahiti und in die Südsee, 1772–1775* (Berlin: Neues Leben, 1979); Sujit Sivasundaram, *Nature and the Godly Empire: Science and Evangelical Mission in the Pacific, 1795–1850* (Cambridge: Cambridge University Press, 2005), 123–124.

5. Hermann Keyserling, *Das Reisetagebuch eines Philosophen* (Darmstadt: Reichl, 1919), 295.

6. Lora Wildenthal, "Notes on a History of 'Imperial Turns' in Modern Germany," in *After the Imperial Turn: Thinking with and through the Nation,* ed. Antoinette Burton (Durham, NC: Duke University Press, 2003), 144–156.

7. Norbert Elias, *The Germans* (New York: Columbia University Press, 1996), 23–119.

8. Karl Bleibtreu, *Von Robespierre zu Buddha* (Leipzig: Friedrich, 1900).

9. Ibid., 27, 279.

10. Walter Leifer, *Indien und die Deutschen* (Tübingen: Erdmann, 1969), 300. See the works of Elisabeth Sass-Brunner and her daughter, Eliza-

beth, as well as Irmgard Burchard-Simaica, Nicolai Roerich, and Oswald Malura.

11. Peter Hansen, "Confetti of Empire: The Conquest of Everest in Nepal, India, Britain and New Zealand," *Comparative Studies in Society and History* 42 (2000): 307–332; David Thomas Murphy, *German Exploration in the Polar World* (Lincoln: University of Nebraska Press, 2002).

12. Heinrich Harrer, *Sieben Jahre in Tibet* (Vienna: Ullstein, 1952); Willy Merkl, *Nanga Parbat* (Munich: Lehmanns, 1953).

13. Kurt Boeck, *Indische Gletscherfahrten* (Stuttgart: Deutsche Verlags-Anstalt, 1900). Compare with British Himalaya films, as discussed by Peter Hansen, "The Dancing Lamas of Everest: Cinema, Orientalism, and Anglo-Tibetan Relations in the 1920s," *American Historical Review* 101 (1996): 712–747.

14. Fritz Stern, *Politics of Cultural Despair* (Berkeley: University of California Press, 1961), 134, 140; Ulrich Linse, *Barfüßige Propheten* (Berlin: Siedler, 1983), 19, 20; Corinna Treitel, *A Science for the Soul* (Baltimore: Johns Hopkins University Press, 2004), 102–107.

15. This is the classic *Sonderweg* argument.

16. Mary Louise Pratt, *Imperial Eyes* (London: Routledge, 1992), 5–9.

17. Matthew P. Fitzpatrick, *Liberal Imperialism in Germany: Expansion and Nationalism, 1848–1884* (New York: Berghahn Books, 2008), 20; Jens-Uwe Guettel, "From the Frontier to German South-West Africa," *Modern Intellectual History* 7 (2010): 523–552.

18. Friedrich Daab, Introduction to *Paul de Lagarde, Deutscher Glaube—Deutsches Vaterland—Deutsche Bildung: Das Wesentliche aus seinen Schriften,* ed. Daab (Jena: Diederichs, 1914).

19. Bradley Naranch, "Beyond the Fatherland, Colonial Visions, Overseas Expansion, and German Nationalism, 1848–1885," PhD diss., Johns Hopkins University, 2007.

20. Woodruff Smith, "The Ideology of German Colonialism, 1840–1906," *Journal of Modern History* 46 (1974): 641–662.

21. Arne Perras, *Carl Peters and German Imperialism, 1856–1918* (Oxford: Oxford University Press, 2004), 20; Uwe Wieben, *Carl Peters: das Leben eines deutschen Kolonialisten* (Rostock: Neuer Hochschulschriftenverlag, 2000), 24–26.

22. Maximilian von Hagen, *Bismarcks Kolonialpolitik* (Stuttgart: Friedrich Andrews Perthes, 1923), 20, 28, 33; W. O. Henderson, *The German Colonial Empire, 1884–1919* (London: F. Cass, 1993), 61.

23. Wilhelm Hübbe-Schleiden, *Überseeische Politik, eine culturwissenschaftliche Studie mit Zahlenbildern* (Hamburg: Friederichsen, 1881), 66–74.

24. Ulrike Kirchberger, "Deutsche Naturwissenschaftler im britischen Empire," *Historische Zeitschrift* 271 (2000): 621–660.

25. Dirk van Laak, *Imperiale Infrastruktur: Deutsche Planungen für eine Erschließung Afrikas 1880 bis 1960* (Paderborn, Germany: Schöningh, 2004), 52.

26. Rüdiger vom Bruch, *Weltpolitik als Kulturmission* (Paderborn, Germany: Schöningh, 1982), 69, 90.

27. Laak, *Imperiale Infrastruktur*, 87–93.

28. Paul Rohrbach, *Der deutsche Gedanke in der Welt* (Düsseldorf: Langewiesche, 1912), 49–82.

29. Kurt Düwell, *Deutschlands auswärtige Kulturpolitik, 1918–1932* (Vienna: Böhlau Verlag, 1976), 1–27.

30. Stanley Rice, "A German on India," *Calcutta Review* 4 (1916): 17.

31. Ibid.

32. Volker Berghahn, *Der Tirpitz-Plan* (Düsseldorf: Droste, 1971), 173–201; Lewis Pyenson, *Cultural Imperialism and Exact Sciences* (New York: Lang, 1985), 253.

33. Alfred Gollin, *Balfour's Burden: Arthur Balfour and Imperial Preference* (London: Anthony Blond, 1965), 263.

34. Kaushik Bagchi, "An Orientalist in the Orient: Richard Garbe's Indian Journey, 1885–1886," *Journal of World History* 14 (2003): 281–325.

35. Arthur Holitscher, *Das unruhige Asien* (Berlin: Fischer, 1926), 45; Waldemar Bonsels, *Indienfahrt* (Frankfurt: Rütten, 1912), 32; Egon Erwin Kisch, *Asien gründlich verändert* (Berlin: Reiss, 1932), 107.

36. Fitzpatrick, *Liberal Imperialism*, 208; see also William Shanahan, "Liberalism and Foreign Affairs: Naumann and the Prewar German View," *View of Politics* 21 (1959): 188–223.

37. Keyserling, *Reisetagebuch*, 203, 284.

38. Bernhard Kellermann, *Der Weg der Götter* (Berlin: Fischer, 1929), 96.

39. Holitscher, *Unruhige Asien*, 159–161.

40. Arthur Schopenhauer, *Die Welt als Wille und Vorstellung* (Leipzig: Brockhaus, 1819). See Raymond Schwab, *Renaissance Orientale* (Paris: Payot, 1950), 427.

41. John H. Smith, *Dialogues between Faith and Reason* (Ithaca, NY: Cornell University Press, 2011), 136–141.

42. Rüdiger Safranski, *Schopenhauer und die wilden Jahre der Philosophie* (Munich: Hanser, 1987), 200.

43. Eda Sagarra, *Tradition and Revolution* (New York: Basic Books, 1971), 160, 185; Angela Sendlinger, *Lebenspathos und Décadence um 1900* (Frankfurt: Lang, 1994), 79, 151.

44. Kris Manjapra, "Schopenhauer, Schopenhauerians and the German Appropriation of Eastern Thought." Thesis, Harvard University Archives, 2001.

45. Eduard von Hartmann, *Philosophie des Unbewussten, Versuch einer Weltanschauung* (Berlin: Duncker, 1869). Philip Mainländer, *Die Philosophie der Erlösung*, 2 vols. (Berlin: Grisebach, 1886). For commentary on their interpretations of Schopenhauer, see Johann Gestering, *German Pessimism and Indian Philosophy: A Hermeneutic Reading* (Delhi: Ajanta, 1986), 150–258.

46. Hans Rollmann, "Deussen, Nietzsche, and Vedanta," *Journal of the History of Ideas* 39 (1978): 125–132.

47. See Richard Garbe, *Indien und das Christentum* (Tübingen: Mohr, 1914); see also Max Müller, *India: What Can It Teach Us?* (London: Longmans, 1883).

48. Safranski, *Schopenhauer,* 483–508.

49. Christopher Ryan, *Schopenhauer's Philosophy of Religion* (Leuven, Belgium: Peeters, 2010).

50. Sascha Hesse, *Schopenhauer und das Christentum* (Berlin: Wissenschaftlicher Verlag, 2006).

51. Suzanne Marchand, *German Orientalism in the Age of Empire* (New York: Cambridge University Press, 2010), 105–112.

52. Safranski, *Schopenhauer,* 200–204.

53. Paul de Lagarde, *Erinnerungen an Friedrich Rückert* (Göttingen: Dietrich, 1886), 96; Max Müller, *Auld Lang Syne* (New York: Scribner's, 1898), 81.

54. Stern, *Politics of Cultural Despair,* 61, 66–69.

55. Daab, ed., *Paul de Lagarde, Deutscher Glaube,* 3.

56. Treitel, *Science for the Soul,* 30–32; Andreas Daum, *Wissenschaftspopularisierung im 19. Jahrhundert* (Munich: Oldenbourg, 1998), 195–202.

57. Treitel, *Science for the Soul,* 30–32.

58. Ibid., 7.

59. Gerhard Klamp, "Schopenhauertradition und Forschung im zwanzigsten Jahrhundert," *Zeitschrift für philosophische Forschung* 14 (1960): 438–452; Ulrich Linse, *Ökopax und Anarchie: eine Geschichte der ökologische Bewegungen in Deutschland* (Munich: Deutscher Taschenbuch, 1986), 125–152.

60. Norbert Klatt, *Theosophie und Anthroposophie* (Göttingen: Klatt, 1993), 39–60.

61. Ibid., 62.

62. Pierre Bourdieu, *Homo academicus* (Paris: Éditions de Minuit, 1984).

63. Konrad Jarausch, *Students, Society, and Politics* (Princeton, NJ: Princeton University Press, 1982), 134–159.

64. Ibid., 75.

65. Thomas Nipperdey, *Deutsche Geschichte, 1866–1918* (Munich: Beck, 1983), 2:10.

66. Nipperdey, *Deutsche Geschichte*, 1:498–533.

67. F. Charles Thwing, *The American and the German University* (New York: Macmillan, 1928), 42, 43; Daniel Rodgers, *Atlantic Crossings: Social Politics in a Progressive Age* (Cambridge, MA: Belknap Press of Harvard University Press, 1998), 33–75.

68. Jarausch, *Students,* 38.

69. Marchand, *German Orientalism,* 270.

70. See "Dissertantinnen von Josef Strzygowski," *Rigorosenprotokoll der Phil. Fakultät*, Ph 59 1910–1934, Archives of Vienna University.

71. From Klaus Ludwig Janert, *Verzeichnis indienkundlicher Hochschul-schriften* (Wiesbaden: Harrassowitz, 1961). Number of dissertations by time period: 1800–1829: 4; 1830–1849: 5; 1850–1869: 27; 1870–1889: 95; 1890–1909: 146; 1910–1933: 243; 1933–1953: 167; 1953–1964: 55.

72. Maureen Healy, "Becoming Austrian: Women, the State, and Citizenship in World War I," *Central European History* 25 (2002): 1–35.

73. Astrid Kury, *Heiligenscheine eines elektrischen Jahrhundertendes sehen anders aus* (Vienna: Passagen, 2000), 29; Carl Schorske, *Fin-de-Siècle Vienna* (New York: Knopf, 1979), 117.

74. Cemil Aydin, *The Politics of Anti-Westernism in Asia* (New York: Columbia University Press, 2007), 122; Kumari Jayawardena, *The White Woman's Other Burden* (New York: Routledge, 1995), 207–217.

75. Dianne Howe, "The Notion of Mysticism in the Philosophy and Choreography of Mary Wigman, 1914–1931," *Dance Research Journal* 19 (1987): 19–24. See Anne Braude, *Radical Spirits: Spiritualism and Women's Rights* (Boston: Beacon, 1989), 197–202.

76. Jarausch, *Students,* 7; Friedrich Meineke, *Weltbürgertum und National-staat* (Munich: Oldenbourg, 1908).

77. Ute Mehnert, "German Weltpolitik and the American Two-Front Dilemma: The 'Japanese Peril' in German–American Relations, 1904–1917," *Journal of American History* 82 (1996): 1452–1477; Heinz Gollwitzer, *Geschichte des weltpolitischen Denkens* (Göttingen: Vandenhoeck, 1982), 42–43; Barbara Tuchman, *The Zimmermann Telegram* (London: Constable, 1958), 55; see Sebastian Conrad, *Globalisation and the Nation State in Imperial Germany* (Cambridge: Cambridge University Press, 2011), 222–225.

78. Regina Höfer, ed., *Imperial Sightseeing: Die Indienreise von Erzherzog Franz Ferdinand* (Vienna: Museum für Völkerkunde, 2010).

79. Ernst Ludwig von Hessen-Darmstadt, *Staatsbesuch im Indien der Maharajas: Tagebücher zur indischen Reise Grossherzog Ernst Ludwigs von Hessen und bei Rhein* (Darmstadt: Hessische Historische Kommission, 2003).

80. "Nixon Report," in A. K. Samanta, *Terrorism in Bengal* (Calcutta: Government of Bengal, 1995), 2:625.

81. The *Frankfurter Zeitung* noted the arrival of the crown prince in Bombay (January 10, 1911), as well as his visits to Haiderabad and Jaipur (January 24, 1911).

82. Oscar Bongard, *Die Reise des deutschen Kronprinzen durch Ceylon und Indien* (Berlin: Schwetschke, 1911); W. Heichen, *Unseres Kronprinzen Fahrt nach Indien* (Berlin: Phönix, 1911); Hans Zache, *Mit dem Kronprinzen durch Indien* (Berlin: Süd-West, 1913); Annie Sprecht-Blaurock, *Die Reise des deutschen Kronprinzen nach dem Fernen Osten* (Berlin: F. Schulze, 1912); Max Korten, *Die Reise des Kronprinzen nach Ceylon* (Düsseldorf: Schwann, 1911).

83. Hans Molisch, *Als Naturforscher in Indien* (Jena: Gustav Fischer, 1930).

84. Heisenberg visited India in 1928 and Sommerfeld visited in 1929.

85. See Edgar Reitz's *Heimat: eine deutsche Chronink,* miniseries, 1979–1984, Episode 1: "Fernweh 1919–1928" (Leipzig: Kinowelt Home Entertainment, 2006) on the theme of "Fernweh." Compare with Katinka Kocks, *Indianer im Kaiserreich* (Frankfurt: Spiegel, 2004).

86. See Wilhelm von Polenz, *Das Land der Zukunft* (Leipzig: F. Fontante, 1904); J. L. Neve, *Charakterzüge des amerikanischen Volkes* (Leipzig: Wallmann, 1902); Ludwig Fulda, *amerikanische Eindrücke* (Stuttgart: J. G. Cotta, 1906); George von Skal, *Das amerikanische Volk* (Berlin: E. Fleischel, 1908); Ernest Bruncken, *Die amerikanische Volkseele* (Gotha: Perthes, 1911).

87. And Keyserling also published *South American Meditations* (orig. *Südamerikanische Meditationen*) (London: Harper, 1932).

88. Keyserling, *Reisetagebuch,* 2:810–827.

89. Jürgen Offermanns, *Der lange Weg des Zen-Buddhismus nach Deutschland* (Lund: Lunds universitet, 2002); Douglas McGetchin, *Indology, Indomania, and Orientalism* (Madison, NJ: Fairleigh Dickinson University Press, 2009), 126.

90. Helmuth von Glasenapp, *Die fünf großen Religionen* (Düsseldorf: Diederich, 1951).

91. Max Weber, *Gesammelte Aufsätze zur Religionssoziologie: Hinduismus und Buddhismus,* vol. 2 (Tübingen: J. C. B. Mohr, 1920); Helmuth Glasenapp, *Der Jainismus, eine indische Erlösungsreligion* (Berlin: Häger, 1925).

92. Karl Seidenstücker's German Buddhist community was involved in a virulent critique of Theosophy in the 1920s. See discussion by Perry Myers, *German Visions of India, 1871–1914* (New York: Palgrave Macmillan, 2013), 25–53.

93. Hermann Oldenberg, "Die Religion des Veda und der Buddhismus," in *Aus Indien und Iran* (Berlin: Wilhelm Hertz, 1899), 42; Martin Bauman, "Culture Contact and Valuation: Early German Buddhists and the Creation of a 'Buddhism in Protestant Shape,'" *Numen* 44 (1997): 275–277.

94. Karl Seidenstücker, *Buddhistische Evangelien* (Leipzig: Fänrich, 1909); Paul Dahlke, *Buddhismus als Weltanschauung* (Breslau: Markgraf, 1912).

95. Hermann Oldenberg, "Die Orientalische Philosophie, indische und iranische," *Kultur der Gegenwart*, vol. 1, nos. 5 and 6 (Teubner: Berlin, 1909), 32–44.

96. Hermann Oldenberg, *Buddha: Seine Leben, seine Lehre, seine Gemeinde* (Berlin: Hertz, 1881).

97. Linse, *Barfüßige Propheten*, 56.

98. Max Vogrich, *Buddha* (Leipzig: Hofmeister, 1901); Adolf Vogl, *Maja* (Stuttgart: Feuchtinger, 1908).

99. On Weber's reading of the "Orient," see Ronald Inden, "Orientalist Constructions of India," *Modern Asian Studies* 20 (1986): 401–446.

100. Hermann Keyserling, *The Recovery of Truth* (London: Harper, 1929).

101. Hans Ludwig Held, *Deutsche Bibliographie des Buddhismus* (Leipzig: Hans Sachs, 1916), viii.

102. Ibid., vii.

103. On the "furor orientalis," see Marchand, *German Orientalism*, 216–251.

104. Ibid., 276–277; Michael Kater, "The Work Student: A Socio-Economic Phenomenon of Early Weimar Germany," *Journal of Contemporary History* 10 (1975): 71–94.

105. See Glasenapp's overview of popular Buddhism in Germany. "Influence of Indian Thought," *Calcutta Review* 29 (1928): 189–209.

106. Kalidas Nag, *Memoirs* (Calcutta: Writers Workshop, 1991; orig. 1921–1923), 45.

107. Baumann, "Culture Contact and Valuation: Early German Buddhists and the Creation of a 'Buddhism in Protestant Shape,'" *Numen* 44 (1997): 273.

108. McGetchin, *Indology*, 131.

109. Nyanaponika Thera, ed., *Nyanatiloka Centenary Volume* (Kandy: Buddhist Publication Society, 1978).

110. Bhikku Bodhi, *Nyanaponika: A Farewell Tribute* (Kandy: Buddhist Publication Society, 1995).

111. Leifer, *Indien und die Deutschen*, 136.

112. Ken Winkler, *A Thousand Journeys: The Biography of Lama Anagarika Govinda* (Longmead, Dorset, UK: Element, 1990), 12–19.

113. Sri Aturugiriya Gnanawimala, *50 Jahre Buddhistisches Haus* (Berlin: Buddhistisches Haus Frohnau), 1974.

114. Anagarika Govinda, *Der Weg der weissen Wolken: Erlebnisse eines buddhistischen Pilgers in Tibet* (Stuttgart: Rascher, 1969).

115. Bhakti Hridaya Bon, *My Lectures in England and Germany* (Vrindaban: Bhajan Kutir, 1984).

116. Nyanatusita and Hellmuth Hecker, *The Life of Nyanatiloka Thera: The Biography of a Western Buddhist Pioneer* (Kandy: Buddhist Publication Society, 2008), 340.

117. C. F. Andrews, *Sadhu Sundar Singh: A Personal Memoir* (New York: Harper, 1934).

118. See the discussion of Indologist work in Held, *Deutsche Bibliographie des Buddhismus*, iii.

119. Irmgard Heidler, *Der Verleger Eugen Diederichs und seine Welt* (Wiesbaden: Harrassowitz, 1998), 44ff.

120. Ibid., 512ff.

121. Martin Kämpchen, *Rabindranath Tagore in Germany: Four Responses to a Cultural Icon* (Shimla: Indian Institute of Advanced Study, 1999), 58–84.

122. See Mark Morrisson, "The Periodical Culture of the Occult Revival: Esoteric Wisdom, Modernity and Counter-Public Spheres," *Journal of Modern Literature* 31 (2007), 1–22.

123. Heinz Sarkowski, *Der Insel Verlag, 1899–1999* (Frankfurt: Insel-Verlag, 1999), 260–264.

124. Vridhagiri Ganeshan, *Das Indienerlebnis Hermann Hesses* (Bonn: Bouvier Verlag, 1975), 27–30.

125. Hermann Keyserling's *Reisetagebuch eines Philosophen* was another popular success, reaching its seventh edition in four years.

126. Reeta Sanatani, *Rabindranath Tagore und das deutsche Theater der 20e Jahre* (Berlin: Lang, 1983).

127. Alexander Zemlinsky, *Lyrische Symphonie: In sieben Gesängen nach Gedichten von Rabindranath Tagore* (Vienna: Universal Edition, 1924); Hans Gal, *Phantasien: nach Gedichten von Rabindranath Tagore* (Vienna: Universal Edition, 1923). See Roger Oliver, "Hans Gal at 95," *Tempo* 155 (1985): 2–7; Carlo Coppola, "Rabindranath Tagore and Western Composers: A Preliminary Essay," *Journal of South Asian Literature* 19 (1984): 41–61.

128. Krimhild Stöver, *Witte-Lenoir* (Oldenburg: Paape, 1980).

129. Rainer Maria Rilke, poems on the Buddha, *Neue Gedichte* (Leipzig: Insel-Verlag, 1907), 46.

130. Christiane Günther, *Aufbruch nach Asien: Kulturelle Fremde in der deutschen Literatur um 1900* (Munich: Iudicium, 1988), 27; Stefan Zweig, *Amok* (Leipzig: Insel-Verlag, 1922); Lion Feuchtwanger, *Kalkutta, 4. Mai* (Berlin: Drei Masken, 1925).

131. Otto de Fries, *Indien—das Wunderland* (Dresden: Reissner, 1921); Kurt Boeck, *Indische Wunderwelt* (Leipzig: Haessel, 1925); Oscar Kauffmann, *Aus Indiens Dschungels* (Leipzig: Klinkhardt und Bierman, 1911); Immanuel Pfleiderer, *Volkstypen aus Indien* (Stuttgart: Th. Benzinger, 1924); Irma Prinzessin Odescalchi, *Durch Dschungel und Tempel* (Berlin: Paetel, 1927); Lola Kreutzberg, *Tiere, Tänzerin und Dämonen* (Dresden: Carl Reissner, 1929); Alfons Nobel, *Tempel, Paläste und Dschungel* (Bonn: Verleih der Buchgemeinde, 1929); E. Litzmann, *Aus dem Lande der Märchen und Wunder* (Berlin: D. Reimer, 1914); R. Ribbeck, *Im Wunderlande Indien* (Bonn: Verlag der Buchgemeinde, 1925); H. von de Gablentz, *Steinerne Wunder* (Leipzig: Heiling, 1935).

132. Peter Jelavich, *Berlin Cabaret* (Cambridge, MA: Harvard University Press, 1993), 26–33.

133. Ibid., 130.

134. Treitel, *Science for the Soul*, 130.

135. Detlev Peukert, *The Weimar Republik* (London: Allen Lane, 1987), 161–167.

136. See Hanns Heinz Ewers, *Indien und Ich* (Munich: Müller, 1919).

137. Hilmar Teske, *Das heutige Indien und seine Freiheitsbewegung* (Plauen: Selbstverlag, 1930).

138. Ibid., 5.

139. Larry Jones, *German Liberalism and the Dissolution of the Weimar Party System* (Chapel Hill: University of North Carolina Press, 1988), 225–229.

140. Max Weber, *Hinduismus und Buddhismus* (Tübingen: Mohr, 1921).

141. Professor Rudolf Otto, "Parallelen und Wertunterschiede im Christentum und Buddatum," lecture delivered at Göttingen, January 14, 1913. See Otto, *Die Gnadenreligion Indiens und deas Christentum: Vergleich und Unterscheidung* (Gotha: Klotz, 1930).

142. Otto, *Gnadenreligion*, 1–12.

143. Rudolf Otto, "Religiöser Menschheitsbund," *Deutsche Politik* 6 (1921): 237.

144. Hans-Martin Barth, "Die Bedeutung Rudolf Ottos für den ökumenischen und den interreligiösen Dialog," in Barth and Christian Elsas, *Bild und Bildlosigkeit. Beiträge zum interreligiösen Dialog* (Hamburg: Universität Marburg, 1994).

145. See Dorothy Figueira, *Aryans, Jews, Brahmins* (Albany: State University of New York Press, 2002), 50–63.

146. Celia Applegate, *A Nation of Provincials* (Berkeley: University of California Press, 1990), 7.

147. Svoboda Dimitrova-Moeck, *Women Travel Abroad 1925–1932* (Berlin: Weidler, 2009); Mary Nolan, *Visions of Modernity: American Business and the Modernization of Germany* (New York: Oxford University Press, 1994), 1–13.

148. Kris Manjapra, *M. N. Roy: Marxism and Colonial Cosmopolitanism* (Delhi: Routledge, 2010), 31–55.

149. Brian Houghton Hodgson, "Ethnography and Geography of the Sub-Himalayas," *Journal of the Asiatic Society of Bengal* 16 (1847): 44–45.

150. Tony Ballantyne, *Orientalism and Race* (Houndmills, UK: Palgrave, 2002), 49.

151. Thomas Trautmann, *Aryans and British India* (Berkeley: University of California Press, 1997), 172–178; Leon Poliakov, *The Aryan Myth: A History of Racist and Nationalist Ideas in Europe* (London: Chatto and Windus, 1971).

152. Arthur Gobineau, *Sur l'inégalité des races humaines* (Paris: Librairie de Firmin Diot, 1853), 162–162.

153. Trautmann, *Aryans,* 200.

154. Ballantyne, *Orientalism,* 120.

155. Sheldon Pollock, "Deep Orientalism: Notes on Sanskrit and Power Beyond the Raj," in *Orientalism and the Postcolonial Predicament,* ed. Carol Breckenridge and Peter van der Veer (Philadelphia: University of Pennsylvania Press, 1993), 83.

156. See Thomas Mann, *Doctor Faustus: The Life of the German Composer Adrian Leverkühn,* trans. H. T. Lowe-Porter (New York: Knopf, 1948; orig. 1947); Friedrich Nietzsche, *The Genealogy of Morals,* trans. Horace Samuel (Mineola, NY: Dover, 2003; orig. 1887).

157. Stefan Arvidsson, "Aryan Mythology as Science and Ideology," *Journal of the American Academy of Religion* 67 (1999): 327–354.

158. Barbara Besslich, *Faszination des Verfalls* (Berlin: Akademie Verlag, 2002).

159. Oswald Spengler, *Der Untergang des Abendlandes* (Munich: Beck, 2011), 400.

160. Ibid., 450.

161. Hans-Georg Gadamer, *Philosophical Apprenticeships* (Cambridge, MA: MIT Press, 1985), 45.

162. Spengler, quoted in Prasenjit Duara, *Decolonization: Perspectives from Now and Then* (London: Routledge, 2004), 1.

163. Suzanne Marchand, *Down from Olympus* (Princeton, NJ: Princeton University Press, 1996), 306–309.

164. Spengler, *Untergang,* 840–879.

165. Wolfe Schmokel, *Dream of Empire: German Colonialism, 1919–1945* (New Haven, CT: Yale University Press, 1964), 46–75; Roger

Chickering, *We Men Who Feel Most German* (Boston: Allen and Unwin, 1984), 78.

166. Wolfgang Bialas and Anson Rabinbach, eds., *Nazi Germany and the Humanities* (Oxford: Oneworld, 2007); Jeffrey Herf, *Reactionary Modernism* (Cambridge: Cambridge University Press, 1984); Sebastian Maass, *Die andere deutsche Revolution: Edgar Julius Jung und die metaphysischen Grundlagen der konservativen Revolution* (Kiel: Regin-Verlag, 2009); Armin Mohler, *Die konservative Revolution in Deutschland 1918–1932* (Stuttgart: Vorwerk-Verlag, 1950).

167. Sabine Mangold, *Eine "weltbürgerliche Wissenschaft"* (Stuttgart: Steiner, 2004), 115.

168. Hermann Beck, "Between the Dictates of Conscience and Political Expediency," *Journal of Contemporary History* 41 (2006): 611–640. For example, Edgar Jung was murdered in the Night of the Long Knives, and Leopold Ziegler, his friend, emigrated from Germany soon thereafter; Suzanne Marchand, "Nazism, Orientalism and Humanism," in Bialas and Rabinbach, *Nazi Germany,* 296; Helmut Schörer, *Leopold Zielger: Leben und Werk in Dokumenten* (Karlsruhe: Badische Landesbibiothek, 1979), 114.

169. Andrew von Hendy, *The Modern Construction of* Myth (Bloomington: Indiana University Press, 2002). For the later period, see Charles Maier, "The End of Longing? (Notes toward a History of Postwar German National Longing)," in *The Postwar Transformation of Germany,* ed. John Brady et al. (Ann Arbor: University of Michigan Press, 1999), 271–285.

170. Johann Bachofen, *Das Mutterrecht* (Stuttgart: Krais and Hoffman, 1861); Alfred Baeumler, *Das mythsiche Weltalter* (Munich: Beck, 1965).

171. Heinz Grünert, *Gustaf Kossinna* (Rahden, Germany: Leidorf, 2002).

172. Gusaf Kossinna, *Die Herkunft der Germanen: Zur Methode der Siedlungsarchäologie* (Leipzig: Kabitzsch, 1920), 3; Marchand, *Olympus,* 185.

173. Edgar Dacqué, *Organische Morphologie und Paläontologie* (Berlin: Gebrüder Borntraeger, 1935).

174. Wolf-Ernst Reif, "The Search for a Macroevolutionary Theory in German Paleontology," *Journal of the History of Biology* 19 (1986): 79–130.

175. Pollock, "Deep Orientalism," 93.

176. Karl Joël, *Seele und Welt* (Jena: Diederichs, 1912); Leopold Ziegler, *Der ewige Buddho* (Darmstadt: Reichl, 1922).

177. Arthur Moeller van den Bruck, *Das dritte Reich* (Hamburg: Hanseatische Verlagsanstalt, 1923).

178. Nabaneeta Sen, "The 'Foreign Reincarnation' of Rabindranath Tagore," *Journal of Asian Studies* 25 (1966): 275–286; Paul Natorp, *Stunden mit Rabindranath Thakkur* (Jena: Diederichs, 1921).

179. Leopold von Schroeder, *Arische Religion* (Leipzig: Haessel Verlag, 1914).

180. Leopold von Schroeder, *Mysterium und Mimus im Rigveda* (Leipzig: Philo Press, 1908), xi.

181. Strzygowski to Tagore, Vienna, June 18, 1921, Visva Bhārati University Archives (VBU), EC 387.

182. Josef Strzygwoski, *Die Krisis der Geisteswissenschaften* (Vienna: Schroll, 1923); On "crisis" as a Weimar-era concept, see Rüdiger Graf, *Die Zukunft der Weimarer Republik* (Munich: Oldenbourg, 2008).

183. See discussion in Colin Eisler, "Kunstgeschichte American Style," in *The Intellectual Migration,* ed. Donald Fleming and Bernard Bailyn (Cambridge, MA: Harvard University Press, 1969), 560; Strzygowski, *Krisis,* 29.

184. Talinn Grigor, "'Orient oder Rom?' Qajar 'Aryan' Architecture and Strzygowski's Art History," *Art Bulletin* 89 (2007): 562–590.

185. Susannah Heschel, *Aryan Jesus* (Princeton, NJ: Princeton University Press, 2008), 166–200.

186. See Benedict Anderson's concept of "imagined communities," in *Imagined Communities: Reflections on the Origin and Spread of Nationalism* (London: Verso, 1983), 6. By the late 1930s, Strzygowski's interest resolutely turned to Central Europe's purported Aryan cultural advantage over western Europe. See *Das indogermanische Ahnenerbe des deutschen Volkes und die Kunstgeschichte der Zukunft* (Vienna: Deutscher Verlag für Jugend und Volk, 1941); Josef Strzygowski, *Europas Machtkunst im Rahmen des Erdkreises* (Vienna: Wiener Verlag, 1943).

187. Suzanne Marchand, "The Rhetoric of Artifacts and the Decline of Classical Humanism: The Case of Josef Strzygowski," *History and Theory* 33 (1994): 106–130.

188. Hartmut Behr, *A History of International Political Theory: Ontologies of the International* (Basingstoke, UK: Palgrave Macmillan, 2010).

189. Erez Manela, *The Wilsonian Moment* (Oxford: Oxford University Press, 2007); Kevin McDermott and Jeremy Agnew, *The Comintern: A History of International Communism from Lenin to Stalin* (London: Macmillan Press, 1996), 1–40.

190. See Ernst zu Reventlow, "Versailles 1870/71," in *Von Potsdam nach Doorn* (Berlin: Klieber, 1940), 7.

191. Richard Evans, *The Coming of the Third Reich* (London: Allen Lane, 2003), 34–41; Heschel, *Aryan Jesus,* 20–25.

192. Otto Henne am Rhyn, *Kulturgeschichte des deutschen Volkes* (Berlin: Historischer Verlag Baumgaertel, 1903), i.

193. Bettina Arnold, "'Arierdämmerung': Race and Archaeology in Nazi Germany," *World Archaeology* 28 (2006): 8–31.

194. Egon Freiherr von Eickstedt, *Rassenkunde und Rassengeschichte der Menschheit* (Stuttgart: Ferdinand Enke, 1934), 14.

195. Klemens von Klemperer, *Konservative Bewegungen zwischen Kaiserreich und Nationalsozialismus* (Vienna: R. Spies, 1957), 148.

196. Geoffrey Field, "Nordic Racism," *Journal of the History of Ideas* 38 (1977): 523–540.

197. William Bossenbrook, *The German Mind* (Detroit: Wayne State University Press, 1961); George Santayana, *The German Mind* (New York: Crowell, 1968).

198. Stefan Arvidsson, *Aryan Idols* (Chicago: University of Chicago Press, 2006), 178–238; Thomas Trautmann, *The Aryan Debate* (Delhi: Oxford University Press, 2005), xxix.

199. Marchand, *German Orientalism*, 66–71.

200. Intro by Sven Hedin in Herbert Tichy, *Zum Heiligsten Berg der Welt* (Vienna: Seidel, 1937), 10.

201. Arthur Drews, "Das Licht des Ostens," *Tat* 15 (1923): 692.

202. Kevin Repp, *Reformers, Critics and the Paths of German Modernity* (Cambridge, MA: Harvard University Press, 2000), 53; Volker Berghahn, *Europe in the Era of Two World Wars* (Princeton, NJ: Princeton University Press, 2006): 33–47; Robert Chickering, *We Men Who Feel Most German;* Stanley Suval, "Overcoming Kleindeutschland: The Politics of Historical Mythmaking in the Weimar Republic," *Central European History* 2 (1969): 312–330.

203. Mike Tydesley, "The German Youth Movement and National Socialism," *Journal of Contemporary History* 41 (2006): 21–34; Peukert, *Weimar Republik*, 242: Schorske, *Fin-de-Siècle Vienna*, 62.

204. Bundesarchiv SS Parteikarten.

205. Pollock, "Deep Orientalism," 94; Michael H. Kater, *Das Ahnenerbe der SS* (Stuttgart: Deutsche Verlags-Anstalt, 1974): 43.

206. See Valentina Stache-Rosen, *German Indologists: Biographies of Scholars in Indian Studies Writing in Germany* (Delhi: Max Müller Bhavan, 1981).

207. See biographies of the main figures discussed in the online *Deutsche Biographie* of the Bavarian State Library (Bayerischen Staatsbibliothek), www.deutsche-biographie.de/index.

208. Kater, *Ahnenerbe*, 65; Anke Oesterle, "John Meier und das SS-Ahnenerbe," in *Volkskunde und Nationalsozialismus,* ed. Helge Gerndt (Munich: Münchner Beiträge zur Volkskunde, 1987), 83–93; Heschel, *Aryan Jesus*, 21.

209. Margarete Dierks, *Jakob Wilhelm Hauer* (Heidelberg: Schneider, 1986), 208–274; Schaul Baumann, *Die Deutsche Glaubensbewegung* (Marburg: Diagonal-Verlag, 2005).

210. Pollock, "Deep Orientalism," 94.

211. Bialas and Rabinbach, *Nazi Germany,* xxxii-xlii; Willi Oberkrome, "German Historical Scholarship under National Socialism," in Bialas and Rabinbach, *Nazi Germany,* 207–237.

212. Walter Ruben, "Autobiography," handwritten manuscript, Archiv der Berlin-Brandenburgischen Akademie der Wissenschaften (BBAW), Box 11, unnumbered files, no date.

213. For example, Wüst studied with Geiger; Breloer studied with Hermann Jacobi, and Ludwig Alsdorf studied under Heinrich Lüders.

214. Walther Wüst, *Stilgeschichte und Chronologie des RgVeda* (Leipzig: Deutsche morgenländische Gesellschaft, 1928), published on the literary style of the Rg-Veda.

215. Erich Frauwallner, *Geschichte der indischen Philosophie* (Salzburg: Otto Müller, 1956).

216. E. H. Johnston, "Hermann Jacobi," *Journal of the Royal Asiatic Society of Great Britain and Ireland* (1938), 346.

217. Ludwig Alsdorf, *The History of Vegetarianism and Cow-Veneration in India* (London: Routledge, 2010; orig. 1961).

218. Ludwig Alsdorf, *Deutsch-Indische Geistesbeziehungen* (Heidelberg: Kurt Vowinckel Verlag, 1944).

219. Horst Junginger, "From Buddha to Adolf Hitler: Walther Wüst and the Aryan Tradition," in *The Study of Religion under the Impact of Fascism,* ed. Juninger (Leiden: Brill, 2008), 107–178.

220. Bernhard Breloer, *Die Grundelemente der altindischen Musik* (Bonn: Bonner Universitäts-Buchdruckerei, 1922), 13.

221. Herman Lommel, *Religion und Kultur der alten Arier* (Frankfurt, 1935); Johannes Hertel, *Die arische Feuerlehre* (Leipzig: Haessel, 1925).

222. Helmuth von Glasenapp, *Der Hinduismus* (Munich: Wolff, 1922).

223. Franz Altheim, *Die Krise der Alten Welt* (Berlin: Ahnenerbe-Stiftung Verlag, 1943).

224. Ibid.

225. Hermann Güntert, *Der Ursprung der Germanen* (Heidelberg: Carl Winter, 1934).

226. Ibid., 137–157.

227. Hans F. K. Guenther, *The Racial Elements of European History* (London: Methuen, 1927), 152.

228. Hans F. K. Guenther, *Die Nordische Rasse bei den Indogermanen Asiens: Zugleich ein Beitrag zur Frage nach der Urheimat und Rassenherkunft der Indogermanen* (Jena: J. F. Lehmanns Verlag, 1934).

229. See Egon von Eickstedt, *Grundlagen der Rassenpsychologie* (Stuttgart: Ferdinand Enke, 1936), 103.

230. Oswald Menghin, *Einführung in die Urgeschichte Böhmens und Mährens* (Reichenberg: Sudetendeutscher Verlag Franz Kraus, 1926).

231. "Prehistoric" scholarship had reached a peak. Johan Callmer, ed., *Die Anfänge der ur- und frühgeschichtlichen Archäologie als akademisches Fach (1890–1930)* (Rahden, Germany: Leidorf, 2006).

232. The publishing of Buddhist texts, whether canonical or popular works, fell sharply in Germany in the 1930s. Heinz Sarkowski, *Der Insel Verlag, 1899–1999* (Frankfurt am Main: Insel, 1999).

233. Mitchell Ash, ed., *Forced Migration and Scientific Change* (Washington, DC: German Historical Institute, 1996); David Kettler, *The Liquidation of Exile* (London: Anthem, 2011); Volkmar von Sühlsdorff, *Deutsche Akademie im Exil* (Berlin: EMV, 1999).

234. Heinrich Robert Zimmer, *Kunstform und Yoga im indischen Kultbild* (Berlin: Frankfurter Verlags-Anstalt, 1926). See introduction by Joseph Campbell, ed., *Myths and Symbols in Indian Art and Civilization* (New York: Pantheon, 1972), v; Lucian Scherman, ed., *Kleine Schriften* (Stuttgart: F. Steiner, 2000); J. Scheftelowitz, *Die Zeit als Schicksalsgottheit in der indischen und iranischen Religion* (Stuttgart: Kohlhammer, 1929).

235. Erich von Hornbostel, *Music of the Orient* (New York: Decca, 1940); Dieter Christensen, "Erich von Hornbostel, Carl Stump, and the Institutionalization of Comparative Musicology," in *Comparative Musicology and Anthropology of Music*, ed. Bruno Nettl et al. (Chicago: University of Chicago Press, 1991), 201–209; Vanessa Agnew, "The Colonialist Beginnings of Comparative Musicology," in *Germany's Colonial Pasts*, ed. Eric Ames et al. (Lincoln: University of Nebraska Press, 2005), 41; Introduction by Barbara Stoler-Miller, ed., *Exploring India's Sacred Art: Selected Writings of Stella Kramrisch* (Philadelphia: University of Pennsylvania Press, 1983), 3–35.

236. Ash and Söllner, eds., *Forced Migration,* 6.

237. Martin Kern, "Die Emigration der Sinologen 1933–1945: Zur ungeschriebenen Geschichte der Verluste," in *Chinawissenschaften,* ed. Helmut Martin and Christiane Hammer (Hamburg: Istitut für Asienkunde, 1999), 222–242.

238. Skuli Sigurdsson, "Physics, Life, and Contingency: Born, Schroedinger, and Weyl in Exile," in Ash and Söllner, eds., *Forced Migration,* 48–70.

239. Kurt Walf, "Reading and Meaning of Daoist Texts in Nazi Germany," in *At Home in Many Worlds*, ed. Raoul Findeisen et al. (Wiesbaden: Harrassowitz, 2009), 152; see Steve Hochstadt, *Shanghai-Geschichten: die jüdische Flucht nach China* (Berlin: Hentrich and Hentrich, 2007).

240. Karl Löwith, *Reisetagebuch 1936 und 1941* (Marbach: Deutsche Schillergesellschaft, 2001), 79–95.

241. Alvin Mars, "A Note on Jewish Refugees in Shanghai," *Jewish Social Studies* 31 (1969): 286–291.

242. Anil Bhatti and Johannes Voigt, eds., *Jewish Exile in India* (Delhi: Manohar, 1999); see Muhammad Asad (previously Leopold Weiss), *Islam und Abendland* (Olten, Switzerland: Walter, 1960).

243. Bhatti and Voigt, *Jewish Exile,* 9–24.

244. Hermann Goetz, "Notes on the Maharaja Fatesingh Museum, Baroda," *East and West* 12 (1961): 254–255.

245. Thomas Lawton, "Dr. Stella Kramrisch," *Artibus Asiae* 53 (1993): 499–500.

246. Horst Krüger, *Neue Indienkunde* (Berlin: Akademie Verlag, 1970); Johannes Voigt, *Die Indienpolitik der DDR* (Cologne: Böhlau, 2008), 241; Friedrich Wilhelm, "The German Response to Indian Culture," *Journal of the American Oriental Society* 81 (1961): 395–405.

247. Walter Ruben, "Autobiography," unpublished manuscript, NL Ruben, BBAW. The result of the trip was an essay on the religion of the Asur tribe. Ruben, *Eisenschmiede und Dämonen in Indien* (Leiden: Brill, 1939), 102ff.

248. Ruben, "Autobiographie" in Walter Ruben Nachlass, BBAW, Berlin, Case 11, uncataloged.

249. Renate Heuer, ed., "Betty Heimann," *Lexikon deutsch-jüdischer Autoren*, vol. 10 (Munich: K. G. Saur, 2002), 353–355.

250. Linda Kerber, "The Stateless as the Citizen's Other: A View from the United States," *American Historical Review* 112 (2007): 1–34.

251. Tom Ambrose, *Hitler's Loss* (London: Chester Springs, 2001); Claus Dieter Krohn, *Intellectuals in Exile* (Amherst: University of Massachusetts Press, 1993); Fleming and Bailyn, *Intellectual Migration,* 8.

252. The case of Adorno in America provides a classic touchstone for the study of German methodology "in exile." See Theodor Adorno, "A European Scholar in America," trans. Donald Fleming, in Fleming and Bailyn, *Intellectual Migration,* 222–242. Franz Neumann, the political scientist living for some time in the United States, also wrote about the exile of German "theory and history" in the land of American "empiricism and pragmatism." Franz Neumann et al., *The Cultural Migration* (Philadelphia: University of Pennsylvania Press, 1953); Leo Spitzer's inquiry into the memory work of exiled Jewish communities, *Hotel Bolivia* (New York: Hill and Wang, 1998).

253. Anthony Heilbut, *Exiled in Paradise: German Refugee Artists and Intellectuals in America* (New York: Viking, 1983), 119, 438–468.

254. Scholars such as Hermann Goetz, Muhammad Asad (aka Leopold Weiss), Agehananda Bharati (aka Leopold Fischer), Stella Kramrisch, Walter Kaufmann, Otto Königsberger, all of Central European Jewish descent, made major contributions to the knowledgeable nationalism in India.

4. INDIAN VISIONS OF A GERMANIC HOME

1. Radhakamal Mukherjee, "Indian Emigration," in *Economic Problems of Modern India,* vol. 1 (London: Macmillan, 1939), 100; Eric Hobsbawn,

Industry and Empire: From 1750 to the Present Day (Harmondsworth, UK: Penguin, 1969), 207.

2. On Abinash Chandra Bhattacharya's previous career as a revolutionary terrorist in Bengal, see Samaren Roy, *The Restless Brahmin: Early Life of M. N. Roy* (Bombay: Allied Publishers, 1970), 19. See Abinash Chandra Bhattacharyya to Clemens Delbrück, August 11, 1914, AA, R21070–1, 28–30. Also see Bhattacharya's history of the diasporic nationalist movement, *Iyurōpe Bhāratiya Biplaber Sādhanā* (Calcutta: Bandana Impression, 1949).

3. Karl Emil Schabinger's report on the "Nachrichtenstelle für den Orient" includes a description of the twenty-three-room office at Tauentziener-straße 19a. III, September 21, 1915, AA, R1502, 13643.

4. Kris Manjapra, "Illusions of Encounter," *Journal of Global History* 1 (2006): 363–382.

5. On "sojourning," see Sunil Amrith, *Migration and Diaspora in Modern Asia* (Cambridge: Cambridge University Press, 2011), 22–37.

6. Lala Hardayal, *Forty-four Months in Germany and Turkey, February 1915 to October 1918* (London: P. S. King, 1920), 20.

7. Ibid., 17.

8. On the Hindustan Haus dormitory on Uhlandstraße, and the Association of Indians in Central Europe house on Knesebeckstraße, and on places of worship: Ausländer Kartei-Indien, 1928–1938, HUA; Cricket field at Baumschulenweg: I.B. Orientals in Berlin, India Office Library, L/P&J/12/102, September 3, 1923; homes of senior émigrés on Georg-Wilhelm-Straße: Orientals in Berlin, India Office Library, L/P&J/12/102, May 22, 1923.

9. Kris Manjapra, "From Imperial to International Horizons," *Modern Intellectual History* 8 (2011), 327–359.

10. Devesh Kapur and John McHale, *Give Us Your Best and Brightest: The Global Hunt for Talent and Its Impact on the Developing World* (Washington, DC: Center for Global Development, 2005), 105.

11. Giuseppe Flora, *Benoy Kumar Sarkar (1887–1949)* (Delhi: Center for Contemporary Studies, 1998), 14.

12. B. K. Sarkar, "The Making of Naren Sengupta," *Indian Journal of Psychology* 19 (1944): 125–134.

13. Benoy Kumar Sarkar, *Duniyār Ābhāōyā* (Calcutta: Raychaudhuri, 1926).

14. Benoy Kumar Sarkar, "Social Metabolism in Its Bearings on Progress," *Social Forces* 16 (1937): 169–177.

15. Flora, *Sarkar,* 12–17.

16. Benoy Kumar Sarkar, *Parājita Jārmānī* (Calcutta: Oriental Book Agency, 1932), 11.

17. Benoy Kumar Sarkar, *Economic Development* (Madras: B. G. Paul, 1926), i.

18. Sarkar, *Parājita Jārmānī*, i.

19. Sarkar, *Duniyār Ābhāōyā*, iv.

20. The series consisted of the following volumes: vol. 1 Egypt, vol. 2 Great Britain and Ireland, vol. 3 The Great War, vol. 4 United States of America, vol. 5 Japan, vol. 6 China, vol. 7 France, vol. 8 Germany, vol. 9 Austria, Vol. 10 Switzerland, vol. 11 Italy, and vol. 12 Atmosphere of the World.

21. Sarkar, *Parājita Jārmānī*, 14.

22. See Kshitish Chandra Banerjee's travelogue, *My Travels in the East* (Calcutta: Shailen, 1936); David Motadel, "Qajar Shahs in Imperial Germany," *Past and Present* 213 (2011): 191–235; Julie Codell, "Reversing the Grand Tour: Guest Discourse in Indian Travel Narratives," *Huntington Library Quarterly* 70 (2007): 173–189.

23. Kalidas Nag, *Memoirs* (Calcutta: Writers Workshop, 1991; orig. 1921–1923), 55.

24. Jacques Rancière, *Politics of Aesthetics* (London: Continuum, 2004).

25. "Orientals in Berlin," APAC: L/PJ/12/102. British intelligence reports on Indian life in Berlin held at the British Library.

26. Kris Manjapra, *M. N. Roy: Marxism and Colonial Cosmopolitanism* (Delhi: Routledge, 2010), 31–62.

27. Compare Omkar Goswami, "Sahibs, Babus, and Banias: Changes in Industrial Control in Eastern India," in *Entrepreneurship and Industry*, ed. Rajat Ray (Delhi: Oxford University Press, 1993), 228–259.

28. Uma Das Gupta, "Rabindranath Tagore on Rural Reconstruction: The Shriniketan Programme, 1921–1941," *Indian Historical Review* 5 (1978): 354–378.

29. Britain remained the most important center for Indian education overseas, in terms of numbers. Rozina Visram, *Ayahs, Lascars, and Princes* (London: Pluto, 1986); Sumita Mukherjee et al., "'The Land of Gold and Silver': Indian Students and Their Perceptions of Britain," *Historical Studies*, no. 26 (2009): 135–150.

30. "Indian Information Bureau and Chattopadhyaya," May 15, 1930, APAC, L/PJ/12/233, 79–81.

31. A. C. N. Nambiar to Nehru, Document regarding the founding of the Indian Information Bureau, March 20, 1929, ZMO Krüger Archive, Item 59; The Indian Information Bureau in Berlin, run by Virendranath Chattopadhyaya and A. C. N. Nambiar, facilitated the study of Indian students in Berlin. The organization leaders sent monthly reports to Nehru, and received funds from the coffers of the Indian National Congress beginning in 1928.

32. A. C. N. Nambiar to Jawaharlal Nehru, January 4, 1929, ZMO Krüger Archiv, Item 59.

33. Nehru to Chattopadhyaya, April 25, 1929, NAI Nehru Correspondence, ZMO Krüger Archive, Item 47.

34. "Indian Information Bureau and Chattopadhyaya," May 15, 1930, APAC, L/PJ/12/223: 79–81.

35. Eckard Michels, "Deutsch als Weltsprache?" *German History* 22 (2004): 206–228; Kurt Düwell, *Deutschlands auswärtige Kulturpolitik, 1918–1932* (Vienna: Böhlau Verlag, 1976), 379–384; Volkhard Laitenberger, *Akademischer Austausch und auswärtige Kulturpolitik* (Göttingen: Musterschmidt, 1976).

36. Nambiar to Nehru, August 27, 1929, ZMO Krüger Archive, Item 179.

37. Haushofer Nachlass N1122/115, January 31, 1936, Bundesarchiv Koblenz.

38. Nirode Barooah, *Chatto: The Life and Times of an Indian Anti-Imperialist in Europe* (Oxford: Oxford University Press, 2004), 178–224.

39. Thomas Fraser, "Germany and Indian Revolution, 1914–1918," *Journal of Contemporary History* 12 (1977): 255–272; Daniel Brückenhaus, "Every Stranger Must Be Suspected: Trust Relationships and the Surveillance of Anticolonialists in Early Twentieth-Century Western Europe," *Geschichte und Gesellschaft* 36 (2010): 525.

40. Barooah, *Chatto*, 7.

41. British surveillance file, APAC, L/PJ/12/667.

42. P. C. Ray, *Life and Experiences of a Bengali Chemist* (Calcutta: Chuckervertty, Chatterjee, 1932), 132.

43. Margit Pernau, "Schools for Muslim Girls: A Colonial or an Indigenous Project?" *Oriente Moderno* 23 (2004): 271; Sheela Raj, *Mediaevialism to Modernism* (Bombay: Popular Prakashan, 1987), 240; Tara Ali Baig, *Sarojini Naidu* (Delhi: Ministry of Information and Broadcasting, 1974).

44. Sarojini Naidu studied at King's College London and at Cambridge; Kamaladevi completed a course of study at the University of London; Virendranath studied at Oxford; Barooah, *Chatto*, 7–10.

45. Mrinalini Sinha, "Refashioning Mother India," *Feminist Studies* 26 (2000): 623–644.

46. Sibnarayan Ray, *In Freedom's Quest* (Calcutta: Minerva, 2002), 2:31–34.

47. M. Saha, "Facilities for Study in Germany," *Modern Review* 31 (1922): 157ff.

48. Sehri Saklatvala, *The Fifth Commandment: A Biography of Shapurji Saklatvala* (Salford, UK: Miranda, 1991); Mike Squires, *Saklatvala* (London: Lawrence and Wishart, 1990), 140, 144–157.

49. In 1923, British Intelligence reported more than 200 politically active students in Berlin. "Orientals in Berlin," APAC, January 13, 1923, L/PJ/12/102, 9,10.

50. Ausländerkartei Indien, 1928–1938, HUA. This source consists of enrollment cards of Indian students to the university in these years.

51. See Ausländerkartei Indien, 1928–1938, HUA.

52. Vivendranath Chattopadhyaya's house on Georg-Wilhelm-Straße served as the social epicenter. APAC, September 3, 1923, L/P&J/12/102.

53. Report on Indians, L/PJ/12/102, 1923.

54. Orientals in Berlin, APAC, May 22, 1923, L/PJ/12/102.

55. Hoi-eun Kim, "Physicians on the Move; German Physicians in Meiji Japan and Japanese Medical Students in Imperial Germany, 1868–1914," PhD diss., Harvard University, 2006; Meng Hong and Dagmar Yue-Dembski, *Chinesen in Berlin* (Berlin: Verwaltungsdrückerei Berlin, 1996), 32; Marilyn Levine, *The Found Generation: Chinese Communists in Europe during the Twenties* (Seattle: University of Washington Press, 1993), 147–149; Thomas Harnisch, *Chinesische Studenten in Deutschland: Geschichte und Wirkung ihrer Studienaufenthalte in den Jahren von 1860 bis 1945* (Hamburg: Institut für Asienkunde, 1999), 205.

56. See notes on immatriculation, December 4, 1923, *Mitteilungen des Deutschen Instituts für Ausländer,* HUA; Klaus Bade ed., *Deutsche im Ausland—Fremde in Deutschland* (Munich: Beck, 1992), 24.

57. "Berlin Pictorial," *Calcutta Review*, series 3, 7 (1923), 465.

58. "Berlin Pictorial."

59. Ibid.

60. See the Ausländer Kartei-Indien, 1928–1938, HUA.

61. The Siemensstadt, located in Spandau district, was established in 1899. Indian engineering students completed internships there in the 1930s. For example, N. G. Swami of Madras (1931), M. H. Advani (1929), Manmohan Lal Gauba (1929). See Siemens Aktenarchiv (SAA), Ausländerkartei nos. 9, 56, 168.

62. SAA, Munich, Akte 1291. In 1935, Siemens in Calcutta became the regional office for all of Asia.

63. SAA, Akte 9463, describes the visits of Indian nationalists to the Siemensstadt in 1936. Indian students also trained in engineering while living there, see the Humboldt Universität Ausländer Kartei Indien.

64. File 9463, SAA, Catalog no. 13139.

65. File 9463, SAA.

66. Daniel Rodgers, *Atlantic Crossings: Social Politics in a Progressive Age* (Cambridge, MA: Belknap Press of Harvard University Press, 1998); Hoi-Eun Kim, "Physicians on the Move."

67. Vivendranath Chattopadhyaya's house on Georg-Wilhelm-Straße served as the social epicenter of the Indian émigré community. APAC, September 3, 1923, L/P&J/12/102.

68. Sugata Bose, *His Majesty's Opponent* (Cambridge, MA: Belknap Press of Harvard University Press, 2011), 91.

69. "Indian Students in Germany at Home to German Professors," *Modern Review* 40 (1926): 229–231.

70. Sunil Kumar Ghosh, *Bhupendranath* (Kolkata: Madanmohan Library, 1971); Bhupendranath Datta, "Eine Untersuchung der Rassenelemente in Belutchistan, Afghanistan und den Nachbarländern des Hindukusch," PhD diss., University of Hamburg, 1921.

71. Interview with A. C. N. Nambiar, Oral History Collection at the Nehru Memorial Museum and Library (NMML), November 18, 1972.

72. "Indians and Germany" in *Sind Observer,* ZMO Krüger Archive, October 25, 1922, Item 50.

73. Amit Das Gupta, *Handel, Hilfe, Hallstein-Doktrin* (Husum: Matthiesen, 2004), 30.

74. In October 1922, Chattopadhyaya started the Indian News Service and Information Bureau in Berlin with support from Moscow. Lohani, Khankoji, and Abani Mukherjee, all three of whom were present at the original competition for Soviet support in early 1921, were apparently also being individually provided with financial support from the Soviet government to carry on communist activities outside M. N. Roy's circle. Das Gupta, December 24, 1923, NAI, Home Department Political, 1924 File 21/1.

75. Cecil Kaye, *Communism in India* (Calcutta: Editions Indian, 1971), 11.

76. Jawaharlal Nehru, in his *Autobiography* (London: John Lane, 1936), 161, records having been in Berlin at the end of 1926.

77. The League against Imperialism was originally called the "League against Cruelties and Oppression in the Colonies," Report on League Activities, APAC, June 2, 1927, L/PJ/12/267. This was a Soviet-sponsored organization established to increase Russian influence in the colonial world.

78. Surveillance report to Petrie, APAC, April 9, 1927, L/PJ/12/266.

79. Bornell, "Passports of Indians for Germany," APAC, September 7, 1922, L/PJ/12/98: 4, 5.

80. "List of Suspect Civilian Indians on the Continent of Europe," APAC, February 1944, L/PJ/12/659: 55.

81. A. M. Bose, AA, File 21090, August 25, 1916.

82. "Statement of Nalini Bhusan Das Gupta," NAI, Home Department, Political 1924, File 21/1.

83. APAC, L/PJ/12/462; Ray, *In Freedom's Quest*, 3:181.

84. Sheikh Ali, *Zakir Husain* (Delhi: Vikas, 1991).

85. Joachim Oesterheld, "Lohia as a Doctoral Student in Berlin," *Economic and Political Weekly* 45 (2010): 85–91.

86. Amar Farooqui, *Remembering Dr. Gangadhar Adhikari* (Delhi: People's Publishing House, 1998), 5–9.

87. Jyotirmoy Gupta, ed., *M.N. Saha in Historical Perspective* (Calcutta: Thema, 1994).

88. Virendranath Chattopadhyaya married Agnes Smedley, then, after their divorce, Lidiia Kazunovskaia. M. N. Roy married Evelyn Trent, and then Ellen Gottschalk after their divorce. Subhas Chandra Bose married Emilie Schenkel, while Benoy Kumar Sarkar married Ida Steiler. A. C. N. Nambiar, after his divorce from Suhasini Chattopadhyaya, married a German woman. See Manjapra, *M. N. Roy,* 119.

89. Vikram Seth, *Two Lives* (London: Little, Brown, 2005).

90. "CIB's Reports on Activities of Germans, Italians and Japanese," APAC, L/PJ/12/506, 79.

91. Ibid., 93.

92. Nina Berman, *Orientalismus, Kolonialismus und Moderne* (Stuttgart: M&P Verlag, 1997), 35.

93. Jon Jacobson, *Locarno Diplomacy: Germany and the West, 1925–1929* (Princeton, NJ: Princeton University Press, 1972), 35–46; John Lowe, *The Great Powers, Imperialism, and the German Problem* (London: Routledge, 1994), 251–253.

94. Wolfe Schmokel, *Dream of Empire: German Colonialism, 1919–1945* (New Haven, CT: Yale University Press, 1964), 76–89; Roger Chickering, *We Men Who Feel Most German* (Boston: Allen and Unwin, 1984), 56–62.

95. Agnes Smedley, "Indians in European Zoological Gardens," October 10, 2006, newspaper clipping in Krüger Nachlass, Box 59, Zentrum Moderner Orient (henceforth ZMO).

96. See Rachel Holmes, *The Hottentot Venus* (New York: Random House, 2006); Sander Gilman, "Black Bodies, White Bodies: Towards an Iconography of Female Sexuality in Late Nineteenth-Century Art, Medicine, and Literature" in *Race, Writing and Difference,* ed. Henry Gates (Chicago: University of Chicago Press, 1986), 223–261.

97. See Robert Rydell, *All the World's a Fair: Visions of Empire in American International Expositions, 1876–1916* (Chicago: University of Chicago Press, 1984), 22–32; Alexander Honold, "Ausstellung des Fremden— Menschen- und Völkerschau um 1900," in *Das Kaiserreich transnational,* ed. Sebastian Conrad and Jürgen Osterhammel (Göttingen: Vandenhoeck und Ruprecht, 2004), 170–190.

98. Lothar Dittrich, *Carl Hagenbeck (1844–1913): Tierhandel und Schaustellungen im Deutschen Kaiserreich* (Frankfurt am Main: Peter Lang, 1998); Carl Hagenbeck, *Von Tieren und Menschen: Erlebnisse und Erfahrungen* (Berlin: Vita, 1909); Klaus-Dieter Kürschner, *Von der Menagerie zum größten Circus Europas: Krone* (Berlin: Ullstein, 1998).

99. Mutius to Foreign Office, September 6, 1915, AA, 21089–1: 129, 130.

100. *Berliner Tageblatt*, March 21, 1927.

101. Virendranath Chattopadhyaya, "Der Zoo, ein neuer Lunapark. Der Schwindel der Indienschau," *Welt am Abend*, July 3, 1926.

102. Ibid.

103. See Chandana Mozumdar, "Swastika and Tiranga: Subhas Bose and Indian Nationalism's Connection with the Third Reich," PhD diss., Auburn University, 1999, 23, which references an article by Rudolf Olden in the files of the German Foreign Office.

104. Report, F. 15 XLV 28 Pol, NAI, reproduction in Krüger Nachlass, ZMO.

105. See reports of Tagore in the British press in Kalyan Kundu et al., *Imagining Tagore* (Calcutta: Shishu Sahitya Samsad, 2000), 120ff.

106. Martin Kämpchen, *Rabindranath Tagore and Germany* (Calcutta: Max Müller, 1991), 9; Rita Panesar, "Der Hunger nach dem Heiland," MA thesis, University of Hamburg, 2004.

107. Kämpchen, *Tagore and Germany*, 84ff.

108. Ketaki Kushar Dyson, *Ranger Rabindranath* (Kolkata: Ananda, 1997), 130.

109. Humboldt University, Musikwissenschaftliches Seminar, Lautarchiv, LA 346. This is a recording at the Berlin Staatsbibliothek by Wilhelm Doegen on Tagore's first visit to Germany in 1921. Recordings of an English and a Bengali address by Benoy Kumar Sarkar made in 1921, a poetry reading by Dwijendralal Ray, an address by the Maharaja of Baroda (LA 71) and by Keramat Ali are also stored in the archive.

110. Friedrich Raff, "Tagore-Aktien," *Vossische Zeitung*, December 15, 1921; Kurt Düwell, "Staat und Wissenschaft in der Weimarer Epoche: Zur Kulturpolitik des Ministers C. H. Becker," *Historische Zeitschrift* 1 (1971): 31–74.

111. Partha Mitter, *The Triumph of Modernism* (London: Reaktion, 2007); Kris Manjapra, "Stella Kramrisch and the Bauhaus in Calcutta," in *The Last Harvest*, ed. R. Sivakumar (Delhi: NGMA, 2011), 34–40.

112. Friedrich Raff, "Tagore-Aktien," *Vossische Zeitung*, December 15, 1921; Dr. E. R. Filcher, "Tagore und wir. Ein Schlußwort zur Tagore 'Mache,'" *Allgemeine Zeitung Chemnitz*, March 7, 1921; Alex Aronson, *Brief Chronicles of the Time: Personal Recollections of My Stay in Bengal* (Calcutta: Writers Workshop, 1990), 22.

113. Lewis Hyde, *The Gift: Imagination and the Erotic Life of Property* (New York: Random House, 1983), 56; Marcel Mauss, *Essai sur le Don* (Paris: Alcan, 1925).

114. Rabindranath Tagore to C. F. Andrews, May 10, 1921, Zurich, in C. F. Andrews, ed., *Letters to a Friend* (London: George Allen, 1931), 163.

115. Prasanta Kumar Pal, *Rabijibanī* (Kolkata: Bhurjapatra, 1988), 4:195.

116. Georg Lukàcs describes Tagore as a "a wholly insignificant figure," and criticizes the German fascination as a thirst for "spiritual substitutes" in

his review of *Gora*, "Tagore's Gandhi Novel" (1922), in *Reviews and Articles for Die Rote Fahne*, trans. Peter Palmer (London: Merlin Press, 1983), 8–11.

117. "Rabindranath Pratyābartan," *Prabāsī* 21 (1921): 763–764.

118. Ibid.

119. Ketaki Kushari Dyson, *Ranger Rabindranath* (Kolkata: Ananda, 1997), 130.

120. Ute Gahlings, *Hermann Keyserling* (Darmstadt: Liebig Verlag, 1996).

121. David Gosling, *Science and the Indian Tradition: When Einstein Met Tagore* (London: Routledge, 2007). The conversation between the two was published as Rabindranath Tagore, *The Religion of Man* (New York: Macmillan, 1930).

122. W. G. Archer, "The Paintings of Tagore," *East and West* 12 (1961): 147–151; Ananda Coomaraswamy, "Drawings by Rabindranath Tagore," *Rupam*, nos. 42-44, 1930, 73–75.

123. Stella Kramrisch, "Indische Malerei der Gegenwart: zur XV. Jahresausstellung der India Society of Oriental Art," *Der Cicerone* 16 (1924): 954–962.

124. Ratan Parimoo, *Paintings of Three Tagores* (Baroda: University of Baroda, 1973).

125. "Tagore als Maler," in *Der Tag*; "Ausstellung in der Galerie Moeller" by KZ, "Tagore als Maler" by WG. These clippings from 1930 are in File 1436 "Tagore, Rabindranath" at the Zentralarchiv der Staatlichen Museen zu Berlin (ZSMB).

126. Tagore to Justi, ZSMB, August 15, 1930, File 1436, p. 1.

127. Stella Kramrisch, "Form Elements in the Visual Work of Rabindranath Tagore," *Lalit Kala Contemporary*, 2 (1964): 37–39.

128. Fritz Wartenweiler, *Indiens Not, Indiens Ringen; Hinweis auf neuere Schriften über Indien und Gandhi* (Erlenbach: Rotapfel, 1932), 123–126.

129. Josef Strzygowski to Rabindranath Tagore, April 4, 1922, Vienna, Visva Bhārati Archive (VBA), Shantiniketan, EC 387.

130. Alik Akhtar Ansari, "Tadsch Mahal und seine Bedeutung für die Geschichte der indische Baukunst," PhD diss., Fachbibliotek Kunstgeschichte, Vienna University, 1926. Accompanying images in Fotosammlung Box 28; Josef Strzygowski, *The Influences of Indian Art* (London: India Society, 1925).

131. See Kalidas Nag, "Dr. Sten Konow and the Via-Bharati," *Modern Review* 36 (1924): 721–722.

132. Moriz Winternitz, *Rabindranath Tagore* (Prague: Calve in Komm, 1936).

133. Rabindranath Tagore to Nirmalkumari Mahalanobis, July 15, 1927, in Tagore, *Jāvā Yātrīr Patra,* quoted in Sugata Bose, *A Hundred Horizons* (Cambridge, MA: Harvard University Press, 2006), 245.

134. Hermann Weber, *Der deutsche Kommunismus* (Cologne: Kiepenheuer und Witsch, 1963), 101.

135. Peel, "Memorandum on V. Chattopadhyaya," APAC, January 1929, L/PJ/12/280.

136. See the Richthofen report, Bundesarchiv, Reichskommissariat für Überwachung der öffentlichen Ordnung, R1507/67299/650, October 17, 1924, 11, 12. Meanwhile in India, von Collenberg was also busy trying to obtain new permissions for German traders. In an interview for the *Industrie und Handelszeitung* of May 1925, no. 1, 245, 246, the German consul general of India said that Germany's trade aims must take pride of place.

137. "Orientals in Berlin," APAC, September 3, 1923, L/PJ/12/102.

138. "Communiste (Internationale)," GA C3, and "Au Sujet du Mouvement Nationaliste Hindou," B2184 148.800-C, Prefecture de Policier, Paris. These files recount the efforts of French police to track and expel M. N. Roy in 1925.

139. Benoy Kumar Sarkar returned to India on September 18, 1925. He was hailed in the local press, the *Indian Daily Mail* and the *Bombay Chronicle,* as the ambassador of new India. See Giuseppe Flora, *Benoy Kumar Sarkar (1887–1949)* (Delhi: Center for Contemporary Studies, 1998), 17. Bhupendranath Datta returned in 1927. See "Bhupendranath Datta Returning to India," *Modern Review,* May 1927, 289–290. On the Kheiri brothers' petition to return to India, see the letter from Madeleine Slade to Alexander Muddmann, NAI, January 12, 1926, "Jabbar and Sattar Kheiri," Political File no. 39.

140. See the recollections of Lucie Hecht, Chattopadhyaya's secretary, in her letter to Horst Krüger, "Memories of Chattopadhyaya," 1967, ZMO Archive, Krüger Nachlass, Item 41.

141. Ibid.

142. Ibid.

143. Evelyn Roy to Henk Sneevliet [Jack Horner], March 13, 1927, International Institute for Social History (IISH), Sneevliet Files 362.

144. Agnes Smedley, "European Quest" in *Battle Hymn of China* (New York: Knopf, 1943), 150.

145. Ruth Price, *The Lives of Agnes Smedley* (New York: Oxford University Press, 2005), 141–144.

146. "Die Ermordung des Inders Singh von seiner Frau und Mörderin, Hilde Singh-Aluwaliya," *Welt am Abend,* September 27, 1926.

147. Prittwitz, "Sketch of Har Dayal," AA, March 19, 1918, R21112–2: 134–137; Dharmavira, *Lala Har Dayal and Revolutionary Movements of His Times* (Delhi: India Book Company, 1970).

148. Dharmavira, *Har Dayal*.

149. Ray, *In Freedom's Quest*, 3:53, 54.

150. See, for example, the report about Abdussattar Siddiqi, AA, July 31, 1915, R21087. Subhas Chandra Bose would also suffer from chronic stomach ailments. See Leonard A. Gordon, *Brothers against the Raj: A Biography of Indian Nationalists Sarat and Subhas Chandra Bose* (New York: Columbia University Press, 1990), 257.

151. Nayan Shah, "Between 'Oriental Depravity' and 'Natural Degenerates': Spatial Borderlands and the Making of Ordinary Americans," *American Quarterly* 57 (2005): 703–725.

152. Lucie Hecht to Horst Krüger, August 10, 1967, ZMO. She said that "Chatto was essentially on the run." Chattopadhyaya, in a letter to Nehru, wrote, "My health has been causing me some anxiety . . . My nerves are in a terrible condition." Chattopadhyaya to Nehru, January 23, 1929, NAI Nehru Correspondence, photocopied in ZMO, Krüger Nachlass, Item 43.

153. Letter from Lidiia Kazunovskaia, Chattopadhyaya's Russian wife, to Horst Krüger, June 13, 1965, "Memories of Chattopadhyaya," ZMO, Krüger Nachlass, Item 59.

154. Chattopadhyaya writes to Jawaharlal Nehru, May 1928: "The work of the Secretariat (of the League against Imperialism) is extremely heavy and I sometimes feel like giving it up. But then what will I do? . . . I feel very tired—and dreadfully home-sick." Chattopadhyaya to Nehru, NAI: Nehru Correspondence, photocophy in Krüger Nachlass, ZMO, Item 130.

155. He became a professor of anthropology in Moscow in the early 1930s, but was charged with advancing views that were not in line with party discipline. Virendranath Chattopadhyaya was likely executed in one of Stalin's purges in 1936. See Barooah, *Chatto*, 300.

156. "Archie Phinney," RGASPI, Fund 100, Item 109.

157. Barooah, *Chatto*, 309.

158. Adolf Hitler, *Mein Kampf* (Boston: Houghton Mifflin, 1999), 1:150–155.

159. Tapan Mukherjee, *Taraknath Das* (Calcutta: Jadavpur, 1998), 201.

160. On the arrest of Nambiar and Naidu, see British intelligence report, APAC, March 8, 1933, L/PJ/12/73. The communists were banned in March 1933, and the SPD in June 1933. But the conflict between the socialists and communists, on one hand, and the Nazis, on the other, had already begun to intensify by early 1931. On large-scale arrests of Nazis see Detlev Peukert, *Inside Nazi Germany* (New Haven, CT: Yale University Press, 1987), 89–95; Ossip Flechtheim, *Die KPD in der Weimarer Republik* (Frankfurt am Main: Europäische Verlangsanstalt, 1969), 283–288; William Allen, *The Nazi Seizure of Power* (Chicago: Quadrangle Books, 1965), 34.

161. See the report by the British ambassador in Berlin, Horace Rumbold, APAC, March 8, 1933, L/PJ/12/73.

162. "Nazi Imprisonment," APAC, L/PJ/12/73.

163. Taraknath Das, "A Memorandum on the Possibility of Establishing a School of Oriental Studies in Munich," Institut für Zeitgeschichte Archive (IZA), November 1, 1931, MA 1190/3.

164. See Nicholas Goodricke-Clarke, *Hitler's Priestess: Savitri Devi, the Hindu-Aryan Myth, and Neo-Nazism* (New York: New York University Press, 1998), 80–91; on German Indology in the Nazi period, see also Sheldon Pollock, "Deep Orientalism: Notes on Sanskrit and Power Beyond the Raj," in *Orientalism and the Postcolonial Predicament,* ed. Carol Breckenridge and Peter van der Veer (Philadelphia: University of Pennsylvania Press, 1993), 86; Karl Haushofer was the president of the Deutsche Akademie, and like many intellectuals in the party did not see the alliance between India and Germany through the lens of occultism or spiritual yearning, but believed in a geopolitical alliance.

165. The most important sources on Subhas Chandra Bose in Germany are Gordon, *Brothers against the Raj*, and Bose, *His Majesty's Opponent;* Trott zu Solz, "Notriz für Herrn Luther," NA-UK, January 28, 1943, Catalog no. 349596, GFM 33/564.

166. Trott zu Solz, "Notriz für Herrn Luther," NA-UK GFM 33/564.

167. His first preserved letter from the continent is dated March 1933. See Subhas Chandra Bose, *Letters, Articles, Speeches and Statements, 1933–1937,* ed. Sisir Kumar Bose and Sugata Bose (Calcutta: Netaji Research Bureau, 1994), 1. Nazi intelligence kept a close watch on Bose's activities in 1933. German agents referred to him as the "presumptive successor of Mahatma Gandhi." See Report by Emil Gassner, October 22, 1933, Bundesarchiv, R1501/125746: 44, 45.

168. Gordon, *Brothers against the Raj,* 269; Anton Pelinka, *Demokratie in Indien* (Vienna: Studienverlag, 2005), 81–105.

169. "Deutsch-Indische Gesellschaft," Österreichisches Staatsarchiv, AdR/BPO Wien, Vereinsbüro XVIII/11809; APAC, CIB Report, Survey no. 10 of 1939, 26.

170. "CIB's Reports on Activities of Germans, Italians and Japanese," APAC, L/PJ/12/506, 111.

171. APAC, L/PJ/12/506.

172. Johannes Voigt, "Hitler und Indien," *Vierteljahrshefte für Zeitgeschichte* 19 (1971): 33–63.

173. See quote in Gassner report, Bundesarchiv, October 22, 1933, R1501/125746: 44, 45.

174. Gordon, *Brothers against the Raj,* 283.

175. Subhas Chandra Bose to Dyckhoff, April 5, 1934, quoted in Gordon, *Brothers against the Raj,* 283.

176. Durlab Singh, *Formation and Growth of the Indian National Army* (Lahore: Hero Publications, 1946), 24–26.

177. After strong pressure from the British government, the "Hindoo-German Conspiracy Case" in San Francisco ran from November 1917 to April 1918.

178. APAC, May 21, 1940, L/PJ/12/163, 100.

179. Shedai to Doertenbach, National Archivs UK, E233877–83 (4757), GFM 33/2110.

180. "List of Suspect Civilian Indians on the Continent of Europe," APAC, L/PJ/12/659. Of the 116 names on the surveillance list, 24 were recorded as having come to Central Europe before the rise of the Nazis. The list is not complete, and does not offer comparable information for each individual recorded.

181. Eric Phipps, "Indian Societies and Associations in Germany," 1939, APAC, L/P&J/12/410.

182. "Indian Communist Party," August 18, 1922, APAC, L/PJ/12/46, 3.

183. Gerhard Höpp, ed., *Blind für die Geschichte? Arabische Begegnungen mit dem Nationalsozialismus* (Berlin: Klaus Schwarz, 2004), 55; Gerhard Höpp, *Mufti-Papiere: Briefe, Memoranden, Reden und Anrufe Amin al-Husaini* (Berlin: Schwarz, 2001), 105.

184. Francis Nicosia, "Arab Nationalism and National Socialist Germany, 1933–39: Ideological and Strategic Incompatibility," *International Journal of Middle East Studies* 12 (1980): 351–372.

185. Höpp, *Mufti-Papiere,* 170.

186. Noor-Aiman Khan, *Egyptian-Indian Nationalist Collaboration* (New York: Palgrave Macmillan, 2011).

187. Jakob Hauer became the leader of the Nazi Glaubensbewegung, and advanced notions of the Aryan brotherhood of Germans and Indians. See Goodricke-Clarke, *Hitler's Priestess,* 71–79; Margaret Dierks, *Hauer,* 208.

188. Phipps, "Indian Societies and Associations in Germany," APAC, September 8, 1939, L/P&J/12/410, 10–15.

189. Ludwig Alsdorf, "Zu schaffendes Organ für die Indo-Germanische Arbeitsgemeinschaft," an Trott and Staatssekretär Keppler, National Archive UK, 1942, GFM, 599–602, 16.

190. Ibid.

191. Gordon, *Brothers against the Raj,* 524; N. G. Ganpuley, *Netaji in Germany* (Bombay: Bharatiya Vidya Bhavan, 1959), 151ff.

192. "CIB's Reports on Activities of Germans, Italians and Japanese," APAC, L/PJ/12/506.

193. Ibid.

194. Ibid.

195. Delhi Intelligence Bureau Reports, January 20, 1940, APAC, L/PJ/ 12/507, 26.

196. "CIB's Reports on activities of Germans, Italians and Japanese," APAC, L/PJ/12/506.

197. Bose, *His Majesty's Opponent*; Johannes Voigt, *Indien im Zweiten Weltkrieg* (Delhi: Arnold-Heinemann, 1987), 150–159.

5. THE PHYSICAL COSMOS

1. Carl Schorske, *Fin-de-Siècle Vienna* (New York: Knopf, 1979), xix.

2. Paul Forman, "Scientific Internationalism and the Weimar Physicists," *Isis* 64 (1973): 154; John Cornwell, *Hitler's Scientists* (New York: Viking, 2003), 93–110.

3. Ashis Nandy, "Defiance and Conformity in Science: The Identity of Jagadis Chandra Bose," *Science Studies* 2 (1972): 31–85.

4. Saha established the *Science and Culture Journal* in 1934.

5. Benjamin Zachariah, "Uses of Scientific Argument: The Case of 'Development' in India, 1930–1950," *Economic and Political Weekly* 36 (2001): 3689–3702.

6. Deepak Kumar, "Reconstructing India: Disunity in the Science and Technology for Development Discourse, 1900–1947," *Osiris* 15 (2000): 241–257.

7. Erwin Schrödinger, "Ist die Naturwissenschaft milieubedingt?" February 18, 1932, Berlin, in *Über Indeterminismus in der Physik* (Leipzig: Barth, 1932), 35–36.

8. Henning Eichberg, "On Olympic Sport," in *Fin de Siècle and Its Legacy*, ed. Mikulas Teich and Roy Porter (Cambridge: Cambridge University Press, 1990), 115–131; Dikaia Chatziefstathiou, *Discourses of Olympism: From the Sorbonne 1894 to London 2012* (Hampshire, UK: Palgrave Macmillan, 2012), 28–31.

9. Walter John Moore, *Schrödinger, Life and Thought* (Cambridge: Cambridge University Press, 1989), 9.

10. Russell McCormmach, "On Academic Scientists in Wilhelmian Germany," *Daedalus* 130 (1974): 157–171.

11. Lewis Pyenson and Douglas Skopp, "Educating Physicists in Germany circa 1900," *Social Studies of Science* 7 (1977): 329–366.

12. Brigitte Schroeder-Gudehus, "Challenge to Transnational Loyalties: International Scientific Organizations after the First World War," *Science Studies* 3 (1973): 93–118.

13. Jagdish Mehra, *The Golden Age of Theoretical Physics* (Singapore: World Scientific, 2001), 1:404–458.

14. Ian Hacking, *The Emergence of Probability* (London: Cambridge University Press, 1975), 63–72.

15. Subrata Dasgupta, *Jagadis Chandra Bose and the Indian Response to Western Science* (Oxford: Oxford University Press, 1999); Ashis Nandy, *Alternative Sciences: Creativity and Authenticity in Two Indian Scientists* (Delhi: Allied, 1980), 20.

16. Jagadish Chandra Bose, "Inauguration of the Bose Institute," November 30, 1917; J. C. Bose, *Sir Jagadish Chander Bose: His Life, Discoveries and Writings* (Madras: G. A. Natesan, 1921): 90–110; Patrick Geddes, *The Life and Work of Sir Jagadis C. Bose* (London: Longmans, Green, 1920).

17. Jagadish Chandra Bose, "Reply to Calcutta Citizens' Address," *Sir Jagadish Chander Bose*, 117; On J. C. Bose, see the recent work by Pratik Chakrabarti, *Western Science in Modern India: Metropolitan Methods, Colonial Practices* (Delhi: Permanent Black, 2004): 180–218.

18. Quote of Jagadananda Roy, Visvapriya Mukherjee, *Jagadish Chandra Bose* (Delhi: Ministry of Information and Broadcasting, 1983), 29.

19. See Jagadis Chandra Bose's world travels, Monoranjon Gupta, *Jagadishchandra Bose* (Delhi: Bharatiya Vidya Bhavan, 1964); Subrata Dasgupta, *Jagadish Chandra Bose and the Indian Response to Western Science* (Delhi: Oxford University Press, 2000).

20. Srinivasa Ramanujan (1918, mathematics); J. C. Bose (1920, physics); Chandrasekhar Venkata Raman (1924, physics); Meghnad Saha (1927, physics); Birbal Sahni (1936, palaeobotany); Kariamnikkam Krishnan (1940, physics); Homi Jehangir Bhabha (1941, physics); Shanti Swarup Bhatnagar (1943, chemistry); Subhramanyam Chandrasekhar (1944, astrophysics); P. C. Mahalanobis (1945, statistics); Darashaw Nosherwan Wadia (1957, geology); Satyendranath Bose (1958, physics). See *Current Science* 80 (2001): 721.

21. C. V. Raman was elected fellow in 1924, Meghnad Saha was elected in 1927, and S. N. Bose elected in 1958. See S. Bhagavantam, "C. V. Raman (1888–1970)," *Biographical Memoirs of Fellows of the Royal Society* 17 (1971): 564–592; D. S. Kothari, "Meghnad Saha (1893–1956)," *Biographical Memoirs of Fellows of the Royal Society* 5 (1959): 217–236; J. Mehra, "Satyendra Nath Bose, 1894–1974," *Biographical Memoirs of Fellows of the Royal Society* 21 (1975): 116–126.

22. Elisabeth Crawford, J. L. Heilbron, and Rebecca Ullrich, *The Nobel Population 1901–1937: A Census of the Nominators and Nominees for the Prizes in Physics and Chemistry* (Berkeley: University of California Press,

344 • Notes to Pages 116–119

1987); Singh Rajinder, "India's Physics and Chemistry Nobel Prize Nominators and Nominees," *Notes and Records of the Royal Society* 61 (2007): 333–345.

23. Brigitte Schroeder-Gudehus, "Division of Labour and the Common Good," in *Science, Technology and Society in the Time of Alfred Nobel,* ed. Carl Gustaf Bernhard et al. (Oxford: Pergamon, 1982), 14.

24. Erez Manela, *The Wilsonian Moment* (Oxford: Oxford University Press, 2007).

25. B. D. Nag, "India and Intellectual Co-operation," *India and the World Journal* 1 (1932): 213.

26. A. G. Cock, "Chauvinism and Internationalism in Science: The International Research Council, 1919–1926," *Notes and Records of the Royal Society* 37 (1983): 249–288.

27. Cock, "Chauvinism."

28. See Dhruv Raina, *Images and Contexts: The Historiography of Science and Modernity in India* (Delhi: Oxford University Press, 2003), which presents Indians as engaged in a dialogue with new methods.

29. Abha Sur, "Scientism and Social Justice: Meghnad Saha's Critique of the State of Science in India," *Historical Studies in the Physical and Biological Sciences* 33 (2002): 87–105.

30. P. C. Ray, *Autobiography of a Bengali Chemist* (Calcutta: Orient Book, 1932).

31. "Development of Chemical Industries and Its Necessity," *Calcutta Review,* 3rd series, 5 (1922): 137, 138.

32. John Loudusamy, "The Indian Association for the Cultivation of Science," *Journal of Science Education and Technology* 12 (2003): 381–396.

33. Meghnad Saha, autobiographical note, in *Collected Works,* ed. Shanitmay Chatterjee (Delhi: Government of India, 1986), 1:103.

34. Johann Heinrich von Thünen, *Der isolierte Staat in Beziehung auf Land, Wirtschaft und Nationalökonomie* (Berlin: Akademie-Verlag, 1835), 160.

35. Mokshagundam Visvesvaraya, *Memoirs of My Working Life* (Bangalore: Visvesvaraya, 1951), 30.

36. Shiv Visvanathan, *Organizing for Science: The Making of an Industrial Research Laboratory* (Delhi and Oxford: Oxford University Press, 1985), 49–89.

37. *Indian Industrial Commission 1916–1918* (Delhi: Agricole Publishing Academy, 1980).

38. Arnold, *New Cambridge History of India,* 166.

39. Chakrabarti, *Western Science in Modern India,* 296.

40. Shiv Visvanathan, *Organizing for Science* (Delhi: Oxford University Press, 1985), 50.

41. Rajani Palme Dutt, *India Today* (London: n.p., 1940), 144.

42. Quoted in B. R. Tomlinson, *The Economy of Modern India* (Cambridge: Cambridge University Press, 1993), 120.

43. P. C. Ray, *Essays and Discourses: with a Biographical Sketch* (Madras: Natesan, 1918), 15; Arnold, *New Cambridge History of India,* 162.

44. Ray, *Essays and Discourses,* 240.

45. Ibid., 70.

46. Santimay Chatterjee, "Introduction," in Saha, *Collected Works,* 1:4.

47. S. N. Bose, quoted in Jagdish Mehra, S. N. Bose obituary, *Biographical Memoirs of Fellows of the Royal Society* 21 (1975): 120.

48. Meghnad Saha, "On Maxwell's Stresses," *Philosophical Magazine* 33, nos. 193–198 (1917), 256–261; Meghnad Saha, "On Radiation-Pressure and the Quantum Theory," *Astrophysical Journal* 50 (1919): 220–226.

49. Ben Almassi, "Trust in Expert Testimony: Eddington's 1919 Eclipse Expedition and the British Response to General Relativity," *Studies in History and Philosophy on Modern Physics* 40 (2009): 57–67.

50. Alex Soojung-Kim Pang, "The Social Event of the Season: Solar Eclipse Expeditions and Victorian Culture," *Isis* 84 (1993): 125–177.

51. Saha, *Collected Works,* 2:450.

52. "The Eclipse of the Sun," *London Times,* June 5, 1919.

53. "Time and Space—The New Scientific Theory," *Statesman* (Calcutta), November 4, 1919.

54. Jagadish Mehra, "S. N. Bose," *Biographical Memoirs of Fellows of the Royal Society* 21 (1975): 117–122.

55. See Saha's autobiographical note in *Collected Works of Meghnad Saha,* 1:7.

56. The notation of Meghnad Saha's ionization equation is:

$$\frac{n_{i+1} n_e}{n_i} = \frac{2}{\Lambda^3} \frac{g_{i+1}}{g_i} \exp\left[-\frac{\varepsilon_{i+1} - \varepsilon_i}{k_B T} \right].$$

57. Robert Anderson, *Building Scientific Institutions in India: Saha and Bhabha* (Montreal: McGill University Press, 1975), 12.

58. Diana Barkan, *Walther Nernst and the Transition to Modern Physical Science* (Cambridge: Cambridge University Press, 1999), 23; Hans-Georg Bartel and Rudolf Hübener, *Walther Nernst: Pioneer of Physics and of Chemistry* (Hackensack, NJ: World Scientific, 2007), 194.

59. Meghnad Saha to Ashutosh Mukherjee, August 20, 1921, Berlin, Nehru Memorial Museum and Library, List 92; K. Mendelssohn, *The World of Walther Nernst: The Rise and Fall of German Science, 1864–1941* (Pittsburgh: University of Pittsburgh Press, 1973), 68.

60. M. N. Saha, "Versuch einer Theorie der physikalischen Erscheinungen bei hohen Temperaturen mit Anwendungen auf die Astrophysik" (Attempt at

a Theory of Physical Occurrences at High Temperatures with Implications for Astrophysics), *Zeitschrift für Physik A: Hadrons and Nuclei* 6 (1921): 40–55. He published a subsequent important article, "Über einen experimentellen Nachweis der thermischen Ionisierung der Elemente," *Zeitschrift für Physik* 40 (1926): 648–651.

61. Meghnad Saha, "Facilities for Study in Germany," *Modern Review* 31 (1922): 157.

62. British surveillance reports asserted M. N. Saha's contacts to M. N. Roy during the former's stay in Berlin. "Activities of Roy's Agents in India," APAC, L/PJ/12/54, 15–19.

63. Subhas Chandra Bose and Meghnad Saha called a conference of the Bengal Young Men's Conference on Bow Street in 1922. See Meghnad Saha Files, Bengal State Archives, 100; Sambit Mallick et al., "Debates on Science and Technology in India: Alliance Formation between the Scientific and Political Elite during the Inter-War Period," *Social Scientist* 33 (2005): 49–75.

64. Saha, "Address as President, Physics and Mathematics Section", *13th Indian Science Congress: Papers and Abstracts* (Kolkata: Indian Science Congress Association, 1926).

65. Abinash Chandra Bhattacharaya, *Bahirbhārate Bhārater Muktiprayās* (Kolkata: Firma Mukhopadhyaya, 1962), 104.

66. S. N. Bose, quoted in Jagdish Mehra, *S. N. Bose* obituary, 122–124.

67. S. N. Bose, "Plancks Gesetz und Lichtquantenhypothese," *Zeitschrift für Physik* 26 (1924): 178–181.

68. Mehra, *S. N. Bose*, 136.

69. David Rowe and Robert Schulmann, *Einstein on Politics* (Princeton, NJ: Princeton University Press, 2007), 204–215.

70. Einstein Papers, Boston University Archive Papers, Box 13; Gandhi–Einstein correspondence in Control no. 587–623, Einstein Papers, Boston University Library; Nehru–Einstein correspondence in Control no. 725–52, Einstein Papers, Boston University Library; Tagore–Einstein correspondence in folder EC104 of Visva Bhārati Archives, Shantiniketan; on Einstein's correspondence with M. N. Roy, see Sibnarayan Ray, *In Freedom's Quest* (Calcutta: Minerva, 2002), 3:284n31.

71. Hubert Goenner, *Einstein in Berlin* (Munich: Beck, 2005), 291–305.

72. Adolf von Harnack, "Denkschrift Seiner Majestät dem deutschen Kaiser unterbreitet, 1909," in *Wissenschaftspolitische Reden und Aufsätze*, ed. Bernhard Fabian (Hildesheim, Germany: Olms-Weidmann, 2001), 12.

73. Elisabeth Crawford, *Nationalism and Internationalism in Science, 1880–1939* (Cambridge: Cambridge University Press, 1992), 106–124.

74. Schroeder-Gudehus, "Division of Labour," 6.

75. H. Kellermann, *Der Krieg der Geister* (Weimar: Duncker, 1915); Jürgen von Ungern-Sternberg and Wolfgang von Ungern-Sternberg, *Der Aufruf "An die Kulturwelt!" Das Manifest der 93 und die Anfänge der Kriegspropaganda im Ersten Weltkrieg* (Stuttgart: Steiner, 1996); Stefan Wolff, "Physicists in the 'Krieg der Geister': Wilhelm Wien's 'Proclamation,'" *Historical Studies in the Physical and Biological Sciences* 33 (2003): 337–368.

76. Bartel and Hübener, *Walther Nernst*, 251.

77. Robert Anderson, *Building Scientific Institutions in India: Saha and Bhabha* (Montreal: McGill University, 1975), 12.

78. Humboldt Universität Archiv, Phil Fak. 312. Chakravarty wrote his dissertation paper "Über Anthrapyridone."

79. Suman Seth, *Crafting the Quantum* (Cambridge, MA: MIT Press, 2010), 73, 79–84.

80. Jeffrey Johnson, *The Kaiser's Chemists: Science and Modernization in Imperial Germany* (Chapel Hill: University of North Carolina Press, 1990), 124.

81. Max Born, *My Life and My Views* (New York: Scribner, 1968), 169–173.

82. Bartel and Huebener, *Walther Nernst,* xi.

83. Forman, "Scientific Internationalism," 161.

84. Kevin Repp, *Reformers, Critics and the Paths of German Modernity* (Cambridge, MA: Harvard University Press, 2000), 12–13.

85. Forman, "Scientific internationalism," 151–180.

86. Repp, *Reformers*, 215–312.

87. Hans Hartmann, *Max Planck als Mensch und Denker* (Basel: Ott, 1953), 32–33.

88. Frank-Rutger Hausmann, "Auch im Krieg schweigen die Musen nicht," in *Die deutschen wissenschaftlichen Institute im Zweiten Weltkrieg* (Göttingen: Vandenhoeck und Rupprecht, 2001).

89. Nadine Rossol, *Performing the Nation in Interwar Germany: Sport, Spectacle and Political Symbolism* (Basingstoke, UK: Palgrave Macmillan, 2010), 26–36.

90. Brigitte Schroeder-Gudehus, *Deutsche Wissenschaft und internationale Zusammenarbeit* (Geneva: Dumaret & Golay, 1966), 204.

91. Fritz Haber to H. R. Kruyt, July 7, 1926, quoted in Forman, "Scientific Internationalism," 163.

92. Pamela Spencer Richards, *Scientific Information in Wartime: The Allied-German Rivalry, 1939–1945* (Westport, CT: Greenwood Press, 1994), 46.

93. "Die deutsche Chemie in den letzten 10 Jahren," 13 Mai 1924, *Mitteilungen des Deutschen Instituts für Ausländer,* HUA.

94. "Denkschrift der Kartellierten Akademien über den Conseil International de Recherches," 1927, Berlin-Brandenburg Academie der Wissenschaft Archiv (BBAW), PAW Abschnitt II (1812–1945), II-XII-7, F. 59, 60.

95. *Kaiser-Wilhelm-Gesellschaft Mitteilungen* (Dahlem: MPI), 1931–1932; 1932–1933.

96. Michael Eckert, *Die Atomphysiker: Eine Geschichte der theoretischen Physik am Beispiel der Sommerfeldschule* (Braunschweig: Vieweg, 1993), 119–121; Rajinder Singh, "Arnold Sommerfeld: The Supporter of Indian Physics in Germany," *Current Science* 81 (2001): 1489–1494. On Sommerfeld, see Seth, *Crafting the Quantum,* 71–94.

97. Kurt Düwell, *Interne Faktoren auswärtiger Kulturpolitik im 19. und 20. Jahrhundert* (Stuttgart: Institut für Auslandsbeziehungen, 1981), 10–14.

98. J. L. Heilbron, *The Dilemmas of an Upright Man* (Cambridge, MA: Harvard University Press, 2000), 149.

99. Max Planck Archives, January 12, 1930, No. 1049, 283.

100. Helmuth Albrecht and Armin Hermann, "Kaiser Wilhelm Gesellschaft im Dritten Reich," in *Forschung im Spannungsfeld,* ed. Rudolf Vierhaus and Bernhard vom Brocke (Stuttgart: Deutsche Verlags-Anstalt, 1990), 364.

101. Mark Mazower, *Dark Continent: Europe's Twentieth Century* (New York: Knopf, 1988).

102. Hans A. Bethe, "The Happy Thirties," in *Nuclear Physics in Retrospect,* ed. Roger H. Stüwer (Minneapolis: University of Minnesota Press, 1979), 11–31.

103. D. P. Ray Chaudhuri, "The Cyclotron," *Science and Culture* 5 (1940): 403–409.

104. Eckert, *Die Atomphysiker,* 119.

105. Jahnavi Phalkey, "Big-science, State-formation and Development: The Organisation of Nuclear Research in India, 1938–1959," PhD diss., Georgia Institute of Technology, 1997, 224; Hans-Joachim Bieber, "Zur Frühgeschichte der indischen Nuclearpolitik," *Geschichte und Gesellschaft* 31 (2005): 379.

106. David Cassidy, *Heisenberg: A Bibliography of His Writings* (Berkeley: University of California Press 1984), 548; Dieter Hoffmann and Mark Walker, *The German Physical Society in the Third Reich,* trans. Ann Hentschel (Cambridge: Cambridge University Press, 2012), 1–22.

107. Letter from Reichs- und Preußischen Minister für Wissenschaft to the director of the Kaiser-Wilhelm-Institut, Dr. W. Bothe, December 13, 1937, Max Planck Institute Microfiche, Dok I Abt. Rep 000 1A no. 1056; Alan Beyerchen, *Scientists under Hitler* (New Haven, CT: Yale University Press, 1977), 58–60, 62–78.

108. Friedrich Herneck, *Max von Laue* (Leipzig: Teubner, 1979), 60.

109. Heilbron, *Dilemmas*, 154, 193.

110. Saha, "Need for a Hydraulic Research Laboratory," *Collected Works*, 1:34.

111. Saha, "The All India Radio: What Are Its Defects and How to Remedy Them," *Modern Review* 62 (1937): 693.

112. Bieber, "Frühgeschichte," 379.

113. Phalkey, *Nuclear India*, 231.

114. Saha to Nehru, October 27, 1941, NMML, Jawaharlal Nehru Papers, File 90.

115. Meghnad Saha, "The River Physics Laboratories of the World," *Collected Works*, 2:44.

116. Meghnad Saha, "Need for a Hydraulic Research Laboratory," *Collected Works*, 2:34.

117. D. M. Bose, "Meghnad Saha Memorial Lecture, 1965" (Calcutta: Bose Institute, 1967), 118–120.

118. Meghnad Saha, "Flood," *Science and Culture* 9 (1943): 92.

119. Saha to Nehru, Jawaharlal Nehru Papers, December 5, 1953.

120. G. Venkataraman, *Journey into Light* (Bangalore: IAS, 1988), 186.

121. G. H. Keswani, *Raman and His Effect* (New Delhi: National Book Trust, 1980), 61.

122. Abha Sur has collected these references. Sur, "Aesthetics, Authority, and Control in an Indian Laboratory: The Raman-Born Controversy on Lattice Dynamics," *Isis* 90 (1999): 25–49; C. V. Raman and K. S. Krishnan, "A New Type of Secondary Radiation," *Nature* 1928 (121): 501; "The Optical Analogue of the Compton Effect," *Nature* 121 (1928): 711; *Indian Journal of Physics* 2 (1928): 387, 399; "The Negative Absorption of Radiation," *Nature* 122 (1928): 12; "Polarization of Scattered Light-quanta," *Nature*, 122 (1928): 168; "Molecular Spectra in the Extreme Infra-Red," *Nature* 122 (1928): 278; "Radiation of Molecules Induced by Light," *Nature* 122 (1928): 822.

123. See the 1929 volume of *Nature*. Ernst Rutherford contributed "Recent Reactions between Theory and Experiment. The Raman Effect: The Constitution of Hydrogen Gas," 127 (1929): 878–880.

124. "Raman Light Thesis Stirs Physicists," *New York Times*, June 28, 1931; "India's Men of Science Leading a Renaissance: Raman, Bose and Ray," *New York Times*, January 31, 1932.

125. Wilhelm Füßl, *Oskar von Miller 1855–1934* (Munich: Deutsches Museum, 2005).

126. "Korrespondierende Mitglieder," Karl Haushofer Nachlass, files of the Deutsche Akademie, Bundesarchiv Koblenz, N1122/109.

127. D. E. Wacha, *The Life and Life Work of J. N. Tata* (Madras: Ganesh and Co., 1914), 139.

128. Max Planck Institute Archives, December 1930.
129. On invitations to Schrödinger and Born, see Max Born, *My Life*, 366.
130. Sitzung des Indischen Ausschusses der DA, October 23, 1934, Haushofer Nachlass, Bundesarchiv Koblenz, N1122/115.
131. Keswani, *Raman and His Effect*, 103.
132. Born to Lindemann, Bangalore, November 14, 1935, quoted in Skuli Sigurdsson, "Physics, Life, and Contingency," in *Forced Migration*, ed. Mitchell G. Ash and Alfons Söllner (Washington: German Historical Institute, 1996), 55.
133. Nancy Thorndike Greenspan, *The End of the Certain World* (New York: Basic Books, 2005), 207.
134. *The Second Quinquennial Reviewing Committee of the Indian Institute of Science* (Bangalore: Manager of Publications, 1936).
135. Meghnad Saha, "The Indian Institute of Science," *Science and Culture* 1 (1936): 523.
136. Quoted in Greenspan, *End of the Certain World*, 206.
137. Born, *My Life*, 273–274.
138. Greenspan, *End of the Certain World*, 206.
139. Ibid.
140. S. Bhagavantam, "C. V. Raman," *Biographical Memoirs of Fellows of the Royal Society* 17 (1971): 573.
141. Abha Sur, "Aesthetics, Authority, and Control," 32.
142. See Raman's vigorous arguments about crystal structures between 1945 and 1948 in the journal *Nature*: for example, "Scattering of Light in Crystals," *Nature* 155 (1945): 396–397; "Infra-Red Absorption Spectra of Crystals," *Nature* 161 (1948): 165–166.
143. Abha Sur, "Aesthetics, Authority, and Control," 33.
144. Eric Hobsbawm, *Age of Extremes* (New York: Pantheon, 1994), 229.
145. Bieber, "Zur Frühgeschichte der indischen Nuclearpolitik."

6. INTERNATIONAL ECONOMIES

1. Erik Grimmer-Solem, *The Rise of Historical Economics and Social Reform in Germany 1864–1894* (Oxford: Clarendon Press, 2003); Erik Grimmer-Solem, "German Social Science, Meiji Conservatism, and the Peculiarities of Japanese History," *Journal of World History* 16 (2005): 187–222.
2. As in the case of Kolwey's reading of Radhakamal Mukherjee.
3. D. E. Wacha, *The Life and Life Work of J. N. Tata* (Madras: Ganesh, 1914), 180.

4. Raj Chandavarkar, *Origins of Industrial Capitalism in India* (Cambridge: Cambridge University Press), 58–71.

5. Wacha, *J. N. Tata*, 2.

6. R. M. Lala, *Beyond the Last Blue Mountain* (Delhi: Penguin Books, 1991).

7. Blair Kling, "Paternalism in Indian Labour: The Tata Iron and Steel Company of Jamshedpur," *International Labor and Working-Class History* 53 (1998): 69–87.

8. Satyabrata Datta, "Role of Indian Worker in Early Phase of Industrialisation," *Economic and Political Weekly* 20 (1985); "Jāmshedpurē ārō Iyurōpiyō āmdāni," *Prabāsī* (1924), 717.

9. "Jāmshedpurē," *Prabāsī*.

10. Tirthankar Roy, *The Economic History of India, 1857–1947* (Oxford: Oxford University Press, 2000), 225.

11. Note from September 22, 1932, SAA, File 4286, 5.

12. Chronology of Siemens in India, SAA, 68.Li156.

13. Walter Leifer, *Indien und die Deutschen* (Tübingen: Erdmann, 1969), 267.

14. D. R. Gadgil, *Imperial Preference for India* (Bombay: Gokhale Institute, 1932), quoting Ainscough, 29.

15. Thomas Ainscough, *Report on the Conditions and Prospects of British Trade in India 1926–1927* (London: His Majesty's Stationery Office, 1927), 65.

16. Anne McClintock on "commodity racism," in *Imperial Leather* (London: Routledge, 1995), 32–33, 207–231.

17. Balkrishna Madan, *India and Imperial Preference: A Study in Commercial Policy* (Oxford: Oxford University Press, 1939), 46.

18. Gadgil, *Imperial Preference for India*, 31.

19. Königliches Institut für Seeverkehr und Weltwirtschaft an der Christian-Albrechts-Universität zu Kiel.

20. Bernhard Harms, *Rede gehalten bei der Eröffnungsfeier February 24, 1911* (Kiel: Institut für Weltwirtschaft, 1911), 36.

21. Friedrich von Lupin, *Die indische Textilindustrie als Industrie eines kolonialen Rohstofflandes* (Jena: Fischer, 1931).

22. Paul Kennedy, "Finance and Strategy in Twentieth-Century Great Britain," *International History Review* 13 (1981): 44–61.

23. Emma Rothschild, *Economic Sentiments: Adam Smith, Condorcet, and the Enlightenment* (Cambridge, MA: Harvard University Press, 2001), 224–227; Jeffrey Young, *Economics as a Moral Science: The Political Economy of Adam Smith* (Chelthenham, UK: Edward Elgar, 1997), 157, 163–176.

24. Deborah Redman, *The Rise of Political Economy as a Science* (Cambridge, MA: MIT Press, 1997), 208–215.

25. Adam Smith's *Theory of Moral Sentiments* quoted in Rothschild, *Economic Sentiments,* 122; and see Rothschild's excellent exposition, 116–146.

26. Emma Rothschild, "Smithianismus and Enlightenment in 19th Century Europe" (1998), in The Rise and Fall of Historical Political Economy, unpublished conference proceedings held at the Center for History and Economics, Cambridge University.

27. Raymond James Sontag, *Germany and England: Background of Conflict 1848–1894* (New York: Appleton-Century, 1938), ix.

28. Keith Tribe, *Strategies of Economic Order* (Cambridge: Cambridge University Press, 1995), 44.

29. Friedrich List, *Gesammelte Schriften,* vol. 2 (Stuttgart: Cotta, 1850), 103.

30. Tribe, *Strategies,* 55; List, *Schriften,* 2:105.

31. M. G. Ranade, *Essays on Indian Economics* (Madras: Natesan, 1920), 189.

32. Romesh Chunder Dutt, *The Economic History of British India* (London: Kegan Paul, Trench, Truebner, 1902), 296; Manu Goswami, *Producing India: From Colonial Economy to National Space* (Chicago: University of Chicago Press, 2004), 231, 280.

33. Dutt, *Economic History,* 299.

34. M. G. Ranade, *Essays on Indian Economics,* 18.

35. Ibid., 20.

36. Roman Szporluk, *Communism and Nationalism* (New York: Oxford University Press, 1988), 140.

37. Ranade, *Essays on Indian Economics,* 189.

38. V. G. Kale, *India and Imperial Preference* (Trichinopoly: S. M. Raja Rao, 1910), 3, 25.

39. Ibid., 27.

40. Joseph Schumpeter, *Epochen der Dogmen- und Methodengeschichte* (Tübingen: Mohr, 1914), 6; Pramatha Nath Banerjea's *Study of Indian Economics* (London: Macmillan, 1911).

41. Volker Berghahn, ed., *Quest for Economic Empire* (Providence, RI: Berghahn Books, 1996), 7. On the need for colonies as outlets of German surplus power, see Maximilian von Hagen, *Bismarcks Kolonialpolitik* (Stuttgart: Gotha, 1923), 13; on colonial dreams in the interwar years, see Wolfe Schmockel, *Dream of Empire: German Colonialism, 1919–1945* (New Haven, CT: Yale University Press, 1964), 2.

42. Bernhard Harms, *Volkswirtschaft und Weltwirtschaft: Versuch der Begründung einer Weltwirtschaftslehre* (Jena: Fischer, 1912), 10.

43. Heinrich Dietzel, *Weltwirtschaft und Volkswirtschaft* (Dresden: Zahn und Jaensch, 1900), 119.

44. Arthur Dix, *Deutschland auf den Hochstraßen des Weltwirtschafs- verkehrs* (Jena: Fischer, 1901); Harms, *Volkswirtschaft und Weltwirtschaft,* 44.

45. Friedrich Hoffmann, *Die Geschichte des Instituts für Weltwirtschaft* (Kiel: Institut für Weltwirschaft, 1960), 257.

46. Benoy Kumar Sarkar's Address, 1922, Musikwissenschaftliche Abteilung, Lautarchiv, Humboldt University, LA 346.

47. Brij Narain, "Indian Exchange and Currency During 1920," *Weltwirtschaftliches Archiv* 17 (1921): 67–74; V. G. Kale, "Small Indus- tries in India," *Weltwirtschaftliches Archiv* 19 (1923): 153–160; Sudhir Sen, "Die Goldbewegung aus Britisch-Indien," in *Weltwirtschaftliches Archiv* 39 (1934): 186–216.

48. Adam Tooze, *Statistics and the German State* (Cambridge: Cambridge University Press, 2001), 103.

49. Benoy Kumar Sarkar, "Economic Planning for Bengal," *Insurance and Finance Review* 4 (1936): 25–42.

50. Bernhard Harms, *Weltwirtschaftliche Aufgaben der deutschen Verwal- tungspolitik: Zugleich als ein Beitrag für die Reform des Konsulatswesens* (Jena: Fischer, 1911), 14.

51. Rudolf Kobatsch, *Internationale Wirtschaftspolitik* (Vienna: Manz, 1907), 11–14.

52. Bernhard Harms, "Das Objekt der Sozialwirtschaftslehre: Wesen und Begriff," *Allgemeine Sozialwirtschaftslehre* (1919), 17.

53. David Dyzenhaus, *Legality and Legitimacy: Carl Schmitt, Hans Kelsen and Herman Heller in Weimar* (Oxford: Clarendon Press, 1997), 50.

54. Anonymous, "Industrial Methods and Commercial Policies in Modern Economic Development," *Bengal National Chamber of Commerce Journal* 2 (1927–1928): 230.

55. Benoy Kumar Sarkar, "Financial Germany since Stabilization," *Journal of the Bengal National Chamber of Commerce* 1 (1926–1927): 24.

56. "Chemical Combines of France and Great Britain," *Bengal National Chamber of Commerce Journal* 2 (1927–1928): 14.

57. *Bangiya Jārmān Vidya Pariṣad* Annual Reports (Calcutta, 1933–1938), File 149.B.311 at National Library of India, Kolkata.

58. Giuseppe Flora, *Benoy Kumar Sarkar and Italy* (New Delhi: Italian Embassy Cultural Center, 1994), 71.

59. "Introduction," *Ārthīk Unnati* 1 (1931): 36.

60. Benoy Kumar Sarkar, *Futurism of Young Asia* (Berlin: Springer, 1922), 82.

61. "Seven Postulates of Arthasastra," *Journal of the Bengal Chamber of Commerce* (1927–1928), 79.

62. Sarkar, *Baṅgīya Jārmān Vidyā Saṃsad* (Calcutta: Calcutta Oriental Book Agency, 1937), 8.

63. "German Electrical Engineer on Tour in India," 1926–1928, *Journal of the Bengal Chamber of Commerce*, 274; Oskar von Miller Archive, Deutsches Museum, VB1926/27.

64. Sarkar, *Futurism*, 200.

65. Benoy Kumar Sarkar, "Die Entwicklung und weltwirtschaftliche Bedeutung des modernen Indien," in *Indien in der modernen Weltwirtschaft und Weltpolitik* (Stuttgart: Fleischhauer und Spohn, 1931), 37–54.

66. Benoy Kumar Sarkar, "Das technische Studium in Indien und seine Bedeutung für die deutsch-indischen Wirtschaftsbeziehungen," *Sonderdruck aus der Bayerischen Industrie- und Handelszeitung* 49 (1930).

67. Benoy Kumar Sarkar, "Economic Planning for Bengal," *Insurance and Finance Review* 4 (1933): 42.

68. Anonymous, "Bata Shoe Factory, Konnagore," *India and the World* 3 (1934): 56.

69. Benoy Kumar Sarkar, *Parājita Jārmānī*, 34.

70. Ibid., 103.

71. Ibid., 660.

72. P. C. Ray, *The Industrial Development of India* (Nagpur: Nagpur University Press, 1932), 1, 24–26.

73. David Ludden, *Agrarian History of South Asia* (Cambridge: Cambridge University Press, 1999), 18.

74. Karl Kolwey, "Zwei Indier über ökonomische Probleme in Indien," *Archiv für Sozialwissenschaft und Sozialpolitik* 52 (1924): 177–195.

75. Radhakamal Mukherjee, *Principles of Comparative Economics* (London: P. S. King), xxiv.

76. Ibid., xxv.

77. Ibid., xxvi.

78. Ibid., xxvi.

79. Padmanabha Pillai, *Economic Conditions in India* (London: Routledge, 1925), 154; C. F. Strickland, *An Introduction to Co-operation in India* (London: Humphrey Milford, 1922), 42.

80. Radhakamal Mukherjee, *Groundwork of Economics* (London: Longmans, Green, 1925), 235.

81. M. L. Darling, *Some Aspects of Co-operation in Germany, Italy and Ireland* (Lahore: Superintendent, Government Printing, Punjab, 1922), 1,

4; Henry Wolff, *Rambles in the Black Forest* (London: Longmans, Green, 1890), 42.

82. Patrick Geddes, *Town Planning in Theory and Practice* (London: Garden City Association, 1908).

83. Mukherjee, *Groundwork*, 196.

84. Ibid.

85. Ibid., 155.

86. J. C. Kumarappa, *Why the Village Movement?* (Rajahmundry: Hindustan Publishing, 1939).

87. Mukherjee, *Groundwork*, 328.

88. Radhakamal Mukerjee, ed., *Economic Problems of Modern India* (London: Macmillan, 1939–1941), 204.

89. Mukherjee, *Groundwork*, 196.

90. Mukherjee, *Regional Sociology* (New York: Century, 1926), v.

91. Mukherjee, *Groundwork*, 208.

92. Radhakamal Mukerjee and Narendra Nath Sen-Gupta, *Introduction to Social Psychology: Mind in Society* (London: Heath, 1929), 255.

93. Gary Herrigel, *Industrial Constructions* (Chicago: University of Chicago Press, 1996), 74–85.

94. Schorr, "Zakir Husain," ZMO, Krüger Nachlass (Berlin, undated), Item 88, 2.

95. Gustav Schmoller, *Die Volkswirtschaft, die Volkswirtschaftslehre und ihre Methode* (Frankfurt am Main: Klostermann, 1893), 71.

96. Michael Appel, *Werner Sombart: Historker und Theoretiker des modernen Kapitalismus* (Marburg: Metropolis-Verlag, 1992), 15.

97. Joachim Zweynert and Daniel Riniker, *Werner Sombart in Russland* (Marburg: Metropolis, 2004), 21.

98. Jabbar Kheiri to Sombart, Sombart Nachlass, Geheimes Staatsarchiv Preussischer Kulturbesitz (GStAPK) PGStA, Rep. VI NL Sombart 6a. 23 March 1928; Paul Kara Mursa December 8, 27; Achmed Halid July 22, 1929; Chaoi Feng of China February 19, 1924; Kimosuke Otsukda December 28, 1923, Tsunao Miyajima from Japan October 14, 1928, M. Baba of Japan; Achmed Naim Hakimbay from Turkistan May 20, 1927; S. Mukacs also of Japan March 3, 1921; Sombart corresponded with the Japanese scholar M. Baba throughout the 1930s.

99. Friedrich Lenger, *Werner Sombart, 1863–1941: eine Biographie* (Munich: Beck, 1994), 184.

100. See GStPk, Correspondence, Rep VI, Nl. Sombart.

101. Ziyaettin Fahri, "Mes Souvenirs autour de W. Sombart," *Revue de la Faculté des Sciences Économiques de l'Université d'Istanbul* 3 (1942): 68;

see Appel, *Werner Sombart,* 78: "Werner Sombart scheint als Hoschulleh-
rer zahlreiche ausländische Studenten angesprochen zu haben . . ."

102. British intelligence reported the number of Indian students, see "Orientals in Berlin," September 3, 1923, APAC: L/PJ/12/102.

103. File on "Zakir Husain" in HUA, Phil. Fak. 699.

104. Werner Sombart, *Die römische Campagna* (Leipzig: Suncker and
Humblot, 1888).

105. Erik Grimmer-Solem, "Imperialist Socialism of the Chair: Gustav
Schmoller and the German *Weltpolitik, 1897–1905,*" in *Wilhelminism and
its Legacies,* ed. Eley et al. (New York: Berghahn, 2003), 107–122;
Andrew Zimmerman, *Alabama in Africa: Booker T. Washington, the
German Empire, and the Globalization of the New South* (Princeton, NJ:
Princeton University Press, 2010), 80–92.

106. Werner Sombart, *Das Wirtschaftsleben im Zeitalter des Hochkapitalismus* (Munich: Duncker & Humblot, 1928), 2:967.

107. See, for example, Freiherr von Freytag-Loringhoven, "Versailles, Spa und
die Zeitrichtung," *Preußische Kreuzzeitung,* 351, July 23, 1920, 1. These
authors imagined themselves in league with anticolonial activists.

108. For example, "Indisches Volkstum," in *Deutsche Volkstum,* 2 (1926):
491–497, in which Indians are portrayed as rising, revolutionary
people.

109. On Reventlow and Oppenheim, see Gerhard Höpp, *Araber in Berlin*
(Berlin: Ausländerbeauftrage des Senats, 1998), 14. British intelligence
reported the attendance of Adolf Hitler at an anticolonial meeting of
Egyptian, Turkish, Indian, and Irish revolutionaries on December 22,
1922, approximately one year before the Munich Putsch. See "Orientals in
Berlin," APAC, August 1, 1923, L/PJ/12/102.

110. "Die aussenpolitische Orientierung der Rechtsverbände," Bundesarchiv,
Microfiche, R43 I/2696, 1926, Fiche 2, 37, 38.

111. Dirk von Laak, *Über alles in der Welt: Deutscher Imperialismus im 19.
und 20. Jahrhundert* (Munich: Beck, 2005), 104–129.

112. Ernst Bloch, *Das Prinzip Hoffnung,* vol. 4 (Frankfurt am Main:
Suhrkamp, 1959), 798.

113. Arthur Mitzman, *Sociology and Estrangement: Three Sociologists of
Imperial Germany* (New York: Knopf, 1973), 136–143.

114. Appel, *Werner Sombart,* 233.

115. Lenger, *Werner Sombart,* 247.

116. Sombart, *Die deutsche Volkswirtschaft im 19. Jahrhundert,* 1:71.

117. Kevin Repp, *Reformers, Critics and the Paths of German Modernity*
(Cambridge, MA: Harvard University Press, 2000), 171.

118. Werner Sombart, *Luxus und Kapitalismus* (Munich: Duncker und
Humblot, 1913), 169.

119. Werner Sombart, *Der Moderne Kapitalismus* (Munich: Duncker und Humblot, 1902), 2:422–475.

120. Ibid., 50.

121. Sombart began by studying Italian society before changing his focus to the study of Germany. His dissertation was on the economy of the ancient Roman countryside. "Die römische Campagna" (1888).

122. Werner Sombart, "Der Kampf um die Edelmetalle im Zeitalter des Frühkapitalismus," *Weltwirtschaftliches Archiv* 11 (1913), 147–170.

123. Werner Sombart, *Der Bourgeois* (Munich: Duncker und Humblot, 1920), 213.

124. Gerhard Schacher, "Die national-wirtschaftliche Emanzipation des Orients," *Zeitschrift für Geopolitik* 9 (1932): 393, quotes Werner Sombart's book to support the thesis that the East was rising in terms of economic power.

125. Sombart, *Luxus*, 35.

126. Ibid., 36.

127. Ibid., 43.

128. Ibid., 46.

129. Werner Sombart, *Händler und Helden* (Munich: Duncker und Humblot, 1915), 130.

130. *Weltbürgerlichkeit*, "cosmopolitanism," was seen by many Germans as a particularly Germanic quality beginning with Immanuel Kant's famous *Idee zu einer allgemeinen Geschichte in weltbürgerlicher Absicht* (1784), and *Zum ewigen Frieden* (1795); see Susan Meld-Shell on Kant's readings of French philosophers, especially Rousseau, in the development of his views, *The Embodiment of Reason* (Chicago: University of Chicago Press, 1996), 81. See the insightful article by Karl Guthke, "Die Entdeckung der Welt um 1800. Die Geburt der globalen Bildung aus dem Geist der Geographie und Ethnologie," in *Jahrbuch des freien deutschen Hochstifts* (2003): 134–208; Friedrich Meinecke, *Weltbürgertum und Nationalstaat* (Munich: Oldenbourg, 1908).

131. Meinecke, *Weltbürgertum*, 135–136.

132. Sombart, *Händler und Helden*, 47.

133. Karl Hardach, *The Political Economy of Germany in the Twentieth Century* (Berkeley: University of California Press, 1976), 12.

134. Zakir Husain, "Die Agrarverfassung Britisch-Indiens," PhD diss., Friedrich-Wilhelms-Universität zu Berlin, 72.

135. Ibid., 113.

136. Ibid., 80.

137. Ibid., 2:135.

138. Zakir Husain, *Capitalism: Essays in Understanding* (London: Asia Publishing House, 1944), 25.

139. Ibid., 127.
140. Ibid., 200.
141. Majid Hayat Siddiqi, "Bluff, Doubt and Fear: The Kheiri Brothers and the Colonial State, 1904–45," *Indian Economic and Social History Review* 24 (1987): 233–263.
142. "Reports on Activities of Germans, Italians and Japanese," September 9, 1938, APAC, L/PJ/12/506.
143. Abdul Jabbar Kheiri, "Indien und seine Arbeiterschaft: Ihre Entstehung und Bewegung," PhD diss., Humboldt Universität, 1927, HUA, Phil. Fak. 658, 13.
144. Ibid., 14.
145. Ibid., 19.
146. Ibid., 22.

7. MARXIST TOTALITY

1. Georg Lukàcs, "What Is Orthodox Marxism?" *History and Class Consciousness*, trans. Rodney Livingstone (Cambridge: MIT Press, 1971; orig. 1919), 1–26.
2. Partha Chatterjee, *Arms Alliances and Stability* (New York: Wiley, 1975), 30–32.
3. Gareth Stedman Jones, "Radicalism and the Extra-European World," in *Victorian Visions of the Global Order* (Cambridge: Cambridge University Press, 2007), 199; Kevin Anderson, *Marx at the Margins* (Chicago: University of Chicago Press, 2010), 182–195, 217; Bryan Turner, *Marx and the End of Orientalism* (London: Allen and Unwin, 1978), 7.
4. Eric Hobsbawm, *Age of Extremes* (New York: Pantheon, 1994), 57.
5. V. I. Lenin, "On the National pride of the Great Russians," *Sotsial-Demokrat*, 21 (1914), 102.
6. V. I. Lenin, "The Awakening of Asia" (*Pravda*, no. 103, 1913), trans. George Hanna, *Lenin Collected Works,* vol. 19 (Moscow: Progress Publishers, 1977), 85–86; Sanjay Seth, *Marxist Theory and Nationalist Politics* (Delhi: Sage, 1995), 38.
7. Dadabhai Naoroji and Bikhaji Cama represented India. See Peter Grohmann et al., *Der Internationale Sozialistenkongress Stuttgart 1907: Protokoll* (Stuttgart: Selbstverlag der Studiengruppe, 1977), 36.
8. Karl Kautsky, *Sozialismus und Kolonialpolitik* (Berlin: Buchhandlung Vorwärts, 1907), 21.
9. Ibid., 27.
10. Ibid., 24.
11. This is how colonial people particularly of Africa were referred to during the 1907 Stuttgart debate. See Kautsky, *Sozialismus und Kolonialpolitik*;

see Christian Koller, "Eine Zivilisierungsmission der Arbieterklasse? Die Diskussion über eine 'sozialistische Kolonialpolitik' vor dem Ersten Weltkrieg," in *Zivilisierungsmissionen: Imperiale Weltverbesserung seit dem 18. Jahrhundert,* ed. Jürgen Osterhammel and Boris Barth (Konstanz, Germany: UK Verlagsgesellschaft, 2005), 229–235; Andrew Zimmerman, "Ethnologie im Kaiserreich. Natur, Kultur und 'Rasse' in Deutschland und seinen Kolonien," in *Kaiserreich Transnational,* ed. Sebastian Conrad and Jürgen Osterhammel (Göttingen: Vandenhoeck und Ruprecht, 2004), 191–212.

12. Thomas Nipperdey, *Deutsche Geschichte 1866–1918,* vol. 2 (Munich: Beck, 1983), 630–645. The influential liberal publicist Paul Rohrbach was a proponent of German economic and territorial expansion, primarily into Southeast Europe, but also abroad in Africa; Paul Dehn, *Von deutscher Kolonial- und Weltpolitik* (Berlin: Allgemein Verein für Deutsche Literatur, 1907), 31. Philipp Ther, "Deutsche Geschichte als imperiale Geschichte. Polen, slawophone Minderheiten und das Kaiserreich als kontinentales Empire," in Conrad and Osterhammel, *Kaiserreich Transnational,* 129–148.

13. The critiques of Luxemburg's book were ample. See reviews by Otto Bauer in *Die Neue Zeit,* no. 24, 1913; Anton Pannekoek in *Bremer Bürgerzeitung,* January 29, 1913; and G. Eckstein in *Vorwärts,* February 16, 1913.

14. Such inverted geometry also interested Leon Trotsky around the same time, in his *Permanent Revolution* (1906) in which he too searched for a theory to explain why revolution began in the less capitalist regions of the world and spread to those that were more capitalistically developed.

15. Georg Lukàcs, "The Marxism of Rosa Luxemburg," in *History and Class Consciousness* (Cambridge, MA: MIT Press, 1971), 27–45.

16. August Thalheimer, "Bietrag zur Kenntnis der Pronomina personalia und possessiva der Sprachen Mikronesien," noted in Jürgen Kästner, *Die politische Theorie August Thalheimers* (Frankfurt: Campus, 1982), 17.

17. August Thalheimer, *Einführung in den dialektischen Materialismus* (Berlin: Verleih für Literatur und Politik, 1928), 35.

18. See Arthur Holitscher's transcription of Chinese revolutionary songs, "Aus den Gesängen der Chinesischen Revolution," *Weltbühne* 27 (1931): 676. See also Franz Carl Enders, "Der neue Orient," *Weltbühne* 21 (1925): 564.

19. Theodor Lessing, *Europa und Asien* (Hannover: W. A. Adam, 1924), 18.

20. Lawrence Baron, "Discipleship and Dissent: Theodor Lessing and Edmund Husserl," *Proceedings of the American Philosophical Society* 183 (1983): 32–49; Robert Ruig, *Theodor Lessing* (Soesterberg: Aspekt, 2010).

21. Hans-Georg Gadamer, "Selbstdarstellung," in *Gesammelte Werke* (Tübingen: Mohr-Siebeck, 1990), 480.

22. Rainer Marwedel, *Theodor Lessing: Eine Biographie* (Darmstadt: Luchterhand, 1987), 258.

23. Ibid., 257, 309.

24. On Marxist anthropology, see Andre Gingrich, "From the Late Imperial Era to the End of the Republican Interlude: Creative Subaltern Tendencies, Larger and Smaller Schools of Anthropology," in *One Discipline, Four Ways: British, German, French and American Anthropology*, ed. Fredrik Barth (Chicago: University of Chicago Press, 2005), 96–97.

25. Otto Corbach, "Das erwachende China," *Weltbühne* 22 (1926): 34.

26. Arthur Holitscher, *Das unruhige Asien* (Berlin: Fischer, 1926), 21.

27. Egon Erwin Kisch, *Asien gründlich verändert* (Berlin: Aufbau-Verlag, 1980), 227.

28. Paul Zils, "Ten Years," *Indian Documentary* 2 (1955): 7. Documentaries on India by Zils are stored at the Deutsches Filminstitut Filmarchiv in Wiesbaden.

29. Egon Erwin Kisch, *China Geheim* (Berlin: E. Reiss, 1933).

30. Karl Schlögel, *Berlin, Ostbahnhof Europas* (Berlin: Siedler, 1998), 356.

31. "IAH Filmprogram,"1930, Bundesarchiv, RY 9/I 6/7/15, 53.

32. Alexander Watlin, *Die Komintern: 1919–1929* (Mainz: Deacton, 1993), 513.

33. "'Das Schanghai-Dokument' Der große China-Film des Volks-Film-Verbandes," *Arbeiter Illustrierte Zeitung* 7 (1928): 2.

34. Cemil Aydin, *The Politics of Anti-Westernism in Asia* (New York: Columbia University Press, 2007), 142–168.

35. Morgan Philips Price's *My Reminiscences of the Russian Revolution* (London: G. Allen & Unwin, 1921) was the first book available in India on the Russian Revolution. See Satyabrata Rai Chowdhuri, *Leftist Movements in India* (Calcutta: Minerva Association, 1976), 67.

36. *Report of Indian Constitutional Reform* (HMSO, Cmd. 9109, 1918, 14), cited in B. R. Nanda, *Socialism in India* (Delhi: Vikas, 1972), 41.

37. Ranajit Guha, "A Colonial City and Its Times," *Indian Economic and Social History Review* (IESHR) (2008): 329–351.

38. Home Political File 27, NAI, Binder 4, 1921.

39. Fischer-Tiné, Harald, and Carolien Stolte, "Imagining Asia in India: Nationalism and Internationalism (ca. 1905–1940)," *Comparative Studies in Society and History* 54 (2012): 65–92.

40. S. A. Dange, "The Asiatic International," *Socialist*, October 7, 1922. Dange founded this journal in August 1922.

41. Branko Lazic, *Biographical Dictionary of the Comintern* (Stanford, CA: Hoover Institution Press, 1973).

42. See August 18, 1922, APAC, L/PJ/12/46. On the historical place of Berlin as an alternation point between West and East Europe, see Schlögel, *Berlin Ostbahnhof Europas*, 152.

43. Sean McMeekin, *The Red Millionaire: A Political Biography of Willi Münzenberg* (New Haven, CT: Yale University Press, 2003), 156; Ulrich Weitz, *Salonkultur und Proletariat: Eduard Fuchs, Sammler, Sittenge-schichtler, Sozialist* (Stuttgart: Stöffler und Schütz, 1991).

44. Roy was provided with £200 per month from the WES for the publication of the *Vanguard*. See Public Record Office (hereafter PRO), London, F. O. 371/8170: 248–272.

45. R. P. Dutt, *The Two Internationals* (Westminster: Allen and Unwin, 1920).

46. Jan Lucassen, "Brickmakers' Strikes on the Ganges Canal," in *Coolies, Capital and Colonialism,* ed. Rana Partap Behal et al. (Cambridge: Cambridge University Press, 2006), 48.

47. Rajani Kanta Das, preface, *India and a New Civilisation* (Calcutta: N. C. Das, 1942).

48. IOR/L/E/7/1331, File 544, September 20, 1923–March 19, 1930.

49. Rajani Kanta Das, *The Industrial Efficiency of India* (London: P. S. King & Sons, 1930); R. J. Das, *History of Indian Labour Legislation* (Calcutta: University of Calcutta, 1941); R. J. Das and Ruth Sklar Das, *India and New Civilisation* (Calcutta: N. C. Das, 1942).

50. Yogendra Yadav, "What Is Living and What Is Dead in Rammanohar Lohia?" *Economic and Political Weekly* 45 (2010): 92–107.

51. See British intelligence report, "Dr. R. M. Lohia's Lectures on Socialism," November 11, 1935, NAI, File no. 800 (78) A III; Rai Akhilendra Prasad, *Socialist Thought in Modern India* (Delhi: Meenakshi Prakashan, 1974), 126; Nanda, *Socialism in India,* 153.

52. Kris Manjapra, *M. N. Roy: Marxism and Colonial Cosmopolitanism* (Delhi: Routledge, 2010), 86; Odd Arne Westad, *The Global Cold War* (Cambridge: Cambridge University Press, 2005), 54.

53. A. K. Hindi, *M. N. Roy: The Man Who Looked Ahead* (Bombay: Modern Publishing House, 1938), 220–221.

54. Dipesh Chakrabarty, *Provincializing Europe* (Princeton, NJ: Princeton University Press, 2000); Hans-Georg Gadamer, *Philosophische Lehrjahre* (Frankfurt: Vittorio Klostermann, 1977), 11.

55. S. Ani Mukherji, "The Anti-colonial Imagination: The Exilic Productions of American Radicalism in Interwar Moscow," PhD diss., Brown University, 2011; Michael Adas, "Contested Hegemony: The Great War and the Afro-Asian Assault on the Civilizing Mission," in *Making a World after Empire*, ed. Christopher Lee (Athens: Ohio University Press, 2010), 69–106.

56. Fenner Brockway, "The Coloured People's International," *New Leader* 2 (1927).

57. *Rote Fahne*, February 19, 1927. Hans Piazza, "Jawaharlal Nehru und die Antiimperialistische Liga," *Wissenschaftliche Zeitschrift für Geschichte*

19 (1970): 397. H. Krüger, "Zum Einfluss internationaler Faktoren auf die Herausbildung und Entwicklung der antiimperialistischen Haltung Jawaharlal Nehrus," in *Politik und Ideologie im gegenwärtigen Indien* (Berlin: Schriften des Zentralinstituts f'r Geschichte, 1975). 308. W. Münzenberg, *Solidarität: Zehn Jahre Internationale Arbeiterhilfe*, 1921–1931 (Berlin: Neuer Deutscher Verlag, 1931), 333.

58. Nehru cited this earliest meeting as free from Soviet designs. But he noted that the league increasingly suffered Soviet imposition in coming years. Jawaharlal Nehru, *Autobiography* (Oxford: Oxford University Press, 1980), 161–166.

59. Michele Louro, "At Home in the World: Jawaharlal Nehru and Global Anti-Imperialism," PhD diss., Salem State University, 2011; League against Imperialism, IISH, October 2, 1927, File 1–13.

60. For example, the 1929 Youth Conference in Amsterdam, the War Resister's Internationals of 1931 and 1932, and the Peace Congress of 1936. See Vijay Prashad, *The Darker Nations: A People's History of the Third World* (New York: New Press, 2007), 16–50.

61. The Bandung "Asian-African Conference" was held in April 1955.

62. Frantz Fanon, "The Algerian War and Man's Liberation," in *Toward the African Revolution*, trans. Haakon Chevalier (New York: Monthly Review Press, 1964), 145.

63. The Kuomintang and the Chinese Communist Party battled for control of the mainland, and Indian insurgency reached an unprecedented peak in British India; Kris Manjapra, "Transcolonial Recognition" in *Cosmopolitan Thought Zones*, ed. Sugata Bose and Kris Manjapra (Houndmills, UK: Palgrave Macmillan, 2010), 159–177.

64. Jawaharlal Nehru, "Der Britische Imperialismus in Indien, Persien und Mesopotamien," *Das Flammenzeichen vom Palais Egmont: Offizielles Protokoll des Kongresses gegen koloniale Unterdrückung, Brüssel, 10.-15. Februar 1927* (Berlin: Neuer Deutscher Verlag, 1927), 55–61; Jean Jones *The League against Imperialism* (Preston: Socialist History Society, 1996), 5; Hans Piazza, ed., *Die Liga gegen Imperialismus und für nationale Unabhängingkeit* (Leipzig: Karl Marx Universität, 1987).

65. *Offizielles Protokol des Kongresses,* 78.

66. Indian National Congress Report of the Proceedings of the Forty-third Session of the Indian National Congress (Calcutta, 1928), 97.

67. Nehru, *Autobiography,* 161.

68. Franz Josef Furtwängler, "Gandhi oder MacDonald? Zur Gewissenskrise des internationalen Sozialismus," *Das Freie Wort* 24 (1930): 7; Max Baumann, "Gandhi und die deutsche Jugend," *Das Freie Wort* 28 (1930): 19; Ingolf Askvald, "Furtwängler und die indischen Parias," *Das Freie*

Wort 28 (1930): 22; Hans Neisser, "England und Indien," *Das Freie Wort* 28 (1930): 24; Hermann Kranold, "Die britische Politik der britsichen Arbeiterregierung," *Sozialistische Monatshefte* 36 (1930): 1092; Viktor Schiff, "Der Heilige und sein Nahrr," *Das Freie Wort* 26 (1930), 27.

69. Friedrich Heiler, *Christlicher Glaube und indisches Geistesleben* (Munich: Reinhardt, 1926); Zakir Husain, *Die Botschaft des Mahatma Gandhi* (Berlin: Volkserzieher Verlag, 1924); Helmuth von Glasenapp, *Von Buddha zu Gandhi: indisches Denken im Wandel der Jahrhunderte* (Tübingen: J. C. B. Mohr, 1934).

70. "Lebenslauf Selbstdarstellung," Box 1, File 1, Furtwängler Nachlass, Friedrich-Ebert-Stiftung Archive (FESA-FN), Bonn.

71. "Charakter der deutschen Gewerkschaftsbewegung," Furtwängler Nachlass, FESA-FN, Box 6, 1947.

72. Mary Nolan, *Visions of Modernity: American Business and the Modernization of Germany* (New York and Oxford: Oxford University Press, 1994), 65–80.

73. Ibid., 113–149; Daniel Rodgers, *Atlantic Crossings: Social Politics in a Progressive Age* (Cambridge: Cambridge University Press, 1998), 112–149.

74. Willy Buschak, *Franz Josef Furtwängler: Gewerkschafter, Indien-Reisender, Widerstandskämpfer. Eine politische Biografie* (Essen: Klartext Verlag, 2011), 55.

75. Ibid., 55; Franz Josef Furtwängler, "Die Zukunft der indischen Arbeiterbewegung und der IGB," *Die Arbeit* 7 (1927): 458.

76. Lebenslauf, Selbtdarstellung, FESA-FN, Box 1, File 1.

77. Karl Schrader and Franz Josef Furtwängler, *Das werktätige Indien* (Berlin: Deutscher Textilarbeiter-Verband, 1928), 157.

78. Franz Josef Furwängler, "Der Maertyrer von Bengalen," *Vorwärts,* June 9, 1927; Buschak, *Furtwängler,* 189.

79. Wilhelm Filchner, "Britisch-Indien," *Kölnische Zeitung,* July 14, 1928.

80. "Indiens Freiheitskampf und die Weltwirtschaft," May 15, 1930, *Deutsche Wirtschafts-Zeitung,* 200.

81. Franz Josef Furtwängler, *Die weltwirtschaftliche Konkurrenz des indischen Industriearbeiters* (Leipzig: Deutsche wissenschatliche Buchhandlung, 1929); *Die Zukunft der indischen Arbeiterbewegung und der internationale Gewerkschaftsbund; Indien: Das Brahmanenland im Frühlicht* (Berlin: Büchergilde Gutenberg, 1931).

82. Franz Josef Furtwängler, *Indien: Das Brahmanenland im Frühling* (Leipzig: Büchergilde Gutenberg, 1931).

83. "Die Drachensaat," FESA-FN, Box, 1, File 3, uncataloged.

84. Buschak, *Furtwängler,* 90.

85. Ibid., 91.

86. Ibid., 129–164.

87. Christopher Sykes, *Troubled Loyalty: A Biography of Adam von Trott zu Solz* (London: Collins, 1968), 332–347.

88. Milan Hauner, *India in Axis Strategy* (Stuttgart: Klett-Cotta, 1981), 359. See Leonard A. Gordon's authoritative account, *Brothers against the Raj* (New York: Columbia University Press, 1990), 446–462.

89. Buschak, *Furtwängler,* 186.

90. Karl Haushofer, "Mitarbeiter der Geopolitik," Institut für Zeitgeschichte Archiv MA 618, 1941.

91. Thalheimer to Karnik, Paris, May 24, 1934, NMML, M. N. Roy Archives, Karnik Files.

92. Ibid.

93. Ibid.

94. Collected by A. K. Pillai and published after Roy's release as M. N. Roy, *Letters to Congress Socialists* (Calcutta: Renaissance, 1937).

95. M. N. Roy, "To the Executive Committees of the Congress Socialist party," NMML, Roy Papers, 42, February 1936.

96. John Patrick Haithcox, *Communism and Nationalism: M. N. Roy and Comintern Policy* (Princeton, NJ: Princeton University Press), 1971, 250.

97. Quoted in Jane Degras, *The Communist International, 1919–1943* (London: Oxford University Press, 1960), 1:138–144.

98. Robert Alexander, *The Right Opposition: The Lovestoneites and the International Communist Opposition of the 1930s* (Westport, CT: Greenwood Press, 1981), 292–294.

99. Jon Wilson, *The Domination of Strangers* (Basingstoke, UK: Palgrave Macmillan, 2008), 190–192.

8. GEOCULTURAL WHOLES

1. Margaret MacMillan, *Paris 1919: Six Months that Changed the World* (New York: Random House, 2002), 219–223.

2. The term "subaltern" was glossed in German as "untergeordnet, ohne eigene Verantwortung" in the *Große Brockhaus* dictionary of 1928. While the term did not have great resonance in the German language in the 1920s, it was used widely in English to refer not to colonial populations, as it has come to be used in postcolonial literature, but rather to those in a subordinate military rank. See, for example, Charles Carrington, *A Subaltern's War* (London: P. Davies, 1929), about experience at the front, or Max Plowman, *A Subaltern on the Somme in 1916* (Uckfield, UK: Naval & Military Press, 2001).

3. Susan Pedersen, "Settler Colonialism at the Bar of the League of Nations," in *Settler Colonialism in the Twentieth Century*, ed. Caroline Elikins and Susan Pedersen (New York: Routledge, 2005), 113–134.

4. Dipesh Chakrabarty, *Provincializing Europe* (Princeton, NJ: Princeton University Press, 2000), 2–36.

5. Ramananda Chattopadhyaya, "Mahattvar Bhārat," *Prabāsī* 25 (1925): 119–124.

6. Rabindranath Tagore, *Greater India* (Madras: S. Ganesan, 1921). See Benoy Sarkar, *Baithakē* (Kolkata: Chakrabarty Chatterjee, 1945), 181.

7. Volker Ullrich, *Die nervöse Großmacht, Aufstieg und Untergang des deutschen Kaiserreichs, 1871–1918* (Frankfurt: Fischer, 1997).

8. Thomas Nipperdey, *Deutsche Geschichte*, vol. 2 (Munich: Beck, 1983), 621; A. J. P. Taylor, *The Struggle for Mastery in Europe 1848–1918* (Oxford: Clarendon Press, 1954).

9. Jacob Burckhardt, *Weltgeschichtliche Betrachtungen*, 3rd ed. (Stuttgart: Verlag von W. Spemann, 1918), 12.

10. Friedrich Meinecke, *Cosmopolitanism and the National State* (Princeton, NJ: Princeton University Press, 1970; orig. 1908), ix.

11. See Willi Oberkrome, *Volksgeschichte: Methodische Innovation und völkische Ideologisierung in der deutschen Geschichtswissenschaft 1918–1945* (Göttingen: Vandenhoeck und Ruprecht, 1993), 126–146.

12. Celia Applegate, *A Nation of Provincials: The German Idea of Heimat* (Berkeley: University of California Press, 1990), 30.

13. Ibid., 79.

14. Ibid., 155.

15. Rabindranath Tagore, "Śikṣār Bāhan" (1915), in *Rabindra Racanābalī*, vol. 12 (Kolkata: Viśvabhāratī, 1947–1966), 635–647.

16. Bankim Chandra Chattopadhyaya, "Bangadeśer Kṛṣak" (1872), in *Sāhitya Samagra* (Kolkata: Tuli-Kalam, 2004), 288.

17. Dadabhai Naoroji, *Poverty and Un-British Rule in India* (London: Swan Sonnenschein, 1901), 33; Romesh Dutt, *The Economic History of British India* (London: Kegan Paul, 1902), xiii.

18. Rama Mantena, *The Origins of Modern Historiography in India* (New York: Palgrave, 2012), 44–55.

19. E. J. Rapson, *Ancient India* (Cambridge: Cambridge University Press, 1914), 122–126.

20. V. A. Smith, *Ancient India* (London: Luzac, 1911), 336–400.

21. D. D. Kosambi, "The Basis of Ancient Indian History," *Journal of the American Oriental Society* 75 (1955): 226–237.

22. Ranabir Samaddar, "Territory and People: The Disciplining of Historical Memory," in *Texts of Power: Emerging Disciplines in Colonial Bengal*, ed.

Partha Chatterjee (Minneapolis: University of Minnesota Press, 1995), 167–200.

23. Alan Trevithick, *The Revival of Buddhist Pilgrimage at Bodh Gaya* (Delhi: Shri Jainendra Press, 2006), 44–58.

24. J. W. De Jong, *A Brief History of Buddhist Studies in Europe and America* (Delhi: Satguru, 1987), 38.

25. The *Arthashastra* was rediscovered in 1905 by R. Shamasastry, chief librarian of the Mysore Government Oriental Library. He began publishing it in serialized form in 1905, and the first English translation appeared in 1915. It was later shown that the Arthashastra was the product of multiple authors writing over the course of many centuries. See Thomas Trautmann, *Kautilya and the Arthashastra: A Statistical Investigation of the Authorship and Evolution of the Text* (Leiden: Brill, 1971), 48, 65. The Sukraniti was shown to be a text written in the nineteenth-century. Lallanji Gopal, "The Sukraniti: A Nineteenth-Century Text," *Bulletin of the School of Oriental and African Studies* 25 (1962): 524–556.

26. Kashi Prasad Jayaswal's influential talk in 1912 on "Introduction to Hindu Polity," based on the *Arthashastra*, reprinted in *Modern Review* 13 (1913): 535–541, 664–668, and 14 (1913): 77–83, 201–206, 288–291. See Johannes H. Voigt, "Nationalist Interpretations of Arthasastra in Indian Historical Writing" in *South Asian Affairs,* ed. S. N. Mukherjee (St. Anthony's Papers no. 18) (Oxford: Oxford University Press, 1966), 52.

27. Pramatha Nath Banerjea, *Public Administration in Ancient India* (London: Macmillan, 1916); N. N. Law, *Studies in Ancient Hindu Polity* (London: Longmans, Green, 1914); R. C. Majumdar, *Corporate Life in Ancient India* (Calcutta: Surendra Nath Sen, 1918); U. N. Ghoshal, *The History of Hindu Political Theories from the Earliest Times to the End of the First Quarter of the Seventeenth Century* (London: H. Milford, 1923).

28. V. D. Savarkar, *Hindu-Pad-Padashahi* (Madras: B. G. Paul, 1925), 249.

29. Hemchandra Ray, "Was State-Socialism Known in Ancient India? A Study in Kautilya's Arthasastra," in *Sir Asutosh Mookerjee Silver Jubilee Volumes* (Calcutta: Calcutta University, 1922), 429–446.

30. Hemchandra Ray, "Economic Policy and Functions of the Kautiliyan State," *Journal of the Department of Letters of University of Calcutta* 13 (1926): 29.

31. Kalidas Nag, "Greater India," *Calcutta Review,* January 1926, 17.

32. Moriz Winternitz, "Kautilya and the Art of Politics in Ancient India," *The Visva Bharati Quarterly* 1 (1923): 261.

33. P. C. Bagchi wrote *India and China* (Calcutta: Greater India Society, 1927); Niranjan Prasad Chakravarti published *India and Central Asia* (Calcutta: Abinash Chandra Sarkar, 1927); Bijan Raj Chatterji wrote

Indian Culture in Sumatra and Java (Calcutta: A. C. Sarkar, 1927); R. C. Majumdar published *Ancient Indian Colonies in the Far East* (Lahore: Punjab Sanskrit Book Depot, 1927); Phanindranath Bose wrote *Indian Teachers in China* (Madras: S. Ganesan, 1923); and Upendranath Ghoshal penned *Ancient Indian Culture in Afghanistan* (Calcutta: Prabāsī Press, 1928).

34. For example, Beni Barua, *The Religion of Asoka* (Calcutta: Maha Bodhi Society, 1927).

35. B. K. Sarkar, R. K. Mukherji, Dhiren Roy, N. R. Ray, I. H. Baqai, H. B. Sarkar, Keshab Gupta, Amar Lahiri, Vivekanadna Mukerji, Rajnarayan Gupta, Arun Datta-Majumdar, Mahan Raychaudhuri, Kshitish Banerji, Manoranjan Chowdhury, Ajit Ghosh, and other members of the second-generation movement in the 1920s and 1930s.

36. See the discussion of Islamic Universalism in Ayesha Jalal, *Self and Sovereignty* (London: Routledge, 2000), 189–211.

37. Sheldon Pollock, *The Language of Gods in the World of Men* (Berkeley: University of California, 2006), 23.

38. Bhupendranath Datta, *Bāṃlār Itihāsa* (Kolkata: Nababhārata Publishers, 1977), 25–49.

39. Rabindranath Tagore, *Bhāratvarse Itihāser Dhārā* (Calcutta: Jivansmriti, 1912), 250; Vasant Kaiwar, "The Aryan Model of History and the Oriental Renaissance," in *Antinomies of Modernity,* ed. Vasant Kaiwar and Sucheta Mazumdar (Durham, NC: Duke University Press, 2003), 30–51.

40. Tagore, *Java Yatrir Patra,* quoted in Sugata Bose, *Hundred Horizons* (Cambridge: Cambridge University Press, 2006), 258.

41. Hans Adolf Jacobsen, *Karl Haushofer,* vol. 1 (Boppard: Boldt, 1979), 88.

42. Haushofer Nachlass, Bundesarchiv Koblenz, 1909, N1122/153, part 2.

43. David Thomas Murphy, *The Heroic Earth: Geopolitical Thought in Weimar Germany, 1918–1933* (Kent, OH: Kent State University Press, 1997), 277.

44. Norbert Krebs, "Der Bereich der deutschen Ausstrahlung im Osten," in *Deutsche Ostforschung,* ed. Hermann Aubin et al. (Leipzig: Hirzel, 1942), 12–30.

45. Michael Burleigh, *Germany Turns Eastwards* (Cambridge: Cambridge University Press, 1988), 78–147; David Blackbourn, *The Conquest of Nature* (London: Jonathan Cape, 2006), 249–265.

46. Fritz Hesse, "Geopolitische Probleme Englands im vorderen Orient," *Zeitschrift für Geopolitik* 7 (1930): 662.

47. Friedrich Ratzel, *Politische Geographie* (Munich: R. Oldenbourg, 1897), 21–39.

48. Karl Haushofer, *Zur Geopolitik der Selbst-Bestimmung* (Munich: Roesl, 1923), 161.

49. Ibid., 11.

50. Ibid., 23.

51. Michael Ash et al., *Geisteswissenschaften im Nationalsozialismus* (Göttingen: V&R Press, 2010), 18.

52. Karl Haushofer, "Bericht über den indopazifischen Raum," *Zeitschrift für Geopolitik* 9 (1932): 45.

53. Karl Haushofer, *Geopolitik der Pan-Ideen* (Berlin: Zentral-Verlag GmBH, 1931), 15.

54. Haushofer, "Bericht über den Indopazifische Raum," *Zeitschrift für Geopolitik*, 8 (1931): 930.

55. Andrew Zimmermann, *Alabama in Africa: Booker T. Washington, the German Empire, and the Globalization of the New South* (Princeton, NJ: Princeton University Press, 2010), 173–198.

56. Graf Bethlen, "Nationalismus und Kosmopolitismus," *Zeitschrift für Geopolitik* 7 (1929): 517.

57. Hans Freyer, *Herrschaft und Planung* (Hamburg: Hanseatische Verlagsanstalt, 1933), 39.

58. Charles S. Maier, "Consigning the Twentieth Century to History," *American Historical Review* 105 (2000): 807–831.

59. Ernst Tiessen, "Der Friedensvertrag von Versailles und die politische Geographie," *Zeitschrift für Geopolitik* 1 (1924): 203–220.

60. Hermann Aubin, *Grundlagen und Perspektiven geschichtlicher Kulturraumforschung und Kulturmorphologie* (Bonn: Ludwig Röhrscheid, 1965), 17–26.

61. Haushofer, *Zur Geopolitik der Selbst-bestimmung Südostasiens* (Munich: Rösl, 1923), 50.

62. Benoy Kumar Sarkar, *Chinese Religion through Hindu Eyes* (Shanghai: Shanghai Commercial Press, 1916), 236.

63. Benoy Kumar Sarkar, *Benoy Kumar Sarkarer Baithake,* ed. Haridas Mukhopadhyaya, vol. 1 (Calcutta: De's Publishing, 2002), 18.

64. "Report of the Deutsche Akademie," IfZ-M, 1931, MA 1190/3.

65. For example, "Indisches Volkstum," in *Deutsches Volkstum* 2 (1926): 491–497, in which Indians are portrayed as rising, revolutionary people.

66. Erich Obst, "Wir fordern unsere Kolonien zurück!," *Zeitschrift für Geopolitik* 3 (1926): 153.

67. "Die außenpolitische Orientierung der Rechtsverbände," 1926, Bundesarchiv, Microfiche, R43 I/2696, Fiche 2, 37, 38. One of the most colorful titles from the war years, *Der Vampir der Festlandes* [The vampire of the Continent] (Berlin: E. S. Mittler, 1939), on the history of what he called "English world power."

68. "Deutsche Akademie," Bundesarchiv, R51 FB 3240.

69. "Sitzung des indischen Ausschusses der Deutschen Akademie am 23. Oktober 1934," N1122/115.

70. E. Michels, "Deutsch als Weltsprache? Franz Thierfelder, the Deutsche Akademie in Munich and the Promotion of the German Language Abroad, 1923–1945," *German History* 22 (2004): 206–228.

71. Franz Thierfelder, "Die Arbeit der Deutschen Akademie im Jahre 1926/27," Bundesarchiv N1122/109.

72. "Report on Indian Committee," IfZ-M, 1936, MA 1190/3.

73. A delegation of German scientists traveled to Calcutta in 1938 to give presentations at Benoy Kumar Sarkar's German Institute. See Report on the Bangiya Jarman Vidya Samsad, File 149.B.311 at the National Library of India, Kolkata.

74. German Indologists with a "spiritualist" bent, such as Jakob Hauer at the University of Tübingen, also worked with the Deutsche Akademie, for example. Bundesarchiv Koblenz, Haushofer Nachlass, N1122/47.

75. Tapan Mukhejee, *Taraknath Das: Life and Letters of a Revolutionary in Exile* (Calcutta: National Council of Education, 1998), 8–10, 184–189.

76. Taraknath Das, *India's Position in World Politics* (Calcutta: Sarawaty Library, 1922), 64.

77. Nathaniel Curzon, *Persia and the Persian Question* (London: Longmans, Green, 1892): 555–585.

78. Taraknath Das, "India and the British Commonwealth of Nations," *Calcutta Review* (1928): 143–153.

79. Eugene D'souza, "Nazi Propaganda in India," *Social Scientist* 28 (2000): 77–90.

80. Ibid., 78. International Railway Information Bureau of Madras, the Bombay Press Service, the IndoGerman News Exchange of New Delhi, the German Society of Aligarh University, the Bhatachar Movement in Bengal, Khaksar Movement in the United Provinces, the German Institute of Bombay, the German Institute of Calcutta, and branches of the Hindu Mahasabha.

81. Letter from Commissioner of Police to the Secretary to the Government of Bombay, NAI, July 21, 1939, Home Department (Special), File No. 830(A), 37; D'souza, "Nazi Propaganda," 84.

82. Ludwig Alsdorf, "Zu schaffendes Organ für die Indo-Germansiche Arbeitsgemeinschaft," GFM 33/564, NA-UK.

83. "CIB's Reports on Activities of Germans, Italians and Japanese," APAC, L/PJ/12/506, 52.

84. Ibid., 58.

85. Ibid., 64.

86. CIB Reports, L/PJ/12/506, Survey 12 1939, 46.

87. CIB Reports, L/PJ/12/506, 94.

88. Ibid., 158; Maria Casolari, "Hindutva's Foreign Tie-up in the 1930s," *Economic and Political Weekly* 35 (2000): 218–228.

89. Savarkar, *Hindu-Pad-Padashahi*, 1.

90. Ibid., 254.

91. Nicholas Goodrick-Clarke, *Hitler's Priestess* (New York: New York University, 1998), 50–57.

92. Ibid., 60.

93. Ibid., 61.

94. Ibid., 67.

95. Elaine Scarry, *The Body in Pain* (New York: Oxford University Press, 1985); Ranajit Guha, *Dominance without Hegemony* (Cambridge, MA: Harvard University Press, 1997).

96. CIB Reports, L/PJ/12/506.

97. Anita Desai, *Baumgartner's Bombay* (London: Heinemann, 1988), 125.

9. THE PSYCHOANALYTIC UNIVERSE

1. Ashis Nandy provided the classic study, *The Savage Freud* (Princeton, NJ: University Press, 1995), 81. Also see Ranjana Khanna, *Dark Continents* (Durham, NC: Duke University Press, 2003), 1, 66; Purnima Mehta, "The Import and Export of Psychoanalysis to India," *Journal of the American Academy of Psychoanalysis and Dynamic Psychiatry* 25 (1997): 455–471; Kalpana Seshadri-Crooks, "The Primitive as Analyst: Postcolonial Feminism's Access to Psychoanalysis," *Cultural Critique* 28 (1994): 175–213.

2. See Matt Ffytche's discussion of Freud as a "post-Enlightenment" thinker, in *The Foundation of the Unconscious* (Cambridge: Cambridge University Press, 2012), 272.

3. Peter Gay, *A Godless Jew: Freud, Atheism, and the Making of Psychoanalysis* (New Haven: Yale University Press, 1987), 72–113.

4. Mitchell G. Ash, *Gestalt Psychology in German Culture, 1890–1967* (Cambridge: Cambridge University Press, 1995), 36.

5. David Meskill, *Optimizing the German Workforce* (New York: Berghahn Books, 2010), 42.

6. Ash, *Gestalt Psychology*, 28–50, 103–108; On Freud's "devastating" positivism, see David Lindenfeld, *The Transformation of Positivism* (Berkeley: University of California Press, 1980), 1–10.

7. Anne Harrington, *Reenchanted Science* (Cambridge, MA: Harvard University Press, 1996), 25; Ash, *Gestalt Psychology*, 72, 287–291.

8. See Narendra Nath Sengupta File, UAIII 15.88.10, 1890–1968, Box 4486, Harvard University Archives.

9. Mou Banerjee, "Rabindranath at Harvard, An Enquiry," unpublished essay.

10. Ibid.

11. Durganand Sinha, *Psychology in a Third World Country: The Indian Experience* (New Delhi: Sage), 13–16.

12. Suhrit Chandra Mitra File, Leipzig University Archives, PhilFakProm 10035.

13. Benoy Kumar Sarkar, "The Making of Naren Sengupta, the Pioneer of Experimental Psychology in India," *Indian Journal of Psychology* 19 (1944): 133.

14. Mitra File, UAL PhilFakProm 10035.

15. Stanley Hall, *Founders of Modern Psychology* (New York: Appleton, 1912), v–vi.

16. N. N. Sengupta, "Psychology, Its Present Development and Outlook," *Indian Journal of Psychology* 1 (1926): 1–25.

17. Ibid., 23.

18. Radhakamal Mukerjee and Narendra Nath Sengupta, *Introduction to Social Psychology: Mind in Society* (London: D. C. Heath, 1929), 255.

19. M. N. Banerji, "Reaction Time as an Indicator of Onset of Fatigue," *Indian Journal of Psychology* 10 (1935): 69–71.

20. Petra Rösgen, "Kripal Singh Sodhi: Leben und Werk eines indischen Psychologen in Deutschland," MA thesis, Universität Koblenz, 2003; "Indian Civilians Known or Believed to be on the Continent of Europe," APAC: L/P&J/12/762, 51–68.

21. Kripal Singh Sodhi, *Urteilsbildung im sozialen Kraftfeld* (Göttingen: C. J. Hogrefe, 1953).

22. N. N. Sengupta, "On Gestalt Theory," *Journal of Indian Psychology* 2 (1927): 55–59.

23. Overview of *Indian Journal of Psychology 1926–1937* (150 total articles): 16 articles on workforce experiments, fatigue, and efficiency; 33 articles on intelligence experiments and memory; 22 articles on emotion, instinct, attention, and religious feeling; 12 articles on discussions about the field; 24 articles on the physiology of perception; 9 articles on group, language, identity, and sociability; 3 articles on child psychology; 16 articles on psychoanalysis; and 2 articles on gestalt psychology.

24. Carl Jung, "Reise nach Afrika 1925/26," Hs 10455: 45, University of Zurich Jung Archiv. The connection between Freud's psychoanalysis and archaeological methodology has been explored recently by Khanna, *Dark Continents*, 33–65

25. Sigmund Freud, *New Introductory Lectures on Psychoanalysis* (London: Hogarth Press, 1933), 181.

26. Sigmund Freud to Romain Rolland, January 19, 1930, in *Letters of Sigmund Freud,* ed. Ernst Freud (New York: Basic Books, 1960), 392–393.

27. Edward Said, *Culture and Imperialism* (New York: Knopf, 1993), 239.

28. Romain Rolland, *Mahatma Gandhi,* trans. Emil Roniger (Zurich: Rotapfel Verlag, 1924); Rolland, *Essai sur la mystique et l'action de l'Inde vivante* (Paris: Stock, 1929); Rolland, *La vie de Vivekananda et l'évangile universel* (Paris: Stock, 1930).

29. Freud to Rolland, *Letters,* July 14, 1929, 388.

30. Sigmund Freud to Romain Rolland, *Letters,* March 4, 1923.

31. Ibid.

32. Carl Schorske, *Fin-de-Siècle Vienna* (New York: Knopf, 1979), 185; John Boyer, *Political Radicalism in Late Imperial Vienna* (Chicago: University of Chicago Press, 1981), 316.

33. Freud to Rolland, January 19, 1930, in *Sigmund Freud et Romain Rolland correspondance, 1923–1936,* ed. Henri Vermorel (Paris: Presses Universitaires de France, 1993), 313.

34. Sigmund Freud, *Civilization and Its Discontents* (London: Hogarth Press, 1930), 47, 61.

35. Girindrasekhar Bose, "Scope of Psychology," *Indian Journal of Psychology* 7 (1932): 29.

36. Christiane Hartnack, *Psychoanalysis in Colonial India* (Delhi: Oxford University Press, 2001), 107.

37. The two most important classic analyses are provided by Hartnack, *Psychoanalysis in Colonial India,* 107–130; and Nandy, *Savage Freud,* 95–115.

38. In *Freud and the Non-European* (London: Verso, 2003), 27, Edward Said wrote, "Freud is a remarkable instance of a thinker for whom scientific excavation of the buried, forgotten, repressed and denied past. Not for nothing was Schliemann a model for him"; Richard H. Armstrong, "Freud: 'Schliemann of the Mind,'" *Biblical Archaeology Review* 4 (April 2001): 17.

39. Girindrasekhar Bose, *The Concept of Repression* (Calcutta: S. C. Majumdar, 1921), 32.

40. Nandy, *Savage Freud,* 95–115.

41. Bose, *Concept of Repression,* 32.

42. "An Indian Psychoanalyst," *Modern Review* (May 1922): 637.

43. Freud to Girindrasekhar Bose, October 27, 1922, *The Bose-Freud Correspondence* (Calcutta: Indian Psycho-analytical Society, 1964), 12.

44. Paul Ricoeur, *Freud and Philosophy* (New Haven, CT: Yale University Press, 1970), 87–102.

45. See Hartnack, *Psychoanalysis in Colonial India,* 204.

46. Girindrasekhar Bose, "Ambivalence," *Sankhya* 3 (1949): 5.

47. Bose, *Concept of Repression,* 32ff.

48. Pierre Sabourin, *Sandor Ferenczi: Un pionnier de la clinique* (Paris: Campagne Première, 2011), 149–172.

49. Girindrasekhar Bose, "Opposite Fantasies in the Release of Repression: A New Psycho-Analytic Technique," *Indian Journal of Psychology* 7 (1932): 31.

50. Owen Berkeley-Hill, *All too Human: An Unconventional Autobiography* (London: Peter Davies, 1939), 40.

51. Ibid., 64.

52. Owen Berkeley-Hill, "The Anal-Erotic Factor in the Religion, Philosophy and Character of the Hindus," *International Journal of Psycho-Analysis* 2 (1921): 306; "A Short Study of the Life and Character of Mohammed," *International Journal of Psycho-Analysis* 2 (1921): 31; "The 'Color Question' from a Psychoanalytic Standpoint," *Collected Papers of Owen Berkeley-Hill* (London: Book Company, 1933), 139–148.

53. Owen Berkeley-Hill, "Psychology and Pedagogy," *Collected Papers* (Calcutta: Book Company, 1933), 172.

54. "Business Meeting Report," *International Psychoanalytic Association,* Business Meeting 10 (1929): 510–526.

55. See Hartnack's nuanced discussion of Berkeley-Hill's work, in *Psycho-analysis in Colonial India,* 55.

56. Girindrasekhar Bose, "The Reliability of Psychoanalytic Findings," *British Journal of Medical Psychology* 3 (1923): 105–115. Christiane Hartnack, "The Uses of Psychoanalysis in the Treatment of Indian Patients," in *Psychoanalysis in Colonial India,* 144–162.

57. Girindrasekhar Bose, "Psychological Outlook in Hindu Philosophy," *Modern Review* (January 1931): 16.

58. Girindrasekhar Bose quoted in D. Ganguly, "Girindrasekhar," *Samīkṣa: Journal of the Indian Psychoanalytical Society* 9 (1955): 38.

59. Girindrasekhar Bose, "Gītā," *Prabāsī* 31 (1931): 9, 251, 340, 473, 667, 837.

60. Ibid., 349.

61. Girindrasekhar Bose, "The Yoga Sutras," *Samīksa: Journal of the Indian Psychoanalytical Society* 11 (1957): 45–51.

62. Partha Chatterjee, *Lineages of Political Society* (New York: Columbia University Press, 2011), 50.

63. Bose, "Gītā," 255.

64. Ibid.

65. Girindrasekhar Bose, "Yoga Sutras," *Indian Journal of Psychology* 6 (1931): 139.

66. Girindrasekhar Bose, "Psychology and Psychiatry," *Indian Journal of Psychology* 5 (1930): 145.

67. Girindrasekhar Bose, "The Rishi's Mind," *Indian Journal of Psychology* 5 (1930): 126.

68. Jay Sherry, *Carl Gustav Jung: Avant-Garde Conservative* (London: Palgrave, 2010), 70.

69. His interest in occultism is seen in his attendance to various "Spiritische Experimente" in 1895; see "Protokoll der Sitzung," JAZ, Hs 1055:1a, Carl Jung Archiv, Zurich. For his interest in flying saucers, see the correspondence between Carl Jung and Fowler McCormick, March 20, 1953.

70. Carl Jung, "Reise-Reminiszenzen Indienreise Dezember 37-Februar 38," JAZ, Hs 1057, S. P. Mukherjee to Dr. Jung, informs him that he will receive an honorary doctorate.

71. Carl Jung, "Concerning Mandala Symbolism," first published in 1950, *Carl Jung Collected Works,* vol. 10 (New York: Pantheon, 1953), 355.

72. Jung's sketches of mandalas from Ajanta, and sketches of the temple design at Amarkantak, Reise-Reminiszenzen, are stored in his archive, JAZ, Hs 1057.

73. David L. Hart, "The Classical Jungian School," in *The Cambridge Companion to Jung,* ed. Polly Young-Eisendrath and Terence Dawson (Cambridge: Cambridge University Press, 2008), 95.

74. Petteri Pietikainen, "The 'Volk' and Its Unconscious: Jung, Hauer and the 'German Revolution,'" *Journal of Contemporary History* 35 (2000), 523–539; Walter Kaufmann, *Freud versus Adler and Jung* (New York: McGraw-Hill, 1980), 292.

75. Michael Vannoy Adams, "The Archetypal School," in *Cambridge Companion to Jung* (Cambridge: Cambridge University Press, 1997), 102.

76. Carl Jung, "What India Can Teach Us," originally published in 1939, reprinted in *Civilization in Transition, C. G. Jung Collected Works,* vol. 10, trans. R. F. C. Hull (Princeton, NJ: Princeton University Press, 1978), 525–532.

77. Review of C. G. Jung, *Two Essays on Analytical Psychology,* in *Indian Journal of Psychology* 3 (1929): 75.

78. Freud, *Civilization and Its Discontents,* 72.

79. David Dollenmayer, "The Advent of Döblinism: *Wang-Lun and Wadzek,"* in *A Companion to the Works of Alfred Döblin,* ed. Roland Albert Dollinger (Rochester: Camden House, 2004), 60.

80. Ibid., 60.

81. Christiane Günther, *Aufbruch nach Asien* (Munich: Iudicium, 1988), 78.

82. Jung, "Concerning Mandala Symbolism," 356.

83. Jakob Wilhelm Hauer, *Die Anfänge der Yogapraxis in alten Indien* (Stuttgart: Kohlhammer, 1921).

84. Thomas Colebrooke, "On the *Vedas* or Sacred Writings of the Hindus," *Asiatic Researches* 8 (1808): 390; Nirad Chaudhuri, *Scholar Extraordi-*

nary: The Life of Friedrich Max Müller (New York: Oxford University Press, 1974), 137.

85. Hauer dedicated *Das Lankavatara-Sutra und Das Samkhya* (Stuttgart: Kohlhammer, 1927) to Garbe in addition to *Yogapraxis* (Berlin: Kohlhammer, 1921).

86. See K. R. Dhawan to Hauer, 1932, and K. A. Bhatta to Hauer, 1942, in Hauer Nachlass, Bundesarchiv Koblenz, N1131/179.

87. Shyamsundar Goswami to J. K. Hauer, Bundesarchiv Koblenz, November 9, 1932, N1131/137.

88. Ibid.

89. J. K. Hauer to Shyamsundar Goswami, Bundesarchiv Koblenz, December 27, 1932, N1131/137.

90. Magnus Hirschfeld, *Men and Women: The World Journey of a Sexologist* (New York: Putnam's, 1935), 141.

91. Ibid., 149.

92. Jung to Zimmer, December 12, 1938, Correspondence Files in Jung Archive, ETH, 205.

93. Jung, "What India Can Teach Us," 203.

94. See Kurt Köster, *Johan Huizinga, 1872–1945* (Oberursel: Verlag Europa, Archiv, 1947).

95. Mircea Eliade, *Bengal Nights* (Manchester: Carcanet, 1993). See Mac Ricketts, *Mircea Eliade*, vol. 1 (Boulder: East European Monographs, 1988), 464–486.

96. Maitraye Devi, *Na Hanyante, It Does not Die* (Calcutta: Writers Workshop, 1976), 235, 255.

97. Freud, *Civilization and Its Discontents,* 74.

98. "Indian Psycho-Analytical Society Annual Report for 1948," *Samīkṣa* 3 (1948): iv.

99. Ibid., 202.

100. Girindrasekhar Bose, "Everyday Psychoanalysis," *Samīkṣa* (1945). See T. G. Vaidyanathan and Jeffrey Kripal, eds., *Vishnu on Freud's Desk* (Delhi: Oxford University Press, 1999).

10. WORLDS OF ARTISTIC EXPRESSION

1. Krishna Bose and Sugata Bose, introduction to Rabindranath Tagore, *Purabi*, trans. Charu Chowdhuri (London: Seagull, 2007).

2. Ashish Rajadhyaksha, *Indian Cinema in the Time of Celluloid* (Bloomington: Indiana University Press, 2009), 69ff.

3. William Petig, "The Birth of a New Realism: Photography, Painting and the Advent of Documentary Cinema," *Film History* 10 (1998): 165–187;

Christopher Pinney, *The Coming of Photography in India* (London: British Library, 2008), 3, 4.

4. Jacques Rancière, *Politics of Aesthetics* (London: Continuum, 2004).

5. Pinney, *Coming of Photography,* 103–160.

6. Choodamani Nandagopal, *Impressions: Devika Rani Roerich* (Bangalore: International Roerich Memorial Trust, 1992), 25–45. A Joseph Wirsching Foundation has been established in Goa.

7. Partha Mitter, *Art and Nationalism in Colonial India* (Cambridge: Cambridge University Press, 1994), 308–309.

8. Roger Lipsey, *Coomaraswamy: His Life and Work* (Princeton, NJ: Princeton University, 1977), 87.

9. Ananda Coomaraswamy, *La Sculpture de Bodhgaya* (Paris: Editions d'Art et d'Histoire, 1935).

10. Stella Kramrisch, *The Presence of Śiva* (Princeton, NJ: Princeton University Press, 1981).

11. Stella Kramrisch, "Untersuchungen zum Wesen frühbuddhistischen Bildnerei Indiens," PhD diss., University of Vienna, 1919.

12. Willy Rotzler, *Johannes Itten. Werke und Schriften* (Zurich: Orell Füssli, 1972), Itten's diary entry, 108.

13. Barbara Stoler Miller, "A Biographical Essay," in *Exploring India's Sacred Art: Selected Writings of Stella Kramrisch,* ed. Stoler Miller (Philadelphia: University of Pennsylvania, 1983), 5; Wassily Kandinsky, *Über das Geistige in der Kunst* (Munich: Piper, 1912), 18–35.

14. Max Dvořák, *Idealismus und Naturalismus in der gotischen Skulptur und Malerei* (Munich: Oldenbourg, 1918), 19.

15. "Stella Kramrisch" File, Vienna University Archives, PH RA 4727.

16. Rabindranath Tagore, *The Center of Indian Culture* (Madras: Society for the Promotion of National Education, 1919), 13. This text is an inauguration speech for Viśva Bhārati University.

17. This was on June 19, or 20, 1920. Ketaki Kushari Dyson and Sushobhan Adhikary, *Raṅger Rabindranath* (Calcutta: Ananda, 1997), 401; Prasanta Kumar Pal, Rabijībanī, vol. 4 (Calcutta: Ananda, 1989), 17.

18. Stella Kramrisch to O. C. Gangoly, London, June 15, 1921, quoted in R. K. Das Gupta, "Philosopher of Indian Art," *Statesman,* June 25, 1996.

19. See Josef Strzygowski to Rabindranath Tagore, Vienna, June 15, 1921, EC 387, Visva Bhārati Archives.

20. William Rothenstein to Rabindranath Tagore, Letter 143, in Mary Lago, ed., *Imperfect Encounter: Letters of William Rothenstein and Rabindranath Tagore* (Cambridge, MA: Harvard University Press, 1972), 281.

21. Ibid.

22. Stella Kramrisch, "The Expressiveness of Indian Art," *Calcutta Review* (October 1922): 1–46.

23. In the end, Strzygowski did not come to Shantiniketan. Strzygowski to Rabindranath Tagore, VBA, April 4, 1922, EC 387.

24. C. A. Bayly, "The Origins of Swadeshi," in *The Social Life of Things: Commodities in Cultural Perspective,* ed. Arjun Appadurai (Cambridge: Cambridge University Press, 1986), 310.

25. Ananda Coomaraswamy, *Introduction to Indian Art* (Adyar: Theosophical Publishing, 1923), vii.

26. Saloni Mathur, *India by Design* (Berkeley: University of California Press, 2007), 49–55.

27. Mitter, *Art and Nationalism,* 248.

28. Ananda Coomaraswamy, *Geschichte der indischen und indonesischen Kunst* (Leipzig: Verlag Karl Hiersemann, 1927); Ananda Coomaraswamy, *Art and Swadeshi* (Madras: Ganesh, n.d.), 116.

29. Mitter, *Art and Nationalism,* 267.

30. Tapati Guha-Thakurta, *Art, Artists and Aesthetics in Bengal, c. 1850–1920: Westernising Trends and Nationalist Concerns in the Making of a New "Indian" Art* (Oxford: Oxford University Press, 1988), 190.

31. Stella Kramrisch, "The Significance of Indian Art (in Indian Arts and Art-Crafts) Recent Movements in Western Art," in *Indian Art and Art-Crafts: Five Lectures,* ed. W. D. S. Brown (Adyar: Theosophical Publishing House, 1922) given in connection with the Arts and Art-Crafts Exhibition held during the Theosophical Society's Annual Convention.

32. Nandalal Bose, *Vision and Creation* (Calcutta: Viśva Bharati, 1999).

33. Panchanan Mandal, *Bhāratśilpi Nandalal,* vol. 2 (Shantiniketan: Rarh-Gabesana, 1988), 121.

34. Binode Bihari Mukherjee comments on this in "On Ramkinkar Baij," *Chitrakar* (Kolkata: Seagull, 2006), 86. Soon after Kramrisch's arrival, she delivered a series of lectures in Shantiniketan titled "The Tendencies of Modern European Art." See the announcement in, "Ourselves," *Rupam,* no. 10 (1922): 69.

35. Mandal, *Bhāratśilpi Nandalal,* 2:121.

36. Kramrisch delivered six lectures on "The Expressiveness of Indian Art," beginning July 1922. See PMA-Kram, Box 25 "SK Calcutta" folder, uncataloged.

37. Kramrisch, "The Expressiveness of Indian Art"; "The Aesthetics of Young India: A Rejoinder," *Rupam,* no. 10 (1922): 66–67; "Indian Art and Europe," *Rupam,* no. 11, 81–86; "An Indian Cubist," *Rupam,* no. 11 (1922): 107–109; "The Significance of Indian Art"; and "The New Art in Europe," *The Visva Bharati Quarterly* 1 (April 1923): 69–75.

38. Ibid., 22.

39. Abanindranath Tagore published *Sadanga: The Six Limbs of Painting* (Calcutta: Indian Society of Oriental Art, 1921), as a reconstruction of the ancient Indian aesthetic tradition.

40. The subtlety of this argument receives masterful exposition in Partha Mitter, "Bauhaus in Kalkutta," unpublished manuscript in a volume by Annemarie Jäggi on Global Bauhaus, forthcoming from the Bauhaus-Archiv, Berlin.

41. Stella Kramrisch, "Indian Art and Europe," *Rupam,* no. 11 (1922): 81–85.

42. Kramrisch, "The Expressiveness of Indian Art"; "The Aesthetics of Young India: A Rejoinder," *Rupam,* no. 9 (1922): 66–67; "Indian Art and Europe," 81–86.

43. Barbara Stoler Miller, "Introduction," in Miller, *Exploring India's Sacred Art.*

44. Mitter, "Bauhaus in Kalkutta," 4.

45. Kramrisch to Itten, May 5, 1922, Thuringia Hauptarchiv (THA), Fiche 130, File 57, 1.

46. Ibid.

47. Itten's letter to Klee, copied to Feininger, Marcks, and Schlemmer. Itten to Klee, THA August 7, 1922, Fiche 130, File 57, 5.

48. Hirschfeld to Klee, THA, August 23, 1922, Fiche 130, File 57, 5.

49. THA, Lists No. II, VIII, and IX, THA Fiche 130, File 57, 35–58.

50. THA, Lists No. I, III, IV, V, VI, VII, X, THA Fiche 130, File 57, 35–58.

51. Kramrisch to Itten, August 31, 1922, THA Fiche 130, File 57, 26.

52. Anonymous, "The Fourteenth Annual Exhibition of the Indian Society of Oriental Art," *Rupam,* nos. 13–14 (1923): 14–18.

53. *Rupam,* January–June 1923, contains an excerpt from the introductory note to the catalog.

54. Abany C. Bannerjee, "Gaganendranath Tagore's New Indian Art," *Visva Bharati Quarterly* 2 (1924): 298–301.

55. See report from April 25, 1923, ZSMB (henceforth ZSMB), I/NG 603, 8. After Berlin it went on to exhibit at the Leipzig Art Association.

56. See the list of artwork sent, Zentral Staatliche Museen zu Berlin Archive, I/NG 603, 16–12.

57. Tagore, as a rule, did not name his paintings. "Sonderausstellungen," ZSMB, I/NG 603, 1923–24, 50. Item 50 is labeled: "Die javanische Schauspielerin," by Mr. Rabendra Nath Tagore. Compare with Sarkar's catalog listing of "Nabendranath Tagore." "Ausstellung Moderner Indischer Aquarelle in der Nationalgalerie," Indo-European Trading Company, Berlin, 1, 4.

58. Benoy Kumar Sarkar, *Economic Development* (Madras: B. G. Paul, 1926), xiii.

59. Kramrisch, "The Aesthetics of Young India," *Rupam*, no. 10 (1922): 66–67; B. K. Sarkar, "Social Philosophy in Aesthetics," *Rupam*, nos. 15–16 (1923): 88.

60. Both Kramrisch and a scholar with the pen name "Agastya" wrote critical rejoinders to Benoy Sarkar's essay on "futurism." Their essays appear in the April, July, and October issues of *Rupam* in 1922, nos. 10–12. Sarkar responds in his 1923 essay, "Social Philosophy in Aesthetics," *Rupam*, nos. 15–16 (1923): 88–99.

61. Benoy Kumar Sarkar, "Ausstellung Moderner Indischer Aquarelle in der Nationalgalerie." A copy of this catalog is available under call number V-Ind wd 8 at the Ibero-American Institute of the Preußischer Kulturbesitz, Berlin.

62. Kramrisch and "Agastya" start the dispute with Sarkar in *Rupam*. See the April, July, and October issues of 1922. Sarkar responds in his 1923 essay, "Social Philosophy in Aesthetics," *Rupam*, nos. 15–16 (1923): 88–99.

63. Stella Kramrisch, "Indische Malerei der Gegenwart," *Der Cicerone* 16 (1924): 954–962; repr. in *Jahrbuch der jungen Kunst*, 4 (1924): 234–242.

64. Stella Kramrisch, "The New Art in Europe," *Visva Bharati Quarterly* (April 1923): 68.

65. O. C. Ganguly, "Movements in European Art," *Journal of the Society of Oriental Art* 1(1923): 493.

66. Kalidas Nag, *India and the Pacific World* (Calcutta: Book Company, 1941), 1.

67. Pramatha Nath Bose, *Degeneration: A World Problem* (Calcutta: Newman, 1924).

68. B. K. Sarkar called Tilak the "Goethe of Poona" in *Futurism of Young Asia* (Berlin: Springer, 1922). Tilak's thesis about the Arctic Aryans was argued in *The Arctic Home in the Vedas: being also a new key to the interpretation of many Vedic texts* (Pune: Kesari, 1903).

69. Geeta Kapur, "Contemporary Practice: Some Polemical Categories," *Third Text* 11 (1990): 111.

70. Kramrisch, "Expressiveness," 1–46, 8.

71. Stella Kramrisch, "The Present Movement of Art, East and West," *Visva Bharati Quarterly* 1 (October 1923): 225.

72. Mondal, *Bhāratśilpi Nandalal*, 121–123.

73. Ibid., 18.

74. Stella Bloch, "Intuition," *Rupam*, no. 3 (1920): 25–26.

75. Hermann Goetz, "The Relations between Indian Painting and Indian Sculpture," *Rupam*, nos. 22–23 (1925): 46–53; William Cohn, "Problems of Indian Art," *Rupam*, no. 3 (July 1920): 2–10; William Cohn, "Buddhistische Skupturen aus Japan," *Berliner Museen: Berichte aus den Preußischen Kunstsammlungen* 43, no. 7/8 (1922): 75.

76. Josef Strzygowski, "India's Position in the Art of Asia," *Journal of the Indian Society of Oriental Art* 1 (1933): 7–17.

77. Josef Strzygowski, "Three Northern Currents in the Art of the Chinese People," *Journal of the Indian Society of Oriental Art* 5 (1937): 42–57; Heinrich Zimmer, "Trees, Huts and Temples," *Journal of the Indian Society of Oriental Art* 5 (1937): 111–121.

78. Betty Heimann, "Significance of Numbers in Hindu Philosophical Texts," *Journal of the Indian Society of Oriental Art* 6 (1938): 88–93.

79. See the cataloging of Indian art objects in Siam, at Amaravati, in Berlin, Calcutta, and Lahore in the *Rupam Magazine,* 1929.

80. Max Osborn, "The Indian Exhibition in Berlin," *Rupam,* nos. 15–16 (July and December 1923): 74–82.

81. Valentina Stache-Rosen, "Hermann Goetz," in *German Indologists* (New Delhi: Goethe Institut, 1981).

82. See "Meine Bilder," Tagore's introduction to the exhibition, dated July 2, 1930. ZSMB, File 1436 "Tagore, Rabindranath."

83. See the article "Mit und Ohne Schleier," *Berlin Zeitung am Abend,* October 14, 1981.

84. "Tagore als Maler," in *Der Tag;* "Ausstellung in der Galerie Moeller," by KZ; "Tagore als Maler," by WG. These clippings from 1930 are in File 1436 "Tagore, Rabindranath" at the ZSMB.

85. Review by Ferdinand Eckhardt, ZSMB, August 30, 1930, in File 1436 "Tagore, R." at ZSMB.

86. Tagore to Jüsti, ZSMB, August 15, 1930, File 1436, 1.

87. Paul Ortwin Rave, *Kunstdiktatur im Dritten Reich* (Berlin: Argon, 1988), 28.

88. "Beschlagnahme 1937," ZSMB, I/NG 863, p. 382.

89. Annegret Janda and Jörn Grabowski, *Kunst in Deutschland 1905–1937* (Berlin: Staatliche Museen zu Berlin, Berlin), 202, 203.

90. Stella Kramrisch, *Grundzüge der indischen Kunst* (Dresden: Avalun-Verlag, 1924), 87.

91. Donald Fleming and Bernard Bailyn, *The Intellectual Migration: Europe and America, 1930–1960* (Cambridge, MA: Harvard University Press, 1969), 37.

92. Aby Warburg, *Gesammelte Schriften* (Berlin: Akademic Verlag, 1998), 104; Frances Yates, *Giordano Bruno and the Hermetic Tradition* (Chicago: University of Chicago Press, 1964).

93. "Kramrisch at Courtauld Institute in London," uncataloged. Public Lectures 1936–1937; 1938–1939; 1939, Courtauld Institute.

94. Ananda Coomaraswamy, *The Transformation of Nature in Art* (Cambridge, MA: Harvard University Press, 1934), 157ff.

95. Francis Younghusband, "Kramrish Exhibition of 1940," in File titled: "Papers re. proposed exhibition of photographs, 'Aspects of Indian Art' to be held at Warburg Institute," Warburg Institute Archive (WIA), July 12, 1940.

96. Stella Kramrisch to William Rothenstein, August 2, 1937, APAC HOU B MS Eng 1148.

97. Review of the Exhibition, *Listener,* London, November 21, 1940.

98. Stella Kramrisch to Frank Richter, February 2, 1941, Kramrisch Correspondence, APAC, Mss Eur F 147/70.

99. Younghusband, "Kramrish Exhibition of 1940," 3.

100. Ibid.

101. "Exhibition of Indian Art at the Warburg Institute," Exhibition Catalogue, 1, in the collection of the WIA.

102. See a continuation of this method in Diana Eck, *Darśan, Seeing the Divine Image in India* (Chambersburg, PA: Anima Books, 1981), 9.

103. Stella Kramrisch Papers, Philadelphia Museum of Art Archive (SK-PMA), Box 40, Item 24.

104. Stella Kramrisch alludes to the unpleasant parting in her June 20, 1973, letter to Niharranjan Ray, a former student who assumed her chair after she left Calcutta. See the SK-PMA, uncataloged correspondence.

105. Brigitte Schulze, *Humanist and Emotional Beginnings of a Nationalist Indian Cinema in Bombay* (Berlin: Avinus, 2003), 51.

106. "Indien produziert," *Kinematograph* 22 (June 1928).

107. Miriam Hansen, "The Mass Production of the Senses: Classical Cinema as Vernacular Modernism," *Modernism/Modernity* 6 (1999): 59–77; Rajadhyaksha, *Indian Cinema,* 39.

108. Priti Ramamurthy, "The Modern Girl in India in the Interwar Years," *Women's Studies Quarterly* 34 (2006): 213; Neepa Mujumdar, *Wanted Cultured Ladies Only! Female Stardom and Cinema in India, 1930s–1950s* (Chicago: University of Illinois Press, 2009), 17–49.

109. Babli Sinha, "Entertaining the Raj: Cinema and Cultural Intersections of the United States, Britain and India in the Early Twentieth Century," PhD diss., University of Chicago, 2006.

110. A. F. Stenzel, "Franz Osten und das indische Filmwesen," *Deutsche Filmzeitung,* no. 29 (1929): 30.

111. Himanshu Rai, "Der nationale Film in Indien," *UFA-Feuilleton,* no. 47 (November 19, 1919): 4–5; Brigitte Schulze, *Kino im interkulturellen Kontext* (Nordhausen, Germany: Traugott Bautz, 2008), 38–40.

112. Ausländer Kartei-Indien, 1928–38, HUA.

113. Zohra Segal, *Close-Up: Memoirs of a Life on Stage and Screen* (Delhi: Women Unlimited, 2010).

114. Mihir Bose, *Bollywood: A History* (Stroud: Tempus, 2006), 105.
115. "Criminal Investigation Department Reports on activities of Germans, Italians and Japanese," APAC, L/PJ/12/506, 53.
116. *Illustrated Weekly of India* (1939), 20.
117. Ramamurthy, "The Modern Girl in India," 210.
118. Erik Bournow, "Acquisition File for Indian Film Collection," 1977, Library of Congress, FEB 8068, 2.
119. Choodamani Nandagopal, *Impressions, Devika Rani Roerich* (Bangalore: International Roerich Memorial Trust, 1992).
120. Madhavi Kale, "Screening Empire from Itself: Imperial Preference, Represented Communities, and the Decent Burial of the Indian Cinematograph Committee Report (1927–28)," in *Beyond Sovereignty: Britain, Empire and Transnationalism, c. 1880–1950*, ed. Kevin Grant (London: Palgrave), 191–213.
121. Priya Jaikumar, *The End of Empire: Politics of Transition in Britain and India* (Durham, NC: Duke University Press, 2006), 65–106; Jaikumar, "More than Morality: The Indian Cinematograph Committee Interviews (1927)," *Moving Image* 3 (2003): 82–109.
122. Sinha, "Entertaining the Raj."
123. B. Jha, "Patriarchs of Indian Cinema," in *70 Years of Indian Cinema*, ed. T. M. Ramachandran (Bombay: Cinema India-International, 1985), 54–60.
124. Niranjan Pal, *Such Is Life: An Autobiography*, ed. Kushum Pant Joshi and Lalit Mohan Joshi in *Niranjan Pal: A Forgotten Legend and Such Is Life* (London: South Asian Cinema Foundation, 2012), 57–75. See the oral history with Niranjan Pal's son, Colin Pal, included in Amrit Gangar, *Franz Osten and the Bombay Talkies* (Bombay: Max Müller Bhavan, 2000), 12; Erik Barnow and S. Krishnaswamy, *Indian Film* (New York: Columbia University Press, 1963), 89; Kushum Pant Joshi, *Niranjan Pal: A Forgotten Legend and Such Is Life* (London: South Asian Cinema Foundation, 2012).
125. "Evidence from the India Cinematograph Committee," British Library Social Sciences Collection, V/26/970/2.
126. Joshi, *Niranjan Pal.*
127. On Indian humanism, see Schulze, *Humanist and Emotional Beginnings*, 54–66. For example, Louis Brody, born M'bebe Mpessa in Cameroon, acted in *Dad Indische Grabmal*. See Tobias Nagl, "Von Kamerun nach Babelsberg—Louis Brody und die schwarze Präsenz im deutschsprachigen Kino vor 1945," in *Kolonialmetropole Berlin*, ed. Ulrich van der Heyden and Joachim Zeller (Berlin: Berlin-Edition, 2002), 220–225.

128. The "mythological" was one of the standard genres.

129. The film was remade by Richard Eichberg in 1938.

130. Richard John Ascarate, "Cinematic Enlightenment: Franz Osten's *Die Leuchte Asiens*," *Quarterly Review of Film and Video* 25 (2008): 357–367.

131. Brigitte Schulze, "Land des Grauens und der Wunder," in *Triviale Tropen: Exotische Reise- und Abenteurfilme aus Deutschland 1919–1939* (Hamburg: CineGraph, 1997), 72–84.

132. Suresh Chabria, ed., *Light of Asia: Indian Silent Cinema* (Delhi: Wiley Eastern, 1994).

133. Gerhard Koch, "Von der Münchener Lichtspielkunst zu den Bombay Talkies," in *Kino in Indien,* ed. Chidananda das Gupta and Werner Kobe (Freiburg: Mersch, 1986), 134.

134. Peter Jelavich, *Munich and Theatrical Modernism* (Cambridge, MA: Harvard University Press, 1985), 9.

135. Jan-Christopher Horak and Jennifer Bishop, "German Exile Cinema, 1933–50," *Film History* 8 (1966): 373–389; Kristin Thompson, "Early Alternatives to the Hollywood Mode of Production: Implications for Europe's Avant-Gardes," *Film History* 4 (1993): 392.

136. Anton Kaes, Martin Jay et al., eds. *The Weimar Republic Sourcebook* (Berkeley: University of California Press, 1994), 367.

137. Carl-Erdman Schönfeld, "Franz Osten's 'Light of Asia' (1926): A German-Indian Film of Prince Buddha," *Historical Journal of Film, Radio and Television* 15 (1995): 556.

138. Barnouw and Krishnaswamy, *India Film,* 92.

139. "Report of the Indian Cinematograph Committee, 1927–28," V/26/970/1 (APAC) (Madras: Superintendent, Goverment Press, 1928), 1005.

140. Ibid.

141. Ashish Rajadhyaksha, "The Phalke Era: Conflict of Traditional Form and Modern Technology," in *Interrogating Modernity: Culture and Colonialism in India,* ed. Tejaswini Niranjana et al. (Calcutta: Seagull Books, 1993), 47–82.

142. Naval Gandhi, "The Film Market in India," *Lichtbild-Bühne* 39 (1925).

143. "Report of the India Cinematograph Committee," 1004.

144. Franz Osten, "Franz Osten und das indische Filmwesen," *Süddeutsche Filmzeitung* 8 (1929): 16. see Jessica Elizabeth Kamm, "German Film, World Travel," PhD diss., University of Illinois, Urbana-Champaign, 2011.

145. Franz Osten, "The Love of Buddha," *Lichtbild-Bühne* (1925), no. 129.

146. Ibid.; Thomas Brandlemeir, "Franz Osten, a Bavarian in Bombay," *Griffithiana,* no. 53 (May 1995): 83.

147. Also see Veronika Feuchtner, "The International Project of National(ist) Film: Franz Osten in India," in *The Many Faces of Weimar Cinema*, ed. Christian Rogowski (Rochester, NY: Camden House, 2010), 179.

148. Koch, "Von der Münchener Lichtspielkunst zu den Bombay Talkies," 125–144.

149. Osten, "Franz Osten und das indische Filmwesen."

150. Franz Osten, *Elisabeth von Österreich* (1931).

151. Bundesarchiv Filmarchiv, Prüf-Nummer 21334, Microfiche 771.

152. Horak and Bishop, "German Exile Cinema," 376.

153. "Franz Osten" Personalakte, Bundesarchiv RFA-Film A46, 286, 288.

154. Frank Leberecht and Franz Schröder, *Kampf um den Himalaja* (Degeto Kulturfilm, 1938).

155. Günter Oskar Dyhrenfurth, *Dämon Himalaya. Bericht der internationalen Karakoram-Expedition* (Basel: Schwabe, 1935).

156. "Gustav Ucicky" in Hans-Michael Bock and Tim Bergfelder, *The Concise Cinegraph: Encyclopaedia of German Cinema* (New York: Berghahn Books, 2009), 490.

157. "About Colin Ross," APAC, December 7, 1939, L/PS/12/4076.

158. Bobo-Michael Baumunk, "Ein Pfadfinder der Geopolitik: Colin Ross und seine Reisefilme," in *Triviale Tropen: Exotische Reise- und Abenteurfilme aus Deutschland 1919–1939,* ed. Jörg Schöning (Hamburg: CineGraph, 1997), 86.

159. Louis Ralph, *Emden: Unsere Emden* (Bavaria Film, 1926); Franz Osten, *Die kleine Inge und ihre drei Väter* (EMELKA, 1926); James Bauer, *Mein Heidelberg, ich kann dich nicht vergessen* (EMELKA, 1927); Karl Grune, *Waterloo* (EMELKA, 1929).

160. Tagore, *Pūrabī*, trans. Charu Chowdhuri, ed. Krishna Bose and Sugata Bose in *Purabi: The East in Its Feminine Gender* (Calcutta: Seagull Books, 2007), 1–43.

161. Ravi Vasudevan, *The Melodramatic Public* (New York: Palgrave, 2011), 51, 104.

162. Ibid., 100.

163. Rachel Dwyer and Divia Patel, *Cinema India* 9 (New Brunswick, NJ: Rutgers University Press, 2002), 161.

164. Sudhir Bose, "On Cinema in Calcutta," *Ananda Bazaar Patrika,* August 15, 1933.

165. Ute Poiger, "Imperialism and Empire in Twentieth-Century Germany," *History and Memory* 17 (2005): 134.

166. Baburao Patel, "The Foreigners Insult the Indians!," *Filmindia* 4 (September 1938): 1–5.

167. Saadat Hasan Manto, "Ashok Kumar," *Journal of South Asian Literature* 20 (1995): 113–120.

168. Carl-Erdmann Schönfeld, "Das wahre Märchen vom Prinzen Buddha: Franz Ostens indische Stummfilme," *EPD Film* 7 (1996): 28–33.
169. Choodamani Nandagopal, ed., *Impressions, Devika Rani Roerich* (Bangalore: International Roerich Memorial Trust, 1992), 25–24, 145.
170. Koch, "Von der Münchener Lichtspielkunst zu den Bombay Talkies," 125–144.
171. Bose, *Bollywood,* 129
172. Sharmistha Gooptu, *Bengali Cinema: An Other Nation* (London: Routledge, 2001), 140.
173. "Himanshu Rai," *Film-Kurier* 22 (1940): 3.

11. A NEW ORDER

1. Mark Mazower, "An International Civilization? Empire, Internationalism and the Crisis of the Mid-Twentieth Century," *International Affairs* 82 (2006): 553–566.
2. Fred Taylor, *Exorcising Hitler* (London: Bloomsbury, 2011); Siegfried Kupper, *Zone, Macht Staat* (Schkeuditz: Schkeuditzer Buchverlag, 2010); Matthias Uhl, *Die Teilung Deutschlands* (Berlin: Be.Bra, 2009); Henry Wend, *Recovery and Restoration* (Westport, CT: Praeger, 2001).
3. Jennifer Fay, *Theaters of Occupation* (Minneapolis: University of Minnesota Press, 2008), xiii–xx.
4. Philip Mosely, "Dismemberment of Germany: The Allied Negotiations from Yalta to Potsdam," *Foreign Affairs* 28 (1950): 487–498; Manfred Müller, *Die USA in Potsdam 1945* (Berlin: Fides, 1996).
5. Harald Hagemann, "Dismissal, Expulsion, and Emigration of German-Speaking Economists after 1933," *Journal of the History of Economic Thought* 27 (2005): 416.
6. Hans Ulrich Esslinger, *Entwicklungsökonomisches Denken in Großbritannien* (Marburg: Metropolis, 1999).
7. Hagemann, "Dismissal," 405–420.
8. Karl Jaspers, *The Question of German Guilt* (New York: Capricorn Books, 1961), 18; Mark Clark, *Beyond Catastrophe: German Intellectuals and Cultural Renewal* (Lanham, MD: Lexington Books, 2006), 53.
9. Alexander Gerschenkron, *Bread and Democracy in Germany* (Berkeley: University of California Press, 1943), 212.
10. Alexander Gerschenkron, "Economic Backwardness in Historical Perspective," in *The Progress of Underdeveloped Areas,* ed. Bert Hoselitz (Chicago: University of Chicago Press, 1952), 6.
11. Gerald Feldman, *Vom Weltkrieg zur Weltwirtschaftskrise* (Göttingen: Vandenock und Ruprecht, 1984).

12. Albert Harvey Leibenstein, *Economic Backwardness and Economic Growth* (New York: Wiley, 1957), 111ff.
13. Gunnar Myrdal, *Asian Drama* (New York: Twentieth Century Fund, 1968), 3.
14. Ibid., 12.
15. Marjorie Lamberti, "Returning Refugee Political Scientists and America's Democratization Program in Germany after the Second World War," *German Studies Review* 31 (2008): 263–284.
16. Corinna Unger, "Modernization a la mode. West German and American Development Plans for the Third World," *Bulletin of the German Historical Institute* 40 (2007): 143–159; Bodo Sperling, *Die Rourkela-Deutschen* (Bonn: Eichholz, 1963).
17. Surendra Chopra, *Pakistan's Thrust in the Muslim World* (New Delhi: Deep and Deep, 1992); G. L. Mehta, "Asian Nationalism vis-à-vis other Asian Nations," *Annals of the American Academy of Political and Social Science* 318 (1958): 89–96; Marvin Weinbaum, "Pakistan and Afghanistan: The Strategic Relationship," *Asian Survey* 31 (1991): 496–511.
18. K. M. Panikkar, *Asia and Western Dominance* (London: Allen and Unwin, 1953).
19. Rahul Mukherji, "Appraising the Legacy of Bandung," in *Bandung Revisited,* ed. See Seng Tan and Amitav Acharya (Singapore: NUS Press, 2008), 167.
20. Akhil Gupta, *Postcolonial Development: Agriculture in the Making of Modern India* (Durham, NC, and London: Duke University Press, 1998), 49.
21. Christopher Lee, *Making a World after Empire* (Athens: Ohio University Press, 2010), 35.
22. Kweku Ampiah, *Political and Moral Imperatives of Bandung* (Folkesone: Global Oriental, 2007); Vijay Prasad, *The Darker Nations* (New York: Norton, 2007); Jamie Mackie, *Bandung 1955: Non-alignment and Afro-Asian Solidarity* (Singapore: Editions Didier Millet, 2005); Antonia Finnane and Derek McDougall, eds., *Bandung 1955: Little Histories* (Melbourne: Monash Asia Institute, 2010).
23. James Brennan, "Radio Cairo and the Decolonization of East Africa, 1953–64," in Lee, *Making a World after Empire,* 173–195.
24. Ang Cheng Guan, "The Bandung Conference and the Cold War International History of Southeast Asia," in Tan, *Bandung Revisited,* 39.
25. Odd Arne Westad, *The Global Cold War* (Cambridge: Cambridge University Press, 2005), 34.
26. Michael J. Montesano, "Bandung 1955 and Washington's Southeast Asia," in Tan, *Bandung Revisited,* 211; Randall Stone, *Strategy and Conflict in*

the Politics of Soviet-Bloc (Princeton: Princeton University Press, 1996), 33ff.

27. Quinn Slobodian, *Foreign Front: Third World Politics in Sixties West Germany* (Durham, NC: Duke University Press, 2012), 15.

28. Martin Klimke et al., eds. *1968 in Europe* (New York: Palgrave, 2008).

29. Akhil Gupta, *Postcolonial Development: Agriculture in the Making of Modern India* (Durham, NC: Duke University Press, 1998), ix; Ward Morehouse, *Science and the Human Condition in India and Pakistan* (New York: Rockefeller University Press, 1968).

30. Jonathan Parry and Christian Struempell, "On the Desecration of Nehru's 'Temples': Bhilai and Rourkela Compared," *Economic and Political Weekly* 43 (2008): 47–57.

31. Paul Zils, "Ten Years: Documentary-Making in India I," *Indian Documentary: A Quarterly* 2 (1955): 8.

32. Ibid., 1.

33. Paul Zils, *Rourkela—Stahl für Indien* (1963).

34. For example, Zils's documentary, *Auf einer Teeplantage in Dardschiling* (1962).

35. Theodor Heuss, *Kräfte und Grenzen einer Kulturpolitik* (Tübingen: Wunderlich, 1951), 39, 64.

36. Omkar Goswami, "Sahibs, Babus, and Banias: Changes in Industrial Control in Eastern India," in *Entrepreneurship and Industry,* ed. Rajat Ray (Delhi: Oxford University Press, 1993), 256–258.

37. Zils, *Rourkela,* 40 Brochure, AA Archive.

38. Bosch GmbH opened its Bangalore branch in 1953. Daimler-Benz of Germany opened an office in Bombay in 1954. Hindustan Machine Tools and MAN Machine Works in Jabalpur were established with German aid. The German AEG had its headquarters in Bangalore in the Government Electric Factory. In 1957 came Troisdorfer Dynamit Nobel AG, a company founded by Alfred Nobel himself. Westfälische Metall-Industrie and Albert Chemical Works of Wiesbaden-Biebrich opened up branches in Delhi. Kugelfischer Georg-Schaefer and Co. operated from Bombay beginning in 1960. BASF, Bayer, Krupp, and Kraus-Maffei all had business in India by the 1960s.

39. Ravi Kalia, *Bhubaneswar: From a Temple Town to a Capital City* (Carbondale: Southern Illinois University Press, 1994).

40. Otto Koenigsberger, "New Towns in India," *Planning Review* 23 (1952): 95–132; Rhodri Windor Liscombe, "In-dependence: Otto Koenigsberger and Modernist Urban Resettlement in India," *Planning Perspectives* 21 (2006): 157–178.

41. Volker Berghahn, *America and the Intellectual Cold Wars in Europe* (Princeton, NJ: Princeton University Press, 2001), 26–51, 250–283.

42. "Großer Erfolg des 'Tages der DDR,'" *Neues Deutschland* 8 (February 1960).

43. Johannes Voigt, *Die Indienpolitik der DDR: Von den Anfängen bis zur Anerkennung* (Cologne: Böhlau Verlag, 2008), 241.

44. Voigt, *Indienpolitik,* 254.

45. "Walter Ruben Autobiographical Note," NL Ruben, Box 11, BBAW Archive.

46. Ibid.

47. Walter Ruben, *Kulturgeschichte Indiens: Ein Versuch der Darstellung ihrer Entwicklung* (Berlin: Akademie Verlag, 1978).

47. Ibid., 343.

48. Walter Ruben, *Rabindranath Tagores Weltbedeutung* (Berlin: Akademie Verlag, 1962), 1.

49. Ibid., 25.

50. Walter Ruben, "Die Perspektiven der Indologie in der Deutschen Demokratischen Republik," Ruben Papers, uncatalogued, BBAW, Box 4, 1960.

51. Walter Ruben, Box 2, File 3, August 28, 1956, BBAW Archive.

52. Ludwig Alsdorf, "Der Stand der Indologie in Deutschland," Binder B2, AA, January 1960.

53. Walter Ruben, *Über die Aufklärung in Indien* (Berlin: Akademie Verlag, 1959).

53. Ibid., 10.

54. Walter Ruben, "Indology in Berlin after the War," Ruben Papers, uncatalogued, BBAW, Box 13, 12.

55. Ashis Nandy, "The First Non-Western Psychoanalyst in Colonial India," in *The Savage Freud* (Princeton, NJ: Princeton University Press, 1995), 105; A. G. Hopkins, "Development and the Utopian Ideal, 1960–1999," in *Oxford History of the British Empire,* ed. Robin Winks (Oxford: Oxford University Press, 1999), 643.

56. E. M. Butler, *The Tyranny of Greece over Rome* (Boston: Beacon Press, 1958).

57. Carl Schmitt, *Der Nomos der Erde: im Völkerrecht des Jus Publicum Europaeum* (Cologne: Greven Verlag, 1950), 207; see also George Mosse, *The Crisis of German Ideology* (New York: Fertig, 1998), 283.

58. Stephen Legg, ed., *Spatiality, Sovereignty and Carl Schmitt* (London: Routledge, 2011).

EPILOGUE

1. Francoise Lionnet and Shu-mei Shih, *Minor Transnationalism* (Durham, NC: Duke University Press, 2005); Durba Ghosh and Dane Kennedy,

Decentering Empire (New Delhi: Orient Longman, 2006); Gilles Deleuze and Felix Guattari, *A Thousand Plateaus* (Minneapolis: University of Minnesota Press, 1987); Ernesto Laclau and Chantal Mouffe, *Hegemony and Social Strategy* (London: Verso, 1985); Michael Hardt and Antonio Negri, *Empire* (Cambridge, MA: Harvard University Press, 2009).

2. Eduard Glissant, *Poetics of Relation* (Ann Arbor: University of Michigan, 1997), 137–140, 159–161.

3. Michael Hardt and Antonio Negri, *Commonwealth* (Cambridge, MA: Harvard University Press, 2009), 206.

Glossary of Bengali and German Names and Keywords

AUTHORITATIVE NAME	VARIANTS	IDENTIFICATION
Bose, J. C.	Jagadish Chandra Bose Jagadis Chandra Bose Jagadish Chunder Bose	Physicist, biologist (1858–1937)
Bose, S. N.	Satyendranath Bose Satyendra Nath Bose	Physicist (1894–1974)
Chattopadhyaya, Bankim Chandra	Bankim Bankim Chunder Bankimchandra Bankim Chandra Chatterji Bankim Chandra Chatterjee	Poet, philosopher (1838–1894)
Chattopadhyaya, Virendranath	Viren Virendranath	Diasporic nationalist leader (1880–1837)
Das, Taraknath	Tarak Nath Das	Diasporic nationalist leader (1884–1958)
Datta, Bhupendranath	Bhupendra Nath Datta	Diasporic nationalist leader (1880–1961)
Derozio	Henry Derozio Henry Louis Vivian Derozio	Poet, reformer (1809–1831)
Devika Rani	a.k.a Devika Chaudhuri	Film actress (1908–1994)
Ghosh, Aurobindo	Aurobindo Sri Aurobindo	Spiritual leader, nationalist leader (1872–1950)
Mukherjee, Asutosh	Asutosh Ashutosh Asutosh Mukhopadhyaya Ashutosh Mookerjee Asutosh Mukherji	Educational reformer, nationalist leader, lawyer (1864–1924)

AUTHORITATIVE NAME	VARIANTS	IDENTIFICATION
Mukherjee, Radhakamal	Radhakamal Radhakamal Mookerjee R. K. Mukherjee	Economist, social theorist (1889–1968)
Mukhopadhyaya, Bhudev	Bhudev Bhudeb Bhudev Mukherjee	Historian, social thinker (1827–1894)
Osten, Franz	a.k.a. Franz Ostermayr	Filmmaker (1876–1956)
Raman, C. V.	Chandrasekhara Vekanta Raman	Physicist (1888–1970)
Ray, P. C.	Prafulla Chandra Ray	Chemist (1861–1944)
Roy, M. N.	Manabendranath Roy a.k.a. Narendranath Bhattacharya	Philosopher, diasporic nationalist leader (1887–1954)
Roy, Rammohan	Rammohan Roy Rommohun Roy Ram Mohan Roy	Philosopher, reformer (1772–1833)
Saha, Meghnad	M. N. Saha	Physicist (1893–1956)
Sarkar, Benoy Kumar	B. K. Sarkar Sarkar	Sociologist, philosopher, diasporic nationalist leader (1887–1949)
Seal, Brajendranath	Brajendra Nath Seal	Philosopher (1864–1938)
Sengupta, Narendranath Nath	N. N. Sengupta	Psychologist (1889–1944)
Tagore, Rabindranath	Rabindra Rabindranath Rabindranath Thakkur	Poet, artist, philosopher (1861–1941)

BENGALI KEYWORDS	DEFINITION
Āntarjātik	International
Ārthīk	Relating to finance or economy
Bhārat	A Bengali word for India
Bideś	Foreign, foreign land, a foreign country
Bilāt	Great Britain, the West
Biplab	Revolt, revolution
Cakravartī	Ruler

Charka	The spinning wheel, a symbol for "self-rule" in M. K. Gandhi's thought and political practice
Dāsatva	Slaver
Deś	Land, country
Dhanavijñān, Dhana-Vijñān	Economics
Digvijaya	Conquest
Gōlāmi	Slavery
Hindustān	A Bengali word for India
Jāti	A national people, also a kinship or caste community
Madhyasthā	The middling classes in colonial Bengali society
Parājita	The state of being conquered
Prabāsī	A Bengali individual living outside the region of Bengal
Pracestā	Endeavor, pursuit
Rāj	Rule
Rūpam	Form
Śakti	Strength
Sarvabhauma	Emperor
Shantiniketan	The village in Bengal where Rabindranath Tagore established his institutions for rural reconstruction, and for international education
Śiksā	Learning, education
Śilpa	Art
Svadeśi, also often, *Swadeshi*	For the native land, for the home country
Svarāj	Self-rule
Viśva	World
Viśvakabi	World poet
Viśvaśakti	World force
Yugāntar	New Age

GERMAN KEYWORDS	DEFINITIONS
Ahnenerbe	"Ancestor Research" associated with the Aryanism of the Nazi Regime
Genie	Genius, the propensity for profundity and deep understanding
Kultur	In its nationalistic sense: A concept of national exceptionalism based on ideas about the superiority of high and folk cultures
Kulturpolitik	Cultural diplomacy
Lehrfreiheit	The freedom of instructors to teach a curriculum of their choice, associated with reforms in higher education in the time of Wilhelm von Humboldt (1767–1835)
Macht	Political or martial power
Mitteleuropa	The German imperialist concept of Central Europe
Ostforschung	Research on the contiguous countries and terrains to the East of German-speaking Europe
Raum	Space, terrain
Volk	A national people
Volkswirtschaft	Political economy, national economy
Weltbürgerlichkeit	German word for "world citizenship," often presented as different from and superior to British or French "cosmopolitanism"
Weltpolitik	The pursuit of power in international affairs

Selected Bibliography

ARCHIVES

Archive of the Eidgenössische Technische Hochschule (ETH), Carl Jung Papers, Zurich.
Archives of Vienna University.
Asia, Pacific and African Collections (APAC) of the British Library, London.
Auswärtiges Amt (AA), the Foreign Office of Germany, Berlin.
Berlin-Brandenburgische Akademie der Wissenschaften (BBAW) Archives, Berlin.
Boston University Archives, Einstein Papers.
British Film Archives, London.
Bundesarchiv, Berlin.
Bundesarchiv, Koblenz.
Bundesarchiv Filmarchiv, Berlin.
Courtauld Institute Archive, London.
Deutsches Filminstitut Filmarchiv, Wiesbaden.
Friedrich-Ebert-Stiftung Archives Josef Furtwängler Nachlass (FESA-FN), Bonn.
Geheimes Staatsarchiv Preußischer Kulturbesitz (GStPK), Potsdam.
Harvard University Archives, Cambridge, MA.
Hoover Institute Archives, Stanford, CA.
Humboldt University Archives (HUA), Berlin.
Institute for Social History (IISH), Amsterdam.
Institut für Weltwirtschaft, Kiel.
Institut für Zeitgeschichte (IfZ), Munich.
Jawaharlal Nehru University Archives, Delhi.
Landesarchiv, Berlin.

Landesarchiv, Bremen.
Landesarchiv, Hamburg.
Library of Congress, Washington, DC.
National Archives of India, Delhi.
National Archives of the United Kingdom (NA-UK), London.
National Library of India, Kolkata.
Nehru Memorial Museum and Archives, Delhi.
Österreichisches Staatsarchiv, Vienna.
Philadelphia Museum of Art Archives, Stella Kramrisch Papers (PMA-SK).
Rabindra Bhawan, Viśva Bhārati University Archives, Shantinikentan.
Russian State Archive of Socio-Political History (RGASPI), The Comintern
    Archive, Moscow.
Siemens Aktenarchiv (SAA), Munich.
Thüringisches Hauptarchiv (THA), Weimar.
Warburg Institute Archive (WIA), London.
West Bengal State Archives, Kolkata.
Zentralarchiv der Staatlichen Museen zu Berlin (ZSMB).
Zentrum Moderner Orient (ZMO), Berlin.

PRIMARY SOURCES

Acharya, M. P. T. *Reminiscences of an Indian Revolutionary.* Edited by Bishamber Dayal Yadav. Delhi: Anmol, 1991.

Ainscough, Thomas. *Report on the Conditions and Prospects of British Trade in India 1926–27.* London: His Majesty's Stationery Office, 1927.

Alsdorf, Ludwig. *Deutsch-Indische Geistesbeziehungen.* Heidelberg: Kurt Vowinckel Verlag, 1944.

———. *The History of Vegetarianism and Cow-Veneration in India.* London: Alsdof, 2010; orig. 1961.

Arnold, Matthew. *Higher Schools and Universities in Germany.* London: Macmillan, 1874.

Aronson, Alex. *Brief Chronicles of the Time: Personal Recollections of My Stay in Bengal.* Calcutta: Writers Workshop, 1990.

Ball, V. *Scientific Results of The Second Yarkand Mission: Memoir of the Life and Works of Ferdinand Stoliczka.* London: Eyre and Spottiswoode, 1886.

Banerjea, Pramatha Nath. *Public Administration in Ancient India.* London: Macmillan and Co., 1916.

Bhattacharaya, Abinash Chandra. *Bahirbhārate Bhārater Muktiprayās.* Kolkata: Firma Mukhopadhyaya, 1962.

————. *Iyurōpe Bhāratiya Bilplaber Sādhanā*. Calcutta: Bandana Impression, 1949.

Bleibtreu, Karl. *Von Robespierre zu Buddha*. Leipzig: Friedrich, 1800.

Boeck, Kurt. *Indische Gletscherfahrten*. Stuttgart: Deutsche Verlags-Anstalt, 1900.

Bonsels, Waldemar. *Indienfahrt*. Frankfurt: Rütten, 1912.

Bopp, Franz. Preface to *Comparative Grammar*. Translated by Edward Eastwick. London: Madden and Malcolm, 1845.

Bose, Girindrasekhar. "The Aim and Scope of Psychology." *Indian Journal of Psychology* 7 (1932): 11–29.

————. *The Concept of Repression*. Calcutta: S. C. Majumdar, 1921.

Bose, Nandalal. *Vision and Creation*. Calcutta: Visva Bharati, 1999.

Bühler, Georg. *Report on Sanskrit MSS 1874–75*. Bombay: Education Department of the Presidency of Bombay, 1875.

Burckhardt, Jacob. *Weltgeschichtliche Betrachtungen*. Stuttgart: Verlag von W. Spemann, 1918.

Chattopadhyaya, Bankimchandra. *Vijñānrahasya*. Edited by Brajendra Nath Bandyopadhyay. Calcutta: Bangiya Sāhitya Pariṣat, 1938.

Coomaraswamy, Ananda. *Art and Swadeshi*. Madras: Ganesh, 1912.

————. *Geschichte der Indischen und Indonesischen Kunst*. Leipzig: Verlag Karl Hiersemann, 1927.

————. *The Transformation of Nature in Art*. Cambridge, MA: Harvard University Press, 1934.

Creuzer, Friedrich. *Symbolik und Mythologie der alten Völker*. Leipzig: Leske, 1810.

Das, Taraknath. *India in World Politics*. New York: Huebsch, 1924.

————. *India's Position in World Politics*. Calcutta: Sarawaty Library, 1922.

Dasgupta, Hemchandra. *Bhārater Biplabkāhini*. Calcutta, 1948.

Datta, Bhupendranath. *Āmār Āmērikay Abhijñatā*. Calcutta: Metcalf Press, 1926.

Devi, Maitraye. *Na Hanyante, It Does Not Die*. Calcutta: Writers Workshop, 1976.

Dietrich, Brandis et al. *Report on the Deodar Forests of Bashahr Punjab*. Simla: Forestry Department, 1865.

Duhem, Pierre. *German Science*. La Salle, IL: Open Court, 1991; orig. 1915.

Dvořák, Max. *Idealismus und Naturalismus in der gotischen Skulptur und Malerei*. Munich: Oldenbourg, 1918.

Dyhrenfurth, Günter Oskar. *Dämon Himalaya: Bericht der internationalen Karakoram-Expedition*. Basel: Schwabe, 1935.

Eickstedt, Egon Freiherr von. *Rassenkunde und Rassengeschichte der Menschheit*. Stuttgart: Ferdinand Enke, 1934.

Eliade, Mircea. *Bengal Nights*. Manchester, UK: Carcanet, 1993.

Frauwallner, Erich. *Geschichte der indischen Philosophie.* Salzburg: Otto Müller, 1956.

Freud, Sigmund. *Civilization and Its Discontents.* London: Hogarth Press, 1930.

———. *Letters of Sigmund Freud.* Edited by Ernst Freud. New York: Basic Books, 1960.

Frobenius, Leo. *Indische Reise: Ein unphilosophisches Reisteagebuch aus Südiniden und Ceylon.* Berlin: Hobbing, 1930.

Fuchs, Eduard. *Illustrierte Sittengeschichte: Das bürgerliche Zeitalter.* Munich: Langen, 1912.

Gadgil, D. R. *Imperial Preference for India.* Bombay: Gokhale Institute, 1932.

Gobineau, Arthur. *Sur l'inégalité des races humaines.* Paris: Librairie de Firmin Diot, 1853.

Goetz, Hermann. "The Relations between Indian Painting and Indian Sculpture." *Rupam,* no. 22–23, 1925, 46–53.

Gopal, Lallanji. "The 'Sukraniti': A Nineteenth-Century Text." *Bulletin of the School of Oriental and African Studies, University of London* 25 (1962): 524–556.

Görres, Josef. *Mythengeschichte der asiatischen Welt.* Heidelberg: Mohr und Zimmer, 1810.

Grierson, George. "Report on the Linguistic Survey of India." *Journal of the Royal Asiatic Society of Great Britain and Ireland* (1908): 1127–1131.

Guenther, Hans F. K. *Die Nordische Rasse bei den Indogermanen Asiens: Zugleich ein Beitrag zur Frage nach der Urheimat und Rassenherkunft der Indogermanen.* Jena: J. F. Lehmanns Verlag, 1934.

Güntert, Hermann. *Der Ursprung der Germanen.* Heidelberg: Carl Winter, 1934.

Harms, Bernhard. *Volkswirtschaft und Weltwirtschaft: Versuch der Begründung einer Weltwirtschaftslehre.* Jena: Fischer, 1912.

Hauer, Jakob Wilhelm. *Die Anfänge der Yogapraxis in alten Indien.* Stuttgart: Kohlhammer, 1921.

Haushofer, Karl. *Geopolitik der Pan-Ideen.* Berlin: Zentral-Verlag GmBH, 1931.
———. *Zur Geopolitik der Selbst-Bestimmung.* Munich: Roesl, 1923.

Heine, Heinrich. *Deutschland, a Winter's Tale,* trans. T. J. Reed. London: Angel Books, 1986; orig. 1844.

Held, Hans Ludwig. *Deutsche Bibliographie des Buddhismus.* Leipzig: Hans Sachs, 1916.

Hindi, A. K. *M. N. Roy: The Man Who Looked Ahead.* Bombay: Modern Publishing House, 1938.

Hirschfeld, Magnus. *Men and Women: The World Journey of a Sexologist.* New York: Putnam's, 1935.

Holitscher, Arthur. *Das unruhige Asien.* Berlin: Fischer, 1926.

Humboldt, Alexander von. *Central-Asien: Untersuchungen.* Leipzig: Brockhaus, 1863.

Husain, Zakir. *Capitalism: Essays in Understanding.* London: Asia Publishing House, 1944.

Jolly, Julius. *Georg Bühler 1837–1898.* Strassburg: Trübner, 1899.

Jung, Carl. *Civilization in Transition, C.G. Jung Collected Works.* Vol. 10, translated by R. F. C. Hull, 525–532. Princeton: Princeton University Press, 1970.

———. *Collected Works.* London: Routledge, 1970.

Kandinsky, Wassily. *Über das Geistige in der Kunst.* Munich: Piper, 1912.

Kanungo, Hemchandra. *Bāṃlāy Biplab Pracesṭā.* Calcutta: Kamala Book Depot, 1928.

Kautsky, Karl. *Sozialismus und Kolonialpolitik.* Berlin: Buchhandlung Vorwärts, 1907.

Kaye, Cecil. *Communism in India.* Calcutta: Editions Indian, 1971.

Keyserling, Hermann. *Das Reisetagebuch eines Philosophen.* Darmstadt: Reichl, 1919.

Kipling, Rudyard. "In the Rukh." In *All the Mowgli Stories.* London: Macmillan, 1993.

Kisch, Egon Erwin. *Asien gründlich verändert.* Berlin: Reiss, 1932.

Klemperer, Klemens von. *Konservative Bewegungen zwischen Kaiserreich und Nationalsozialismus.* Vienna: R. Spies, 1957.

Kramrisch, Stella. *Exploring India's Sacred Art: Selected Writings of Stella Kramrisch.* Edited by Barabara Stoler-Miller. Philadelphia: University of Pennsylvania, 1983.

———. *The Hindu Temple.* Calcutta: University of Calcutta, 1946.

———. "The Present Movement of Art, East and West." *Visva Bharati Quarterly* 1 (1923): 221–225.

Lessing, Theodor. *Europa und Asien.* Hannover: W. A. Adam, 1924.

Löwith, Karl. *Reisetagebuch 1936 und 1941.* Marbach: Deutsche Schillergesellschaft, 2001.

Lukács, Georg. *History and Class Consciousness.* Cambridge, MA: MIT Press, 1971.

Madan, Balkrishna. *India and Imperial Preference: A Study in Commercial Policy.* Oxford: Oxford University Press, 1939.

Maine, Henry. "The Effect of Observation on India on Modern European Thought." *The Rede Lecture.* Cambridge: Cambridge University Press, 1875.

Makinder, H. J. *India.* London: George Philip, 1910.

Mayhew, Arthur. *The Education of India.* London: Faber and Gwyer, 1928.

Meinecke, Friedrich. *Cosmopolitanism and the National State.* Princeton, NJ: Princeton University Press, 1970; orig. 1908.

———. *Weltbürgertum und Nationalstaat.* Munich: Oldenbourg, 1908.

Molisch, Hans. *Als Naturforscher in Indien.* Jena: Gustav Fischer, 1930.

Mookerjee, Asutosh. *Addresses: Literary and Academic.* Calcutta: R. Cambray & Co., 1915.

———. *A Diary of Sir Asutosh Mookerjee.* Calcutta: Asutosh Mookerjee Institute, 1998.

Mosse, George. *The Crisis of German Ideology.* New York: Fertig, 1998.

Mukerjee, Radhakamal. *Principles of Comparative Economics.* London: P. S. King, 1922.

———. *Regional Sociology.* New York: Century, 1926.

Mukerjee, Radhakamal, and Narendra Nath Sengupta. *Introduction to Social Psychology: Mind in Society,* London: D. C. Heath, 1929.

Mukherjee, Asutosh. *University Convocation.* Calcutta: University of Calcutta, 1915.

Müller, Max. *Auld Lang Syne.* New York: Scribner's, 1898.

———. *Chips from a German Workshop.* London: Longmans, 1867.

Münzenberg, W. *Solidarität: Zehn Jahre Internationale Arbeiterhilfe, 1921–1931.* Berlin: Neuer Deutscher Verlag, 1931.

Nag, Kalidas. *Memoirs.* Calcutta: Writers Workshop, 1991; orig. 1921–1923.

Naoroji, Dadabhai. *Poverty and Un-British Rule in India.* London: Swan Sonnenschein, 1901.

Natorp, Paul. *Stunden mit Rabindranath Tagore.* Jena: Eugen Diederichs, 1921.

Oldenberg, Hermann. *Buddha: Sein Leben, Sene Lehre, Seine Gemeinde.* Berlin: Hertz, 1881.

Otto, Rudolf. *Die Gnadenreligion Indiens und deas Christentum: Vergleich und Unterscheidung.* Gotha: Klotz, 1930.

Phalkey, Jahnavi. "Big-science, State-formation and Development: The Organisation of Nuclear Research in India, 1938–1959." PhD diss., Georgia Institute of Technology, 1997.

Ratzel, Friedrich. *Politische Geographie.* Munich: R. Oldenbourg, 1897.

Ray, Hemchandra. "Economic Policy and Functions of the Kautiliyan State." *Journal of the Department of Letters of University of Calcutta* 13 (1926): 1–30.

Ray, P. C. *Autobiography of a Bengali Chemist.* Calcutta: Orient Book, 1932.

———. *Life and Experiences of a Bengali Chemist.* Calcutta: Chuckervertty, Chatterjee, 1932.

Ribbentrop, Berthold. *Forestry in British India.* Calcutta: Superintendent of Government Printing, 1900.

Rohrbach, Paul. *Der deutsche Gedanke in der Welt.* Düsseldorf: Langewiesche, 1912.

Ruben, Walter. *Rabindranath Tagores Weltbedeutung.* Berlin: Akademie-Verlag, 1962.

Saha, Meghnad. *Collected Works.* Vols. 1 and 2. Edited by Shantimay Chatterjee. Delhi: Government of India, 1986.

Sarkar, B. K. *Education for Industrialization.* Calcutta: Chuckervertty, Chatterjee, 1946.

Sarkar, Benoy Kumar. *Chinese Religion through Hindu Eyes.* Shanghai: Shanghai Commercial Press, 1916.

——. *Duniyār Ābhāōyā.* Calcutta: Raychaudhuri, 1926.

——. *Economic Development.* Madras: B. G. Paul, 1926.

——. *Futurism of Young Asia.* Berlin: Springer, 1922.

——. *Parājita Jārmānī.* Calcutta: Oriental Book Agency, 1932.

Savarkar, V. D. *Hindu-Pad-Padashahi.* Madras: B. G. Paul, 1925.

Scharder, Karl, and Josef Furtwängler. *Das Werktätige Indien.* Berlin: Deutscher Textilarbeiter-Verband, 1928.

Schlagintweit, Hermann, Adolphe Schlagintweit, and Robert Schlagintweit. *Results of a Scientific Mission to India and High Asia, Undertaken between the Years 1854 and 1858.* Leipzig: F. A. Brockhaus, 1863.

Schmitt, Carl. *Der Nomos der Erde: Im Völkerrecht des Jus Publicum Europaeum.* Cologne: Greven Verlag, 1950.

Segal, Zohra. *Close-Up: Memoirs of a Life on Stage and Screen.* Delhi: Women Unlimited, 2010.

Sengupta, N. N. "On Gestalt Theory." *Journal of Indian Psychology* 2 (1927): 59–73.

——. "Psychology, Its Present Development and Outlook." *Indian Journal of Psychology* 1 (1926): 1–25.

Smith, Swire. *Educational Comparison on Industrial Schools in England, Germany and Switzerland.* London: Simpkin, 1873.

Sodhi, Kripal Singh. *Urteilsbildung im sozialen Kraftfeld.* Göttingen: C. J. Hogrefe, 1953.

Sombart, Werner. *Der Moderne Kapitalismus.* Vol. 2. Munich: Duncker und Humblot, 1902.

——. *Händler und Helden.* Munich: Duncker und Humblot, 1915.

——. *Luxus und Kapitalismus.* Munich: Duncker und Humblot, 1913.

Spengler, Oswald. *Der Untergang des Abendlandes.* Munich: Beck, 2011; orig. 1918.

Stein, Aurel. *Innermost Asia: Its Geography as a Factor in History.* London: Royal Geographical Society, 1925.

Strzygowski, Josef. "India's Position in the Art of Asia." *Journal of the Indian Society of Oriental Art* 1 (1933): 7–18.

——. *Die Krisis der Geisteswissenschaften.* Vienna: Schroll, 1923.

Suess, Eduard. *Das Antlitz der Erde.* Prague: Tempsky, 1883–1909.

Tagore, Abanindranath. *Sadanga: The Six Limbs of Painting.* Calcutta: Indian Society of Oriental Art, 1921.

Tagore, Rabindranath. *The Center of Indian Culture*. Madras: Society for the Promotion of National Education, 1919.

———. *Nationalism*. New York: Macmillan, 1917.

———. *The Oxford India Tagore: Selected Writings on Education and Nationalism*. Edited by Uma Dasgupta. Delhi: Oxford University Press, 2009.

———. *Purabi*. Translated by Charu Chowdhuri. London: Seagull Books, 2007.

Teske, Hilmar. *Das heutige Indien und seine Freiheitsbewegung*. Plauen: Selbstverlag, 1930.

Tollmann, Alexander. *Eduard Süss, Forscher und Politiker*. Vienna: Österreichische Geologische Gesellschaft, 1981.

Visvesvaraya, Mokshagundam. *Memoirs of My Working Life*. Bangalore: Visvesvaraya, 1951.

Walker, Campbell. *Reports on Forest Management in Germany, Austria, and Great Britain*. London: George Eyre, 1873.

Wartenweiler, Fritz. *Indiens Not, Indiens Ringen; Hinweis auf neuere Schriften über Indien und Gandhi*. Erlenbach, Switzerland: Rotapfel, 1932.

Weber, Max. *From Max Weber*. Edited by Bryan Turner. London: Routledge, 1991.

———. *Gesammelte Aufsätze zur Religionssoziologie*. Tübingen: J. C. B. Mohr, 1920.

Wunderlich, Erich. *Indien in der modernen Weltwirtschaft und Weltpolitik*. Stuttgart: Fleischhauer und Spohn, 1931.

Ziegler, Leopold. *Der ewige Buddho*. Darmstadt: Reichl, 1922.

Zimmer, Heinrich Robert. *Kunstform und Yoga im indischen Kultbild*. Berlin: Frankfurter Verlags-Anstalt, 1926.

SECONDARY SOURCES

Adas, Michael. "Contested Hegemony: The Great War and the Afro-Asian Assault on the Civilizing Mission." In *Making a World after Empire*, edited by Christopher Lee, 169–106. Athens: Ohio University Press, 2010.

Ali, Sheikh. *Zakir Husain*. Delhi: Vikas, 1991.

Allen, Charles. *The Buddha and the Sahibs*. London: John Murray, 2002.

Allen, William. *The Nazi Seizure of Power*. Chicago: Quadrangle Books, 1965.

Anderson, Kevin. *Marx at the Margins*. Chicago: University of Chicago Press, 2010.

Anderson, Robert. *Building Scientific Institutions in India: Saha and Bhabha*. Montreal: McGill University Press, 1975.

———. *Nucleus and Nation: Scientists, International Networks, and Power in India*. Chicago: University of Chicago Press, 2010.

Appadurai, Arjun, ed. *The Social Life of Things: Commodities in Cultural Perspective.* New York: Cambridge University Press, 1986.

Appel, Michael. *Werner Sombart: Historiker und Theoretiker des modernen Kapitalismus.* Marburg: Metropolis-Verlag, 1992.

Applegate, Celia. *A Nation of Provincials.* Berkeley: University of California Press, 1990.

Armstrong, Richard H. "Freud: Schliemann of the Mind." *Biblical Archeology Review* 4 (2001): 17–25.

Arnold, David. *The New Cambridge History of India: Science, Technology and Medicine.* Cambridge: Cambridge University Press, 2000.

———. *Science, Technology and Medicine.* Cambridge: Cambridge University Press, 2000.

Arvidsson, Stefan. "Aryan Mythology as Science and Ideology." *Journal of the American Academy of Religion* 67 (1999): 337–354.

Ash, Mitchell, Wolfram Niess, and Ramon Pils, eds. *Geisteswissenschaften im Nationalsozialismus.* Göttingen: V&R Press, 2010.

Ash, Mitchell, and Alfons Söllner, eds. *Forced Migration and Scientific Change: Emigre German-Speaking Scientists and Scholars after 1933.* Washington, DC: German Historical Institute, 1996.

———. *Gestalt Psychology in German Culture, 1890–1967.* Cambridge: Cambridge University Press, 1995.

Aydin, Cemil. *The Politics of Anti-Westernism in Asia.* New York: Columbia University Press, 2007.

Bagchi, Kaushik. "An Orientalist in the Orient: Richard Garbe's Indian Journey, 1885–1886." *Journal of World History* 14 (2003): 281–325.

Baha, Lal. "The Hijrat Movement and the Northwest Frontier Province." *Islamic Studies* 18 (1979): 231–242.

Bakhtin, Mikhail. *The Dialogic Imagination.* Austin: University of Texas Press, 1981.

Ballantyne, Tony. *Orientalism and Race.* Houndmills, UK: Palgrave, 2002.

Banerjee, Kalyan Kumar. *Indian Freedom Movement.* Calcutta: Jijnasa, 1969.

Barooah, Nirode. *India and the Official Germany.* Frankfurt: Peter Lang, 1977.

Bartel, Hans-Georg, and Rudolf Hübener. *Walther Nernst.* Leipzig: Teubner, 1989.

Bartky, Ian. *One Time Fits All.* Stanford, CA: Stanford University Press, 2007.

Basu, Aparna. *Essays in the History of Indian Education.* Delhi: Concept, 1982.

Baumann, Schaul. *Die Deutsche Glaubensbewegung.* Marburg: Diagonal-Verlag, 2005.

Bayly, C. A. *Empire and Information.* Cambridge: Cambridge University Press, 1996.

————. *Imperial Meridian: the British Empire and the World, 1780–1830*. London: Longman, 1989.

————. *Recovering Liberties: Indian Thought in the Age of Liberalism and Empire*. Cambridge: Cambridge University Press, 2012.

————. *Rulers, Townsmen and Bazaars*. Cambridge: Cambridge University Press, 1983.

Behr, Hartmut. *A History of International Political Theory: Ontologies of the International*. Basingstoke, UK: Palgrave Macmillan, 2010.

Bell, Duncan. *The Idea of Greater Britain*. Princeton, NJ: Princeton University Press, 2007.

————. *Victorian Visions of the Global Order*. Cambridge: Cambridge University Press, 2007.

Berghahn, Volker. *Europe in the Era of Two World Wars*. Princeton, NJ: Princeton University Press, 2006.

————, ed. *Quest for Economic Empire*. Providence, RI: Berghahn Books, 1996.

————. *Der Tirpitz-Plan*. Düsseldorf: Droste, 1971.

Berman, Morris. "'Hegemony' and the Amateur Tradition in British Science." *Journal of Social History* 8 (1975): 30–50.

Berman, Nina. *German Literature of the Middle East*. Ann Arbor: University of Michigan Press, 2011.

————. *Orientalismus, Kolonialimus und Moderne*. Stuttgart: M&P, 1997.

Berman, Russell. *Enlightenment or Empire*. Lincoln: University of Nebraska Press, 1998.

Bhagavan, Manu. "The Rebel Academy: Modernity and the Movement for a University in Princely Baroda, 1908–1949." *Journal of Asian Studies* 61 (2002): 919–947.

Bhagavantam, S. "C. V. Raman." *Biographical Memoirs of Fellows of the Royal Society* 17 (1971): 568–592.

Bhattacharya, Tithi. *The Sentinels of Culture: Class, Education, and the Colonial Intellectual in Bengal*. Delhi: Oxford University Press, 2005.

Bialas, Wolfgang, and Anson Rabinbach, eds. *Nazi Germany and the Humanities*. Oxford: Oneworld, 2007.

Bieber, Hans-Joachim. "Zur Frühgeschichte der indischen Nuklearpolitik." *Geschichte und Gesellschaft* 31 (2005): 373–414.

Blackbourn, David. *The Conquest of Nature*. London: Jonathan Cape, 2006.

————. *The Long Nineteenth Century*. London: Fontana, 1997.

Bluche, Lorraine et al. *Der Europäer–Ein Konstrukt*. Göttingen: Wallstein, 2009.

Boelcke, Willi. *So kam das Meer zu uns*. Frankfurt: Ullstein, 1981.

Born, Max. *My Life and My Views*. New York: Scribner, 1968.

Bose, Mihir. *Bollywood: A History*. Stroud, UK: Tempus, 2006.

Bose, Sugata. *His Majesty's Opponent.* Cambridge, MA: Belknap Press of Harvard University Press, 2011.

———. *A Hundred Horizons.* Cambridge, MA: Harvard University Press, 2006.

Bose, Sugata, and Kris Manjapra, eds. *Cosmopolitan Thought Zones.* Houndmills, UK: Palgrave Macmillan, 2010.

Bourdieu, Pierre. *Homo academicus.* Paris: Éditions de Minuit, 1984.

Boyer, John. *Political Radicalism in Late Imperial Vienna.* Chicago: University of Chicago Press, 1981.

Brady, John et al., eds. *The Postwar Transformation of Germany.* Ann Arbor: University of Michigan Press, 1999.

Bruch, Rüdiger vom. *Weltpolitik als Kulturmission.* Paderborn, Germany: Schöningh, 1982.

Brückenhaus, Daniel. "Every Stranger Must Be Suspected: Trust Relationships and the Surveillance of Anticolonialists in Early Twentieth-Century Western Europe." *Geschichte und Gesellschaft* 36 (2010): 523–566.

———. "The Transnational Surveillance of Anticolonialist Movements in Western Europe, 1905–1945." PhD diss., Yale University, 2011.

Burleigh, Michael. *Germany Turns Eastwards.* Cambridge: Cambridge University Press, 1988.

Buschak, Willy. *Franz Josef Furtwängler: Gewerkschafter, Indien-Reisender, Widerstandskämpfer. Eine politische Biografie.* Essen: Klartext Verlag, 2011.

Callmer, Johan, ed. *Die Anfänge der ur- und frühgeschichtlichen Archäologie als akademisches Fach (1890–1930).* Rahden, Germany: Leidorf, 2006.

Cannadine, David. *Ornamentalism: How the British Saw Their Empire.* Oxford: Oxford University Press, 2001.

Casanova, Pascale. *The World Republic of Letters.* Cambridge, MA: Harvard University Press, 2004.

Chabria, Suresh, ed. *Light of Asia: Indian Silent Cinema.* Delhi: Wiley Eastern, 1994.

Chakrabarti, Pratik. *Western Science in Modern India: Metropolitan Methods, Colonial Practices.* Delhi: Permanent Black, 2004.

Chakrabarty, Dipesh. *Provincializing Europe.* Princeton, NJ: Princeton University Press, 2000.

Chandavarkar, Raj. *The Origins of Industrial Capitalism in India.* Cambridge: Cambridge University Press, 1994.

Chatterjee, Partha. *Arms, Alliances, and Stability.* New York: Wiley, 1975.

———. *Lineages of Political Society.* New York: Columbia University Press, 2011.

———. *Nationalist Thought and the Colonial World.* Minneapolis: University of Minnesota Press, 1986.

———. *Texts of Power: Emerging Disciplines in Colonial Bengal.* Minneapolis: University of Minnesota Press, 1995.

Chatziefstathiou, Dikaia, and Ian P. Henry. *Discourses of Olympism: From the Sorbonne 1894 to London 2012.* Hampshire, UK: Palgrave Macmillan, 2012.

Chickering, Roger. *We Men Who Feel Most German.* Boston: Allen and Unwin, 1984.

Christensen, Dieter. "Erich von Hornbostel, Carl Stump, and the Institutionalization of Comparative Musicology." In *Comparative Musicology and Anthropology of Music,* edited by Bruno Nettl et al., 201–209. Chicago: University of Chicago Press, 1991.

Clark, Ian. *Hegemony in International Society.* Oxford: Oxford University Press, 2011.

Clark, Mark. *Beyond Catastrophe: German Intellectuals and Cultural Renewal.* Lanham, MD: Lexington Books, 2006.

Cock, A. G. "Chauvinism and Internationalism in Science: The International Research Council, 1919–1926." *Notes and Records of the Royal Society of London* 37 (1983): 249–288.

Codell, Julie. "Reversing the Grand Tour: Guest Discourse in Indian Travel Narratives." *Huntington Library Quarterly* 70 (2007): 173–189.

Cohn, Bernard. *An Anthropologist among the Historians and Other Essays.* Delhi: Oxford University Press, 1987.

Colley, Linda. *Britons: Forging the Nation, 1707–1837.* New Haven, CT: Yale University Press, 1992.

Conrad, Sebastian. *Globalisation and the Nation State in Imperial Germany.* Cambridge: Cambridge University Press, 2011.

Conrad, Sebastian, and Dominic Sachsenmaier. *Competing Visions of World Order.* New York: Palgrave, 2007.

Conrad, Sebastian, and Jürgen Osterhammel, eds. *Das Kaiserreich transnational.* Göttingen: Vandenhoeck und Ruprecht, 2004.

Cornwell, John. *Hitler's Scientists.* New York: Viking, 2003.

Crawford, Elisabeth. *Nationalism and Internationalism in Science, 1880–1939.* Cambridge: Cambridge University Press, 1992.

Crawford, Elisabeth, J. L. Heilbron, and Rebecca Ullrich. *The Nobel Population, 1901–1937: A Census of the Nominators and Nominees for the Prizes in Physics and Chemistry.* Berkeley: University of California Press, 1987.

Crystal, David. *English as a Global Language.* Cambridge: Cambridge University Press, 1997.

Dandekar, R. N., ed. *Ramakrishna Gopal Bhandarkar as an Indologist.* Poona, India: Bhandarkar Oriental Research Institute, 1976.

Daniels, Roger. *History of Indian Immigration to the United States.* Cambridge, MA: Belknap Press of Harvard University Press, 1998.

Das Gupta, Amit. *Handel, Hilfe, Hallstein-Doktrin.* Husum, Germany: Matthiesen, 2004.

Daum, Adreas. *Wissenschaftspopularisierung im 19. Jahrhundert.* Munich: Oldenbourg, 1998.

Davis, Mike. *Late Victorian Holocausts.* London: Verso, 2001.

Deghaye, Pierre. *De Paracelse a Thomas Mann: Les avatars de l'hermétisme allemande.* Paris: Editions Dervy, 2000.

De Grazia, Victoria. *Irresistible Empire.* Cambridge, MA: Belknap Press of Harvard University Press, 2005.

Deleuze, Gilles, and Felix Guattari. *A Thousand Plateaus.* Minneapolis: University of Minnesota Press, 1987.

Desai, Anita. *Baumgartner's Bombay.* London: Heinemann, 1988.

Dharmavira, *Lala Har Dayal and Revolutionary Movements of His Times.* Delhi: India Book Company, 1970.

Dierks, Margarete. *Jakob Wilhelm Hauer.* Heidelberg: Schneider, 1986.

Dimitrova-Moeck, Svoboda. *Women Travel Abroad, 1925–1932.* Berlin: Weidler, 2009.

Dollenmayer, David. "The Advent of Döblinism: *Wang-Lun and Wadzek.*" In *A Companion to the Works of Alfred Döblin,* edited by Roland Albert Dollinger, 55–74. Rochester, NY: Camden House, 2004.

Driver, Felix. *Geography Militant: Cultures of Exploration and Empire.* Oxford: Blackwell, 2001.

D'Souza, Eugene. "Nazi Propaganda in India." *Social Scientist* 28 (2000): 77–90.

Düwell, Kurt. *Deutschlands auswärtige Kulturpolitik, 1918–1932.* Vienna: Böhlau Verlag, 1976.

———. *Interne Faktoren auswärtiger Kulturpolitik im 19. und 20. Jahrhundert.* Stuttgart: Institut für Auslandsbeziehungen, 1981.

———. "Staat und Wissenschaft in der Weimarer Epoche: Zur Kulturpolitik des Ministers C. H. Becker." *Historische Zeitschrift* 1 (1971): 31–74.

Dyson, Ketaki Kushari. *Ranger Rabindranath.* Kolkata: Ananda, 1997.

Dyzenhaus, David. *Legality and Legitimacy: Carl Schmitt, Hans Kelsen and Herman Heller in Weimar.* Oxford: Clarendon Press, 1997.

Eck, Diana. *Darśan, Seeing the Divine Image in India.* Chambersburg, PA: Anima, 1981.

Eckert, Michael. *Die Atomphysiker: Eine Geschichte der theoretischen Physik am Beispiel der Sommerfeldschule.* Braunschweig: Vieweg, 1993.

Elias, Norbert. *The Germans.* New York: Columbia University Press, 1996.

———. *Über den Prozess der Zivilisation.* Basel: Haus zum Falken, 1939.

Epkenhans, Tim. *Die iranische Moderne im Exil.* Berlin: Klaus Schwarz, 2000.

Esleben, Jörg. "'Indisch lesen': Conceptions of Intercultural Communication in Georg Forster's and Johann Gottfried Herder's Reception of Kalidasa's 'Sakuntala.'" *Monatshefte* 95 (2003): 217–229.

Espagne, Marc, and Michael Werner, eds. *Transferts: les relations interculturelles dans l'espace franco-allemand.* Paris: Editions Recherche sur les civilisations, 1988.

Evans, Richard. *Rethinking German History.* London: Allen and Unwin, 1987.

Fabian, Johannes. *Time and the Other.* New York: Columbia University Press, 1983.

Fanon, Frantz. "The Algerian War and Man's Liberation." In *Toward the African Revolution,* translated by Haakon Chevalier, 44–150. New York: Monthly Review Press, 1964.

Feuchtner, Veronika. "The International Project of National(ist) Film: Franz Osten in India." In *The Many Faces of Weimar Cinema,* edited by Christian Rogowski, 167–181. Rochester, NY: Camden House, 2010.

Ffyth, Matt. *The Foundation of the Unconscious.* Cambridge: Cambridge University Press, 2012.

Field, Geoffrey. "Nordic Racism." *Journal of the History of Ideas* 38 (1977): 523–540.

Figueira, Dorothy. *Aryans, Jews, Brahmins.* Albany: State University of New York Press, 2002.

Findeisen, Raoul et al., eds. *At Home in Many Worlds.* Wiesbaden: Harrassowitz, 2009.

Fischer, Fritz. "World Policy, World Power and German War Aims." In *The Origins of the First World War,* edited by H. W. Koch, 128–188. London: Macmillan, 1984.

Fischer-Tiné, Harald. "Indian Nationalism and the 'World Forces.'" *Journal of Global History* 2 (2007): 325–344.

Fischer-Tiné, Harald, and Carolien Stolte. "Imagining Asia in India: Nationalism and Internationalism (ca. 1905–1940)." *Comparative Studies in Society and History* 54 (2012): 65–92.

Fitzpatrick, Matthew P. *Liberal Imperialism in Germany: Expansionism and Nationalism, 1848–1884.* New York: Berghahn Books, 2008.

Flechtheim, Ossip. *Die KPD in der Weimarer Republik.* Frankfurt am Main: Europäische Verlangsanstalt, 1969.

Fleming, Donald, and Bernard Bailyn, eds. *The Intellectual Migration.* Cambridge, MA: Harvard University Press, 1969.

Flora, Giuseppe. *Benoy Kumar Sarkar (1887–1949).* Delhi: Center for Contemporary Studies, 1998.

Forman, Paul. "Scientific Internationalism and the Weimar Physicists." *Isis* 64 (1973): 151–180.

Foucault, Michel. *The Order of Things.* New York: Pantheon, 1970.

Fraser, Thomas. "Germany and Indian Revolution, 1914–1918." *Journal of Contemporary History* 12 (1977): 255–272.

Fritzsche, Peter. *A Nation of Fliers.* Cambridge, MA: Harvard University Press, 1992.

Frost, Mark Ravinder. "The Great Ocean of Idealism: Calcutta, the Tagore Circle, and the Idea of Asia, 1900–1920." In *Indian Ocean Studies,* edited by Shanti Moorthy and Ashraf Jamal, 251–279. New York: Taylor and Francis, 2010.

———. "Wider Opportunities: Religious Revival, Nationalist Awakening and the Global Dimension." *Modern Asian Studies* 36 (2002): 937–967.

Füßl, Wilhelm. *Oskar von Miller 1855–1934.* Munich: Deutsches Museum, 2005.

Gadamer, Hans-Georg. *Philosophische Lehrjahre.* Frankfurt: Vittorio Klostermann, 1977.

Gahlings, Ute. *Hermann Graf Keyserling: Ein Lebensbild.* Darmstadt: Liebig Verlag, 1996.

Galison, Peter. *Image and Logic.* Chicago: University of Chicago Press, 1997.

Ganeshan, Vridhagiri. *Das Indienerlebnis Hermann Hesses.* Bonn: Bouvier Verlag, 1975.

Gangar, Amrit. *Franz Osten and the Bombay Talkies.* Bombay: Max Müller Bhavan, 2000.

Ganpuley, N. G. *Netaji in Germany.* Bombay: Bharatiya Vidya Bhavan, 1959.

Gerndt, Helge, ed. *Volkskunde und Nationalsozialismus.* Munich: Münchner Beiträge zur Volkskunde, 1987.

Ghosh, Durba, and Dane Kennedy. *Decentering Empire.* New Delhi: Orient Longman, 2006.

Glissant, Eduard. *Poetics of Relation.* Ann Arbor: University of Michigan Press, 1997.

Goenner, Hubert. *Einstein in Berlin.* Munich: Beck, 2005.

Gollwitzer, Heinz. *Geschichte des weltpolitischen Denkens.* Göttingen: Vandenhoeck, 1982.

Goodrick-Clarke, Nicholas. *Hitler's Priestess: Savitri Devi, the Hindu-Aryan Myth, and Neo-Nazism.* New York: New York University Press, 1998.

Gooptu, Sharmistha. *Bengali Cinema: An Other Nation.* London: Routledge, 2001.

Gordon, Andrew. *The Modern History of Japan.* New York: Oxford University Press, 2003.

Gosling, David. *Science and the Indian Tradition: When Einstein Met Tagore.* London: Routledge, 2007.

Goswami, Omkar. "Sahibs, Babus, and Banias: Changes in Industrial Control in Eastern India." In *Entrepreneurship and Industry in India*, edited by Rajat Kanta Ray. 228–259. Oxford: Oxford University Press, 1992.

Grant, Kevin, Philippa Levine, Frank Trentmann et al., eds. *Beyond Sovereignty*. New York: Palgrave Macmillan, 2007.

Green, Abigail. "Representing Germany? The Zollverein at the World Exhibitions, 1851–1862." *Journal of Modern History* 75 (2003): 836–863.

Greenspan, Nancy Thorndike. *The End of a Certain World*. New York: Basic Books, 2005.

Grimmer-Solem, Erik. "German Social Science, Meiji Conservatism, and the Peculiarities of Japanese History." *Journal of World History* 16 (2005): 187–222.

———. *The Rise of Historical Economics and Social Reform in Germany 1864–1894*. Oxford: Clarendon Press, 2003.

Grohmann, Peter et al. *Der Internationale Sozialistenkongress Stuttgart 1907: Protokoll*. Stuttgart: Selbstverlag der Studiengruppe, 1977.

Grout, Andrew. "Geology and India, 1775–1805: An Episode in Colonial Science." *South Asian Research* 10 (1990): 1–18.

Guettel, Jens-Uwe. "From the Frontier to German South-West Africa." *Modern Intellectual History* 7 (2010): 523–552.

Guha, Ramachandra. *Forestry and Social Protest in British Kumaun, c. 1893–1921*. Calcutta: Centre for Studies in Social Sciences, 1985.

———. *Sociology and the Dilemmas of Development*. Delhi: Oxford University Press, 1994.

Guha, Ranajit. "A Colonial City and Its Times." *Indian Economic and Social History Review* 45 (2008): 329–351.

———. *Dominance without Hegemony*. Cambridge, MA: Harvard University Press, 1997.

Guha-Thakurta, Tapati. *The Making of a New "Indian" Art: Art, Artists, Aesthetics and Nationalism in Bengal, c. 1850–1920*. Cambridge: Cambridge University Press, 1992.

Gupta, Akhil. *Postcolonial Development: Agriculture in the Making of Modern India*. Durham, NC: Duke University Press, 1998.

Gupta, Amit Kumar. "Defying Death: Nationalist Revolution in India, 1897–1938." *Social Scientist* 25 (1997): 3–27.

Guthke, Karl. *Die Erfindung der Welt: Globalität und Grenzen in der Kulturgeschichte der Literatur*. Tübingen: Francke, 2005.

Habib, Irfan, and Dhruv Raina, "Copernicus, Columbus, Colonialism and the Role of Science in Nineteenth Century India." *Social Scientist* 17 (1989): 50–66.

Hacking, Ian. *The Emergence of Probability*. Cambridge: Cambridge University Press, 1975.

Haithcox, John Patrick. *Communism and Nationalism: M. N. Roy and Comintern Policy.* Princeton, NJ: Princeton University Press, 1971.

Halbfass, Wilhelm. *India and Europe: An Essay in Understanding.* Albany: State University of New York Press, 1988.

Hale, Matthew. *Human Science and Social Order.* Philadelphia: Temple University Press, 1980.

Hansen, Peter. "Confetti of Empire: The Conquest of Everest in Nepal, India, Britain and New Zealand." *Comparative Studies in Society and History* 42 (2000): 307–332.

Hardach, Karl. *The Political Economy of Germany in the Twentieth Century.* Berkeley: University of California Press, 1976.

Hardt, Michael, and Antonio Negri. *Commonwealth.* Cambridge, MA: Harvard University Press, 2009.

Harnisch, Thomas. *Chinesische Studenten in Deutschland: Geschichte und Wirkung ihrer Studienaufenthalte in den Jahren von 1860 bis 1945.* Hamburg: Institut für Asienkunde, 1999.

Harper, T. N. "Empire, Diaspora and the Languages of Globalism, 1850–1914." In *Globalization in World History,* edited by A. G. Hopkins, 141–166. New York: Norton, 2002.

Harrington, Anne. *Reenchanted Science.* Cambridge, MA: Harvard University Press, 1997.

Hartmann, Hans. *Max Planck als Mensch und Denker.* Basel: Ott, 1953.

Hartnack, Christiane. *Psychoanalysis in Colonial India.* Delhi: Oxford University Press, 2001.

Haupt, Gerhard, and Jürgen Kocka, eds. *Geschichte und Vergleich.* Frankfurt: Campus, 1996.

Heehs, Peter. "Foreign Influences on Bengali Revolutionary Terrorism, 1902–1908." *Modern Asian Studies* 28 (1994): 533–556.

———. *The Bomb in Bengal.* Delhi: Oxford University Press, 1993.

Heidler, Irmgard. *Der Verleger Eugen Diederichs und seine Welt.* Wiesbaden: Harrassowitz, 1998.

Heilbron, J. L. *The Dilemmas of an Upright Man.* Cambridge, MA: Harvard University Press, 2000.

Herbert Hobbs, William. "Eduard Suess." *Journal of Geology* 22 (1914): 811–817.

Herf, Jeffrey. *Reactionary Modernism.* Cambridge: Cambridge University Press, 1984.

Herling, Bradley. *The German Gita.* New York: Routledge, 2006.

Herneck, Friedrich. *Max von Laue.* Leipzig: Teubner, 1979.

Herrigel, Gary. *Industrial Constructions.* Chicago: University of Chicago Press, 1996.

Heschel, Suzannah. *Aryan Jesus.* Princeton, NJ: Princeton University Press, 2008.

Hesmer, Herbert. *Leben und Werk von Dietrich Brandis.* Opladen: Westdeutscher Verlag, 1975.

Hobsbawm, Eric. *Age of Extremes.* New York: Pantheon, 1994.

Hochstadt, Steve. *Shanghai-Geschichten: Die jüdische Flucht nach China.* Berlin: Hentrich and Hentrich, 2007.

Hoffmann, Dieter, and Mark Walker. *The German Physical Society in the Third Reich,* translated by Ann Hentschel. Cambridge: Cambridge University Press, 2012.

Hoffmann, Friedrich. *Geschichte des Instituts für Weltwirtschaft: Von der Gründung bis zum Ausscheiden des Gründers.* Kiel, Germany: Seminar, 1962.

Hopkins, Anthony, and P. J. Cain. *British Imperialism: 1688–2000.* London: Longman, 2002.

Höpp, Gerhard, ed. *Blind für die Geschichte? Arabische Begegnungen mit dem Nationalsozialismus.* Berlin: Klaus Schwarz, 2004.

———. *Mufti-Papiere: Briefe, Memoranden, Reden und Anrufe Amin al-Husaini.* Berlin: Schwarz, 2001.

———. *Muslime in der Mark: Als Kriegsgefangene und Internierte in Wünsdorf und Zossen, 1914–1924.* Berlin: Das Arabische Buch, 1997.

Howe, Dianne. "The Notion of Mysticism in the Philosophy and Choreography of Mary Wigman, 1914–1931." *Dance Research Journal* 19 (1987): 19–24.

Howse, Derek. *Greenwich Time and the Discovery of the Longitude.* Oxford: Oxford University Press, 1980.

Hughes, Stuart J. *Consciousness and Society.* New York: Knopf, 1958.

Huxley, Andrew. "Dr. Fuehrer's Wanderjahre: The Early Career of a Victorian Archaeologist." *Journal of the Royal Asiatic Society of Great Britain and Ireland* 20 (2010): 489–502.

Hyam, Ronald. *Britain's Imperial Century.* London: Batsford, 1976.

Hyde, Lewis. *The Gift: Imagination and the Erotic Life of Property.* New York: Random House, 1983.

Iklé, Frank. "Sir Aurel Stein: A Victorian Geographer in the Tracks of Alexander." *Isis* 59 (1968): 144–155.

Inkster, Ian, and Jack Morrell, eds. *Metropolis and Province: Science and British Culture.* Philadelphia: University of Pennsylvania Press, 1982.

Ion, Hamish. *American Missionaries, Christian Oyatoi, and Japan, 1859–1873.* Vancouver: University of British Columbia Press, 2010.

Jacobson, Jon. *Locarno Diplomacy: Germany and the West, 1925–29.* Princeton, NJ: Princeton University Press, 1972.

Jaikumar, Priya. "More than Morality: The Indian Cinematograph Committee Interviews (1927)." *Moving Image* 3 (2003): 82–109.

Jalal, Ayesha. *Self and Sovereignty.* London: Routledge, 2000.

Jarausch, Konrad. *Students, Society, and Politics.* Princeton, NJ: Princeton University Press, 1982.

Jasanoff, Maya. *Edge of Empire: Lives, Culture, and Conquest in the East, 1750–1850.* New York: Knopf, 2005.

Jaspers, Karl. *The Question of German Guilt.* New York: Capricorn Books, 1961.

Jay, Martin. *Marxism and Totality.* Berkeley: University of California Press, 1984.

Johnson, Donald Clay. "German Influences on the Development of Research Libraries in Nineteenth-Century Bombay." *Journal of Library History* 21 (1986): 215–227.

Johnson, Jeffrey. *The Kaiser's Chemists: Science and Modernization in Imperial Germany.* Chapel Hill: University of North Carolina Press, 1990.

Jones, Larry. *German Liberalism and the Dissolution of the Weimar Party System.* Chapel Hill: University of North Carolina Press, 1988.

Joshi, Kushum Pant. *Niranjan Pal: A Forgotten Legend and Such is Life.* London: South Asian Cinema Foundation, 2012.

Judson, Pieter. *Exclusive Revolutionaries.* Ann Arbor: University of Michigan Press, 1996.

Juninger, Horst. *The Study of Religion under the Impact of Fascism.* Leiden: Brill, 2008.

Kaes, Anton, and Martin Jay et al., eds. *The Weimar Republic Sourcebook.* Berkeley: University of California Press, 1994.

Kakar, Sudhir. *Culture and Psyche.* Karachi: Oxford University Press, 1997.

Kale, Madhavi. *Fragments of Empire.* Philadelphia: University of Pennsylvania Press, 1998.

Kämpchen, Martin. *Rabindranath Tagore and Germany.* Calcutta: Max Müller, 1991.

———. *Rabindranath Tagore and Germany: A Documentation,* edited by Jeanne Openshaw, translated by S. V. Raman and Martin Kämpchen. Kolkata: Max Mueller Bhavan, 1991.

Kapila, Shruti. "The Enchantment of Science in India." *Isis* 101 (2010): 120–132.

Kapur, Devesh, and John McHale. *Give Us Your Best and Brightest: The Global Hunt for Talent and Its Impact on the Developing World.* Washington, DC: Center for Global Development, 2005.

Kater, Michael. "The Work Student: A Socio-Economic Phenomenon of Early Weimar Germany." *Journal of Contemporary History* 10 (1975): 71–94.

Kaviraj, Sudipta. *The Unhappy Consciousness: Bankimchandra Chattopadhyay and the Formation of Nationalist Discourse in India.* Oxford: Oxford University Press, 1995.

Keller, Richard. "Madness and Colonization: Psychiatry in the British and French Empires." *Journal of Social History* 35 (2001): 295–326.

Kelly, John, and Martha Kaplan, *Represented Communities*. Chicago: University of Chicago Press, 2001.

Keswani, G. H. *Raman and His Effect*. Delhi: National Book Trust, 1980.

Khan, Noor-Aiman. *Egyptian–Indian Nationalist Collaboration and the British Empire*. New York: Palgrave Macmillan, 2011.

Khanna, Ranjana. *Dark Continents*. Durham, NC: Duke University Press, 2003.

Kirchberger, Ulrike. *Aspekte deutsch-britischer Expansion: Die Überseeinteressen der deutschen Migranten in Großbritannien in der Mitte des 19. Jahrhunderts*. Stuttgart: Franz Steiner Verlag, 1999.

———. "Deutsche Naturwissenschaftler im britischen Empire." *Historische Zeitschrift* 271 (2000): 621–660.

Kling, Blair. "Paternalism in Indian Labour: The Tata Iron and Steel Company of Jamshedpur." *International Labor and Working-Class History* 53 (1998): 69–87.

Kontje, T. *German Orientalisms*. Ann Arbor: University of Michigan Press, 2004.

Korom, Frank. "Of Navels and Mountains." *Asian Folklore Studies* 51 (1992): 103–125.

Kumar, Deepak. "The 'Culture' of Science and Colonial Culture, India 1820–1920." *British Journal for the History of Science* 29 (1996): 195–209.

Kumarappa, J. C. *Why the Village Movement?* Rajahmundry, India: Hindustan Publishing, 1939.

Laak, Dirk van. *Imperiale Infrastruktur: Deutsche Planungen für eine Erschließung Afrikas 1880 bis 1960*. Paderborn, Germany: Schöningh, 2004.

———. *Über alles in der Welt: Deutscher Imperialismus im 19. und 20. Jahrhundert*. Munich: Beck, 2005.

Lago, Mary, ed. *Imperfect Encounter: Letters of William Rothenstein and Rabindranath Tagore*. Cambridge, MA: Harvard University Press, 1972.

Laitenberger, Volkhard. *Akademischer Austausch und auswärtige Kulturpolitik*. Göttingen: Musterschmidt, 1976.

Lala, R. M. *Beyond the Last Blue Mountain*. Delhi: Penguin Books, 1991.

Langewiesche, Dieter. *Europa zwischen Restauration und Revolution, 1815–1849*. Munich: Oldenbourg, 1985.

———. *Liberalismus in Deutschland*. Frankfurt am Main: Suhrkamp, 1988.

———. *Nation, Nationalismus, Nationalstaat*. Munich: Beck, 2000.

Langhorne, Richard. *The Collapse of the Concert of Europe*. Basingstoke, UK: Macmillan, 1981.

La Vopa, Anthony. *Prussian Schoolteachers: Profession and Office, 1763–1848*. Chapel Hill: University of North Carolina Press, 1980.

———. "Specialists against Specialization: Hellenism as Professional Ideology in German Classical Studies." In *German Professions,* edited by Jeffrey Cocks and Konrad Jarausch, 27–46. New York: Oxford University Press, 1990.

Lefmann, Salomon. *Franz Bopp: Sein Leben und seine Wissenschaft.* Vol. 1. Berlin: Reimer, 1891.

Leifer, Walter. *Indien und die Deutschen.* Tübingen: Erdmann, 1969.

Lenger, Friedrich. *Werner Sombart, 1863–1941: Eine Biographie.* Munich: Beck, 1994.

Levine, Marilyn. *The Found Generation: Chinese Communists in Europe during the Twenties.* Seattle: University of Washington Press, 1993.

Lincicome, Mark. "Nationalism, Imperialism, and the International Education Movement in Early Twentieth-Century Japan." *Journal of Asian Studies* 58 (1999): 338–360.

Lindenfeld, David. *The Transformation of Positivism.* Berkeley: University of California Press, 1980.

Lindenlaub, Dieter. *Richtungskämpfe im Verein für Sozialpolitik.* Wiesbaden: Steiner, 1967.

Linse, Ulrich. *Barfüßige Propheten.* Berlin: Siedler, 1983.

Lionnet, Francoise, and Shu-mei Shih. *Minor Transnationalism.* Durham, NC: Duke University Press, 2005.

Liu, Lydia. *Translingual Practice: Literature, National Culture, and Translated Modernity—China 1900–1937.* Stanford: Stanford University Press, 1995.

Lowe, John. *The Great Powers, Imperialism, and the German Problem.* London: Routledge, 1994.

Lowe, Lisa. *Critical Terrains: French and British Orientalisms.* Ithaca, NY: Cornell University Press, 1991.

Lubrich, Oliver. "Alexander von Humboldt: Revolutionizing Travel Literature." *Monatshefte* 96 (2004): 360–387.

MacMillan, Margaret. *Paris 1919: Six Months that Changed the World.* New York: Random House, 2002.

Mah, Harold. *Enlightenment Phantasies: Cultural Identity in France and Germany, 1750–1914.* Ithaca, NY: Cornell University Press, 2003.

Maier, Charles. "Consigning the Twentieth Century to History: Alternative Narratives for the Modern Era." *American Historical Review* 105 (2000): 807–831.

Mandal, Panchanan. *Bhāratśilpi Nandalal.* Vol. 2. Shantiniketan: Rarh-Gabesana, 1988.

Mandler, Peter. "'Race' and 'Nation' in Mid-Victorian Thought." In *History, Religion, Culture: British Intellectual History, 1750–1950,* edited by Stefan Collini, 224–244. Cambridge: Cambridge University Press, 2000.

Manela, Erez. *The Wilsonian Moment.* Oxford: Oxford University Press, 2007.

Mangold, Sabine. *Eine "weltbürgerliche Wissenschaft."* Stuttgart: Steiner, 2004.

Manjapra, Kris. "From Imperial to International Horizons." *Modern Intellectual History* 8 (2011): 327–359.

———. "Knowledgeable Internationalism and the Swadeshi Movement." *Economic and Political Weekly* 47 (2012): 53–62.

———. *M. N. Roy: Marxism and Colonial Cosmopolitanism.* Delhi: Routledge, 2010.

———. *Schopenhauer, Schopenhauerians and the German Appropriation of Eastern Thought.* Thesis, Harvard University, 2001.

———. "Stella Kramrisch and the Bauhaus in Calcutta." In *The Last Harvest,* edited by R. Sivakumar, 34–40. Delhi: NGMA, 2011.

Mantena, Karuna. *Alibis of Empire: Henry Maine and the Ends of Liberal Imperialism.* Princeton, NJ: Princeton University Press, 2010.

Marchand, Suzanne. *German Orientalism in the Age of Empire.* New York: Cambridge University Press, 2010.

———. "Nazism, 'Orientalism' and Humanism." In *Nazi Germany and the Humanities,* edited by Wolfgang Bialas and Anson Rabinbach, 267–305. Oxford: Oneworld, 2007.

———. "The Rhetoric of Artifacts and the Decline of Classical Humanism: The Case of Josef Strzygowski." *History and Theory* 33 (1994): 106–130.

Marshall, P. J. *Bengal: The British Bridgehead.* Cambridge: Cambridge University Press, 1987.

———. *The British Discovery of Hinduism in the Eighteenth Century.* Cambridge: Cambridge University Press, 1970.

Marwedel, Rainer. *Theodor Lessing: Eine Biographie.* Darmstadt: Luchterhand, 1987.

Mathur, Saloni. *India by Design.* Berkeley: University of California Press, 2007.

Maurer, Michael. *Aufklärung und Anglophilie in Deutschland.* London: DHI, 1987.

Mauss, Marcel. *Essai sur le Don.* Paris: Alcan, 1925.

Mazower, Mark. *Dark Continent: Europe's Twentieth Century.* New York: Knopf, 1988.

———. "An International Civilization? Empire, Internationalism and the Crisis of the Mid-Twentieth Century." *International Affairs* 82 (2006): 553–566.

———. "Travellers and the Oriental City, c. 1840–1920." *Transactions of the Royal Historical Society* 12 (2002): 59–111.

McClintock, Anne. *Imperial Leather.* New York: Routledge, 1995.

McGetchin, Douglas. *Indology, Indomania, and Orientalism.* Madison, NJ: Fairleigh Dickinson University Press, 2009.

McMeekin, Sean. *The Red Millionaire: A Political Biography of Willi Münzenberg.* New Haven, CT: Yale University Press, 2003.

Mehra, Jagdish. *The Golden Age of Theoretical Physics.* Singapore: World Scientific, 2001.

———. "S. N. Bose." *Biographical Memoirs of Fellows of the Royal Society* 21 (1975): 116–126.

Mehta, Purnima. "The Import and Export of Psychoanalysis to India." *Journal of the American Academy of Psychoanalysis and Dynamic Psychiatry* 25 (1997): 455–471.

Mehta, Uday. *Liberalism and Empire.* Chicago: University of Chicago Press, 1999.

Meld-Shell, Susan. *The Embodiment of Reason.* Chicago: University of Chicago Press, 1996.

Meskill, David. *Optimizing the German Workforce.* New York: Berghahn Books, 2010.

Metcalf, Thomas. *Imperial Connections.* Berkeley: University of California Press, 2007.

Meyer, Karl, and Shareen Blair Brysac. *Tournament of Shadows: The Great Game and Race for Empire in Central Asia.* Washington, DC: Counterpoint, 1999.

Michels, Eckard. "Deutsch als Weltsprache?" *German History* 22 (2004): 206–228.

Mignolo, Walter. *Local Histories/Global Designs: Coloniality, Subaltern Knowledges, and Border Thinking.* Princeton, NJ: Princeton University Press, 2000.

Mirsky, Jeannette. *Sir Aurel Stein, Archaeological Explorer.* Chicago: University of Chicago Press, 1977.

Mitter, Partha. *Art and Nationalism in Colonial India.* Cambridge: Cambridge University Press, 1994.

———. *The Triumph of Modernism.* London: Reaktion, 2007.

Mitzman, Arthur. *Sociology and Estrangement: Three Sociologists of Imperial Germany.* New York: Knopf, 1973.

Mohler, Armin. *Die konservative Revolution in Deutschland 1918–1932.* Stuttgart: Vorwerk-Verlag, 1950.

Mommsen, Wolfgang, ed. *Max Weber and His Contemporaries.* London: Allen and Unwin, 1987.

Moore, Walter John. *Schrödinger, Life and Thought.* Cambridge, Cambridge University Press, 1989.

Morrisson, Mark. "The Periodical Culture of the Occult Revival: Esoteric Wisdom, Modernity and Counter-Public Spheres." *Journal of Modern Literature* 31 (2007): 1–22.

Mukherjee, Haridas, and Uma Mukherjee. *Origins of the National Education Movement, 1905–1910.* Calcutta: Jadavpur University Press, 1957.

Mukherjee, Sumita. *Nationalism, Education, and Migrant Identities.* London: Routledge, 2010.

Mukherjee, Tapan. *Taraknath Das.* Calcutta: Jadavpur, 1998.

Murphy, David Thomas. *German Exploration in the Polar World.* Lincoln: University of Nebraska Press, 2002.

———. *The Heroic Earth: Geopolitical Thought in Weimar Germany, 1918–1933.* Kent, OH: Kent State University Press, 1997.

Murti, Kamakshi. *India: The Seductive and Seduced "Other" of German Orientalism.* Westport, CT: Greenwood, 2000.

Myers, Perry. *German Visions of India, 1871–1918.* New York: Palgrave Macmillan, 2013.

Myrdal, Gunnar. *Asian Drama.* New York: Twentieth Century Fund, 1968.

Naginsky, Erica. "Riegl, Archaeology, and the Periodization of Culture." *Anthropology and Aesthetics* 40 (2001): 135–152.

Nagl, Tobias. "Von Kamerun nach Babelsberg—Louis Brody und die schwarze Präsenz im deutschsprachigen Kino vor 1945." In *Kolonialmetropole Berlin,* edited by Ulrich van der Heyden and Joachim Zeller, 220–225. Berlin: Berlin-Ed., 2002.

Nandagopal, Choodamani, ed. *Impressions, Devika Rani Roerich.* Bangalore: International Roerich Memorial Trust, 1992.

Nandy, Ashis. *Alternative Sciences: Creativity and Authenticity in Two Indian Scientists.* Delhi: Allied, 1980.

———. *The Savage Freud.* Princeton, NJ: Princeton University Press, 1995.

Naranch, Bradley. "Beyond the Fatherland, Colonial Visions, Overseas Expansion, and German Nationalism, 1848–1885." PhD diss., Johns Hopkins University, 2007.

Neumann, Franz et al. *The Cultural Migration.* Philadelphia: University of Pennsylvania Press, 1953.

Nipperdey, Thomas. *Deutsche Geschichte 1866–1918.* Vol. 2. Munich: Beck, 1983.

Niranjana, Tejaswini et al., eds. *Interrogating Modernity: Culture and Colonialism in India.* Calcutta: Seagull Books, 1993.

Nolan, Mary. *Visions of Modernity: American Business and the Modernization of Germany.* New York: Oxford University Press, 1994.

Northrup, David. *Indentured Labor in the Age of Imperialism.* Cambridge: Cambridge University Press, 1995.

Oberkrome, Willi. *Volksgeschichte: Methodische Innovation und völkische Ideologisierung in der deutschen Geschichtswissenschaft 1918–1945.* Göttingen: Vandenhoeck und Ruprecht, 1993.

Oesterheld, Joachim. "Lohia as a Doctoral Student in Berlin." *Economic and Political Weekly* 45 (2010): 85–91.

Oesterheld, Joachim et al. *Inder in Berlin.* Berlin: Ausländerbeauftragte des Senats, 1997.

Osterhammel, Jürgen. "Alexander von Humboldt: Historiker der Gesellschaft, Historiker der Natur." *Archiv für Kulturgeschichte* 81 (1999): 105–131.

Otte, T. G. "Great Britain, Germany, and the Far-Eastern Crisis of 1897–98." *English Historical Review* 110 (1995): 1157–1179.

Pal, Prasanta Kumar. *Rabijibanī.* Vol. 4. Kolkata: Bhurjapatra, 1988.

Palit, Chitabrata. *Science and Nationalism in Bengal, 1876–1947.* Kolkata: Institute of Historical Studies, 2004.

Palladino, Paola, and Michael Worboys. "Science and Imperialism." *Isis* 84 (1993): 91–102.

Pandita, S. N. *Aurel Stein in Kashmir: The Sanskritist of Mohand Marg.* Delhi: Om, 2004.

———. *Western Indologists and Sanskrit Savants of Kashmir.* Delhi: Siddharth, 2000.

Parimoo, Ratan. *Paintings of Three Tagores.* Baroda: University of Baroda, 1973.

Parthsarathi, Ashok. "Leadership in Science and Technology." *Economic and Political Weekly* 36 (2001): 3843–3851.

Pedersen, Susan. "Settler Colonialism at the Bar of the League of Nations." In *Settler Colonialism in the Twentieth Century,* edited by Caroline Elikins and Susan Pedersen. 113–134. New York: Routledge, 2005.

Pennybacker, Susan. *From Scottsboro to Munich: Race and Political Culture in 1930s Britain.* Princeton, NJ: Princeton University Press, 2009.

Perras, Arne. *Carl Peters and German Imperialism, 1856–1918.* Oxford: Oxford University Press, 2004.

Petig, William. "The Birth of a New Realism: Photography, Painting and the Advent of Documentary Cinema." *Film History* 10 (1998): 165–187.

Peukert, Detlev. *Inside Nazi Germany.* New Haven, CT: Yale University Press, 1987.

———. *Weimar Republik.* London: Allen Lane, 1987.

Pillai, Padmanabha. *Economic Conditions in India.* London: Routledge, 1925.

Pinney, Christopher. *The Coming of Photography in India.* London: British Library, 2008.

Pitts, Jennifer. *A Turn to Empire: The Rise of Imperial Liberalism.* Princeton, NJ: Princeton University Press, 2005.

Poliakov, Leon. *The Aryan Myth: A History of Racist and Nationalist Ideas in Europe.* London: Chatto and Windus, 1971.

Pollock, Sheldon. "Deep Orientalism: Notes on Sanskrit and Power Beyond the Raj." In *Orientalism and the Postcolonial Predicament,* edited by Carol

Breckenridge and Peter van der Veer, 76–133. Philadelphia: University of Pennsylvania Press, 1993.

———. *The Language of the Gods in the World of Men.* Berkeley: University of California Press, 2006.

Prashad, Vijay. *The Darker Nations: A People's History of the Third World.* New York: New Press, 2007.

Pratt, Mary Louise. *Imperial Eyes.* London: Routledge, 1992.

Price, Ruth. *The Lives of Agnes Smedley.* New York: Oxford University Press, 2005.

Pyenson, Lewis. *Cultural Imperialism and Exact Sciences.* New York: Lang, 1985.

Rai Chowdhuri, Satyabraha. *Leftist Movements in India.* Calcutta: Minerva Association, 1976.

Raina, Dhruv. *Images and Contexts: The Historiography of Science and Modernity in India.* Delhi: Oxford University Press, 2003.

Raina, Dhruv, and Irfan Habib. "Technical Institutes in Colonial India Kala Bhavan, Baroda (1890–1990)." *Economic and Political Weekly* 26 (1991): 2619–2624

Raj, Kapil. *Relocating Modern Science.* Houndmills, UK: Palgrave Macmillan, 2007.

Rajadhyaksha, Ashish. *Indian Cinema in the Time of Celluloid.* Bloomington: Indiana University Press, 2009.

Ramamurthy, Priti. "The Modern Girl in India in the Interwar Years." *Women's Studies Quarterly* 34 (2006): 197–226.

Ramnath, Maia. *Hajj to Utopia.* Berkeley: University of California Press, 2011.

Rave, Paul Ortwin. *Kunstdiktatur im Dritten Reich.* Berlin: Argon, 1988.

Ray, Sibnarayan. *In Freedom's Quest.* Vols. 1–3. Calcutta: Minerva, 1998–2007.

Raychaudhuri, Tapan. *Europe Reconsidered: Perceptions of the West in Nineteenth Century Bengal.* Delhi: Oxford University Press, 1988.

Repp, Kevin. *Reformers, Critics and the Paths of German Modernity.* Cambridge, MA: Harvard University Press, 2000.

Richards, Pamela Spencer. *Scientific Information in Wartime: The Allied-German Rivalry, 1939–45.* Westport, CT: Greenwood Press, 1994.

Ricoeur, Paul. *Freud and Philosophy.* New Haven, CT: Yale University Press, 1970.

Rocher, Rosane. "Sanskrit for Civil Servants, 1806–1818." *Journal of the American Oriental Society* 122 (2002): 381–390.

Rodgers, Daniel. *Atlantic Crossings: Social Politics in a Progressive Age.* Cambridge, MA: Belknap Press of Harvard University Press, 1998.

Rossol, Nadine. *Performing the Nation in Interwar Germany: Sport, Spectacle and Political Symbolism.* Basingstoke: Palgrave Macmillan, 2010.

Rotzler, Willy. *Johannes Itten: Werke und Schriften*. Zurich: Orell Füssli, 1972.

Rueschemeyer, Dietrich, and Theda Skocpol, eds. *States, Social Knowledge, and the Origins of Modern Social Policies*. Princeton, NJ: Princeton University Press, 1996.

Said, Edward. *Culture and Imperialism*. New York: Knopf, 1993.

———. *Freud and the Non-European*. London: Verso, 2003.

———. *Orientalism*. New York: Pantheon, 1978.

Saldanha, Indra. "Colonialism and Professionalism: A German Forester in India." *Economic and Political Weekly* 31 (1996): 1265–1273.

Sanatani, Reeta. *Rabindranath Tagore und das deutsche Theater der 20e Jahre*. Berlin: Lang, 1983.

Sarkar, Sumit. *The Swadeshi Movement in Bengal*. New Delhi: People's Publishing House, 1973.

Sarkowski, Heinz. *Der Insel Verlag, 1899–1999*. Frankfurt am Main: Insel, 1999.

Sartori, Andrew. *Bengal in Global Concept History*. Chicago: University of Chicago Press, 2008.

Scarry, Elaine. *The Body in Pain*. New York: Oxford University Press, 1985.

Schacher, Gerhard. "Die national-wirtschaftliche Emanzipation des Orients." *Zeitschrift für Geopolitik* 9 (1932): 393–397.

Schmokel, Wolfe. *Dream of Empire: German Colonialism, 1919–1945*. New Haven, CT: Yale University Press, 1964.

Schmoller, Gustav. *Die Volkswirtschaft, die Volkswirtschaftslehre und ihre Methode*. Frankfurt am Main: Klostermann, 1893.

Schöning, Jörg, ed. *Triviale Tropen: Exotische Reise- und Abenteurfilme aus Deutschland 1919–1939*. Hamburg: CineGraph, 1997.

Schorske, Carl. *Fin-de-Siècle Vienna*. New York: Knopf, 1979.

Schroeder, Paul. "Did the Vienna Settlement Rest on a Balance of Power?" *American Historical* Review 97 (1992): 683–706.

Schroeder-Gudehus, Brigitte. "Challenge to Transnational Loyalties: International Scientific Organizations after the First World War." *Science Studies* 3 (1973): 93–118

———. *Deutsche Wissenschaft und internationale Zusammenarbeit*. Geneva: Dumaret and Golay, 1966.

———. "Division of Labour and the Common Good." In *Science, Technology and Society in the Time of Alfred Nobel*, edited by Carl Gustaf Bernhard et al., 3–20. Oxford: Pergamon, 1982.

———. "Internationale Wissenschaftsbeziehungen und auswärtige Kulturpolitik, 1919–1933." In *Forschung im Spannungsfeld von Politik und Gesellschaft*, edited by Rudolf Vierhaus et al., 858–885. Stuttgart: Deutsche Verlags-Anstalt, 1990.

Schulze, Brigitte. *Humanist and Emotional Beginnings of a Nationalist Indian Cinema in Bombay.* Berlin: Avinus, 2003.

Sengupta, Indra. *From Salon to Discipline.* Würzburg: Ergon, 2005.

Seshadri-Crooks, Kalpana. "The Primitive as Analyst: Postcolonial Feminism's Access to Psychoanalysis." *Cultural Critique* 28 (1994): 175–218.

Seth, Suman. *Crafting the Quantum.* Cambridge, MA: MIT Press, 2010.

Seth, Vikram. *Two Lives.* London: Little, Brown, 2005.

Shanahan, William. "Liberalism and Foreign Affairs: Naumann and the Prewar German View." *View of Politics* 21 (1959): 188–223.

Sheehan, James. *German Liberalism.* Chicago: University of Chicago Press, 1978.

Sherry, Jay. *Carl Gustav Jung: Avant-Garde Conservative.* London: Palgrave, 2010.

Sigurdsson, Skuli. "Physics, Life, and Contingency: Born, Schroedinger, and Weyl in Exile." In *Forced Migration and Scientific Change: Emigre German-Speaking Scientists and Scholars after 1933,* edited by Mitchell G. Ash and Alfons Söllner, 48–70. Washington, DC: GHI, 1996.

Singh, Rajinder. "Arnold Sommerfeld—The Supporter of Indian Physics in Germany." *Current Science* 81 (2001): 1489–1494.

Sinha, Babli. "Entertaining the Raj: Cinema and Cultural Intersections of the United States, Britain and India in the Early Twentieth Century." PhD diss., University of Chicago, 2006.

Sinha, Durganand. *Psychology in a Third World Country: The Indian Experience.* New Delhi: Sage, 1986.

Slobodian, Quinn. *The Other Alliance: Student Protest in West Germany and the United States in the Global Sixties.* Princeton, NJ: Princeton University Press, 2011.

Sontag, Raymond James. *Germany and England: Background of Conflict, 1848–1894.* New York: Appleton-Century, 1938.

Spitzer, Leo. *Hotel Bolivia.* New York: Hill and Wang, 1998.

Stache-Rosen, Valentina. *German Indologists: Biographies of Scholars in Indian Studies Writing in Germany.* Delhi: Max Müller Bhavan, 1981.

Staub, Nicole, and Kathrin Jost, eds. *Humboldt International: Der Export des deutschen Universitätsmodells im 19 und 20. Jahrhundert.* Basel: Schwabe, 2001.

Stein, Aurel. *Serindia: Detailed Report on Explorations in Central Asia.* Oxford: Clarendon Press, 1921.

Stern, Philip. *The Company-State: Corporate Sovereignty and the Early Modern Foundation of the British Empire in India.* Oxford: Oxford University Press, 2011.

Stewart, Gordon T. *Journeys to Empire: Enlightenment, Imperialism and the British Encounter with Tibet, 1774–1904.* Cambridge: Cambridge University Press, 2009.

Stoler, Ann Laura. *Carnal Knowledge and Imperial Power: Race and the Intimate in Colonial Rule.* Berkeley: University of California Press, 2002.

Strickland, C. F. *An Introduction to Co-operation in India.* London: Humphrey Milford, 1922.

Struwe, Ruth. "An Ambitious German in Early Twentieth Century Tasmania: The Collections Made by Fritz Noetling." *Australian Archaeology* 62 (2006): 31–37.

Stüwer, Roger H., ed. *Nuclear Physics in Retrospect.* Minneapolis: University of Minnesota Press, 1979.

Sühlsdorff, Volkmar von. *Deutsche Akademie im Exil.* Berlin: EMV, 1999.

Sur, Abha. "Aesthetics, Authority, and Control in an Indian Laboratory: The Raman-Born Controversy on Lattice Dynamics." *Isis* 90 (1999): 25–49.

———. "Scientism and Social Justice: Meghnad Saha's Critique of the State of Science in India." *Historical Studies in the Physical and Biological Sciences* 33 (2002): 87–105.

Tanaka, Stefan. *New Times in Modern Japan.* Princeton, NJ: Princeton University Press, 2004.

Taylor, A. J. P. *The Struggle for Mastery in Europe, 1848–1918.* Oxford: Clarendon Press, 1954.

Thackray, Arnold. "Nature Knowledge in a Cultural Context: The Manchester Model." *American Historical Review* 79 (1974): 672–709.

Thünen, Johann Heinrich von. *Der isolierte Staat in Beziehung auf Land, Wirtschaft und Nationalökonomie.* Berlin: Akademie-Verlag, 1835.

Tinker, Hugh. *A New System of Slavery.* London: Oxford University Press, 1974.

Tooze, Adam. *Statistics and the German State.* Cambridge: Cambridge University, 2001.

Trautmann, Thomas. *Aryans and British India.* Berkeley: University of California Press, 1997.

———. *Kautilya and the Arthashastra: A Statistical Investigation of the Authorship and Evolution of the Text.* Leiden: Brill, 1971.

Treitel, Corinna. *A Science for the Soul.* Baltimore: Johns Hopkins University Press, 2004.

Tribe, Keith. *Strategies of Economic Order.* Cambridge: Cambridge University Press, 1995.

Trivedi, Lisa. *Clothing Gandhi's Nation.* Bloomington: Indiana University Press, 2007.

Tull, Herman W. "F. Max Mueller and A. B. Keith: 'Twaddle,' and 'Stupid' Myth, and the Disease of Indology." *Numen* 28 (1991): 27–58.

Turner, Bryan. *Marx and the End of Orientalism*. London: Georg Allen and Unwin, 1978.

Tzoref-Ashkenazi, Chen. "India and the Identity of Europe: The Case of Friedrich Schlegel." *Journal of the History of Ideas* 67 (2006): 713–734.

Ullrich, Volker. *Die nervöse Großmacht, Aufstieg und Untergang des detuschen Kaiserreichs, 1871–1918*. Frankfurt: Fischer, 1997.

Umbach, Maiken. "Visual Culture, Scientific Images and German Small-State Politics in Late Enlightenment." *Past and Present* 158 (1998): 110–145.

Vasudevan, Ravi. *The Melodramatic Public*. New York: Palgrave, 2011.

Veblen, Thorstein. *The Theory of the Leisure Class*. London: Macmillan, 1899.

Veer, Peter van der. *Nation and Migration: The Politics of Space in the South Asian Diaspora*. Philadelphia: University of Pennsylvania Press, 1995.

Venkataraman, G. *Journey into Light*. Bangalore: Indian Academy of Sciences, 1988.

Visram, Rozina. *Ayahs, Lascars, and Princes*. London: Pluto, 1986.

Visvanathan, Shiv. *Organizing for Science: The Making of an Industrial Research Laboratory*. Delhi and Oxford: Oxford University Press, 1985.

Voigt, Johannes. *Die Indienpolitik der DDR*. Cologne: Böhlau, 2008.

———. *Indien im Zweiten Weltkrieg*. Delhi: Arnold-Heinemann, 1987.

———. *Max Mueller: The Man and His Ideas*. Calcutta: Firma K. L. Mukhopadhyay, 1967.

Voigt, Johannes, and Anil Bhatti, eds. *Jewish Exile in India*. Delhi: Manohar, 1999.

Wacha, D. E. *The Life and Life Work of J. N. Tata*. Madras: Ganesh, 1914.

Walker, Annabel. *Aurel Stein: Pioneer of the Silk Road*. London: John Murray, 1995.

Wallerstein, Immanuel. *The Modern World-System*. New York: Academic Press, 1974.

Weil, Benjamin. "Conservation, Exploitation, and Cultural Change in the Indian Forest Services, 1875–1927." *Environmental History* 11 (2006): 319–343.

Weinreich, Max. *Hitler's Professors*. New York: Yiddish Scientific Institute, 1946.

Weitz, Ulrich. *Salonkultur und Proletariat: Eduard Fuchs, Sammler, Sittengeschichtler, Sozialist*. Stuttgart: Stöffler und Schütz, 1991.

Westad, Odd Arne. *The Global Cold War*. Cambridge: Cambridge University Press, 2005.

Wieben, Uwe. *Carl Peters: das Leben eines deutschen Kolonialisten*. Rostock: Neuer Hochschulschriftenverlag, 2000.

Wilhelm, Friedrich. "The German Response to Indian Culture." *Journal of the American Oriental Society* 81 (1961): 395–405.

Williamson, George. *Longing for Myth*. Chicago: University of Chicago Press, 2004.

Wilson, Jon. *The Domination of Strangers*. Basingstoke, UK: Palgrave Macmillan, 2008.

Winkler, Ken. *A Thousand Journeys: The Biography of Lama Anagarika Govinda*. Longmead, Dorset, UK: Element, 1990.

Winternitz, Moriz. *Georg Bühler und die Indologie*. Munich: n.p., 1898.

Wolff, Henry. *Rambles in the Black Forest*. London: Longmans, Green, 1890.

Wolff, Stefan. "Physicists in the 'Krieg der Geister': Wilhelm Wien's 'Proclamation.'" *Historical Studies in the Physical and Biological Sciences* 33 (2003): 337–368.

Zachariah, Benjamin. *Developing India*. Delhi: Oxford University Press, 2005.

———. *Nehru*. London: Routledge, 2004.

Zantop, Susan. *Colonial Fantasies*. Durham, NC: Duke University Press, 1997.

Zimmermann, Andrew. *Alabama in Africa: Booker T. Washington, the German Empire, and the Globalization of the New South*. Princeton, NJ: Princeton University, 2010.

Zinnes, Dina. "Coalition Theories and the Balance of Power." In *The Study of Coalition Behavior*, edited by Sven Groennings et al., 351–368. New York: Rinehart and Winston, 1970.

Zweynert, Joachim, and Daniel Riniker. *Werner Sombart in Russland*. Marburg: Metropolis, 2004.

Acknowledgments

This book took a long time to write, and I have benefited from much generosity along the way. If all those who have helped me could see in this book an impress of what they shared, it would be my greatest reward. During those periods when I felt the writing too daunting, I thought of all those colleagues, mentors, and friends who have supported me. Those moments of reflection and gratitude propelled me forward. For the errors and imperfections that remain in this work, I bear sole responsibility.

I thank David Blackbourn for providing a model of scholarship, and for his sustained encouragement. I have learned as much from Sugata Bose, who has offered much guidance and intellectual stimulation, and has been a kind mentor and friend. To Peter Gordon, I extend my sincerest thanks for all our enriching interactions. I am deeply indebted to my teachers. Without the aid and encouragement of Louis Miller, I would never have gotten started on this road. Thanks too to the late Donald Fleming—a maestro at the podium, and a brilliant and kind mentor.

Research and writing for this book was completed thanks to a postdoctoral fellowship from the Alexander von Humboldt Foundation and a fellowship from the Deutscher Akademischer Austausch Dienst (DAAD). Sebastian Conrad served as my host at the Free University during the Humboldt fellowship year, and to him I am indebted on many counts. A Mellon Postdoctoral Fellowship at UCLA provided me needed time to work on this manuscript. The guidance and support of Françoise Lionnet and Shu-mei Shih at UCLA meant a great deal to me. Affiliations with the Institute of Commonwealth Studies at the University of London and a visiting fellowship at the History Department of University College London helped me complete my work. I heartily thank the library and archival staff at the many institutions that facilitated my research. The names of institutions are listed in the bibliography. I only wish I could have included the names of all the people who made those institutions so accessible and friendly.

I benefited from presenting parts of this work at various venues. To the audiences at Cambridge University, Witswatersrand University, Harvard University, Viswa Bharati University, BRAC University, Humboldt University, and the Free University, I salute you for your critical engagement. Your questions moved this project forward.

This research required me to trespass foolhardily across a number of fields. Thanks to Skúli Sigurdsson, Kamal Datta, Matthew Povich, and Jahnavi Phalkey for generous guidance in my venture into the history of physics. Thanks to Debashree Banerjee for help in film studies. To scholars who read chapters of my work and offered helpful and profound comments, I express my sincere gratitude. Andrew Zimmerman, Nina Berman, Sheldon Pollock, Christiane Hartnack, and Susannah Heschel offered especially important feedback. My greatest debt of gratitude, however, is to Suzanne Marchand for our many invigorating conversations, for the much-needed encouragement she provided when times got tough, and for attentively reading my full manuscript and helping me to get to the heart of the matter.

The insightful comments by Adam McKeown on the manuscript were of indispensable value. Cemil Aydin helped me to take important steps forward in completing this book. Thanks also to other scholars who offered encouragement and food for thought, especially Tim Harper, Javed Majeed, Dilip Menon, Kiran Patel, Neilesh Bose, Iftekhar Iqbal, C. A. Bayly, Anthony La Vopa, Dhruv Raina, Bruce Mazlish, Joya Chatterji, Anthony Grafton, Olivier Remaud, Astrid Eckert, Pieter Judson, Quinn Slobodian, Andreas Eckert, Sanjay Subrahmaniam, Aamir Mufti, and Vinayak Chaturvedi. Björn Blass worked with alacrity and precision on aspects of my manuscript preparation.

Without the friendship of many individuals the research and writing of this book would have been too heavy a load. Thanks for making things lighter: Zeenat Potia, Abby Collins, Guenther Bisges, Miguel de Baca, Lambert Williams, Nico Slate, Stephan Link, Shirley Ye, Andrew Rueb, Howard Axelrod, Robert Fanion, Radiclani Clytus, Randy Sachs, James Savage, Thomas Brennan, Martin Kämpchen, and Monika Golembiewski. In preparing this work, I benefited from fortifying discussions at the coffee or dining tables of many generous mentors. I thank Partha Mitter, Uma Dasgupta, and Leonard Gordon especially. Leonard Gordon read a penultimate draft of the full manuscript and offered important feedback, and his kind words of support made a big difference in the final stages. Space does not allow me to complete the list, but I hope to find a way to thank the many friends who have gone unnamed here.

Andrew Kinney, my editor at Harvard University Press, has seen the best in my work and helped me bring it to the surface. This book has greatly benefited from his penetrating comments and his perceptive guidance. Thanks to the other editors and employees at the Press, as well as to the anonymous reviewers for their commitment to this project.

I am fortunate to work in the wonderfully collegial history department at Tufts University with such inspiring colleagues. Thanks especially to Jeanne Penvenne for her friendship. Sol Gittelman always knew what to say at the right time. And a special note of gratitude to Ayesha Jalal, who has supported me throughout, and with whom I have shared so many important conversations and collaborations.

The members of my family have sustained me and increased my joy. Although words cannot do justice to how I feel, I must try. I could not have done this without Saugato Datta, who kept me steady throughout all the challenges. My mother, Jeanile, always reminded me of what was most important. And Lucia Volk has long been a dear friend, a big sister, and a source of light.

This work is dedicated to my father. In many ways, it began with him. Although he died many years ago, I felt him unusually close in the final stages of preparing this manuscript. I often recall one of his favorite proverbs: "First live, and then philosophize!" I have learned that to be a good historian is to take that piece of wisdom seriously.

Index